INTERNATIONAL

International Migration Law

VINCENT CHETAIL

OXFORD
UNIVERSITY PRESS

Great Clarendon Street, Oxford, OX2 6DP,
United Kingdom

Oxford University Press is a department of the University of Oxford.
It furthers the University's objective of excellence in research, scholarship,
and education by publishing worldwide. Oxford is a registered trade mark of
Oxford University Press in the UK and in certain other countries

First Edition published in 2019

Impression: 1

Published in the United States of America by Oxford University Press
198 Madison Avenue, New York, NY 10016, United States of America

British Library Cataloguing in Publication Data
Data available

Library of Congress Control Number: 2019931642

ISBN 978–0–19–966827–4 (pbk.)
ISBN 978–0–19–966826–7 (hbk.)

Printed and bound by
CPI Group (UK) Ltd, Croydon, CR0 4YY

Acknowledgements

A book is never finished; it is abandoned. This one is not an exception. This book is the result of a long process of reflection and discussion that started in 1999. At that time, I was apparently the first to give a course on international migration law in a post-graduate curriculum. Since then, I have realized the need for a textbook that provides a comprehensive and didactic immersion into the rich body of international legal norms governing the movement of persons across borders.

While students have been supportive and passionate about this topic from the outset, the interest of international legal scholars has drastically evolved during the last two decades. The reactions of the profession have steadily moved from scepticism to enthusiasm. There is some exaggeration in both postures. Minds have become so imbued by immigration control that even international lawyers have quite lately (re)discovered the relevance of their discipline. This relative indifference has now given way to an unprecedented interest fueled by the sudden politicization of migration. Discussions on migration and international law are today commonplace, be it in the media, political spheres, or academic circles.

The label 'international migration law' is relatively new, but its substance is as old as international law. The movement of persons across borders is inter-national by essence and it has always been a question of international law. Addressing migration through the prism of international law discloses a global vision that is based on the mutual interests of states and the rights of the individuals. It provides a nuanced and rational account of migration as a topical issue of international concern. International law has become a counter-narrative to populism and the last limit to unilateralism, although there is nothing comforting in this.

Whether one likes it or not, international law is not politically neutral. It is primarily created by states and informed by an international legal system that is grounded on cooperation, sovereignty, and the rule of law. However, international migration law is neither the new utopia of a globalized world nor the outdated apology of the sovereign state. International migration law is grounded on existing rules and principles that are legally binding for states. It thus reflects the potential and the limit of our current international legal system.

From this systemic perspective, international migration law represents a self-evident catch-word to encapsulate the broad variety of international legal norms within a common framework of analysis. This framework of analysis is informed by the sources and actors of public international law. Its main objective is not to create another subfield of specialization. Instead this book revisits the long-standing relationships between migration and international law from the perspective of a generalist. Despite the rapid evolution of this field, I did my very best to update the state of international law until the delivery of my manuscript to OUP in October 2018.

Writing this book would not have been possible without the support and advice of many people. I am indebted, first of all, to the generations of students from the

Graduate Institute of International and Development Studies, who have attended my course years after years and expressed their enthusiasm for this topic. The ideas developed in this book have been further refined through intense discussions with many scholars and lawyers who cannot be listed here at the risk of missing anyone. I also had the chance to test my main arguments in several lectures I gave as visiting professor in various inspiring places, such as Boston (Harvard Law School), Brussels (Université libre de Bruxelles), Florence (European University Institute), the Hague (Hague Academy of International Law), London (Queen Mary University; King's College London), Paris (Université Paris II Panthéon-Assas; Université Paris XI Jean Monnet), and Tunis (Faculté des sciences juridiques, politiques et sociales de Tunis). I am indebted to the research assistants and colleagues who have worked at the Global Migration Centre, which I created in 2012 at the Graduate Institute of International and Development Studies. I would like to thank in particular: Alexandra Goossens, Júlia Miklasová, Vera Piovesan, Giulia Raimondo, Géraldine Ruiz, and Allegra Sary for their assistance and support.

Finally, my deepest thanks and gratitude go to my wife and soulmate Céline and my children, Edouard and Quentin, for their love, patience, and support. From the bottom of my heart, thank you.

Vincent Chetail
Professor of International Law
Director of the Global Migration Centre
Head of the International Law Department
Graduate Institute of International and Development Studies

Table of Contents

PART II. THE TREATY REGIMES OF
INTERNATIONAL MIGRATION LAW

PART III. SOFT LAW AND GLOBAL
MIGRATION GOVERNANCE

Table of Cases

EUROPEAN COURT OF JUSTICE

INTER-AMERICAN COMMISSION OF HUMAN RIGHTS

INTER-AMERICAN COURT OF HUMAN RIGHTS

INTERNATIONAL COURT OF JUSTICE

INTERNATIONAL CRIMINAL TRIBUNAL FOR THE FORMER YUGOSLAVIA

INTERNATIONAL CRIMINAL COURT

IRAN-UNITED STATES CLAIMS TRIBUNAL

PERMANENT COURT OF ARBITRATION

PERMANENT COURT OF INTERNATIONAL JUSTICE

NATIONAL JUDGMENTS

Australia

Canada

France

UNITED NATIONS TREATY BODIES

Human Rights Committee (HRC)

Table of Instruments

BILATERAL AGREEMENTS

REGIONAL INSTRUMENTS

Africa

List of Abbreviations

AALCO	Asian-African Legal Consultative Organization
Abu-Dhabi Dialogue	Ministerial Consultations on Overseas Employment and Contractual Labour for Countries of Origin and Destination in Asia
ACHPR	African Charter on Human and Peoples' Rights
AComHPR	African Commission of Human and Peoples' Rights
ACHR	American Convention on Human Rights
ACP	African, Caribbean, and Pacific Group of States
ACTIP	ASEAN Convention against Trafficking in Persons, especially Women and Children
AFDI	Annuaire français de droit international
AIDI	Annuaire de l'Institut de Droit International
AJIL	American Journal of International Law
AJIL Unbound	American Journal of International Law Unbound
Alb Govt L Rev	Albany Government Law Review
Almaty Process	Almaty Process on Refugee Protection and International Migration
Am J Comp L	American Journal of Comparative Law
Am Political Science Rev	American Political Science Review
Am UL Rev	American University Law Review
AMU	Arab-Maghreb Union
Amsterdam LF	Amsterdam Law Forum
APD	Archives de philosophie du droit
APEC	Asia-Pacific Economic Cooperation
Arch VR	Archiv des Völkerrechts
ARIEL	Austrian Review of International and European Law
ARCP	Arab Regional Consultative Process on Migration and Refugee Affairs
ASDI	Annuaire suisse de droit international
ASEAN	Association of Southeast Asian Nations
ASEM	Asia-Europe Meeting
ASIL Proc	American Society of International Law Proceedings
ASLP	Association of Special Libraries of the Philippines
AU	African Union
Aust YBIL	Australian Yearbook of International Law
AVRR	Assisted Voluntary Return and Reintegration
AWR Bulletin	Association for the Study of World Refugee Problem Bulletin
Bali Process	Bali Process on People Smuggling, Trafficking in Persons and Related Transnational Crime
BC Int'l & Comp L Rev	Boston College International and Comparative Law Review

Berk J Int'l L	Berkeley Journal of International Law
BOND	British Overseas NGOs for Development
BYIL	British Yearbook of International Law
BSEC	Organisation of the Black Sea Cooperation
BU Int'l LJ	Boston University International Law Journal
CAIS	Central American Integration System
CAN	Andean Community of Nations
CARICOM	Caribbean Community
CASCTHB	Comprehensive Arab Strategy for Combating Trafficking in Human Beings
CAT	Convention against Torture and Other Cruel, Inhuman or Degrading Treatment or Punishment
CAT Committee	Committee against Torture
CCEAC	Communauté Economique des Etats de l'Afrique Centrale
Cde D	Les Cahiers de Droit
CEDAW	Convention on the Elimination of Discrimination against Women
CEDAW Committee	Committee on the Elimination of Discrimination against Women
CEACR	Committee of Experts on the Application of Conventions and Recommendations
CEN-SAD	Community of Sahel-Saharan States
CERD	Committee on the Elimination of Racial Discrimination
CESCR	Committee on Economic, Social and Cultural Rights
CETS	Council of Europe Treaty Series
CIS	Commonwealth of Independent States
CIS Convention	Commonwealth of Independent States Convention on Human Rights and Fundamental Freedoms
CLB	Commonwealth Law Bulletin
CMC	Caribbean Migration Consultations
CMW	Committee on the Protection of the Rights of All Migrant Workers
COE	Council of Europe
Colombo Process	Ministerial Consultation on Overseas Employment and Contractual Labour for Countries of Origin in Asia
Colum J of Transnat'l L	Columbia Journal of Transnational Law
Columb L Rev	Columbia Law Review
COMESA	Common Market for Eastern and Southern Africa
Comp Lab L & Pol'y J	Comparative Labor Law & Policy Journal
Cornell L Rev	Cornell Law Review
CRC	Convention on the Rights of the Child
CRC Committee	Committee on the Rights of the Child
CRPD Committee	Committee on the Rights of Persons with Disabilities
CRRF	Comprehensive Refugee Response Framework
CSCE	Commission on Security and Cooperation in Europe
CTS	Consolidated Treaty Series
CUP	Cambridge University Press

Denv J Int'l L & Pol'y	Denver Journal of International Law and Policy
Droits Rev Fr	Droits: Revue Francaise de Théorie Juridique
Duke J Comp & Int'l L	Duke Journal of Comparative & International Law
EAC	East African Community
EaPPMA	Eastern Partnership Panel on Migration and Asylum
EC	European Commission
ECAC	European Civil Aviation Conference
ECCAS	Economic Community for Central African States
ECGLC	Economic Community of the Great Lake Countries
ECHR	European Convention on Human Rights
ECtHR	European Court of Human Rights
ECO	Economic Cooperation Organization
ECOSOC	Economic and Social Council
ECOWAS	Economic Community of West African States
ECJ	European Court of Justice
ECR	European Court Reports
EEA	European Economic Area
EFTA	European Free Trade Agreement
EJIL	European Journal of International Law
EJML	European Journal of Migration & Law
EHRR	European Human Rights Reports
EMCCA	Economic and Monetary Community of Central Africa
EPC	European Policy Centre
ETS	European Treaty Series
EU	European Union
EUI	European University Institute
EURASEC	Eurasian Economic Community
EXCOM	Executive Committee (UNHCR)
FAO	Food and Agriculture Organization of the United Nations
FIDH	International Federation of Human Rights Leagues
FOM	Federal Office for Migration
Fordham Int'l LJ	Fordham International Law Journal
Fordham L Rev	Fordham Law Review
Fourth Geneva Convention	Geneva Convention Relative to the Protection of Civilian Persons in Time of War
GA	General Assembly
Ga J Int'l & Comp L	Georgia Journal of International and Comparative Law
GATS	General Agreement on Trade and Services
GAOR	General Assembly Official Records
GCC	Gulf Cooperation Council
GCIM	Global Commission on International Migration
GDP	Gross Domestic Product
Geneva Convention	Convention relating to the Status of Refugees
Geo Immigr L J	Georgetown Immigration Law Journal
Geo J Int'l L	Georgetown Journal of International Law

Germ Yrbk Int'l L	German Yearbook of International Law
GFMD	Global Forum on Migration and Development
GMG	Global Migration Group
Goettingen J Int'l L	Goettingen Journal of International Law
Harv CR-CLL Rev	Harvard Civil Rights – Civil Liberties Law Review
Harv Hum Rts J	Harvard Human Rights Journal
Harv Int'l L J	Harvard International Law Journal
Hofstra L Rev	Hofstra Law Review
HRC	Human Rights Committee
HRLJ	Human Rights Law Journal
HRQ	Human Rights Quarterly
HRW	Human Rights Watch
IAComHR	Inter-American Commission of Human Rights
IACtHR	Inter-American Court of Human Rights
IAEA	International Atomic Energy Agency
IASC	Inter-Agency Standing Committee
ICAO	International Civil Aviation Organization
ICCPR	International Covenant on Civil and Political Rights
ICEM	Intergovernmental Committee for European Migration
ICERD	International Convention on the Elimination of All Forms of Racial Discrimination
ICESCR	International Covenant on Economic, Social and Cultural Rights
ICHRP	International Council on Human Rights Policy
ICJ	International Court of Justice
ICLQ	International & Comparative Law Quarterly
ICRC	International Committee of the Red Cross
ICRMW	International Convention on the Protection of the Rights of All Migrant Workers and Members of Their Families
ICRPD	International Convention on the Rights of Persons with Disabilities
IDC	International Detention Coalition
IDF	Israel Defence Forces
IFAD	International Fund for Agricultural Development
IGAD	Intergovernmental Authority on Development
IGAD-RCP	Intergovernmental Authority on Development – Regional Consultative Process on Migration
IHRDA	Institute for Human Rights and Development in Africa
IHRR	International Human Rights Reports
IJCLLIR	International Journal of Comparative Labour Law and Industrial Relations
IJHR	International Journal of Human Rights
IJMS	International Journal on Multicultural Societies
IJRL	International Journal of Refugee Law
ILA	International Law Association

ILC	International Law Commission
ILC session	International Labour Conference session
Illinois L Rev	Illinois Law Review
ILM	International Legal Materials
ILO	International Labour Organization
Im&NatL Rev	Immigration and Nationality Law Review
IMF	International Monetary Fund
IMI	International Migration Institute
IML	International Migration Law
IMO	International Maritime Organization
Int'l J Soc L	International Journal of the Sociology of Law
Int'l Lab Rev	International Labour Review
Int'l Rev Soc Hist	International Review of Social History
Int'l Soc Sci J	International Social Science Journal
Int'l J Child Rts	The International Journal of Children's Rights
IOE	International Organization of Employers
IOM	International Organization for Migration
IOM MRS	International Organization for Migration's Migration Research Series
Iran-USCTR	Iran-United States Claims Tribunal
IRO	International Refugee Organization
Israel L Review	Israel Law Review
Israel Yrbk Hum Rts	Israel Yearbook on Human Rights
ISMU	Iniziative e Studi sulla Multietnicità
J Dev Stud	Journal of Development Studies
J Europ Integration	Journal of European Integration
J Hist Int'l L	Journal of the History of International Law
J Hist Philosophy	Journal of the History of Philosophy
J Imp & Commonwealth Hist	The Journal of Imperial and Commonwealth History
JL and Society	Journal of Law and Society
J Legal Anal	Journal of Legal Analysis
JCL	Journal of Criminal Law
JDI	Journal du droit international
JEPP	Journal of European Public Policy
JHRE	Journal of Human Rights and the Environment
JICJ	Journal of International Criminal Justice
JMHS	Journal on Migration and Human Security
JPL	Journal of Public Law
JRS	Journal of Refugee Studies
LAS	League of Arab States
LCP	Law and Contemporary Problems
LHR	Law and History Review
LJIL	Leiden Journal of International Law
LN	League of Nations
LNOJ	League of Nations Official Journal
LNTS	League of Nations Treaty Series

Loyola Int'l & Comp L Rev	Loyola of Los Angeles International and Comparative Law Review
LQR	Law Quarterly Review
MADE Network	Migration and Development Civil Society Network
Max Planck UNYB	Max Planck Yearbook of United Nations Law
Mcgill LJ	McGill Law Journal
Melb J Int'l L	Melbourne Journal of International Law
Melb UL Rev	Melbourne University Law Review
MERCOSUR	Mercado Común del Sur (Southern Common Market)
Mich J Int'l L	Michigan Journal of International Law
Mich L Rev	Michigan Law Review
Michigan YB Int'l Leg Studies	Michigan Yearbook of International Legal Studies
MICIC	Migrants in Countries in Crisis
MIDCAS	Migration Dialogue for Central African States
MIDCOM	Migration Dialogue from the Common Market for Eastern and Southern Africa Member States
MIDSA	Migration Dialogue for Southern Africa
MIDWA	Migration Dialogue for Western Africa
Minn L Rev	Minnesota Law Review
Mode 4	GATS Annex 4 on the Movement of Natural Persons Supplying Services
MTM	Mediterranean Transit Migration Dialogue
MRS	See IOM MRS
NAFTA	North American Free Trade Agreement
Nord J Int'l L	Nordic Journal of International Law
NORDIC	Nordic Common Labour Market
NQHR	Netherlands Quarterly of Human Rights
Neth Yearbook Int'l L	Netherlands Yearbook of International Law
NYL Forum	New York Law Forum
NYL Sch L Rev	New York Law School Law Review
NYU	New York University
NYUJ Int'l Law & Pol	New York University Journal of International Law and Politics
NYU Rev L & Soc Change	New York University Review of law
NZL Rev	New Zealand Law Review
OAS	Organization of American States
OASGA	Organization of American States General Assembly
OAU	Organization of African Unity
OAU Convention	Convention Governing the Specific Aspects of Refugee Problem in Africa
OCHA	United Nations Office for the Coordination of Humanitarian Affairs
ODI	Overseas Development Institute
OECD	Organisation for Economic Co-operation and Development
OECS	Organisation of Eastern Caribbean States

OHCHR	Office of the High Commissioner for Human Rights
OSCE	Organization for Security and Co-operation in Europe
OUP	Oxford University Press
Oxford J Legal Stud	Oxford Journal of Legal Studies
PCIJ	Permanent Court of International Justice
Penn St Int'l L	Penn State International Law Review
Perm Ct Arb	Permanent Court of Arbitration
Philip LJ	Philippine Law Journal
PIDC	Pacific Immigration Directors' Conference
PIF	Pacific Island Forum
Pol Theory	Political Theory
PTA	Preferential Trade Agreement
RADDH	Rencontre africaine pour la défense des droits de l'homme
RBDI	Revue belge de droit international
RCADI	Recueil des cours de l'Académie de droit international
RCM	Regional Conference on Migration
Rev Int'l Stud	Review of International Studies
RGDIP	Revue générale de droit international public
RIAA	Reports of International Arbitral Awards
RQDI	Revue québécoise de droit international
RSCAS	Robert Schuman Centre for Advanced Studies
RSDIE	Revue suisse de droit international et européen
RSO	Regional Support Office
RSQ	Refugee Survey Quarterly
RTDH	Revue trimestrielle des droits de l'homme
SAARC	South Asian Association for Regional Cooperation
SACM	South America Conference on Migration
SADC	Southern Africa Development Community
SAR Convention	International Convention on Maritime Search and Rescue
Sc St L	Scandinavian Studies in Law
SDGs	Sustainable Development Goals
S Ill ULJ	Southern Illinois University Law Journal
Soc Res	Social Research
SOLAS Convention	International Convention for the Safety of Life at Sea
Stud Transnat'l Legal Pol'y	Studies in Transnational Legal Policy
Suffolk Transnat'l L Rev	Suffolk Transnational Law Review
SWP	Stiftung Wissenschaft und Politik
Syracuse J Int'l L &Com	Syracuse Journal of International Law and Commerce
Syd LR	Sydney Law Review
Tex Int'l LJ	Texas International Law Journal
Third Geneva Convention	Geneva Convention Relative to the Treatment of Prisoners of War
Tul L Rev	Tulane Law Review

U Pa L Rev	University of Pennsylvania Law Review
UEMOA	Union Economique et Monétaire Ouest Africaine
UCLA L Rev	UCLA Law Review
UDHR	Universal Declaration of Human Rights
UM-ICVA	University of Michigan/International Council of Voluntary Agencies
UK	United Kingdom
UKSLR	UK Law Student Review
UN	United Nations
UNAIDS	Joint United Nations on HIV/AIDS
UNASUR	Pacific Alliance South American Union of Nations
UNCTAD	United Nations Conference on Trade and Development
UNDESA	United Nations Department of Economic and Social Affairs
UNDP	United Nations Development Programme
UNEP	United Nations Environment Programme
UNESCAP	United Nations Economic and Social Commission for Asia and the Pacific
UNESCO	United Nations Educational, Scientific and Cultural Organization
UNFCCC	United Nations Framework Convention on Climate Change
UNFPA	United Nations Population Fund
UNICEF	United Nations International Children's Emergency Fund
UNIDO	United Nations Industrial Development Organization
UNISDR	United Nations Office for Disaster Risk Reduction
UNITAR	United Nations Institute for Training and Research
UNGA	United Nations General Assembly
UNHCR	United Nations High Commissioner for Refugees
UNODC	United Nations Office on Drugs and Crime
UNRWA	United Nations Relief and Works Agency for Palestine Refugees in the Near East
UNSC	United Nations Security Council
UNSCEB	United Nations System Chief Executives Board for Coordination
UNSW	University of New South Wales
UNTS	United Nations Treaty Series
UNU	United Nations University
UNU-CRIS	United Nations University–Institute on Comparative Regional Integration Studies
UNU-WIDER	United Nations University–World Institute for Development Economics Research
UN Women	United Nations Entity for Gender Equality and the Empowerment of Women
UNWTO	United Nations World Tourism Organization
US	United States
USSR	Union of the Soviet Socialist Republics
USUN	United States Mission to the United Nations

Va J Int'l L	Virginia Journal of International Law
Vand J Transnat'l L	Vanderbilt Journal of Transnational Law
VCLT	Vienna Convention on the Law of the Treaties
WAEMU	West African Economic and Monetary Union
W Eur Pol	West European Politics
WEF GFCM	World Economic Forum Global Future Council on Migration
WFP	World Food Programme
WHO	World Health Organization
Willamette J Int'l L and Dis Res	Willamette Journal of International Law and Dispute Resolution
Windsor YB Access Just	Windsor Yearbook of Access to Justice
WIPO	World Intellectual Property Organization
Wis Int'l L J	Wisconsin International Law Journal
Wm & Mary L Rev	William and Mary Law Review
Wm Mitchell L Rev	William Mitchell Law Review
WMO	World Meteorological Organization
WTO	World Trade Organization
Yale J Int'l L	Yale Journal of International Law
YBILC	Yearbook of the International Law Commission
ZaöRV	Zeitschrift für ausländisches und öffentliches Recht und Völkerrecht

Introduction

Mass hysteria has taken over migration. Migration is everywhere in the media, be it in newspapers, television, radio, or social media. It dominates headlines to such an extent that no one today can escape daily reports on migration. The pervasiveness of migration is not only dictated by the magnitude of information the public is confronted with in quantitative terms. It is also nurtured by the type of information conveyed and the manner in which it is portrayed by mass media. Migration is often depicted in alarming and emotional terms as an unstoppable massive influx threatening national values, identity, and security.[1] As a result of this effervescence, 'the worldwide fear of terror has overlapped and intertwined with the fear of illegal migration. The prosperous West is under siege, this popular refrain tells us; the hordes are ascending.'[2]

Beyond media coverage, this narrative has been compounded by the hijacking of migration by politicians. In an era where globalization has destabilized the economic, social, cultural, and political foundations of nation-states, migrants have appeared as the ideal scapegoat for the failures of national politics. Redirecting the attention and the fault to the 'other', the foreigner, has provided politicians with a formidable avenue to conceal their own deficiencies and galvanize their nationals in some exclusionary form of social cohesion. This politicization of migration has not only been fuelled by the rise of populism, but also tends more broadly to permeate different spheres of politics through a growing racialization of the political

---

[1] Among the vast literature on the representation of migration and migrants, see for instance the special issue guest edited by M Krzyzanowski, A Triandafyllidou, and R Wodak, 'The Mediatization and the Politicization of the "Refugee Crisis" in Europe' (2018) 16(1–2) Journal of Immigrant & Refugee Studies; VM Esses, LK Hamilton, and D Gaucher, 'The Global Refugee Crisis: Empirical Evidence and Policy Implications for Improving Public Attitudes and Facilitating Refugee Resettlement' (2017) 11(1), Social Issues and Policy Review 78–123; L Nguyen and K McCallum, 'Drowning in our Own Home: A Metaphor-Led Discourse Analysis of Australian News Media Reporting on Maritime Asylum Seekers' (2016) 2(2) Communication Research and Practice 159–176; W Allen and S Blinder, *Migration in the News: Portrayals of Immigrants, Migrants, Asylum Seekers and Refugees in National British Newspapers, 2010–2012* (University of Oxford, Centre on Migration, Policy and Society 2013); JD Cisneros, 'Contaminated Communities: The Metaphor of "Immigrant as Pollutant" in Media Representations of Immigration' (2008) 11(4) Rhetoric and Public Affairs 569–601; A Buonfino, 'Between Unity and Plurality: The Politicization and Securitization of the Discourse of Immigration in Europe' (2004) 26(1) New Political Science 23–49.

[2] C Dauvergne, 'Sovereignty, Migration and the Rule of Law in Global Times' (2004) 67(4) The Modern Law Review 588, 588.

discourse. As a result, migration has become today an intrinsic component of any political parties' agenda for electioneering.

The moral panic spurred by extensive media coverage and the politicization of migration lacks rationality. Emotions and perceptions have taken over facts and reality. Everyone has an opinion about migration, but very few really know what migration actually is. This disjuncture between reality and representation is well illustrated by the perception Europeans have of migration. In 2018, 38 per cent of Europeans considered immigration to constitute the most important challenge over and above terrorism for the European Union (EU) in 21 EU Member States.[3] A majority of 52 per cent of respondents reported having negative feelings about migration,[4] even though Europeans overestimate the proportion of immigrants in their countries: 'in 19 of the 28 Member States the estimated proportion of the population who are immigrants is at least twice the size of the actual proportion of immigration'.[5] This gap between perception and reality calls for demystifying migration as the evil of the century.

Demystifying Migration: Facts and Figures

Much is to be learnt from data and statistics to inform and objectivize the debate. Three main lessons can be drawn therefrom with respect to the magnitude of the movement of persons across borders, the types and patterns of migration, and the contribution of migrants to host countries and societies.

First, while movements of persons across borders have increased and will likely continue to do so in an ever-more globalized world, this phenomenon is not a crisis of numbers. Migrants only accounted for 3.4 per cent of the world's population in 2017, with some 258 million migrants globally.[6] Although the relative number of migrants has increased since 1990 when they represented 2.9 per cent of the world's population, an increase of 0.5 per cent is still very far from representing the invasion of the Global North so frequently depicted by mass media and politicians. In fact, '[s]ince 2000, 60 per cent of the increase of the total number of international migrants reflected movements between countries located in the South'.[7]

---

[3] European Commission, *Standard Eurobarometer 89. First Results: Public Opinion in the European Union* (European Union 2018) 6 concerning extra-EU migration, that is, migration of non-EU nationals. According to the Eurobarometer, terrorism ranked only at the second position, being mentioned by 29 per cent of Europeans surveyed: ibid. The survey was conducted in March 2018 in 34 countries and territories, including the 28 EU Member States and five candidate countries.

[4] European Commission, *Standard Eurobarometer 89. Report: The Views of Europeans on the European Union's Priorities* (European Union 2018) 37.

[5] European Commission, *Special Eurobarometer 469. Report: Integration of Immigrants in the European Union* (European Union 2018) 20. The report notes that '[i]n some countries, the ratio is much higher: in Romania, Bulgaria and Poland, the estimated proportion of immigrants is over eight times greater than the actual figure, and in Slovakia it is nearly 14 times the actual figure': ibid 21.

[6] United Nations Department of Economic and Social Affairs (UNDESA), Population Division, *International Migration Report 2017* (United Nations 2017) ST/ESA/SER.A/403, 1 and 2.

[7] ibid 1.

South-South migration is thus more important than South-North migration, the former having even surpassed the pace of increase of the latter.[8] In the period 2010–2017, the average annual rate of migrants in the North declined to 1.6 per cent whereas, in the South, it increased to 3.2 per cent.[9] In 2017, Europe was hosting 30.23 per cent of the worldwide share of migrants, a majority of whom came from developed countries,[10] while 22.39 per cent were in North America and 3.26 per cent in Oceania.[11] The region with the highest share of migrants was Asia with some 79.6 million migrants, accounting for 30.89 per cent of the global migrant stock.[12] This global picture accordingly unveils an unjustified bias on—and incorrect account of—the situation of Western countries.

Second, in contrast to the disproportionate focus on irregular migration and the so-called refugee crisis by the media and politicians, the overwhelming majority of migrants around the world are travelling in a safe and regular manner. Albeit impossible to quantify with accuracy, irregular migrants do not make up the greatest share of migrants worldwide. Most estimates suggest that 10–15 per cent are in an irregular situation,[13] while the highest projections do not go above some 22.5 per cent in 2017.[14] Similarly, the prevailing rhetoric of the refugee crisis in the Global North is far from representing the reality and the actual issues at stake. According to UN statistics, by the end of 2016, 82.5 per cent of the world's refugees and asylum seekers were hosted in the Global South.[15] Furthermore, the total number of refugees and asylum seekers in the world accounted for 25.9 million, representing 10.1 per cent of all international migrants.[16]

If migrant workers represent the greatest share—around two-thirds—of international migrants globally,[17] the enduring myth of the male migrant from a developing country, leaving his family behind in pursuit of a better life, does not reflect reality. Males are far from representing the global migrant population. In

---

[8] ibid 1–2.   [9] ibid 1.

[10] ibid 2, Table I.2, according to which 43.3 million migrants in Europe were from developed regions, while 34.6 million were from developing regions. In fact, Europe is the only region where migrants from developed regions outnumbered migrants from developing regions.

[11] ibid 1, Table I.1, with 77.9 million migrants in Europe, 57.7 million in North America, and 8.4 million in Oceania.

[12] ibid.

[13] IOM, *World Migration Report 2010. The Future of Migration: Building Capacities for Change* (IOM 2010) 29. Regional estimates in Europe similarly suggest that: 'They were 1.9 to 3.8 million irregular migrants in the EU in 2008—7 to 13 per cent of the foreign-born population.' As further noted by IOM, 'In 2017, the total number of irregular border-crossings into the EU dropped to its lowest in four years. The annual 204,719 marked a 60 per cent decrease compared to the 511,047 apprehensions of 2016.' See: IOM, *Global Migration Indicators 2018* (IOM 2018) 30.

[14] IOM, *Global Migration Indicators 2018* (n 13). See also: United Nations Development Programme (UNDP), *Human Development Report 2009. Overcoming Barriers: Human Mobility and Development* (Palgrave Macmillan 2009) 2.

[15] UNDESA, *International Migration Report 2017: Highlights* (United Nations 2017) ST/ESA/SER.A/404, 7.

[16] ibid.

[17] International Labour Organization (ILO), *ILO Global Estimates on Migrant Workers, Results and Methodology* (ILO 2015) 5. A share of these migrant workers may however be refugees as statistical categories are overlapping. For the definition of migrant workers used by ILO for statistical purposes, see ibid 28.

2017, women accounted for 48.4 per cent of the international migrant stock,[18] with higher percentages in Europe, North America, and Oceania.[19] While this 'feminization of migration' is not a recent development in quantitative terms,[20] women are today not only migrating as part of a household but also on their own, playing an increasingly important role as remittance senders.[21]

Third, the current narrative spread by mass media and political discourses obstructs the important contributions made by migrants to host societies and countries of origin. Contrary to what is often claimed, evidence highlights that the overall economic contributions of migrants to host and origin countries are positive, rather than negative. Among many other similar accounts, a 2016 study suggested that, in advanced economies, 'a 1 percentage point increase in the share of migrants in the adult population […] can raise GDP per capita by up to 2 percent' over the long run.[22] Migrants indeed raise labour productivity, often filling gaps in the labour market, especially in countries with ageing population.[23] They work in sectors where both low-skilled and highly skilled workers are in short supply, such as in farms, nursing, highly-skilled manufacturing, and technology.[24] Migrants also contribute to the economies of host countries by paying taxes and spending some 85 per cent of their salaries therein.[25] The remaining 15 per cent of their earnings is sent

---

[18] UNDESA, Population Division, *International Migration Report 2017* (n 6) 9.

[19] ibid. The percentage of women migrants in these regions was 52 per cent in Europe, 51.5 per cent in North America, and 51 per cent in Oceania.

[20] UNDESA accounts for a decrease in the percentage of women migrants in developing regions from 1990 to 2017 (from 47 to 43.9 per cent) and for only a slight increase in the North over the same period (from 51.1 to 51.8 per cent): ibid 9. On the relativity of the feminization of migration in quantitative terms, see for instance D Paiewonsky, 'The Feminization of International Labour Migration' (2009) United Nations International Research and Training Institute for the Advancement of Women, Gender, Migration and Development Series, Working Paper 1, 4; KM Donato and D Gabaccia, 'Global Feminization of Migration: Past, Present, and Future' (1 June 2016) Migration Policy Institute, available at <https://www.migrationpolicy.org/article/global-feminization-migration-past-present-and-future> accessed 12 October 2018.

[21] See United Nations General Assembly (UNGA), 'Making Migration Work for All, Report of the Secretary-General' (12 December 2017) UN Doc A/72/643, para 28; Paiewonsky, 'The Feminization of International Labour Migration' (n 20) 4.

[22] F Jaumotte, K Koloskova, and SC Saxena, *Impact of Migration on Income Levels on Advanced Economies*, (Spillover Task Force / International Monetary Fund 2016) 2.

[23] See, for instance, ILO, Organisation for Economic Co-operation and Development (OECD), and World Bank Group, 'The Contribution of Labour Mobility to Economic Growth' (2015) Joint paper for the 3rd meeting of G20 Employment Working Group, Cappadocia, Turkey, 23–25 July 2015; T Sobotka, V Skirbekk, and D Philipov, 'Economic Recession and Fertility in the Developed World' (2011) 37(2) Population and Development Review 267–306.

[24] Among the abundant literature on migrant workers filling gaps in labour markets, see for instance WR Kerr, 'US High-Skilled Immigration, Innovation and Entrepreneurship: Empirical Approaches and Evidence' (2014) WIPO Economics and Statistics Series, Economic Research Working Paper No 16; B Rijks, *Mobility of Health Professionals to, from and within the European Union* (IOM 2014); M Zavodny and T Jocaby, *Filling the Gap: Less-Skilled Immigration in a Changing Economy* (Immigration Works USA 2013); DM West, 'The Paradox of Worker Shortages at a Time of High National Unemployment' (2013) Governance Studies at Brookings; Information Technology Industry Council, Partnership for a New American Economy, and US Chamber of Commerce, 'Help Wanted: The Role of Foreign Workers in the Innovation Economy' (2012) Report; Y Takeno, 'Facilitating the Transition of Asian Nurses to Work in Australia' (2010) 18(2) Journal of Nursing Management, 215–24.

[25] UNGA, 'Making Migration Work for All, Report of the Secretary-General' (n 21) para 20.

as remittances to their country of origin. These remittances amounted to some 613 billion US dollars globally in 2017, among which 466 billion was sent to low- and middle-income countries, representing more than three times the total of development assistance.[26]

While statistics and facts speak for themselves, the current misperceptions and manipulations say more about the vacuity of the mass media and the mediocrity of the politics than they do about the reality of migration. Migration has been polarized and instrumentalized, before being analysed and understood. Although migration is not a problem to be solved, it constitutes both a challenge and an opportunity for migrants themselves as well as for their countries of origin and destination. As a permanent and worldwide phenomenon, it calls for a sound understanding and a global vision. There is more than ever a crucial need for developing a pedagogy of migration through evidence-based knowledge. Lawyers should play a role in this endeavour to dispel the complexity of international law and to promote a more rational, balanced, and comprehensive narrative of migration.

Dispelling the Complexity of International Law and Migration

The role of international law in the field of migration is complex and frequently misunderstood. This complexity is inherent in the dual nature of migration as a question of both domestic and international concern. On the one hand, any discussion about migration inexorably starts by acknowledging the centrality of territorial sovereignty and the correlative right of states to control and regulate the movement of persons across their borders. While no other basic concept has raised as much controversy as the one of territorial sovereignty, its traditional function is to 'mark a link between a particular people and a particular territory, so that within that area that people may exercise through the medium of the state its jurisdiction while being distinguished from other peoples exercising jurisdiction over other areas'.[27] This reflects the basic axiom of classical international law built on nation-states as the paradigmatic units of the Westphalian order.

On the other hand, the movement of persons across borders is international in essence: it presupposes a triangular relationship between a migrant, a state of origin, and a state of destination. Migration is, thus, a matter of common interest that cannot be managed on a purely unilateral basis. As notably acknowledged by the New York Declaration for Refugees and Migrants, the movements of persons across borders 'are global phenomena that call for global approaches and global solutions. No one State can manage such movements on its own.'[28] As further underlined by states in the Global Compact for Migration, 'it is crucial that the challenges and

---

[26] World Bank, 'Migration and Remittances: Recent Developments and Outlook, Transit Migration' (2018) Migration and Development Brief 29, 3.

[27] MN Shaw, 'Territory in International Law' (1982) XIII NYIL 61, 73.

[28] UNGA Res 71/1 (19 September 2016) UN Doc A/RES/71/1, para 7.

opportunities of international migration unite us, rather than divide us'.[29] Because migration is a shared responsibility of all states, 'a comprehensive approach is needed to optimize the overall benefits of migration, while addressing risks and challenges for individuals and communities in countries of origin, transit and destination'.[30]

From this international perspective, no one today can contest that territorial sovereignty is relative and not absolute. This evolution is not peculiar to migration; it mirrors a broader transformation of the international legal order which has evolved from a law of coexistence into a law of interdependence. As a result of the systemic evolution of international law, territorial sovereignty is both a competence and a responsibility. When transposed in this particular field, the competence of states to regulate migration at the domestic level shall be exercised in due accordance with the binding rules of international law.

In recognition thereof, the movement of persons across borders has been internationalized by a wide array of legal norms that are firmly anchored in the sources of public international law. Even the most sceptical positivists cannot fail to acknowledge the significant body of international rules that govern migration and constrain states' sovereignty. This development has however been achieved in a piecemeal fashion over a long process of incremental consolidation. As a result, the current international legal framework governing migration consists of an eclectic set of superimposed norms that are scattered throughout a vast number of overlapping fields (such as human rights law, trade law, humanitarian law, labour law, refugee law, maritime law, air law, consular law, criminal law, etc). As described by Richard Lillich, the overall framework resembles 'a giant unassembled juridical jigsaw puzzle', for which 'the number of pieces is uncertain and the grand design is still emerging'.[31] The great diversity of applicable rules and their dispersion across a broad range of professional silos clearly undermine both the understanding and implementation of international law. This represents the most important challenge for scholars and practitioners who are willing to understand and use international law in this area.

Against such a normative background, the broad variety of legal rules calls for a principled and global approach to conceptualize migration as a discrete field of international law with a view to promoting a comprehensive and coherent frame of analysis. As Martti Koskenniemi recalls, 'the emergence of new "branches" of the law ... is a feature of the social complexity of a globalizing world. If lawyers feel unable to deal with this complexity, this is not a reflection of problems in their "toolbox" but in their imagination about how to use it.'[32] Although the fragmentation of

---

[29] Global Compact for Safe, Orderly and Regular Migration (13 July 2018) para 9 available at https://refugeesmigrants.un.org/sites/default/files/180713_agreed_outcome_global_compact_for_migration.pdf accessed 12 October 2018.

[30] ibid para 11.

[31] R Lillich, *The Human Rights of Aliens in Contemporary International Law* (Manchester University Press 1984) 122.

[32] International Law Commission, 'Fragmentation of International Law: Difficulties Arising from the Diversification and Expansion of International Law. Report of the Study Group of the International Law Commission' (13 April 2006) UN Doc A/CN.4/L.682, 115.

international legal rules is far from being specific to this particular field, the overall framework governing migration still requires some imagination as the great diversity of applicable rules and their overlapping with other areas of international law may disturb or disconcert some. This heterogeneity is inevitable and intrinsic: it reflects the multifaceted dimensions of migration and its cross-cutting character which transcends existing silos of international law.

International Migration Law as a Global Framework of Analysis

Conceptualizing the great variety of applicable rules and principles within the generic label of 'international migration law' is critical to assembling the dispersed pieces of this jigsaw puzzle. This exercise of reconstruction follows the threefold purpose of providing a framework of analysis which is comprehensive, coherent, and contextual.

First, comprehensiveness is inherently achieved through the design of this discrete field of international law, since its primary rationale is to gather the fairly substantial, albeit eclectic, applicable legal norms. International migration law thus provides the global picture encompassing the broad variety of rules regulating the movement of persons across borders.

Second, the blend of these rules within the same normative frame of reference promotes a more coherent approach for the purpose of articulating the various legal norms among themselves. While applicable rules are located at the intersection of several branches of international law, they remain closely interconnected. None of them can be assessed in isolation. They make sense only when understood in relation to one another.

Third, and perhaps more fundamentally, bringing these rules together under the auspices of international migration law paves the way for their contextualized application in order to better take into account the specificities of migration. In sum, the main virtue of international migration law is a methodological—if not pedagogical—one: it encourages a more systemic and cogent approach in apprehending migration as a topic of analysis on its own.

With this aim in mind, international migration law may be defined as the set of international rules and principles governing the movement of persons between states and the legal status of migrants within host countries. It is meant to gather all relevant international legal norms that apply to individuals who are leaving their own country, entering another one, and/or staying therein. This working definition encompasses the whole continuum of migration: departure from the country of origin, entry into a foreign country and stay therein, as well as return into one's own country. It accordingly embraces emigration and immigration as the two sides of the migration cycle. Moreover, while the specific legal regimes may vary from one group of persons to another, the scope of international migration law is deliberately inclusive. It covers all migrants irrespective of their motivations and grounds for admission (such as labour, family reunification, asylum, study), their legal status (documented or not), and the duration of their stay (transit, temporary stay, long-term residence).

Following this stance, an inclusive and factual understanding of the term 'migrant' better reflects the reach of international law as well as its unity and diversity to regulate the movement of persons across borders. By definition, a migrant is a person who has crossed an international border to live in a state other than that of his or her nationality. The United Nations Department of Economic and Social Affairs observes in this sense that: 'while there is no formal legal definition of an international migrant, most experts agree that an international migrant is someone who changes his or her country of usual residence, irrespective of the reason for migration or legal status'.[33] This definition has been notably endorsed by the International Organization for Migration (IOM) in the following terms:

IOM defines a migrant as any person who is moving or has moved across an international border or within a State away from his/her habitual place of residence, regardless of (1) the person's legal status; (2) whether the movement is voluntary or involuntary; (3) what the causes for the movement are; or (4) what the length of the stay is.[34]

Instead of establishing another subfield of specialization, international migration law provides a holistic frame of analysis which places migrants at its centre. When assessed as a whole, international law—as notably enshrined in human rights treaties—provides the common legal framework that applies to all migrants. These general legal norms are further supplemented by more specialized conventional regimes focusing on specific categories of persons (such as migrant workers, refugees, smuggled migrants, and victims of human trafficking).

Migration studies have long suffered from a compartmentalized approach based on the simplistic and Manichean opposition between forced and voluntary migration alongside the priorities and policies of destination states. In practice however, the distinction between refugees and migrant workers is a legal fiction that fails to capture the complex reality of migration. Research in sociology, anthropology, and political science has unveiled the inadequacy of this binary categorization given that the movement of persons across borders is triggered by a combination of many different causes, aspirations, motivations, and factors that overlap and are not mutually exclusive.[35]

---

[33] See <https://refugeesmigrants.un.org/definitions> accessed 12 October 2018.

[34] IOM, 'Key Migration Terms' (IOM) <https://www.iom.int/key-migration-terms> accessed 12 October 2018. One should notice that IOM includes internally displaced persons within this definition to reflect its broad mandate that encompasses both international migration and internal displacement. Although this approach is understandable from the angle of the organization and its mandate, to include internally displaced persons within the definition of migrants goes against the ordinary meaning of the very term 'migrant'. It also fails to reflect the legal specificities that apply to the movement of persons across borders. While the causes of international migration and internal displacement largely coincide in practice, internally displaced persons are governed by a distinct legal regime that is addressed to the state of origin. By contrast, migration involves, by definition, at least two states and this represents its defining feature under international law.

[35] Among a vast literature, see for instance H Crawley and D Skleparis, 'Refugees, Migrants, Neither, Both: Categorical Fetishism and the Politics of Bounding in Europe's "Migration Crisis"' (2018) 44(1) Journal of Ethnic and Migration Studies 48–64; H Crawley and others, 'Destination Europe? Understanding the Dynamics and Drivers of Mediterranean Migration in 2015' (2016) Unravelling the Mediterranean Migration Crisis (MEDMIG) Final Report; SM Holmes and H Castaneda, 'Representing the "European Refugee Crisis" in Germany and Beyond: Deservingness and

From a legal perspective, the distinction between refugees and migrant workers has also represented an enduring misunderstanding about the reach of international law based on the wrong premise that the latter's fate is left to states' discretion contrary to the former who are entitled to international protection. While this misperception has no legal rationale, focusing too much on the specific categories of migrants detracts attention from their wider normative context. This does not mean that categories as legal constructions of states shall be disregarded by international lawyers. Instead, they must be seen as part and parcel of a much broader and more nuanced legal framework.

The role of international law cannot be fully appraised without a holistic perspective which takes into account the fluidity of legal categories and encapsulates them within their broader normative ecosystem. From this angle, international migration law is an umbrella term which comprises both general and specific legal norms that apply to the movement of persons across borders. This characteristic is not unique to migration but inherent in international law:

All legal systems are composed of rules and principles with greater and lesser generality and speciality in regard to their subject-matter and sphere of applicability. Sometimes they will point in different direction and if they do, it is the task of legal reasoning to establish meaningful relationships between them so as to determine whether they could be applied in a mutually supportive way or whether one rule or principle should have definite priority over the other. This is [...] called 'systemic integration'.[36]

Difference, Life and Death' (2016) 43(1) American Ethnologist 12; C Mainwaring and N Brigden, 'Beyond the Border: Clandestine Migration Journeys' (2016) 21(2) Geopolitics 243–62; K Yarris and H Castaneda, 'Special Issue Discourses of Displacement and Deservingness: Interrogating Distinctions between "Economic" and "Forced" Migration' (2015) 53(3) International Migration 64–69; K Long, 'When Refugees Stopped Being Migrants: Movement, Labour and Humanitarian Protection' (2013) 1(1) Migration Studies 4–26; O Bakewell, 'Conceptualising Displacement and Migration: Processes, Conditions and Categories' in K Koser and S Martin (eds), *The Migration–Displacement Nexus: Patterns, Processes and Policies* (Berghahn Books 2011) 14–28; A Monsutti, 'Afghan Migratory Strategies and the Three Solutions to the Refugee Problem' (2008) 27(1) RSQ 58–73; KE Cortes, 'Are Refugees Different from Economic Immigrants? Some Empirical Evidence on the Heterogeneity of Immigrant Groups in the United States' (2004) 86(2) Review of Economics and Statistics 465–80; J Hein, 'Refugees, Immigrants, and the State' (1993) 19(1) Annual Review of Sociology 43–59; A Richmond, 'Sociological Theories of International Migration: The Case of Refugees' (1988) 36(7) Current Sociology 7–25.

[36] International Law Commission, 'Fragmentation of International Law' (n 32) 114. For further discussion about the notion of systemic integration, see among a vast literature: A Rachovitsa, 'The Principle of Systemic Integration in Human Rights Law' (2017) 66(3) ICLQ 557; CI Fuentes, *Normative Plurality in International Law. A Theory in the Determination of Applicable Rules* (Springer 2016); P Merkouris, *Article 31(3)(c) VCLT and the Principle of Systemic Integration. Normative Shadows in Plato's Cave* (Brill | Nijhoff 2015); E De Wet and J Vidmar, 'Conflicts between International Paradigms: Hierarchy Versus Systemic Integration' (2013) 2(2) Global Constitutionalism 196; M Prost, *The Concept of Unity in Public International Law* (Hart Publishing, 2012); J D'Aspremont, 'The Systemic Integration of International Law by Domestic Courts: Domestic Judges as Architects of the Consistency of the International Legal Order' in A Nollkaemper and OK Fauchaud (eds) *The Practice of International and National Courts and the (De-)Fragmentation of International Law* (Hart Publishing 2012); G Orellana-Zabalza, *The Principle of Systemic Integration: Towards a Coherent International Legal Order* (Lit Verlag 2012); A Young (ed), *Regime Interaction in International Law: Facing Fragmentation* (CUP 2012); C MacLachlan, 'The Principle of Systemic Integration and Article 31(3)(c) of the Vienna Convention' (2005) 54(2) ICLQ 279; P-M Dupuy, 'L'unité de l'ordre juridique international: cours général de droit international public' (2000) 297 Collected Courses of the Hague Academy of International Law 1.

International migration law is an attempt to provide a systemic integration of the broad variety and number of rules governing the movement of persons across borders. It does not supersede the other branches of international law, nor does it constitute a so-called 'self-contained regime'. On the contrary, it is built on norms existing in different legal fields with a view to articulating them through a comprehensive approach to international law.

Similar to many other disciplines (such as environmental law or trade law), international migration law is primarily a doctrinal construction inferred from the traditional sources and actors of international law. The very expression 'international migration law' is not a new term in legal scholarship. It was first coined in 1927 by Louis Varlez.[37] He explained in his course at the Hague Academy of International Law that studying the rules of international law governing migration 'shows an extremely lively and fertile legislative activity, where it is possible, perhaps better than for any other phenomenon, to follow the life of law in constant evolution'.[38] As Varlez cogently underlined, international migration law 'is not an abstract law but a living one that constantly acts and reacts on a phenomenon that is bound to regulate'.[39]

Forty-five years later, in 1972, Richard Plender published a seminal book called *International Migration Law* which was re-edited in 1988.[40] Although this burgeoning field has been largely eclipsed by the extensive focus of scholarship on international refugee law, a significant number of edited books has been devoted to international migration law since the beginning of the 21st century.[41] Its epistemic community is growing quite rapidly, be it to map its main features under general international law[42] or to focus on more specific issues (such as the human rights of

---

[37] L Varlez, 'Les migrations internationales et leur réglementation' (1927) 20 RCADI 165, 171.
[38] ibid 343.   [39] ibid 344.
[40] R Plender, *International Migration Law* (Sijthoff 1972). Another pioneer reference book was published in 1978 by GS Goodwin-Gill, *International Law and the Movement of Persons between States* (Clarendon Press 1978).
[41] See especially in the chronological order of their publications: TA Aleinikoff and V Chetail (eds), *Migration and International Legal Norms* (TMC Asser Press 2003); R Cholewinski, R Perruchoud, and E MacDonald (eds), *International Migration Law: Developing Paradigms and Key Challenges* (TMC Asser Press 2007); V Chetail (ed) *Globalization, Migration and Human Rights: International Law Under Review* (Bruylant 2007); B Opeskin, R Perruchoud, J Redpath-Cross (eds), *Foundations of International Migration Law* (CUP 2012); V Chetail and C Bauloz (eds), *Research Handbook on International Law and Migration* (Edward Elgar Publishing 2014); R Plender (ed), *Issues in International Migration Law* (Brill 2015); GS Goodwin-Gill and P Weckel (eds), *Migration and Refugee Protection in the 21st Century: International Legal Aspects*, Hague Academy of International Law (Martinus Nijhoff 2015); V Chetail (ed), *International Law and Migration* (Edward Elgar Publishing 2016). Several collections of international migration law instruments have also been published: V Chetail (ed), *Code de droit international des migrations* (Bruylant 2008); R Plender (ed), *Basic Documents on International Migration Law* (3rd revised edn, Martinus Nijhoff 2007); R Perruchoud and K Tomolova, *Compendium of International Migration Law Instruments* (TMC Asser Press 2007).
[42] In addition to the edited volumes quoted before, see for instance C Thomas, 'Mapping Global Migration Law, or the Two Batavias' (2017) 111 AJIL Unbound 504–08; V Chetail, 'The Architecture of International Migration Law: A Deconstructivist Design of Complexity and Contradiction' (2017) 111 AJIL Unbound 18–23; V Chetail, 'Conceptualizing International Migration Law' (2017) ASIL Proc of the one hundred tenth annual meeting 201–04; PJ Spiro, 'The Possibilities of Global Migration Law' (2017) 111 AJIL Unbound 3–7; J Ramji-Nogales, 'Moving Beyond the Refugee Law Paradigm' (2017) 111 AJIL Unbound 8–12; F Mégret, 'Transnational Mobility, the International Law of Aliens, and the Origins of Global Migration Law' (2017) 111 AJIL Unbound 13–17; E Borgnas, 'An Overview

migrants,[43] irregular migration,[44] or interception at sea).[45] However, despite the unprecedented interest of the legal doctrine, international migration law is still a work in progress and it is not always recognized as a discrete field on its own.

Whether labelled or not as international migration law, a systemic and decompartmentalized approach to international law is crucial to identify the broad variety of rules governing migration and to assess their potential and limits. International migration law can be compared to a pointillist painting whose clarity is only realized from a distance. As one approaches more closely, the picture becomes a juxtaposition of coloured dots which unveil the diversity of international law. The plasticity of international law opens up new avenues for rethinking migration as a global phenomenon that calls for collective action. While positivism is inevitable to take stock of existing rules, international law can be deconstructed through various perspectives, including critical studies, legal pluralism, gender and Third World approaches.[46]

---

of the Model Convention Commentaries' (2017) 56 Colum J of Transnat'l L 238; MW Doyle, 'The Model International Mobility Convention Commentaries' (2017) 56 Colum J of Transnat'l L 219; M Panizzon and others (eds), *The Palgrave Handbook of International Labour Migration: Law and Policy Perspectives* (Springer 2016); C Thomas 'What Does the Emerging International Law of Migration Mean for Sovereignty' (2013) 14 Melb J Int'l L 392; SS Juss (ed), *The Ashgate Research Companion to Migration Law, Theory and Policy* (Routledge 2013); C Thomas, 'Convergences and Divergences in International Legal Norms on Migrant Labor Law and Development: Perspectives on Labor Regulation in Africa and the African Diaspora' (2010) 32 Comparative Labor Law & Policy Journal 405; B Opeskin, 'The Influence of International Law on the International Movement of Persons' (2009) Human Development Research paper 2009/18; J Bhabha, ' "More than their Share of Sorrows": International Migration Law and the Rights of Children' (2003) 22 Saint Louis University Public Law Review 253–74.

[43] See among many other books: E Guild, S Grant, and CA Groenendijk (eds), *Human Rights of Migrants in the 21st Century* (Routledge 2017); T Gammeltoft-Hansen and J Vedsted-Hansen (eds), *Human Rights and the Dark Side of Globalisation: Transnational Law Enforcement and Migration Control* (Routledge 2016); C Dauvergne, *The New Politics of Immigration and the End of Settler Societies* (CUP Press 2016); M Crock (ed), *Migrants and Rights* (Routledge 2016); C Costello, *The Human Rights of Migrants and Refugees in European Law* (OUP 2015); M-B Dembour, *When Humans Become Migrants: Study of the European Court of Human Rights with an Inter-American Counterpoint* (OUP 2015); R Rubio-Marin (ed), *Human Rights and Immigration* (OUP 2014); G Cornelisse, *Immigration Detention and Human Rights: Rethinking Territorial Sovereignty* (Martinus Nijhoff 2010); R Cholewinski, P de Guchteneire, and A Pécoud (eds), *Migration and Human Rights: The United Nations Convention on Migrant Workers' Rights* (CUP 2009); DS Weissbrodt, *The Human Rights of Non-Citizens* (OUP 2008); S Saroléa, *Droits de l'homme et migrations. De la protection du migrant aux droits de la personne migrante* (Bruylant 2006); C Tiburcio, *The Human Rights of Aliens under International and Comparative Law* (Martinus Nijhoff 2001).

[44] See notably AT Gallagher and F David, *The International Law of Migrant Smuggling* (CUP 2014); B Ryan and V Mitsilegas (eds), *Extraterritorial Immigration Control* (Martinus Nijhoff 2010); C Dauvergne, *Making People Illegal: What Globalization Means for Migration and Law* (CUP 2009); B Bogusz and others (eds), *Irregular Migration and Human Rights: Theoretical, European and International Perspectives* (Martinus Nijhoff 2004).

[45] See especially I Mann, *Humanity at Sea: Maritime Migration and the Foundations of International Law* (CUP 2016); F Ippolito and S Trevisanut (eds), *Migration in the Mediterranean: Mechanisms of International Cooperation* (CUP 2015); V Moreno-Lax and E Papastavridis (eds), *'Boat Refugees' and Migrants at Sea: A Comprehensive Approach: Integrating Maritime Security with Human Rights* (Brill | Nijhoff 2016).

[46] See especially J Bhabha, 'Human Mobility and the Longue Durée: The Prehistory of Global Migration Law' (2017) 111 AJIL Unbound 136; J Ramji-Nogales, 'Migration Emergencies' (2017) 68 Hastings Law Journal 609; E Tendayi Achiume, 'The Fatal Flaw in International Law for Migration' (2018) 56 Colum J of Transnat'l L 257; and S Juss and T Zartaloudis, 'Introduction: Critical Approaches

International migration law is clearly an imperfect law for a world of imperfect states. It mirrors the contradictions of our world composed of both independent and interdependent nations. Yet, despite its shortcomings, international law represents a vital source of legally binding commitments which constrain and channel states in relation to the movement of persons across borders.

Objective and Structure of the Textbook

The aim of this textbook is to clarify the role of international law in migration by providing a comprehensive and accessible overview of the main applicable legal norms. It combines two different levels of analysis. At the macro level, the textbook has been conceived to offer a didactic mapping of international migration law, by unveiling its main features and developments within the international legal system. At the micro level, it discusses and details the content of the most relevant rules as well as the articulations between themselves, be they general or specific to this field. It thus provides an immersion into the very substance of international law as applied to migration.

Against this twofold level of analysis, the textbook is structured in three parts addressing respectively: 1) the origins and foundations of international migration law, 2) the specialized treaty regimes governing the movement of persons across borders, and 3) the role of soft law in global migration governance. Each part sheds light on one particular facet of a much broader field. As choices inevitably had to be made, this overview does not pretend to be exhaustive. This textbook is nothing more than a first step in the development of a thorough account of the reach of international law in this composite and multifaceted area. Its main objective is to cut through the complexity of this field by demonstrating what current international law is, and assessing how it operates. This textbook accordingly maps the evolution and the present state of international law, by providing a didactic analysis of the various applicable legal norms and suggesting how they interact and may continue to develop in the future.

Following this systemic perspective, the book departs from the narrative of abuses and the rhetoric of crisis to highlight the normality of migration as a long-standing human phenomenon. Like many human activities, leaving one country for another is not outside the realm of international law. As observed by Aleinikoff, 'there is both more and less international law than might be supposed'.[47] There is more international law than politicians presume, but there is less international law than activists may desire. Despite the limits inherent to our current inter-state legal system, international law offers a counter narrative to unilateralism that is grounded on binding rules of law. The virtue of international law is twofold: it provides a nuanced

---

to Migration Law Special Issue: Critical Approaches to Migration Law' (2015) 22 International Journal on Minority and Group Rights 1.

[47] A Aleinikoff, 'International Legal Norms and Migration: A Report' in Aleinikoff and Chetail (eds), *Migration and International Legal Norms* (n 41) 1, 2.

and rational account of migration as a traditional topic of international concern, and it unveils a comprehensive and global vision based on the mutual interests of states and the basic rights of individuals.

In Part I, the origins and foundations of international migration law remind us that migration is and has always been framed by international law. Chapter 1 sketches the long and turbulent history of international migration law from the 16th to the 20th century. History proves to be much more refreshing and subversive than is the current narrative of migration control. The free movement of persons has long been the rule in the history of international law and was not held incompatible with territorial sovereignty for a long time. Migration control is indeed a recent invention of states which was generalized at the turn of the 20th century. Meanwhile, the notion of territorial sovereignty has been rediscovered to justify border controls, even though the former was not concomitant with the latter.

However, this late resurgence of sovereignty has not eclipsed international law. The treatment of foreigners in their host states remained a classical question of international law through the law of state responsibility for injuries committed to aliens. During the second half of the 20th century, the traditional law of aliens was then reframed by the normative expansion of human rights law which has eventually become the main source of migrants' protection. As a result of this evolution, the ethos of migration control coexists with the one of human rights as the two defining features of international migration law.

Chapter 2 focuses on the foundational principles of international migration law that are grounded on a dense and superimposed network of customary and conventional rules. This chapter thus provides the general normative framework and unveils its internal logic by governing the three constitutive components of the migration process: departure, admission, and stay of migrants. As far as the first component is concerned, departure from the country of origin is enshrined in the right to leave any country, subjected to the traditional lawful restrictions to protect national security and public order. This fundamental freedom has been acknowledged in a broad range of conventions and constitutes today an integral part of customary international law.

The absence of a symmetric right to enter another state under human rights instruments does not mean that access into the territory operates in a legal vacuum. The admission of non-nationals is primarily governed, at the conventional level, by a plethoric number of regional agreements endorsing the right to free movement in various parts of the world. The competence of states to regulate the admission of migrants is further limited by treaty law and customary law through both substantive and procedural requirements (including in particular the principle of *non-refoulement*, the prohibitions of collective expulsion and arbitrary detention, and access to consular protection). Finally, the sojourn of migrants in host countries is framed by the customary law principle of non-discrimination, prohibiting any difference of treatment that is not reasonable, objective, and proportionate. As a result of this fundamental principle, most human rights apply to all migrants irrespective of their nationality and migration status.

The general principles of international migration law are supplemented and de-tailed by more specialized treaty regimes that are analysed in Part II. The conventions adopted in this field under the auspices of the United Nations (UN) focus on specific categories of migrants, namely, refugees (Chapter 3), migrant workers (Chapter 4), and trafficked or smuggled migrants (Chapter 5). While disclosing the categorization scheme of international migration law, these UN instruments provide a more nuanced picture when they are assessed from a systemic perspective. First, none of them may be understood outside the broader normative framework of international law. They must be interpreted and applied in accordance with other general conventions that shape and inform their content alongside a complex and rich normative continuum between generality and speciality. Second, the scope and content of these specialized conventions are closely interrelated and not mutually exclusive. They overlap in a significant way to provide incremental protection. Depending on the relevant instruments, the same migrant may fit in several legal categories, either simultaneously or consecutively.

The third and last part of the textbook explores the rise of global migration governance through the proliferation of non-legally binding instruments and other related consultative processes. Though not a source of law per se, soft law has been instrumental in building confidence among states and creating a routine of inter-governmental dialogue within the UN. This evolution has culminated with the adoptions, in 2016, of the New York Declaration for Refugees and Migrants[48] and, in 2018, of the Global Compact for Safe, Orderly and Regular Migration and the Global Compact on Refugees.[49]

This renewed commitment to multilateralism opens up new perspectives for apprehending migration as a common good through a comprehensive and balanced approach among states and international organizations. Although global migration governance has reached a new turning point that was hardly imaginable a few years ago, the expanded use of non-binding instruments remains a truly ambivalent phenomenon. While acknowledging migration as a discrete field of international co-operation, soft law reflects the reluctance of states towards legally binding rules. In order to better understand the limit and potential of this trend, Chapter 6 assesses the function and the evolution of soft law in international migration law and Chapter 7 focuses on its impact on the overall architecture of global migration governance at the multilateral level.

---

[48] UNGA Res 71/1 (n 28).
[49] Global Compact for Safe, Orderly and Regular Migration (n 29); and Global Compact on Refugees (Report of the United Nations High Commissioner for Refugees: Part II, Global Compact on Refugees) (2 August 2018, reissued 13 September 2018) UN Doc A/73/12.

PART I

ORIGINS AND FOUNDATIONS OF INTERNATIONAL MIGRATION LAW

Introduction to Part I

'Whether migration is controlled by those who send, by those who go, or by those who receive, it mirrors the world as it is at the time.'

Kingsley Davis[1]

Migration is a permanent feature of history that has been framed by international law for ages. One can even assert that, from its inception, international law has had a symbiotic relationship with migration. The very term *jus gentium* designated a set of customary rules governing the legal status of aliens under the law of Ancient Rome.[2] As far back as the 16th century, this Latin expression was specifically used to refer to the Law of Nations, before Jeremy Bentham coined the term 'international law' in 1789.[3]

The origin of international migration law is inseparable from the broader history of international law and mirrors its evolution. With the rise of nation-states, the partition of the world into a vast juxtaposition of independent territorial units made migration more acute. The movement of persons across borders has become an issue of both international and domestic concern. To better capture and understand this duality, Chapter 1 revisits the long history of international law through the dialectic between the territorial sovereignty of states and the free movement of persons. These two foundational concepts raised longstanding discussions in legal scholarship and their interaction drastically evolved through the practice of states.

This ongoing tension between sovereignty and migration explains in turn the complexity and contradiction of contemporary international law. The trivialization of immigration control has contributed to obscuring the role of international legal norms to such an extent that migration is frequently confused with domestic jurisdiction. However, when approached from a distance, the current state of international law provides a much more nuanced picture. The notion of domestic jurisdiction is indeed the starting point but cannot be the last word, since its very content depends on the development of international law.[4]

---

[1] K Davis, 'The Migrations of Human Populations' (1974) 231(3) Scientific American 92, 96.

[2] DJ Bederman, *International Law in Antiquity* (CUP 2004) 85.

[3] J Bentham, *Introduction to the Principles of Morals and Legislation* (1789) chap XVII, para 1, sec XXV, fn 143.

[4] *Nationality Decrees Issued in Tunis and Morocco*, Advisory Opinion [1923] PCIJ Series B, No 4, 24.

From this angle, the movement of persons across borders is governed by an increasingly detailed range of rules that are solidly anchored in the sources of international law. Chapter 2 presents and analyses this rich and complex body of customary and conventional rules alongside the migration cycle. This exercise of reconstruction unveils the founding principles of international migration law governing, respectively, departure from the country of origin, admission into the territory of the destination state, and sojourn therein.

1

History of International Migration Law

International law has forged the key concepts at stake in migration through the enduring dialectic between the free movement of persons and the territorial sovereignty of states. This ongoing tension and the ways to articulate its two opposite poles have dramatically evolved during the history of international law. Free movement had long been the rule in the doctrine and practice of international law, while territorial sovereignty was initially conceived as an exception to this principle with a view to protecting some essential interests of the states. The hierarchical order between these two founding notions of international migration law has progressively been inverted with the result of establishing state sovereignty as the primary rule in this field.

From a chronological perspective, this process may be schematically approached through three main stages in the history of international law. Each phase highlights the prevailing ethos of its time and constitutes a main section of this chapter. Following this three-tiered periodization, the movement of persons across borders firstly emerged as a typical subject of discussion among the founding fathers of international law from the 16th century to the 18th century (section 1.1).

Secondly, the subsequent legal practice and scholarship witnessed the rise and fall of free movement during the 19th and the 20th centuries, when the prevailing *laissez faire-laissez passer* was progressively replaced by restrictive domestic legislation on immigration (section 1.2). The spread of migration control accordingly occurred quite recently in the history of humanity, at the beginning of the last century.

Thirdly and lastly, this new pattern of state practice emerged in parallel with a growing recognition of migrants' rights in their host states as a side effect of the normative expansion of human rights law throughout the 20th century and the beginning of the 21st century (section 1.3). As a result of this evolution, the pervasiveness of immigration control coexists with the one of human rights. This balancing act between migration control and migrants' rights has become a defining feature of contemporary international migration law that unveils its complexities and contradictions.

1.1 The Movement of Persons in the Doctrine of the Law of Nations (16th Century to 18th Century)

From the 16th to the 18th century, the early doctrine of the Law of Nations played a critical role in conceptualizing the fabric of public international law, its foundations, and basic notions. During this precursory period, the movement of persons across borders was at the heart of the first discussions about the Law of Nations.[1] In schematic terms, this typical issue of international law was understood by early scholars according to three main schools.

The free movement of persons was first acknowledged by Vitoria and Grotius as a rule of international law through the right of communication between peoples. Following this stance, sovereignty was held compatible with hospitality. By contrast, subsequent scholars (such as Pufendorf and Wolff) insisted on state discretion to refuse admission of aliens as a consequence of its territorial sovereignty. Hospitality accordingly became charity. Yet, between these two different poles—hospitality versus sovereignty—Vattel later represented a middle ground according to which the sovereign power of the state to decide upon the admission of foreigners was counterbalanced by a qualified freedom of entry based on the right of necessity.

1.1.1 The right of communication between peoples by Vitoria and Grotius

The free movement of persons across borders has a long pedigree in the history of international law. It was first acknowledged and conceptualized by Vitoria through the right of communication, before Grotius reaffirmed it as a key principle of international law deriving from the law of hospitality.

Vitoria and the right of communication

Francisco de Vitoria (1480–1546)—who is frequently portrayed as 'the founder of the modern *Law of Nations*'[2]—played an influential role in establishing the free

---

[1] This section is partially based on V Chetail, 'Sovereignty and Migration in the Doctrine of the Law of Nations: An Intellectual History of Hospitality from Vitoria to Vattel' (2016) 27(4) EJIL 901. See also on this topic: G Baker, 'Right of Entry or Right of Refusal? Hospitality in the Law of Nature and Nations' (2011) 37 Rev Intl Stud 1423; G Cavallar, 'Immigration and Sovereignty: Normative Approaches in the History of International Legal Theory (Pufendorf–Vattel–Bluntschli–Verdross)' (2006) 11 ARIEL 3; V Chetail, 'Migration, droits de l'homme et souveraineté: Le droit international dans tous ses états' in V Chetail (ed), *Mondialisation, migration et droits de l'homme: Le droit international en question/Globalisation, Migration and Human Rights: International Law under Review* (Bruylant 2007) 23; G Cavallar, *The Rights of Strangers: Theories of International Hospitality, the Global Community, and Political Justice since Vitoria* (Ashgate/Aldershot 2002); JAR Nafziger, 'The General Admission of Aliens under International Law' (1983) 77(4) AJIL 804, 810.

[2] JB Scott, *The Spanish Origins of International Law: Francisco de Vitoria and his Law of Nations* (OUP 1934) 68. See also: J Barthélemy, 'François de Vitoria' in *Les fondateurs du droit international* (first published 1904, Edition Panthéon-Assas 2014) 39–60; P Zapatero, 'Legal Imagination in Vitoria: The Power of Ideas' (2009) 11 J Hist Intl L 221; L Valenzuela-Vermehren, 'Empire, Sovereignty, and Justice

movement of persons as a cardinal principle of international law. His notion of *ius communicationis* was developed in his well-known lecture *On the American Indians* delivered at the University of Salamanca in 1539, when he discussed the most controversial issue of his time: the legitimacy of the Spanish conquest in the New World. Vitoria first asserted that the Indians were the true masters of their land and thus had a right of ownership (*dominium*).[3] Therefore, 'they could not be robbed of their property, either as private citizens or as princes', by the Spaniards.[4] Then, Vitoria meticulously refuted the various grounds generally invoked to justify the colonization of the New World, such as the universal authority of the Emperor and the Pope,[5] the right of discovery,[6] or the refusal of the Christian faith.[7] He accordingly concluded that 'the Spaniards, when they first sailed to the land of the barbarians, carried with them no right at all to occupy their countries',[8] before inquiring into the legitimate grounds that could justify the Spanish conquest.

The 'first just title', identified by the Professor of Salamanca as a justification for the Spanish conquest, relies on 'the right of natural partnership and communication' (*naturalis societas et communicationis*).[9] The free movement of persons derived from his *ius communicationis* as a basic axiom of international law. Vitoria conceptualized the principle of free movement as a truly universal norm binding every state (whether European or not), grounded in the natural sociability of human beings, and acknowledged by the time-honoured tradition of hospitality. According to this principle, 'the Spaniards have the right to travel and dwell in those countries, so long as they do no harm to the barbarians'.[10] Such a right to travel is founded on international law: it 'comes from the law of nations (*ius gentium*), which either is or derives from natural law'.[11] For Vitoria, all nations acknowledged the right to travel

---

in Francisco de Vitoria's International Thought: A Re-interpretation of *De Indis*' (2013) 40(1) Revista Chilena de Derecho 259. For a more critical and convincing account of his stance as a founding father, see however: P Haggenmacher, 'La place de Francisco de Vitoria parmi les fondateurs du droit international' in *Actualité de la pensée juridique de Francisco de Vitoria* (Bruylant 1988) 27.

[3] 'The conclusion of all that has been said is that the barbarians undoubtedly possessed as true dominion, both public and private, as any Christians': F de Vitoria, 'On the American Indians' in A Pagden and J Lawrance (eds), *Francisco de Vitoria: Political Writings* (CUP 1992) 250. For Vitoria, 'this is self-evident, because they have some order (*ordo*) in their affairs: they have properly organized cities, proper marriages, magistrates and overlords (*domini*), laws, industries, and commerce, all of which require the use of reason. They likewise have a form (*species*) of religion and they correctly apprehend things which are evident to other men, which indicates the use of reason'. ibid.

[4] ibid 250–51.   [5] ibid 252–64.   [6] ibid 264–65.   [7] ibid 265–75.

[8] ibid 264.

[9] According to the historian Anthony Pagden, the right of communication as defined by the Spanish Jesuit 'seems to have been Vitoria's own creation' although St Augustine had suggested before him that denying a right of passage might justify a just war: A Pagden, 'Human Rights, Natural Rights, and Europe's Imperial Legacy' (2003) 31(2) Pol Theory 171, 197, fn 30.

[10] Vitoria, 'On the American Indians' (n 3) 278.

[11] ibid. The conception of Vitoria is subtler than this assimilation between *ius naturale* and *ius gentium*. According to him, in most cases, the binding force of the law of nations derives from natural law and, when this is not the case, its authority comes from the universal consent of the nations: 'And there are certainly many things which are clearly to be settled on the basis on the law of nations (*ius gentium*), whose derivation from natural law is manifestly sufficient to enable it to enforce binding rights. But even on the occasions when it is not derived from natural law, the consent of the greater part of the world is enough to make it binding, especially when it is for the common good of all men.' ibid 280–81.

as a rule of international law given that '[a]mongst all nations it is considered [...] humane and dutiful to behave hospitably to strangers'.[12] He further asserted that this rule existed since the beginning of the world and it was not called into question by the division of the world into different nations:

[I]n the beginning of the world, when all things were held in common, everyone was allowed to visit and travel through any land he wished. This right was clearly not taken away by the division of property (*diuisio rerum*); it was never the intention of nations to prevent men's free mutual intercourse with one another by this division.[13]

Following this stance, the right of communication is grounded in the natural sociability of mankind and the correlative duty of friendship between human beings: 'it is a law of nature to welcome strangers' because 'amity (*amicitia*) between men is part of natural law'.[14] Indeed, 'nature has decreed a certain kinship between all men,' and 'man is not a "wolf to his fellow man" as Ovid says, but a fellow'.[15] While quoting St Augustine, Vitoria reasserted that 'every man is your neighbour'[16] before concluding that 'hospitality is commended in Scripture: "use hospitality one to another without grudging" (1 Pet. 4:9) [...]. It follows that to refuse to welcome strangers and foreigners is inherently evil.'[17] In sum, for Vitoria, free movement derived from the duty of hospitality as a principle of international law grounded in the natural sociability of human beings.

  While outlining the legal and moral foundations of free movement, Vitoria further refined its scope in a rather balanced way. Indeed, the right to travel and the duty of hospitality are not absolute. Vitoria stressed on several occasions that they were no longer binding 'if travellers were doing something evil by visiting foreign nations'.[18] His *ius communicationis* accordingly equates with a qualified right of entry: the admission of foreigners into the territory of another state is mandatory as long as it does not harm the host society. In his words, it is 'lawful' only if it is 'neither harmful nor detrimental to the barbarians'.[19] Though he did not detail the exact content of this exception, Vitoria made clear that foreigners who did not commit any crime were free to enter another country: 'it is not lawful to banish visitors who are innocent of any crime'.[20] The importance he assigned to this right of entry shall not be underestimated. Refusing such admission is not only a violation of international law; it can also be considered as an act of war.[21]

  Although his right of communication can be derogated from when it is harmful or detrimental to the host society, it remains a truly universal rule binding all nations. It is thus applicable to both Christians and Indians on an equal footing: '[I]t would not be lawful for the French to prohibit Spaniards from travelling or even living in France, or vice versa, so long as it caused no sort of harm to themselves; therefore it is not lawful for the barbarians either.'[22] As exemplified by this last quotation, the right of communication reflects a broader conception of international law grounded in

---

[12] ibid.   [13] ibid.   [14] ibid 279.   [15] ibid 280.   [16] ibid 279.
[17] ibid 281.   [18] ibid 278.   [19] ibid 278.   [20] ibid 278.   [21] ibid 278.
[22] ibid 278. He added that 'the barbarians themselves admit all sorts of other barbarians from elsewhere, and would therefore do wrong if they did not admit the Spaniards'. ibid 279.

reciprocity and equality between foreign nations. This twofold notion of reciprocity and equality between foreign nations represents a central contribution of Vitoria that prefigured classical international law.

Interestingly, his *ius communicationis* was not limited to the right to travel and the duty of hospitality. It was a much broader principle of international law that also included free trade,[23] freedom of navigation,[24] and *ius soli*.[25] The right of communication between peoples is accordingly at the heart of his whole conception of the Law of Nations: such a right is not only grounded in international law; it is the essence thereof. Following this stance, the right of communication is the necessary precondition for establishing international relations between equal nations, and, by the same token, constitutes the *raison d'être* of international law as a whole.

While conceptually sound and attractive, Vitoria's construction suffered from one major paradox: his *ius communicationis* was the founding principle of a universal society composed of equal nations on the one hand, and the main legal ground for justifying the colonization of the New World on the other hand. This ambiguity explains why Vitoria has been condemned by several authors for 'outlining, in clear and stark terms, the colonial origins of international law'[26] and praised by others for his 'moral cosmopolitism'[27] and his modern notion of international community.[28] There is arguably some exaggeration in both positions. At the time of his lecture *On the American Indians*, the colonization of the New World was already a *fait accompli*. His ambition was not to legitimize it, but instead to constrain and regulate this reality within a general system based on moral and legal precepts.

---

[23] 'In the first place, the law of nations (*ius gentium*) is clearly that travellers may carry on trade so long as they do no harm to the citizens; and second, in the same way it can be proved that this is lawful in divine law. Therefore any human enactment (*lex*) which prohibited such trade would indubitably be unreasonable.' ibid, 279–80.

[24] '[T]he jurist's determination that by natural law running water and the open sea, rivers, and ports are the common property of all, and by the law of nations (*ius gentium*) ships from any country may lawfully put in anywhere (Institutions II.1.1-4)'. ibid 279.

[25] '[I]f children born in the Indies of a Spanish father wish to become citizens (*cives*) of that community, they cannot be barred from citizenship or from the advantages enjoyed by the native citizens born of parents domiciled in that community.' ibid 281.

[26] A Anghie, *Imperialism, Sovereignty and the Making of International Law* (CUP 2004) 9. See also C Miéville, *Between Equal Rights: A Marxist Theory of International Law* (Brill 2005) 173–78; A Anghie, 'Francisco de Vitoria and the Colonial Origins of International Law' (1996) 5(3) Social and Legal Studies 321; RA Williams Jr, *The American Indian in Western Legal Thought: The Discourses of Conquest* (OUP 1990) 96–107; H Méchoulan, *Le sang de l'autre ou l'honneur de Dieu: Indiens, juifs et morisques au Siècle d'Or* (Fayard 1979) 62–67 and 85–90.

[27] G Cavallar, 'Vitoria, Grotius, Pufendorf, Wolff and Vattel: Accomplices of European Colonialism and Exploitation or True Cosmopolitans?' (2008) 10 J Hist Intl L 181, 191. See also: P Niemelä, 'A Cosmopolitan World Order? Perspectives on Francisco de Vitoria and the United Nations' (2008) 12 Max Planck UNYB 301.

[28] Zapatero, 'Legal Imagination in Vitoria' (n 2) 227; N Lewkowicz, 'The Spanish School as a Forerunner to the English School of International Relations' (2007) 6 Estudios Humanisticos Historia 85–96; A Gòmez Robledo, 'Le *ius cogens* international: sa genèse, sa nature, ses fonctions' (1981) 172(III) Collected Courses of the Hague Academy of International Law 9, 23–25 and 189–91; F de Los Rio, 'Francisco de Vitoria and the International Community' (1947) 14(4) Soc Res 488–507; Barthélemy, 'François de Vitoria' (n 2) 42–43.

Within such a construction, the right of communication established the missing link between sovereign entities that are bound to interact and develop relationships. In turn, it represented a common good of a world composed of equal nations. While it provided an entry point for Europeans into the New World, the general principle of free communication was unable to justify colonization on its own. Indeed, one cannot contend that colonization did not harm the host society in accordance with his own exception to the right to travel and stay in a foreign nation.[29] As a result, Vitoria had to resort to several other 'just titles' to justify the conquest of the New World. They primarily rely on the spread of Christianity, the defence of the innocents against tyranny, as well as the need for a true and voluntary election.[30]

Although this colonial bias undermined his very notion of equality between nations, Vitoria wrote the prologue of international law by drawing the contours of an international society governed by universal norms.[31] His main ambition was to demonstrate that international law was both binding and universal for any nation:

[T]he law of nations (*ius gentium*) does not have the force merely of pacts and agreements between men, but has the validity of a positive enactment (*lex*). The whole world, which is in a sense a commonwealth, has the power to enact laws which are just and convenient to all men; and these make up the law of nations. From this it follows that those who break the law of nations, whether in peace or in war, are committing moral crimes [. . .]. No kingdom may choose to ignore this law of nations, because it has the sanction of the whole world.[32]

Grotius and the law of hospitality

The *ius communicationis* of Vitoria was upheld and developed by Hugo Grotius (1583–1645). Grotius did not only endorse the view of Vitoria, he also refined and enriched the principle of free movement by delineating its key components—the right to leave one's own country and the right to remain in a foreign country—as two sides of the same coin. Hence, while Vitoria set the scene for the free movement of persons under international law, Grotius consolidated and detailed its very content.

---

[29] The destruction of the Aztec empire on the Yucatán peninsula by Cortés and his troops in 1519–1521 was a well-known example of the violence perpetrated by the *conquistadores*.

[30] Vitoria, *On the American Indians* (n 3) 284–91. He also referred to the mental incapacity of the natives, although he expressed his scepticism about this last title.

[31] As rightly observed by Joe Verhoeven, '[i]l ne faut certes pas demander à Vitoria plus qu'il ne peut donner. Le droit des gens est encore à ses balbutiements. L'essentiel est néanmoins en place. Tel est sans doute l'intérêt de [son] œuvre [. . .]. Vitoria a planté les éléments du décor, et il les a plantés de telle façon que la pièce qui allait s'y dérouler fût largement "prédestinée". Mais il n'en a écrit que le prologue.': J Verhoeven, 'Vitoria ou la matrice du droit international' in *Actualité de la pensée juridique de Francisco de Vitoria* (n 2) 127.

[32] F de Vitoria, *On Civil Power* in Pagden and Lawrance (eds), *Francisco de Vitoria: Political Writings* (n 3) para 21, 40. For further discussion about his conception of international law, see most notably: A Wagner, 'Francisco de Vitoria and Alberico Gentili on the Legal Character of the Global Commonwealth' (2011) 31(3) Oxford J Legal Stud 565; R Lesaffer, 'The Grotian Tradition Revisited: Change and Continuity in the History of International Law' (2002) BYIL 121–28; D Kennedy, 'Primitive Legal Scholarship' (1986) 27(1) Harvard Intl L J 13, 13–40.

The Dutch jurist first discussed the general notion of *ius communicationis* in *The Free Sea* (1609), which is considered 'an icon in international law'.[33] He reaffirmed free communication in particularly straightforward terms as a fundamental principle inherent in international law: 'every nation is free to travel to every other nation' as an 'unimpeachable rule of the law of nations [...] which is self-evident and immutable'.[34] While referring to Vitoria, he recalled that this basic rule of international law was truly universal[35] and relied on 'the sacrosanct law of hospitality'.[36] Grotius further underlined that such a rule was not limited to common properties (such as the sea), but also applied to the territories possessed by states: 'even in the case of the land that has been assigned as private property, whether to nations or to single individuals, it is nevertheless unjust to deny the right of passage (that is to say, of course, unarmed and innocent passage) to men of many nations'.[37]

The right of innocent passage was further refined in his masterwork *The Rights of War and Peace* (1625), which has been praised as 'the first systematic treatment of international law'.[38] When discussing 'things which belong in common to all Men',[39] Grotius reaffirmed that 'a free Passage ought to be granted to Persons where just Occasion shall require, over any Lands and Rivers, or such Parts of the Sea as belong to any Nation'.[40] In line with Vitoria, he concluded that the right of passage can be claimed by force if refused.[41] Yet, Grotius' conception differed starkly from Vitoria's in that the former conceived the right of communication outside any colonial context. Within such a de-colonized version, the principle of free movement became more powerful and universal than Vitoria's right of communication.

---

[33] E Gordon, 'Grotius and the Freedom of the Seas in the Seventeenth Century' (2008) 16 Willamette J Intl L and Dis Res 252. For further discussion about his *Mare Liberum*, see G van Nifterik and J Nijman, 'Introduction: *Mare Liberum* Revisited (1609–2009)' (2009) 30 Grotiana 3–19; M J van Ittersum, 'Preparing *Mare Liberum* for the Press: Hugo Grotius' Rewriting of Chapter 12 of *De iure praedae* in November-December 1608' (2005–2007) 26–28 Grotiana 246–80; P Borschberg, 'Hugo Grotius's Theory of Trans-Oceanic Trade Regulation: Revisiting Mare Liberum (1609)' (2006) International law and Justice Working Papers, New York University School of Law; I Shearer, 'Grotius and the Law of the Sea' (1983) 26 ASLP Bulletin 46–65; A Reppy, 'The Grotian Doctrine of the Freedom of the Seas Reappraised' (1950) 19(3) Fordham L Rev 243.

[34] H Grotius, *Mare Liberum 1609–2009* (edited and annotated by R Feenstra, Brill 2009) 25.

[35] It 'pertains equally to all peoples' because 'nature has granted every nation access to every other nation'. ibid 27.

[36] ibid 29.   [37] ibid 93.

[38] DJ Bederman, 'Grotius and his Followers on Treaty Construction' (2001) 3 J Hist Intl L 18. For Lauterpacht, his treatise 'became identified with the idea of progress in international law': H Lauterpacht, 'The Grotian Tradition in International Law' (1946) 23 BYIL 1, 52. See also: Lesaffer, 'The Grotian Tradition Revisited' (n 32) 103–39; R Higgins, 'Grotius and the United Nations' (1985) 37(1) Intl Social Science J 119–27; CF Murphy, 'The Grotian Vision of World Order' (1982) 76(3) AJIL 477–98; H Bull, 'The Grotian Conception of International Society' in H Butterfield and M Wight (eds), *Diplomatic Investigations: Essays in the Theory of International Politics* (Harvard University Press 1966) 51–73. For a more nuanced and thorough account of Grotius as a transitional figure and his debt toward Vitoria and the Scholastic, see however P Haggenmacher, *Grotius et la doctrine de la guerre juste* (Presses universitaires de France 1983) 615–29; Kennedy, 'Primitive Legal Scholarship' (n 32) 76–81.

[39] H Grotius, *The Rights of War and Peace* (edited with an introduction by R Tuck, Liberty Fund 2005) Book II, ch II, at 420.

[40] ibid para XIII.1 at 439.

[41] '[T]he liberty of passing ought first to be demanded, and if that be denied, it may be claimed by force.' ibid para XIII.3 at 441.

In addition, Grotius went one step further by delineating two crucial notions—the right to leave one's own country and the right to remain in a foreign country—in clear and somehow modern terms. Concerning the first notion, Grotius devoted particular attention 'to the Case [...] when a single Person leaves his Country'.[42] While endorsing Cicero's view of freedom to leave as 'the foundation of liberty', Grotius recognized that the right to leave one's own country was not absolute given that it could be subjected to restrictions in the interest of society for debtors as well as in times of war.[43] Except for such cases, the principle remained that 'Nations leave to every one the Liberty of quitting the State'.[44]

The right to leave one's own country is supplemented and reinforced by a right to remain in a foreign country. This represents another key added value of Grotius compared to Vitoria who did not delve into the stay of non-nationals in a foreign country as a consequence of free movement. The Dutch lawyer underlined that:

Persons also that pass either by Land or Water, may, on Account of their Health, or for any other just Cause, make some Stay in the Country; this being likewise an innocent Utility. [...] So likewise, a fixed Abode ought not to be refused to Strangers, who being expelled their own Country, seek a Retreat elsewhere: Provided they submit to the Laws of the State, and refrain from every Thing that might give Occasion to Sedition.[45]

Similarly to the right to leave, the right to remain in a foreign country is not absolute: it presupposes a 'just cause' to stay therein and foreigners' respect for the laws of the host state.[46] For Grotius—a refugee himself—a typical instance of such a 'just cause' could be found in '[t]he so much revered Rights of Suppliants or Refugees, and the many Precedents of *Asylums* [...]; for they are intended only for the Benefit of them who suffer undeservedly, and not for such whose malicious Practices have been injurious to any particular Men, or to human Society in general'.[47] Quoting Cicero, the Dutch lawyer recalled that '*It is our Duty to have Compassion on such*

---

[42] Emigration of individuals is distinguished from the case of a large portion of the population leaving the state, which may thus imperil the very *raison d'être* of the civil society: 'That we ought not to go out in Troops or large Companies, is sufficiently evident from the End and Design of Civil Society, which could not subsist if such a Permission were granted; and in Things of a moral Nature, what is necessary to obtain the End has the Force of a Law'. ibid Book II, ch V, para XXIV.2 at 553–54.

[43] '[I]t is no Ways for the Benefit of a Civil Society, if there be any great publick Debt contracted, for an Inhabitant to leave it, unless he be ready to pay down his Proportion towards it: Or if a War be undertaken upon a Confidence in the Number of Subjects to support it, and especially if a Siege be apprehended, no Body ought to quit the Service of his Country, unless he substitutes another in his Room, equally qualified to defend the State'. ibid para XXIV.2 at 55–55.

[44] ibid para XXIV.3 at 555.

[45] ibid Book II, ch II, para XV.1 at 446 and para XVI at 447. While repeating that 'those People who refuse to admit Foreigners amongst them, are very much to blame', he further added that: 'And if there be any waste or barren Land within our Dominions, that also is to be given to Strangers, at their Request, or may be lawfully possessed by them, because whatever remains uncultivated, is not to be esteemed a Property, only so far as concerns Jurisdiction, which always continues the Right of the antient People'. ibid para XVI at 447 and para XVII at 448.

[46] For Grotius as for Vitoria, this duty of hospitality did not apply in times of war: 'And without doubt Strangers, that come into an Enemy's Country after a War is proclaimed, and begun, are liable to be treated as Enemies' because 'when War is proclaimed against a Nation, it is at the same Time proclaimed against all of that Nation'. ibid Book III, ch IV, para VI at 1281 and para XVIII.1 at 1282.

[47] ibid Book II, ch XXI, para V.1 at 1067–68.

whose Misery is owing not to their Crimes but Misfortune.'[48] In Grotius' own words, '[r]efugees are [...] entitled to Protection',[49] because they are 'innocent of [any] Crimes'.[50] By contrast, for the one who has committed a crime, the host state 'must either punish him or deliver him up' to the injured state according to his well-known maxim *aut dedere aut judicare*.[51]

In drawing the line between those who deserve protection and those who do not, his distinction between victims and criminals clearly prefigured the modern definition of refugees.[52] Yet, his contribution is not confined to asylum. Grotius considerably enriched the debate initiated by Vitoria. Not only did he reassert the right of communication between peoples as a universal rule of international law binding all nations, but he further strengthened and refined this principle by outlining two related rights: departure (from one's own country) and admission (into another country) as the key tenets of free movement.

1.1.2 State sovereignty and the admission of aliens by Pufendorf and Wolff

In stark contrast to Vitoria and Grotius, subsequent scholars of the Law of Nations insisted on states' discretion to refuse the admission of foreigners. This change of paradigm obviously coincided with the rise of state sovereignty as endorsed in 1648 in the Peace of Westphalia.[53] Within the doctrine of the Law of Nations, the primary rationale underlying the sovereign power to refuse admission of aliens was based on two mutually reinforcing notions: the reason of state as presumed by Pufendorf and the patrimonial conception of the state as elaborated by Wolff.

Pufendorf and the reason of state

Samuel Pufendorf (1632–1694) is one of the first scholars who departed from the right of communication between peoples inherited from Vitoria and developed by

---

[48] ibid para V.1 at 1068–69 (original emphasis).   [49] ibid para VI.1 at 1075.
[50] ibid para VI.1 at 1070.
[51] ibid para IV.3 at 1063. He explained that 'since for one State to admit within its Territories another foreign Power upon the Score of exacting Punishment is never practised, nor indeed convenient, it seems reasonable, that that State where the convicted Offender lives or has taken Shelter, should, upon Application being made to it, either punish the demanded Person according to his Demerits, or else deliver him up to be treated at the Discretion of the injured Party'. ibid para IV.1 at 1062.
[52] The refugee definition enshrined in Article 1 of the United Nations Convention relating to the Status of Refugees meticulously distinguishes between inclusion clauses (a well-founded fear of being persecuted) and exclusion clauses (mainly grounded on serious crimes). For further discussion about the early doctrine of the law of nations and its impact on asylum and refugee law, see V Chetail, 'Théorie et pratique de l'asile en droit international classique: étude sur les origines conceptuelles et normatives du droit international des réfugiés' (2011) 115(3) RGDIP 625.
[53] The Peace of Münster: Treaty of Peace between Spain and the Netherlands (signed 30 January 1648) (1648) 1 CTS 1. The Treaties of Münster: Treaty of Peace between the Holy Roman Empire and France (signed 24 October 1648) (1648) 1 CTS 271; and Osnabrück: Treaty of Peace between the Holy Roman Empire and Sweden (signed 24 October 1648) (1648) 1 CTS 198. Together, these treaties form the Peace of Westphalia.

Grotius. The German Professor distinguished departure from admission as two opposite notions governed by different sets of norms. As far as emigration is concerned, Pufendorf reasserted in *The Law of Nature and Nations*, published in 1672, that 'every Man reserved to himself the Liberty to remove at discretion'.[54] As for Grotius, the freedom of emigration can be subjected to legitimate restrictions mainly for debtors or in case of war.[55] With Pufendorf, however, the right to leave is divorced from the general principle of free movement. Departure from one's own country becomes a distinctive right on its own, whereas admission into another country falls into the realm of the sovereign:

[I]t is left in the Power of all States, to take such Measures about the Admission of Strangers, as they think convenient; those being ever excepted, who are driven on the Coasts by Necessity, or by any Cause that deserves Pity and Compassion. Not but that it is barbarous to treat, in the same cruel Manner, those who visit us as Friends, and those who assault us as Enemies.[56]

As a result of the state's power to decide upon the admission of foreigners, the freedom to leave one's own country did not coincide with a correlative right to enter another country. The former is a right of individuals, while the latter is a right of states. Although this distinction eventually became conventional wisdom, Pufendorf did not explain the exact rationale and motives for such a departure from his predecessors. His insistence on the reason of state and the influence of Thomas Hobbes are probably the main reasons.[57]

The thought of Pufendorf was nevertheless more nuanced than it may have appeared at first sight. His primary concern focused on unbridled access to all kinds of foreigners. While criticizing the *ius communicationis* of Vitoria, he argued that:

[I]t seems very gross and absurd, to allow others an indefinite or unlimited Right of travelling and living amongst us, without reflecting either on their Number, or on the Design of their coming; whether, supposing them to pass harmlessly, they intend only to take a short View of our Country, or whether they claim a Right of fixing themselves with us for ever. And that he who will stretch the Duty of Hospitality to this extravagant Extent, ought to be rejected as a most unreasonable, and most improper Judge of the Case.[58]

He expressed the same concern on several occasions. Although the Ancients conceived 'the Right of Hospitality [. . .] [as] the most Sacred Friendship', 'to give a natural Right to these Favours, it is requisite that the Stranger be absent from his own House on an honest, or on a necessary Account; as, also, that we have no Objection

---

[54] S Pufendorf, *The Law of Nature and Nations or a General System of the Most Important Principles of Morality, Jurisprudence and Politics* (first published 1672, 5th edn, J & J Bonwicke 1749) Book VIII, ch XI, para II at 873.

[55] ibid para III at 874.   [56] ibid Book III, ch III, para IX at 252–53.

[57] For further discussion about the influence of Hobbes on Pufendorf see: T Toyoda, *Theory and Politics of the Law of Nations: Political Bias in International Law Discourse of Seven German Court Councillors in the Seventeenth and Eighteenth Centuries* (Martinus Nijhoff 2011) 30–39; F Palladini, 'Pufendorf Disciple of Hobbes: The Nature of Man and the State of Nature: The Doctrine of *Socialitas*' (2008) 34 History of European Ideas 26–60; E Jouannet, *Emer de Vattel et l'émergence doctrinale du droit international classique* (Pedone 1998) 283–86 and 361–63; M Nutkiewicz, 'Samuel Pufendorf: Obligation as the Basis of the State' (1983) 21(1) J Hist Philosophy 15–29.

[58] Pufendorf, *The Law of Nature and Nations* (n 54) Book III, ch III, para IX at 252.

against his Integrity, or Character, which might render our Admission of him, either dangerous or disgraceful'.[59] His criticism of Vitoria and Grotius was hardly justifiable since, for both of them, the free movement of persons was not absolute and could be restricted in the interest of the host society. Furthermore, as was the case with his predecessors, Pufendorf had to equally acknowledge that 'Inhospitality [is] commonly, and for the most Part, justly censured, as the true Mark of a savage and inhuman Temper.'[60] The resulting tension between sovereignty and hospitality thus framed and constrained the admission of aliens.

While rejecting free movement as a rule of international law, Pufendorf inverted the terms of the debate: sovereignty became the principle and hospitality an exception. He thus prioritized the former over the latter, although the two notions were not necessarily incompatible. For Pufendorf, the admission of foreigners had to be encouraged not only as an office of humanity, but also in the interest of the state in accordance with an early conception of utilitarianism:

Humanity, it is true, engages us to receive a small Number of Men expelled their Home, not for their own Demerit and Crime; especially if they are eminent for Wealth or Industry, and not likely to disturb our Religion, or our Constitution. And thus we see many States to have risen to a great and flourishing Height, chiefly by granting Licence to Foreigners to come and settle amongst them; whereas others have been reduced to a low Condition, by refusing this Method of Improvement.[61]

However, it remains that with Pufendorf the admission of foreigners became a favour granted by the host state, because the primary consideration for allowing their admission is determined by its own interest:

[E]very State may be more free or more cautious in granting these Indulgences, as it shall judge proper for its Interest and Safety. In order to which Judgment, it will be prudent to consider, whether a great Increase in the Number of Inhabitants will turn to Advantage; whether the Country be fertile enough to feed so many Mouths; whether upon Admission of this new Body, we shall be strained for Room; whether the Men are industrious, or idle; whether they may be so conveniently placed and disposed, as to rend them incapable of giving any Jealousy to the Government. If on the whole, it appears that the Persons deserve our Favour and Pity, and that no Restraint lies on us from good Reasons of State, it will be an Act of Humanity to confer such a Benefit on them.[62]

Hospitality must therefore be granted when humanitarian considerations coincide with states' interests. If not, Pufendorf considered the reason of state to be self-evident enough to discard any sense of duty.

Wolff and the patrimonial state

The shift from the right of communication between peoples to the discretionary power of the state was endorsed and reinforced by Christian Wolff (1679–1754).

---

[59] ibid 251–52. See also: ibid para V at 245 and para VIII at 251, where he discusses the right of passage by Grotius.
[60] ibid Book III, ch III, para IX at 252.   [61] ibid para X at 253.   [62] ibid.

The German philosopher was even more radical than Pufendorf in vindicating the authority of the state in the field of admission. He reaffirmed in particularly strong and categorical terms that a state can forbid the entry of foreigners into its own territory. He explained in his *Jus Gentium Methodo Scientifica Pertractatum* (1749) that '[n]o nation nor any private person who is a foreigner can claim any right for himself in the territory of another'.[63] As a result, 'no foreigner is in any way permitted, contrary to the prohibition of the ruler, to enter the latter's territory, even for some definite purpose, as the prohibition may have set forth'.[64] In such a case, the state could even 'impose a penalty upon the one entering or forbid it under a definite penalty'.[65] Wolff thereby confirmed and exacerbated the departure from Vitoria and Grotius initiated by Pufendorf: admission of foreigners became a discretionary competence of the state that could be enforced by criminal sanctions.

Such a discretionary competence was grounded in a patrimonial conception of the state whereby ownership of its territory equated with sovereignty. Wolff developed this analogy in considerable detail. For him, 'there is a natural connexion of the ownership of a nation with the sovereignty so that if ownership is established, sovereignty is likewise established, but if sovereignty is taken away, ownership also is taken away'.[66] Thus, 'the ruler of the state may be called the lord (or owner) of the territory [...] because, of course, he has ownership over the nation'.[67] This assimilation between property right and territorial sovereignty triggered the discretionary power of excluding foreigners from the state's territory in a self-referential logic: 'A nation has the same power of ownership as a private person. Therefore, just as the owner of a private estate can prohibit any other person from entering upon the same, a thing which no one denies, so also the ruler of a territory can prohibit any foreigner from entering upon it.'[68]

According to this absolute conception of territorial sovereignty, it is up to each state to decide if, and under which conditions, foreigners may be permitted to enter the territory. Indeed, 'since an owner can dispose of the use of his property according to his liking, the conditions under which the ruler of a territory desires to permit approach to foreigners, depend altogether upon his will'.[69] Hence, the grounds for refusing admission must be left to the discretion of the sovereign state depending upon various considerations, such as the number of foreigners, their difference of religion and morality, their criminal convictions, and any other reasons which are justified by public welfare.[70] Emigration is not an exception to this system entirely

---

[63] C Wolff, *Jus Gentium Methodo Scientifica Pertractatum*, vol 2 (trans J H Drake, Clarendon Press/ Humphrey Milford 1934) ch III, para 293 at 149.

[64] ibid para 295 at 149–50. See also: C Wolff, *Principes du droit de la nature et des gens* (first published 1758, trans S Formey, Université de Caen 1988) Tome III, Book IX, ch IV, para XV at 278: 'Si quelque puissance juge qu'il convient à la sûreté de son Etat de n'en permettre l'entrée à aucun étranger, il dépend d'elle de l'interdire, et d'attacher des peines à la violation de cette loi.'

[65] Wolff, *Jus Gentium Methodo Scientifica Pertractatum* (n 63) ch III, para 296 at 150.

[66] ibid para 305 at 154.   [67] ibid para 307 at 155.   [68] ibid para 295 at 150.

[69] ibid para 298 at 150–51.

[70] '[T]here may be several reasons on account of which admittance may be denied and [...] they must be determined by the state. [...] Here properly belongs the fact that the number of subjects is greater than can be provided for adequately from the things which are demanded for the needs, comforts, and pleasure of life, both as regards the people in general and also as regards the class of people

based on the discretionary power of the state. Contrary to Pufendorf, Wolff argued that 'in a state of nature there is no right to emigrate'.[71] As a result, emigration is nothing more than a 'permission to go into voluntary exile'[72] which 'depends upon the law of the state'.[73]

In order to mitigate the drastic consequences of his own conception, Wolff counterbalanced the discretion of the state by a reminiscence of the right to free passage. He reasserted, in line with the Scholastic tradition of natural law, that ownership of the territory—and by extension sovereignty—did not prejudice the 'right of harmless use'.[74] Such a right includes the right 'of passage for proper causes over lands and rivers, [...] the right of remaining in lands which are subject to the ownership of a nation, [and the right] of the admittance of those who have been expelled from their own homes'.[75] Wolff deduced from the right of harmless use that 'foreigners must be allowed to stay with us for the purpose of recovering health',[76] 'of study',[77] or 'for the sake of commerce.'[78]

This duty of admission is nevertheless an imperfect right and, as such, cannot be enforced.[79] The limit of such an imperfect right is graphically illustrated by the admission of refugees. For Wolff, '[w]e ought to be compassionate toward exiles'[80] and, as a result, '[a] permanent residence in its territory cannot be denied to exiles by a nation, unless special reasons stand in the way'.[81] However, 'since nations are free, the decision concerning these matters must be left to the nations themselves, and that decision must be respected. [...] And if this right should be claimed as regards these lands, it is imperfect, consequently no nation can be compelled to receive exiles.'[82]

The enduring dialectic between state sovereignty and free movement is accordingly rephrased and captured through the distinction between perfect and imperfect rights. The German Professor underlined this tension on several occasions:

[S]ince it depends altogether on the will of the people, or on the will of the one who has the right of the people, whether or not he desires to receive an outsider into his state, an exile is allowed to ask admittance, but he cannot assuredly according to his liking determine domicile for himself, wherever he shall please, and if admittance is refused, that must be endured.[83]

Against such a framework, foreigners have a right to claim admission, but not a right to be granted it. Because of its imperfect nature, the right of admission is accordingly

---

who follow the same pursuit of life. Here also belongs the reason that there is fear lest the morals of the subjects may be corrupted, or lest prejudice may be aroused against religion, or even lest criminals be admitted, because of whom injury threatens the state, and other things which are detrimental to public welfare.' ibid ch I, para 148 at 81.

[71] ibid para 154 at 83.   [72] ibid para 153 at 83.   [73] ibid para 154 at 83.
[74] '[O]wnership of things could not have been introduced unless the right of harmless use had been reserved'. ibid ch III para 343 at 175. In other words, 'the right of harmless use, [...] as a residue from the primitive joint holding remains common to nations after the introduction of ownership'. ibid para 349 at 179.
[75] ibid para 343 at 175.   [76] ibid para 345 at 177.   [77] ibid para 344 at 176.
[78] ibid para 346 at 177.
[79] For further discussion on the distinction between perfect and imperfect rights by Wolff, see Jouannet, *Emer de Vattel* (n 57) 211–13.
[80] Wolff, *Jus Gentium Methodo Scientifica Pertractatum* (n 63) ch I para 150 at 81.
[81] ibid para 149 at 81.   [82] ibid para 149 at 81.   [83] ibid para 148 at 80.

confined to a moral duty. In other words, hospitality becomes charity and the discretionary competence of the state in the field of admission is thus preserved. For Wolff, the difference between perfect and imperfect rights relied on the distinction between justice and charity: 'it is against charity and not justice, if one nation fails in its duty toward another. Therefore although it does no wrong, nevertheless it sins.'[84] In sum, the state is morally bound to admit foreigners but legally free to refuse them.

1.1.3 The synthesis of Vattel: sovereignty versus necessity

No other treatise on international law has been more widely read and cited than *The Law of Nations* by Emer de Vattel (1714–1767).[85] Published in 1758, his treatise acquired an unrivalled and durable influence during the following centuries. In an early 20th-century study on 'The Authority of Vattel', Fenwick wrote:

Vattel's treatise on the law of nations was quoted by judicial tribunals, in speeches before legislative assemblies, and in the decrees and correspondence of executive officials. It was the manual of the student, the reference work of the statesman, and the text from which the political philosopher drew inspiration. Publicists considered it sufficient to cite the authority of Vattel to justify and give conclusiveness and force to statements as to the proper conduct of a state in its international relations.[86]

Although courts and commentators have frequently misconstrued his views, Vattel represents the middle ground between the partisans of free movement and the proponents of state sovereignty. On the one hand, the Swiss author endorsed and framed emigration and immigration in somewhat conventional terms when compared to the contemporary understanding of these issues. On the other hand, he counterbalanced and qualified state sovereignty in the field of admission by two substantial caveats: innocent passage and necessity.

---

[84] ibid para 159 at 86.
[85] E de Vattel, *The Law of Nations or, Principles of the Law of Nature, Applied to the Conduct and Affairs of Nations and Sovereigns* (B Kapossy and R Whatmore (eds), Liberty Fund 2008). Among the numerous books devoted to Vattel, see notably: V Chetail and P Haggenmacher (eds), *Vattel's International Law in a XXIst Century Perspective / Le droit international de Vattel vu du XXIeme siècle* (Martinus Nijhoff 2011); S Beaulac, *The Power of Language in the Making of International Law: The Word Sovereignty in Bodin and Vattel and the Myth of Westphalia* (Martinus Nijhoff 2004); Jouannet, *Emer de Vattel* (n 57); FS Ruddy, *International Law in the Enlightenment: The Background of Emmerich de Vattel's 'Le Droit des Gens'* (Oceana 1975); JJ Manz, *Emer de Vattel, Versuch einer Wurdigung: Unter besonderer Berucksichtigung der individuellen Freiheit und der souveranen Gleichheit* (Schulthess Polygraphischer Verlag 1971); PP Remec, *The Position of the Individual in International Law According to Grotius and Vattel* (Martinus Nijhoff 1960); P Guggenheim, *Emer de Vattel et l'étude des relations internationales en Suisse* (Libraire de l'Université 1956).
[86] CG Fenwick, 'The Authority of Vattel' (1913) 7 Am Political Science Rev 395. For further discussion about the influence of Vattel, see besides the references quoted above: V Chetail, 'Vattel and the American Dream: An Inquiry into the Reception of the *Law of Nations* in the United States' in V Chetail and P-M Dupuy (eds), *The Roots of International Law: Liber Amicorum Peter Haggenmacher* (Martinus Nijhoff 2013) 251–300; FS Ruddy, 'The Acceptance of Vattel' (1972) Grotian Society Papers 177–96; H Thévenaz, 'Vattel ou la destinée d'un livre' (1957) 14 ASDI 9–16.

Emigration and immigration by Vattel

Contrary to Wolff, his master, Vattel devoted lengthy passages to 'the liberty of emigration'.[87] He acknowledged as a principle that 'every man has a right to quit his country, in order to settle in any other, when by that step he does not endanger the welfare of his country'.[88] This qualified right to leave a country applies to both citizens and foreigners alike.[89] Nonetheless, the freedom of emigration is only applicable in times of peace and public interest may require return.[90] As a witness of his time, Vattel provided a nuanced account of the prevailing practice. While observing that 'the political laws of nations vary greatly in this respect', he distinguished three types of state practice:

> In some nations, it is at all times, except in case of actual war, allowed to every citizen to absent himself, and even to quit the country altogether, whenever he thinks proper, without alleging any reason for it. [...] In some other states, every citizen is left at liberty to travel abroad on business, but not to quit his country altogether, without the express permission of the sovereign. Finally, there are states where the rigour of the government will not permit any one whatsoever to go out of the country, without passports in form, which are even not granted without great difficulty. In all these cases it is necessary to conform to the laws, when they are made by a lawful authority. But in the last-mentioned case, the sovereign abuses his power, and reduces his subjects to an insupportable slavery, if he refuses them permission to travel for their own advantage, when he might grant it to them without inconvenience, and without danger to the state.[91]

To support his stance against undue restrictions of free emigration, the Swiss author strongly reaffirmed that 'there are cases in which a citizen has an absolute right to renounce his country, and abandon it entirely—a right founded on reasons derived from the very nature of the social compact'.[92] Such a fundamental right is triggered in three cases: when the state is unable to provide subsistence to its own citizens, fails to discharge its obligations toward its citizens, or enacts intolerant laws (such as those interfering with freedom of conscience).[93] Although his rationale primarily

---

[87] Vattel, *The Law of Nations* (n 85) Book I, ch XIX, para 225 at 224.

[88] ibid para 220.2 at 221.

[89] To Vattel, a foreigner 'is free at all time to leave it; nor have we a right to detain him, except for a time, and for very particular reasons, as, for instance, an apprehension, in war time, lest such foreigner, acquainted with the state of the country and of the fortified places, should communicate his knowledge to the enemy'. ibid Book II, ch VIII, para 108 at 315.

[90] 'In a time of peace and tranquillity, when the country has no actual need of all her children, the very welfare of the state, and that of the citizens, requires that every individual be at liberty to travel on business, provided that he be always ready to return, whenever the public interest recalls him.' ibid Book I, ch XIX, para 221 at 222.

[91] ibid para 222 at 222.   [92] ibid para 223 at 223.

[93] '1. If the citizen cannot procure subsistence in his own country, it is undoubtedly lawful for him to seek it elsewhere. For political or civil society being entered into only with a view of facilitating to each of its members the means of supporting himself, and of living in happiness and safety, it would be absurd to pretend that a member, whom it cannot furnish with such things as are most necessary, has not a right to leave it.

2. If the body of the society, or he who represents it, absolutely fail to discharge their obligations towards a citizen, the latter may withdraw himself. For if one of the contracting parties does not observe his engagements, the other is no longer bound to fulfil his; for the contract is reciprocal between

relied on natural law, Vattel further observed that freedom of emigration may derive from several sources of positive law, such as the constitution of the state, the explicit permission granted by the sovereign, and international treaties.[94]

In contrast to the freedom of emigration, admission of foreigners falls within the competence of the host state as a consequence of its territorial sovereignty. Vattel reaffirmed, in line with Wolff, that:

The sovereign may forbid the entrance of his territory either to foreigners in general, or in particular cases, or to certain persons, or for certain particular purposes, according as he may think it advantageous to the state. There is nothing in all this, that does not flow from the rights of domain and sovereignty.[95]

Following the same premise, the sovereign state may subject the entry of foreigners to specific conditions it sees fit: 'since the lord of the territory may, whenever he thinks proper, forbid its being entered [. . .], he has no doubt a power to annex what conditions he pleases to the permission to enter'.[96] The two passages quoted above have frequently been heralded by Anglo-American courts to substantiate an un-qualified discretion of states to refuse admission of foreigners. The oft-quoted case *Nishimura Ekiu v United States* in 1892 provided the best illustration:

It is an accepted maxim of international law, that every sovereign nation has the power, as inherent in sovereignty, and essential to its self-preservation, to forbid the entrance of foreigners within its dominions, or to admit them only in such cases and upon such conditions as it may see fit to prescribe. Vattel, lib. 2, §§ 94, 100; 1 Phillimore (3d ed.) c. 10, § 220.115.[97]

At the time of this judgment, the authority of Vattel proved to be instrumental in justifying a radical shift from the time-honoured tradition of free movement. However, as James Nafziger demonstrates, the famous dictum of the US Supreme Court was based on a biased and selective reading of Vattel.[98] In fact, the two quoted

---

the society and its members. It is on the same principle also that the society may expel a member who violates its laws.

3. If the major part of the nation, or the sovereign who represents it, attempt to enact laws relative to matters in which the social compact cannot oblige every citizen to submission, those who are averse to these laws have a right to quit the society, and go settle elsewhere. For instance, if the sovereign, or the greater part of the nation, will allow but one religion in the state, those who believe and profess another religion have a right to withdraw, and to take with them their families and effects. For they cannot be supposed to have subjected themselves to the authority of men, in affairs of conscience; and if the society suffers and is weakened by their departure, the blame must be imputed to the intolerant party: for it is they who fail in their observance of the social compact,—it is they who violate it, and force the others to a separation.' ibid para 223 at 223–24.

[94] ibid para 225 at 224–25.   [95] ibid Book II, ch VII, para 94 at 309.
[96] ibid Book II, ch VIII, para 100 at 312.
[97] *Nishimura Ekiu v United States* [1892] 142 US 651, Gray J, 659. See also *Attorney-General for Canada v Cain* [1906] AC 542, 546: 'One of the rights possessed by the supreme power in every State is the right to refuse to permit an alien to enter that State, to annex what conditions it pleases to the permission to enter it, and to expel or deport from the State, at pleasure, even a friendly alien, especially if it considers his presence in the State opposed to its peace order, and good government, or to its social or material interest: Vattel, Law of Nations, book 1, s 231; book 2, s 125.'
[98] Nafziger, 'The General Admission of Aliens under International Law' (n 1) 811–15. As explained in the subsequent section the *Ekiu* case was also heavily drawn from Judge Robert Phillimore.

passages above were taken out of context, with the overall result of providing a distorted and partial account of Vattel's views on the admission of foreigners. This misreading of Vattel still prevails today among US judges.[99]

It is true that the ambiguity of his Law of Nations is prone to this sort of manipulation; the nuanced and sometimes contradictory statements of Vattel contributed a lot to his enduring success by providing a powerful rhetorical tool for justifying various kinds of actions. As observed by many scholars, 'it is easy to find in his book detached passages in favour of either side of any question'.[100] This is hardly surprising. On the one hand, the very notion of national sovereignty constitutes the driving force of his law of nations, which in turn explains both his ambiguity and enduring influence in the next centuries.[101] On the other hand, Vattel provides a synthesis between the tradition of natural law and an early form of positivism.[102]

---

[99] *Arizona v United States*, 567 US (2012), Dissenting Opinion of Justice Antonin Scalia: 'As a sovereign, Arizona has the inherent power to exclude persons from its territory, subject only to those limitations expressed in the Constitution or constitutionally imposed by Congress. That power to exclude has long been recognized as inherent in sovereignty. Emer de Vattel's seminal 1758 treatise on the Law of Nations stated: "The sovereign may forbid the entrance of his territory either to foreigners in general, or in particular cases, or to certain persons, or for certain particular purposes, according as he may think it advantageous to the state."'

[100] R Wildman, *Institutes of International Law*, vol 1 (Benning 1849) 32. For a similar account see also M Koskenniemi, *From Apology to Utopia: The Structure of International Legal Argument* (CUP 2005) 112; M Wight, 'Western Values in International Relations' in H Butterfield and M Wight (eds), *Diplomatic Investigations: Essays in the Theory of International Politics* (Allen and Unwin 1966) 119; C Parry, 'The Function of Law in the International Community' in M Sørensen (ed), *Manual of Public International Law* (Macmillan/St Martin's Press 1968) 25; and Thévenaz, 'Vattel ou la destinée d'un livre' (n 86) 13. For further discussion about the ambiguity of Vattel as a key factor of his enduring success see: V Chetail, 'Vattel et la sémantique du droit des gens: une tentative de reconstruction critique' in Chetail and Haggenmacher, *Vattel's International Law in a XXIst Century Perspective* (n 85) 387–434.

[101] On the extensive literature devoted to Vattel's conception of the sovereign state, see: Chetail, 'Vattel et la sémantique du droit des gens' (n 100) 402–13; B Holland, 'The Moral Person of the State: Emer de Vattel and the Foundations of International Legal Order' (2011) 37(4) History of European Ideas 438–45; T Tetsuya, 'La doctrine vattelienne de l'égalite souveraine dans le contexte neuchâtelois' (2009) 11 J Hist Intl L 103; T Christov, 'Liberal Internationalism Revisited: Grotius, Vattel, and the International Order of States' (2005) 10(7) The European Legacy 561; Beaulac, *The Power of Language* (n 85) 138–79; Jouannet, *Emer de Vattel* (n 57) 319–40; NG Onuf, *The Republican Legacy in International Thought* (CUP 1998) 118, 123, 139–40; P Haggenmacher, 'L'Etat souverain comme sujet du droit international de Vitoria à Vattel' (1992) 16 Droits Rev Fr 11; FG Whelan, 'Vattel's Doctrine of the State' (1988) 9 History of Political Thought 59; H Muir-Watt, 'Droit naturel et souveraineté de l'Etat dans la doctrine de Vattel' (1987) 32 APD 71; PF Butler, 'Legitimacy in a State-System: Vattel's Law of Nations' in M Donelan (ed), *The Reason of States: A Study in International Political Theory* (Allen and Unwin 1978) 45–63.

[102] For further discussion about Vattel as a transitional figure, see most notably E Jouannet, 'Les dualismes du *Droit des gens*' in Chetail and Haggenmacher, *Vattel's International Law in a XXIst Century Perspective* (n 85) 133–50; I Nakhimovsky, 'Vattel's Theory of the International Order: Commerce and the Balance of Power in the Law of Nations' (2007) 33 History of European Ideas 157–73; Jouannet, *Emer de Vattel* (n 57) 249–50, 419–25; DJ Bederman, *The Spirit of International Law* (University of Georgia Press 2002) 55–56; NG Onuf, '"Tainted by Contingency": Retelling the Story of International Law' in R Falk, LEJ Ruiz, and RBJ Walker (eds), *Reframing the International. Law, Culture, Politics* (Routledge 2002) 28.

Innocent passage and the dual law of nations

The great ambition of Vattel was to reconcile state sovereignty with natural law. The dialectic between power and justice is illustrated by his distinction between the internal law of nations (also called necessary law) and the external law of nations (labelled voluntary law). The former 'is just and good in itself'[103] and as such it 'is always obligatory on the conscience',[104] whereas 'voluntary law tolerates what cannot be avoided without introducing greater evils'.[105] Vattel explained in his Preface that:

> The necessary and the voluntary law of nations are therefore both established by nature, but each in a different manner; the former as a sacred law which nations and sovereigns are bound to respect and follow in all their actions; the latter, as a rule which the general welfare and safety oblige them to admit in their transactions with each other. […] This double law, founded on certain and invariable principles, is susceptible of demonstration, and will constitute the principal subject of this work.[106]

When transposed to the admission of foreigners, his dual law of nations provides a nuanced account that is far from endorsing an unqualified discretion of the state. On the contrary, the external, or voluntary, right to refuse admission is qualified by the internal, or necessary, duty of innocent passage:

> In explaining the effects of domain we have said above […] that the owner of the territory may forbid the entrance into it, or permit it on such conditions as he thinks proper. We were then treating of his external right,—that right which foreigners are bound to respect. But now that we are considering the matter in another view, and as it relates to his duties and to his internal right, we may venture to assert that he cannot, without particular and important reasons, refuse permission, either to pass through or reside in the country, to foreigners who desire it for lawful purposes. For, their passage or their residence being in this case an innocent advantage, the law of nature does not give him a right to refuse it: and though other nations and other men in general are obliged to submit to his judgment […], he does not the less offend against his duty, if he refuses without sufficient reason: he then acts without any true right; he only abuses his external right.[107]

Thus, while the external law of nations acknowledges the state's competence to decide upon the admission of foreigners, the internal law of nations requires a right of innocent passage that cannot be refused without solid reasons. Otherwise, the state is committing an abuse of its external right to control entry into its territory. Indeed, 'his duty towards all mankind obliges [the owner of the territory] […] to allow a free passage through, and a residence in, his state'.[108] Vattel's right of free passage relied on the scholastic tradition of natural law:

> The introduction of property cannot be supposed to have deprived nations of the general right of traversing the earth for the purposes of mutual intercourse, of carrying on commerce with each other, and for other just reasons. It is only on particular occasions when the owner of a country thinks it would be prejudicial or dangerous to allow a passage through it, that

---

[103] Vattel, *The Law of Nations* (n 85) Preface at 16.   [104] ibid Preliminaries, para 28 at 79
[105] ibid Book III, ch XIII, para 192 at 593.   [106] ibid Preface at 17.
[107] ibid Book II, ch X, para 135 at 328.   [108] ibid Book II, ch VIII, para 100 at 312.

he ought to refuse permission to pass. He is therefore bound to grant a passage for lawful purposes, whenever he can do it without inconvenience to himself. And he cannot lawfully annex burthensome conditions to a permission which he is obliged to grant, and which he cannot refuse if he wishes to discharge his duty, and not abuse his right of property.[109]

Although this crucial feature of the Vattelian thought has frequently been ignored, both internal and external laws bound each nation. The two laws are not necessarily incompatible nor exclusive, but instead mutually reinforcing. As a result of this dual law, state competence must be exercised in accordance with the right of innocent passage. However, if such admission is prejudicial or dangerous to the host state, its external right to refuse entry must prevail over its internal duty of innocent passage. In such a case, even refugees must comply with a refusal of admission, when the safety of the territorial state requires them to do so.[110] One could concede that the practical result of his subtle construction is not so detached from that of Wolff. However, Vattel distinguishes himself from his master with a major feature: necessity triggers a right to illegal entry and, accordingly, trumps the sovereign power to refuse admission.

Necessity: a right to illegal entry

The key contribution and modernity of Vattel lie in the right of necessity as a way to reconcile the external right to refuse admission with the internal duty to allow innocent passage. Courts and commentators alike have long neglected this crucial aspect because of an enduring misperception that Vattel endorsed 'an early triumph of state sovereignty'.[111] Even the very few authors who have noticed his right of necessity concluded that 'Vattel ultimately cannot decide between right of communication and right of property.'[112] This assertion is arguably incorrect, since Vattel attributes great value to the right of necessity in order to resolve the tension between sovereignty and hospitality. Indeed, necessity imposes a major restriction on state sovereignty and paves the way for a right to illegal entry.

According to Vattel, the right of necessity overrules the prevalence of the external right to refuse admission over the internal duty to allow innocent passage. He

[109] ibid Book II, ch X, para 132 at 327.

[110] 'For, on the other hand, every nation has a right to refuse admitting a foreigner into her territory, when he cannot enter it without exposing the nation to evident danger, or doing her a manifest injury. What she owes to herself, the care of her own safety, gives her this right; and in virtue of her natural liberty, it belongs to the nation to judge, whether her circumstances will or will not justify the admission of that foreigner (Prelim. §16). He cannot then settle by a full right, and as he pleases, in the place he has chosen, but must ask permission of the chief of the place; and if it is refused, it is his duty to submit. However, as property could not be introduced to the prejudice of the right acquired by every human creature, of not being absolutely deprived of such things as are necessary,—no nation can, without good reasons, refuse even a perpetual residence to a man driven from his country. But if particular and substantial reasons prevent her from affording him an asylum, this man has no longer any right to demand it,—because, in such a case, the country inhabited by the nation cannot, at the same time, serve for her own use, and that of this foreigner'. ibid Book I, ch XIX, paras 230–31 at 226–27.

[111] Cavallar, 'Immigration and Sovereignty' (n 1) 9.

[112] Baker, 'Right of Entry or Right of Refusal? Hospitality in the Law of Nature and Nations' (n 1) 1430.

defined the right of necessity as 'the right which necessity alone gives to the performance of certain actions that are otherwise unlawful, when, without these actions, it is impossible to fulfil an indispensable obligation'.[113] As a result, the right of necessity allows foreigners to force the passage denied by the state. He explained that:

The right of passage is also a remnant of the primitive state of communion, in which the entire earth was common to all mankind, and the passage was everywhere free to each individual according to his necessities. Nobody can be entirely deprived of this right (§117); but the exercise of it is limited by the introduction of domain and property: since they have been introduced, we cannot exert that right without paying due regard to the private rights of others. The effect of property is to give the proprietor's advantage a preference over that of all others. When, therefore, the owner of a territory thinks proper to refuse you admission into it, you must, in order to enter it in spite of him, have some reason more cogent than all his reasons to the contrary. Such is the right of necessity: this authorises an act on your part, which on other occasions would be unlawful, viz. an infringement of the right of domain.[114]

As a result of this balancing act between territorial sovereignty and the right of necessity, Vattel concluded:

When a real necessity obliges you to enter into the territory of others,—for instance, if you cannot otherwise escape from imminent danger, or if you have no other passage for procuring the means of subsistence, or those of satisfying some other indispensable obligation,—you may force a passage when it is unjustly refused.[115]

Instead of acknowledging an unbridled discretion of the state, Vattel endorsed in a rather modern fashion a right to irregular entry when there is no other means to flee from a danger or to procure one's own means of subsistence. Even more strikingly, such a right of necessity is a perfect right, which can be enforced against the will of the state.[116] This represents a major difference from innocent passage as, contrary to the latter, necessity leaves no room of appreciation for the state, which is accordingly bound and forced to admit foreigners: 'th[e] right of innocent use is not a perfect right like that of necessity; for it belongs to the owner to judge whether the use we wish to make of a thing that belongs to him will not be attended with damage or inconvenience'.[117] Accordingly, Vattel's notion of necessity has two particularly straightforward implications: first, the judgment as to whether there is a state of necessity lies with the person seeking entry and not with the state and, second, necessity truly confers an individual right and is not a mere defence to a claim.

The threshold triggering the right of necessity remains high and requires a casuistic approach that is quite similar to a proportionality test: necessity prevails over sovereignty if, and only if, irregular entry is the only way to safeguard an essential interest of the foreigner. As Vattel cautiously underlined, 'in such a case, the

---

[113] Vattel, *The Law of Nations* (n 85) Book II, ch IX, para 119 at 320.
[114] ibid Book II, ch IX, para 123 at 322.   [115] ibid.
[116] ibid Book II, ch IX, para 128 at 324. To Vattel, '[t]he *perfect right* is that which is accompanied by the right of compelling those who refuse to fulfil the correspondent obligation; the *imperfect* right is unaccompanied by that right of compulsion. The *perfect obligation* is that which gives to the opposite party the right of compulsion; the *imperfect* gives him only a right to ask'. ibid Preliminaries, para 17 at 75.
[117] ibid Book II, ch IX, para 128 at 324.

obligation must really be an indispensable one, and the act in question the only means of fulfilling that obligation. If either of these conditions be wanting, the right of necessity does not exist on the occasion'.[118]

Against this framework, one could be tempted to conclude that Vattel's right of necessity prefigures a post-modern duty of *non-refoulement* where there is a risk of serious violations of human rights (whether civil, political, economic, or social). His right of necessity remains, however, an exception to the principle of state competence to decide upon the admission of foreigners. His system accordingly contrasts with the regime of free movement developed by Vitoria and Grotius. His innovative construction based on the right of necessity was thus primarily bound to apply only to very few states—like China and Japan—that forbade the entrance of foreigners without express permission.[119] Vattel observed that, in the practice of many other states, for instance in the European continent, free movement of persons remained the rule: 'in Europe the access is every where free to every person who is not an enemy of the state, except, in some countries, to vagabonds and outcasts'.[120]

1.2 The Rise and Fall of Free Movement (19th Century to 20th Century)

As exemplified by Vitoria, Grotius, and Vattel, early scholars of international law were far from acknowledging an absolute discretion of the state in the field of migration. On the contrary, the very notion of state sovereignty was held compatible with a qualified right of entry, whether grounded in the right of necessity or the right of communication between peoples. Paradoxically, the doctrine of the Law of Nations was distorted and instrumentalized in order to justify immigration restrictions as a natural consequence of territorial sovereignty. This narrative of immigration control has become commonplace today. For instance, in 2004, the British Supreme Court asserted in its famous *Prague Airport* case that '[t]he power to admit, exclude and expel aliens was among the earliest and most widely recognised powers of the sovereign State'.[121]

However, this conventional wisdom is grounded on false premises for both historical and normative reasons. Indeed, assuming the power to exclude aliens as the earliest prerogative of the state is inaccurate and highly disputable.[122] On the

---

[118] ibid Book II, ch IX, para 119 at 320. According to this proportionality test, 'if an equal necessity obliges the proprietor to refuse you entrance, he refuses it justly; and his right is paramount to yours. Thus a vessel driven by stress of weather has a right to enter, even by force, into a foreign port. But if that vessel is infected with the plague, the owner of the port may fire upon it and beat it off, without any violation either of justice, or even of charity, which, in such a case, ought doubtless to begin at home'. ibid Book II, ch IX, para 123 at 322.

[119] ibid Book II, ch VIII, para 100 at 312; ch VII, para 94 at 309.

[120] ibid Book II, ch VIII, para 100 at 312.

[121] *European Roma Rights Centre and Others v Immigration Officer at Prague Airport* [2004] UKHL 55, 11 (Lord Bingham).

[122] As underlined by R Plender, 'the right to exclude aliens has not always been regarded as an essential attribute of a State's sovereignty' R Plender, *International Migration Law* (Martinus Nijhoff 1988) 62. For a similar account, see notably S Saroléa, *Droits de l'homme et migrations. De la protection du*

contrary, free movement across borders has long been the rule, rather than the exception, in the history of humanity.[123] Furthermore, from the 16th to the end of the 18th century, the rise of the nation-state and its implicit corollary—territorial sovereignty—did not coincide with the introduction of border controls. For a long time, restrictions were instead primarily imposed on the internal movement of both nationals and non-nationals within the territory of each state (mainly for tax purposes). In contrast, the admission of foreigners was traditionally viewed as a means of strengthening the power of host states (primarily for demographic and economic reasons). This attitude prevailed during most of the 19th century until the introduction of immigration controls at the turn of the 20th century.

1.2.1 The climax of free movement in the 19th century

The 19th century is commonly depicted as the golden age of free movement. This understanding is firmly grounded on transatlantic migration from Europe to the Americas from 1850 to 1914 which is conventionally labelled as 'the age of free mass migration'.[124] This, however, was only one form of migration among many others. The 19th century witnessed a great diversity of migratory flows, including intra-European migration, colonial migration in Africa and Asia, forced migration of slaves, and its replacement by indentured workers through the so-called 'coolie system'.[125] Not only did migration happen at a massive scale, but it was also a worldwide phenomenon which affected many regions, including Asia. A historical survey carried out by Adam McKeown has highlighted that long-distance migratory flows

migrant aux droits de la personne migrante (Bruylant 2006) 442ff; G Fourlanos, *Sovereignty and the Ingress of Aliens: With Special Focus on Family Unity and Refugee Law* (Almqvist and Wiksell International 1986) 9ff; Nafziger, 'The General Admission of Aliens under International Law' (n 1) 807ff.

[123] For an historical overview of global migrations, see most notably MH Fisher, *Migration: A World History* (OUP 2014); P Manning, *Migration in World History* (Routledge 2005); and W Gungwu (ed), *Global History and Migrations* (Westview Press 1997).

[124] TJ Hatton and JG Williamson, *The Age of Mass Migration: Causes and Economic Impact* (OUP 1998) 3. Among a plethoric literature, see also RL Cohn, *Mass Migration under Sail: European Immigration to the Antebellum United States* (CUP 2009); EJ Errington, *Emigrant Worlds and Transatlantic Communities: Migration to Upper Canada in the First Half of the Nineteenth Century* (McGill-Queen's University Press 2007); KH O'Rourke and JG Williamson, *Globalization and History: The Evolution of a Nineteenth-Century Atlantic Economy* (MIT Press 1999); C Strikwerda, 'Tides of Migration, Currents of History: The State, Economy, and the Transatlantic Movement of Labor in the Nineteenth and Twentieth Centuries' (1999) 44 Intl Rev Soc Hist 367; W Nugent, *Crossings: The Great Transatlantic Migrations, 1870–1914* (Indiana University Press 1992).

[125] For an historical overview of these different migratory flows during the 19th century, see especially Manning, *Migration in World History* (n 123) 132–56; U Bosma, 'Beyond the Atlantic: Connecting Migration and World History in the Age of Imperialism, 1840–1940' (2007) 52(1) Intl Rev Soc Hist 116–23; D Hoerder, *Cultures in Contact: World Migrations in the Second Millennium* (Duke University Press 2002) 135–442; R Cohen (ed), *The Cambridge Survey of World Migration* (CUP 1995) 11–222; D Northrup, *Indentured Labor in the Age of Imperialism, 1834–1922* (CUP 1995); L P Moch, *Moving Europeans: Migration in Western Europe since 1650* (Indiana University Press 1992) 102–60; PC Emmer and M Mörner (eds), *European Expansion and Migration: Essays on the Intercontinental Migration from Africa, Asia, and Europe* (Berg 1992); R Vecoli and S Sinke (eds), *A Century of European Migrations, 1830–1930* (University of Illinois Press 1992); L Potts, *The World Labour Market: A History of Migration* (Zed Books Ltd 1990) 38–154.

in Asia were largely similar to the transatlantic migration both in size and timing.[126] The historian further argues that most Asian migrants moved freely and for the same reasons as Europeans to areas where labour was in high demand.[127]

This period of mass migration—also labelled as the 'proletarian mass migration'[128]—coincided with the rise of legal positivism and the celebration of state sovereignty.[129] But, at that time, migration was not held incompatible with sovereignty. *Laissez faire-laissez passer* was indeed the prevailing rule during most of the 19th century. It was even encouraged by states primarily to attract a cheap and docile labour force or to populate new territories. One could contend that states generally abstained from carrying out immigration controls because they simply did not have the effective and practical means to do so. This view is incorrect and fails to reflect the acknowledgement of the right of entry in the practice of states. The United Kingdom provided a convincing counter-example, although it was one of the rare states which was able to carry out immigration control as a result of its insularity. From the end of the Napoleonic Wars until 1905, no aliens were excluded or expelled from its territory.[130] The British Foreign Secretary explained in 1852: 'By the existing law of Great Britain, all foreigners have the unrestricted right of entrance and residence in this country; and while they remain in it, are, equally with British subjects, under the protection of the law.'[131]

The right of entry was even enshrined in the constitutions of several other states,[132] as well as in a number of bilateral

---

[126] A McKeown, 'Global Migration, 1846–1940' (2004) 15 Journal of World History 155–89; A McKeown, *Melancholy Order: Asian Migration and the Globalization of Borders* (Columbia University Press 2008) 43–89.

[127] ibid. For further discussion and studies on Asian migration, see J Lucassen and L Lucassen (eds), *Globalising Migration History: The Eurasian Experience (16th–21st Centuries)* (Brill 2014); DR Gabaccia and D Hoerder (eds), *Connecting Seas and Connected Ocean Rims: Indian, Atlantic, and Pacific Oceans and China Seas Migrations from the 1830s to the 1930s* (Brill 2011); PA Kuhn, *Chinese Among Others: Emigration in Modern Times* (Rowman and Littlefield 2008); L Lucassen, 'Migration and World History: Reaching a New Frontier' (2007) 52(1) Intl Rev Soc Hist 89–96; PP Mohapatra, 'Eurocentrism, Forced Labour, and Global Migration: A Critical Assessment' (2007) 52(1) Intl Rev Soc Hist 110–15; S Mazumdar, 'Localities of the Global: Asian Migrations between Slavery and Citizenship' (2007) 52(1) Intl Rev Soc Hist 124–33.

[128] Hoerder, *Cultures in Contact* (n 125) 344.

[129] For a thorough analysis on the rise of positivism during the 19th century see most notably, Anghie, *Imperialism, Sovereignty and the Making of International Law* (n 26) 32–114; M Koskenniemi, *The Gentle Civilizer of Nations: The Rise and Fall of International Law 1870–1960* (CUP 2001) 11–178; D Kennedy, 'International Law and the Nineteenth Century: History of an Illusion' (1996) 65 Nordic J Intl Law 385–420; A Carty, *The Decay of International Law? A Reappraisal of the Limits of Legal Imagination in International Affairs* (Manchester University Press 1986) 43–64.

[130] B Porter, *The Refugee Question in Mid-Victorian Politics* (CUP 1979) 1.

[131] 'Circular Dispatch to H.M. Representatives in European Capitals, January 13, 1852' (1852–1853) *State Papers* 42. See also: WF Craies, 'The Right of Aliens to Enter British Territory' (1890) 6(21) LQR 27.

[132] See in particular the 1876 Constitution of Spain (art 2) quoted in A Jeancourt-Galignani, *L'immigration en droit international* (Rousseau 1908) 128. In Latin American states, see also among other instances the 1860 Constitution of Bolivia (art 4); the 1879 Constitution of Guatemala (art 19); the 1853 Constitution of Argentina (art 25); and the 1891 Constitution of Brazil (art 72), quoted in P Fauchille, *Traité de droit international public* (Rousseau 1922) 897–98.

treaties.[133] Occasionally, domestic law provided for the right of the state to deport aliens, but it was rarely applied in practice and generally limited to troublemakers and other enemies of the nation.[134] Some states were of course less liberal than others with regard to immigrants: some of them—such as France[135] and Germany[136]— had already experimented with an embryonic form of bureaucratic interventionism to control the foreign population with few concrete results. This emerging process has been notably documented by John Torpey in his book *The Invention of the Passport: Surveillance, Citizenship and the State*. The historian contends that the first attempts to control the identity and mobility of foreigners were part of the broader evolution of modern European states and 'the institutionalization of the idea of the "nation-state" as a prospectively homogenous ethnocultural unit'.[137] He maintains, however, that this slow and gradual process was not effective for a while because it 'required the creation of elaborate bureaucracies and technologies that only gradually came into existence, a trend that intensified toward the end of the nineteenth century.'[138]

Free movement and sovereignty in the legal doctrine of the 19th century

While reflecting the conventional view of the time, the legal doctrine of the 19th century was used to discuss the role of international law in migration and the relations between the free movement of persons and the sovereignty of states. Until the end of the 19th century, most scholars acknowledged free movement as an established practice despite the recognition of state sovereignty as a founding principle of international law.

While admitting that the state could prohibit the entry of aliens by virtue of its territorial sovereignty, the German jurist and diplomat Georg Friedrich von Martens (1756–1821) observed that freedom of entry remained the rule in Europe:

Nowadays, however, no power in Europe refuses, in time of peace, to grant such permission to the subjects of another power; nor is it even necessary for such subjects to ask permission to enter a state, and bring their property into it. Thus, then the liberty of entry and passage may be considered as generally established between powers of Europe.[139]

---

[133] See for instance the 1860 Convention of Friendship (Britain-China), *II Hertslet's Commercial Treaties* 112 and the 1873 Treaty of Friendship (France-Burma), published in *Recueil des traités conclus par la France en Extrême-Orient (1684–1902)* (Leroux 1902) 113.

[134] For an overview of the law and practice governing expulsion at the time see notably A Chantre, *Du séjour et de l'expulsion des étrangers* (Aubert-Schuchardt 1890); L von Bar, 'L'expulsion des étrangers' (1886) JDI 1.

[135] G Noiriel, *La tyrannie du national. Le droit d'asile en Europe (1793-1993)* (Calmann-Lévy 1991) 45–93.

[136] J Torpey, *The Invention of the Passport: Surveillance, Citizenship and the State* (CUP 2000) 57–92.

[137] ibid 1.

[138] ibid 7. For further interesting studies on the first experimentations of immigration control see also McKeown, *Melancholy Order* (n 126) 121ff; A Fahrmeir, O Faron, and P Weil (eds) *Migration Control in the North Atlantic World: The Evolution of State Practices in Europe and the United States from the French Revolution to the Inter-War Period* (Berghahn Books 2003).

[139] GF von Martens, *The Law of Nations* (4th edn, William Cobbett 1829) 83.

The same observation was made by many other scholars, such as the German Theodor von Schmalz (1760–1831),[140] the Englishman James Reddis (1773–1852),[141] or the Argentinian Carlos Calvo (1824–1905).[142] The peaceful coexistence between state sovereignty and free movement constituted the common understanding of scholars, even if some nuances can be discerned between Continental authors and Anglo-American ones.

One of the most prominent international lawyers of the 19th century,[143] the Swiss Johann Caspar Bluntschli (1808–1881), devoted lengthy discussions to the rights and duties of states toward foreigners in his seminal book *Le droit international codifié*.[144] The Professor of Heidelberg University first observed that freedom of emigration was recognized by most European states and, as a result, both nationals and foreigners were free to leave their state of residence.[145] When discussing admission, he further affirmed that: 'no state has the right to prohibit in an absolute way the entry of foreigners onto its territory'.[146] Such a rule is grounded in 'civilized international law [which] is bound to protect the peaceful relations between men'.[147]

For Bluntschli, 'states are members of mankind; they are bound to respect the links that unite nations between themselves; their sovereignty is not an absolute right; it is limited by international law'.[148] While celebrating the free movement of his time,[149] he had to admit that states could still prohibit entry to some foreigners

---

[140] T von Schmalz, *Le droit des gens européen* (Maze 1823) 165: 'Aucune nation européenne n'interdit à un étranger, non suspect, l'entrée de son territoire. Mais c'est un droit généralement reconnu de ne pas admettre ceux dont la présence pourrait compromettre la sureté publique.' See also his German fellow: L Neumann, *Eléments du droit des gens modernes européen* (trans MA de Riedmatten, Rousseau 1886) 37: 'Aucun état civilisé ne refuse de nos jours l'entrée de son territoire à l'étranger dûment légitimé et non suspect. Mais le rapatriement ou le renvoi des vagabonds suspects ou sans ressource fait l'objet de nombreux traités entre les états européens.'

[141] J Reddie, *Inquiries in International Law* (2nd edn, Blackwood and Sons 1851) 204–05: 'The exclusive rights of dominion and property, over, and to its own territory, would authorize the denial of entry, or passage to all foreigners, either by land or sea. But, with respect to their European possessions, all the powers now generally accord to each other, in time of peace, the liberty of entry, passage and residence, as well by land as by sea, and upon most rivers; subject of course to such conditions and regulations, as the security and internal tranquillity of the state may require.'

[142] C Calvo, *Le droit international: Théorie et pratique* (4th edn, Durant et Peonde-Lauriel/Guillaumin 1888) 189: 'Tout Etat est libre d'admettre les étrangers sur son territoire ou de les en exclure, en cas de nécessité, pour motifs d'ordre public; à plus forte raison est-il libre de ne les admettre qu'à certaines conditions, sous certaines restrictions. Toutefois l'usage généralement suivi par les gouvernements permet, en temps de paix, aux étrangers l'entrée sur leur territoire, la liberté d'y faire du commerce, le passage, le séjour temporaire, l'établissement […]'.

[143] For further discussion about the thought and influence of JC Bluntschli, see: Koskenniemi, *The Gentle Civilizer of Nations* (n 129) 42–54 and 80–85.

[144] See especially JC Bluntschli, *Le droit international codifié* (trans MC Lardy, Guillaumin 1895) 26–28 and 218–37.

[145] ibid para 370 at 224–25 and para 392 at 232.

[146] ibid para 381 at 228 (author's translation).   [147] ibid (author's translation).

[148] ibid (author's translation).

[149] ibid. He wrote with the typical lyricism of his time that: 'Dans le monde civilisé, on respecte envers les étrangers les droits de l'humanité, et sur tous les points importants du droit privé, ils sont complètement assimilés aux nationaux. […] [U]n grand nombre de traités ont eu pour but d'abolir les droits à payer en cas d'émigration, et garantissent le libre établissement. Le Français vit à New York, Berlin ou Calcutta tout aussi en sûreté qu'à Paris ou à Lyon. Une quantité énorme d'étrangers venus de tous pays demeurent sur toute la terre, en paix les uns à côté des autres […]. Le développement de principes communs aux différents peuples n'est point resté en arrière de l'extension des moyens de transport.

on specific grounds.[150] Such a refusal of admission nevertheless had to be duly justified by considerations of public order and public safety because, otherwise, it would be in contradiction with the principle of freedom in international relations among nations.[151] In short, free movement had to remain the rule, but state sovereignty could justify an exception to this reminiscent right of communication between peoples.[152]

This balancing act between state sovereignty and free movement reflected the prevailing stance even among Anglo-American scholars. However, the insistence of the latter on state sovereignty considerably changed the terms of the debate by relegating free movement to the remote realm of natural law. The correlative rise of legal positivism provided an additional justification for derogating from what came to be characterized as a mere moral duty of admission. The most influential US scholar of the 19th century, James Kent (1763–1847), provided a persuasive illustration of this shift in his *Commentaries on American Law*. While referring to Pufendorf and Vattel, Kent reaffirmed the duty to grant free passage, but he recognized that it could be refused when admission was contrary to the interest of the host state:

Every nation is bound, in time of peace, to grant a passage, for lawful purposes, over their lands, rivers, and seas, to the people of other states, whenever it can be permitted without inconvenience; and burdensome conditions ought not to be annexed to the transit of persons and property. If, however, any government deems the introduction of foreigners, or their merchandise, injurious to the interests of their own people, they are at liberty to withhold the indulgence. The entry of foreigners and their effects is not an absolute right, but only one of imperfect obligation, and it is subject to the discretion of the government which tolerates it.[153]

It is not difficult to see that such an emphasis on states' discretion would eventually lay the grounds for justifying the introduction of immigration control in the US at the end of the century. Some authors were even more straightforward in asserting a total discretion of states without any reference to free passage as a moral or imperfect duty. An English Judge and politician, Robert Phillimore (1810–1885), affirmed in his *Commentaries upon International Law*:

It is a received maxim of International Law, that the Government of a State may prohibit the entrance of strangers into the country, and may therefore regulate the conditions under which they shall be allowed to remain in it, or may require and compel their departure from it.[154]

Ces principes communs ont brisé l'isolement de certaines nations; ils constituent aujourd'hui un droit auquel aucun état ne peut se soustraire car cet état attirerait sur lui non seulement la désapprobation du monde civilisé, mais encore le danger d'être appelé à rendre compte de sa conduite et de payer cher sa manière d'agir; les autres nations chercheraient évidemment à lui apprendre à respecter en l'étranger l'homme, à voir dans les relations commerciales ou autres une conséquence de la communauté d'intérêt des peuples. La qualité de citoyens du monde, que Kant envisageait d'un côté comme une condition essentielle, de l'autre comme un idéal impossible à atteindre, est devenue aujourd'hui plus ou moins une vérité.' Bluntschli, *Le droit international codifié* (n 144) 27.

[150] ibid para 382 at 228.   [151] ibid.
[152] See also in this sense: Cavallar, 'Immigration and Sovereignty' (n 1) 13–14.
[153] J Kent, *Commentaries on American Law*, vol 1 (11th edn, Little and Brown Company 1866) 35.
[154] R Phillimore, *Commentaries upon International Law*, vol 1 (3rd edn, Butterworths 1879) 320.

His view was endorsed in 1892, almost verbatim, by the US Supreme Court in the famous *Ekiu* case to justify the exclusion of a Japanese immigrant.[155] Curiously enough, Phillimore did not elaborate further on his shift from other scholars of the time, including the continental ones.[156] His postulation was clearly influenced by his absolute conception of state sovereignty. The above quotation is tellingly drawn from a chapter devoted to the right of self-preservation 'which prevents, as well as [...] repels, attack' and constitutes, for Phillimore, 'the first law of nations'.[157] It is true that the rhetoric of war is not rare in the narrative of migration control. Nonetheless, it would perhaps be excessive to infer from his reasoning an implicit equation of immigration with invasion.

Instead, his main justification for advocating for states' discretion to refuse admission of foreigners relied on an uninhibited understanding of territorial sovereignty. He defined it as an 'absolute and uncontrolled power of jurisdiction over all Persons, and over all Things, within [the] territorial limits' of the state.[158] Phillimore accordingly endorsed the patrimonial conception of the state inherited from Wolff. Following this approach, he underlined that each state possesses 'an exclusive right of property' of its territory and, as a result, 'no stranger can be entitled, without [its] permission, to enter within [its] boundaries'.[159]

A similar yet much more balanced account can be found in the work of the English lawyer William Edward Hall (1835–1894), who has been portrayed by Martti Koskenniemi as 'an avowed positivist and a pragmatist, the author of perhaps the most influential English-language textbook of the period'.[160] Hall wrote in his well-known *Treaties on International Law* first published in 1880 that:

> [Because] a state may do what it chooses within its own territory so long as its conduct is not actively injurious to other states, it must be granted that in strict law a country can refuse the hospitality of its soil to any, or to all, foreigners; but the exercise of the right is necessarily tempered by the facts of modern civilization. For a state to exclude all foreigners would be to withdraw from the brotherhood of civilized peoples; to exclude any without reasonable or at least plausible cause is regarded as so vexatious and oppressive, that a government is thought to have the right of interfering in favour of its subjects in cases where sufficient cause does not in its judgement exist.[161]

Accordingly, Hall agreed with Bluntschli that a state cannot exclude all foreigners without isolating itself from the club of the so-called civilized nations. However, for the English positivist, such a rule pertained to natural law: it derived from 'the

---

[155] ibid. The relevant extract and reference of this case are mentioned above in section 1.1.3.

[156] He simply mentioned that: 'During periods of revolutionary disturbances both on the Continent and within this kingdom, it has been customary to pass Acts of Parliament authorizing certain high officers of the State to order the departure of aliens from the realm within a specified time, and their imprisonment in case of refusal. These Acts have generally been limited in their duration: the operation of the last was confined to the period of one year.' ibid 320. This argument is however not convincing for the relevant acts adopted in 1793 and then in 1848 remained the exception rather than the rule: they were adopted for a very short period as an emergency legislation in times of revolutionary turmoil.

[157] ibid 312.   [158] ibid 443.   [159] ibid 221.

[160] Koskenniemi, *The Gentle Civilizer of Nations* (n 129) 81. See also Anghie, *Imperialism, Sovereignty and the Making of International Law* (n 26) 39, fn 12.

[161] WE Hall, *A Treatise on International Law* (3rd edn, Clarendon Press 1890) 211.

duty of sociability' between nations that belonged to 'purely moral obligations' rather than to binding duties under positive international law.[162] While criticizing the right of communication promoted by Vitoria and Bluntschli, Hall argued that:

[This] doctrine is no doubt limited by the qualification that a state may take what measures of precaution it considers needful to prevent the right of access and intercourse from being used to its injury, and may subject foreigners and foreign trade to regulation in the interest either of its own members or of states which it wishes to favour.[163]

Hall concluded that the sovereign will of the state to refuse admission of foreigners had to take priority over the natural right of communication:

If a country decides that certain classes of foreigners are dangerous to its tranquillity, or are inconvenient to it socially or economically or morally, and if it passes general laws forbidding the access of such persons, its conducts affords no ground for complaint. Its fears may be idle; its legislation may be harsh; but its action is equal.[164]

The codification of the right to admission by the Institute of International Law

While witnessing a period of transition, the positivist claim in favour of the sovereign state was yet to be the conventional wisdom of the legal profession. Indeed, the resolutions adopted by the Institute of International Law provided a different picture which fairly reflected the prevailing view of the time.[165] In 1892, the Institute adopted a set of *International Rules on the Admission and Expulsion of Aliens* in order to formulate 'some constant principles' on this topical issue of international law.[166] Article 6 of these international rules affirmed as a general principle of international law that 'free entrance of aliens into the territory of a civilized state cannot be prohibited in a general and permanent manner other than in the interest of public welfare and on extremely serious grounds'.[167] The right to enter into a foreign country thus remained the rule and could be derogated from by states only in exceptional circumstances as a last resort.

Following the typical Western-centric approach of the time, the 'extremely serious grounds' elaborated in Article 6 included 'a fundamental difference of morals or civilisation' and 'a dangerous accumulation of aliens' at a massive scale. The first ground raised some controversy during the drafting of the *International Rules on the*

---

[162] ibid 58.   [163] ibid, 58–59.

[164] ibid, 211. The state's discretion to refuse admission of immigrants is distinguished from its right of expulsion. Hall further added that: 'The matter is different where for identical reasons individual foreigners, or whole classes of foreigners, who have already been admitted into the country, or who are resident there, are subjected to expulsion. In such cases the propriety of the conduct of the expelling government must be judged with reference to the circumstances of the moment. Instances have occurred in which the rights of expulsion have been seriously strained.' ibid.

[165] According to its own statute, the Institute was established in 1873 'to promote the progress of international law' through 'the gradual and progressive codification of international law' in line with 'the legal conscience of the civilized world'.

[166] 'Règles internationales sur l'admission et l'expulsion des étrangers. Session de Genève, 1892' (1892–1894) 12 Annuaire de l'Institut du droit international 220, 3rd preambular para.

[167] ibid 220 (author's translation).

Admission and Expulsion of Aliens, because the initial version mentioned a difference of races to justify a refusal of admission.[168] Any reference to race was eventually deleted because such insertion was 'in contradiction with all the ideas of this century'.[169] Nonetheless, it was clear that the 'fundamental difference of morality or civilization' primarily related to the US measures adopted at the time against what was considered by one of the rapporteurs 'the progressive invasion of Chinese on its territory'.[170]

The other grounds of exclusion laid down in Articles 8 and 12 were more conventional. Under the former provision, states retained the right to restrict or temporarily prohibit the entry of aliens in times of war, domestic turmoil, or epidemic. Besides these exceptional circumstances, Article 12 permitted the exclusion of three specific types of immigrants: vagabonds and beggars; those who suffered from a disease which could endanger public health; and individuals who were strongly suspected of or condemned for having committed a serious crime abroad. While reflecting the state of domestic legislation at the end of the 19th century, the grounds of exclusion laid down by the *International Rules on the Admission and Expulsion of Aliens* were considered as an exception to the general principle of free admission. In support of this principle, Article 7 further underlined that 'the protection of national labour force is not in itself a sufficient ground of non-admission'.

In 1897, the Institute of International Law adopted a draft convention on emigration for the purpose of restating the prevailing practice.[171] Its first article reaffirmed that 'Contracting States recognise freedom to emigrate and to immigrate, whether by individuals or groups, without any distinction based on nationality.'[172] It further specified that 'this freedom can be only restricted by decision duly published by governments and in the strict limits of social and political necessities'. However, this draft convention came out during a period of drastic change in state practice. It eventually remained a dead letter and the last remnant of the 19th century, when free movement and state sovereignty were still not mutually exclusive. At the turn of the 20th century, the growing rise of immigration control progressively became the rule and no longer the exception.

1.2.2 The invention of immigration control and the turn of the 20th century

Immigration control is a relatively recent invention of states. With a few exceptions,[173] immigration controls mainly emerged at the end of the 19th century in some countries and for specific categories of aliens. The US was among the first

---

[168] (1892–1894) 12 AIDI 133–36.   [169] ibid 134 (author's translation).

[170] ibid 133 (author's translation).

[171] The rapporteurs underlined that the draft convention broadly reflected the common principles acknowledged in most domestic legislations: (1897) AIDI 57–58.

[172] 'Principes recommandés par l'Institut de droit international, en vue d'un projet de convention en matière d'émigration' (1897) AIDI 262–63 (author's translation).

[173] Like China and Japan, or in times of war and domestic turmoil— such as during the French revolution and the Napoleonic wars.

states to depart from the time-honoured tradition of immigration liberalism.[174] In 1875, the Congress prohibited the entry of non-national convicts and prostitutes.[175] A few years later, the Chinese Exclusion Act of 1882 suspended the immigration of Chinese labourers for ten years and forbade any court to grant citizenships to Chinese immigrants.[176] This temporary exclusion was perpetuated and strengthened by subsequent statutes,[177] and further grounds of exclusion were introduced in 1891 for nationals of other countries (including persons with mental or physical incapacities, those suffering from contagious diseases and persons likely to become a public charge).[178] Although both the Senate and the House of Representatives recently expressed their regret with regard to the Chinese Exclusion Act,[179] this first battery of domestic legislation engendered a disastrous domino effect on other traditional countries of immigration: Australia,[180] Canada,[181] and many Latin American states[182] considerably hardened their legislation along the US line.

[174] See also for similar immigration restrictions and the racial context underpinning them in the British Empire and Australia A Bashford, 'Immigration Restriction: Rethinking Period and Place from Settler Colonies to Postcolonial Nations' (2014) 9 Journal of Global History 26–48; McKeown, *Melancholy Order* (n 126) 185–214; M Lake and H Reynolds, *Drawing the Global Colour Line: White Men's Countries and the International Challenge of Racial Equality* (CUP 2008); J Martens, 'A Transnational History of Immigration Restriction: Natal and New South Wales, 1896–97' (2006) 34 J Imp & Commonw Hist 323–44; RA Huttenback, *Racism and Empire: White Settlers and Colored Immigrants in the British Self-governing Colonies, 1830–1910* (Cornell University Press 1976); C Price, *The Great White Walls Are Built: Restrictive Immigration to North America and Australasia, 1836–1888* (Australian National University Press 1974); AT Yarwood, *Asian Migration to Australia: The Background to Exclusion* (Melbourne University Press 1964).
[175] Immigration Act of 1875, 18 Stat 477. For previous immigration regulations adopted at the state level see however: GL Neuman, 'The Lost Century of American Immigration Law (1776–1875)' (1993) 93(8) Colum L Rev 1833–1901. See more generally about the introduction of immigration control in the US: AR Zolberg, *A Nation by Design: Immigration Policy and the Fashioning of America* (Harvard University Press 2006); D King, *Making Americans: Immigration, Race, and the Origins of Diverse Democracy* (Harvard University Press 2000); A Gyory, *Closing the Gate: Race, Politics, and the Chinese Exclusion Act* (University of North Carolina Press 1998); AR Zolberg, 'The Great Wall Against China: Responses to the First Immigration Crisis, 1885–1925' in J Lucassen and L Lucassen (eds), *Migration, Migration History, History: Old Paradigms and New Perspectives* (Peter Lang 1997) 291–315; S Chan (ed), *Entry Denied: Exclusion and the Chinese Community in America, 1882–1943* (Temple University Press 1991); V M Briggs, *Immigration Policy and the American Labor Force* (Johns Hopkins University Press 1984); K Calavita, *US Immigration Law and the Control of Labor, 1820–1924* (Academic Press 1984); MS Seller, 'Historical Perspectives on American Immigration Policy: Case Studies and Current Implications' (1982) 45 LCP 137–62.
[176] Chinese Exclusion Act of 1882, 22 Stat 58.
[177] The Chinese Exclusion Act was made permanent in 1902 and repealed only in 1943: Chinese Exclusion Repeal Act of 1943, 64 Stat 427.
[178] Immigration Act of 1891, 26 Stat 1084.
[179] H Res 683, 112th Congress, Jun 2012; S Res 201, 112th Congress, May 2011.
[180] See in particular Immigration Restriction Act of 1901, No 17, which was regularly amended and reinforced until 1949.
[181] Chinese Immigration Act of 1885, 48–49 Vict, c 71. This act was further strengthened in 1900, 1903, and 1923 before it was repealed in 1947. See also with regard to other non-citizens: Immigration Act of 1906, 6 Edward VII, c 19 and Immigration Act of 1910, 9–10 Edward VII, c 27.
[182] See especially the restrictive immigration laws introduced by Ecuador in 1889, Venezuela in 1894, Costa Rica in 1896 and 1905, Uruguay in 1890 and 1907, Bolivia in 1907, Honduras in 1906, Mexico in 1908, Guatemala and Peru in 1909, quoted in *Conférence internationale de l'émigration et de l'immigration, Rome 15–31 mai 1924*, vol 1 (Imprimerie de la Chambre des députés 1925) 246–304.

In Europe, the new era of immigration control was inaugurated by the UK at the beginning of the 20th century with a view to restricting Jewish immigration from Eastern Europe.[183] According to the Alien Act of 1905, 'undesirable immigrants' were not permitted to enter: (a) if they did not have the means of decently supporting themselves and their dependants; (b) if they were insane or were likely to become a public charge owing to disease or infirmity; (c) if they had been sentenced in a foreign country for a non-political crime; or (d) if an expulsion order had been made against them.[184] During the First World War, immigration controls became generalized in the domestic law of many other countries and reinforced by the introduction of passport requirements.[185] This wartime legislation was then maintained after the First World War and perpetuated due to the Great Depression of 1929.[186] Commentators of the time observed that 'the doors which once were opened wide are now but slightly ajar'.[187]

In short, one can advance without too much exaggeration that, from the end of the 19th century until the mid-20th century, immigration controls were primarily introduced for racial reasons, then generalized as wartime legislation and further reinforced by the economic crisis to become the standard of so-called modern states. The correlative rise of the welfare state and political suffrage has further strengthened the perception that the domestic labour market needed to be protected from foreign workers.[188] Still today, the vicious circle of armed conflicts, terrorism, economic recession, and electoral politics constitutes an influential factor for justifying

---

[183] On the political context prevailing at the time and the rise of anti-Semitism, see: T Kushner, 'Racialisation and "White European" Immigration to Britain' in K Muri and J Solomos (eds), *Racialization: Studies in Theory and Practice* (OUP 2005) 207–25; A Lee, 'Aspects of the Working Class Response to the Jews in Britain 1880–1914' in K Lunn (ed), *Hosts, Immigrants and Minorities: Historical Responses to Newcomers in British Society, 1870–1914* (St Martin's Press 1980) 134–59; B Gainer, *The Alien Invasion: The Origins of the Alien Act of 1905* (Heinemann 1972); L P Gartner, *The Jewish Immigrant in England, 1870–1914* (Allen and Unwin 1960).

[184] Aliens Act 1905, Sec 1(3), 5 Edward 7, c 13. For further comments see: A Bashford and J McAdam, 'The Right to Asylum: Britain's 1905 Aliens Act and the Evolution of Refugee Law' (2014) 32(2) LHR 309–50; H Wray, 'The Alien Act 1905 and the Immigration Dilemma' (2006) 33(2) J L and Society 302–23; N-W Sibley and A Elias, *The Aliens Act and the Right of Asylum* (Clower and Sons 1906); E Pépin, *L'Aliens Act de 1905: Causes et résultats* (Rousseau 1913).

[185] For further discussion about the generalization of passports after the First World War, see especially: Torpey, *The Invention of the Passport* (n 136) 111–21; E Reale, 'Le problème des passeports' (1934) 50 Collected Courses of the Hague Academy of International Law 85–188; E Reale, *Le régime des passeports et la Société des Nations* (2nd edn, Rousseau 1931).

[186] For an overview of the numerous immigration legislations at the time, see: International Labour Office, *Emigration and Immigration: Legislation and Treaties* (International Labour Office 1922) 167–226; *Conférence internationale de l'émigration et de l'immigration* (n 182) 241–304.

[187] H Fields, 'Closing Immigration throughout the World' (1932) 26 AJIL 671. For a similar account, see for instance: L Varlez, 'Migration Problems and the Havana Conference of 1928' (1929) 19(1) Intl Labour Rev 1, 9: 'Under the influence of many causes, accentuated by the war frame of mind, the freedom to migrate has disappeared almost everywhere.'

[188] McKeown, *Melancholy Order* (n 126) 321; L Lucassen, 'The Great War and the Origins of Migration Control in Western Europe and the United States (1880–1920)' in A Böcker and others (eds), *Regulation of Migration. International Experiences* (Het Spinhuis 1998) 45–72. For further developments on the racial context in the interwar period and the hostility toward Asian migrants, see especially among the references quoted above: Lake and Reynolds, *Drawing the Global Colour Line* (n 174) 310–31.

immigration control. Meanwhile, on a more conceptual plane, immigration control has become conventionally associated with territorial sovereignty. Though the former is not concomitant with the latter, the very notion of territorial sovereignty has proven to be a powerful tool not only for vindicating a radical break from the past, but also for ensuring the perpetuation of immigration control.

However, immigration controls did not arise without debate among international lawyers. This was graphically illustrated by the divide between Anglo-American authors and those in continental Europe. Manifestly influenced by the practice of their own states, the former endorsed and justified immigration control as a natural consequence of territorial sovereignty. The most famous British positivist of the early 20th century, Lassa Oppenheim (1858–1919), was the most ardent supporter of states' discretion in the field of migration, though he had to concede that a state cannot exclude all foreigners without questioning its membership in the international community of nations. Following the path of Hall, he wrote in his *International Law: A Treatise* first published in 1905 that:

Many writers maintain that every member of the Family of Nations is bound by International Law to admit all foreigners into its territory for all lawful purposes, although they agree that every State could exclude certain classes of foreigners. This opinion is generally held by those who assert that there is a fundamental right of intercourse between States. It will be remembered that no such fundamental right exists, but that intercourse is a characteristic of the position of the States within the Family of Nations and therefore a presupposition of the international personality of every State. A State, therefore, cannot exclude foreigners altogether from its territory without violating the spirit of the Law of Nations and endangering its very membership of the Family of Nations. But no State actually does exclude foreigners altogether. The question is only whether an international legal duty can be said to exist for every State to admit all unobjectionable foreigners to all parts of its territory. And it is this duty which must be denied as far as the customary Law of Nations is concerned. It must be emphasised that, apart from general conventional arrangements, as, for instance, those concerning navigation on international rivers, and apart from special treaties of commerce, friendship and the like, no State can claim the right for its subjects to enter into and reside on the territory of a foreign State. The reception of foreigners is a matter of discretion, and every State is by reason of its territorial supremacy competent to exclude foreigners from the whole or any part of its territory.[189]

---

[189] L Oppenheim, *International Law: A Treatise*, vol 1 (Longmans, Green and Co 1905) 369 (footnotes omitted). His colleague at Cambridge University, John Westlake, came to the same conclusion as Oppenheim, albeit with a slightly different reasoning which unveiled the racial, if not racist, prejudices surrounding discussions about immigration control: 'Between states of the white race, the entire exclusion of the subjects of any from the territory of any other at peace with the former has scarcely been attempted within historical times. If such an attempt could be imagined, it would be defeated by the stipulations in favour of mutual intercourse usual in the network of commercial treaties by which the white world is bound together, and which may be taken as expressing a general sentiment requiring that free intercourse shall be the rule. But those stipulations are vague, and are not understood to prevent the exclusion of individuals or even of classes for special reasons. The power to exclude individuals deemed undesirable is assumed in the passport system [...] [and] in the legislative exclusion of pauper aliens or of aliens arriving under contracts for employment, of which the United States furnish an example, and the adoption of which system so far as concerns the former class is urged by many in England, without its being suggested that in either country it is or would be a violation of international duty towards the states from which such aliens might come. Thus a clause providing for free intercourse in the common

The state's discretion to refuse admission of foreigners as inherent in its territorial sovereignty was further upheld by a large number of US scholars and practitioners, such as the Professor of political science and international law, Amos S Hershey (1867–1933),[190] John B Moore (1860–1947)—the first American judge to serve on the Permanent Court of International Justice[191]—Ewin Borchard (1884–1951)—law Professor at Yale University[192]—and Charles G Fenwick (1880–1973)—one of the most influential US international lawyers of the first half of the 20th century.[193] While referring to Vattel and the *Nishimura Ekiu* case of the US Supreme Court, Fenwick asserted that, as 'a well-established general principle', 'a state may forbid the entrance of aliens into its territory, or admit them only in such cases as commend themselves to its judgement'.[194]

In stark contrast to Anglo-American authors, many continental European lawyers postulated the right of mutual intercourse between nations as a general principle of international law and inferred from this basic rule a legal duty of admission. This was acknowledged by several authorities of international law, such as the Belgian Ernest Nys (1851–1920),[195] the Italian Pasquale Fiore (1837–1914),[196]

---

form of commercial treaties would scarcely seem sufficient to compel a state which regarded Jews as a special and inferior class to receive them from a country in which they enjoy the full rights of citizenship. […] As between states of the white race and orientals, the former […] have for the better part of a century past demanded freer admission for them. […] On the other hand, the United States and the Australasian colonies of Great Britain have directed against the yellow races legislation which, being based on the national character of the immigrants, cannot be compared with such special exclusions as those of Jews, paupers or persons under contract for employment.' See J Westlake, *International Law*, part 1 (CUP 1904) 208–09.

[190] AS Hershey, *The Essentials of International Public Law and Organization* (Macmillan 1927) 369.

[191] JB Moore, *A Digest of International Law*, vol 4 (Government Printing Office 1906) 67.

[192] EM Borchard, *The Diplomatic Protection of Citizens Abroad or the Law of International Claims* (Banks Law 1915) 45–46.

[193] Among many other similar assertions by US scholars, see: HW Bowen, *International Law: A Simple Statement of its Principles* (GP Putnam's Sons 1896) 53; H Taylor, *A Treatise on International Public Law*, (Callaghan and Co 1901) 231–32; GB Davis, *The Elements of International Law* (Harper and Brothers 1908) 118–19; CL Bouvé, *A Treatise on the Laws Governing Exclusion and Expulsion of Aliens in the United States* (John Byrne and Co 1912) 3–9; RR Foulke, *A Treatise on International Law*, vol 1 (John C Winston and Co 1920) 8–9. See however EC Stowell, *International Law: A Restatement of Principles in Conformity with Actual Practice* (Henry Holt and Co 1931) 137–39 and 279 (who asserts a duty of admission for alien merchants as a consequence of the right of commercial intercourse).

[194] CG Fenwick, *International Law* (first published in 1924, 3rd edn, Appleton-Century-Crofts 1948) 267. He continued by acknowledging that '[t]he right of total exclusion is, however, more theoretical than real. As a practical issue, no state can be assumed to be desirous of cutting itself off from all intercourse with the outside world; and should it do so it might reasonably be held to have forfeited its position as a member of the international community'. ibid 267–68. He concluded nevertheless that '[t]otal exclusion of immigrants may at any time become a necessity for those states of the Western Hemisphere which feel that the number of immigrants to their territories has exceeded the capacity for beneficial assimilation'. ibid 268. See also: CG Fenwick, 'The New Immigration Law and the Exclusion of Japanese' (1924) 18(3) AJIL 518–23.

[195] E Nys, *Le droit international. Les principes, les théories, les faits*, vol 2 (Weissenbruch 1912) 263.

[196] P Fiore, *Le droit international codifié et sa sanction juridique* (Pedone 1911) 314. However, while recognizing that the duty of admission is acknowledged by the great majority of authors, Anzilotti expressed his doubt about such a duty without justifying further his assertion: D Anzilotti, 'La responsabilité internationale des Etats à raison des dommages soufferts par des étrangers' (1906) 13 RGDIP 5, 17–18.

the German Franz von Liszt (1851–1919),[197] and the French Marcel Sibert (1884–1957).[198] Nonetheless, the duty of admission was not conceived as an absolute rule. The French scholar Paul Fauchille (1858–1926)—founder of the *Revue générale de droit international public*—tempered the principle of free admission with an exception based on the self-preservation of the state:

Two rules may be laid down for immigration. (1) Every state has a legal duty to admit to its territory nationals of other states who arrive at its frontiers. (2) It may escape this duty and impose prohibitions or restrictions only if its right of self-preservation necessitates this. In other words, foreigners have a right of access to the territory of a state, but this right is limited by the state's right of self-preservation.[199]

Fauchille explained in terms that could have been written today that free movement is triggered by the economic interdependence of states and the liberty of individuals.[200] As a result of these two influential factors, he further observed that:

[S]overeignty is not absolute but only relative; every state must take into account the rights of other states. The rights of a state include the right of protecting its own subjects as well as the right to reciprocal trade, but this certainly does not mean that the rights of the individual should take precedence of the rights of the state. The liberty of action of the individual is no more absolute than the sovereignty of the state. It finds its limits in the incontestable right of self-preservation appertaining to every state.[201]

Both continental European and Anglo-American lawyers thus concurred in acknowledging the competence of the state to regulate the admission of foreigners. However, the former envisaged it as an exception to the principle of free movement that could only be triggered when the preservation of the state was at stake. By contrast, and in line with the voluntarist theory of international law, the latter relied on an absolute conception of state sovereignty that could only be restricted by treaties. This professional—if not cultural—divide between Anglo-American and continental European lawyers echoed the ambiguous practice of the time and the growing opposition between countries of immigration and countries of emigration during the interwar period.

---

[197] F von Liszt, *Le droit international. Exposé systématique* (Pedone 1927) 204–05. In contrast to the other scholars, Liszt considered that free access was limited to so-called civilized states, whereas immigration could be restricted for nationals of states, such as China, which were not considered part of the international community.

[198] M Sibert, *Traité de droit international public*, vol 1 (Dalloz 1951) 575–76.

[199] P Fauchille, 'The Rights of Emigration and Immigration' (1924) 9 Intl Labour Rev 324. This article is in fact a translation of his chapter devoted to immigration in his *Traité de droit international public* (n 132) 888–922. For a similar account see also: J Thomas, 'La condition des étrangers et le droit international' (1897) 4 RGDIP 620, 623–27.

[200] Fauchille, 'The Rights of Emigration and Immigration' (n 199) 324.

[201] ibid 324–25.

1.2.3 Inter-state cooperation and the emergence of global migration governance

The interwar period unveils some striking analogies with our time, which highlight the complexity and ambiguity of international law when it comes to migration. Since the end of the First World War, immigration has been increasingly considered a matter of domestic jurisdiction (also referred to as 'reserved domain'), which is by definition not governed by international law. In fact, the very notion of domestic jurisdiction was literally invented by the US with a view to avoiding any interference in its sovereign right to decide on the admission of foreigners. Indeed, during the drafting of the Covenant of the League of Nations, President Wilson requested the insertion of a provision preserving states' domestic jurisdiction in order to make sure that immigration would fall under the exclusive control of each state.[202]

This safeguard clause was however phrased in very abstract terms and its impact was mainly procedural: according to Article 15(8) of the Covenant, the Council of the League was prohibited from making recommendations on 'a matter which by international law is solely within the domestic jurisdiction' of a state involved in a dispute with another Member State of the League. Furthermore, and more fundamentally, international law determines whether or not a matter falls within the domestic jurisdiction of states. In 1923, the Permanent Court of International Justice confirmed that the extent of the reserved domain depended on international law and varied according to its development.[203] In other words, domestic jurisdiction finishes where international law starts.

From the perspective of international law, the interwar period witnessed several initiatives carried out with the purpose of regulating migration at the multilateral level. This was a period of intense intergovernmental cooperation which laid down the basis of the current legal framework for migration. The interwar period experimented with many important features which now have become integral parts of contemporary international law, such as the organization of intergovernmental

---

[202] S Brawley, *The White Peril: Foreign Relations and Asian Immigration to Australasia and North America 1919–1978* (University of New South Wales Press 1995) 36–55; HH Jones, 'Domestic Jurisdiction—From the Covenant to the Charter' (1951–1952) 46 Illinois L Rev 219, 222–23; T Marbug and HE Flack (eds), *Taft Papers on League of Nations* (Macmillan 1920) 322. In parallel with the introduction of a specific provision endorsing the notion of domestic jurisdiction, President Wilson—with the support of Australia, Canada, and the UK—opposed a Japanese amendment in the preamble of the Covenant according to which: 'The equality of nations being a basic principle of the League of Nations, the High Contracting Parties agree to accord as soon as possible to all alien nationals of states who are members of the League, equal and just treatment in every respect, making no discrimination in law or in fact on account of their race or nationality.' DH Miller, *The Drafting of the Covenant* (GP Putnam's Sons 1928) 183. The diplomatic manoeuvrings carried out by Anglo-American states for neutralizing this proposal is well-documented in ibid 9–35. In particular '[w]hen Wilson called for the amendment to be put, 11 of the possible 17 votes supported the amendment, including Japan, France, Italy, Brazil, China, Greece, Yugoslavia and Czechoslovakia. In a last-ditch effort to exclude the clause, Wilson, who chaired the session, took the unprecedented step of claiming the motion had not been carried because the decision had not been unanimous. Earlier majority vote decisions were entered, he claimed, because the minority had allowed them to be passed without objection.' ibid 26.

[203] *Nationality Decrees Issued in Tunis and Morocco* (Advisory Opinion) [1923] PCIJ Series B No 4, 23.

consultative processes, the use of soft law standards, the development of bilateral treaties for governing labour migration, and the adoption of multilateral conventions for protecting refugees and migrant workers. Meanwhile, this period of experimentation unveiled the difficulties in promoting inter-state cooperation and in gaining the acceptance of states to be bound by international legal norms at the multilateral level. These difficulties were notably exemplified by the obstacles encountered by the International Labour Organization (ILO) in regulating the movement of persons between states.

Established in 1919 by the Treaty of Versailles, the ILO is the first international organization with a specific mandate on migration.[204] The ILO Constitution entrusted the organization to promote the 'protection of the interests of workers when employed in countries other than their own'.[205] The first International Labour Conference, held in Washington in 1919, further decided to establish 'an international commission to regulate the migration of workers' (also referred to as the 'International Emigration Commission').[206] According to its terms of reference, 'while giving due regard to the sovereign rights of each State, [this international commission] shall consider and report what measures can be adopted to regulate the migration of workers out of their own States and to protect the interests of wage earners residing in States other than their own'.[207]

Despite this broad mandate, the work of the International Emigration Commission proved to be very limited. It only adopted non-binding recommendations, and most of them were devoted to technical and practical issues, such as the exchange of information on statistics and employment opportunities, hygiene, insurance, and education of emigrants or state supervision of emigration agents.[208] Some recommendations nevertheless addressed more substantial issues, such as the need to protect women and children from trafficking.[209] The Commission also recommended that ILO Member States promote equality of treatment between foreign and national workers in respect to labour and social insurance legislation, relief, and the right of association for trade union purposes.[210] The Commission was however much more timorous regarding the admission of foreign workers. It simply acknowledged the rise of restrictive legislations and advised states to take precautions to avoid any vexatious consequences on emigrants.[211]

---

[204] For an instructive overview of ILO's activities during the interwar period, see especially SF Martin, *International Migration. Evolving Trends from the Early Twentieth Century to the Present* (CUP 2014) 26–48; R Böhning, *A Brief Account of the ILO and Policies on International Migration* (International Institute for Labour Studies 2012) 4–13.
[205] Constitution of the International Labour Organization (adopted 1 April 1919, entered into force 28 June 1919 as Part XIII of the Treaty of Versailles) 15 UNTS 40, preamble.
[206] *International Labor Conference, First Annual Meeting, October 29, 1919–November 29, 1919* (Government Printing office 1920) Appendix, 276.
[207] ibid. Its membership included both countries of immigration and emigration: the first chairman was a former Secretary of State for Home Affairs in the British government and the vice-chairman was from Italy, a major sending country at the time.
[208] International Emigration Commission, *Report of the Commission* (International Labour Office 1921) 3–8.
[209] ibid 5.   [210] ibid 4.
[211] Its resolution entitled *Application of Laws Restricting Emigration and Immigration* recommended that: 'Whenever a State makes a considerable modification in its legislation with regard to emigration

Due to the very few achievements of the International Emigration Commission, Italy convened the International Conference on Emigration and Immigration in Rome in May 1924. This intergovernmental conference took place outside the auspices of the ILO and the League of Nations, even though representatives of both organizations were invited as observers to this state-owned consultation process. The conference gathered 57 state representatives in order to promote a balanced approach to migration based on the mutual interests of both countries of emigration and immigration.[212] The International Conference on Emigration and Immigration constituted the first comprehensive attempt to draw soft law standards in the field of migration through a multilateral process of intergovernmental negotiation. From this angle, it was a forerunner of the multilateral consultative processes launched at the beginning of the 21st century, including most notably the UN Global Compact for Migration. Retrospectively, the recommendations adopted at the Rome Conference in 1924 are quite similar to the ones of the Global Compact for Migration, although the former is more ambitious and comprehensive than the latter with regards to the rights of migrants.

The International Conference on Emigration and Immigration approved a detailed and wide-ranging set of 49 recommendations on a broad variety of issues, such as transportation of migrants, health, sanitary and housing services, specific assistance for women and children, exchange of information and statistics, respect for the religion and traditional customs of immigrants, legal and judicial assistance, exchange of skilled workers, or the adoption of uniformed passports, and simplification of consular visas.[213] In order to address the concerns of immigration countries, the Final Act of the Rome Conference further underlined 'the necessity of repressing clandestine emigration and immigration' and recommended that 'all States should severely punish those who encourage or abet the infraction of the laws and regulations promulgated for this purpose in emigration or immigration countries'.[214]

The most remarkable outcome of the Rome Conference was the adoption of an 'Emigrants' Charter', which identified 'the general principles which should govern national legislation and international agreements'.[215] This charter delineated the basic rights of migrants through an ambitious and far-reaching set of standards. Not only did it acknowledge the right to emigrate (subject to legitimate restrictions based on public order),[216] but it also proclaimed a qualified right to immigrate:

---

or immigration, it is desirable that in applying any provisions made in this respect it should take such precautions as may be possible to avoid any vexations consequence to emigrants which might result from too sudden an application of such measures.' ibid 7. Pre-departure control of emigrants before their embarkation was further recommended in order to assess whether they satisfied the requirements governing entry into countries of immigration: ibid 5.6.

[212] Because of the large number of states' representatives, the Rome Conference was a truly universal forum as in 1924 the League of Nations counted 55 Member States.

[213] 'Final Act of the International Conference on Emigration and Immigration' in *Conférence internationale de l'émigration et de l'immigration, Rome 15–31 mai 1924*, vol 3 (Commissariat général italien de l'émigration 1925).

[214] ibid 152.   [215] ibid 159.   [216] ibid 160, para 1.

[T]he right of immigration should be recognized, without prejudice to international agreements and subjects to the restrictions imposed in the interests of public order or for economic or social reasons, particularly the state of the labour market and the protection of the public health and morals of the immigration country.[217]

The charter also endorsed a right to family reunification,[218] as well as a right to equal treatment between nationals and foreigners with regard to both civil and labour rights (including access to trade unions and social insurance benefits).[219] Likewise, access to work opportunities was to be granted under the same conditions as for nationals, although subject to exceptions based on national security, public order, and the state of the labour market.[220] This extensive catalogue of migrants' rights was supplemented by two provisions related to criminal matters: the duty to prosecute and punish those who encouraged or abetted violations of domestic legislation was restated alongside a more general call addressed to both immigration and emigration countries to cooperate in the prohibition and prevention of such violations.[221]

Although the Emigrants' Charter was approved by a large majority of states, the US, Australia, and New Zealand refused to vote favourably as they did for most of the numerous resolutions adopted at the International Conference on Emigration and Immigration. In fact, a few days before the adoption of the Final Act of the Rome Conference, the US enacted the Immigration Act of 1924[222] to harshen and perpetuate the immigration quotas which were initially introduced by the Emergency Quota Act of 1921 as a temporary legislation.[223] The divorce between countries of emigration and immigration was even more apparent at the Second International Conference on Emigration and Immigration held in Havana from 31 March to 17 April 1928. The US made clear that the admission of foreigners was a domestic affair: its representative declared that 'each migration-controlling country has the right to determine the conditions under which aliens may immigrate into or otherwise enter its territories'.[224]

As a matter of fact, one month before the Havana Conference, the Sixth International Conference of American States adopted the Convention on the Status of Aliens, which reaffirmed in its first article that: 'states have the right to establish by means of laws the conditions under which foreigners may enter and reside in their territory'.[225] Such an acknowledgement in a binding treaty considerably undermined the negotiations at the Second International Conference on Emigration and Immigration, where only a few recommendations on technical issues (such as transportation,

---

[217] ibid para 2.
[218] '[I]n order to maintain family unity in the interest of public and social morals, the right of the other members of an immigrant's family to emigrate and immigrate should be recognized where there are no personal reasons for excluding them on grounds of public order, health or morals'. ibid para 4.
[219] ibid paras 9 and 13.   [220] ibid para 10.   [221] ibid paras 7 and 8.
[222] Pub L 68-39, 43 Stat 153, enacted May 26, 1924.
[223] Ch 8, 42 Stat 5 of May 19, 1921.
[224] C-2-5:11, Laughlin Papers, quoted in A Zampogna-Krug, 'Immigration vs. Emigration: The Internationality of US Immigration Policy' (2012) 27 49th Parallel 4 available at <http://49thparalleljournal.org/2014/07/12/issue-27-winter-2012/> accessed 29 February 2016.
[225] This convention was ratified by the US in 1930 and it is still binding today on its 15 States Parties, see <http://www.oas.org/Juridico/english/sigs/a-22.html> accessed 16 October 2018.

recruitment, and vaccination of emigrants) were adopted.[226] The overall result of the Havana Conference was to shed light on the diverging views between countries of immigration and emigration on this new field of inter-state cooperation.

In the meantime, because of the impossibility to reach a consensus between immigration and emigration countries, the ILO focused on some specific aspects of labour migration with the view to promoting the progressive development of international law. During the interwar period, it adopted four migration-related conventions addressing three particular issues: social security, emigration, and employment of migrant workers. They are (in chronological order): the 1925 Convention concerning Equality of Treatment for National and Foreign Workers as regards Workmen's Compensation for Accidents (C 19); the 1926 Convention concerning the Simplification of the Inspection of Emigrants on Board Ship (C 21); the 1935 Convention concerning the Establishment of an International Scheme for the Maintenance of Rights under Invalidity, Old-Age and Widows' and Orphans' Insurance (C 48); and the 1939 Convention concerning the Recruitment, Placing and Conditions of Labour of Migrants for Employment (C 66).[227] In practice, however, these treaties were ratified by an uneven number of states. In 1939, the first two conventions were respectively ratified by 34 and 21 states, whereas only four states ratified the Maintenance of Migrants' Pension Rights Convention, and the last one never came into force because of the Second World War. In order to compensate for the limited impact of multilateral conventions, a growing number of bilateral treaties were concluded between sending and receiving countries to manage labour migration and to protect the rights of foreign workers.[228]

A similar mixed picture can be observed with regard to refugee protection.[229] On the one hand, the interwar period was a particularly prolific one for the development

---

[226] The text of the resolutions adopted at the Havana Conference is available in: *Monthly Record of Migration*, vol 3 (International Labour Office 1928) 205. For a critical comment on the results of the Havana Conference, see: Varlez, 'Migration Problems and the Havana Conference of 1928' (n 187) 1–19.

[227] Though not specific to migrants, the 1919 Convention concerning Unemployment (C 2) also provided that States Parties 'shall, upon terms being agreed between the Members concerned, make arrangements whereby workers belonging to one Member and working in the territory of another shall be admitted to the same rates of benefit of such insurance as those which obtain for the workers belonging to the latter' (art 3). More generally ILO treaties were supplemented by a substantial number of recommendations on various issues related to migration. See most notably: Reciprocity of Treatment Recommendation, 1919 (No 2); Migration Statistics Recommendation, 1922 (No 19); Equality of Treatment (Accident Compensation) Recommendation, 1925 (No 25); Migration (Protection of Females at Sea) Recommendation, 1926 (No 26); Migration for Employment Recommendation, 1939 (No 61); and Migration for Employment (Cooperation between States) Recommendation, 1939 (No 62).

[228] For an overview of these bilateral treaties, see especially: International Labour Office, *Emigration and Immigration: Legislation and Treaties* (n 186) 366–98; M Thibert, 'Emigration et immigration' in A De Lapradelle and J-P Niboyet (eds), *Répertoire de droit international*, vol 7 (Sirey 1930) 565–77.

[229] For an historical overview of refugee protection during the interwar period see especially CM Skran, *Refugees in Inter-War Europe: The Emergence of a Regime* (Clarendon Press 1995); MR Marrus, *The Unwanted European Refugees in the Twentieth Century* (OUP 1985); JC Hathaway, 'The Evolution of Refugee Status in International Law: 1920–1950' (1984) ICLQ 348–80; RY Jennings, 'Some International Law Aspects of the Refugee Question' (1939) BYIL 98–114; JH Simpson, *The Refugee Problem: Report of a Survey* (OUP 1939); LW Holborn, 'The Legal Status of Political Refugees, 1920–1938' (1938) AJIL 680–730.

of this area of international law: from 1922 to 1939, seven international arrangements, two conventions, and one additional protocol were concluded under the auspices of the League of Nations for the purpose of protecting refugees.[230] On the other hand, the League of Nations opted for a piecemeal approach focusing on specific categories of refugees identified on the basis of their national origin. The first instrument concluded in 1922 was limited to Russian refugees, with subsequent instruments progressively extended to Armenians in 1924, Turkish, Assyrian, Assyro-Chaldean and assimilated refugees in 1928, and German refugees in 1938.

With the rise of immigration control, the priority was to assure that these refugees received a certificate of identity, the so-called 'Nansen passport'.[231] When states realized that repatriation of refugees in their countries of origin was not a viable option (mainly because most were stateless), they further adopted in 1928 an international legal status for the purpose of facilitating local integration in asylum countries. The refugee status was then consolidated by two conventions adopted in 1933 and 1938, which notably acknowledged the principle of *non-refoulement* as the main legal norm governing admission of refugees.[232] Nevertheless, while the interwar instruments framed the basic tenets of contemporary international refugee law, they suffered from a conspicuous lack of effectiveness: the various arrangements were indeed not binding but merely recommendatory, and the two refugee conventions of 1933 and of 1938 were only ratified by a few states.[233]

Despite its modest impact on the actual practice of states, the interwar period was a time of intense legal experimentation that prefigured the subsequent developments of international law. While becoming a topic of international concern, the protection of refugees and that of migrant workers emerged as two distinct legal categories, before this distinction turned into a defining feature of international law after the Second World War. The ILO mandate toward migrant workers was confirmed by

---

[230] Arrangement with regard to the Issue of Certificates of Identity to Russian Refugees (5 July 1922) 13 LNTS 238 (No 355); Plan for the Issue of a Certificate of Identity to Armenian Refugees (31 May 1924) LN Doc CL 72(a); Arrangement relating to the Issue of Identity Certificates to Russian and Armenian Refugees, Supplementing and Amending the Previous Arrangements (12 May 1926) 89 LNTS 47 (No 2004); Arrangement relating to the Legal Status of Russian and Armenian Refugees (30 June 1928) 89 LNTS 53 (No 2005); Arrangement concerning the Extension to Other Categories of Refugees of Certain Measures taken in Favour of Russian and Armenian Refugees (30 June 1928) 89 LNTS 63 (No 2006); Agreement concerning the Functions of the Representatives of the League of Nations' High Commissioner for Refugees (30 June 1928) 93 LNTS 377 (No 2126); Convention relating to the International Status of Refugees (28 October 1933) 159 LNTS 199 (No 3663); Arrangement relating to the Issue of a Certificate of Identity to Refugees from the Saar (24 May 1935) Judgment No 10–12 at 1681; Provisional Arrangement concerning the Status of Refugees coming from Germany (4 July 1936) 171 LNTS 75 (No 3952); Convention concerning the Status of Refugees coming from Germany (10 February 1938) 192 LNTS 59 (No 4461); and Additional Protocol to the Provisional Arrangement and to the Convention concerning the Status of Refugees coming from Germany (14 September 1939) 198 LNTS 141 (No 4634).

[231] Most of the relevant instruments specified that this certificate of identity did not prejudice 'the laws and regulations in force in a state with regard to the control of foreigners'.

[232] Article 3 of the Convention relating to the International Status of Refugees of 28 October 1933 (CLIX LNTS (No 3663)); Article 5 of the Convention concerning the Status of Refugees coming from Germany of 10 February 1938 (CXCII LNTS 59 (No 4461)).

[233] In 1939, the Refugee Convention of 1933 was ratified by eight states and the 1938 one by two states only.

the 1944 Declaration of Philadelphia and the Geneva-based international organization adopted in July 1949 the Convention concerning Migration for Employment (C 97). In parallel, the protection of refugees became the distinct prerogative of one single UN specialized agency: the International Refugee Organization (1946–1952) which was explicitly mandated to focus on 'genuine refugees' as opposed to 'persons who intend to settle in other countries for purely economic reasons, thus qualifying as emigrants'.[234] This agency was then replaced by the United Nations High Commissioner for Refugees (UNHCR), established on 14 December 1950, which was to become the lead UN agency in charge of refugees.[235] The year following the creation of UNHCR, on 28 July 1951, the UN Convention relating to the Status of Refugees was adopted as the main legal instrument of refugee protection.

Tracing the historical origins of this dual regime distinguishing refugees from migrant workers, Rieko Karatani asserts that 'the distinction between "migrants" and "refugees", and the institutional setting which flowed from that division, was inadvertent rather than deliberate, resulting from the desire of the US to limit the involvement of international institutions'.[236] The author highlights that the current patchwork of international norms and institutions resulted from the 'battle' between the US and the relevant international organizations (ILO and UN) over the question of how to deal with displaced persons in Europe after the Second World War: 'The US government favoured an institution which had specifically designed functions based on intergovernmental negotiations, whereas the ILO-UN plan recommended international cooperation under the leadership of a single international organisation. The US eventually won the debate and the development of the fragmented regimes subsequently followed.'[237] After two international conferences organized in Naples and Brussels in 1951, the US plan was accepted and the Provisional Intergovernmental Committee for the Movement of Migrants from Europe—now renamed the International Organization for Migration—was created outside the UN with a mandate concurrent to those of UNHCR and ILO.[238]

---

[234] Constitution of the International Refugee Organization (adopted 15 December 1946, entered into force 20 August 1948) 18 UNTS 3, Annex I(I)(e). Prior to the International Refugee Organization, the United Nations Relief and Rehabilitation Administration was taking care of the assistance and repatriation of refugees, as part of its broader mandate to arrange and provide 'relief of victims of war in any area under the control of any of the United Nations through the provision of food, fuel, clothing, shelter and other basic necessities, medical and other essential services' (art I(2)(a), Agreement for the United Nations Relief and Rehabilitation Administration, 57 Stat 1164 (adopted 9 November 1943, entered into force 9 November 1943)).

[235] See Statute of the Office of the United Nations High Commissioner for Refugees, UNGA Res 428(V) (14 December 1950). In parallel to UNHCR, the United Nations Relief and Works Agency for Palestine Refugees was established by UNGA Res 302(IV) of 8 December 1949 to carry out direct relief and works programmes for Palestinian refugees.

[236] R Karatani, 'How History Separated Refugee and Migrant Regimes: In Search of Their Institutional Origins' (2005) 17 IJRL 517, 519.

[237] ibid.

[238] ibid 532–38. G Loescher further explains in his seminal book *The UNHCR and World Politics*: 'In contrast to the UNHCR, the PICME, later to be renamed the Intergovernmental Committee for European Migration (ICEM), was designed to be operational in order to enable national states to manage and structure migration flows. By including both labour migrants and refugees under its mandate, the establishment of ICEM also killed any prospects for the creation of a labour migration programme at the ILO. [. . .] The ICEM was established as a multilateral institution outside the United

1.3 The Human Rights of Migrants: From Minimum Standards to Fundamental Rights (20th Century to 21st Century)

Immigration controls emerged at the turn of the 20th century in parallel with the growing recognition of the rights of migrants in their host states.[239] This uneasy coexistence between migration control and migrants' rights has become a defining feature of contemporary international law originating from the traditional law of state responsibility for injuries committed to aliens. The treatment of foreigners in their host states has indeed been a classic question of international law, which was crystallized through the notion of international minimum standard at the end of the 19th century and in the first half of the 20th century.

Since then, international human rights law has progressively encapsulated the notion of minimum standard before constituting the primary source of protection. As a result of this longstanding process, the legal protection of migrants has evolved from this notion of a minimum standard based on state responsibility to that of fundamental rights embedded in human rights law. This development highlights the extent to which migrants' rights are anchored in international law and reflects its broader evolution whereby human rights are reframing the basic tenets of general international law.

1.3.1 The origins of the international minimum standard in the law of state responsibility

Since the 19th century, the responsibility of states for injuries to aliens was a branch of international law on its own and, in fact, one of the most important.[240] From 1840 to 1940, some 60 mixed-claims commissions were set up to deal with disputes

Nations, with an American Director, and a board composed entirely of democratic nations friendly to the United States.' G Loescher, *The UNHCR and World Politics: A Perilous Path* (OUP 2001) 59. For further discussion about the origins of IOM, see notably: M Ducasse-Rogier, *The International Organization for Migration 1951–2001* (IOM 2001).

[239] This section is partially based on: V Chetail, 'The Human Rights of Migrants in General International Law: From Minimum Standards to Fundamental Rights' (2013) 28(1) Geo Immigr L J 225.

[240] Among a rich literature, see CF Amerasinghe, *State Responsibility for Injuries to Aliens* (Clarendon Press 1967); Anzilotti, 'La responsabilité internationale des États à raison des dommages soufferts par les étrangers' (n 196) 5–29 and 110–30; Borchard, *The Diplomatic Protection of Citizens Abroad* (n 192); A Decencière-Ferrandière, *La responsabilité internationale des États à raison des dommages subis par des étrangers* (Rousseau 1925); F Sherwood Dunn, *The Protection of Nationals: A Study in the Application of International Law* (The Johns Hopkins Press 1932); J Dumas, 'La responsabilité des Etats à raison des crimes et délits commis sur leur territoire au préjudice d'étrangers' (1931) 36 Collected Courses of the Hague Academy of International Law 183; FV Garcia-Amador, L Sohn, and R Baxter, *Recent Codification of the Law of State Responsibility for Injuries to Aliens* (Oceana 1974); FV Garcia-Amador, 'State Responsibility: Some New Problems' (1958) 94 Collected Courses of the Hague Academy of International Law 365; RB Lillich (ed), *International Law of State Responsibility for Injuries to Aliens* (University Press of Virginia 1983).

arising in this field.[241] The influential US scholar Philip Jessup (1897–1986) observed in 1948 that '[t]he international law governing the responsibility of states for injuries to aliens is one of the most highly developed branches of that law'.[242] Its primary rationale was based on the well-known fiction of Vattel: 'Whoever uses a citizen ill, indirectly offends the State, which is bound to protect this citizen.'[243]

According to this traditional stance, aliens are worthy of protection as nationals because they personify their own state. The legal status of aliens under classical international law is the result of a purely inter-state relationship: both in practice and principle, aliens are under the dual dependency of the territorial state (where they sojourn) and of the personal state (of which they have the nationality). This traditional account is well-synthesized by the arbitral award delivered in 1928 in the famous *Island of Palmas* case: 'Territorial sovereignty [...] involves the exclusive right to display the activities of a State. This right has as corollary a duty: the obligation to protect within the territory the rights [...] each State may claim for its nationals in foreign territory.'[244]

This overlap between territorial and personal jurisdictions is inherent in alienage. It further explains the longstanding interest of international law regarding aliens. By contrast, classical international law has long been indifferent to the treatment of nationals within their own country. Until the first half of the 20th century, migrants were thus more protected than nationals living in their own state. The leading British scholar Hersch Lauterpacht (1897–1960) observed in 1950 that 'the individual in his capacity as an alien enjoys a larger measure of protection by international law than in his character as the citizen of his own State'.[245]

This paradox corresponded to a specific stage in the evolution of international law when the individual was considered an object of international law and not a subject in his own right.[246] The treatment reserved for aliens was not an exception; on the contrary, it was a confirmation of this purely inter-state legal system. Individuals could be protected abroad only because they embodied their state of nationality. This was epitomized by the *Mavrommatis* judgment delivered in 1924 by the Permanent Court of International Justice:

It is an elementary principle of international law that a State is entitled to protect its subjects, when injured by acts contrary to international law committed by another State, from whom they have been unable to obtain satisfaction through the ordinary channels. By taking up the case of one of its subjects and by resorting to diplomatic action or international judicial

[241] I Brownlie, *Principles of Public International Law* (6th edn, OUP 2003) 500; MO Hudson, *International Tribunals: Past and Future* (Carnegie Endowment for International Peace and Brookings Institution 1944) 196.

[242] PC Jessup, *A Modern Law of Nations: An Introduction* (MacMillan 1948) 94.

[243] Vattel, *The Law of Nations* (n 85) Book II, ch VI, para 71 at 298.

[244] *Island of Palmas (US v Netherlands)*, Hague Ct Rep 2d (Scott) 83, 93 (Perm Ct Arb 1928).

[245] H Lauterpacht, *International Law and Human Rights* (Stevens 1950) 121.

[246] See WGF Phillimore, 'Droits et devoirs fondamentaux des Etats' (1923) 1 Collected Courses of the Hague Academy of International Law 25, 63. For further references and discussion see V Chetail, 'Le droit d'avoir des droits en droit international public: Réflexions sur la subjectivité internationale de l'individu' in MC Caloz-Tschopp (ed), *Lire Hannah Arendt aujourd'hui: Pouvoir, guerre, pensée, jugement politique* (L'Harmattan 2008) 217.

proceedings on his behalf, a State is in reality asserting its own rights—its right to ensure, in the person of its subjects, respect for the rules of international law.[247]

This inter-state monologue was further exacerbated by the discretionary nature of diplomatic protection. As restated by the International Court of Justice (ICJ), '[t]he State must be viewed as the sole judge to decide whether its protection will be granted, to what extent it is granted, and when it will cease'.[248]

Against this framework, one should not be surprised that diplomatic protection has been a persistent source of tension among states—especially between Western states and newly independent ones (notably in Latin America). Aliens involved in such disputes were generally entrepreneurs from industrialized countries in search of new markets abroad. From this angle, 'the history of the rights of non-citizens began as the history of the rights of the privileged'.[249] Furthermore, diplomatic protection was used as a common pretext for justifying intervention in disregard of the principles of sovereign equality and non-interference in the domestic affairs of foreign states. As acknowledged by Jessup, '[t]he history of the development of the international law on the responsibility of states for injuries to aliens is thus an aspect of the history of "imperialism", or "dollar diplomacy" '.[250] Among other well-known instances, the Boer War from 1899 to 1902 was officially justified by the UK in order to protect the British mine owners of Witwatersrand.[251]

The conflicting interests underlying the law of state responsibility were reflected by two opposite conceptions of the applicable standard of treatment granted to aliens. Developing states advanced the doctrine of national treatment: aliens had to be treated on an equal footing with nationals (with the obvious exception of political rights).[252] As a result, aliens could not claim more rights than those granted to nationals and only a difference of treatment might trigger the responsibility of the

---

[247] *Mavrommatis Palestine Concessions (Greece v UK)* (Judgment) [1924] PCIJ Rep Series B No 3, para 21. See also *Panevezys-Saldutiskis Railway (Estonia v Lithuania)* (Judgment) [1939] PCIJ Rep Series A/B No 76 at 16.

[248] *Barcelona Traction Light and Power Company (Belgium v Spain)* (Judgment) [1970] ICJ Rep 3, para 79.

[249] D Weissbrodt, *The Human Rights of Non-citizens* (OUP 2008) 36.

[250] Jessup, *A Modern Law of Nations* (n 242) 96. Among other similar observations, see also *Barcelona Traction Light and Power Company* (n 248) 246 (Separate Opinion of Judge Padilla-Nervo): 'The history of the responsibility of States in respect to the treatment of foreign nationals is the history of abuses, illegal interference in the domestic jurisdiction of weaker States, unjust claims, threats and even military aggression under the flag of exercising rights of protection, and the imposing of sanctions in order to oblige a government to make the reparations demanded.'

[251] ILC, 'First Report on Diplomatic Protection by Special Rapporteur John R Dugard' (2000) UN Doc A/CN.4/506, 212. The Special Rapporteur further observed that more recently the US military interventions were carried out in Grenada in 1983 and Panama in 1989 on the pretext of defending their nationals in Latin America: ibid.

[252] C Calvo, *Le droit international: Théorie et pratique*, vol 6 (5th edn, Rousseau 1896) 230, para 256. For further discussion, see also A Guani, 'La solidarité internationale dans l'Amérique latine' (1925) 8 Collected Courses of the Hague Academy of International Law 203, 287; J De Louter, *Le droit international public positif*, vol 1 (OUP 1920) 296–98; Nys, *Le droit international: Les principes, les théories, les faits* (n 195) 266; JM Yepes, 'Les problèmes fondamentaux du droit des gens en Amérique' (1934) 47 Collected Courses of the Hague Academy of International Law 1, 106; H Arias, 'The Non-Liability of States for Damages Suffered by Foreigners in the Course of a Riot, an Insurrection, or a Civil War' (1913) 7 AJIL 724.

host state. The doctrine of national treatment was endorsed at the First International Conference of American States held in Washington in 1889–1890.[253] It was re-inforced at the regional level in several treaties, including the 1902 Convention relative to the Rights of Aliens,[254] the 1928 Convention on the Status of Aliens,[255] as well as the famous Montevideo Convention on the Rights and Duties of States adopted in 1933.[256]

Nonetheless, international initiatives carried out by Latin American states were primarily confined to their own region. At the universal level, the first Conference for the Codification of International Law, held in 1930 under the auspices of the League of Nations, demonstrated the absence of a broader consensus. The Conference was unable to adopt the draft Convention on Responsibility of States for Damage done in their Territory to the Person or Property of Foreigners mainly because of the two different conceptions regarding the applicable standard: 17 states supported the doctrine of national treatment, whereas 23 others were opposed thereto.[257]

In contrast to national treatment, Western states promoted the notion of a min-imum international standard as traditionally defined in the following terms:

Each country is bound to give to the nationals of another country in its territory the benefit of the same laws, the same administration, the same protection, and the same redress for injury which it gives to its own citizens, and neither more nor less: provided the protection which the country gives to its own citizens conforms to the established standard of civilization. There is a standard of justice, very simple, very fundamental, and of such general acceptance by all civilized countries as to form a part of the international law of the world. [...] If any country's system of law and administration does not conform to that standard, although the people of the country may be content or compelled to live under it, no other country can be compelled to accept it as furnishing a satisfactory measure of treatment to its citizens.[258]

Thus, aliens shall not be treated below a minimum standard, which is required by general international law regardless of how a state treats its nationals. This doc-trine has been endorsed in a substantial number of treaties and in jurisprudence.[259] The very content of the international minimum standard was, however, particularly vague. It raised many controversies among states, some of them considering the ambiguity of the notion as the perfect excuse for justifying arbitrary interferences

---

[253] JB Scott (ed), *The International Conferences of American States 1889–1928* (OUP 1931) 45.
[254] ibid 415–16.   [255] ibid.
[256] Convention on Rights and Duties of States (adopted 26 December 1933, entered into force 26 December 1934) 165 LNTS 19. As under the previous convention, the US made a reservation to the relevant article on national treatment.
[257] *Acts of the Conference for the Codification of International Law, Volume IV: Minutes of the Third Committee on the Responsibility of States* (1930) LN Doc C 351(c) M 145(c) 1930 V, at 188.
[258] E Root, 'The Basis of Protection to Citizens Residing Abroad' (1910) 4 ASIL Proceedings 16, 20–21.
[259] Among numerous arbitral awards, see most notably *Hopkins v United Mexican States (US v Mexico)*, 4 RIAA 41, 47 (Perm Ct Arb 1926); *Neer v United Mexican States (US v Mexico)*, 4 RIAA 60, 64, 65 (Perm Ct Arb 1926); *Roberts v United Mexican States (US v Mexico)*, 4 RIAA 77, 79–80 (Perm Ct Arb 1926); and *British Claims in Spanish Zone of Morocco (UK v Spain)*, 2 RIAA 615, 635, 644 (Perm Ct Arb 1925). See also Treaty of Friendship and Establishment, Egypt-Persia (adopted 28 November 1928) 93 LNTS 381, arts IV-VI; Convention Respecting Conditions of Residence and Business and Jurisdiction (adopted 24 July 1923) 28 LNTS 151, arts 1, 2, 13, 14, 17.

in host states. Nevertheless, as a result of these inter-state disputes, a considerable body of arbitral awards has progressively identified and refined the international minimum standard on a case-by-case basis.

This incremental process has been crystallized in a core set of fundamental guarantees, including the right to life and respect for physical integrity, the right to recognition as a person before the law, freedom of conscience, the prohibition of arbitrary detention, the right to a fair trial in civil and criminal matters, and the right to property (save for public expropriation with fair compensation).[260] As is apparent from this enumeration, the minimum standard of treatment was the forerunner of human rights law at the international level. The traditional law of aliens has constituted the normative and conceptual laboratory of international human rights law. The duty of the host state to respect aliens as nationals of their own states progressively moved from a purely inter-state logic to a human rights-based approach premised on the idea that some basic rights are inalienable to every human being and must be granted to foreigners as well.

A telling illustration of such a shift is provided by Alfred Verdross (1890–1980), who has been portrayed as a precursor of the constitutionalist approach to international law.[261] The Austrian scholar observed in 1931 that 'states are bound by international law to respect in foreigners the dignity of human personality in recognizing them the rights necessary to this end. This principle is absolute and suffers from no exception.'[262] According to the Professor of Vienna University, this fundamental principle reflected the prevailing view of the doctrine as notably exemplified by the Institute of International Law: it acknowledged at its first session in 1874 that states were bound to grant foreigners the benefit of civil rights and the legal capacity to exercise such rights.[263] For Verdross, the legal personality of foreigners and the rights attached to such status were then confirmed by the general practice of states and endorsed by a significant number of bilateral treaties.[264] He concluded that, even in the absence of such treaties, customary international law obliged states to grant foreigners a minimum of fundamental rights.[265]

[260] See S Basdevant, *Théorie générale de la condition de l'étranger* in A De Lapradelle and J P Niboyet (eds), *Répertoire de droit international*, vol 8 (Sirey 1930) 31–61; AV Freeman, *The International Responsibility of States for Denial of Justice* 507–30 (1st edn, Longmans 1938); AH Roth, *The Minimum Standard of International Law Applied to Aliens* (AW Sijthoff's Uitgeversmaatschappij NV 1949) 185–86; A Verdross, 'Les règles internationales concernant le traitement des étrangers' (1931) 37 Collected Courses of the Hague Academy of International Law 323, 353–406.

[261] T Kleinlein, 'Alfred Verdross as a Founding Father of International Constitutionalism?' (2012) 4 Goettingen J Intl L 385–416 and the references quoted therein. For further discussion about the thought of Verdross, see most notably: B Simma, 'The Contribution of Alfred Verdross to the Theory of International Law' (1995) 6(1) EJIL 33–54; A Truyol y Serra, 'Verdross et la théorie du droit' (1995) 6(1) EJIL 55–69; B Conforti, 'The Theory of Competence in Verdross' (1995) 6(1) EJIL 70–77; A Carty, 'Alfred Verdross and Othmar Spann: German Romantic Nationalism, National Socialism and International Law' (1995) 6(1) EJIL 78–97.

[262] Verdross, '*Les règles internationales concernant le traitement des étrangers*' (n 260) 350 (author's translation).

[263] ibid 349.   [264] ibid.   [265] ibid.

Verdross represents a pioneer of international migration law. The 'international law of aliens'—as he called it—was grounded in customary international law establishing universal rules binding all states.[266] Such rules were not only confined to the notion of minimum standard. He envisaged the international law of aliens as a 'system' encompassing three main components: the admission of foreigners, their treatment in host countries, and their expulsion from the states of sojourn.[267] His view on the admission of foreigners is particularly worth mentioning, as he arguably prefigured the current stance of international law. His nuanced position fell in-between the absolutists of state sovereignty and the champions of free movement. Verdross claimed that in practice:

[N]one of these opinions are recognised in an absolute way. Because all agree that States can refuse admission of dangerous aliens. On the other hand, no State of the international community pretends to have the right to arbitrarily close its borders to foreigners. All States have in fact followed the principle according to which each refusal of admission must be based on a reasonable ground to be legitimate under international law.[268]

The reasonable grounds for justifying a refusal of admission can be either subjective or objective. The subjective grounds relate to the character of the foreigner: when he constitutes a danger to the state or its population because of his destitution, illness, criminal background, political activities or any other related reasons.[269] The objective grounds of non-admission can be triggered by an exceptional situation, such as a pandemic, domestic turmoil or social crisis.[270] Verdross concluded that 'the questions of immigration are not at all left to the arbitrary power of one single state, because international law limits its competence in this field for the sake of the common good of humanity'.[271]

The views of Verdross on the admission of foreigners and their treatment in host countries clearly reflected the future development of international law, even if he was probably ahead of his time. This was particularly the case concerning the international minimum standard, which proved to be more controversial than he assumed. Divergences among states are exemplified by the failure of the Conference organized in 1930 by the League of Nations to codify the law of states' responsibility for injuries committed to aliens. Nonetheless, the very notion of international minimum standard played a critical role in diffusing the idea promoted by Verdross that 'rights must be granted by States to foreigners by virtue of their quality as human beings'.[272] This acknowledgement eventually came to embody the current state of international law. Nowadays, while it still retains some residual value, the international minimum standard is to a large extent absorbed by human rights treaties and customary law.

---

[266] ibid 330–31.   [267] ibid 337.   [268] ibid 343–44 (author's translation).
[269] ibid 345.   [270] ibid.   [271] ibid 347 (author's translation).
[272] ibid 389 (author's translation).

1.3.2 The emergence of international human rights law as the primary source of protection for migrants

The law of aliens inherited from the traditional notion of state responsibility has been progressively marginalized and arguably replaced by human rights law.[273] This mirrors a more general and systemic evolution whereby human rights law is profoundly reshaping general international law.[274] Even the ICJ acknowledged in the *Diallo* judgment of 2007 that:

Owing to the substantive development of international law over recent decades in respect of the rights it accords to individuals, the scope *ratione materiae* of diplomatic protection, originally limited to alleged violations of the minimum standard of treatment of aliens, has subsequently widened to include, *inter alia*, internationally guaranteed human rights.[275]

Upon closer examination, human rights law constitutes a normative synthesis between the two traditional conceptions concerning the treatment of aliens under international law. On the one hand, this branch of law guarantees a core content of basic rights in line with the very notion of a minimum standard. On the other hand, human rights law asserts equality of treatment between citizens and non-citizens in accordance with the national treatment standard. McDougal, Lasswell, and Chen acknowledge in this sense:

In sum, the principal thrust of the contemporary human rights movement is to accord nationals the same protection formerly accorded only to aliens, while at the same time raising the standard of protection for all human beings, nationals as well as aliens, far beyond the minimum international standard developed under the earlier customary law. […] The consequence is thus […] that continuing debate about the doctrines of the minimum international standard and equality of treatment has now become highly artificial; an international standard is now authoritatively prescribed for all human beings.[276]

---

[273] On the impact of human rights law on the law of state responsibility, see notably: TE Carbonneau, 'The Convergence of the Law of State Responsibility for Injury to Aliens and International Human Rights Norms in the Revised Restatement' (1985) 25 Va J Int'l L 99, 100–02, 117, 136, 140; A-C Kiss, 'La condition des étrangers en droit international et les droits de l'Homme' in *Mélanges en l'honneur de M Ganshof van der Meersch*, vol 1 (Bruylant 1972) 499, 509; MS McDougal, HD Lasswell, and L-C Chen, 'Protection of Aliens from Discrimination and World Public Order: Responsibility of States Conjoined with Human Rights' (1976) 70 AJIL 432, 443, 452, 454, 461.

[274] On this evolution, see generally: P-M Dupuy, 'L'individu et le droit international: Théorie des droits de l'Homme et fondements du droit international' (1987) 32 APD 119; MT Kamminga and M Scheinin (eds), *The Impact of Human Rights Law on General International Law* (OUP 2009); T Meron, 'International Law in the Age of Human Rights' (2003) 301 Collected Courses of the Hague Academy of International Law 1; A Augusto Cançado Trindade, *International Law for Humankind: Towards a New Jus Gentium* (Brill 2013); M Virally, 'Droits de l'Homme et théorie générale du droit international' (1972) 4 René Cassin Amicorum Disipulorumque Liber 323, 329; WM Reisman, 'Sovereignty and Human Rights in Contemporary International Law' (1990) 84 AJIL 866, 869, and 876; LB Sohn, 'The New International Law: Protection of the Rights of Individuals Rather than States' (1982) 32 AJIL 6.

[275] *Ahmadou Sadio Diallo (Guinea v Democratic Republic of the Congo)* (Preliminary Objections) [2007] ICJ Rep 582, 599, para 39.

[276] McDougal, Lasswell, and Chen, 'Protection of Aliens from Discrimination and World Public Order' (n 273) 464. Among many other similar accounts, see: CG Fenwick, 'The Progress of International Law During the Past Forty Years' (1951) 79 Collected Courses of the Hague Academy of International Law 1, 44; AV Freeman, 'Human Rights and the Rights of Aliens' (1951) 45 ASIL Proceedings 120, 122–23, 129; RY Jennings, 'The Responsibility of States' (1967) 121 Collected Courses of the Hague

Nevertheless, merging the old law of aliens with the new law of human rights has been gradual and is still an ongoing process. One of the first systematic attempts was carried out by the International Law Commission (ILC). In 1953, the UN General Assembly requested the ILC to 'undertake the codification of the principles of international law governing State responsibility'[277] and appointed Garcia Amador as Special Rapporteur in 1955. From 1956 to 1961, he submitted six reports focusing on the responsibility of states for the injuries caused to aliens within their territory.[278] His great ambition was 'to change and adapt traditional law so that it will reflect the profound transformation which has occurred in international law. In other words, it will be necessary to bring the "principles governing State responsibility" into line with international law at its present stage of development.'[279]

According to Amador, traditional conceptions of the treatment of aliens have shown their limits in establishing clear-cut rules.[280] They must be reassessed in accordance with the dramatic transformation of modern international law deriving from the UN Charter and the international recognition of human rights:

International law is not now concerned solely with regulating relations between States, for one of the objects of its rules is to protect interests and rights which are not truly vested in the State. Hence it is no longer true, as it was for centuries in the past, that international law exists only for, or finds its sole *raison d'être* in, the protection of the interests and rights of the State; rather, its function is now also to protect the rights and interests of its other subjects who may properly claim its protection. [...] International law today recognizes that individuals and other subjects are directly entitled to international rights, just as it places upon them certain international obligations. [...] The basis of this new principle would be the 'universal respect for, and observance of, human rights and fundamental freedoms' referred to in the Charter of the United Nations and in other general, regional and bilateral instruments. The object of the 'internationalization' (to coin a term) of these rights and freedoms is to ensure the protection of the legitimate interests of the human person, irrespective of his nationality. Whether the person concerned is a citizen or an alien is then immaterial: human beings, as such, are under the direct protection of international law.[281]

Given this 'new' normative frame, the Special Rapporteur proposed in 1957 a draft Convention on international responsibility of the state for injuries caused in its

---

Academy of International Law 473, 480, 486–88; Kiss, 'La condition des étrangers en droit international et les droits de l'Homme' (n 273) 509; H Mosler, *The International Society as a Legal Community* (Brill 1980) 72.

[277] UNGA Res 799 (VIII) (7 December 1953) UN Doc A/2630, 52.

[278] See Special Rapporteurs of the International Law Commission (1949–2016) available at http://legal.un.org/ilc/guide/annex3.shtml accessed 16 October 2018.

[279] ILC, 'Special Rapporteur FV Garcia-Amador's International Responsibility' (1956) UN Doc A/CN.4/SER.A/1956/Add.1 (reprinted in (1956) 2 Yearbook ILC 176).

[280] '[T]he subject of responsibility has always been one of the most vast and complex of international law; it would be difficult to find a topic beset with greater confusion and uncertainty. The cause lies not so much in the dominant part played by political factors in the shaping and development of this branch of international law, as in the glaring inconsistencies of traditional doctrine and practice. Perhaps because of the existence and influence of extraneous factors which are not always compatible with the law, artificial legal concepts and principles have been evolved which often appear markedly incongruent.' ibid 175.

[281] ibid 184, 192, 203.

territory to the person or property of aliens.[282] In its final version published in his last Report of 1961, Article 1(1) of the draft postulated that 'aliens enjoy the same rights and the same legal guarantees as nationals', while specifying that as a minimum 'these rights and guarantees shall in no case be less than the "human rights and fundamental freedoms" recognized and defined in contemporary international instruments'.[283] Its second paragraph then offered a non-exhaustive list of such fundamental human rights.[284]

At the time, however, this pioneering work was a 'somewhat revolutionary approach',[285] as Amador himself acknowledged. In fact, his draft received scant attention from the ILC, and several members criticized his approach on the twofold ground that the individual was not a subject of international law and that the identification of human rights pertained to a different topic of codification outside state responsibility.[286] A new Special Rapporteur, Roberto Ago, was designated to focus exclusively on the secondary rules of state responsibility[287] with a view to defining the general conditions for the state to be considered responsible for wrongful actions or omissions, and the legal consequences which follow therefrom.[288] As a result of this new approach, primary rules and, in particular, the substantive and more sensitive obligations regulating the protection of aliens were excluded from the work of the ILC.[289]

---

[282] ILC, 'Special Rapporteur FV Garcia-Amador's International Responsibility: Second Report' (1957) UN Doc A/CN.4/SER.A/1957/Add.1 (reprinted in (1957) 2 Yearbook ILC 127–28).

[283] ILC, 'Special Rapporteur FV Garcia-Amador's International Responsibility: Sixth Report' (1961) UN Doc A/CN.4/SER.A/1961/Add.1 (reprinted in (1961) 2 Yearbook ILC 46).

[284] The 'human rights and fundamental freedoms' referred to in the foregoing paragraph are: '(*a*) The right to life, liberty and security of person; (*b*) The right to own property; (*c*) The right to apply to the courts of justice or to the competent organs of the State, by means of remedies and proceedings which offer adequate and effective redress for violations of the aforesaid rights and freedoms; (*d*) The right to a public hearing, with proper safeguards, by the competent organs of the State, in the substantiation of any criminal charge or in the determination of rights and obligations under civil law; (*e*) In criminal matters, the right of the accused to be presumed innocent until proved guilty; the right to be informed of the charge made against him in a language which he understands; the right to present his defence personally or to be defended by a counsel of his choice; the right not to be convicted of any punishable offence on account of any act or omission which did not constitute an offence, under national or international law, at the time when it was committed; the right to be tried without delay or to be released'. Article 1, paragraph 3 of the final draft further specifies that: '[t]he enjoyment and exercise of the rights and freedoms specified in paragraph 2 (*a*) and (*b*) are subject to such limitations or restrictions as the law expressly prescribes for reasons of internal security, the economic well-being of the nation, public order, health and morality, or to secure respect for the rights and freedoms of others'.

[285] ILC, 'Summary Records of the 416th Meeting' (1957) UN Doc A/CN.4/SR/416 (reprinted in (1957) 1 Yearbook ILC 169).

[286] ILC, 'Special Rapporteur F V Garcia-Amador's International Responsibility: Sixth Report' (n 283); ILC, 'Special Rapporteur FV Garcia-Amador's International Responsibility: Third Report' (1958) UN Doc A/CN.4/SER.A/1958/Add.1 (reprinted in (1958) 2 Yearbook ILC 48–50).

[287] G Nolte, 'From Dionisio Anzilotti to Roberto Ago: The Classical International Law of State Responsibility and the Traditional Primacy of a Bilateral Conception of Inter-State Relations' (2002) 13 EJIL 1083, 1097.

[288] ILC, 'Special Rapporteur Roberto Ago's First Report on State Responsibility' (1969) UN Doc A/CN.4/SER.A/1969/Add.1 (reprinted in (1969) 2 Yearbook ILC 127); ILC, 'Special Rapporteur Roberto Ago's Second Report on State Responsibility' (1970) UN Doc A/CN.4/SER.A/1970/Add.1 (reprinted in (1970) 2 Yearbook ILC 177).

[289] Three succeeding Rapporteurs followed, finally leading to the adoption in 2001 of the Draft Articles on Responsibility of States for Internationally Wrongful Acts. See UNGA Res 56/83 (28 January

This failed attempt to reconcile the old law of aliens with the new law of human rights was primarily due to the political and legal context of the time. During the 1950s and 1960s, Latin American states were reluctant to abandon their own doctrine of national treatment for another one so similar to the notion of international minimum standard. In Africa and Asia, newly independent states were also unwilling to codify the rights of aliens which were associated with imperialism and the diplomacy of their former colonial powers. Furthermore, communist states still viewed human rights as a product of capitalism and thus resisted their international recognition. As a result of the cold war and the decolonisation process, it was not the moment to codify the legal status of aliens, and even less so to relate it to human rights.

These political impediments were indeed reinforced by purely legal ones. In 1961 when Amador submitted his final report,[290] the only universal instrument which comprehensively addressed human rights was the non-binding Universal Declaration of Human Rights.[291] At the regional level, only one treaty had been adopted (the European Convention for the Protection of Human Rights and Fundamental Freedoms).[292] Against such a background, merging the old and controversial law of aliens with the new and emerging field of human rights was bound to fail. It was simply too early.

The history of migrants' rights under international law steadily exemplifies that, in this area as in many others, the *avant-garde* of today frequently becomes the reality of tomorrow. However, quite paradoxically, while the notion of minimum standard was the forerunner of human rights on the international scene, the latter has been emancipated from the former to such an extent that the law of aliens now stands in the shadow of human rights law.

1.3.3 The international protection of migrants: the epitome of human rights

The rights of migrants have been (re)discovered quite recently as a side effect of the normative expansion of human rights law. After a decade of lengthy discussions, the UN General Assembly adopted in December 1985 the Declaration on the Human Rights of Individuals Who Are Not Nationals of the Country in Which They Live.[293] The added value of this Declaration is more symbolic than substantial. While restating the plain applicability of human rights to non-nationals, it signals

---

2002) UN Doc A/RES/56/83, para 1; ILC, 'Report of the Commission to the General Assembly on the Work of Its 53rd Session' (2001) UN Doc A/CN.4/SER.A/2001/Add.1 (Part 2) (reprinted in (2001) 2 Yearbook ILC 26, paras 69–71).

[290] ILC, 'Special Rapporteur F V Garcia-Amador's International Responsibility: Sixth Report' (n 283).

[291] Universal Declaration of Human Rights, UNGA Res 217A (III) (10 December 1948) UN Doc A/810, at 71 (UDHR).

[292] Council of Europe, Convention for the Protection of Human Rights and Fundamental Freedoms (adopted 4 November 1950, entered into force 3 September 1953) 213 UNTS 222, ETS No 005.

[293] UNGA Res 40/144 (13 December 1985) UN Doc A/RES/40/144.

that the international protection of migrants works in tandem with the development of human rights law.

From a systemic perspective, the very term 'human rights of migrants' testifies to the appropriation of alienage by human rights law. Due respect for the human rights of migrants has been restated on multiple occasions. Among the most well-known examples are: the 1993 Vienna Conference on Human Rights;[294] the International Conference on Population and Development held the following year in Cairo;[295] the Summit for Social Development in Copenhagen in March 1995;[296] the fourth World Conference on Women organized in Beijing from 4 to 15 September 1995;[297] and the 2001 World Conference against Racism, Racial Discrimination, Xenophobia and related Intolerance held in Durban.[298] Alongside similar restatements by regional organizations,[299] the UN General Assembly has constantly underlined 'the need for all states to protect fully the universally recognized human rights of migrants, especially women and children, regardless of their legal status'.[300] This

---

[294] World Conference on Human Rights, 14–25 June 1993, 'Vienna Declaration and Programme of Action' (12 July 1993) UN Doc A/CONF.157/23, paras 33–35.

[295] International Conference on Population and Development, Cairo, Egypt, 5–13 September 1994, 'Report of the International Conference on Population and Development' (18 October 1994) UN Doc A/CONF.171/13, 135.

[296] World Summit for Social Development, Copenhagen, Denmark, 6–12 March 1995, 'Report of the World Summit for Social Development' (19 April 1995) UN Doc A/CONF.166/9, 99.

[297] Fourth World Conference on Women, Beijing, China, 4–15 September 1995, 'Report of the Fourth World Conference on Women' (17 October 1995) UN Doc A/CONF.177/20, IV(D).

[298] World Conference against Racism, Racial Discrimination, Xenophobia and Related Intolerance, 31 August–8 September 2001, Durban, South Africa, 'Durban Declaration and Programme of Action' (8 September 2001) UN Doc A/CONF.189/12, para 48.

[299] See African Common Position on Migration and Development, Executive Council of the African Union, 9th Session, 25–29 June 2006 (29 June 2006) Doc EX.CL/277(IX), paras 3.7–3.9; Association of South East Asian Nations (ASEAN) Declaration on the Protection and Promotion of the Rights of Migrant Workers, 12th ASEAN Summit, Cebu, Philippines (13 January 2007) paras 1–4; Inter-American Program for the Promotion and Protection of the Human Rights of Migrants, Including Migrant Workers and Their Families (7 June 2005) Doc AG/RES.2141 (XXXV-O/05), I(A)(1); European Council, 'The Stockholm Programme—An Open and Secure Europe Serving and Protecting Citizens' (4 May 2010) OJ C 115/1, paras 6.1.4–4.1.6.

[300] UNGA Res 54/166 (17 December 2009) UN Doc A/RES/54/166, para 4; UNGA Res 58/190 (22 December 2003) UN Doc A/RES/58/190, para 9; UNGA Res 57/218 (18 December 2002) UN Doc A/RES/57/218, para 7; 'Protection of Migrants', UNGA Res 56/170 (19 December 2001) UN Doc A/RES/56/170, para 5; and UNGA Res 55/92 (4 December 2000) UN Doc A/RES/55/92, para 5. With slight changes in the wording, see 'Declaration of the High-Level Dialogue on International Migration and Development' (1 October 2013) UN Doc A/68/L.5, para 5; UNGA Res 67/172 (20 December 2012) UN Doc A/RES/67/172, para 1; UNGA Res 66/172 (19 December 2011) UN Doc A/RES/66/172, para 1; UNGA Res 65/212 (21 December 2010) UN Doc A/RES/65/212, para 1; UNGA Res 64/166, (18 December 2009) UN Doc A/RES/64/166, para 1; UNGA Res 63/184 (18 December 2008) UN Doc A/RES/63/184, para 1; UNGA Res 62/156 (18 December 2007) UN Doc A/RES/62/156, para 1; UNGA Res 61/165 (19 December 2006) UN Doc A/RES/61/165, para 1; UNGA Res 60/169 (16 December 2005) UN Doc A/RES/60/169, para 5; and UNGA Res 59/194 (20 December 2004) UN Doc A/RES/59/194, para 7. The Millennium Declaration also endorses such a position. See 'United Nations Millennium Declaration', UNGA Res 55/2 (8 September 2000) UN Doc A/RES/55/2, paras 24–25. For earlier resolutions inviting states to take all necessary and appropriate measures to ensure that the fundamental human rights, irrespective of their immigration status, are fully respected under their national legislation, see also 'Measures to Improve the Situation and Ensure the Human Rights and Dignity of All Migrant Workers', UNGA Res 32/120 (16 December 1977) UN Doc A/RES/32/120, para 2(c); and 'Measures to Improve the Situation and Ensure the Human Rights

evolution has culminated in 2016 with the adoption of the New York Declaration
for Refugees and Migrants. Migrants are explicitly recognized as 'rights holders' and
all UN Member States reaffirm their commitments 'to protecting the safety, dignity
and human rights and fundamental freedoms of all migrants, regardless of their migratory status, at all times'.[301]

Notwithstanding its widespread acknowledgement, the appropriation of alienage
by human rights law is far from providing a cogent and uniform pattern. The human
rights of migrants are governed by two distinctive sets of legal norms that are unequally endorsed by states. Specialized treaties devoted to migrant workers are still
poorly ratified, whereas general treaties on human rights have been widely recognized as the main source of protection of the rights of migrants. Despite the ancient
lineage of migrants' rights in international law, it was not until 1990 that the UN
adopted a specific convention on migrant workers: the International Convention on
the Protection of the Rights of All Migrant Workers and Members of Their Families
(ICRMW).[302] Although it mainly restates and sometimes specifies the rights already
enshrined in more general instruments,[303] this convention is conspicuously confronted with a slow ratification process. It experienced the longest period before entry
into force in comparison to the other core UN human rights instruments: adopted in
December 1990, the ICRMW entered into force almost 13 years later in July 2003.
Even today, it remains the least ratified instrument among the core human rights
treaties: as of October 2018, the Convention counts 54 States Parties and is yet to be
ratified by Western countries.[304] A similarly limited number of ratifications can be
observed with regard to the two migrant workers conventions adopted by ILO: the
1949 Convention concerning Migration for Employment (Revised) (No 97)[305]
is ratified by 49 states, whereas the 1975 Convention concerning Migrations in
Abusive Conditions and the Promotion of Equality of Opportunity and Treatment
of Migrant Workers (No 143)[306] counts only 23 States Parties.[307]

However, this modest number of ratifications does not reflect the normative
density surrounding the rights of migrant workers. Looking at all three specialized

and Dignity of All Migrant Workers', UNGA Res 31/127 (16 December 1976) UN Doc A/RES/31/
127, para 2(c).

[301] UNGA Res 71/1(19 September 2016), paras 5 and 41.

[302] International Convention on the Protection of the Rights of All Migrant Workers and Members of
Their Families (adopted 18 December 1990, entered into force 1 July 2003) 2220 UNTS 3 (ICRMW).

[303] For a similar account, see UN Human Rights Office of the High Commissioner, Europe
Regional Office, 'Rights of Migrant Workers in Europe' (2011) 11; AT Gallagher, *The International Law
of Human Trafficking* (CUP 2010) 169; VA Leary, 'Labour Migration' in T A Aleinikoff and V Chetail
(eds), *Migration and International Legal Norms* (TMC Acer Press 2003) 227 and 235; D Weissbrodt and
S Meili, *Human Rights and Protection of Non-Citizens: Whither Universality and Indivisibility of Rights?*
(2010) 28 RSQ 34, 43–44.

[304] This number is still far from reaching the 196 states that have ratified the Convention on the
Rights of the Child, which was adopted only one year before the ICRMW.

[305] Convention concerning Migration for Employment (No 97) (adopted 1 July 1949, entered into
force 22 January 1952) 120 UNTS 70.

[306] Convention concerning Migrations in Abusive Conditions and the Promotion of Equality of
Opportunity and Treatment of Migrant Workers (No 143) (adopted 24 June 1975, entered into force
9 December 1978) 1120 UNTS 323.

[307] For further discussion on the content and ratification of the migrant worker conventions concluded by the UN and ILO see Chapter 4.

conventions together provides a different picture regarding the ratification status. Cholewinski rightly observes that:

To contend [...] that these instruments are irrelevant because they have not been widely ratified is somewhat of a myth, especially when again they are considered together. Eighty-three countries—nearly two-thirds of the some 130 countries for which international labour migration is an important feature —have ratified at least one of these three complementary conventions.[308]

Since then, the total number of State Parties has grown to 90. From this angle, the spread of ratifications is noteworthy and encompasses both countries of immigration and of emigration (including 17 Western states).[309] Despite this significant number of ratifications, these three specialized treaties fall short of providing a uniform source of protection across the world.

As a result, specialized treaties on migrant workers have been eclipsed by general human rights conventions that are widely ratified. Though drafted for a broader purpose, these general treaties offer a vital source of protection for the rights of migrants. They are generally applicable to everyone irrespective of nationality and they frequently include specific provisions for non-citizens. Besides the general principle of non-discrimination and equality before the law,[310] these instruments notably enshrine the right to leave any country and to return to one's own country,[311] the right of children to acquire a nationality,[312] due process guarantees governing expulsion,[313] and protection against *refoulement*.[314] General comments adopted by UN treaty bodies have further restated the plain applicability of human rights to non-citizens and usually devote particular attention to migrants.[315]

---

[308] R Cholewinski, 'Migration for Employment' in R Plender (ed), *Issues in International Migration Law* (Brill/Nijhoff 2015) 55.

[309] Western states having ratified at least one of these specialized treaties are mainly European ones but not exclusively. They include Belgium, Bosnia-Herzegovina, Cyprus, France, Germany, Israel, Italy, the FYR of Macedonia, the Netherlands, New Zealand, Norway, Portugal, Serbia, Slovenia, Spain, Sweden, and the United Kingdom. A ratification table of the three instruments is provided in the last section of Chapter 4.

[310] See Convention on the Rights of Persons with Disabilities (adopted 13 December 2006, entered into force 3 May 2008) 2515 UNTS 3 (ICRPD) arts 1, 3(a), 4, and 5; Convention on the Rights of the Child (adopted 20 November 1989, entered into force 2 September 1990) 1577 UNTS 3 (CRC) art 2; Convention on the Elimination of All Forms of Discrimination against Women (adopted 18 December 1979, entered into force 3 September 1981) 1249 UNTS 13 (CEDAW) arts 1, 2, and 15(1); International Covenant on Civil and Political Rights (adopted 16 December 1966, entered into force 23 March 1976) 999 UNTS 171 (hereinafter ICCPR) arts 2(1) and 26; International Convention on the Elimination of All Forms of Racial Discrimination (adopted 21 December 1965, entered into force 4 January 1969) 660 UNTS 195 (ICERD) arts 1, 2, and 5(a).

[311] See ICRPD art 18(1)(d); CRC art 10(2); CEDAW art 15(4); ICCPR arts 12(2) and 4; ICERD art 5(d)(ii).

[312] See ICRPD art 18(1)(a-b), (2); CRC art 7; CEDAW art 9; ICCPR arts 24(2) and 3; ICERD art 5(d)(iii).

[313] See ICCPR art 13. See also CRC art 10(1) (regarding family reunification).

[314] See International Convention for the Protection of All Persons from Enforced Disappearances (adopted 20 December 2006, entered into force 23 December 2010) 2716 UNTS 3, art 16; Convention against Torture and Other Cruel, Inhuman, or Degrading Treatment or Punishment (adopted 10 December 1984, entered into force 26 June 1987) 1465 UNTS 85 (Convention against Torture) art 3.

[315] See among many other instances: CEDAW Committee, 'General Recommendation No 26: Women Migrant Workers' (5 December 2008) UN Doc CEDAW/C/2009/WP.1/R, para 27; CERD, 'General Recommendation No 30: Discrimination Against Non-Citizens' (27 May 2008) UN Doc HRI/GEN/1/Rev.9; HRC, 'General Comment No 15: The Position of Aliens under the

The added value of general human rights treaties is not only normative but also institutional: their treaty bodies constitute an important means for advancing the protection of migrants within their respective mandates and instruments.[316] Their concluding observations on states' reports frequently address the rights of migrants as inferred from their relevant instrument. Although the Human Rights Committee (HRC) is less systematic than the others,[317] the Committee on Economic, Social and Cultural Rights (CESCR),[318] the Committee on the Elimination of Racial Discrimination (CERD),[319] the Committee on the Elimination of Discrimination against Women (CEDAW Committee),[320] and the Committee on the Rights of the Child (CRC Committee)[321] regularly insist on the need to protect the rights of migrants under their respective instruments. The critical role played by general human rights instruments does not disqualify the need for a more specific treaty devoted to

Covenant' (27 May 2008) UN Doc HRI/GEN/1/Rev.9; and CRC Committee, 'General Comment No 6: Treatment of Unaccompanied and Separated Children Outside Their Country of Origin' (1 September 2005) UN Doc CRC/GC/2005/6, para 27.

[316] For a similar account, see D Weissbrodt and J Rhodes, 'UN Treaty Bodies and Migrant Workers' in V Chetail and C Bauloz (eds), *Research Handbook on International Law and Migration* (Edward Elgar Publishing 2014) 303–28. But see I Slinckx, 'Migrants' Rights in UN Human Rights Conventions' in R Cholewinski, P de Guchteneire, and A Pécoud (eds), *Migration and Human Rights: The United Nations Convention on Migrant Workers' Rights* (CUP 2009) 143–48.

[317] See mainly HRC, *Norway*, CCPR/C/70/Add.27 (4 Nov 1993), para 4; *Slovenia*, A/49/40 (21 Sep 1994), paras 12–13; *Italy*, A/49/40 (21 Sep 1994), para 2; *Kuwait*, CCPR/C/KWT/CO/2 (18 Nov 2011), para 18.

[318] See for instance: CESCR, *Kazakhstan*, E/C.12/KAZ/CO/1 (1 Jul 2010), paras 20 and 27; *United Kingdom*, E/C.12/GBR/CO/5 (12 Jun 2009), para 22; *Cyprus*, E/C.12/CYP/CO/5 (12 Jun 2009), paras 14–15, 18 and 21–22; *Canada*, E/C.12/CAN/CO/4 and E/C.12/CAN/CO/5 (22 May 2006), paras 22 and 49; *China*, E/C.12/1/Add.107 (13 May 2005), paras 24, 53, 89, 114, 116, 124, and 126; *Norway*, E/C.12/1/Add.109 (23 Jun 2005), paras 10–11 and 27–29; *Italy*, E/C.12/1/Add.103 (14 Dec 2004), paras 17 and 36; *Russian Federation*, E/C.12/1/Add.94 (12 Dec 2003), para 17; *Poland*, E/C.12/1/Add.82 (19 Dec 2002), paras 15 and 37; *Dominican Republic*, E/C.12/1/Add.16 (12 Dec 1997), para 34.

[319] See notably: CERD, *China*, CERD/C/CHN/CO/10–13 (15 Sep 2009), paras 30 and 33; *Nigeria*, CERD/C/NGA/CO/18 (27 Mar 2007), para 12; *Ireland*, CERD/C/IRL/CO/2 (14 Apr 2005), paras 15, 23, and 25; *Bahrain*, CERD/C/BHR/CO/7 (14 Apr 2005), para 14; *Lebanon*, CERD/C/64/CO/3 (28 Apr 2004), para 10; *Libya*, CERD/C/64/CO/4 (10 May 2004), paras 7 and 10–11; *Republic of Korea*, CERD/C/63/CO/9 (10 Dec 2003), paras 4 and 10; *Saudi Arabia*, CERD/C/62/CO/8 (21 Mar 2003), paras 16–20; *Chile*, CERD/C/304/Add.81 (12 Apr 2001), paras 12 and 17; *Spain*, A/49/18 (8 Oct 1994), paras 479–511, esp. paras 484, 499, and 503; *Czech Republic*, CERD/C/CZE/CO/8-9 (2 Sep 2011), para 20; *Maldives*, CERD/C/MDV/CO/5-12 (14 Sep 2011), para 11; *Iceland*, CERD/C/ISL/CO/19-20 (25 Mar 2010), para 18; *Kazakhstan*, CERD/C/KAZ/CO/4-5 (6 Apr 2010), paras 16 and 22.

[320] See especially: CEDAW Committee, *Albania*, CEDAW/C/ALB/CO/3 (16 Sep 2010), paras 19 and 40–41; *Australia*, CEDAW/C/AUS/CO/7 (30 Jul 2010), paras 44–45; *Egypt*, CEDAW/C/EGY/CO/7 (5 Feb 2010), paras 35–36; *United Arab Emirates*, CEDAW/C/ARE/CO/1 (5 Feb 2010), paras 10, 26–27 and 36–37(a); *Bahrain*, CEDAW/C/BHR/CO/2 (14 Nov 2008), paras 34–35; *Netherlands*, CEDAW/C/NLD/CO/4 (2 Feb 2007), paras 15–19, 21 and 27–28; *Philippines*, CEDAW/C/PHI/CO/6 (25 Aug 2006), paras 21–22; *Kuwait*, A/59/38 (18 Mar 2004), paras 76–77 and 79; *Costa Rica*, A/58/38 (18 Jul 2003), paras 62–63; and *China*, A/54/38 (5 Feb 1999), paras 326–28.

[321] See notably: CRC Committee, *Honduras*, CRC/C/HND/CO/3 (3 May 2007), paras 70–71; *Chile*, CRC/C/CHL/CO/3 (23 Apr 2007), paras 29 and 63; *Republic of Oman*, CRC/C/OMN/CO/2 (29 Sep 2006), paras 24–25 and 59–60; *Panama*, CRC/C/15/Add.233 (30 Jun 2004), paras 24–25; *Japan*, CRC/15/Add.231 (26 Feb 2004), paras 24–25; *Republic of Korea*, CRC/C/15/Add.197 (18 Mar 2003), paras 31–32 and 58–59; *Spain*, CRC/C/15/Add.185 (13 Jun 2002), para 27; *Demark*, CRC/C/15/Add.151 (17 Jul 2001), paras 26–27; *Palau*, CRC/C/15/Add.149 (21 Feb 2001), para 32; *Kuwait*, CRC/C/15/Add.88 (5 Jun 1998), para 18; *Iceland*, CRC/C/ISL/CO/3-4 (6 Oct 2011), paras 36–37;

migrant workers. Monitoring bodies are aware of such a need and they regularly call for the ratification of the ICRMW.[322]

Moreover, migrants can bring individual complaints to seven UN treaty bodies,[323] as well as to the special procedures established by the Human Rights Council, in particular, the Special Rapporteur on the human rights of migrants.[324] The Committee against Torture (CAT Committee) is by far the most solicited UN treaty body. It has even become an anti-deportation committee given that between 80 per cent and 90 per cent of all individual complaints submitted thereto concern alleged violations of the principle of *non-refoulement* enshrined in Article 3 of the Convention.[325] At the regional level, the European Court of Human Rights is another particularly active treaty body whose judgments are binding on Contracting States. It has regularly sanctioned violations of human rights committed against migrants.[326] The European Court of Human Rights is not the only regional body addressing the protection of the human rights of migrants. Indeed, virtually all are concerned with violations by states against non-nationals, such as the Inter-American and African Courts of Human Rights.[327]

To conclude, as a result of a longstanding evolution, the traditional law of aliens grounded in diplomatic protection and state responsibility has been progressively marginalized and absorbed to a large extent by human rights law. This process is not

Italy, CRC/C/ITA/CO/3-4 (31 Oct 2011), para 62; *Republic of Korea*, CRC/C/KOR/CO/3-4 (6 Oct 2011), paras 36 and 68–69; *Costa Rica*, CRC/C/CRI/CO/4 (17 Jun 2011), paras 10 and 29–30; and *Japan*, CRC/C/JPN/CO/3 (20 Jun 2010), paras 37 and 45.

[322] CERD, *Lebanon*, A/59/18 (2004) 18, para 83; *Spain*, A/59/18 (2004) 32, para 171; *Portugal*, A/59/18 (2004) 66, para 371; CESCR, *Republic of Moldova*, E/2004/22 (2003) 49, para 326; *Russian Federation*, E/2004/22 (2003) 64, para 487; CESCR, *Kuwait*, E/2005/22 (2004) 29, para 205; *Italy*, E/2005/22 (2004) 54, para 447; CRC Committee, *Israel*, CRC/C/121 (2002) 131, para 577; CRC, *Republic of Korea*, CRC/124 (2003) 24, para 137; CEDAW Committee, *France*, CEDAW/C/FRA/CO/6 (8 Apr 2008), para 44; *Mauritius*, CEDAW/C/MUS/CO/6-7 (8 Nov 2011), para 39; *Australia*, CEDAW/C/AUS/CO/7 (30 Jul 2010), para 49; *United Arab Emirates*, CEDAW/C/ARE/CO/1 (5 Feb 2010), para 53; and *Bahrain*, CEDAW/C/BHR/CO/2 (14 Nov 2008), para 45.

[323] They are the HRC, the CESCR, the CERD, the Committee against Torture (CAT Committee), the CEDAW Committee, the Committee on the Rights of Persons with Disabilities (CRPD Committee), and the Committee on Enforced Disappearances.

[324] The mandate of the Special Rapporteur on the Human Rights of Migrants was created in 1999 by the Commission on Human Rights pursuant to resolution 1999/44. Since then, his/her mandate has been extended by Commission on Human Rights resolutions 2002/62 and 2005/47 and Human Rights Council resolutions 8/10, 17/12, and 26/19, each for a period of three years. The mandate of the Special Rapporteur covers all countries, irrespective of whether a state has ratified any relevant treaty, including the ICRMW. In contrast to the procedure before UN treaty bodies, communications submitted to the Special Rapporteur do not require prior exhaustion of domestic remedies.

[325] V Chetail, 'Le Comité des Nations Unies contre la torture et l'expulsion des étrangers: Dix ans de jurisprudence' (2006) 26 RSDIE 63, 66; M Nowak and E McArthur (eds), *The United Nations Convention Against Torture: A Commentary* (OUP 2008) 159.

[326] For recent condemnations see, for example, *Othman (Abu Qatada) v the United Kingdom* App No 8139/09 (ECtHR 17 January 2012); *Hirsi Jamaa et al v Italy* App No 27765/09 (ECtHR 23 February 2012); and *MSS v Belgium and Greece* App No 30696/09 (ECtHR 21 January 2011).

[327] For recent condemnations pronounced by the Inter-American Court of Human Rights see, for example, *Nadege Dorzema et al v Dominican Republic* Series C No 12,688 (IACtHR 24 October 2012); and *Veles Loor v Panama* Series C No 12,581 (IACtHR 23 November 2010). Though the newly established African Court has not yet delivered a judgment in the field, the African Commission has already developed a substantial jurisprudence on the rights of migrants. See for instance *Kenneth Good v Botswana* Report No 313/05 (AComHPR 26 May 2010); and *John K Modise v Botswana* Report No 97/93 (AComHPR 6 November 2000).

confined to the specific situation of migrants, but reflects a broader evolution of general international law during the last century.[328] The consequences of this phenomenon are both normative and institutional. Migrants' rights have become the epitome of human rights for better or for worse. The international protection of migrants is now anchored in human rights law through its existential premise: the universality of human rights. From this stance, 'migrants' rights today are more clearly recognizable as human and labour rights'.[329] At the same time, the universality of human rights is plagued by endemic violations against migrants.[330] Migration exemplifies the limits of human rights law more than any other field. The vertiginous gap between proclaimed rights and actual violations represents the sad reality of many migrants across the world.[331]

Although the rights of migrants remain the poor cousins of human rights at the domestic plane, international human rights law offers new remedies and enforcement mechanisms to address their violations. Already in 1984, Richard B Lillich observed that:

What the international community is witnessing today is a major change—the significance of which cannot be overstated—in the way in which the rights of aliens are protected: from the classic system of diplomatic protection by the alien's state of nationality, invoking the traditional international law governing the treatment of aliens, to the direct protection of the individual alien's rights through his use of national and international procedures to enforce a set of reformulated international norms [. .].[332]

This does not mean that diplomatic protection has no role to play in contemporary international law.[333] In our current state system, countries of origin remain an

---

[328] On the impact of human rights law on diplomatic protection, see generally ST Pesch, 'The Influence of Human Rights on Diplomatic Protection: Reviving an Old Instrument of Public International Law' in N Weiss and J-M Thouvenin (eds), *The Influence of Human Rights on International Law* (Springer 2015) 55–67; A Vermeer-Künzli, 'Diplomatic Protection as a Source of Human Rights Law' in D Shelton (ed), *The Oxford Handbook of International Human Rights Law* (OUP Press 2013) 251–74; RP Mazzeschi, 'Impact on the Law of Diplomatic Protection' in Kamminga and Scheinin (eds), *The Impact of Human Rights Law on General International Law* (n 274) 211–33; E Milano, 'Diplomatic Protection and Human Rights Before the International Court of Justice: Re-fashioning Tradition?' (2004) 35 Neth Yearbook Intl L 85–142.

[329] R Cholewinski, 'Human Rights of Migrants: The Dawn of a New Era?' (2010) 24 Geo Immigr L J 585, 614.

[330] For a critique of the universality of human rights when confronted with undocumented migrants, see J Ramji-Nogales, 'Undocumented Migrants and the Failures of Universal Individualism' (2014) 47 Vanderbilt J Trans L 699–763.

[331] See for instance among many other official reports of violations: Human Rights Council, 'Report of the Special Rapporteur on the Human Rights of Migrants, François Crépeau. Labour Exploitation of Migrants' (3 April 2014) UN Doc A/HRC/26/35; Human Rights Council, 'Report of the Special Rapporteur on the Human Rights of Migrants, François Crépeau. Regional Study: Management of the External Borders of the European Union and its Impact on the Human Rights of Migrants' (24 April 2013) UN Doc A/HRC/23/46; and Human Rights Council, 'Report of the Special Rapporteur on the Human Rights of Migrants, François Crépeau' (2 April 2012) UN Doc A/HRC/20/24.

[332] RB Lillich, *The Human Rights of Aliens in Contemporary International Law* (Gillian M White 1984) 3. For a general appraisal of this evolution, see also: B Simma, 'From Bilateralism to Community Interest in International Law' (1994) 250 Collected Courses of the Hague Academy of International Law 217–384.

[333] For a general account of diplomatic protection under contemporary international law, see in addition to the references already quoted: CF Amerasinghe, *Diplomatic Protection* (OUP 2008); A

important means for protecting the rights of their nationals abroad. The traditional institution of diplomatic protection thus coexists with national and supranational procedures in order to ensure due respect for the rights of migrants. It is true that the latter's procedures are more reliable than the former's because, as a method of enforcement, they are not discretionary and more objective.[334] UN human rights treaty bodies are nevertheless not the panacea. Contrary to regional courts, their views are not formally binding, even if a duty to give them effect can be inferred from the twofold obligation to provide an effective remedy and to respect in good faith the procedure of individual communication.[335] Diplomatic protection accordingly retains a residual role when access to human rights treaty bodies is not possible or ineffective for practical or legal reasons. John R Dugard, the ILC Special Rapporteur on diplomatic protection, observes in this sense that:

This starkly illustrates the current position: that aliens may have rights under international law as human beings, but they have no remedies under international law—in the absence of a human rights treaty—except through the intervention of their national state. Until the individual acquires comprehensive procedural rights under international law, it would be a setback for human rights to abandon diplomatic protection.[336]

Pellet, 'The Second Death of Euripide Mavrommatis? Notes on the International Law Commission's Draft Articles on Diplomatic Protection' (2008) 7(1) The Law and Practice of International Courts and Tribunals 33–58; S Touzé, *La protection des droits des nationaux à l'étranger: Recherche sur la protection diplomatique* (Pedone 2007); A Vermeer-Künzli, *The Protection of Individuals by Means of Diplomatic Protection: Diplomatic Protection as a Human Rights Instrument* (Leiden University Press 2007); ILC, 'Draft Articles on Diplomatic Protection with Commentaries. Report of the International Law Commission on the Work of its 58th Session' (2006) UN Doc A/61/10; and M Zieck, 'Codification of the Law on Diplomatic Protection: The First Eight Draft Articles' (2001) 14(1) Leiden J Intl L 209–32.

[334] The Draft Articles on Diplomatic Protection adopted by the ILC in 2006 confirm in Article 2 that diplomatic protection is a right of the state, not a duty. Article 19 merely advises as a 'recommended practice' that a state 'should [. . .] give due consideration to the possibility of exercising diplomatic protection, especially when a significant injury has occurred'.

[335] See for instance: HRC, 'General Comment No 33: The Obligations of States Parties under the Optional Protocol to the International Covenant on Civil and Political Rights' (5 November 2008) UN Doc CCPR/C/GC/33, paras 14–20; HRC, *Weiss v Austria* Communication No 1086/2002 (24 May 2002) UN Doc CCPR/C/77/D/1086/2002, para 11.1. For further developments on the legal nature of the views adopted by UN treaty bodies, see notably A Nollkaemper and R Van Alebeek, 'The Legal Status of Decisions by Human Rights Treaty Bodies in National Law' (11 April 2011) Amsterdam Center for International Law, Research Paper No 2011-02, at 2; E Rieter, *Preventing Irreparable Harm, Provisional Measures in International Human Rights Adjudication* (Intersentia 2010) 886; M Nowak, *UN Covenant on Civil and Political Rights: A Commentary* (Engel 2005) 893; M Scheinin, 'International Mechanisms and Procedures for Implementation' in R Hanski and S Markku (eds) *An Introduction to the International Protection of Human Rights: A Textbook* (2nd edn, Åbo Akademi University Press 1999) 444.

[336] ILC, 'First Report on Diplomatic Protection by Special Rapporteur John R Dugard' (n 251) 214. For further discussion related to the diplomatic protection of migrants, see A Vermeer-Künzli, 'Diplomatic Protection and Consular Assistance of Migrants' in Chetail and Bauloz (eds), *Research Handbook on International Law and Migration* (n 316) 265–80.

2

Founding Principles of International Migration Law

The legal stance of migrants under international law unveils the dual nature of the world legal system. Contemporary international law is both a law of coexistence between sovereign states and a law of interdependence, whereby common concerns call for a global response that transcends the state. International migration law is not an exception to this dialectic between these two faces of public international law.

On the one hand, immigration controls remind us that states have created the world to fit their own image by distinguishing their nationals from the 'others'. Such a distinction mirrors the structural feature of an international society composed of nation-states. From this standpoint, the ambivalent notion of national sovereignty represents both the basis and the limit of public international law. As a vessel of power, state sovereignty is as much an instrument of domination over individuals as an instrument of emancipation of peoples.

On the other hand, the unprecedented expansion of human rights law has substantially eroded state's sovereignty and now constitutes the primary source of protection for asserting the rights of migrants. As a result of this schizophrenic evolution, the ethos of immigration control coexists with that of human rights. These two conflicting driving forces frame the overall scheme and the very content of international migration law. The complexity inherent in this existential tension is exacerbated by the dispersion of applicable rules across a vast number of general and specialized treaties that have informed, in turn, the development of customary international law.

However, when international law is assessed with some distance through a systemic approach, some general and well established principles may be identified from the significant—albeit eclectic—body of legal norms governing the movement of persons across borders. These founding principles provide the benchmark for apprehending international migration law as a global set of legal norms. They shed light on the internal logic of this field in regulating the three constitutive components of the migration process: departure from the country of origin (section 2.1), admission into the territory of the destination state (section 2.2), and sojourn therein (section 2.3). Each of its core components is governed by several norms of customary international law which interact and overlap with treaty law through a dense and subtle continuum of mutual interaction. Following this integrated approach, this chapter provides the general picture of international migration law by inquiring into its founding principles, their respective content, and legal basis.

2.1 Departure of Migrants

Departure is the prerequisite to migration. It has been acknowledged in contemporary international law as the right to leave any country. Freedom to leave—whether for travel, emigration, or expatriation purposes—constitutes the founding act of international migration law for, without such a basic freedom, there is no room for international rules applicable to the transnational movement of persons. The right to leave any country is not only the very first right of potential migrants. It is more fundamentally at the heart of the theory of human rights.

Freedom to leave is traditionally considered an essential attribute to personal liberty. It is regarded as 'the first and most fundamental of man's liberties',[1] 'the right of personal self-determination',[2] 'an indispensable condition for the free development of a person',[3] and 'a necessary prerequisite to the enjoyment of a number of other human rights'.[4] From this last stance, 'there is no doubt that the right to "vote with one's feet"—whether to escape persecution, seek a better life, or for purely personal motives having nothing to do with larger political or economic issues—may be the ultimate means through which the individual may express his or her personal liberty.'[5] The right to leave any country accordingly constitutes both the prerequisite and the product of human rights. Against such a frame, it is not surprising that the freedom to leave has been endorsed by a wide range of human rights instruments before maturing into a norm of customary international law.

[1] M Cranston, 'The Political and Philosophical Aspects of the Right to Leave and to Return' in K Vasak and S Liskofsky (eds), *The Right to Leave and to Return: Papers and Recommendations of the International Colloquium held in Uppsala, Sweden, 19–20 June 1972* (The American Jewish Committee 1976) 21.

[2] JD Inglès, Special Rapporteur of the Sub-Commission on Prevention of Discrimination and Protection of Minorities 'Study of Discrimination in Respect of the Right of Everyone to Leave Any Country, Including his Own, and to Return to his Country' (1963) UN Doc E/CN.4/Sub.2/220/Rev.1, 9.

[3] Human Rights Committee (HRC), 'General Comment No 27 (67): Freedom of Movement (article 12)' (1 November 1999) UN Doc CCPR/C/21/Rev.1/Add.9.

[4] E Guild, 'The Right to Leave a Country' (2013) Issue Paper by the Council of Europe Commissioner for Human Rights, 5. For further discussion about the historical origins of the right to leave, see V Chetail, 'The Transnational Movement of Persons under General International Law: Mapping the Customary Law Foundations of International Migration Law' in V Chetail and C Bauloz (eds), *Research Handbook on International Law and Migration* (Edward Elgar Publishing 2014) 10–15; J McAdam, 'An Intellectual History of Freedom of Movement in International Law: The Right to Leave as a Personal Liberty' (2011) 12 Melb J Int'l L 27–56; SF Jagerskiold, 'Historical Aspects of the Right to Leave and to Return' in Vasak and Liskofsky (eds), *The Right to Leave and to Return* (n 1) 3–17.

[5] H Hannum, *The Right to Leave and Return in International Law and Practice* (Martinus Nijhoff 1987) 4.

2.1.1 The international recognition of the right to leave any country

Under contemporary international law, the right to leave any country was first endorsed in the Universal Declaration of Human Rights adopted by the UN General
Assembly in December 1948.[6] Its Article 13(2) unequivocally proclaims: 'Everyone
has the right to leave any country, including his own, and to return to his country.'
During the drafting of this provision, most of the states' representatives acclaimed
the right to leave any country as 'a fundamental human right'.[7] As stressed by the
Belgian delegate, its recognition by the Universal Declaration of Human Rights 'was
of vital importance'.[8] The Haitian delegation further recalled that this principle was
'recognized before national states had reached their present stage of development'.[9]
While highlighting the close relations between freedom to leave and other basic
rights, the representative of Chile underlined that 'the right to personal liberty [...]
includes [...] the right to leave the state itself'.[10] He accordingly considered the
right to leave as 'the sacred right of every human being' and further declared '[t]hat
principle should be defended and maintained as an element necessary to progress
and to civilization'.[11]

Though acknowledged by most delegates, this view was not unanimous. The
exact scope and content of the right to leave was a contentious issue because of the
political context of the Cold War. The Union of Soviet Socialist Republics (USSR)
argued that 'every sovereign state should have the right to establish whatever rules
it considered necessary to regulate movement on its territory and across its borders. Recognition of that right was based on respect for the principle of national
sovereignty embodied in the United Nations Charter.'[12] Hence, acknowledging an
individual right to leave without any reference to domestic legislation of the states
'would be to distort the normal relations between the citizen and the state', as 'besides rights, people had certain obligations which they had to fulfill'.[13] Otherwise,
'individuals could leave their country at will, forgetting duty to the fatherland. The

---

[6] Universal Declaration of Human Rights (adopted 10 December 1948) UNGA Res 217A(III)
(UDHR).

[7] Commission on Human Rights, 'Summary Record of the Fifty-Fifth Meeting' Third Session of 2
June 1948 (15 June 1948) UN Doc E/CN.4/SR.55. For the statement of the Indian delegation, see ibid
6. See also ibid 9 and ibid 11 for statements by the representatives of Chile and Australia respectively.
The French delegation, in line with the representative of the United Kingdom, equally considered that
'any restriction of the freedom to emigrate might be a flagrant form of persecution', see Commission on
Human Rights, Sub-Commission on the Prevention of Discrimination and the Protection of Minorities
'Summary Record of the Eight Meeting' First Session (28 November 1947) UN Doc E/CN.4/Sub.2/
SR.8, 20.

[8] UNGA, Third Committee 'Summary Record of the Hundred and Twentieth Meeting' Third
Session (2 November 1948) UN Doc A/C.3/SR.120, 322.

[9] ibid 318.

[10] Commission on Human Rights, Drafting Committee on an International Bill of Human Rights
'Documented Outline' First Session (11 June 1947) UN Doc E/CN.4/AC.1/3/Add.1, 73. A draft proposal submitted by Ecuador even explicitly stated that 'the right to personal liberty includes [...] the
right to leave', see Commission on Human Rights 'Draft Charter of International Human Rights and
Duties, Note by the Secretary-General' Second Session (12 November 1947) UN Doc E/CN.4/32, 2.

[11] UNGA, 'Summary Record of the Hundred and Twentieth Meeting' (n 8) 316.

[12] Commission on Human Rights, 'Summary Record of the Fifty-Fifth Meeting' (n 7) 7.

[13] ibid.

war had produced numerous examples of the result of such negligence. It would be morally wrong and contrary to democratic ideals to encourage such disregard of duty.'[14]

This view, however, was discarded by the great majority of states' representatives on the ground that any amendment referring to domestic legislation 'would nullify the meaning of article [13]'.[15] It 'would imply the renunciation of the inherent rights of mankind. A document drawn up in that sense would be a declaration of the absolute rights of the state and not a declaration of human rights.'[16] As summed up by the Australian delegation, the right to leave any country 'was unquestionably one of the fundamental rights of man, and it should form the subject of a statement of principle. To subject it to reservations would be to deprive the Declaration of all its force.'[17] Freedom to leave any country was eventually endorsed without any specific qualification, although the general limitation clause contained in article 29 of the Universal Declaration was deemed applicable to it in the same way as to the other fundamental rights proclaimed therein.

Although the Universal Declaration is a resolution of the General Assembly without legally binding force, most of the rights enshrined therein are currently considered as being part of customary international law.[18] This raises the question whether the right to leave any country proclaimed by its Article 13 has matured into a norm of customary international law. Before inquiring into the existence of such a customary norm, one should first observe that the freedom to leave is firmly grounded in treaty law.

The right to leave any country constitutes a prevalent feature of international human rights law restated in a wide range of universal and regional treaties. At

[14] Commission on Human Rights, Drafting Committee on an International Bill of Human Rights 'Summary Record of the Thirty-Sixth Meeting' Second Session (19 May 1948) UN Doc E/CN.4/AC.1/SR.36, 8.

[15] See the statement of the Philippines delegation, UNGA, 'Summary Record of the Hundred and Twentieth Meeting' (n 8) 318.

[16] See the statement by the Chilean representative ibid 316. For a similar account, see also the statements of the delegations of India, the United States of America, Lebanon, Belgium, the United Kingdom, Uruguay, and Ecuador, ibid 317–26. The USSR amendment was finally rejected by 24 votes to 7 with 13 abstentions.

[17] Commission on Human Rights, 'Summary Record of the Fifty-Fifth Meeting' (n 7) 11.

[18] See, among many others, S Joseph and J Kyriakakis, 'The United Nations and Human Rights' in S Joseph and A McBeth (eds), *Research Handbook on International Human Rights Law* (Edward Elgar 2010) 2; O De Schutter, *International Human Rights Law* (CUP 2010) 50; JG Merrills and AH Robertson, *Human Rights in the World: An Introduction to the Study of the International Protection of Human Rights* (4th edn, Manchester University Press 2001) 29; A Eide and G Alfredsson, 'Introduction' in A Eide and G Alfredsson (eds), *The Universal Declaration of Human Rights: A Common Standard of Achievement* (Martinus Nijhoff 1999) xxv, xxxi–ii; L Henkin, *The Age of Rights* (Columbia University Press 1990) 19; NS Rodley, 'Human Rights and Humanitarian Intervention: The Case Law of the World Court' (1989) 38(2) ICLQ 321–33; T Meron, *Human Rights and Humanitarian Norms as Customary Law* (Clarendon Press 1989) 106; F Kirgis, 'Custom on a Sliding Scale' (1987) 81 AJIL 146, 146–48; LB Sohn, 'The New International Law: Protection of the Rights of Individuals Rather than States' (1982) 32 Am UL Rev 1, 15–17; KMG Nayar, 'Human Rights: The UN and US Foreign Policy' (1978) 19 Harv Int'l LJ 813, 816–17; H Waldock, 'Human Rights in Contemporary International Law and the Significance of the European Convention' (1965) 11 ICLQ 1–23; JP Humphrey, 'The International Bills of Rights: Scope and Implementation' (1976) 17 Wm & Mary L Rev 527.

the universal level, the most influential instrument is the International Covenant on Civil and Political Rights (ICCPR), which is currently ratified by 172 states from all regions of the world. Its Article 12(2) reiterates in line with the Universal Declaration of Human Rights that '[e]veryone shall be free to leave any country, including his own'. During the drafting of the Covenant, several delegations 'emphasized the importance of the right recognized in that article, particularly in view of the great human migrations that had recently taken place'.[19]

As it was the case during the drafting of the Universal Declaration, discussions mainly focused on the range of permissible limitations. A few delegates argued that the legitimate restrictions were so many and so varied that a meaningful assertion of this right could not be provided in the Covenant.[20] This argument, however, was resoundingly rejected by most state representatives. Indeed, 'the importance of a provision in the covenant on the right to liberty of movement was stressed by many representatives, who regarded such a right as a necessary complement of the other rights recognized in the covenant on civil and political rights and in the covenant on economic, social and cultural rights'.[21] As underscored by the Lebanese delegate, the right to leave any country was 'an important right' which constituted 'an essential part of the right to personal liberty'.[22] Thus, 'deprivation of that right would considerably limit the exercise of all the other human rights'.[23]

The right to leave any country was finally reaffirmed in the Covenant on the ground that it was one of the 'fundamental human rights'.[24] Like many other rights (such as freedom of religion or the right to peaceful assembly), it may be submitted to lawful restrictions. The main concern of the drafters was to formulate them in order to ensure that the exercise of the right to leave remained the rule and limitations of this right the exception. The limitation clause contained in Article 12(3)

---

[19] See the statement of Pakistan, Commission on Human Rights 'Summary Record of the Three Hundred and Fifteenth Meeting' Eighth Session (17 June 1952) UN Doc E/CN.4/SR.315, 10; and the statement of Sweden ibid, 7. See also the statement of the Lebanese delegation, Commission on Human Rights, 'Summary Record of the Hundred and Fiftieth Meeting' Sixth Session (17 April 1950) UN Doc E/CN.4/SR.150, 12. For statements by the Indian and French delegations, see ibid 13 and ibid 14.

[20] See the statement of USSR delegate, Commission on Human Rights, 'Summary Record of the Hundred and Sixth Meeting' (8 June 1949) UN Doc E/CN.4/SR.106, 7. For similar assertions by the delegations of the UK and Australia, see Commission on Human Rights, 'Summary Record of the Three Hundred and Fifteen Meeting' (n 19) 5–6.

[21] Commission on Human Rights, 'Report to the Economic and Social Council on the Eighth Session of the Commission, held in New York, from 14 April to 14 June 1952' Supp No 4, Eighth Session (1952) UN Doc E/2256; E/CN.4/669, 28.

[22] See Commission on Human Rights, 'Summary Record of the Hundred and Fifty-First Meeting' Sixth Session (19 April 1950) UN Doc E/CN.4/SR.151, 12.

[23] See also ibid 8 and ibid 13 for the statements of Lebanon and France.

[24] See ibid 3 for the affirmation of Uruguay. For similar statements, see also Commission on Human Rights, 'Summary Record of the Three Hundred and Fifteenth Meeting' (n 19) 5 (for India) and 8 (for Chile); UNGA, Third Committee 'Official Record of the Fourteenth Session' (12 November 1959) UN Doc A/C.3/SR.954, 232 (for Belgium); UNGA Third Committee 'Official Record of the Fourteenth Session 956th Meeting' (13 November 1959) UN Doc A/C.3/SR.956, 237 (for France), 238 (for Philippines), and 240 (Spain); for Ecuador see UNGA Third Committee, 'Official Record of the Fourteenth Session 957th Meeting' (16 November 1959) UN Doc A/C.3/SR.957, 24.

has accordingly been worded in the same terms as those provided for other human rights.[25]

Though submitted to lawful restrictions, the scope of the right to leave any country is broad and inclusive. As restated by the Human Rights Committee in its General Comment No 27, Article 12(2) applies to everyone—ie both nationals and non-nationals—and its benefit is not restricted to persons lawfully within the territory of a state.[26] The right to leave thus covers undocumented migrants in transit countries as well. The material scope of the right to leave is equally broad as it includes both temporary stay abroad (right to travel) and long-term departure (right to emigrate). The Human Rights Committee recalls in its General Comment No 27 that:

> Freedom to leave the territory of a State may not be made dependent on any specific purpose or on the period of time the individual chooses to stay outside the country. Thus travelling abroad is covered as well as departure for permanent emigration. Likewise, the right of the individual to determine the State of destination is part of the legal guarantee.[27]

Furthermore and more importantly, the right to leave implies a twofold obligation for the state: a negative obligation not to impede departure from its territory and a positive obligation to issue travel documents. The negative duty requires states to 'eliminate the exit visa requirement as a general rule and require it only in individual cases that can be justified in relation to the Covenant' under Article 12(3).[28] Concerning the positive obligations of states, the Human Rights Committee has made clear in several individual communications,[29] as well as in its General Comment No 27,[30] that the right to obtain travel documents is an integral part of the right to leave in order to ensure the effective respect of the latter. More generally, the treaty body of the ICCPR has further underlined that 'the restrictions [under Article 12(3)] must not impair the essence of the right [...]; the relation between right and restriction, between norm and exception, must not be reversed'.[31] In other words, '[l]imits are permissible, but they must not render the right ineffective in practice'.[32]

---

[25] 'The above-mentioned rights shall not be subject to any restrictions except those which are provided by law, are necessary to protect national security, public order (ordre public), public health or morals or the rights and freedoms of others, and are consistent with the other rights recognized in the present Covenant.'

[26] HRC, 'General Comment No 27' (n 3).   [27] ibid.

[28] HRC, 'Concluding observations of the Human Rights Committee: Syrian Arab Republic' (24 April 2001) UN Doc CCPR/CO/71/SYR, para 21. See also HRC 'Concluding observations of the Human Rights Committee: Democratic People's Republic of Korea' (27 August 2001) UN Doc CCPR/CO/72/PRK, para 20; 'Concluding observations of the Human Rights Committee: Gabon' (10 November 2000) UN Doc CCPR/CO/70/GAB, para 16; 'Comments of the Human Rights Committee: Belarus' (25 September 1992) UN Doc CCPR/C/79/Add.5, para 6.

[29] See among others, HRC *Vidal Martins v Uruguay* (1982) Communication No 57/1979 UN Doc CCPR/C/15/D/57/1979 37, 157; HRC *Varela Nunez v Uruguay* (1983) Communication No 108/1981 UN Doc CCPR/C/19/D/108/19981 38, 225; HRC *El Ghar v Libyan Arab Jamahiriva* (2004) Communication No 1107/2002 UN Doc CCPR/C/82/D/1107/2002, paras 7.2–7.3; HRC *Farag El Dernawi v Libyan Arab Jamahiriya* (2007) Communication No 1143/2002 UN Doc CCPR/C/90/D/1143/2002, para 6.2.

[30] HRC 'General Comment No 27' (n 3) para 9.   [31] ibid para 13.

[32] C Harvey and RP Barnidge, 'Human Rights, Free Movement, and the Right to Leave in International Law' (2007) 19(1) IJRL 1, 6.

According to Article 12(3), restrictions are permissible when the following three cumulative conditions are fulfilled: first, restrictions are provided by law; second, they are necessary to protect national security, public order, public health or morals, or the rights and freedoms of others; and finally, they are consistent with the other rights recognized in the Covenant. As restated by the Human Rights Committee, '[t]he application of restrictions in any individual case must be based on clear legal grounds and meet the test of necessity and the requirements of proportionality. These conditions would not be met, for example, if an individual were prevented from leaving a country merely on the ground that he or she is the holder of "state secrets." '[33] Likewise, refusing to issue a passport to a political dissident is undoubtedly a violation of the right to leave any country.[34]

By contrast, during the drafting history of Article 12(3), '[i]t was agreed that the right to leave the country could not be claimed in order to escape legal proceedings or to avoid such obligations as national service, and the payment of fines, taxes or maintenance allowances'.[35] However, even in such cases, restrictive measures must conform to the principle of proportionality.[36] The Human Rights Committee has recalled that:

Restrictive measures [...] must be appropriate to achieve their protective function; they must be the least intrusive instrument amongst those which might achieve the desired result; and they must be proportionate to the interest to be protected. The principle of proportionality has to be respected not only in the law that frames the restrictions, but also by the administrative and judicial authorities in applying the law.[37]

As a foundational instrument of international human rights law, the ICCPR ensures a solid and widespread conventional basis to the right to leave any country, which has been reinforced by many other universal treaties. It has been steadily reaffirmed in more specific UN treaties, such as the 1965 International Convention on the Elimination of all Forms of Racial Discrimination (ICERD) (Article 5(d)(i)); the 1973 Convention on the Suppression and Punishment of the Crime of Apartheid (Article 2(c));[38] the 1989 Convention on the Rights of the Child (CRC) (Article 10(2)); the 1990 International Convention on the Protection of the Rights of all Migrant Workers and Members of their Families (ICRMW) (Article 8(1)); and the 2006 International Convention on the Rights of Persons with Disabilities (ICRPD, Article 18(1)(c)).[39] Furthermore, the plain applicability of freedom to

---

[33] HRC 'General Comment No 27' (n 3) para 16.

[34] HRC, *Bwalya v Zambia* (1993) Communication No 314/1988 UN Doc CCPR/C/48/D/314/1988, para 6.5.

[35] UNGA 'Draft International Covenants on Human Rights. Annotation' Tenth Session (1 July 1955) UN Doc A/2929, 109 para 53.

[36] HRC 'General Comment No 27' (n 3) para 14.

[37] ibid paras 14–15. Although judicial proceedings may justify restrictions to the right to leave, this is no longer the case when such judicial proceedings have been unduly delayed for seven years, see, for example, HRC, *González del Río v Peru* (1992) Communication No 263/1987 UN Doc CCPR/C/46/D/263/1987, para 5.3.

[38] International Convention on the Suppression and Punishment of the Crime of Apartheid (adopted 30 November 1973, entered into force 18 July 1976) 1015 UNTS 243.

[39] Convention on the Rights of Persons with Disabilities (adopted 13 December 2006, entered into force 3 May 2008) 2515 UNTS 3 (ICRPD).

leave in times of armed conflict has also been endorsed by the widely ratified 1949 Geneva Convention relative to the Protection of Civilian Persons in Time of War (Articles 35, 37, and 48).[40]

In addition to this already substantial number of universal treaties, the benefit of the right to leave any country has been restated for several specific categories of persons. This notably concerns the diplomatic, consular, and other related staff, as acknowledged by the 1961 Vienna Convention on Diplomatic Relations (Article 44)[41] and then reiterated in a similar language by other instruments, such as the 1963 Vienna Convention on Consular Relations (Article 26),[42] the 1969 Convention on Special Missions (Article 45(1)),[43] and the 1975 Vienna Convention on the Representation of States in Their Relations with International Organizations of a Universal Character (Article 80).[44] The benefit of the right to leave has been equally restated for another specific—and much more significant—group of persons: refugees and stateless persons. Although the 1951 Convention Relating to the Status of Refugees[45] and the 1954 Convention Relating to the Status of Stateless Persons[46] do not mention the right to leave *expressis verbis*, the obligation to issue travel documents under their common Article 28 'can be regarded as a realization of the principle laid down in Art. 13, para. 2 of the Universal Declaration of Human Rights'.[47]

The right to leave laid down in the Universal Declaration is also reaffirmed in all the regional human rights conventions, thus covering almost all continents. These regional instruments include the 1963 Protocol 4 to the European Convention for the Protection of Human Rights and Fundamental Freedoms (Article 2(2)),[48]

---

[40] Geneva Convention Relative to the Protection of Civilian Persons in Time of War (adopted 12 August 1949, entered into force 21 October 1950) 75 UNTS 287 (Fourth Geneva Convention).

[41] Vienna Convention on Diplomatic Relations (adopted 18 April 1961, entered into force 24 April 1964) 500 UNTS 95.

[42] Vienna Convention on Consular Relations (adopted 24 April 1963, entered into force 19 March 1967) 596 UNTS 261.

[43] Convention on Special Missions (adopted 8 December 1969, entered into force 21 June 1985) 1400 UNTS 231.

[44] Vienna Convention on the Representation of States in their Relations with International Organizations of a Universal Character (adopted 13 March 1975, not yet in force) UN Doc A/CONF.67/16.

[45] Convention Relating to the Status of Refugees (adopted 28 July 1951, entered into force 22 April 1954) 189 UNTS 137 (Refugee Convention).

[46] Convention relating to the Status of Stateless Persons (adopted 28 September 1954, entered into force 6 June 1960) 360 UNTS 117.

[47] J Vedsted-Hansen, 'Article 28/Schedule: Travel Documents/Titres de Voyage' in A Zimmermann (ed), *The 1951 Convention relating to the Status of Refugees and its 1967 Protocol* (OUP 2011) 1201. See also JC Hathaway, *The Rights of Refugees under International Law* (CUP 2005) 851.

[48] Protocol 4 to the European Convention for the Protection of Human Rights and Fundamental Freedoms (adopted 16 September 1963, entered into force 2 May 1968) ETS No 46. For more specific categories of persons, see also European Agreement on Travel by Young Persons on Collective Passports between the Member Countries of the Council of Europe (adopted 16 December 1961, entered into force 17 January 1962) ETS No 037; European Convention on the Legal Status of Migrant Workers (adopted 24 November 1977, entered into force 1 May 1983) ETS No 093. The right to leave any country is surprisingly not mentioned in the Charter of Fundamental Rights of the European Union (18 December 2000, entered into force 1 December 2009) OJ C 326/01.

the 1969 American Convention on Human Rights (ACHR) (Article 22(2)),[49] the
1981 African Charter of Human and Peoples' Rights (ACHPR) (Article 12(2)),[50]
the 1995 Commonwealth of Independent States (CIS) Convention on Human
Rights and Fundamental Freedoms (Article 22(2)),[51] and the 2004 Arab Charter
on Human Rights (Article 27(a)).[52] A substantial number of regional instruments
devoted to refugees as well reiterate the right to leave.[53]

Interestingly, both the Inter-American and European Courts of Human Rights
have endorsed the interpretative framework provided by the Human Rights
Committee in its General Comment No 27.[54] The proportionality of restrictions
has been assessed in an extensive case-law of the European Court on various grounds
such as pending criminal proceedings,[55] refusal to pay a tax debt[56] and a fine for a
customs offence,[57] knowledge of state secrets,[58] or failure to pay judgment debts
to private persons.[59] In most cases, restrictive measures were held disproportionate
because of their excessive duration,[60] their automatic nature,[61] or the failure of the

[49]   American Convention on Human Rights (adopted 22 November 1969, entered into force 18 July
1978) 1144 UNTS 123 (ACHR).
[50]   African Charter on Human and Peoples' Rights (adopted 27 June 1981, entered into force 21
October 1986) 1520 UNTS 217 (ACHPR).
[51]   Commonwealth of Independent States Convention on Human Rights and Fundamental
Freedoms (adopted 26 May 1995, entered into force 11 August 1998) reprinted in 3 International
Human Rights Reports 212 (1996) (CIS Convention on Human Rights and Fundamental Freedoms).
[52]   Arab Charter on Human Rights (adopted 23 May 2004, entered into force 15 May 2008) reprinted in 12 International Human Rights Reports 893 (2005).
[53]   See, especially, European Parliament and Council Directive 2011/95/EU of 13 December 2011
on standards for the qualification of third-country nationals or stateless persons as beneficiaries of
international protection, for a uniform status for refugees or for persons eligible for subsidiary protection, and for the content of the protection granted (recast) [2011] OJ L 337/9 art 25; Convention
on Territorial Asylum (adopted 28 March 1954, entered into force 29 December 1954) OAS Treaty
Series No 19 (1954) art 10; Convention Governing the Specific Aspects of Refugee Problem in Africa
(adopted 10 September 1969, entered into force 20 June 1974) 1001 UNTS 45 (OUA Convention)
art 6; Arab Convention Regulating the Status of Refugees in Arab Countries (adopted by the League of
Arab States in 1994, not yet entered into force) art 10.
[54]   IACtHR, *Case of Ricardo Canese v Paraguay* (Merits, Reparations and Costs) Series C No 111
(IACtHR, 31 August 2004) paras 115–17; ECtHR, *Riener v Bulgaria* App no 46343/99 (ECtHR, 23
May 2006) para 83; *Bartik v Russia* ECHR 2006-XV 111 paras 36 and 46.
[55]   See, among many other examples, *Miażdżyk v Poland* App no 23592/07 (ECtHR, 24 January
2012) paras 33–42; *Prescher v Bulgaria* App no 6767/04 (ECtHR, 7 June 2011) paras 47–52; *Pfeifer v
Bulgaria* App no 24733/04 (ECtHR, 17 February 2011) paras 55–58; *Makedonski v Bulgaria* App no
36036/04 (ECtHR, 20 January 2011) paras 39–46; *Sissanis v Romania* App no 23468/02 (ECtHR, 25
January 2007) paras 66–79; *Ivanov v Ukraine* App no 15007/02 (ECtHR, 7 December 2006) paras
90–97; *Antonenkov and Others v Ukraine* App no 14183/02 (ECtHR, 22 November 2005) paras 59–67;
and *Fedorov and Fedorova v Russia* App no 31008/02 (ECtHR, 13 October 2005) paras 39–47.
[56]   *Riener v Bulgaria* (n 54) paras 118–30.
[57]   *Napijalo v Croatia* App no 66485/01 (ECtHR, 13 November 2003) paras 78–82.
[58]   *Bartik v Russia* (n 54) paras 44–52 and *Soltysyak v Russia* App no 4663/05 (ECtHR, 10 February
2011) paras 46–54. Both judgments came to the same conclusion as the Human Rights Committee
expressed below.
[59]   *Ignatov v Bulgaria* App no 50/02 (ECtHR, 2 July 2009) paras 36–41 and *Gochev v Bulgaria* App
no 34383/03 (ECtHR, 26 November 2009) paras 49–57.
[60]   See notably *Ivanov v Ukraine* (n 55) para 96; *Goffi v Italy* App no 55984/00 (ECtHR, 24 March
2005) para 20; *Luordo v Italy* ECHR 2003-IX 93; and *Bassani v Italy* App no 47778/99 (ECtHR, 11
December 2003) para 24.
[61]   *Riener v Bulgaria* (n 54) para 128; *Nalbantski v Bulgaria* App no 30943/04 (ECtHR, 10
February 2011).

state authorities to give due consideration to the individual circumstances of the applicant.[62] In the Court's view, '[t]he restriction may be justified in a given case only if there are clear indications of a genuine public interest which outweigh the individual's right to freedom of movement'.[63] Accordingly, 'any interference with the right to leave one's country should be justified and proportionate throughout its duration, in the individual circumstances of the case'.[64]

On 27 November 2012, the European Court delivered an important judgment in *Stamose v Bulgaria* according to which travel bans designed to prevent breaches of foreign immigration legislation are not compatible with the right to leave any country. It held that the automatic imposition of such a ban without regard to the individual circumstances of the person concerned was clearly disproportionate:

The Court cannot consider such a blanket and indiscriminate measure to be proportionate. The normal consequences of a serious breach of a country's immigration laws would be for the person concerned to be removed from that country and prohibited (by the laws of that country) from re-entering its territory for a certain period of time. Indeed, the applicant suffered such consequences as a result of the infringement of the terms of his student visa—he was deported from the United States of America [...]. It appears quite draconian for the Bulgarian State—which could not be regarded as directly affected by the applicant's infringement—to have also prevented him from travelling to any other foreign country for a period of two years.[65]

Given the impressive body of treaties and case-law governing the freedom to leave, one can fairly conclude with Colin Harvey and Robert Barnidge that 'the temptation [...] to dismiss the right to leave as of theoretical value only [...] would be a mistake: the right to leave one's own country remains significant in international human rights law. It has potential, and its requirements could usefully be mainstreamed into existing attempts to manage international migration more effectively.'[66]

2.1.2 The right to leave any country in customary international law

The large number of treaties endorsing the right to leave any country, the similarity of their respective wording, their widespread ratification, and the rare reservations have been influential in establishing it as a customary norm. When identifying the usual requirements for considering a conventional rule to have become a custom, the International Court of Justice (ICJ) has underlined in the well-known *North Sea Continental Shelf Cases* that 'even without the passage of any considerable period of time, a very widespread and representative participation in the convention might

---

[62] *Riener v Bulgaria* (n 54) para 128; *Prescher v Bulgaria* (n 55) para 50; and *Pfeifer v Bulgaria* (n 55) para 56.
[63] *Hajibeyli v Azerbaijan* App no 16528/05 (ECtHR, 10 July 2008) para 63.
[64] *Riener v Bulgaria* (n 54) para 128. See also, among other similar restatements, *Makedonski v Bulgaria* (n 55) paras 45–46.
[65] *Stamose v Bulgaria* ECHR 2012-VI 1.
[66] Harvey and Barnidge, 'Human Rights' (n 32) 20. See also among other similar acknowledgements: V Moreno-Lax, *Accessing Asylum in Europe: Extraterritorial Border Controls and Refugee Rights under EU Law* (OUP 2017) 340–50.

suffice of itself, provided it included that of States whose interests were specially affected'.[67] Against such framework, one cannot avoid noticing that participation in the seven UN conventions and five regional human rights conventions is much more than 'very widespread and representative', since all UN Member States have ratified one or more of these twelve conventions.

Beyond its extensive endorsement in treaty law, the fact that states made very few reservations further exemplified the importance of the right to leave.[68] In fact, most of the relevant reservations are not directly addressed to the right to leave as such. Instead, they correspond to lawful restrictions (mainly for preventing tax evasion)[69] or they are primarily aimed at preserving immigration legislation with regard to the distinctive issue of the right to enter and to remain of non-citizens.[70] Besides these cases, reservations specifically excluding the right to leave or subordinating its application to domestic legislation remain extremely rare and they have steadily prompted objections from other States Parties. For instance, several states objected to Pakistan's reservation to Article 12 of the ICCPR and Pakistan eventually withdrew it in June 2011.[71]

As far as UN treaties are concerned, only one state—Malaysia—has maintained its reservation excluding the relevant provision or subordinating it to domestic law. This concerns Article 18 of the ICRPD governing liberty of movement (including the right to leave) and nationality of disabled persons. This reservation has raised objections from other States Parties on the ground that 'Article 18 concerns fundamental provisions of the Convention and is incompatible with the object and purpose of that instrument.'[72] It was even asserted that:

Articles 15 [on freedom from torture, inhuman or degrading treatment] and 18 [on freedom of movement] of the Convention address core human rights values that are not only reflected

---

[67] *North Sea Continental Shelf Cases (Federal Republic of Germany/Denmark; Federal Republic of Germany/Netherlands)* (Judgment) [1969] ICJ Rep 3, para 73.

[68] The text of the reservations to UN treaties are available at https://treaties.un.org accessed 6 October 2018.

[69] See especially the reservations of Belize, and Trinidad and Tobago to Art 12(3) of the International Covenant on Civil and Political Rights (ICCPR) and its ratification status at https://treaties.un.org/pages/ViewDetails.aspx?src=IND&mtdsg_no=IV-4&chapter=4&lang=en accessed 6 October 2018.

[70] See mainly the reservations of the United Kingdom to the ICCPR and the ICRPD, the similar one made by China (with respect to Hong Kong) to the CRC and the ICRPD, as well as those of the Cook Island and Singapore to the CRC and the one of Australia to the ICRPD. For reservations to the ICRPD, see https://treaties.un.org/pages/ViewDetails.aspx?src=TREATY&mtdsg_no=IV-15&chapter=4&clang=_en accessed 6 October 2018. For reservations to the CRC, see https://treaties.un.org/pages/viewdetails.aspx?src=ind&mtdsg_no=iv-11&chapter=4&clang=_en accessed 6 October 2018.

[71] According to the reservation of Pakistan, 'the provisions of Articles 12 shall be so applied as to be in conformity with the Provisions of the Constitution of Pakistan'. It has been objected by Austria, Belgium, Canada, the Czech Republic, Denmark, Estonia, Finland, France, Germany, Hungary, Ireland, Italy, the Netherlands, Norway, Poland, Portugal, Slovakia, Spain, Sweden, Switzerland, the United Kingdom, and the United States of America.

[72] Objection of Belgium to the Malaysian reservation. See also, the similar objection raised by Austria, Germany, Hungary, Portugal, Slovakia, and Sweden. Thailand also formulated a reservation that was objected on the same ground by the Czech Republic, Portugal, Spain, and Sweden. Thailand eventually withdrew its reservation in 2015.

in several multilateral treaties, such as the UN Convention against Torture and Other Cruel, Inhuman or Degrading Treatment or Punishment, and the International Covenant on Civil and Political Rights, but also form part of the international customary law.[73]

The conviction to be bound by a customary norm can be further inferred from non-binding resolutions—particularly those of the General Assembly—adopted by consensus or by a broad and representative majority. While highlighting the interactions between customary international law and non-binding resolutions, the ICJ has acknowledged that 'the effect of consent to the text of such resolutions [...] may be understood as an acceptance of the validity of the rule'.[74] In particular, 'General Assembly resolutions, even if they are not binding, may sometimes have normative value. They can, in certain circumstances, provide evidence important for establishing the existence of a rule or the emergence of an *opinio juris*. To establish whether this is true of a given General Assembly resolution, it is necessary to look at its content and the conditions of its adoption.'[75] This accordingly requires two cumulative conditions: the wording of the relevant resolution is formulated in normative terms that clearly endorse a binding rule and the resolution has been adopted by consensus or a least by a broad and representative majority of states.

In this respect, it is noteworthy that the various resolutions and declarations endorsing the right to leave have been adopted without a vote. Evidence of such *opinio juris* can be found in the Declaration on the Human Rights of Individuals Who Are Not Nationals of the Country in Which They Live, adopted in December 1985 without a vote by the General Assembly. Among other examples, the right to leave any country was restated in the New York Declaration for Refugees and Migrants which was approved by all UN Member States in September 2016.[76]

More generally, all General Assembly resolutions on the protection of migrants ritually start by reaffirming Article 13(2) of the Universal Declaration of Human Rights, before 'request[ing] all Member States, in conformity with their respective constitutional systems, effectively to promote and protect the human rights of all

---

[73] Objection of Hungary to the Malaysian reservation.

[74] *Military and Paramilitary Activities in and against Nicaragua (Nicaragua v United States)* (Merits) [1986] ICJ Rep 14, para 188.

[75] *Legality of the Threat or Use of Nuclear Weapons* (Advisory Opinion) [1996] ICJ Rep 226, para 77.

[76] New York Declaration for Refugees and Migrants, UNGA Res 71/1 (19 September 2016) UN Doc A/RES/71/1, para 42. See also, for instance, principle 15 of the Guiding Principles on Internal Displacement, which have been referred to in various resolutions of the General Assembly available at http://www.unhcr.org/protection/idps/43ce1cff2/guiding-principles-internal-displacement.html accessed 17 October 2018. UNGA Res 66/135 (19 December 2011) UN Doc GA/RES/66/135, para 29; UNGA Res 65/193 (21 December 2010) UN Doc GA/RES/65/193, para 29; UNGA Res 63/149 (18 December 2008) UN Doc GA/RES/63/149, para 28; UNGA Res 62/125 (18 December 2007) UN Doc GA/RES/62/125, para 28; UNGA Res 60/128 (16 December 2005) UN Doc GA/RES/60/128, para 26; UNGA Res 59/172 (20 December 2004) UN Doc GA/RES/59/172, para 25; UNGA Res 58/149 (22 December 2003) UN Doc GA/RES/58/149, para 25; UNGA Res 57/183 (18 December 2002) UN Doc GA/RES/57/183, para 33; UNGA Res 56/135 (19 December 2001) UN Doc GA/RES/56/135, para 29; UNGA Res 55/77 (4 December 2000) UN Doc GA/RES/55/77, para 34; UNGA 54/147 (17 December 1999) UN Doc GA/RES/54/147, para 27; UNGA Res 53/125 (9 December 1998) UN Doc GA/RES/53/125, para 16; and UNGA Res 60/01 (24 October 2005) UN Doc GA/RES/ 60/1, para 132. See also UNSC Res 1286 (19 January 2000) UN Doc S/RES/1286, para 6 (on Burundi).

migrants, in conformity with the Universal Declaration of Human Rights'.[77] While the exact wording may slightly change from one resolution to another, all of them have been adopted by consensus and are conspicuously addressed to *all* Member States without regard to the ratification of the relevant treaties, thus reinforcing the customary law nature of the right to leave any country.[78] Furthermore, this basic right has been restated at the regional level in several declarations, including the 1948 American Declaration of the Rights and Duties of Man (Article VIII),[79] the 1990 Cairo Declaration on Human Rights in Islam (Article 12),[80] and, more recently, the 2012 ASEAN Declaration of Human Rights (Article 15).[81]

Besides this vast breadth of universal and regional endorsements, the end of the persistent objections raised by communist countries was a turning point in this

[77] UNGA Res 65/212 (1 April 2011) Doc GA/RES/65/212, paras 2–3. See also, among many others, UNGA Res 70/147 (25 February 2016) UN Doc GA/RES/70/147, para 4; UNGA Res 69/167 (12 February 2015) UN Doc GA/RES/69/167, para 4; UNGA Res 68/17 (28 January 2014) UN Doc GA/RES/68/17, para 4, wording slightly different; UNGA Res 67/172 (3 April 2013) UN Doc GA/RES/67/172, para 4; UNGA Res 66/172 (29 March 2012) UN Doc GA/RES/66/172, para 4; UNGA Res 64/166 (19 March 2010) UN Doc GA/RES/64/166, para 3; UNGA Res 63/184 (17 March 2009) UN Doc GA/RES/63/184, paras 1 and 3; UNGA Res 62/156 (7 March 2008) UN Doc GA/RES/62/156, paras 1 and 3; UNGA Res 61/165 (23 February 2007) UN Doc GA/RES/61/165, paras 1 and 3; UNGA Res 60/169 (7 March 2006) UN Doc GA/RES/60/169, paras 1 and 5; UNGA Res 59/193 (17 February 2005) UN Doc GA/RES/59/193, para 3; UNGA Res 58/190 (22 March 2004) UN Doc GA/RES/58/190, preamble para 2 and para 2; UNGA Res 57/218 (27 February 2003) UN Doc GA/RES/57/218, preamble para 2 and para 2; UNGA Res 56/170 (28 February 2002) UN Doc GA/RES/56/170, preamble para 2 and para 2; UNGA Res 55/92 (26 February 2001) UN Doc GA/RES/55/92, preamble para 2 and para 2; and UNGA Res 54/166 (24 February 2000) UN Doc GA/RES/54/166, preamble para 1 and para 1.

[78] A similar pattern can be observed with regard to resolutions of the Human Rights Council. See, in particular, Human Rights Council Res 17/22 (19 July 2011) UN Doc A/HRC/RES/17/22, preamble para 5, and Human Rights Council Res 14/16 (23 June 2010) UN Doc A/HRC/RES/14/16, preamble para 5 and para 6. See also, among other endorsements of the right to leave, UNHCR EXCOM Conclusion on the Return of Persons Found Not to Be in Need of International Protection No 96 (LIV) (10 October 2003) para (a); UNHCR EXCOM Conclusion on International Protection No 85 (XLIX) (1998) para (z); UNHCR EXCOM Conclusion on Comprehensive and Regional Approaches within a Protection Framework No 80 (XLVII) (1996) paras (e) and (i); UNHCR EXCOM Family Reunification No 24 (XXXII) (1981) para 4; and UNHCR EXCOM Establishment of the Sub-Committee and General Conclusion on International Protection No 1 (XXVI) (1975) para (f).

[79] American Declaration of the Rights and Duties of Man, OAS Res XXX adopted by the Ninth International Conference of American States (1948) reprinted in Basic Documents Pertaining to Human Rights in the Inter-American System OEA/Ser L V/II.82 Doc 6 Rev 1 at 17 (1992).

[80] Organization of Islamic Cooperation, Cairo Declaration on Human Rights in Islam (adopted 5 August 1990) reproduced in English in Contribution of the Organisation of the Islamic Conference UN Doc A/CONF.157/PC/62/Add.18 (1993).

[81] ASEAN Human Rights Declaration (adopted 18 November 2012), available at http://aichr.org/documents/, accessed 6 October 2018. See, also, Asian-African Legal Consultative Organization (AALCO), Principles concerning admission and treatment of aliens (25 February 1961), art 15, available at www.aalco.int/PRINCIPLES%20CONCERNING%20ADMISSION%20AND%20TREATMENT%20OF%20ALIENS.pdf, accessed 6 October 2018. One should add that several declarations restating the right to leave were also adopted by independent experts from various regions of the world. See especially 'Right to Leave and to Return: A Declaration Adopted by the Uppsala Colloquium, Sweden' (adopted 21 June 1972) reprinted in (1974) 4 Israel Yrbk Hum Rts 432–35; 'Strasbourg Declaration on the Right to Leave and to Return' (adopted 26 November 1986) reprinted in (1987) 8 HRLJ 478–84; and 'Declaration on the Protection of Refugees and Displaced Persons in the Arab World' at the Fourth Seminar of Arab Experts on Asylum and Refugee Law (19 November 1992) YB Int'l Inst HumL 36, art 1.

customary law process, since the traditional opponents to the right to leave eventually acknowledged it as an internationally protected right.[82] This change of behaviour was already perceptible in the Final Act of the Conference on Security and Cooperation in Europe adopted at Helsinki in August 1975.[83] The most evident commitment to the principle of freedom to leave was endorsed later on in the concluding document of the Vienna Conference adopted in January 1989. In a prophetic announcement of what would happen a few months later with the fall of the Berlin Wall, the participating states affirmed in unequivocal terms that 'they will fully respect their obligations under international law [...], in particular that everyone shall be free to leave any country, including his own, and to return to his country'.[84] This formal endorsement by the former communist countries was subsequently restated during several other Conferences on Security and Cooperation in Europe[85] and enshrined in the 1995 CIS Convention on Human Rights and Fundamental Freedoms.

Such an endorsement by the very states which were previously opposed to it has arguably proved to be instrumental in crystallizing a customary law process initiated and consolidated by a wide range of treaties and other similar declarations and resolutions adopted at both the universal and regional levels. The customary law nature of the right to leave finds additional support in the plethoric number of domestic

[82] For a telling description of the domestic legislation and prevailing practice in communist countries at that time, see notably V Chalidze, 'The Right of a Convicted Citizen to Leave his Country' (1973) 8(1) Harv CR-CLL Rev 113; J Toman, 'The Right to Leave and to Return in Eastern Europe' in Vasak and Liskofsky (eds), *The Right to Leave and to Return* (n 1) 119–64; LE Pettiti, 'The Right to Leave and to Return in the USSR' in Vasak and Liskofsky (eds), *The Right to Leave and to Return* (n 1) 171–89.

[83] Among the specific measures consented in the Helsinki Final Act, 35 states—including all European states (except Albania and Andorra), the United States, and Canada—committed to 'favourably consider applications for travel with the purpose of allowing persons to enter or leave their territory temporarily, and on a regular basis if desired,' for family, personal, or professional reasons. See Conference on Security and Cooperation in Europe (CSCE) 'Helsinki Final Act' (1 August 1975) reprinted in (1975) 14 IML 1293. For a comment of the provisions on free movement of persons in the Helsinki Final Act and their subsequent implementation, see VY Ghebali, 'Immigration et émigration dans les rapports Est-Ouest: Les recommandations de la Conférence sur la sécurité et la coopération en Europe' in D Turpin (ed), *Immigrés et réfugiés dans les démocraties occidentales—défis et solutions* (Economica, Presses Universitaires d'Aix-Marseille 1989) 287–97; DC Turack, 'Freedom of Transnational Movement: The Helsinki Accord and Beyond' (1980–1981) 4 Im&NatL Rev 43–66; JAR Nafziger, 'The Right of Migration under the Helsinki Accords' (1980) 5 S Ill ULJ 395–438.

[84] Commission on Security and Cooperation in Europe (CSCE), 'Concluding Document of the Vienna Conference on Security and Cooperation in Europe' (1989) reprinted in 10 HRLJ 270. For an overview of the subsequent changes of the state practice in Eastern countries, see DC Turack, 'The Movement of Persons: The Practice of States in Central and Eastern Europe Since the 1989 Vienna CSCE' (1993) 12 Denv J Int'l L&Pol'y 289–309; FA Gabor, 'Reflections on the Freedom of Movement in Light of the Dismantled "Iron Curtain" ' (1991) 65 Tul L Rev 849–81.

[85] See in particular Organization for Security and Co-operation in Europe (OSCE), 'Document of the Copenhagen Meeting of the Conference on the Human Dimension of the CSCE' (29 June 1990) reprinted in (1990) 29 ILM 1305; OSCE, 'Document of the Moscow Meeting of the Conference on the Human Dimension of the CSCE' (4 October 1991) reprinted in (1991) 30 ILM 1671; Commission on Security and Cooperation in Europe (CSCE), 'Charter of Paris for a New Europe' (21 November 1990) reprinted in (1991) 30 ILM 193, 193–94, and 199–200; CSCE, 'Budapest Document: Towards a Genuine Partnership in a New Era' (adopted 6 December 1994) reproduced in (1995) 34 ILM 773, paras 40–41.

enactments. In particular, no less than 116 states have endorsed the freedom to leave within their own constitutions.[86]

Against such an impressive range of international, regional, and domestic materials, it comes as no surprise that a majority of scholars have acknowledged the customary law nature of the right to leave,[87] even if some others have expressed a more nuanced opinion.[88] It is true that violations are still regularly committed by states in different parts of the world. Nevertheless, it is difficult to conclude that this particular right is more violated than other well-established norms of customary international law, such as the prohibition of torture, inhuman, or degrading treatment. It is equally important to note that, when states are accused of violating the right to leave any country, they either invoke the forthcoming adoption of a legislative act to duly take account of it,[89] or they argue that alleged violations correspond to lawful restrictions based on criminal convictions.[90]

---

[86] These constitutions are listed in V Chetail, 'The Transnational Movement of Persons under General International Law' (n 4) 23, fn 135.

[87] See, among other instances, A Fischer-Lescano, T Löher, and T Tohidipur, 'Border Controls at Sea: Requirements under International Human Rights and Refugee Law' (2009) 21 IJRL 256; G Liu, *The Right to Leave and Return and Chinese Migration Law* (Martinus Nijhoff 2007) 32; R Boed, 'The State of the Right of Asylum in International Law' (1994–1995) 5 Duke J Comp & Int'l L 1, 6; Y Zilbershats, 'The Right to Leave Israel and its Restriction on Security Grounds' (1994) 28 Israel L Rev 626, 682; LB Sohn and T Buergenthal (eds), *The Movement of Persons Across Borders* (ASIL 1992) 7; O Schachter, *International Law in Theory and Practice* (Martinus Nijhoff 1991) 339; T Meron, *Human Rights* (n 18) 23; R Hofmann, *Die Ausreisefreiheit nach Völkerrecht und staatlichen Recht* (Springer-Verlag 1988) 309; Commission on Human Rights, Subcommission on Prevention of Discrimination and Protection of Minorities 'Analysis of the Current Trends and Developments Regarding the Right to Leave Any Country Including One's Own, and to Return to One's Own Country, and Some Other Rights or Consideration Arising Therefrom. Final report, first part prepared by CLC Mubanga-Chipoya' (10 July 1987) UN Doc E/CN.4/Sub.2/1987/10, 11; R Plender, *International Migration Law* (2nd edn, Martinus Nijhoff 1988) 119; J Barist and others, 'Who May Leave: A Review of Soviet Practice Restricting Emigration on Grounds of Knowledge of "State Secrets" in Comparison with Standards of International Law and the Policies of Other States' (1987) 15(3) Hofstra L Rev 381, 384–85; I Cotler, 'The Right to Leave and to Family Reunification' (1987) 28(3) Cde D 625, 627; JAR Nafziger, 'The Right of Migration under the Helsinki Accords' (1980) 5 S Ill ULJ 395, 401; Y Dinstein, 'Freedom of Emigration and Soviet Jewry' (1974) 4 Israel Ybk Hum Rts 266.

[88] See RB Lillich, 'Civil Rights' in T Meron (ed), *Human Rights* (n 18) 151: 'both the right to leave and the right to return seem well-established in conventional and perhaps even customary international human rights law.' See also Statement of W Goralczyk, in 'Open Session Governing Rules Project: Review and Discussion on the Movement of Persons across Borders' (1991) 85 ASIL Proc 51, 56, 'it is not clear whether it also constitutes a general, customary rule, binding all States. The prevailing view is in favor of its customary character.' Among the rare authors denying the customary law nature of the right to leave, see GS Goodwin-Gill, 'The Right to Leave, the Right to Return and the Question of a Right to Remain' in V Gowlland-Debbas (ed), *The Problem of Refugees in the Light of Contemporary International Law Issues* (Martinus Nijhoff 1996) 97; Hannum, *The Right to Leave* (n 5) 126.

[89] See, for instance, the following summary records, HRC 'Summary Record of the 2835th Meeting' One Hundred Third Session (15 May 2012) UN Doc CCPR/C/SR.2835, para 6, for Iran; for the initial report of Armenia, see HRC 'Summary Record of the 1711th Meeting' Sixty-Fourth Session (29 October 1998) UN Doc CCPR/C/SR.1711, para 20; for the initial report of Lithuania, see HRC 'Summary Record of the 1635th' Sixty-first Session (5 November 1997) UN Doc CCPR/C/SR.1635, para 11.

[90] HRC 'Summary Record of the 2236th Meeting' Eighty-Second Session (25 October 2004) UN Doc CCPR/C/SR.2236, para 50 (on Morocco); HRC 'Comments by the Government of the Syrian Arab Republic on the Concluding Observations of the Human Rights Committee' (28 May 2002) UN Doc CCPR/CO/71/SYR/Add.1, para 41; HRC 'Consideration of Reports Submitted by States Parties

Whatever is their real merit, these kinds of justifications must be seen as a confirmation of the existence of a customary norm. While acknowledging that the practice does not have to be entirely consistent with the purported customary rule,[91] the ICJ underlines in this regard that:

If a State acts in a way *prima facie* incompatible with a recognized rule, but defends its conduct by appealing to exceptions or justifications contained within the rule itself, then whether or not the State's conduct is in fact justifiable on that basis, the significance of that attitude is to confirm rather than to weaken the rule.[92]

Besides its customary law nature, the right to leave is frequently conflated and confused with other related but distinct notions, such as freedom of movement and admission in the territory of other states. This is probably the main source of recurrent misunderstandings about the scope and nature of this right. Indeed, scholars— including the present author—often lament that the right to leave any country is an incomplete right without the concomitant obligation of admission to another country. Albeit intellectually grounded,[93] such a *de lege ferenda* assertion does not reflect the specific meaning and normative stance of the right to leave as constantly reiterated by human rights instruments.

The normative asymmetry between exit and entry is the product of contemporary international law. Departure has been divorced from admission to constitute a distinctive norm primarily addressed to the states of origin and reinforced by the right to return. Human rights law recognizes the right to leave any country at one side of the migration continuum, and the right to return to one's own country at the other extreme. In between the two, there is no explicit right of admission into another country. This intentional omission plainly signals that, at its current stage of development, public international law does not guarantee a general freedom of movement. It is against this background that the right to leave any country was conceived, as exemplified in the drafting history of the Universal Declaration of Human Rights. The representative of Lebanon stressed in this respect that:

The ideal would be that any person should be able to enter any country he might choose, but account had to be taken of actual facts. The minimum requirement was that any person should be able to return to his country. If that right were recognized, the right to leave a

---

under Article 40 of the Covenant, Fourth Periodic Reports of States Parties, Cameroon' (11 May 2009) UN Doc CCPR/C/CMR/4, paras 186–89.

[91] 'In order to deduce the existence of customary rules, the Court deems it sufficient that the conduct of States should, in general, be consistent with such rules, and that instances of State conduct inconsistent with a given rule should generally have been treated as breaches of that rule, not as indications of the recognition of a new rule.' See *Nicaragua v USA* (n 74) 98.

[92] ibid.

[93] See, among an abundant literature on free movement, A Pécoud and P de Guchteneire (eds), *Migration without Borders: Essays on the Free Movement of People* (UNESCO and Berghahn Books 2007); M Chemillier-Gendreau, 'Un régime juridique pour l'immigration clandestine' in V Chetail (ed), *Mondialisation, migration et droits de l'homme: Le droit international en question*, vol II (Bruylant 2007) 319 and 327–31; SS Juss, *International Migration and the Global Justice* (Ashgate Publishing 2006) 297; KR Johnson, 'Open Borders?' (2003) 51 UCLA L Rev 193–265; C Wihtol de Wenden, *Faut-il ouvrir les frontières?* (Presses de Sciences Po 1999).

country, already sanctioned in the article, would be strengthened by the assurance of the right to return.[94]

The US Chairman of the Human Rights Commission, Eleanor Roosevelt, 'reiterated that article [13] did not deal with the question of immigration, which was necessarily subject to the national legislation of each State.'[95] Among other similar statements, the French delegate, René Cassin, underscored in the same vein that 'while the problem of free movement involved both emigration and immigration, the present article was only concerned with individuals' right to emigrate'.[96]

The resulting distinction between emigration and immigration represents the core conundrum of international migration law. The right to emigrate has been endorsed and restated as an internationally protected right on its own in numerous treaties, declarations, and constitutional enactments to become a norm of customary international law. By contrast, immigration is primarily—but not exclusively—left to the domestic legislation of each state, which may accordingly vary from one country to another. Despite the practical meddling between the two, departure and admission have been conceived and recognized by international law as two distinct legal spheres governed by their respective set of legal norms and responsibilities. The duty holder of the right to leave is the state of departure, whereas admission remains the responsibility of the state of destination. However, this enduring disjuncture between emigration and immigration does not entail that international law has no say over the admission of migrants. The competence of states in this area has been internationalized in a heteroclite set of conventional and customary rules that unveils the complex articulation between departure and admission under contemporary international law.

2.2 Admission of Migrants

Although the right to leave is not accompanied by a general right to enter any country, international law limits in a rather significant way the competence of states to decide who can be admitted into their territory. In contrast to the customary law nature of the right to leave, the right to enter is first and foremost a product of treaty law. Beyond the plethoric number of bilateral agreements governing admission and readmission, several universal and regional treaties have granted an explicit—albeit qualified—right to enter. The resulting picture still remains contrasted. Universal treaties recognizing a right of entry are marginal in number and they focus on very circumscribed categories of migrants (section 2.2.1). By opposition, a vast number of regional agreements have endorsed such a right in a comprehensive way as an integral component of free movement areas (section 2.2.2).

---

[94] UNGA, Third Committee, 'Summary Record of the 120th Meeting' Third Session (2 November 1948) UN Doc AC.3/SR.120, 316.
[95] Commission on Human Rights, 'Summary Record of the Fifty-Fifth Meeting' (n 7) 11.
[96] Commission on Human Rights, Drafting Committee on an International Bill of Human Rights 'Summary Record of the Thirty-Sixth Meeting' (n 14) 10.

From the perspective of treaty law, the explicit recognition of a right to enter accordingly follows a diverging pattern, which is contingent upon the ratification status of the relevant universal or regional conventions. The right of entry is conceived by the former as a limited exception to the general competence of states to decide upon the admission of foreigners, whereas the latter have endorsed a right to free movement as a principle on its own, subjected to the traditional safeguards aimed at protecting public order and national security. The right to enter may thus be viewed either as a principle or as an exception, depending on whether the relevant conventions are concluded at the regional level or the universal one.

In addition to the right of entry as governed by treaty law, customary international law remains essential in laying down basic tenets that all states have to respect when deciding upon the (non-) admission of migrants. The approach followed by customary law is more indirect and subtle than the one of treaty law. Although they fall short of establishing any explicit right to enter, customary rules of international law provide substantial limits to the refusal of entry (section 2.2.3) and lay down the procedural guarantees governing immigration control (section 2.2.4).

2.2.1 The right to enter under universal treaty law

As a result of the subsequent interpretation and development of treaty law, the right to leave is accompanied at the universal plane by a right to enter for very specific categories of migrants in two main areas. The first one concerns the right to enter as laid down in international human rights law, and more specifically the ICCPR. The second one addresses the specific case of those migrating for service supply which is regulated under trade law, namely by the General Agreement on Trade in Services.

The right to enter under the International Covenant on Civil and Political Rights

The first explicit duty of states to admit non-nationals under universal treaty law relates to the very notion of the right to enter under the ICCPR. As apparent from the wording of its Article 12(4), 'the right to enter his own country' is broader than the one of nationality.[97] When interpreted in good faith in accordance with its ordinary

---

[97] The same expression has been acknowledged in the UDHR (n 6). At the regional level, the ACHPR (n 50) and the Arab Charter on Human Rights (n 52) also refer to 'his country' alongside the ICCPR (Article 12(2) of ACHPR and Article 27(2) of the Arab Charter). Conversely, the other regional human rights conventions expressly limit the right to enter to nationals only. See Article 3(2) of the Protocol 4 to the European Convention for the Protection of Human Rights and Fundamental Freedoms (n 48); Article 22(5) of the ACHR (n 49), and Article 25(2) of the CIS Convention on Human Rights and Fundamental Freedoms (n 51). Against this contrasted legal framework, the right to enter one's own country is based on treaty law, whereas the right of nationals to be admitted in their country of nationality is part of customary international law. Among many acknowledgements of the customary law nature of the right to enter for nationals, see notably: European Court of Justice, Case 41-74 *Van Duyn v Home Office* [1974] ECR 1337, 1351, and, more recently, *Plaintiff M70/2011 v Minister for Immigration and Citizenship* and *Plaintiff M106 of 2011 v Minister for Immigration and Citizenship* (31 August 2011) HCA 32 (High Court of Australia).

meaning, the term 'his own country' encompasses long-term residents who have acquired close and enduring connections with their state of residence. This has been the prevailing view of scholars, such as Rosalyn Higgins[98] and Manfred Nowak.[99] Among many other similar acknowledgements,[100] Judge Cançado Trindade of the ICJ has held in his separate opinion in the *Diallo* case that Article 12(4) of the ICCPR extends to non-nationals who 'have developed such a close relationship with the State of residence that it has practically become his "home country" '.[101]

This interpretation has been formally endorsed by the ICCPR treaty body. The Human Rights Committee explains in its General Comment No 27:

The wording of Article 12, paragraph 4, does not distinguish between nationals and aliens ('no one'). Thus, the persons entitled to exercise this right can be identified only by interpreting the meaning of the phrase 'his own country.' The scope of 'his own country' is broader than the concept 'country of his nationality.' It is not limited to nationality in a formal sense, that is, nationality acquired at birth or by conferral; it embraces, at the very least, an individual who, because of his or her special ties to or claims in relation to a given country, cannot be considered to be a mere alien. This would be the case, for example, of nationals of a country who have there been stripped of their nationality in violation of international law, and of individuals whose country of nationality has been incorporated in or transferred to another national entity, whose nationality is being denied them. The language of Article 12, paragraph 4, moreover, permits a broader interpretation that might embrace other categories of long-term residents, including but not limited to stateless persons arbitrarily deprived of the right to acquire the nationality of the country.[102]

The applicability of the right to enter for long-term residents has been further confirmed and refined in 2011 in two leading cases, where the Human Rights Committee found that:

[T]here are factors other than nationality which may establish close and enduring connections between a person and a country, connections which may be stronger than those of nationality. The words "his own country" invite consideration of such matters as long standing residence, close personal and family ties and intentions to remain, as well as to the absence of such ties elsewhere.[103]

---

[98] R Higgins, 'The Right in International Law of an Individual to Enter, Stay In and Leave a Country' (1973) 49 International Affairs 341, 349–50.

[99] M Nowak, *UN Covenant on Civil and Political Rights CCPR Commentary* (2nd revised edn, NP Engel Publishers 2005) 289.

[100] See for instance R Liss, 'A Right to Belong: Legal Protection of Sociological Membership in the Application of Article 12(4) of the ICCPR' (2014) 46 NYU JILP 1097; M Foster, 'An "Alien" by the Barest of Threads—The Legality of the Deportation of Long-Term Residents from Australia' (2009) 33 Melb UL Rev 483, 519; ECtHR, *Beldjoudi v France* (1992) Series A no 234-A, 33–35 (concurring opinion of Judge Martens); Hannum, *The Right to Leave* (n 5) 56–60; S Jagerskiold, 'The Freedom of Movement' in L Henkin (ed), *The International Bill of Rights. The Covenant on Civil and Political Rights* (Columbia University Press 1981) 180–81.

[101] *Ahmadou Sadio Diallo (Republic of Guinea v Democratic Republic of the Congo)* (Merits, Judgment) [2010] ICJ Rep 639 [781] para 156 (separate opinion of Judge Cançado Trindade).

[102] HRC, 'General Comment No 27' (n 3) para 20. For an earlier acknowledgement of this interpretation see HRC, *Stewart v Canada* (1996) Communication No 538/1993 UN Doc. CCPR/C/102/D/538/1993.

[103] HRC, *Jama Warsame v Canada* (2011) Communication No 1959/2010 UN Doc CCPR/C/102/D/1959/2010, para 8.4; HRC, *Nystrom and Turner v Australia* (2011) Communication No 1557/2007

The entitlement to such a right of entry is however not automatic nor absolute. It requires a subtle case-by-case assessment that depends on the individual ties of long-term residents with their country of establishment. Furthermore, this right is not absolute: its qualified nature is implicit in the very notion of arbitrariness, for Article 12(4) prohibits arbitrary deprivation of the right to enter his own country. As confirmed by the Human Rights Committee, the concept of non-arbitrariness requires, in turn, that lawful restrictions are provided by law, proportionate to the objective pursued by the state, and consistent with the provisions and purposes of the Covenant.[104]

Hence, while being a substantive restriction to states' sovereignty in the field of admission, the scope and impact of the right to enter one's own country under the ICCPR is fairly limited for non-nationals. It is circumscribed to a very narrow category thereof, namely to those who are able to establish a close and enduring connection with their country of residence. Such a right is thus primarily aimed at ensuring a right to remain by protecting the acquired rights of permanent residents.

The movement of persons supplying services under the General Agreement on Trade in Services

At the universal level, the only multilateral treaty specifically addressing admission for labour purposes is the General Agreement on Trade in Services (GATS) and its Annex on the Movement of Natural Persons Supplying Services (also called Mode 4).[105] This Annex was included at the request of developing states during the Uruguay Round. Its potential for both developed and developing countries became apparent when a World Bank simulation estimated that a modest increase of 3 per cent of both skilled and unskilled temporary workers in industrial countries in 2001–2025 would generate a global gain superior to those obtained from the total liberalization of trade.[106] This would yield gains to the global economy of $356 billion.[107]

The potential of Mode 4 is further embodied by its inclusive scope, as exemplified by the very notion of supply of services. Article I.2(d) of the GATS defines it in comprehensive terms as 'the supply of a service […] by a service supplier of

UN Doc CCPR/C/102/D/1557/2007, para 7.4. See however the dissenting opinion of Committee members Neuman and Iwasawa in *Nystrom v Australia*, 22.

[104] According to the Human Rights Committee, '[t]he reference to the concept of arbitrariness in this context is intended to emphasize that it applies to all State action, legislative, administrative and judicial; it guarantees that even interference provided for by law should be in accordance with the provisions, aims and objectives of the Covenant and should be, in any event, reasonable in the particular circumstances. The Committee considers that there are few, if any, circumstances in which deprivation of the right to enter one's own country could be reasonable.': HRC, 'General Comment No 27' (n 3) para 21.

[105] Annex 1B of Marrakesh Agreement establishing the World Trade Organization (adopted 15 April 1994, entered into force 1 January 1995) 1867 UNTS 154.

[106] The World Bank, *Global Economic Prospects. Economic Implication of Remittances and Migration* (The International Bank for Reconstruction and Development/The World Bank 2006), 41.

[107] ibid.

one member, through presence of natural persons of a member in the territory of another member'. It thus covers service suppliers at all skills levels and for any occupations. Furthermore, Mode 4 applies to individuals who are 'employed by a service supplier of a Member', as well as to individuals who are 'service suppliers of a Member' (ie self-employed suppliers).

However, its relatively broad scope is mitigated by three significant qualifications. Firstly, it is limited to the temporary movement of service providers. According to the GATS Annex, it does not apply to 'measures affecting natural persons seeking access to the employment market' and those 'regarding citizenship, residence or employment on a permanent basis'. The temporary presence is thus negatively defined in vague and open-ended terms as being non-permanent, leaving WTO Member States a broad margin of discretion.

Secondly, the Annex adds that the GATS 'shall not prevent a Member from applying measures to regulate the entry of natural persons into, or their temporary stay in, its territory, [...] provided that such measures are not applied in such a manner as to nullify or impair the benefits accruing to any Member under the terms of a specific commitment'. The concrete implications of this balancing exercise are unclear: a footnote of the Annex merely indicates that the sole fact of requiring a visa for natural persons of certain Members and not for those of others shall not be regarded as nullifying or impairing benefits under a specific commitment.

Thirdly, and more importantly, the effectiveness of Mode 4 depends on each Member's specific commitments, subject to any terms and conditions specified therein. From this angle, the GATS has clearly failed to deliver on its promises. The number of specific commitments adopted by WTO Member States is very limited and their scope is particularly narrow.[108] Although Mode 4 covers both unskilled and skilled service suppliers, most specific commitments are limited to higher skilled categories, such as managers, intra-corporate transferees, business visitors, and specialists.[109] As a result of this restrictive trend, trade in Mode 4 represents less than 5 per cent of world services trade.[110]

In short, although the GATS jurisdiction over temporary movement of persons 'may become a fertile source of migration law norms' and 'provides an opportunity

---

[108] For further discussion about the limited reach of specific commitments, see notably J Jacobsson, 'GATS Mode 4 and Labour Mobility: The Significance of Employment Market Access' in M Panizzon, G Zürcher, and E Fornalé (eds), *The Palgrave Handbook of International Labour Migration: Law and Policy Perspectives* (Palgrave 2015) 61–94; LR Dawson, 'Labour Mobility and the WTO: The Limits of GATS Mode 4' (2013) 51(1) International Migration 1–23; J Bast, 'Commentary on the Annex on Movement of Natural Persons Supplying Services Under the Agreement' in R Wolfrum, P-T Stoll, and C Feinaugle (eds), *WTO—Trade in Services* (Martinus Nijhoff 2008) 573–95; A Carzaniga, 'The GATS, Mode 4, and Pattern of Commitments' in A Mattoo and A Carzaniga (eds) *Moving People to Deliver Services* (The World Bank/OUP 2003) 21–26; R Chanda, 'Movement of Natural Persons and the GATS' (2001) 24(5) The World Economy 631–54.

[109] See the references quoted in n 108.

[110] Human Rights Council, 'Report of the Special Rapporteur on the Human Rights of Migrants on the Impact of Bilateral and Multilateral Trade Agreements on the Human Rights of Migrants', Thirty-second Session (4 May 2016) UN Doc A/HRC/32/40, para 25; J Kelsey, 'How "Trade in Services" Transforms the Regulation of Temporary Migration for Remittances in Poor Countries' in M Kolsky Lewis and S Frankel (eds) *International Economic Law and National Autonomy* (CUP 2010) 18.

for the WTO to adopt a more people-centered approach to trade and development',[111] much more remains to be achieved in that direction, particularly by extending specific commitments to broader categories of service providers. Because of the limited achievements of the GATS, the last few decades have witnessed the proliferation of hundreds of bilateral treaties, through the conclusion of preferential trade agreements and other related labour mobility memoranda of understanding.[112] Despite the efforts of international organizations to promote best practices,[113] the bilateralization of labour migration has exacerbated the prevailing fragmentation and complexity of international migration law and reinforced power imbalances between countries of destination and origin to the detriment of migrants' rights. By contrast, the right to enter under treaty law finds a much more robust and clear-cut endorsement at the regional level through the establishment of free movement areas.

2.2.2 The right to free movement under regional treaty law

Although universal treaties do not provide for a general right of entry into a foreign country, a plethoric number of regional agreements across various parts of the world have endorsed a right to free movement. States are indeed more inclined to acknowledge the virtue of free movement as a tool for economic development when it happens regionally, that is, among neighbouring states with similar levels of economic development. Although this phenomenon is frequently underestimated, 'regional international organisations have emerged as powerful and promising vehicles for the construction of areas of human mobility with variable intensity'.[114] Labour

---

[111] S Charnovitz, 'Trade Law Norms on International Migration' in TA Aleinikoff and V Chetail (eds), *Migration and International Legal Norms* (TMC Asser Press 2003) 252. For further discussion about the potential of WTO law, see also JP Trachtman, *The International Law of Economic Migration: Toward the Fourth Freedom* (WE Upjohn Institute for Employment Research 2009).

[112] For an overview, see notably P Wickramasekara, *Bilateral Agreements and Memoranda of Understanding on Migration of Low Skilled Workers: A Review* (International Labour Organization 2015) 7–48; R Cholewinski, 'Evaluating Bilateral Labour Migration Agreements in the Light of Human and Labour Rights' in Panizzon, Zürcher, and Fornalé (eds), *The Palgrave Handbook of International Labour Migration* (n 108) 231–52; SM Stephenson and G Hufbauer, 'Labor Mobility' in J-P Chauffour and J-C Maur (eds), *Preferential Trade Agreement Policies for Development: A Handbook* (The World Bank 2011) 275–306; M Panizzon, 'Trade and Labor Migration: GATS Mode 4 and Migration Agreements' (2010) Dialogue on Globalization, Occasional Papers, Friedrich-Ebert-Stiftung; M Panizzon, 'International Law of Economic Migration: A Menage a Trois? GATS Mode 4, EPAs, and Bilateral Migration Agreements' (2010) 44(6) Journal of World Trade 1207–252; KR Zaidi, 'Harmonizing Trade Liberalization and Migration Policy through Shared Responsibility: A Comparison of the Impact of Bilateral Trade Agreements and the GATS in Germany and Canada' (2010) 37(2) Syracuse J Int'l L & Com 267; C Rupa, 'Mobility of Less-Skilled Workers under Bilateral Agreements: Lessons for the GATS' (2009) 43(3) Journal of World Trade 479–506; A Carzaniga, 'A Warmer Welcome? Access for Natural Persons under PTAs' in J Marchetti and M Roy (eds), *Opening Markets for Trade in Services: Countries and Sectors in Bilateral and WTO Negotiations* (CUP 2008), 475–502; OECD, *Migration for Employment: Bilateral Agreements at a Crossroads* (OECD Publishing 2004).

[113] See for instance Agencia Española Internacional Para El Desarrollo 'Bilateral Temporary Labour Arrangements: Good Practices and Lessons Learnt. Analytical Paper' (10 October 2008) available at <https://www.iom.int/files/live/sites/iom/files/What-We-Do/docs/analytical-paper-bilateral-temporary-labour-arrangements-good-practices-and-lessons-learnt.pdf> accessed 7 October 2018.

[114] S Iglesias Sánchez, 'Free Movement of Persons and Regional International Organisations' in R Plender (ed), *Issues in International Migration Law* (Brill 2015) 257–58.

mobility has long been recognized as a core component of regional economic integration alongside the free movement of services, capital, and goods.

As a result, the regionalization of free movement represents the most significant restriction to states' sovereignty in the field of admission, even though this development is not free from challenges. The multiplication of regional treaty regimes has resulted in an extremely complex and heteroclite network of international legal norms that are poorly understood and defy easy categorization. In order to bring some clarity, this section provides a general overview which unveils the overall pattern and typology of the numerous regional agreements concluded in this area, before presenting the progress accomplished so far in Europe, Africa, Latin America, and the Caribbean.

Overview and typology of regional treaty regimes on the free movement of persons

The regionalization of free movement areas represents a structural feature of international migration law which has been too frequently ignored by international lawyers and decision-makers. To take stock of the magnitude of this phenomenon, Table 2.1 provides a mapping of the main regional organizations that have endorsed mobility in their founding instruments and/or subsequent treaties.

From a purely quantitative perspective, the table identifies a significant number of thirty-three regional organizations that have endorsed free movement of persons as an objective on its own. The geographical coverage of these organizations is equally broad, as they include every region of the world. When assessed by reference to the number of states involved, the overall picture becomes even more impressive: a total of 174 states are members of one or several regional organizations aimed at promoting the free movement of persons. Such a high number of states shows the resilience of free movement as a common value and the instrumental role played by regional economic processes to achieve it. As further discussed below, most of them have adopted a specific treaty aimed at implementing free movement.

This quantitative account obviously calls for several qualitative caveats. This widespread endorsement by states is far from being universal and effective in both law and practice. Besides the manifold challenges raised by domestic implementation, the regionalization of free movement depicts profound disparities at two main levels.

At a macro level, despite its extensive geographical coverage, the proliferation of regional areas of free movement remains unequally distributed across the world. There are indeed considerable variations from one region to another: free movement agreements have proliferated in Europe, Africa, South America, and the Caribbean, whereas such developments have been much more modest in Asia and the Pacific region. From this angle, the sum of the numerous areas of regional mobility is unable on its own to ensure free movement at the universal plane. They form instead an eclectic patchwork of treaty regimes. The complexity of the overall picture is further exacerbated by the fact that they overlap with one another: a substantial number of states is part to several regional agreements and organizations.

Table 2.1 Regional organizations and the free movement of persons

Africa	Americas and Caribbean	Asia-Pacific	Europe	Middle-East
• African Union (AU) • Arab-Maghreb Union (AMU) • Common Market for Eastern and Southern Africa (COMESA) • Economic and Monetary Community of Central Africa (EMCCA) • East African Community (EAC) • Economic Community of Central African States (ECCAS) • Economic Community of the Great Lake Countries (ECGLC) • Economic Community of West African States (ECOWAS) • Intergovernmental Authority on Development (IGAD) • Southern African Development Community (SADC) • Community of Sahel-Saharan States (CEN-SAD) • West African Economic and Monetary Union (WAEMU)	• Andean Community of Nations (CAN) • Caribbean Community (CARICOM) • Central American Integration System (CAIS) • Organization of Eastern Caribbean States (OECS) • Pacific Alliance South American Union of Nations (UNASUR) • Southern Common Market (MERCOSUR)	• Asia-Pacific Economic Cooperation (APEC) • Association of Southeast Asian Nations (ASEAN) • Pacific Island Forum (PIF) • South Asian Association for Regional Cooperation (SAARC)	• Benelux, Community of Independent States (CIS) • Council of Europe (COE) • Economic Cooperation Organization (ECO) • European Economic Area (EEA) • European Free Trade Agreement (EFTA) • European Union (EU) • Eurasian Economic Community (EURASEC) • Nordic Common Labour Market (NORDIC) • Organization of the Black Sea Cooperation (BSEC)	• Gulf Cooperation Council (GCC), • League of Arab States (LAS)

At a micro level, the exact scope and content of these regional agreements governing the movement of persons vary considerably. These treaties contain a broad diversity of features with regard to their respective objectives, content, institutional structure, and legal basis.[115] There is nothing surprising in such legal pluralism. Every region has its own specificities and priorities with regard to economic integration which are contingent upon a broad range of factors including, most notably, the degree of geographical proximity of participating states, the extent of similarities in their levels of development, as well as their common culture, history, and identity. The particular context of each economic integration process inevitably impacts on the way the movement of persons is framed and regulated within regional organizations. Because 'there is not a unique approach towards free movement, nor a unique sequence of events',[116] the overall normative picture is inextricably piecemeal and fragmented.

Despite their great variety, regional agreements and organizations may be classified in two main models in light of the comprehensive or sectorial nature of the conventional regimes of free movement. This basic typology is clearly positively correlated to the degree of regional integration contemplated by States Parties. When this degree is less advanced compared to other regions, sectorial agreements merely allow for the temporary entry of some limited categories of skilled workers and service providers. Unsurprisingly, these sectorial agreements have been primarily concluded in Asia and the Pacific region through an exemption of visa for very limited categories of skilled workers.

The most selective ones have been adopted within the SAARC and APEC. The SAARC Visa Exemption Scheme adopted in 1988 and revised in 2005 only grants a temporary visa exemption for a limited list of highly skilled workers (including most notably 'leading businessmen and industrialists', 'eminent sportspersons', and 'accredited journalists'),[117] while the APEC Business Travel Card introduced in 1997 exempts visa requirement and allows expedited airport processing for intra-company transferees and business visitors.[118] In fact, the rationale and content of

---

[115] For a comparative overview of the numerous regional agreements on free movement, see among the rare studies devoted to this complex and important issue S Nita, 'Free Movement of People within Regional Integration Processes: A Comparative View' in S Nita and others (eds), *Migration, Free Movement and Regional Integration* (UNESCO/UNU-CRIS 2017) 3–46; Iglesias Sánchez 'Free Movement of Persons and Regional International Organisations' (n 114) 223–60; J Nielson, 'Labour Mobility in Regional Trade Agreements' in Mattoo and Carzaniga, *Moving People to Deliver Services* (n 108) 93–112; and IOM, *Free Movement of Persons in Regional Integration Processes* (IOM 2010).

[116] Iglesias Sánchez, 'Free Movement of Persons and Regional International Organisations' (n 114) 258.

[117] SAARC Visa Exemption Scheme (adopted during the leaders' Fourth Summit, Islamabad, 29–31 December 1988), see Islamabad Declaration, para 15 <http://saarc-sec.org/uploads/digital_library_document/04-Islamabad-4thSummit1988.pdf>. Further information is available at < http://www.saarc-sec.org/SAARC-Visa-Exemption-Scheme/100/> and, for updated information on categories of entitled persons, < https://www.saarcchamber.org/index.php?option=com_content&view=article&id=88&Itemid=471> accessed 7 October 2018.

[118] Information is available at < https://www.apec.org/Groups/Committee-on-Trade-and-Investment/Business-Mobility-Group/ABTC>. See also APEC, Meeting Paper, Annual Ministerial Meetings (21 November 1997) <https://www.apec.org/Groups/Committee-on-Trade-and-Investment/Business-Mobility-Group/ABTC> accessed 7 October 2018.

the sectorial approach followed by the SAARC and APEC mainly reproduce the pattern of free trade agreements, such as the NAFTA.[119]

The legal regime governing the movement of persons is slightly more developed in the ASEAN, even if it is still focused on a selective range of beneficiaries. The ASEAN Agreement on the movement of natural persons adopted in 2012 grants a temporary entry or stay to skilled workers exhaustively enumerated therein (business visitors; intra-corporate transferees; contractual service suppliers; and other categories as may be specified by each Member State in the Schedules of Commitments).[120] This Agreement is supplemented by eight Mutual Recognition Agreements that allow for a worker's skills, experiences, and accreditations to be recognized across ASEAN in very specific sectors of activities.[121] Furthermore, the ASEAN Framework Agreement on Visa Exemption of 2006, which is not yet in force, allows citizens of any other Member State to enter and stay without visa for a maximum period of fourteen days provided that such a stay is not used for purposes other than visits.[122]

[119] This agreement concluded in 1993 focuses exclusively on the 'temporary entry for business persons' (namely business visitors, traders and investors, intra-company transferees, and professionals): art 102 (Objectives) and Chapter 16 (Temporary Entry for Business Persons) of the North American Free Trade Agreement Between the Government of Canada, the Government of the United Mexican States, and the Government of the United States, (8–17 December 1992) in (1993) 32 ILM, 289 and 605. See <https://www.nafta-sec-alena.org/Home/Texts-of-the-Agreement/North-American-Free-Trade-Agreement > accessed 7 October 2018. The last category of professionals still requires a specific visa, known as the non-immigrant NAFTA Professional visa or TN visa.

[120] Article 2 of the ASEAN Agreement on the movement of natural persons (adopted 19 November 2012, entered into force 14 June 2016), available at <http://agreement.asean.org/media/download/20140117162554.pdf> accessed 7 October 2018.

[121] ASEAN Mutual Recognition Arrangements on Engineering Services (adopted 9 December 2005, entered into force 9 December 2005), available at<http://agreement.asean.org/media/download/20150119180933.pdf>; ASEAN Mutual Recognition Arrangement on Nursing Services (adopted 8 December 2006, entered into force 8 December 2006), available at <http://agreement.asean.org/media/download/20150119183446.pdf>; ASEAN Mutual Recognition Arrangement on Architectural Services (adopted 19 November 2007, entered into force 19 November 2007), available at <http://agreement.asean.org/media/download/20170217112434.pdf>; ASEAN Framework Arrangement on Mutual Recognition of Surveying Qualifications (adopted 19 November 2007, entered into force 19 February 2008), available at <http://agreement.asean.org/media/download/20150119184022.pdf>; ASEAN Mutual Recognition Arrangement on Dental Practitioners (adopted 26 February 2009, entered into force 26 August 2009), available at <http://agreement.asean.org/media/download/20150119175433.pdf>; ASEAN Mutual Recognition Arrangement on Medical Practitioners (adopted 26 February 2009, entered into force 26 August 2009) available at <http://agreement.asean.org/media/download/20150119183234.pdf>; ASEAN Mutual Recognition Arrangement Framework on Accountancy Services (adopted 26 February 2009, entered into force 26 May 2009), available at <http://agreement.asean.org/media/download/20170217112636.pdf>; and ASEAN Mutual Recognition Arrangement on Tourism Professionals (adopted 9 November 2012, entered into force 8 May 2013), available at <http://agreement.asean.org/media/download/20150119182157.pdf> accessed 7 October 2018.

[122] ASEAN Framework Agreement on Visa Exemption (adopted 25 July 2006, not yet in force), available at <http://agreement.asean.org/media/download/20160831072909.pdf> accessed 7 October 2018. This exemption of visa is qualified by two exceptions. Under its Article 3(1), each Member Country retains the right to refuse admission for citizens of other Member Countries who 'may be considered undesirable'. More generally, States Parties may also suspend temporarily the implementation of the Agreement 'for reasons of national security, public order, and public health by giving other Member Countries immediate notice, through diplomatic channels' (Article 5(1)).

From a comparative angle, sectorial regimes of free movement are far from being representative of the developments achieved in many other regions where economic integration is much more advanced. In fact, the vast majority of regional agreements aims for a comprehensive regime of free movement in the framework of a common market alongside the liberalization of goods, services, and capital. In such cases, the free movement of persons is conceived as an integral component of a much broader process of regional integration. Despite some uneven developments from one integration process to another, considerable progress has been achieved not only in Europe, but also in Africa, Latin America, and the Caribbean. As further detailed in the next sections, more than thirty treaties and fifty instruments of secondary legislation have entered into force during the last two decades in these four regions.

The regional overview developed below also highlights a growing convergence with regard to their respective content, the way they have been established and the challenges they are facing. First, despite their own legal specificities, these comprehensive regimes of free movement follow a common pattern based on three distinctive—albeit mutually reinforcing—pillars:

- right of entry and visa exemption for a maximum period of stay (usually limited to ninety days) for all nationals of States Parties;
- right of residence within the territory of any States Parties, which is frequently conditioned by an employment or by sufficient resources not to become a burden for the host state;
- right of establishment to engage in any economic activities (whether as employed or self-employed workers).

None of these rights is obviously absolute. All regional treaties provide safeguard clauses and lawful restrictions to protect public order, national security, or public health in States Parties.

Second, all the comprehensive regimes of free movement follow a step-by-step process of consolidation. The three pillars mentioned above are indeed frequently dissociated through a sequential approach to allow progressive implementation. The right of entry is usually conceived as the first step towards the gradual realization of the supplementary rights of residence and establishment. This phased approach explains the significant variations from one region to another when it comes to their specific stage of implementation. Their completion clearly depends on the degree of development reached by each integration process: comprehensive regimes of free movement are more likely to be achieved when economic integration is already well advanced. Despite the closed interface between free movement and economic integration, most regional treaties are not confined to the mere facilitation of labour mobility as an economic tool for establishing a common market. Instead, the right of entry without a visa is increasingly considered as a right on its own for all nationals of States Parties. This represents the core content of these comprehensive regimes and the main achievement towards their full realization.

Third, the complexity inherent in these multiple and sometimes overlapping treaty regimes has raised manifold challenges for their domestic implementation.

The weak application of these regional agreements is due to a variety of reasons that are context-specific. Basically, the most common obstacles to their domestic implementation include the lack of capacity, resources, or political will of national governments; the absence of a regional enforcement mechanism and/or secondary legislation; and the persistence of economic and political tensions among Member States. Although the completion of the right to free movement remains a complex and long-term endeavour, the ability of a state to determine who can enter its territory has been considerably eroded in many regions of the world. As demonstrated below, a vast number of free movement treaties are currently binding in Europe, Africa, Latin America, and the Caribbean.

Freedom of movement in Europe

The EU represents the archetype of the right to free movement among the broad number of regional organizations aimed at promoting mobility and economic integration. Free movement has been typically conceived as a means for establishing an internal market among its Member States, before becoming the cornerstone of the whole EU construction and identity.

Although the EU is frequently portrayed as the most advanced regime of free movement, its establishment is the result of a long and gradual process initiated in 1957 by the Rome Treaty establishing the European Economic Community.[123] Free movement was initially circumscribed to workers only and it was not implemented until 1968 after the adoption of several secondary regulations.[124] Then, the right to free movement has been progressively enlarged to include other categories of persons[125] and finally extended to all EU nationals, most notably through the creation of Union citizenship in 1993,[126] as well as the adoption of the Schengen Agreement in 1985 and its integration into EU law in 1999.[127] In parallel with this unprecedented, albeit gradual, process of maturation, the abolition of internal borders

---

[123] Treaty establishing the European Economic Community (adopted 25 March 1957, entered into force 1 January 1958) 298 UNTS 3.

[124] Regulation 1612/68/EEC (15 October 1968) of the Council on freedom of movement for workers within the Community [1968] OJ L 257, 2; Council Directive 68/360/EEC (15 October 1968) on the abolition of restrictions on movement and residence within the Community for workers of Member States and their families [1968] OJ L 257, 13.

[125] Council Directive 90/365/EEC on the right of residence for employees and self-employed persons who have ceased their occupational activity [1990] OJ L 180, 28; Council Directive 90/366/EEC on the right of residence for students [1990] OJ L 180, 30; and Council Directive 90/364/EEC on the right of residence [1990] OJ L 180, 26.

[126] Treaty on the European Union (adopted 7 February 1992, entered into force 1 November 1993) 1757 UNTS 3 (Maastricht Treaty).

[127] Agreement between the Governments of the States of the Benelux Economic Union, the Federal Republic of Germany and the French Republic on the Gradual Abolition of Checks at their Common Borders (adopted 14 June 1985) 30 ILM 68 (Schengen Agreement) and Convention Implementing the Schengen Agreement (adopted 19 June 1990, entered into force 1 September 1993) 329 OJ L 19 (Schengen Acquis or Schengen II); Treaty of Amsterdam Amending the Treaty on European Union, the Treaties Establishing the European Communities and Certain Related Acts of 2 October 1997 (adopted 2 October 1997, entered into force 1 May 1999) OJ C 340.

within the whole EU territory has been supplemented by a myriad of legal instruments to reinforce immigration control at the external borders of the Union.[128]

As a result of this evolution, the right of EU citizens to free movement is currently governed by a complex and frequently misunderstood regime based on a broad number of legal instruments.[129] Despite the politicization of free movement, as exemplified by the UK referendum in 2016, the creation of an area in which the free movement of persons across internal borders is ensured remains one of the main achievements of the EU. If the main challenges are primarily political in nature, from a legal perspective, the EU regime of free movement is apt to address Member States' concerns through a typical balancing act, whereby the principle of free movement is tempered by several conditions and exceptions.

Similarly to many other regional regimes of free movement, the extent of the right to free movement primarily depends on the duration of the stay.[130] The right to enter and move within the territory of any Member State is granted for a period limited to three months to any EU citizen, as well as third country nationals with a valid visa or residence permit. According to the Schengen Borders Code, 'internal

---

[128] See most notably Regulation No 810/2009 of the European Parliament and of the Council of 13 July 2009 establishing a Community Code on Visas (Visa Code) [2009] OJ L 243/1; Directive 2008/115/EC of the European Parliament and of the Council of 16 December 2008 on common standards and procedures in Member States for returning illegally staying third-country nationals [2008] OJ L 348/98 (EU Return Directive); Regulation (EC) No 767/2008 of the European Parliament and of the Council of 9 July 2008 concerning the Visa Information System (VIS) and the exchange of data between Member States on short-stay visas (VIS Regulation) [2008] OJ L 218/60; Council Directive 2004/82/EC of 20 April 2004 on the obligation of carriers to communicate passenger data [2004] OJ L 261/24; Regulation (EU) 2016/1624 of the European Parliament and of the Council of 14 September 2016 on the European Border and Coast Guard and amending Regulation (EU) 2016/399 of the European Parliament and of the Council and repealing Regulation (EC) No 863/2007 of the European Parliament and of the Council, Council Regulation (EC) No 2007/2004 and Council Decision 2005/267/EC [2016] OJ L 251/1; Regulation (EU) 2016/399 of the European Parliament and of the Council of 9 March 2016 on a Union Code on the rules governing the movement of persons across borders [2016] OJ L 77/1 (Schengen Borders Code).

[129] See most notably: Consolidated version of the Treaty on the Functioning of the European Union (adopted 13 December 2007) [2012] OJ C 326/47, arts 20(2)(a) and 21; Directive 2004/38/EC of the European Parliament and of the Council of 29 April 2004 on the right of citizens of the Union and their family members to move and reside freely within the territory of the Member States [2004] OJ L 158/77; Regulation (EU) No 492/2011 of the European Parliament and of the Council of 5 April 2011 on freedom of movement for workers within the Union [2011] OJ L141/1; Directive 2014/54/EU of European Parliament and Council of the European Union of 16 April 2014 on measures facilitating the exercise of rights conferred on workers in the context of freedom of movement for workers [2014] OJ L 128/8; Regulation (EU) 2016/399 the European Parliament and the Council of 9 March 2016 on a Union Code on the rules governing the movement of persons across borders (Schengen Borders Code) [2016] OJ L 77/1.

[130] For a more in-depth analysis about the scope and content of free movement in the EU, see notably among a plethoric literature: E Recchi, *Mobile Europe: The Theory and Practice of Free Movement in the EU* (Palgrave MacMillan 2015); E Guild, S Peers, and J Tomkin (eds), *The EU Citizenship Directive: A Commentary* (OUP 2014); MP Broberg and N Holst-Christensen (eds), *Free Movement in the European Union: Cases, Commentaries and Questions* (4th edn, Djøf 2014); N Rogers, R Scandell, and J Walsh (eds), *Free Movement of Persons in the Enlarged European Union* (Sweet and Maxwell 2012); M Condinanzi and others, *Citizenship of the Union and Free Movement of Persons* (Martinus Nijhoff 2008); E Spaventa, *Free Movement of Persons in the EU: Barriers to Movement and their Constitutional Context* (Kluwer 2007); J-Y Carlier and E Guild (eds), *The Future of Free Movement of Persons in the EU* (Bruylant 2006).

borders may be crossed at any point without a border check on persons, irrespective of their nationality, being carried out'.[131] The abolition of border control within the EU is, however, subjected to several exceptions. In particular, it does not preclude the exercise of police powers by Member States (including in their internal border zones), provided that it does not have an effect equivalent to borders checks.[132]

Furthermore, any Member State may exceptionally reintroduce border controls for a limited period of time, where 'there is a serious threat to public policy or internal security'.[133] Such a serious threat does not only include the typical security concerns (such as the fight against terrorism and organized crime). Since 2013, it may also be invoked 'in exceptional circumstances where the overall functioning of the area without internal border control is put at risk as a result of persistent serious deficiencies relating to external border control'.[134] This happened for instance during the refugee crisis in Greece. However, as an exception to the principle of free movement, the reintroduction of border control at the internal borders shall fulfil other substantive and procedural requirements. Most importantly, border control shall remain 'temporary' and can 'only be reintroduced as a last resort'.[135] The reasons, scope, and duration of this reintroduction 'shall not exceed what is strictly necessary to respond to the serious threat' and shall be notified to Member States and the Commission.[136]

While following a similar pattern, the right of residence for a period of more than three months is governed by a distinctive legal regime primarily grounded on the Directive 2004/38/EC on the right of citizens of the Union and their family members to move and reside freely within the territory of the Member State. According to its Article 7, the right of residence is granted to all EU citizens, as long as they fall within one of the three following categories: they (a) are workers or self-employed persons in the host Member State;[137] or (b) have sufficient resources for themselves

---

[131] Article 22 of the Regulation (EU) 2016/399 the European Parliament and the Council of 9 March 2016 on a Union Code on the rules governing the movement of persons across borders (Schengen Borders Code) (n 129).

[132] ibid art 23. According to this last provision, the exercise of police measures is not equivalent to border check when they: (i) do not have border control as an objective; (ii) are based on general police information and experience regarding possible threats to public security and aim, in particular, to combat cross-border crime; (iii) are devised and executed in a manner clearly distinct from systematic checks on persons at the external borders; (iv) are carried out on the basis of spot-checks. Besides police measures, Article 23 envisages three other exceptions to the absence of border control within the EU territory: security checks at ports and airports, the possibility to impose an obligation to hold or carry papers and documents, as well as the possibility to provide for an obligation for third country nationals to report their presence on the territory of a Member State.

[133] ibid art 25.

[134] ibid art 29. Contrary to the other threats to public policy and internal security, this particular ground presupposes a recommendation from the Council based on a proposal from the Commission. Member States may request the Commission to submit such a proposal to the Council.

[135] ibid arts 25 to 30.   [136] ibid.

[137] Directive 2004/38/EC of the European Parliament and of the Council of 29 April 2004 on the right of citizens of the Union and their family members to move and reside freely within the territory of the Member States [2004] OJ L 158/77. According to its Article 7(3), a Union citizen who is no longer a worker or self-employed person still retains the same right of residence in three main circumstances: he/she is temporarily unable to work as the result of an illness or accident; he/she is in duly recorded involuntary unemployment after having been employed for more than one year (if for less than one year, the status of worker can be retained for a maximum of six month); or he/she embarks on vocational training.

and their family members not to become a burden on the social assistance system of the host Member State and have comprehensive sickness insurance cover in the host Member State; or (c) are students who are enrolled at a private or public establishment, accredited or financed by the host Member State and have comprehensive sickness insurance cover in the host Member State and assure the relevant national authority of sufficient resources for themselves not to become a burden on the social assistance system.[138] In addition, the right of residence and the correlative right to work extend to family members of EU citizens who are not nationals of a Member State.[139]

   Although the right of residence entails equal treatment with nationals of the host state,[140] this extensive regime of free movement is far from being absolute. Two main exceptions are provided by Directive 2004/38. First, in order to combat abuses of free movement, the right of entry and residence may be refused or withdrawn in cases of 'abuse of rights or fraud, such as marriages of convenience'.[141] These notions are left to the appreciation of Member States, provided that their decisions are proportionate and subjected to a right to appeal.[142] Second, Member States may restrict the freedom of movement and residence of EU citizens and their family members 'on grounds of public policy, public security or public health'.[143] In order to preserve the very rationale of free movement within the EU, none of these grounds can be invoked 'to serve economic ends' (such as the protection of the labour market).[144] While the ground of public health is circumscribed to a very limited set of circumstances,[145] Member States enjoy a broader margin of appreciation regarding the notions of public policy and public security. The Directive 2004/38 provides, nevertheless, some guidance to ensure that these restrictions are only taken on a

---

   [138] ibid. The requirements listed in Article 7(1) are no longer applicable when EU citizens and members of their families have been granted a permanent residence after a continuous period of five years in the host state (Article 16).

   [139] ibid arts 7(2) and 23.

   [140] ibid art 24. However, as stressed by this provision, the host Member State shall not be obliged to confer entitlement to social assistance during the first three months of residence, nor to grant maintenance aid for studies prior to acquisition of the right of permanent residence.

   [141] ibid art 35.

   [142] Nevertheless, recital 28 defines marriages of convenience as marriages 'contracted for the sole purpose of enjoying the right of free movement and residence'. According to the Commission, national authorities may take into account the following factors: the spouses have never met before their marriage; the spouses are inconsistent about their respective personal details; the spouses do not speak a language understood by both; evidence of a sum of money or gifts handed over in order for the marriage to be contracted; the past history of one or both of the spouses contains evidence of previous marriages of convenience or other forms of abuse and fraud to acquire a right of residence; development of family life only after the expulsion order was adopted; the spouses divorce shortly after the third country national in question has acquired a right of residence. European Commission, 'Communication from the Commission to the European Parliament and the Council on guidance for better transposition and application of Directive 2004/38/EC on the right of citizens of the Union and their family members to move and reside freely within the territory of the Member States' COM/2009/0313 final, 15–16.

   [143] Directive 2004/38/EC (n 137) art 27(1).   [144] ibid.

   [145] Under Article 29(1) (ibid), the only diseases justifying measures restricting freedom of movement are those with epidemic potential as defined by the relevant instruments of the World Health Organization and other infectious or contagious parasitic diseases if they are the subject of protection provisions applying to nationals of the host Member State.

case-by-case basis. Thus, in addition to the general principle of proportionality, any restrictions based on public policy or public security shall be 'based exclusively on the personal conduct of the individual concerned' who must represent 'a genuine, present and sufficiently serious threat affecting one of the fundamental interests of society'.[146] The 2004 Directive also provides several substantive and procedural guarantees in case of expulsion.[147]

Although most discussions about free movement are focused on the EU, many other comprehensive regimes of mobility have been established across the European continent. They notably include the Benelux,[148] the CoE,[149] the EEA,[150] the EFTA,[151] and the NORDIC.[152] The expansion of free movement areas is far from being circumscribed to Western Europe. The free movement of persons has been acknowledged as an integral component of the CIS from its inception. According to the 1991 Agreement on the Creation of the Commonwealth of Independent States, Member States 'guarantee open borders and the freedom of movement of citizens'.[153] This founding principle of the CIS has been reaffirmed in the 1993

---

[146] ibid art 27(2). Furthermore, 'previous criminal convictions shall not in themselves constitute grounds for taking such measures'.

[147] According to Article 28 (ibid), before taking an expulsion decision on grounds of public policy or public security, the host Member State shall take into account the personal circumstances of each case (including the duration of his/her residence, his/her age, state of health, family and economic situation, social and cultural integration into the host Member State, and the extent of his/her links with the country of origin). Moreover, an expulsion decision may not be taken against EU citizens, except if the decision is based on imperative grounds of public security, as defined by Member States, if they: (a) have resided in the host Member State for the previous ten years; or (b) are a minor (Article 31).

[148] Treaty instituting the Benelux Economic Union (adopted 3 February 1958, entered into force 1 November 1960) 381 UNTS 165; Convention of Application of Articles 55 and 56 of the Treaty Establishing the Benelux Economic Union (adopted 19 September 1960, entered into force 1 October 1963) 480 UNTS 432; Convention on the Transfer of Entry and Exit Controls to the External Frontiers of the Benelux Territory (11 April 1960) 374 UNTS 3; Protocol 2 Concerning the Abolition of Controls and Formalities at the Internal Frontiers of Benelux and the Removal of Restrictions on Free Movement (adopted 29 April 1969, entered into force 29 January 1971) 779 UNTS 435.

[149] European Agreement on Regulations governing the Movement of Persons between Member States of the Council of Europe (adopted 13 December 1957, entered into force 1 January 1958) 25 ETS; European Convention on Establishment (adopted 13 December 1955, entered into force 23 February 1965) 19 ETS.

[150] Agreement on the European Economic Area between the European Communities, their Member States and the Republic of Austria, the Republic of Finland, the Republic of Iceland, the Principality of Liechtenstein, the Kingdom of Norway, the Kingdom of Sweden [1994] OJ L1/1.

[151] Convention establishing the European Free Trade Association (adopted 4 January 1960, entered into force 3 May 1960) 370 UNTS 5.

[152] Agreement on the Nordic Common Labour Market (adopted 6 March 1982, entered into force 1 August 1983) 1347 UNTS 21; Protocol concerning the exemption of nationals of the Nordic countries from the obligation to have a passport or residence permit while resident in a Nordic country other than their own (adopted 22 May 1954, entered into force 1 December 1955) 199 UNTS 29; Convention between Denmark, Finland, Norway, and Sweden concerning the waiver of passport control at the intra-Nordic frontiers (adopted 12 July 1957, entered into force 1 May 1958) 322 UNTS 245, amended by the agreement of 27 July 1979 supplemented by the agreement of 2 April 1973; Agreement of 18 September 2000 between Denmark, Finland, Iceland, Norway, and Sweden supplementing the Nordic Passport Convention of 12 July 1957 (adopted 18 September 1979, entered into force 22 April 2001) 2155 UNTS 20.

[153] Article 5 of the Agreement Establishing the Commonwealth of Independent States (adopted 8 December 1991, entered into force 21 December 1991) in (1992) 31 ILM. 138.

Charter of the Commonwealth of Independent States.[154] According to this last treaty, one of the primary purposes of the CIS is the 'promotion of freedom of communications, contacts and travels in the Commonwealth for the citizens of its member states' (Article 2). With this aim, 'migration policy' is considered a 'joint activity' (Article 4) and Member States are committed to cooperate towards the 'formation of a common economic space' based on the 'free movement of goods, services, capitals and labour resources' (Article 19). This last objective has been further endorsed in the 1993 Treaty on the Creation of an Economic Union with a view to promoting the progressive establishment of a common market for goods, services, capital, and labour.[155] As a first step of this Economic Union, the 1994 Agreement on the creation of a free-trade area provides the gradual elimination of restrictions to the mobility of services within the territory of Member States.[156]

Despite its endorsement within the CIS, the realization of free movement therein has struggled to be translated into a truly effective and common practice among its Member States. The Agreement on Visa-free Movement of Citizens of the CIS Members adopted in 1992 became a dead letter after the withdrawals of Turkmenistan in 1999 and the Russian Federation in 2000, followed by those of Kazakhstan and Uzbekistan in 2001.[157] Because of the poor achievements of the CIS, the free movement of persons between Member States has been primarily regulated by a vast and complex network of bilateral agreements.[158] Despite the large number of these bilateral treaties, their scope and degree of implementation vary considerably from one agreement to another. Against this contrasted picture, some commentators have asserted that 'it is still too early to talk about the formation of a common labour market and free movement between the [CIS] countries'.[159]

[154] Charter of the Commonwealth of Independent States (adopted 22 January 1993, entered into force 22 January 1994) 1819 UNTS 58.
[155] The Commonwealth of Independent States Treaty on Creation of an Economic Union (adopted 24 September 1993) in (1995) 34 ILM. 1298
[156] Arts 1 and 17 of the Agreement on the creation of a free-trade area (adopted 15 April 1994), available at < https://wits.worldbank.org/GPTAD/PDF/archive/CIS.pdf> accessed 7 October 2018.
[157] Likewise, several other agreements were adopted by the CIS, but they remain poorly implemented or have never entered into force because of lack of ratification. See for instance: Agreement on Co-operation in the Field of Labour Migration and Social Protection of Migrant Workers (1994); Agreement on Co-operation between Member States of the Commonwealth of Independent States in Combating Illegal Migration (1998); and the Convention on the Legal Status of Migrant Workers and Members of their Families of the Member States of the Commonwealth of Independent States (2008). For further discussion see especially I Molodikova, 'Two Decades of CIS Coexistence: The Transformation of the Visa-free Movement' in Nita and others (eds), *Migration, Free Movement and Regional Integration* (n 115); L Ormonbekova, 'Freedom of Movement and Labour Migration in the Commonwealth of Independent States Comparative Brief on CIS and EU Legislation' (2012) Comparative Brief on CIS and EU Legislation, Bishkek, Social Research Center.
[158] For a commentary of these numerous and highly complex bilateral agreements, see, in addition to the publications quoted above: V Ni, 'Study of the Laws and Institutional Frameworks Governing International Migration in North and Central Asia from the Perspective of Countries of Origin and Destination' (2016) UN Economic and Social Commission for Asia and the Pacific, Working Paper 4, 29–30; O Choudinovskikh, 'Migration and Bilateral Agreements in the Commonwealth of Independent States' in OECD, *Free Movement of Workers and Labour Market Adjustment: Recent Experiences from OECD Countries and the European Union* (OECD Publishing 2012) 251–68;
[159] Choudinovskikh, 'Migration and Bilateral Agreements in the Commonwealth of Independent States (n 158) 267. See also I Molodikova, 'Two Decades of CIS Coexistence' (n 157) 339–40.

Nonetheless, much more concrete results have been achieved within the EURASEC.[160] Adopted in 2000, the Agreement on mutual visa-free travel of citizens grants all nationals of States Parties the right to enter, move across, and stay without a visa, by simply presenting a national identification document.[161] Another important achievement has been attained through the Eurasian Economic Union which entered into force in 2015 between Russia, Kazakhstan, Kyrgyzstan, Belarus, and Armenia. Largely modelled upon the EU, the *raison d'être* of this Union is to 'ensure free movement of goods, services, capital and labor' within a common market across the territory of its Member States.[162]

While the single market for services should be fully operational in 2025, the most immediate accomplishment of the Treaty establishing the Eurasian Economic Union relates to the free movement of workers. Since 2015, employers are free to recruit any nationals of Member States without the need for a work permit and Member States are not allowed to apply any restrictions to protect their national labour market.[163] Furthermore, workers and members of their families have the right to remain in the host country, as long as they have a valid employment contract, and they enjoy the same treatment as nationals in the fields of social protection, emergency medical care, and primary education.[164]

Freedom of movement in Africa

Africa represents a paradigmatic case that highlights both the potential and the limits of the right to free movement. Regional integration initiatives have a long history that dates back to the establishment of the South African Customs Union in 1910 and the East African Community in 1919.[165] Today, Africa is the region in the world with the greatest number of agreements on the free movement of persons.

Most of these treaties have been concluded at the sub-regional level within eleven regional economic communities.[166] At the continental level, the African Union adopted in January 2018 the Protocol to the Treaty Establishing the African

---

[160] One should add that, among the neighbouring countries of the Black Sea, the BSEC adopted in 2008 two agreements to facilitate visa procedures for business people and professional lorry drivers that are not yet in force.

[161] Article 1 of the Agreement between the Government of the Republic of Belarus, the Government of the Republic of Kazakhstan, the Government of the Kyrgyz Republic, the Government of the Russian Federation, and the Government of the Republic of Tajikistan on mutual visa-free travel of citizens (adopted 30 November 2000, entered into force 7 June 2002) available at <http://www.evrazes.com/docs/view/131> accessed 10 October 2018. This extensive right to free movement does not prejudice the right of States Parties to take 'extraordinary measures to protect their borders and territory in emergency situations'. In such a case, they can only introduce 'temporary restrictions' upon notification to all other Parties.

[162] See Articles 1(1), 4, and 28(2) of the Treaty on the Eurasian Economic Union (adopted 29 May 2014, entered into force 1 January 2015) <https://treaties.un.org/doc/Treaties/2015/07/20150724%2011-42%20AM/1-Treaty-English.pdf> accessed 7 October 2018.

[163] ibid art 97.   [164] ibid art 98.

[165] G Alemayehu and K Kebret, 'Regional Economic Integration in Africa: A Review of Problems and Prospects with a Case Study of COMESA' (2007) 17(3) Journal of African Economies 357, 358.

[166] See the list of these regional economic communities in the recapitulative table above.

Economic Community Relating to Free Movement of Persons, Right of Residence, and Right of Establishment. This long awaited Protocol materializes the commitment made by Member States under the 1991 Treaty establishing the African Economic Community to gradually remove obstacles to the free movement of persons, goods, services, and capital.[167] From this angle, 'free movement of persons underpins all other pillars of an African common market because it is critical for the supply of services, the right of establishment and the movement of capital'.[168] In this view, the Free Movement Protocol is supplemented by the Agreement establishing the African Continental Free Trade Area concluded in March 2018 with the aim of establishing 'a single market for goods, services, facilitated by movement of persons in order to deepen the economic integration of the African continent'.[169]

When—and if—the Free Movement Protocol will enter into force, its implementation will be progressive alongside a typical three-pronged phase (Article 5). The right of entry and abolition of visa requirements will be implemented as a first step for any nationals of Member States with a maximum period of ninety days (Article 6). Then, the right of residence will be secured with the correlative right to family reunification for the spouse and dependants (Article 16), before the right of establishment will be implemented in order to guarantee the right to set up a business, trade, profession, or any other self-employed activity (Article 17).

The progressive realization of this unique area of free movement will be further conditioned by three classic safeguards aimed at protecting the sovereignty of Member States. Entry may be prohibited under their domestic legislation to protect national security, public order, or public health (Article 7(1)(c)), while the rights of residence and establishment will be implemented in accordance with the laws of the host Members States (Articles 16 and 17). Likewise, any State Party will be able to suspend temporarily the implementation of the Protocol in case of grave threats to national security, public order, and public health (Article 37(1)).

Despite these traditional caveats, States Parties are explicitly committed to adopting any necessary legislative and administrative measures to give effect to the Protocol (Article 27(2)) and to provide administrative and judicial remedies for nationals of other Member States affected by their decisions (Article 30(1)). Interestingly, nationals of Member States will also have the possibility of bringing any denial of the right of entry, residence, or establishment before the African Commission on Human and Peoples' Rights (Article 31(2)). The progressive and pragmatic realization of free movement across the continent will be supplemented and reinforced by a broad range of ancillary measures, including the future adoption of an African Passport and other related instruments on the mutual recognition of

---

[167] Articles 4(2)(i) and 43 of the Treaty Establishing the African Economic Community (adopted 3 June 1991, entered into force 12 May 1994) in 30 ILM 1241 (Abuja Treaty).

[168] United Nations Economic Commission for Africa, *Assessing Regional Integration in Africa V, Towards an African Continental Free Trade Area* (United Nations Commission for Africa 2012) 6.

[169] Article 3(a) of the Agreement establishing the African Continental Free Trade Area (adopted 21 March 2018, not yet in force) available at <https://au.int/en/treaties/agreement-establishing-african-continental-free-trade-area> accessed 8 October 2018.

professional qualifications, the transfer of remittances, and the portability of social security benefits.[170]

Although the effective implementation of this Protocol is remote for the time being, it relies on a broad range of regional economic communities that are all aimed at facilitating the free movement of persons.[171] Despite some uneven developments from one regional community to another, many of them have achieved significant progress over the last few years. The EAC is among the most advanced regimes of free movement in Africa.[172] The commitment to achieve a comprehensive regime of free movement has been endorsed in its founding treaty of 1999[173] and became effective in 2010 with the entry into force of the Common Market Protocol[174] and its four Annexes on the free movement of persons.

This particularly detailed legal regime of free movement is typically based on three constitutive components. First, any citizens of States Parties (including visitors, students, and medical patients) have the right to enter and stay without a visa.[175] Second, workers are entitled to apply for and take up employment in the private sector and to stay in the territory for the purpose of employment.[176] Third, the right of establishment is guaranteed for any nationals of States Parties to take up and pursue self-employed activities and to set up and manage economic undertakings in the territory of another state.[177] Both employed and self-employed workers are

---

[170] Articles 10, 18, 19, and 22 of the Protocol to the Treaty Establishing the African Economic Community Relating to the Free Movement of Persons, Right of Residence and Right of Establishment (adopted 29 January 2018, not yet in force) available at <https://au.int/en/treaties/protocol-treaty-establishing-african-economic-community-relating-free-movement-persons> accessed 8 October 2018.

[171] According to Article 28 of the 2018 Protocol, regional economic communities shall be the focal points for promoting, following up, and evaluating the implementation of this Protocol and reporting on the progress toward free movement of persons in their respective regions.

[172] For a similar observation, see: S Iglesias Sanchez, 'Free Movement of Persons and Regional International Organizations' (n 114) 246; E Erasmus (ed), *MME on the Move: A Stocktaking of Migration, Mobility, Employment and Higher Education in Six African Regional Economic Communities* (International Centre for Migration Policy Development 2013) 42; J Thuo Gathii, *African Regional Trade Agreements as Legal Regimes* (CUP 2011) 188.

[173] Treaty for the Establishment of the East African Economic Community (adopted 30 November 1999, entered into force 7 July 2000) 2144 UNTS 255. According to its article 104(1), 'The Partner States agree to adopt measures to achieve the free movement of persons, labour and services and to ensure the enjoyment of the right of establishment and residence of their citizens within the Community.'

[174] Protocol on the Establishment of the East African Community Common Market (adopted 20 November 2009, entered into force 1 July 2010) < http://eacj.org/?page_id=748> accessed 8 October 2018.

[175] Article 7 of Protocol on the Establishment of the East African Community Common Market and Annex I: Free Movement of Persons Regulations < http://www.lrct.go.tz/east-africa-laws/eac-protocols-and-annexes/> accessed 8 October 2018)

[176] Article 10 of Protocol on the Establishment of the East African Community Common Market and Annex II: Free Movement of Workers Regulations <http://www.lrct.go.tz/east-africa-laws/eac-protocols-and-annexes/> accessed 8 October 2018.

[177] Article 13 of Protocol on the Establishment of the East African Community Common Market and Annex III: Right of Establishment Regulations. Free movement of service suppliers is also acknowledged in Article 16 of the Protocol and its Annex V: Schedule of Commitments on the Progressive Liberalisation of Services available at <http://www.lrct.go.tz/east-africa-laws/eac-protocols-and-annexes/> accessed 8 October 2018.

eligible for the right of residence and entitled to family reunification.[178] Similarly to other regional agreements, the threefold right to enter, reside, and work is subject to the usual limitations that each state may impose on the grounds of public policy, public security, or public health.[179]

East Africa is far from being the only region of the continent to have developed a comprehensive regime of free movement. In Central Africa, the EMCCA has recently achieved a significant step forward. Though initially scheduled for 2014, the right to free movement has been effective since 2017.[180] All nationals of Member States have the right to enter and reside within the EMCCA area for a period of ninety days on the mere condition of presenting a valid identity card or passport.[181] Quite noticeably, they also enjoy the same rights and freedoms as nationals (except for political rights).[182] This area of free movement has been further consolidated with the introduction of the EMCCA passport[183] and the adoption of the Revised Treaty establishing the Economic Union of Central Africa.[184] This last treaty has launched a new step towards the establishment of 'a common market based on the free movement of goods, services, capital and persons'.[185] With this aim in mind, the Council of Ministers has to adopt a specific regulation governing the right of residence and establishment on a long-term basis.[186] Until this regulation is adopted, Member States remain committed to adopting national measures with a view to securing the right of residence and establishment for more than ninety days.[187]

In West Africa, ECOWAS has been at the forefront of free movement since the adoption of its founding treaty in 1975.[188] Its long-term objective of abolishing all obstacles to the freedom of movement and residence has triggered the adoption of

---

[178] Article 14 of Protocol on the Establishment of the East African Community Common Market and Annex IV: Right of Residence Regulations available at <http://www.lrct.go.tz/east-africa-laws/eac-protocols-and-annexes/> accessed 8 October 2018.

[179] See Articles 7(5), 10(11), 13(9), and 14(4) of Protocol on the Establishment of the East African Community Common Market. Any limitations related to the free movement of workers as well as the right of residence and establishment shall be notified to all other States Parties.

[180] Session extraordinaire de la conférence des chefs d'Etat de la CEMAC, Communiqué final (31 October 2017) available at <https://www.cemac.int/node/283> accessed 8 October 2018.

[181] Article 2 of Acte additionnel No 01/13-CEMAC-070 U-CCE-SE portant suppression du visa pour tous les ressortissants de la CEMAC circulant dans l'espace communautaire (14 June 2013) available at <http://kalieu-elongo.com/wp-content/uploads/2015/08/Act-Add-N-¦-01_Suppression-visa.pdf> accessed 8 October 2018.

[182] ibid art 3.

[183] Règlement No 01/08-UEAC-042-CM-17 modifiant le Règlement No 1/00-CEMAC-042-CM-04 portant Institution et Conditions de gestion et de délivrance du Passeport CEMAC (20 June 2008) available at <http://www.droit-afrique.com/upload/doc/cemac/CEMAC-Reglement-2008-01-delivrance-passeport-CEMAC.pdf> accessed 8 October 2018.

[184] Revised Treaty establishing the Economic Union of Central Africa (adopted 25 June 2008) available at <http://www.droit-afrique.com/upload/doc/cemac/CEMAC-Traite-revise-UEAC-2008.pdf> accessed 8 October 2018.

[185] ibid arts 2, 4, and 13.   [186] ibid art 27.

[187] Article 3, Décision no 02/08-UEAC-CM-17 portant liste des personnes admises à titre transitoire à circuler sans visa en zone CEMAC (2008). However, this duty is limited to specific categories of persons, including: investors, members of liberal professions, researchers and teachers, manager of companies, students, civil servants, members of governments and parliaments.

[188] Article 27 (1) and (2) of the Treaty of the Economic Community of West African States (adopted 28 May 1975, entered into force provisionally 28 May 1975) 1010 UNTS 17 (ECOWAS).

six protocols from 1979 to 1990. The 1979 Protocol relating to Free Movement of Persons and the Right of Residence and Establishment provided a three-phased approach over a period of fifteen years to implement the right of entry and the abolition of visas (1980–1985), the right of residence (1985–1990), and the right of establishment (1990–1995).[189] The implementation of this gradual approach has been further detailed by four supplementary Protocols respectively adopted in 1985, 1986, 1989, and 1990.[190] Many other measures have been introduced to foster mobility, including most notably the creation of the ECOWAS travel certificate in 1986 and the ECOWAS passport in 2000.[191]

As a result of this extensive and detailed legal regime, all Community nationals have the right to enter and stay without a visa for ninety days, to reside within the territory of any Member States for a renewable period of three years to seek and carry out income earning employment, as well as to establish companies and carry out self-employed activities. Although Member States are legally bound 'to adopt, at national level, all measures necessary for the effective implementation' of this comprehensive regime of free movement,[192] they retain a broad margin of appreciation in refusing the admission of Community nationals who are considered as 'inadmissible immigrants' under their own domestic legislation.[193] While the realization of the third phase governing the right of establishment faces recurrent difficulties of implementation,[194] the progress accomplished so far is still significant and the

[189] Protocol on Free Movement of Persons, Right of Residence and Establishment (adopted 29 May 1979, entered into force 8 April 1980) A/P.1/5/79.

[190] Supplementary Protocol on the Code of Conduct for the Implementation of the Protocol on Free Movement of Persons, the Right of Residence and Establishment (adopted 6 July 1985, entered into force 28 June 1989) A/SP.1/7/85; Supplementary Protocol on the Implementation of the Second Phase (Right of Residence) of the Protocol on Free Movement of Persons, Right of Residence and Establishment (adopted 1 July 1986, entered into force 1989) A/SP.1/7/86; Supplementary Protocol Amending and Complementing the Provisions of Article 7 of the Protocol on Free Movement, Right of Residence and Establishment (adopted 30 June 1989, entered into force 1992) A/SP.1/6/89; Supplementary Protocol on the Implementation of the Third Phase (Right of Establishment) of the Protocol on Free Movement of Persons, Right of Residence and Establishment (adopted 29 May 1990, entered into force 19 May 1992) A/SP.2/5/90.

[191] Decision A/DEC 2/7/85 of the Authority of Heads of State and Government of the Economic Community of West African States Relating to the Establishment of ECOWAS Travel Certificate for Member States (July 1985) OJ ECOWAS 7. ECOWAS, 'Internal Affairs Ministers Record Progress on ECOWAS Passport' (12 May 2000) Press Release no 44.

[192] Article 59(3) of the Revised Treaty of the Economic Community of West African States, 1993 (adopted 24 July 1993, entered into force 23 August 1995) 2373 UNTS 233.

[193] Article 4 of the 1979 Protocol on Free Movement of Persons, Residence and Establishment (n 189).

[194] For further discussion, see L Kabbanji, 'Regional Management of Migration in West Africa: The Case of ECOWAS and UEMOA', in Nita and others (eds), *Migration, Free Movement and Regional Integration* (n 115); AI Adeniran, *Migration and Regional Integration in West Africa: A Borderless ECOWAS* (Palgrave Macmillan 2014); A Adepoju, A Boulton, and M Levin, 'Promoting Integration through Mobility: Free Movement under ECOWAS' (2010) 29(3) RSQ 120–44; A Adepoju, 'Operationalizing the ECOWAS Protocol on Free Movement of Persons: Prospects for Sub-Regional Trade and Development' in Panizzon, Zurcher, and Fornalé, *The Palgrave Handbook of International Labour Migration* (n 108) 441–62; K Touzenis, *Free Movement of Persons in the European Union and Economic Community of West African States: A Comparison of Law and Practice* (UNESCO 2012).

effective application of this comprehensive regime of free movement remains a priority of ECOWAS.

Furthermore, eight ECOWAS Member States have consolidated their commitments towards free movement within the WAEMU. The revised treaty of 2003 establishing the West African Economic and Monetary Union reaffirms the objective of establishing a comprehensive regime of free movement within a common market, which is reinforced by ensuring the right to enter and reside, as well as the right of establishment and freedom to provide services.[195] A broad range of secondary legislation has been further adopted to facilitate the effective realization of free movement for specific categories of workers.[196]

Despite the significant achievements accomplished within the EAC, EMCCA, ECOWAS, and WAEMU, free movement of persons still falls short of being a reality in several other regional economic communities. Within the ECCAS, the adoption and entry into force of a comprehensive regime of free movement have been undermined by a weak implementation and considerable variation from one Member State to another. Entered into force in 1984, the Protocol VII on Freedom of Movement and Rights of Establishment of Nationals of Member States within the Economic Community of Central African States[197] ensures that 'nationals of Member States of the Community may freely enter the territory of any Member State, travel there, establish residence there and leave at any time'.[198] The personal scope of this right of entry and residence is quite extensive: it includes all nationals of Member States travelling as tourists or for any personal reasons, as well as for business and employment.[199] Free movement of workers comprises the right to accept a job offered in a Member State and the right to remain within its territory after termination of employment in order to find another job.[200] In addition, the right of

---

[195] See Articles 91, 92, and 93 of the Traité modifié de l'Union Economique et Monétaire Ouest Africaine (adopted 23 January 2003) available at<http://www.uemoa.int/fr/system/files/fichier_article/traitreviseuemoa.pdf> accessed 8 October 2018.

[196] See in particular: Règlement No 05/2006/CM/UEMOA relatif à la libre circulation et à l'établissement des experts-comptables et des comptables agréés ressortissants de l'Union au sein de l'espace UEMOA (2006); Directive No 06/2005/CM/UEMOA relative à la libre circulation et à l'établissement des médecins ressortissants de l'Union au sein de l'espace UEMOA (2005); Directive No 07/2005/CM/UEMOA relative à la libre circulation et à l'établissement des architectes ressortissants de l'Union au sein de l'espace UEMOA (2005); Directive No 06/2008/CM/UEMOA relative à la libre circulation et à l'établissement des pharmaciens ressortissants de l'Union au sein de l'espace UEMOA (2008); and Directive No 07/2008/CM/UEMOA relative à la libre circulation et à l'établissement des chirurgiens-dentistes ressortissants de l'Union au sein de l'espace UEMOA (2008).

[197] This Protocol is annexed to the founding Treaty Establishing the Economic Community of Central African States (adopted 18 October 1983, entered into force 18 December 1984) available at <http://www.wipo.int/edocs/trtdocs/en/eccas/trt_eccas.pdf> accessed 8 October 2018. According to Article 5(1) of the Protocol, free movement of persons became effective four years after the entry into force of the treaty and the right of establishment twelve years after such date.

[198] Article 2(1) of the Protocol VII on Freedom of Movement and Rights of Establishment of Nationals of Member States within the Economic Community of Central African States available at <http://www.visafree.ccpau.org/wp-content/uploads/2016/12/Protocol-relating-to-Freedom-of-Mvt-and-Right-of-Establishment-in-ECCAS.pdf accessed 17 October 2018>.

[199] ibid art 2(2).

[200] ibid art 3(4). These rights may be subjected to limitations on the grounds of public order, public safety, and public health.

establishment is acknowledged for 'unsalaried liberal or craft work' and the 'establishment and management of enterprises'.[201]

Although this ambitious legal regime has been consolidated through secondary legislation,[202] its implementation has been delayed and remains limited in practice to specific categories of persons. Member States committed in 2009 to ensuring the effective application of free movement for the following categories of persons: students, trainees, researchers, and teaching staff (whose period of residence may exceed three months, based on the duration of their studies, internship, or research project); as well as tourists, professionals, and people residing in border areas (whose period of residence is limited to a maximum of three months).[203] Domestic implementation remains however erratic: some Member States still require a visa as a result of the political instability and armed conflicts in this region, while others have achieved much more concrete results within the EMCCA.[204]

In several other regional economic communities, the objective of abolishing obstacles to the free movement of persons has remained aspirational, either because their founding instrument was not supplemented by any specific instrument of implementation (such as AMU, CEN-SAD, and IGAD),[205] or because they have adopted a Protocol which has not yet entered into force due to lack of ratifications. This last category includes the COMESA,[206] the

[201] ibid art 4(1). The right of establishment does not prejudice 'the sovereign right [...] to expel nationals of another Member States'. In such a case, the latter state shall be 'immediately informed of the action taken against its national by the Government concerned, which shall do everything appropriate to safeguard the property and interests of the expelled person' (Article 4(3)).

[202] See in particular: Décision No 03/CCEG/VI/90 du 26/01/90 relative à la libre circulation de certaines catégories de ressortissants des Etats membres à l'intérieur de la Communauté Economique des Etats de l'Afrique Centrale, (1990); Décision No 04/CEEAC/CCEG/X/02 instituant la Réunion des Responsables des Services d'Immigration des Etats membres de la Communauté Economique des Etats de l'Afrique Centrale (2002); Décision No 02/CEEAC/CCEG/X02 adoptant le carnet de libre circulation comme document de voyage de certaines catégories de ressortissants des Etats membres, à l'intérieur de la Communauté Economique des Etats de l'Afrique Centrale (2002); Décision No 01/CEEAC/CCEG/X/02 portant modification de certaines dispositions de la Décision No 03/CCEG/VI/90 du 26 janvier 1990 relative à la libre circulation de certaines catégories de ressortissants des Etats membres à l'Intérieur de la Communauté Economique des Etats de l'Afrique Centrale (2002); Décision No 11/CCEAC/CCEG/XIV/09 portant modification de certaines dispositions de la Décision No 04/CEEAC/CCEG/X/02 du 17 juin 2002 institutionnalisant la Réunion des Responsables des Services d'Immigration des Etats membres de la Communauté Economique des Etats de l'Afrique Centrale (2009); and Déclaration des Chefs d'Etat et de Gouvernement de la CEEAC sur la libre circulation de certaines catégories de ressortissants des Etats membres à l'intérieur de la CEEAC (2009).

[203] Décision No 12/CEEAC/CCEG/XIV/09 portant adoption du calendrier de démantèlement des entraves administratives à la libre circulation des ressortissants des Etats membres de la CEEAC (2009).

[204] Erasmus, *MME on the Move* (n 172) 61.

[205] At the time of writing, IGAD however started a consultation process, with the support of IOM, with a view to concluding a Protocol on free movement. Furthermore, all IGAD Members, except Somalia, are members of the COMESA, while Kenya and Uganda are also Partner States of the EAC and Djibouti, Eritrea, Kenya, and the Sudan are members of CEN-SAD.

[206] The COMESA Protocol on Free Movement of Persons, Labour, Services and the Rights of Establishment was adopted in 1998 to initiate the progressive removal of restrictions to free movement of persons as scheduled in its founding treaty of 1993. The Protocol is not yet in force because of the limited number of ratifications. As a result, States Parties are only bound by a limited visa exemption under the 1984 Protocol on the Gradual Relaxation and Elimination of Visas. See: Articles 4 and 164(3) of the Treaty Establishing a Common Market for Eastern and Southern Africa (adopted 5 November 1993, entered into force 8 December 1994) in 33 ILM 1067.

ECGLC,[207] and the SADC.[208] The obstacles toward to the realization of free movement in these regions are due to a variety of factors. Besides the typical lack of political will (as exemplified by the reluctance of South Africa toward the SADC Protocol), the main obstacles are primarily due to the limited degree of regional integration achieved by these economic communities, the enduring lack of capacity and resources, as well as the instability prevailing in several Member States.[209] From this angle, the prerequisites for the free movement of persons are intrinsically linked to the much broader challenges of peace, security, and sustainable development.

Freedom of movement in Latin America and the Caribbean

In Latin America and the Caribbean region, the free movement of persons is governed by a well-established and rather dense network of regional agreements and organizations.[210] MERCOSUR represents the most advanced regime of free movement in this hemisphere. Although its founding treaty of 1991 was initially limited to 'the free movement of goods, services and factors of production between

[207] Convention sur la libre circulation des personnes, des biens, des services, des capitaux et sur le droit d'établissement dans les pays membres de la Communauté économique des pays des grands lacs (adopted 1 December 2005).

[208] Protocol on the Facilitation of Movement of Persons (adopted 18 August 2005, not yet in force) available at <https://www.sadc.int/files/9513/5292/8363/Protocol_on_Facilitation_of_Movement_of_Persons2005.pdf> accessed 8 October 2018.

[209] For further discussion, see in addition to the literature already quoted before A Segatti, 'The Southern African Development Community: A Walk Away from the Free Movement of Persons?' in Nita and others (eds), *Migration, Free Movement and Regional Integration* (n 115) 47–94; V Mlambo, 'Cross-border Migration in the Southern African Development Community (SADC): Benefits, Problems and Future Prospects' (2017) 8(4) Journal of Social and Development Sciences 42–56; OA Akinboade, 'A Review of the Status, Challenges and Innovations Regarding Temporary Immigration of Labour in the Regional Economic Areas of Africa' (2014) 15(1) Journal of International Migration and Integration 27–47; S Nita, 'Regional Free Movement of People: The Case of African Regional Economic Communities' (2013) 3(3) Regions & Cohesion 8–29.

[210] For an overview, see especially M Eguiguren, 'Regional Migratory Policies within the Andean Community of Nations: Crisis vs. Reinforcement of Freedom of Movement within the Region' in Nita and others (eds), *Migration, Free Movement and Regional Integration* (n 115); C Gallinati and N Gavazzo 'We are all MERCOSUR': Discourses and Practices about Free Movement in the Current Regional Integration of South-America' in Nita and others (eds), *Migration, Free Movement and Regional Integration* (n 115); N Bernal, MN Prada, and R Urueña, 'Intra-Regional Mobility in South America: The Andean Community and MERCOSUR' in Panizzon, Zurcher, and Fornalé, *The Palgrave Handbook of International Labour Migration* (n 108) 507–34; D O'Brien, 'The Right of Free Movement within Caricom: A Step towards Caribbean "Citizenship"? Lessons from the European Union' (2015) 42(3) Legal Issues of Economic Integration 233–56; D Acosta Arcarazo and A Geddes, 'Transnational Diffusion or Different Models? Regional Approaches to Migration Governance in the European Union and Mercosur' (2014) 16(1) European Journal of Migration and Law 19–44; J Haynes, 'The Right to Free Movement of Persons in Caribbean Community (CARICOM) Law: Towards 'Juridification'?' (2001) 2(2) Journal of Human Rights in the Commonwealth 57–66; S Nonnenmacher, 'Free Movement of Persons in the Caribbean Community' in R Cholewinski, R Perruchoud, and E MacDonald (eds), *International Migration Law: Developing Paradigms and Key Challenges* (TMC Asser Press 2007) 387–405; AM Santestevan, 'Free Movement Regimes in South America: The Experience of the MERCOSUR and the Andean Community' in R Cholewinski, R Perruchoud, and E MacDonald (eds), *International Migration Law: Developing Paradigms and Key Challenges* (TMC Asser Press 2007) 363–87.

countries',[211] the common market has been a powerful catalyst for liberalizing the movement of persons among its Member States. A right of entry has been first acknowledged on a temporary basis for specific categories of service providers in 1997[212] and skilled workers in 2000,[213] before a comprehensive regime of free movement has been established through the 2002 Agreement on Residence for State Party Nationals.[214] According to this last instrument which entered into force in 2009, all MERCOSUR citizens have the right to enter, reside and work for both employed and self-employed activities, provided that they have no criminal record for the past five years.[215]

Within the Andean region, although the Cartagena Agreement of 1969 did not contain any specific provisions on labour mobility, considerable progress has been made in the last decades. In 2001, the right of entry as tourists for a renewable period of ninety days has been granted to all Andean nationals and foreign permanent residents.[216] Its realization has further been reinforced by the creation of the Andean passport.[217] A few years later, in 2003, the Andean Instrument of Labour Migration initially adopted in 1977 was revised to 'gradually permit the unhampered movement and temporary residence of Andean nationals in the subregion as wage workers'.[218] This primarily concerns four categories of wage-earning workers, as well as members of their families: (1) dependent workers (provided they have an offer of employment), (2) company workers, (3) seasonal workers, and (4) border workers.[219]

The Caribbean region has also been particularly proactive in promoting the free movement of persons within the CARICOM and the OECS. The Revised Treaty of 2001 establishing the CARICOM commits its Member States to the goal of

[211] Treaty Establishing a Common Market between the Argentine Republic, the Federal Republic of Brazil, the Republic of Paraguay, and the Eastern Republic of Uruguay (adopted 26 March 1991, entered into force 29 November 1991) 2140 UNTS 257.

[212] Montevideo Protocol on Trade in Services of Mercosur (adopted 15 December 1997, entered into force 7 December 2005) MERCOSUR/CMC/DEC No 13/97 (1997).

[213] Acuerdo sobre Exención de Visas entre los Estados Partes del MERCOSUR (adopted 14 December 2000) Mercosur/CMC/DEC No 48/00. This exemption of visa up to ninety days covers artists, scientists, sportspersons, journalists, specialized professions, and technicians. A similar exemption has been granted to tourists in 2006: Acuerdo para la Concesión de un Plazo de Noventa (90) Días a los Turistas de los Estados Partes del MERCOSUR y Estados Asociados Decisión (adopted 2006) CMC No 10/06.

[214] Acuerdo No 13/02, Residencia para Nacionales de los Estados Partes del MERCOSUR and Acuerdo N0 14/02, Residencia para nacionales de los Estados Partes del MERCOSUR, Bolivia y Chile.

[215] This threefold right of entry, residence and establishment is granted for an initial period of two years and can be then transformed into a permanent residence, provided that the MERCOSUR citizen has no criminal record and sufficient economic means. Another significant step was taken in 2010 to develop a Mercosur Citizenship by 2021: Decisión CMC No 64/10, Estatuto de la Ciudadanía del Mercosur—Plan de Acción.

[216] Andean Council, Dec 503 (2001) Reconocimiento de documentos nacionales de identificación.

[217] Andean Council, Dec 504 (2001) Creación del Pasaporte Andino.

[218] Andean Council, Dec 545 (2003) Instrumento Andino de Migración Laboral.

[219] See also for service providers: Andean Council, Dec 439 (1998) Marco General de Principios y Normas para la Liberalización del Comercio de Servicios en la Comunidad Andina.

free movement for all their nationals.[220] As a first step towards its achievement, the right to enter and seek employment has been endorsed for specific categories of workers upon the basis of a common system of accreditation of professional qualifications.[221] The Revised Treaty of Chaguaramas also acknowledges a right of establishment to create and manage economic enterprises, provide services, and engage in any non-wage-earning activities of a commercial, industrial, agricultural, professional, or artisanal nature.[222]

A new decisive leap towards a comprehensive regime of free movement has been taken in 2007 when the Conference of Heads of Government decided that all CARICOM nationals have the right to enter and stay within the territory of any Member States for a significant period of six months.[223] This right of entry and stay is still 'subject to the rights of Member States to refuse undesirable persons entry and to prevent persons from becoming a charge on public funds'. As stressed by the Caribbean Court of Justice, these two exceptions 'must be interpreted narrowly and strictly in order to avoid an unjustified watering down of the importance of the right it seeks to limit'.[224] Likewise, as 'an exception to this fundamental principle, the burden of proof must rest on the Member State that seeks to invoke either ground for refusing entry'.[225]

The right to freedom of movement seems even more developed within the OECS. According to the Protocol of the Eastern Caribbean Economic Union, 'freedom of movement for citizens of Protocol Member States shall be secured within the Economic Union area'.[226] Entered into force in 2011, this Protocol notably abolishes any discrimination based on nationality between citizens of the Protocol Member States as regards employment, remuneration, and other conditions of work.[227] Furthermore, no restriction may be imposed on the right of establishment and freedom of trade in services.[228]

[220] Article 45 of the Revised Treaty of Chaguaramas Establishing the Caribbean Community including the CARICOM Single Market and Economy (adopted 5 July 2001, entered into force 4 February 2002) 2259 UNTS 293.
[221] ibid. The categories listed in its Article 46 include university graduates, media workers, sportspersons, artists, and musicians, while subsequent extensions have been granted for teachers, nurses, and artisans through the same system of accreditation. See Communiqué issued at the Conclusion of the 27th Meeting of the Conference of Heads of Government (2006) available at<https://caricom.org/communications/view/communique-issued-at-the-conclusion-of-the-twenty-seventh-meeting-of-the-conference-of-heads-of-government-of-the-caribbean-community-caricom-3-6-july-2006-bird-rock-st-kitts-and-nevis>; Communiqué issued at the Conclusion of the 28th Meeting of the Conference of Heads of Government (2007) available at <https://caricom.org/communications/view/communique-issued-at-the-conclusion-of-the-twenty-eighth-meeting-of-the-conference-of-heads-of-government-of-the-caribbean-community-caricom-1-4-july-2007-needham-s-point-barbados> accessed 8 October 2018.
[222] Arts 32 to 37 of the Revised Treaty of Chaguaramas (n 220).
[223] Communiqué issued at the Conclusion of the 28th Meeting of the Conference of Heads of Government (n 221).
[224] Caribbean Court of Justice, *Shanique Myrie v Barbados*, Judgment (4 October 2013) Application No OA 2, para 67.
[225] ibid.
[226] Article 12(1) of the Protocol of Eastern Caribbean Economic Union (adopted 18 June 2010, entered into force 21 January 2011) available at <https://treaties.un.org/doc/Publication/UNTS/No%20Volume/54948/Part/I-54948-08000002804ec2dd.pdf> accessed 8 October 2018.
[227] ibid art 12(2).   [228] ibid art 27.

In contrast to the Caribbean and South America, the facilitation of free movement is much more modest in Central America, where the CAIS has not yet adopted any comprehensive instrument governing labour mobility. Nonetheless, four of its Member States (Guatemala, El Salvador, Honduras, and Nicaragua) established in 2006 an area of free movement which is quite similar to the Schengen Agreement.[229]

As exemplified above, although their content and implementation vary from one region to another, the numerous free movement agreements concluded in Europe, Africa, South America, and the Caribbean represent the most significant source of international migration law with regard to the admission of non-nationals.

2.2.3 Admission under customary international law

In parallel with the proliferation of regional agreements on free movement, another structural trend of international migration law relies on the development of customary international law at the universal level. The growth of customary rules and their intermingling with a broad range of widely ratified conventions have steadily converged on the recognition of two general principles governing respectively *non-refoulement* and family reunification.

In stark contrast to the above mentioned treaty law frameworks, these general principles of customary international law do not provide for a clear cut right of entry. Rather, they operate as an obligation of result, not of means, thus giving states a significant margin of appreciation in their implementation. Despite this normative and conceptual nuance, the concrete result might be similar to the right of entry under treaty law. In other words, states are prohibited to refuse admission, when such a refusal amounts to a violation of the principle of *non-refoulement* or family reunification.

The principle of non-refoulement

The key customary norm governing the admission of non-nationals consists in the principle of *non-refoulement*. The prohibition of removing anyone to a country where there is a real risk of persecution or serious violations of human rights is a common principle endorsed in various branches of international law, namely human rights law,[230] humanitarian law,[231] refugee law,[232] and criminal

---

[229] Resolución en materia de libre transito y facilitación migratoria de personas por la via aerea en los países del CA-4 (16 September 1997, entered into force 1 November 1997); Acta de Acuerdos—Reunión de Directores Generales de Migración y Extranjería de los Países Miembros del CA-4 (2006). This has been accompanied by common measures on border controls as well as a common visa for third country nationals. See Normas de la Politica de libre movilidad de los países del CA-4 (2006); Convenio de creación de la visa unica centroamericana para la libre movilidad de extranjeros entre las Repúblicas de El Salvador, Guatemala, Honduras y Nicaragua (2005).

[230] See the universal and regional human rights treaties listed in Chapter 3.

[231] Fourth Geneva Convention (n 40) art 45(4).

[232] See Convention Relating to the Status of Refugees, as amended by the Protocol Relating to the Status of Refugees (adopted 31 January 1967, entered into force 4 October 1967) 606 UNTS 267 (Protocol) art 33; Protocol Relating to Refugee Seamen (adopted 12 June 1973, entered into force 30

law.[233] This 'principle of civilization'[234] is endorsed in numerous universal, regional, and bilateral conventions.[235] Even in the absence of a specific provision, most general human rights treaties have been interpreted by their treaty bodies as including an implicit prohibition of *refoulement*.[236]

Quite logically, a vast majority of the legal doctrine has acknowledged its customary law nature.[237] This conclusion is based on three main observations. First, the

March 1975) 965 UNTS 445 art 10; and OAU Convention (n 53) art II(3) and the EU Qualification Directive (n 53) art 21.

[233] This primarily concerns trafficking, smuggling, and extradition law. See, notably, the safeguarding clauses contained in Protocol to Prevent, Suppress and Punish Trafficking in Persons, Especially Women and Children, Supplementing the United Nations Convention against Transnational Organized Crime (adopted 15 November 2000, entered into force 25 December 2003) 2237 UNTS 319 (Trafficking Protocol) art 14(1); Protocol against the Smuggling of Migrants by Land, Sea and Air, supplementing the United Nations Convention against Transnational Organized Crime (adopted 15 November 2000, entered into force 28 January 2004) 2241 UNTS 507 art 19(1); Convention on Extradition (adopted 25 February 1981, entered into force 28 March 1993) OAS Treaty Series No 60 (1981) art 4(5); and International Convention against the Taking of Hostages (adopted 17 December 1979, entered into force 3 June 1983) 1316 UNTS 205, arts 9 and 15.

[234] A Grahl-Madsen, 'International Refugee Law Today and Tomorrow' (1982) 20(4) ArchVR 411, 439.

[235] Besides the universal and regional treaties mentioned above, the principle of *non-refoulement* has been also restated in bilateral treaties, including, most notably, in readmission agreements. See, among many other instances, Agreement Concerning the Readmission and Transit of Persons in an Irregular Situation (France-Dominica) (adopted 9 March 2006, entered into force 1 March 2007) 2424 UNTS 57, art 13; Agreement on the Readmission of Persons Residing Illegally (Latvia-Uzbekistan) (adopted 7 April 2004, entered into force 17 June 2004) 2421 UNTS 37, art 8; Agreement on the Readmission of Persons (Germany-Albania) (adopted 18 November 2002) 2432 UNTS 86, art 10; Agreement (Estonia-Hungary) (adopted 13 Mar 2002) 2211 UNTS 66, art 8; Agreement on the Readmission of Persons in Irregular Situation (France-Venezuela) (adopted 25 January 1999, entered into force 30 December 2001) 2345 UNTS 147, art 9.

[236] See Chapter 3.

[237] The customary law nature of the *non-refoulement* duty has been endorsed in several declarations adopted by scholars and independent experts, for instance, San Remo Declaration on the Principle of Non-Refoulement (2001) available at <https://www.peacepalacelibrary.nl/ebooks/files/IIHL1_en.pdf> accessed 8 October 2018; International Law Association Res 6/2002 on Refugee Procedures of the Seventieth Conference (Declaration on Minimum Standards for Refugee Procedures) (2002) available at <http://www.refworld.org/docid/4280b2404.html> accessed 8 October 2018; Declaration on the Protection of Refugees and Displaced Persons in the Arab World (1992) available at <http://www.refworld.org/docid/452675944.html> accessed 8 October 2018. Among many other similar doctrinal acknowledgements, see W Kälin, M Caroni, and L Heim, 'Article 33, para 1 (Prohibition of Expulsion or Return ("Refoulement")/Défense d'expulsion et de refoulement)' in A Zimmermann (ed), *The 1951 Convention Relating to the Status of Refugees and its 1967 Protocol* (OUP 2011) 1343–346; GA Duffy, 'Expulsion to Face Torture? Non-Refoulement in International Law' (2008) 20(3) IJRL 373, 389; S Trevisanut, 'The Principle of Non-Refoulement at Sea and the Effectiveness of Asylum Protection' (2008) 12 Max Planck Yrbk UN L 205, 215; G Goodwin-Gill and J McAdam, *The Refugee in International Law* (OUP 2007) 345–54; R Bruin and K Wouters, 'Terrorism and the Non-Derogability of Non-Refoulement' (2003) 15(1) IJRL 5, 25–26; E Lauterpacht and D Bethlehem, 'The Scope and Content of the Principle of Non-Refoulement: Opinion' in E Feller, V Türk, and F Nicholson (eds), *Refugee Protection in International Law, UNHCR's Global Consultations on International Protection* (CUP 2003) 140–64; CM-J Bostock, 'The International Legal Obligations Owed to the Asylum-Seekers on the MV Tampa' (2002) 14(2-3) IJRL 279, 288–90; V Vevstad, *Refugee Protection: A European Challenge* (Tano Aschehong 1998) 161; F Crépeau, *Droit d'asile: De l'hospitalité aux contrôles migratoires* (Bruylant 1995) 180–81; R Marx, 'Non-Refoulement, Access to Procedures, and Responsibility for Determining Refugee Claims' (1995) 7(3) IJRL 383, 391; Sohn and Buergenthal, *The Movement of Persons* (n 87) 123; G Stenberg, *Non-Expulsion and Non-Refoulement* (University Swedish Institute of International Law, Iustus Förlag 1989) 268–80; Meron, *Human Rights* (n 18) 23; RC Sexton, 'Political

relevant practice is particularly widespread and representative, since more than 90 per cent of UN Member States are party to one or more treaties explicitly endorsing the principle of *non-refoulement*. Furthermore, among these states, only one of them expressed a reservation (namely Pakistan concerning Article 3 of the CAT).[238] This reservation raised objections from several other states and was eventually withdrawn by Pakistan.

Second, of the few states that have not ratified one of these instruments, none claims to possess an unconditional right to return a person to a country where there is a real risk of persecution or other serious violations of human rights. On the contrary, these states have endorsed the principle of *non-refoulement* despite the absence of any explicit duty under treaty law. Myanmar, for instance, declared that it 'respected the principle of non-refoulement'.[239] Bangladesh concurred in the following terms: 'Notwithstanding the fact that it had not yet been a party to the 1951 Convention or the 1967 Protocol, Bangladesh had fulfilled its obligation to protect refugees and observed the principle of *non-refoulement*.'[240] Such a conviction to be bound by the duty of *non-refoulement* is telling, since Bangladesh was not a party to any other treaty at the time this declaration was made. It even endorsed its 'non-derogable'[241] nature and acknowledged 'the fact that countries in general respected the principle of *non-refoulement* when faced with refugee flows, regardless whether they had acceded to instruments concerning refugees'.[242] Inversely, states accused of violating this duty attempt to justify their conduct by alleging that there is no risk of persecution and human rights violations in the country of destination.[243]

Refugees, Non-Refoulement and State Practice: A Comparative Study' (1985)18(4) Vanderbilt J Transnatl L 732, 738; M Pellonpää, *Expulsion in International Law: A Study in International Aliens Law and Human Rights with Special Reference to Finland* (Suomalainen Tiedeakatemia 1984) 332–37; DW Greig, 'The Protection of Refugees and Customary International Law' (1983) 8 Aust YBIL 108, 129 and 132; P Hyndman, 'Asylum and Non-Refoulement—Are these Obligations Owed to Refugees under International Law?' (1982) Philip LJ 43, 68; Plender, *International Migration Law* (n 87) 427. See, however, J-Y Carlier, 'Droit d'asile et des réfugiés: De la protection aux droits' (2007) 332 Collected Courses of the Hague Academy of International Law 9, 123–30; Hathaway, *The Rights of Refugees* (n 47) 363–70; and N Coleman, 'Non-Refoulement Revised: Renewed Review of the Status of the Principle of Non-Refoulement as Customary International Law' (2003) 5(1) EJML 23, 49.

[238] A declaration of interpretation was also submitted by the US to Article 3 of the CAT and by Germany to the last provision and Article 16 of the International Convention for the Protection of All Persons from Enforced Disappearance (adopted 20 December 2006, entered into force 23 December 2010) 2716 UNTS 3.

[239] UNHCR 'Summary Record of the 556th Meeting of the Executive Committee of the High Commissioner's Programme held on 3 October 2001' (9 October 2001) UN Doc A/AC.96/SR.556, para 21.

[240] UNHCR 'Summary Record of the 519th Meeting of the Executive Committee of the High Commissioner's Programme' (28 November 1997) UN Doc A/AC.96/SR.519, para 16.

[241] ibid para 20.

[242] UNHCR 'Summary Record of the 509th Meeting of the Executive Committee of the High Commissioner's Programme' (8 January 1997) UN Doc A/AC.96/SR.509, para 53. Since then Bangladesh has ratified the CAT (but not the Refugee Convention nor the Convention against Enforced Disappearances).

[243] Though not party to the Refugee Convention, 'the Governments approached [by UNHCR] have almost invariably reacted in a manner indicating that they accept the principle of *non-refoulement* as a guide for their action. They indeed have in numerous instances sought to explain a case of actual or intended *refoulement* by providing additional clarifications and/or by claiming that the person in

Third and finally, its customary law nature has been expressed and reiterated in plenty of official statements and other related materials. For instance, speaking on behalf of the EU and thirteen other states (including Turkey), Belgium declared in 2001 that 'the principle of *non-refoulement* had long been part of international customary law'.[244] Other states from various regions of the world made similar statements,[245] in addition to domestic case-law[246] and a substantial number of intergovernmental resolutions that have equally acknowledged its customary law character.[247] Notably, in 2001 a declaration of States Parties to the Refugee Convention and its Protocol reaffirmed the centrality of 'the principle of *non-refoulement*, whose applicability is embedded in customary international law'.[248] The Kampala Declaration adopted

question was not to be considered a refugee. The fact that States have found it necessary to provide such explanations or justifications can reasonably be regarded as an implicit confirmation of their acceptance of the principle': in UNHCR 'Principle of Non-Refoulement as a Norm of Customary International Law, Response to the Questions Posed to UNHCR by the Federal Constitutional Court of the Federal Republic of Germany in Cases 2 BvR 1938/93, 2 BvR 1953/93, 2 BvR 1954/93' (31 January 1994), para 5 available at <http://www.refworld.org/docid/437b6db64.html> accessed 8 October 2018.

[244] UNHCR 'Summary Record of the 552nd Meeting of the Executive Committee of the High Commissioner's Programme' (5 October 2001) UN Doc A/AC.96/SR.552, para 50.

[245] See notably the statements of Canada in UNHCR 'Summary Record of the 571st Meeting of the Executive Committee of the High Commissioner's Programme held in Geneva on 29 September 2003' (16 October 2003) UN Doc A/AC.96/SR.571, para 28; Costa Rica in UNGA '13th Plenary Meeting on 1 October 2001' Fifty-Fifth Session (2001) UN Doc A/56/PV.13, 2; Liechtenstein in UNGA Third Committee 'Discussion in the Social, Humanitarian and Cultural Committee' Sixty-Third Session (2009) UN Doc A/C.3/63/SR.37, para 28; and Switzerland in UNHCR 'Summary Record of the 557th Meeting of the Executive Committee of the High Commissioner's Programme' (6 2002) UN Doc A/AC.96/SR.557, para 33. See also Déclaration du Conseil fédéral à l'occasion de la publication du rapport de la Commission indépendante d'experts sur les réfugiés intitulé 'La Suisse et les réfugiés à l'époque du national-socialisme' (11 December 1999) para 7. For more indirect evidence asserting that the principle of *non-refoulement* applies to all states, see also the statements of Denmark in UNHCR 'Summary Record of the 522nd Meeting of the Executive Committee of the High Commissioner's Programme' (23 October 1997) UN Doc A/AC.96/SR.522, para 65; Bangladesh in UNHCR, 'Summary Record of the 509th Meeting of the Executive Committee of the High Commissioner's Programme' (8 January 1997) para 53; Hungary in UNHCR 'Summary Record of the 501st Meeting of the Executive Committee of the High Commissioner's Programme' (20 October 1995) UN Doc A/AC.96/SR.501, para 22; Austria in UNHCR 'Summary Record of the 600th Meeting of the Executive Committee of the High Commissioner's Programme' (26 October 2006) UN Doc A/AC.96/SR.600, para 17 and South Korea in UNHCR 'Summary Record of the 619th Meeting of the Executive Committee of the High Commissioner's Programme' (10 October 2008) UN Doc A/AC.96/SR.619, para 72.

[246] See especially *Zaoui v Attorney General* (2005) 1 NZLR 690 (New Zealand Court of Appeal) para 34; *C and Others v Director of Immigration and Another* (2011) Civil appeals No 132-137 OF 2008 (Hong Kong High Court) paras 47–67.

[247] See in particular UNHCR EXCOM Conclusions No 17 (XXXI) 'Declaration on Territorial Asylum' (1980), para (b); UNHCR EXCOM Conclusion No 25 (XXXIII) 'Restrictive Asylum Practices' (1982), para (b). See also Cartagena Declaration on Refugees, Colloquium on the International Protection of Refugees in Central America, Mexico and Panama (adopted 22 November 1984) Annual Report of the Inter-American Commission on Human Rights, OAS Doc. OEA/Ser.L/V/II.66/doc.10, rev.1, at 190–93 (1984–1985) para 5; and Mexico Declaration and Plan of Action to Strengthen the International Protection of Refugees in Latin America' (16 November 2004) Recital 7 available at <https://www.oas.org/dil/mexico_declaration_plan_of_action_16nov2004.pdf> accessed 8 October 2018.

[248] UNHCR 'Declaration of States Parties to the 1951 Convention and or its 1967 Protocol relating to the Status of Refugees' (16 January 2002) UN Doc HCR/MMSP/2001/09, 4.

by the African Union in 2009 likewise refers to 'the fundamental principle of *non-refoulement* as recognised in International Customary Law'.[249]

More generally, alongside other intergovernmental bodies,[250] the UN General Assembly has constantly 'urge[d] *all States* to respect the fundamental principle of *non-refoulement*',[251] which is thus presumably binding upon all of them regardless of their respective treaty ratifications. The legal duty of all states to respect this principle has been further reaffirmed in the New York Declaration for Refugees and Migrants,[252] as well as in the Global Compact for Safe, Orderly, and Regular Migration and the Global Compact on Refugees.[253] Though not equating with state practice *stricto sensu*, various international bodies have also confirmed its customary law nature. They do not only include UNHCR,[254] but also IOM,[255] the UN special procedures,[256] as well as

---

[249] Kampala Declaration on Refugees, Returnees and Internally Displaced Persons in Africa, adopted by the African Union at the Special Summit on Refugees, Returnees and Internally Displaced Persons in Africa held in Kampala, Uganda (22–23 October 2009) Ext/Assembly/AU/PA/Draft/Decl. (I) Rev 1 (2009) para 6.

[250] At the universal level, see in particular, HRC, Decision 2/112 'Persons Deprived of their Liberty in the Context of Counter-Terrorism Measures' (27 November 2006) UN Doc A/HRC/DEC/2/11, para 5 and Commission on Human Rights Res 2005/80 on Protection of Human Rights and Fundamental Freedoms while Countering Terrorism (21 April 2005) UN Doc E/CN.4/RES/2005/80, preamble para 7. Regarding regional intergovernmental bodies, see for example, Protection of Asylum-Seekers and Refugees in the Americas, OASGA Resolution adopted by the Forty-first Regular Session in San Salvador, El Salvador (7 June 2011) AG/RES 2678 (XLI-O/11), para 1; Protection of Asylum Seekers and Refugees in the Americas, OASGA Resolution adopted at the fourth plenary session (8 June 2010) AG/RES 2597 (XL-O/10), para 1; OASGA Resolution (6 June 2006) AG/RES 2232 (XXXVI-O/06), para 6; OASGA Resolution (8 June 2004) AG/RES 2047 (XXXIV-O/04), para 4.

[251] UNGA Res 65/225 (21 December 2010) UN Doc A/RES/65/225, para 1(iii) (emphasis added). For similar statements see UNGA Res 66/174 (19 December 2011) UN Doc A/RES/66/174, para 1(a)(iii); UNGA Res 64/175 (18 December 2009) UN Doc A/RES/64/175, para 1(a)(iii); UNGA Res 63/190 (18 December 2008) UN Doc A/RES/63/190, para 1(a)(ii); UNGA Res 55/74 (4 December 2000) UN Doc A/RES/55/74, para 6; UNGA Res 54/146 (17 December 1999) UN Doc A/RES/54/146, para 6; UNGA Res 53/125 (9 December 1998) UN Doc A/RES/53/125, para 5; UNGA Res 52/103 (12 December 1997) UN Doc A/RES/52/103, para 5; UNGA Res 51/75 (12 December 1996) UN Doc A/RES/51/75, para 3; UNGA Res 50/152 (21 December 1995) UN Doc A/RES/50/152, para 3; UNGA Res 49/169 (23 December 1994) UN Doc A/RES/49/169, para 4; UNGA Res 48/116 (20 December 1993) UN Doc A/RES/48/116, para 3; UNGA Res 47/105 (16 December 1992) UN Doc A/RES/47/105, para 4; UNGA Res 46/106 (16 December 1991) UN Doc A/RES/46/106, para 4; and UN Res 44/137 (15 December 1989) UN Doc A/RES/44/137, para 3.

[252] New York Declaration (n 76) paras 24, 58, and 67.

[253] Global Compact for Safe, Orderly and Regular Migration (13 July 2018), para 37, available at https://refugeesmigrants.un.org/sites/default/files/180713_agreed_outcome_global_compact_for_migration.pdf accessed 12 October 2018; and Global Compact on Refugees, para 5 (Report of the United Nations High Commissioner for Refugees—Part II, Global compact on Refugees) (2 August 2018, reissued 13 September 2018) UN Doc A/73/12.

[254] UNHCR 'The Principle of Non-Refoulement' (n 243).

[255] IOM 'Amicus Curiae submitted to the Inter-American Court of Human Rights by the International Organization for Migration' Request for Advisory Opinion on Migrant Children (17 February 2012) CDH-OC-21/272, para 167.

[256] See in particular Human Rights Council, 'Report of the Working Group on Arbitrary Detention, Implementation of General Assembly Resolution 60/251 of 15 March 2006 Entitled "Human Rights Council"' (9 January 2007) UN Doc A/HRC/4/40, para 44; Human Rights Council, 'Joint Study on Global Practices in Relation to Secret Detention in the Context of Countering Terrorism of the Special Rapporteur on the Promotion and Protection of Human Rights and Fundamental Freedoms while

the International Criminal Court[257] and the Inter-American Court of Human Rights.[258]

In sum, the almost universal ratification of treaties, the general practice of states (including from non-States Parties), and the numerous manifestations of *opinio juris* anchor the principle of *non-refoulement* in customary international law. Its core content includes at a minimum the absolute and underogable prohibition of *refoulement* toward a state where there is a real risk of torture, inhuman, or degrading treatment or punishment.[259] As very few norms have attained such a degree of consensus, denying such evidence would negate other well-established rules of customary international law (including the prohibitions of torture and the use of armed force).

The principle of family reunification

Besides the principle of *non-refoulement*, the other crucial norm governing the admission of non-nationals is family reunification. As observed by ILO, '[i]n many countries family reunification remains almost the only legal means of immigration for prospective migrants'.[260] Persons admitted in foreign countries on this ground represent around one-third of the total international population of migrants and even more in some industrialized countries.[261]

The principle of family reunification is based on the right to respect for family life 'as an indispensable component of international migration law'.[262] As codified in a broad range of conventions, the right to respect for family life typically includes both

Countering Terrorism, the Special Rapporteur on Torture and Other Cruel, Inhuman or Degrading Treatment or Punishment, the Working Group on Arbitrary Detention and the Working Group on Enforced or Involuntary Disappearances' Thirteenth Session (19 February 2010) UN Doc A/HRC/13/42, para 43. The same opinion was also expressed by several members of the HRC, see for example HRC 'Consideration of Reports Submitted by States Parties under Article 40 of the Covenant: Uzbekistan' Summary Record of the 1910th Meeting held on 27 March 2001 (4 May 2001) UN Doc CCPR/C/SR.1910, para 18 (Mr Henkin); and HRC 'Consideration of Reports Submitted by States Parties under Article 40 of the Covenant: Hong Kong Special Administrative Region of the People's Republic of China' (31 March 2006) UN Doc CCPR/C/SR.2351, para 53 (Mr Shearer).

[257] *Prosecutor v Germain Katanga and Mathieu Ngudjolo Chui* (2011) (Decision on *Amicus Curiae* Application and on the 'Requête tendant à obtenir présentations des témoins DRC-D02-P-0350, DRC-D02-P-0236, DRC,D-02-P-0228 aux autorités néerlandaises aux fins d'asile') (2011) Case No ICC-01/04-01/07 (Trial Chamber II) para 68.

[258] *Pacheco Tineo Family v Plurinational State of Bolivia* (Preliminary Objections, Merits, Reparations, and Costs) Series C No 272 (IACtHR, 25 November 2013), para 151.

[259] For further discussion about the scope of *non-refoulement* and its impact on admission, see section 3.3 of Chapter 3.

[260] International Labour Conference (87th Session) Report III (1B): Migrant Workers (Geneva 1999), para 472.

[261] Bertelsmann Foundation et al (eds), *Migration in the New Millennium* (Bertelsmann Foundation Publishers 2000) 33. Within OECD countries, in 2012, family reunification constituted the main category of entry accounting for 36 per cent (and 45 per cent if accompanying family members of workers are included), see OECD, *International Migration Outlook 2012* (OECD Publishing 2012) 22. The US had the largest share of family migrants in the OECD, that is, about three out of four new permanent immigrants: see in ibid 33 and 283. They represented around two-thirds in Australia and Canada, ibid 211 and 219.

[262] J Vedsted-Hansen, 'Migration and the Right to Family and Private Life' in V Chetail (ed), *Mondialisation, migration et droits de l'homme* (n 93) 722.

a positive obligation to protect the family[263] and a negative obligation prohibiting any unlawful and arbitrary interference with the exercise of the right to family life.[264] Human rights treaty bodies have made abundantly clear that this twofold obligation may require in some circumstances a correlative duty of family reunification. The general obligation to protect the family enshrined in Article 23 of the ICCPR has been interpreted as including 'the adoption of appropriate measures [...] to ensure the unity or reunification of families, particularly when their members are separated for political, economic or similar reasons'.[265] Furthermore, a refusal of family reunification can be considered as an arbitrary or unlawful interference with the right to family life under Article 17 of the Covenant.[266]

The circumstances in which the right to respect for family life may require family reunification have been considered most comprehensively by the ECtHR.[267] While underlining that Article 8 does not impose a general obligation to authorize family reunion, the court has ruled that there is a positive obligation to facilitate family reunification where there is an objective obstacle preventing the migrant already

---

[263] See notably International Covenant on Civil and Political Rights (adopted 15 December 1966, entered into force 23 March 1976) 999 UNTS 171(ICCPR) art 23; International Covenant on Economic, Social and Cultural Rights (adopted 16 December 1966, entered into force 3 January 1976) 993 UNTS 3 (ICESCR) art 10(1); Charter of Fundamental Rights of the European Union (n 48) arts 7 and 33; ACHPR (n 50) art 18(1); African Charter on the Rights and Welfare of the Child (adopted 11 July 1990, entered into force 29 November 1999) OAU Doc CAB/LEG/24.9/49, art 18(1); Arab Charter (n 52) art 33(2); Covenant on the Right of the Child in Islam (adopted June 2005) OIC/9-IGGE/HRI/2004/Rep. Final, art 8(1); CIS Convention on Human Rights and Fundamental Freedoms (n 51) 212 art 13(3); and ACHR (n 49) art 17(1).

[264] See especially ICCPR (n 263) art 17; Convention on the Rights of the Child (adopted 20 November 1989, entered into force 2 September 1990) 1577 UNTS 3 (CRC) art 16; ACHR (n 49) art 11(2); European Convention on Human Rights (adopted 4 November 1950, entered into force 3 September 1953) 213 UNTS 222 (ECHR) art 8; Arab Charter (n 52) art 21; African Charter on the Rights and Welfare of the Child (n 263) art 10; and CIS Convention (n 51) art 9.

[265] HRC 'General Comment No 19: Protection of the Family, the Right to Marriage and Equality of the Spouses' in 'Note by the Secretariat, Compilation of General Comments and General Recommendations Adopted by Human Rights Treaty Bodies' (1990) UN Doc HRI/GEN/1/Rev.5, art 23, para 5. See also HRC, *Ngambi v France* (2004) Communication No 1179/2003 UN Doc CCPR/C/81/D/1179/2003, para 6.4 ('Article 23 of the Covenant guarantees the protection of family life including the interest in family reunification.')

[266] HRC, 'General Comment No 15: The Position of Aliens Under the Covenant' (11 April 1986) HRI/GEN/1/Rev1 18, paras 5 and 7, 'in certain circumstances an alien may enjoy the protection of the Covenant even in relation to entry or residence, for example, when [...] respect for family life arise. [...] They may not be subjected to arbitrary or unlawful interference with their privacy, family, home or correspondence.'

[267] Regarding the practice of other treaty bodies, see notably UN Committee on the Elimination of Discrimination against Women, 'General Recommendation No 21: Equality in Marriage and Family Relations' in 'General Assembly Official Records, Forty-ninth Session Supplement No 38' (12 April 1994) UN Doc A/49/38, para 10; UN Committee on the Elimination of Racial Discrimination (CERD) 'Concluding Observations: Portugal' (10 December 2004) UN Doc CERD/C/65/CO/6, para 14; CERD 'Concluding Observations of the Committee on the Elimination of Racial Discrimination: Lichtenstein' (2007) UN Doc CERD/C/LIE/CO/3, para 20; Committee on Economic, Social and Cultural Rights (CESCR) 'Concluding Observations: The United Kingdom of Great Britain and Northern Ireland (Hong Kong)' (6 December 1996) UN Doc E/C.12/1/add.10, paras 26 and 34; CESCR 'Concluding Observations: Norway' (13 May 2005) UN Doc E/C.12/1/Add.109, paras 16 and 35.

within the state's jurisdiction from realizing his/her family life in any other place.[268] Though states enjoy a broad margin of appreciation in controlling family immigration, assessing the existence of such an obstacle requires an *in concreto* examination of the circumstances of each particular case (including the age of children, their situation in the country of origin, and their degree of dependence upon their parents).[269]

Against such a framework, family reunification is a positive obligation deriving from the right to respect for family life. The former is a means for implementing the latter. Assuming family reunification as an implicit—albeit integral—component of the right to respect for family life has a quite significant impact on the plane of general international law, for the right to respect for family life is conventionally regarded as a customary norm of international law.[270] Hence, the customary character of the right to respect for family life logically presumes that the same conclusion should apply to the positive obligations inherent in the effective respect for this fundamental right, including the correlative duty of family reunification when there is no other alternative for exercising the right to family life elsewhere. Although the doctrine rarely delves into this line of reasoning, an increasing number of scholars have acknowledged the existence of a customary norm that facilitates reunification of the nuclear family (spouse and minor children) of documented migrants.[271] Other commentators nevertheless have considered it a nascent norm of customary

[268] *Abdulaziz, Cabales and Balkandali v the United Kingdom* App No 15/1983/71/107-109 (ECtHR, 1985) paras 67–68; *Gül v Switzerland* App No 53/1995/559/645 (ECtHR, 1996) paras 38–42; *Ahmut v The Netherlands* App No 73/1995/579/665 (ECtHR, 1996), para 63; *Sen v The Netherlands* App No 31465/96 (ECtHR, 2001) para 31; *Chandra and Others v The Netherlands* App No 53102/99 (ECtHR, 2003) para 32; *Benamar v The Netherlands* App No 43786/04 (ECtHR, 2005) para 30; *Haydarie and Others v The Netherlands* App No 8876/04 (ECtHR, 2005) paras 46 and 48; and *Tuquabo-Tekle and Others v The Netherlands* App No 60665/00 (ECtHR, 2005) para 42.

[269] See for instance *Sen v The Netherlands* (n 268) para 37 and *Tuquabo-Tekle and Others v The Netherlands* (n 268) para 44.

[270] Among other instances, see *Applicability of Article VI, Section 22, of the Convention on the Privileges and Immunities of the United Nations* (Advisory Opinion) [1989] ICJ Rep 177 [210]–[211], see particularly the separate opinion of Judge Evensen. See also for example, L Ayoub and S-M Wong, 'Separated and Unequal' (2006) 32(2) Wm Mitchell L Rev 559, 585–86; CG Blood, 'The "True" Source of the Immigration Power and its Power Consideration in Elian Gonzalez Matter' (2000) 18 BU Int'l LJ 215, 240; J Dugard, 'The Application of Customary International Law Affecting Human Rights by National Tribunals' (1982) 76 ASIL Proc 245, 247.

[271] See, in particular, S Kadidal, 'Federalizing Immigration Law: International Law as a Limitation on Congress's Power to Legislate in the Field of Immigration' (2008) 7(2) Fordham L Rev 501, 515–16; SR Chowdhury, 'Response to the Refugee Problems in Post-Cold War Era: Some Existing and Emerging Norms of International Law' (1995) 7(1) IJRL 100, 114; G Fourlanos, *Sovereignty and the Ingress of Aliens: With Special Focus on Family Unity and Refugee Law* (Almqvist & Wiksell International 1986) 108–18; as well as the legal opinions delivered by Brownlie and Shelton referred in HCJ 13/86, *Adel Ahmed Shahin v Regional Commander of IDF Forces in the West Bank, PD* 41(1)197, 202–04 and discussed in Y Merin, 'The Right to Family Life and Civil Marriage under International Law and its Implementation in the State of Israel' (2005) 28(1) BC Int'l & Comp L Rev 79, 109–10. See also K Jastram, 'Family Unity' in TA Aleinikoff and V Chetail (eds), *Migration and International Legal Norms* (TMC Asser Press 2003) 193 and 195–96. For Hathaway, states have 'the customary international legal duty to avoid unlawful or arbitrary interference with a refugee's family', see Hathaway, *The Rights of Refugees* (n 47) 559. The right to family reunion has been alternatively considered as a general principle of law by M Nys, *L'immigration familiale à l'épreuve du droit. Le droit de l'étranger à mener une vie familiale normale* (Bruylant 2002) 585–606.

international law,[272] whereas some have acknowledged the widespread acceptance of states but still have denied that it had been crystallized into a customary rule.[273]

Beyond the variety of doctrinal views, some strong pieces of evidence support, as a core minimum, the reunification of a minor child with his/her family legally established in a foreign country as a duty of customary international law when there is no reasonable alternative for exercising his/her family life elsewhere. This constitutes the lowest common denominator of state practice among the great diversity of domestic legislations on family reunification.[274] Although states' assertions about the existence of such a customary norm are less widespread than for the principle of *non-refoulement*, the French *Conseil d'Etat* held that the right of documented migrants to be reunited with their children and spouses constitutes a general principle of law.[275] Furthermore, a US federal district court ruled that the best interests of the child must be taken into account in the field of immigration as a principle of customary international law codified in the 1989 CRC.[276] This last acknowledgment is particularly significant given that the US is the only UN Member State which is not a party to this treaty.

While restating the cardinal importance of the best interests of the child, the CRC embodies two main principles. First, Article 9(1) enshrines the obligation not to separate a child from his/her parents against his/her will, except when such separation is necessary for his/her best interests. Second, as a result of this general duty, Article 10(1) specifies that:

In accordance with the obligation of States Parties under article 9, paragraph 1, applications by a child or his or her parents to enter or leave a State Party for the purpose of family reunification shall be dealt with by States Parties in a positive, humane and expeditious manner. States Parties shall further ensure that the submission of such a request shall entail no adverse consequences for the applicants and for the members of their family.[277]

---

[272] S Starr and L Brilmeyer, 'Family Separation as a Violation of International Law' (2003) 21 Berk J Int'l L 213, 229–31; Sohn and Buergenthal, *The Movement of Persons* (n 87) 70; GS Goodwin-Gill, *International Law and the Movement of Persons between States* (OUP 1978) 197.

[273] G Lahav, 'International Versus National Constraints in Family-Reunification Migration Policy' (1997) 3 Global Governance 349, 361; CS Anderfuhren-Wayne, 'Family Unity in Immigration and Refugee Matters: United States and European Approaches' (1996) 8(3) IJRL 347, 350; EF Abram, 'The Child's Right to Family Unity in International Immigration Law' (1995) 17(4) Law and Policy 397, 432; Plender, *International Migration Law* (n 87) 366.

[274] For an overview of domestic legislation on family reunification, see notably International Labour Conference (n 260) paras 475–99; Inter-Governmental Consultations (IGC) on Asylum, Refugee and Migration Policies in Europe, North America and Australia, *Report on Family Reunification: Overview of Policies and Practices in IGC Participating States* (IGC 1997); K Groenendijk and others, *The Family Reunification Directive in EU Member States: The First Year of Implementation* (Wolf Legal Publishers 2007); Plender, *International Migration Law* (n 87) 366–82.

[275] Conseil d'Etat, *GISTI et autres, Rec Lebon,* App Nos 10097, 10677, and 10979 (8 December 1978) 493. See also, with regard to refugees, Conseil d'Etat, *Agyepong, Leb,* Case No 112842 (2 December 1994) 523.

[276] *Beharry v Reno* (2002) 183 FSupp 2d 584 (EDNY). See also *Maria v McElroy* (1999) 68 FSupp2d, 206 (EDNY).

[277] See also art 22(2).

This provision is not a model of legal clarity and reflects states' concerns in the field of immigration control. Nevertheless, Article 10(1) enshrines a mixture of both procedural and substantive obligations. On the one hand, the main procedural requirement is to examine applications submitted by a child or his/her parents 'in a positive, humane and expeditious manner.' In other words, Article 10(1) does not only require a rigorous and independent scrutiny of all the circumstances of each particular case, but the examination process should also be done promptly with particular attention to the best interests of the child and the human dignity of family members. As restated by the Committee on the Rights of the Child, States Parties must 'pay particular attention to the implementation [...] of the general principles of the Convention, in particular the best interests of the child and respect for his or her views, in all matters relating to the protection of refugee and immigrant children'.[278]

On the other hand, and although the procedural guidance enshrined in Article 10(1) does not prejudice the outcome of the final decision on applications for family reunification,[279] some substantive obligations can be inferred from the text of this provision. The explicit link to the obligation under Article 9(1) not to separate a child from his/her parents combined with the additional requirement of avoiding any adverse consequences for family members clearly contemplate a presumption of approval.[280] This presumption of approval mainly operates when there is no reasonable alternative for reuniting the child with his/her parents elsewhere. Any other interpretation would contravene the *effet utile* of Article 10(1) in light of the object and purpose of the Convention as a whole and would further be in contradiction with the best interests of the child. The Committee on the Rights of the Child and the Committee on the Protection of the Rights of All Migrant Workers and Members of Their Families have recalled that:

When the child's relations with his or her parents and/or sibling(s) are interrupted by migration (in both the cases of the parents without the child, or of the child without his or her parents and/or sibling(s)), preservation of the family unit should be taken into account when assessing the best interests of the child in decisions on family reunification.[281]

---

[278] CRC (Ninth Session) 'Concluding Observations of the Committee on the Rights of the Child: Canada' (20 June 1995) UN Doc CRC/C/15/Add.37, para 24.

[279] This was confirmed by the drafters during the *travaux préparatoires* of the Convention. While acknowledging that 'family unity and reunification were basic rights', the US delegate explained, in line with the French representative, that the obligation to deal with applications in a 'positive manner' 'only obliged states to act positively and in no way prejudged the outcome of their deliberations on questions of family reunification'—see CRC 'Report of the Working Group on a Draft Convention on the Rights of the Child' Forty-Third Session (9 March 1987) UN Doc E/CN.4/1987/25, para 10; and CRC 'Report of the Working Group on a Draft Convention on the Rights of the Child' Forty-Fifth Session (2 March 1989) UN Doc E/CN.4 /1989/48, para 216 reprinted in S Detrick (ed), *The United Nations Convention on the Rights of the Child: A Guide to the 'Travaux Préparatoires'* (Martinus Nijhoff 1992) 202–06. See also the reservation to Article 10 formulated by Japan. For further comments, see S Detrick, *A Commentary on the United Nations Convention on the Rights of the Child* (Martinus Nijhoff 1999) 191–94.

[280] For a similar account, see notably IOM, 'Amicus Curiae' (n 255) para 219; P Boeles and others, *European Migration Law* (Intersentia 2009) 176; Jastram, 'Family Unity' (n 271) 195; Abram, 'The Child's Right' (n 273) 423.

[281] CRC and CMW, 'Joint General Comment No 4 (2017) of the Committee on the Protection of the Rights of All Migrant Workers and Members of Their Families and No. 23 (2017) of the Committee

From the perspective of general international law, the prompt and almost universal ratification of the CRC might indicate a major step in the customary law process mentioned above. The very small number of reservations to Article 10(1) provides a further confirmation thereof given that only seven of the 196 States Parties have formulated a reservation on family reunification.[282] Moreover, the existence of a customary norm finds additional support in international humanitarian law. Indeed, the obligation to facilitate the reunion of families dispersed as a result of armed conflicts is enshrined in the two 1977 Additional Protocols[283] and it is currently considered as a norm of customary international law.[284]

This customary principle of international humanitarian law is arguably part of a broader legal norm which applies both in times of war and peace for the purpose of reunifying a child with his/her family when there is no other alternative elsewhere. Such a rule is not only an implicit obligation deriving from the right to respect for family life; it is also explicitly codified in several universal and regional treaties. In addition to the treaties mentioned above, these instruments include most notably the ICRMW (Article 44), the African Charter on the Rights and Welfare of the Child (Article 25(2)(b)), the Covenant on the Right of the Child in Islam (Article 8(4)), the European Social Charter (Article 19(6)),[285] the European

on the Rights of the Child on State Obligations Regarding the Human Rights of Children in the Context of International Migration in Countries of Origin, Transit, Destination and Return' (16 November 2017) UN Doc CMW/C/GC/4-CRC/C/GC/23, para 32. See also, CRC 'Concluding Observations: Thailand' Fifty-Ninth Session (17 February 2012) UN Doc CRC/C/THA/CO/3-4, para 55; CRC 'Concluding Observations: Malaysia' Forty-Fourth Session (25 June 2007) UN Doc CRC/C/MYS/CO/1, para 96(d); CRC 'Concluding Observations: Ireland' Forty-Third Session (29 September 2006) UN Doc CRC/C/IRL/CO/2, para 31(c); CRC 'Concluding Observations: Forty-Sixth Session (30 June 2004) UN Doc CRC/C/15/Add.233, para 36(f). The CRC recalled in its General Comment No 6 that the obligations under Articles 9 and 10 of the Convention come into effect whenever family reunion in the country of origin is not in the best interest of the child. This requires a 'careful balancing of the child's best interests and other considerations, if the latter are rights-based and override best interests of the child. Such may be the case in situations in which the child constitutes a serious risk to the security of the state or to the society. Non-rights-based arguments such as those relating to general migration control, cannot override best interests considerations', see CRC, 'General Comment No 6 (2005): Treatment of Unaccompanied and Separated Children Outside Their Country of Origin' Thirty-Ninth Session (1 September 2005) UN Doc CRC/GC/2005/6, paras 82–83 and 86.

[282] These are China (on behalf of the Hong Kong Special Administrative Region), Cook Islands, the Holy See, Japan, Liechtenstein, Singapore, and Switzerland. Germany and the UK withdrew their general reservation on immigration legislation respectively in 2008 and 2010. The text of the reservations is available at https://treaties.un.org/pages/ViewDetails.aspx?src=IND&mtdsg_no=IV-11&chapter=4&lang=en accessed 8 October 2018.

[283] See Protocol Additional to the Geneva Conventions of 12 August 1949 Relating to the Protection of Victims of International Armed Conflicts (adopted 8 June 1977, entered into force 7 December 1978) 1125 UNTS 3 (Protocol I) art 74; Protocol Additional to the Geneva Conventions of 12 August 1949 and Relating to the Protection of Victims of Non-International Armed Conflicts (adopted 8 June 1977, entered into force 7 December 1978) 1125 UNTS 609 (Protocol II) art 4(3)(b). Protocol I has been ratified by 174 States and Protocol II by 168 States.

[284] J-M Henckaerts and L Doswald-Beck, *Customary International Humanitarian Law*, vol 1 (ICRC/CUP 2005) 381.

[285] European Social Charter (adopted 18 October 1961, entered into force 26 February 1965) ETS No 35; and European Social Charter (Revised) (adopted 3 May 1996, entered into force 1 July 1999) ETS No 163.

Convention on the Legal Status of Migrant Workers (Article 12(1)), and several EU Directives.[286]

Furthermore, an impressive number of soft law instruments have constantly underlined the importance of facilitating family reunification[287] and spelt out guidelines detailing its implementation by states.[288] It is also noteworthy that the

[286] See, in particular, Council Directive 2003/86/EC of 22 September 2003 on the right to family reunification [2003] OJ L 251/12; Council Directive 2003/109/EC of 25 November 2003 concerning the status of third-country nationals who are long-term residents [2004] OJ L 16/44, art 16 (as amended by Parliament and Council Directive 2011/51/EU extending its scope to beneficiaries of international protection [2011] OJ L 132/1); and EU Qualification Directive (n 53) art 23.

[287] See for example 'Plan of Action' (World Population Conference, Bucharest, 19–30 August 1974) para 56; 'Recommendation 49' (International Conference on Population, Mexico, 6–14 August 1984); 'Programme of Action' (International Conference on Population and Development, Cairo, 5–13 September 1994) paras 10.9, 10.12, and 10.13; 'Programme of Action' (Annex II) (World Summit for Social Development, Copenhagen, 6–12 March 1995) paras 39(e) and 77 (b); 'Platform for Action' (Annex II) (Fourth World Conference on Women, Beijing, 4–15 September 1995) para 147(k); 'Key Actions for the Further Implementation of the Programme' (Annex) (Review and Appraisal of the Implementation of the ICPD Programme of Action, New York, 1 July 1999) (ICDP + 5) para 24(a); 'Declaration' and 'Program for Action' (Further Initiative for Social Development, Geneva, 26–30 June 2000) paras 22 and 68; 'Report of the World Conference against Racism, Racial Discrimination, Xenophobia and Related Intolerance' (Durban, 31 August–10 September 2001) UN Doc A/CONF.189/12, paras 49 and 28; 'International Agenda for Migration Management' (Berne Initiative, Bern, 2005) Part III(4)(b)(2). See also, among many other regional resolutions, Final Act of the Helsinki Conference on Security and Cooperation in Europe (1975) Basket III, 1 'Co-operation in Humanitarian and Other Fields: Human Contact' available at <https://www.osce.org/helsinki-final-act?download=true> accessed 8 October 2018; Council of Europe, Committee of Ministers, Resolution (78) 33 on the Reunion of Families of Migrant Workers in Council of Europe Member States, adopted at the 289th meeting of the Ministers' (8 June 1978) available at <https://rm.coe.int/CoERMPublicCo mmonSearchServices/DisplayDCTMContent?documentId=09000016804c35f7> accessed 8 October 2018; and General Assembly of the OAS, 'The Human Rights of All Migrant Workers and their Families' (7 June 2011) OAS Doc AG/RES. 2669 (XLI-O/11). With regard to family reunification of refugees, see Recommendation B of General Assembly, 'Final Act of the Conference of Plenipotentiaries on the Status of Refugees and Stateless Persons' (25 July 1951) available at <http://www.unhcr.org/protection/travaux/40a8a7394/final-act-united-nations-conference-plenipotentiaries-status-refugees-stateless.html> accessed 8 October 2018; Cartagena Declaration on Refugees (n 247) para 13; and the following UNHCR EXCOM Conclusions, No 107 (LVIII) 'Children at Risk' (2007) para (h); UNHCR EXCOM Conclusion No 105 (LVII) 'Women and Girls at Risk' (2006) para (n); UNHCR EXCOM Conclusion No 104 (LVI) 'Local Integration' (2005) para (n); UNHCR EXCOM Conclusion No 103 (LVI) (2005) para (n); UNHCR EXCOM Conclusion No 100 (LV) 'International Cooperation and Burden and Responsibility Sharing in Mass Influx Situations' (2004) para (d); UNHCR EXCOM Conclusion No 91 (LII) 'Conclusion on Registration of Refugees and Asylum Seekers' (2001) para (a); UNHCR EXCOM Conclusion No 88 (L) 'Conclusion on the Protection of the Refugee's Family' (1999) paras (b)(ii) and (c); UNHCR EXCOM Conclusion No 85 (XLIX) 'Conclusion on International Protection' (1998) paras (u) to (x); UNHCR EXCOM Conclusion No 74 (XLV) 'General' (1994) para (gg); UNHCR EXCOM Conclusion No 47 (XXXVIII) 'Refugee Children' (1987) para (i); UNHCR EXCOM Conclusion No 24 (XXXII) 'Family Reunification' (1981) para 1; UNHCR EXCOM Conclusion No 15 (XXX) 'Refugees without an Asylum Country' (1979) para (e); UNHCR EXCOM Conclusion No 9 (XXVIII) 'Family Reunion' (1977) paras (a)–(c); and UNHCR EXCOM Conclusion No 7 (XXVIII) 'Expulsion' (1977) para (a).

[288] See especially ILO Recommendation R086: Migration for Employment Recommendation (Revised) (Recommendation concerning Migration for Employment) (32nd ILC Session Geneva 1 July 1949) paras 15–71; ILO Recommendation R151: Migrant Workers Recommendation (Recommendation concerning Migrant Workers) (60th ILC Session Geneva 24 June 1975) paras 13–19; Parliamentary Assembly of the Council of Europe, Recommendation 1686 on Human Mobility and the Right to Family Reunion (23 November 2004); Council of Europe, Committee of Ministers, 'Recommendation Rec(2002)4 of the Committee of Ministers on the Legal Status of Persons Admitted for Family Reunification' (26 March 2002); and Council of Europe, Committee of Ministers,

great majority of General Assembly resolutions referring to family reunification of children have been adopted by consensus.[289] By contrast, however, more general statements recalling 'the vital importance of family reunification' without specific reference to children have been adopted by vote within the General Assembly with a substantial number of abstentions (mainly from Western states).[290] This suggests that, besides the particular case of children, there is no general duty of family re-unification under customary international law. In other words, the emergence of a customary norm is not yet sanctioned by a widespread *opinio juris* when the interest of the child is not at stake. The relevant state practice is also much less uniform with regard to other dependent relatives or unmarried partners without children.[291] The Global Compact for Migration is however promoting a slightly broader under-standing: while most references to family unity are made with respect to children,[292] the Compact underlines as well the need to 'facilitate access to procedures for family reunification for migrants at all skills levels through appropriate measures that pro-mote the realization of the right to family life and the best interests of the child'.[293] This should notably be achieved 'by reviewing and revising applicable requirements, such as on income, language proficiency, length of stay, work authorization, and ac-cess to social security and services'.[294]

In any event, family reunification may also fall within the ambit of other well-established norms of customary international law. In particular, a refusal of family reunification may constitute in some circumstances a degrading treatment or a vio-lation of the principle of non-discrimination.[295] When there is no applicable rule of customary international law, treaty law still plays a vital role in the field of family reunification, whether as an implicit obligation deriving from the right to respect

---

'Recommendation R(1999)23 of the Committee of Ministers to Member States on Family Reunion for Refugees and Other Persons in Need of International Protection' (15 December 1999).

[289] See, for instance, UNGA Res 66/172 (19 December 2011) UN Doc GA/RES/66/172, para 5(e); UNGA Res 66/141 (19 December 2011) UN Doc GA/RES/66/141, para 17; UNGA Res 65/212 (21 December 2010) UN Doc GA/RES/65/212, para 5(e); UNGA Res 65/197 (21 December 2010) UN Doc GA/RES/65/197, para 16; UNGA Res 64/166 (18 December 2009) UN Doc GA/RES/64/166, para 5(c); UNGA Res 64/146 (18 December 2009) UN Doc GA/RES/64/146, para 14; UNGA Res 60/169 (16 December 2005) UN Doc GA/RES/60/169, para 14; UNGA Res 59/194 (20 December 2004) UN Doc GA/RES/59/194, para 18; UNGA Res 58/190 (22 December 2003) UN Doc GA/RES/58/190, para 18; UNGA Res 57/128 (18 December 2002) UN Doc GA/RES/57/128, para 16; and UNGA Res 56/170 (19 December 2001) UN Doc GA/RES/56/170, para 13.

[290] UNGA Res 63/188 (18 December 2008) UN Doc GA/RES/63/188, para 2, adopted by 121–4 with 60 abstentions; UNGA Res 61/162 (19 December 2006) UN Doc GA/RES/61/162, para 2, adopted by 122–4 with 58 abstentions; UNGA Res 59/203 (20 December 2004) UN Doc GA/RES/59/203, para 2, adopted by 122–3 with 61 abstentions; UNGA Res 55/100 (4 December 2000) UN Doc GA/RES/55/100, para 2, adopted by 106–1 with 67 abstentions; and UNGA Res 51/89 (12 December 1996) UN Doc GA/RES/51/89, para 2, adopted by 89–4 with 76 abstentions. See also, UNCHR Res 1995/62 (7 March 1995) UN Doc E/CN.4/1995/65, 191 para 2, adopted by 27–9, with 17 abstentions.

[291] See, for instance, EU Family Reunification Directive (n 286) art 4(2) and (3).

[292] Global Compact for Safe, Orderly and Regular Migration (n 253) paras 23(f), 27(e), 28(d), 29(h), and 37(g).

[293] ibid para 21(i).   [294] ibid.

[295] On the customary law character of these norms, see section 2.2.2.

for family life under general human rights instruments or as an explicit obligation subscribed in more specific conventions.

Family reunification is, nonetheless, not an absolute duty. Generally speaking, a fair balance has to be struck between the competing interests of the state in controlling immigration and of the individual in exercising his/her family life. Needless to say that states retain a broad margin of appreciation for assessing such a balancing act. This case-by-case examination not only takes into account the particular circumstances of the migrant and his/her family members, but it also includes additional factors, such as potential threats to public order, as well as sufficient resources and adequate housing to support incoming family members.

Moreover, it needs to be acknowledged that family reunification is not only about the human rights of migrants. It is also in the interest of host states themselves for promoting full inclusion and social cohesion. Family reunification is a powerful tool for facilitating integration and social adaptation of migrants within their host countries. The ILO acknowledged in this sense that:

Uniting migrant workers with their families living in the countries of origin is recognized to be essential for the migrants' well-being and their social adaptation to the receiving country. Prolonged separation and isolation lead to hardships and stress situations affecting both the migrants and the families left behind and prevent them from leading a normal life. The large numbers of migrant workers cut off from social relations and living on the fringe of the receiving community create many well-known social and psychological problems that, in turn, largely determine community attitudes towards migrant workers.[296]

The Executive Committee of the UNHCR Programme similarly observed that, 'Experience has shown that the family unit has a better chance of successfully [...] integrating in a new country than do individual refugees. In this respect, protection of the family is not only in the best interests of the refugees themselves, but is also in the best interests of States.'[297]

2.2.4 Immigration control and procedural guarantees under customary international law

Public international law does not only impose some substantive obligations on states in deciding whether to admit non-nationals, it also provides for several procedural guarantees in implementing immigration control. This primarily concerns the detention of undocumented migrants, their removal, and other related measures of enforcement.

---

[296] International Labour Conference (87th Session) Report VI(1) Migrant Workers (Geneva, 1974) 27. Among many other similar acknowledgements, see also ILO, Report of the Tripartite Meeting of Experts on Future ILO Activities in the Field of Migration' (1997) Annex I, para 6.1.
[297] UNHCR EXCOM, Standing Committee, 'Family Protection Issues' (4 June 1999) UN Doc EC/49/SC/CRP.14, para 16.

The prohibition of arbitrary detention

The prohibition of arbitrary detention is a well-established rule of customary international law codified in a broad range of treaties.[298] This basic prohibition applies to all deprivations of liberty, including immigration detention,[299] be it upon arrival, during status determination, or with the view to removal,[300] and regardless of the name of the facility where deprivation of liberty takes place.[301] The UN General Assembly has constantly reminded all states (regardless of their ratification of the relevant treaties) to duly respect this principle with regard to undocumented migrants and 'where necessary, to review detention periods in order to avoid excessive detention of irregular migrants, and to adopt, where applicable, alternative measures to detention'.[302]

---

[298] ICCPR (n 263) art 9; CRC (n 264) art 37(d); International Convention on the Protection of the Rights of All Migrant Workers and Members of their Families (adopted 18 December 1990, entered into force 1 July 2003) 2220 UNTS 3 (ICRMW) art 16; ECHR (n 264) art 5; Charter of Fundamental Rights of the European Union (n 48) art 6; ACHR (n 49) art 7; ACHPR (n 50) art 6; Arab Charter on Human Rights (n 52) art 20; and CIS Convention on Human Rights (n 51) art 5. Among many other restatements of its customary law nature, see notably HRC 'General Comment No 24: Issues Relating to Reservations Made upon Ratification or Accession to the Covenant or the Optional Protocols thereto, or in Relation to Declarations under Article 41 of the Covenant' (4 November 1994) UN Doc CCPR/C/21/Rev.1/Add.6, para 8; HRC 'General Comment No 29 (Article 4): Derogations during a State of Emergency' (31 August 2001) UN Doc CCPR/C/21/Rev.1/Add.11, para 11; Inter-American Commission on Human Rights 'Report on Terrorism and Human Rights' (2002) OAS Doc OEA/Ser.L/V/II.116 Doc 5 Rev 1 Corr 2002, para 38; *Alvarez Machain v United States*, No 99-56762 and 99-56880 (9th Cir 2003) (US Court of Appeal); *MA v Ashcroft* 257 F3d 1095 (9th Cir 2001) (US Court of Appeal) para 65; and Human Rights Council, 'Report of the Working Group on Arbitrary Detention' (24 December 2012) UN Doc A/HRC/22/44, para 75.

[299] See most notably HRC, 'General Comment No 35: Article 9 (Liberty and security of person)' (16 December 2014) UN Doc CCPR/C/GC/35, para 5; HRC, 'General Comment No 8: Right to Liberty and Security of Persons' (1982) UN Doc A/37/40, art 9 in Annex V, para 4; HRC, *Danyal Shafiq v Australia* (13 November 2006) Communication No 1324/2004 UN Doc CCPR/C/88/D/1324/2004, para 7.2; and UN Human Rights Council A/HRC/22/44 (n 298) para 68; and ICJ, *Ahmadou Sadio Diallo* (n 101) [668] para 77.

[300] HRC, 'General Comment No 35' (n 299) paras 9 and 60; HRC, 'General Comment No 15' (n 266) para 9.

[301] The types of places and facilities where migrants are deprived of their liberty, as well as their denomination, vary from one state to another. They include, for instance, places of custody in border areas, police premises, premises under the authority of a prison administration, ad hoc premises, house arrest, international/transit areas in ports and airports, gathering centres, and hospital premises (UN Commission on Human Rights, 'Report of the Working Group on Arbitrary Detention' (19 December 1997) UN Doc E/CN.4/1998/44, paras 38–41), 'confinement on board a ship, aircraft, road vehicle or train' (UN Commission on Human Rights, 'Report of the Working Group on Arbitrary Detention' (28 December 1999) UN Doc E/CN.4/2000/4, Annex: Deliberation No 5, 29) and may be referred to as processing centres, reception centres, retention centres, or hotspots (see for instance Human Rights Council, 'Report of the Working Group on Arbitrary Detention' (10 January 2008) UN Doc A/HRC/7/4, para 43, referring to 'transit centres', 'guest house', or 'retention').

[302] UNGA Res 70/147 (25 February 2016) UN Doc GA/RES/70/147, para 4(a); UNGA Res 69/167 (12 February 2015) UN Doc GA/RES/69/167, para 4(a); UNGA Res 68/1 (28 January 2014) UN Doc GA/RES/68/17, para 4(a); UNGA Res 67/172 (3 April 2013) UN Doc A/RES/67/172, para 4(a); UNGA Res 66/172 (29 March 2012) UN Doc A/RES/66/172, para 4(a); UNGA Res 65/212 (1 Apr. 2011) UN Doc A/RES/65/212, para 4(a); UNGA Res 64/166 (19 March 2010) UN Doc A/RES/64/166, para 4(a); and UNGA Res 63/184 (17 March 2009) UN Doc A/RES/63/184, para 9. For further and more general restatements of states' duty to respect the prohibition of arbitrary detention with regard to migrants, see also UNGA Res 62/156 (7 March 2008) UN Doc A/RES/62/156, para 9; UNGA Res 61/165 (23 February 2007) UN Doc A/RES/61/165, para 8; UNGA Res 60/169 (7 March

Nonetheless, detaining undocumented migrants for the purpose of enforcing immigration control is not considered arbitrary per se. Such a possibility is even explicitly permitted by Article 5(1)(f) of the ECHR 'to prevent [a person from] effecting an unauthorised entry into the country'. The ECtHR held in line with the UK Supreme Court[303] that detention of undocumented immigrants is 'a necessary adjunct' to the 'undeniable sovereign right to control aliens' entry'.[304] The HRC considered in the same vein that there is no basis under both treaty law and customary international law for concluding that it is per se arbitrary to detain individuals requesting asylum.[305]

In fact, the increasing use of detention by states has become the most patent manifestation of immigration control for the twofold purpose of deterring future immigrants and removing those already on their territory.[306] This represents the saddest irony of contemporary movement of persons: for states, the only means for preventing individuals from migrating is to deprive them of one of their most precious freedoms, the right to liberty. However, the widespread practice of detaining undocumented migrants does not mean that the prohibition of arbitrary detention has no role to play in channelling the power of states in the field of immigration control. While preserving states' margin of appreciation, this rule of customary international law embodies three main limitations regarding the legal basis of detention, its grounds, and other related procedural guarantees. Each of them has been notably restated in the Global Compact for Migration alongside a dense and well-established practice.[307]

2006) UN Doc A/RES/60/169, paras 19 and 21; UNGA Res 59/194 (18 March 2005) UN Doc A/RES/59/194, paras 12 and 14; and UNGA Res 59/190 (22 March 2004) UN Doc A/RES/58/190, paras 12 and 19.

[303] *R v Secretary of State for the Home Department, ex parte Saadi and Others* [2002] 4 All ER 785 (HL) 794–95 (per Lord Slynn of Hadley).

[304] *Saadi v the United Kingdom* ECHR 2008-I 31, para 64.

[305] HRC, *A v Australia* (30 April 1997) Communication No 560/1993 UN Doc CCPR/C/59/D/560/1993, para 9.3. See, by contrast, Human Rights Council, 'Report of the Working Group on Arbitrary Detention. Promotion and Protection of All Human Rights, Civil, Political, Economic, Social and Cultural Rights, Including the Right to Development, Report of the Working Group on Arbitrary Detention' (10 January 2008) UN Doc A/HRC/7/4, para 53, 'criminalizing an irregular entry into a country exceeds the legitimate interest of States to control and regulate illegal immigration and leads to unnecessary detention'.

[306] For further discussion, see among an extensive literature: B Saul, 'Indefinite Security Detention and Refugee Children and Families in Australia: International Human Rights Law Dimensions' (2013) 20 Australian International Law Journal 55–75; C Costello, 'Human Rights and the Elusive Universal Subject: Immigration Detention under International Human Rights and EU Law' (2012) 19(1) *Indiana Journal of Global Legal Studies* 257–303; A Edwards, 'Back to Basics: The Right to Liberty and Security of Person and "Alternatives to Detention" of Refugees, Asylum-Seekers, Stateless Persons and Other Migrants' (2011) UNHCR Legal and Protection Policy Research Series, Division of International Protection, PPLA/2011/01.Rev.1; C Galina, *Immigration, Detention and Human Rights: Rethinking Territorial Sovereignty* (Martinus Nijhoff 2010); E Acer and J Goodman, 'Reaffirming Rights: Human Rights Protections of Migrants, Asylum Seekers, and Refugees in Immigration Detention' (2010) 24 Geo Immigr L J 507; S Vohra, 'Detention of Irregular Migrants and Asylum Seekers', in Cholewinski, Perruchoud, and MacDonald (eds), *International Migration Law* (n 210) 49; C Teitgen-Colly, 'La détention des étrangers et les droits de l'homme' in Chetail (ed), *Mondialisation, migration et droits de l'homme* (n 93) 571.

[307] Global Compact for Safe, Orderly and Regular Migration (n 253) objective 13, para 29.

First, any detention must be in accordance with and authorized by law. This reflects the general principle of legal certainty which is inherent in the rule of law and codified in all human rights instruments. This fundamental principle notably includes two basic components: detention of undocumented migrants must not only be in accordance with domestic law and procedures; national legislation must also be sufficiently accessible and precise in order to avoid all risks of arbitrariness.[308]

Second, the prohibition of arbitrary detention is generally understood as requiring deprivation of liberty to be reasonable, necessary, and proportionate.[309] As a result of this case-by-case assessment, automatic detention for mere irregular entry and/or stay is considered arbitrary.[310] As acknowledged by the Human Rights Committee in the leading case of *A v Australia*, additional factors are needed for immigration detention to be considered necessary in a particular case, 'such as the likelihood of absconding and lack of cooperation, which may justify detention for a period'.[311] Moreover, such grounds of detention should persist during the whole period of detention.[312] While indefinite detention has been clearly ruled out,[313] instances of lengthy deprivations of liberty which are not justified anymore and/or proportionate to the objective pursued have been deemed arbitrary.[314]

---

[308] See for instance the following restatements of this twofold principle by the ECtHR: *Khlaifia and Others v Italy*, App No 16483/12 (ECtHR, 15 December 2016) para 91; *AB and Others v France*, App no 11593/12 (ECtHR, 12 July 2016) para 119; *Popov v France*, App nos 39472/07 and 39474/07 (ECtHR, 19 January 2012) para 118; *Abdolkhani and Karimnia v Turkey*, App no 30471/08 (ECtHR, 22 September 2009) para 130; and *A and Others v the United Kingdom*, ECHR 2009-II 137, para 164. For a similar account by other treaty bodies, see notably: IACtHR, *Case of Gangaram-Panday v Surinam* (Merits, Reparations and Costs) OAS Series C No 16 (IACtHR, 21 January 1994) para 47; and Inter-American Commission on Human Rights, *Rafael Ferrer-Mazorra et al v United States*, Case 9.903, Report no 51/01 (4 April 2001) para 211.

[309] Among many other similar acknowledgements, see HRC, *MMM et al v Australia* (25 February 2012) Communication No 2136/2012 UN Doc CCPR/C/108/D/2136/2012, para 10.3. See also HRC, *Van Alphen v The Netherlands* (15 August 1990) Communication No 305/1988 UN Doc CCPR/C/39/D/305/1988, para 5.8; HRC, *Madafferi et al v Australia* (26 August 2004) Communication No 1011/2001 UN Doc CCPR/C/81/D/1011/2001, para 9.2; HRC, *X v Republic of Korea* (15 May 2014) Communication No 1908/2009 UN Doc CCPR/C/110/D/1908/2009, para 10.3; IACtHR, *Case of Gangaram-Panday v Suriname* (n 308) para 47; and IACtHR, *Case of Vélez Loor v Panama* (Preliminary Objections, Merits, Reparations and Costs) OAS Series C No 218 (IACtHR, 23 November 2010) para 166. See also Human Rights Council, A/HRC/7/4 (n 301) para 46.

[310] See for instance: IACtHR, *Case of Vélez Loor v Panama* (n 309) paras 167–69. For a detailed description of this last judgment, see: M-B Dembour, *When Humans Become Migrants: Study of the European Court of Human Rights with an Inter-American Counterpoint* (OUP 2015) 359–74. See also IACtHR, *Rights and Guarantees of Children in the Context of Migration and/or in Need of International Protection* (Advisory Opinion) OC-21/14 (IACtHR, 19 August 2014) para 147; Human Rights Council, 'Report of the Working Group on Arbitrary Detention' (18 January 2010) UN Doc A/HRC/13/30, paras 61 and 62.

[311] HRC, *A v Australia* (30 April 1997) Communication No 560/1993 UN Doc CCPR/C/59/D/560/1993, para 9.4.

[312] ibid.

[313] See most notably Human Rights Council, A/HRC/7/4 (n 301) para 52; UN Human Rights Council A/HRC/22/44 (n 298) para 73.

[314] See for instance: HRC, *Shams v Australia* (20 July 2007) Communications Nos 1255, 1256, 1259, 1260, 1266, 1268, 1270, 1288/2004 UN Doc CCPR/C/90/D/1255, 1256, 1259, 1260, 1266, 1268, 1270, and 1288/2004, para 7.2; HRC, *Bakhtiyari v Australia* (6 November 2003) Communication No 1069/2002 UN Doc CCPR/C/79/D/1069/2002, para 9.3; HRC, *D and E v Australia* (9 August 2006) Communication No 1050/2002 UN Doc CCPR/C/87/1050/2002, para 7.2; HRC, *FKAG*

The general principle of proportionality further requires states to rely on alternatives to detention, that is, 'less invasive means' to achieve the stated objectives without interfering with the right to liberty and security.[315] These include diverse measures which entail varying degrees of control over the individual in three main ways: first, by entrusting a third party with care and/or responsibility for the migrant and his/her case (eg community supervision, case management, provision of a guarantor/surety); second, by requiring the migrant to pay bonds or bail; or, third, by limiting to a lesser or greater extent his/her liberty of movement with reporting requirements, the establishment of a home curfew, electronic monitoring, the placement in (semi-)open centres, designated residence, or house arrest.[316]

This obligation to rely on alternatives to detention is more stringent when it comes to migrant children. Indeed, if the principle of necessity already calls for not detaining migrant children due to their mere migration status or that of their parents,[317] 'the possibility of detaining children as a measure of last resort, which may apply in other contexts such as juvenile criminal justice, is not applicable in immigration proceedings as it would conflict with the principle of the best interests of the child and the right to development'.[318] Hence, as underlined by the CMW and the CRC Committee in their joint General Comment No 4/23, migrant children accompanied by their parents and whose best interest dictates maintaining the family unity shall not be detained together, but 'non-custodial solutions [shall be sought]

---

et al v Australia (20 August 2013) Communication No 2094/2011 UN Doc CCPR/C/108/D/2094/2011, para 9.4; HRC, *Al-Gertani v Bosnia and Herzegovina* (28 November 2013) Communication No 1955/2010 UN Doc CCPR/C/109/D/1955/2010, para 10.4; HRC, *MGC v Australia* (7 May 2015) Communication No 1875/2009 UN Doc CCPR/C/113/D/1875/2009, para 11.6; and HRC, *C v Australia* (28 October 2002) Communication No 900/1999 UN Doc CCPR/C/76/d/900/1999, para 8.2.

[315] HRC, *C v Australia* (n 314) para 8.2. For similar restatements by the HRC, see *Kwok v Australia* (23 November 20009) Communication No 1442/2005 UN Doc CCPR/C/97/D/1442/2005, para 9.3; HRC, *Shams v Australia* (n 314) para 7.2; *D and E v Australia* (n 314) para 7.2; HRC, *Bakhtiyari v Australia* (n 314) para 9.3; and HRC, *Baban v Australia* (18 September 2003) Communication No 1014/2001 UN Doc CCPR/C/78/D/1014/2001 para 7.2.

[316] Some of these alternatives are foreseen in UNHCR, *Detention Guidelines* (UNHCR 2012) 22–24; and UNGA, 'Human Rights of Migrants, Report of the Special Rapporteur on the Human Rights of Migrants' (19 July 2017) UN Doc A/72/173, para 61.

[317] See CRC Committee, 'General Comment No. 6 (2005): Treatment of Unaccompanied and Separated Children Outside their Country of Origin' (1 September 2005) UN Doc CRC/GC/2005/6, para 61; and CRC Committee, 'Report of the 2012 Day of General Discussion: The Rights of All Children in the Context of International Migration' (28 September 2012) para 32; affirmed also by the CMW, 'General Comment No. 2 on the Rights of Migrant Workers in an Irregular Situation and Members of Their Families' (28 August 2013) UN Doc CMW/C/GC/2, para 33. At the regional level, see: IACtHR, *Rights and Guarantees of Children in the Context of Migration* (n 310) para 154; and Council of Europe, European Committee for the Prevention of Torture and Inhuman or Degrading Treatment of Punishment, 'Immigration Detention' Factsheet, CPT/Inf (2017)3 (2017) 9.

[318] CMW and CRC Committee, 'Joint General Comment No 4 (2017) of the Committee on the Protection of the Rights of All Migrant Workers and Members of their Families and No. 23 (2017) of the Committee on the Rights of the Child on State Obligations Regarding the Human Rights of Children in the Context of International Migration in Countries of Origin, Transit, Destination and Return' (16 November 2017) UN Doc CMW/C/GC/4-CRC/C/GC/23, para 10 (hereinafter 'Joint General Comment No 4/23'). See also Human Rights Council, 'Report of the Working Group on Arbitrary Detention' (18 January 2010) UN Doc A/HRC/13/30, para 60.

for the entire family'.[319] In such cases, non-custodial alternatives entailing the least degree of control should be favoured, such as community-based arrangements.[320]

Third, the right to challenge the lawfulness of detention before a court is another well-established principle of customary international law.[321] As restated by human rights treaties, this fundamental right includes the following four key procedural guarantees: the review must be prompt; it must be exercised by an independent and impartial judicial body; the procedure must respect the minimum standards of due process (including the equality of arms and the adversarial principle); and the judicial review must be effective and include the possibility of ordering release. In particular, the court review of the lawfulness of detention is not limited to mere compliance with domestic law, but should assess whether the detention is necessary, proportionate, and reasonable in due accordance with international law.[322]

Besides the fundamental guarantees inherent in the prohibition of arbitrary detention, two other guarantees remain particularly important. On the one hand, the right of non-national detainees to consular access is a well-established norm of customary international law as notably codified in Article 36 of the 1963 Vienna Convention on Consular Relations.[323] On the other hand, the conditions of detention must respect human dignity in conformity with the absolute prohibition of torture or inhuman or degrading treatment or punishment.[324] As restated by the

---

[319] CMW and CRC, 'Joint General Comment No 4/23' (n 318) para 11. According to the two UN Committees, these solutions should 'not imply any kind or child of family deprivation of liberty and should be based on an ethic of care and protection, not enforcement' with the first objective of case resolution in taking due account of their best interest and development: ibid para 12. See also IACtHR, *Rights and Guarantees of Children in the Context of Migration* (n 310) paras 158–60.

[320] CRC Committee, 'Report of the 2012 Day of General' (n 317) paras 18 and 35–36. See also UN Human Rights Council, 'Study of the Office of the United Nations High Commissioner for Human Rights on Challenges and Best Practices in the Implementation of the International Framework for the Protection of the Rights of the Child in the Context of Migration' (5 July 2010) UN Doc A/HRC/15/29, paras 54 and 55. On the types of alternatives to detention for migrant children, see further: UNHCR, 'Options for Governments on Care Arrangements and Alternatives to Detention for Children and Families', Options Paper 1, Global Strategy Beyond Detention 2014–19 (2015); IDC, *Captured Childhood: Introducing a New Model to Ensure the Rights and Liberty of Refugee, Asylum Seeker and Irregular Migrant Children Affected by Immigration Detention* (IDC 2012).

[321] Besides the material already mentioned in n 263 and 265, see for instance: Human Rights Council, A/HRC/7/4 (n 301) para 67.

[322] HRC, *A v Australia* (n 311) para 9.5; HRC, *Shams and Others v Australia* (n 314) para 7.3; HRC, *Danyal Shafiq v Australia* (n 299) para 7.4; ECtHR, *Chahal v The United Kingdom* ECHR 1996-V, para 127; *Dougoz v Greece* App No 40907/98 (ECtHR 2001) para 61; IACtHR, *Vélez Loor v Panama* (n 309) para 142–43.

[323] Among other restatements of its customary law nature, see, US Department of State, *Consular Notification and Access: Instructions for Federal, State, and Local Law Enforcement and Other Officials Regarding Foreign Nationals in the United States and the Rights of Consular Officials to Assist Them* (3rd edn, Department of State Publication 2010) 46; IACtHR, *The Right to Information on Consular Assistance in the Framework of the Guarantees of the Due Process of Law* (Advisory Opinion) OC-16/99 Series A No 19 (IACtHR, 1 October 1999), as requested by the United Mexican States. The right to consular assistance has been most notably reaffirmed in Art 16(5) of the 2000 Migrants' Smuggling Protocol (n 233) and Art 16(7) of the ICRMW (n 298).

[324] Besides the prohibition of torture, inhumane and degrading treatment, all general human rights treaties with the exception of the ECHR recall that 'all persons deprived of their liberty shall be treated with humanity and with respect for the inherent dignity of the human person'. See ICCPR (n 263) art 10; ACHR (n 49) art 5(2); ACHPR (n 50) art 5; and Arab Charter on Human Rights (n 52) art 20.

ICJ in the *Diallo* case, '[t]here is no doubt […] that the prohibition of inhuman and degrading treatment is among the rules of general international law which are binding on states in all circumstances, even apart from any treaty commitments'.[325] This prohibition is absolute, and thereby plainly applicable to immigration detention even in situations of 'an increasing influx of migrants'.[326] As a result, conditions of detention may reach the level of torture, inhuman or degrading treatment or punishment due to, for instance, overcrowding of the place of detention, absence of privacy, lack of appropriate ventilation, insufficient provision of food or water, impossibility of outdoor exercise, or unsanitary/unhygienic conditions.[327]

Due process guarantees and the removal of undocumented migrants

Besides the detention of immigrants, international law provides specific due process guarantees governing expulsion. These procedural guarantees are notably enshrined in Article 13 of the ICCPR:

An alien lawfully in the territory of a State Party to the Present Covenant may be expelled therefrom only in pursuance of a decision reached in accordance with law and shall, except where compelling reasons of national security otherwise require, be allowed to submit the reasons against his expulsion and to have his case reviewed by, and be represented for the purpose before, the competent authority or a person or persons especially designated by the competent authority.

These procedural guarantees have been restated in various instruments[328] and are arguably part of customary international law.[329] Their benefit is however circumscribed to 'aliens lawfully in the territory'[330] of the host state and has thus no impact on the removal process of undocumented migrants.

---

[325] *Ahmadou Sadio Diallo* (n 101) para 87. For similar acknowledgements, see for instance *Prosecutor v Jokić* (Trial Chamber Judgment) IT-02-60 (17 January 2005) para 587; *Abebe-Jira v Negero*, 72 F.3d 844 (11th Cir 1996), cert denied, 519 US 830, 117 SCt 961 (1996); *Najarro de Sanchez v Banco Central de Nicaragua*, 770 F2d 1385 (5th Cir 1985); *Paul v Avril*, 901 F Supp. 330 (SD Fla 1994); *Xuncax v Gramajo*, 886 F. Supp 162 (D Mass 1995). On the peremptory nature of the prohibition of torture, see also *Prosecutor v Furundzija* (Judgment) IT-95-17/1 (10 December 1998) para 144; HRC 'General Comment No 24' (n 298) para 10; *Al-Adsani v United Kingdom* App no 35763/97 (ECtHR, 2001) para 61.

[326] See ECtHR, *Khlaifia and Others v Italy* (n 308) para 184; and *MSS v Belgium and Greece* ECHR 2001-I 121, para 223.

[327] For immigration detention cases, see most notably the following three judgments of the Grand Chamber: ECtHR, *Khlaifia and Others v Italy* (n 308) paras 170–77; *Tarakhel v Switzerland* App No 29217/12 (ECtHR, 4 November 2014) paras 93–122; and *MSS v Belgium and Greece* (n 326) paras 223–34.

[328] Convention Relating to the Status of Refugees (n 45) art 32; Convention Relating to the Status of Stateless Persons (n 46) art 31; ICRMW (n 298) art 22; Protocol I (n 283) art 1 as amended by Protocol II (n 283); ACHR (n 49) art 22(6); ACHPR (n 50) art 12(5); Arab Charter on Human Rights (n 52) art 26(2); and CIS Convention (n 51) art 25(3). See also among non-binding instruments UNGA, 'Declaration on the Human Rights of Individuals Who Are Not Nationals of the Country in which They Live' (13 December 1985) UN Doc A/RES/40/144, art 7.

[329] Plender, *International Migration Law* (n 87) 472.

[330] The only treaty which does not explicitly require a lawful presence within the territory is the ICRMW (n 298).

A more relevant norm can be found in the absolute prohibition of collective expulsion. This prohibition has been endorsed in a substantial number of instruments regardless of the (un)lawful presence of non-nationals.[331] It thus provides a crucial guarantee for undocumented migrants subjected to forced removals. The prohibition of collective expulsion is all the more significant since it arguably binds all states regardless of their ratification of the relevant treaties. There are indeed strong reasons for considering that collective expulsion violates customary international law.[332] In particular, states' participation in the relevant treaties is broad and representative: as of October 2018, 142 states from various regions of the world have ratified at least one of the conventions explicitly prohibiting collective expulsion. More decisively, even states which have not ratified one of these treaties have endorsed the prohibition of collective expulsion. For instance, both China and Iran declared that 'collective expulsion was prohibited under international law since in most cases such action was discriminatory'.[333] This line of argument is probably the most convincing: a collective expulsion will rarely be—if ever—in conformity with the customary law principle of non-discrimination.[334]

---

[331] ICRMW (n 298) art 22(1); ACHR (n 49) art 22(9); ACHPR (n 50) art 12(5); ECHR (n 264) art 4; Arab Charter on Human Rights (n 52) art 26(2); CIS Convention (n 51) art 25(4); EU Charter (n 48) art 19(1). See also Fourth Geneva Convention (n 40) art 49. Furthermore, though not explicitly mentioned in the ICCPR, the HRC considers that such prohibition is implicit in Article 13 because 'it entitles each alien to a decision in his own case and, hence, Article 13 would not be satisfied with laws or decisions providing for collective or mass expulsions', see HRC 'General Comment No 15' (n 266) para 10. Among other soft law restatements, see also Global Compact for Safe, Orderly and Regular Migration (n 253), paras 24(a) and 37; UN Committee on the Elimination of Racial Discrimination (CERD) 'General Recommendation 30: Discrimination against Non-Citizens' (2004) UN Doc CERD/C/64/Misc.11/rev.3, para 26; International Law Association, 'Declaration of Principles of International Law on Mass Expulsion' 62nd International Law Association (Seoul, 23–30 August 1986); and Council of Europe, Committee of Ministers, 'Twenty Guidelines on Forced Return' (2005) Guideline 3.

[332] For a similar account, see notably *Short v Iran* (1987) 16 Iran-USCTR 76; Plender, *International Migration Law* (n 87) 476; J-M Henckaerts, *Mass Expulsion in Modern International Law and Practice* (Martinus Nijhoff 1995) 45; DE Arzt, 'Existing and Emerging International Human Rights and Humanitarian Law Standards Outlawing Forcible Population Transfer and Settler Implantation' Expert Seminar on the Human Rights Dimensions of Population Transfer, Including the Implantation of Settlers and Settlements (14 February 1997) UN Doc HR/SEM.1/PT/1997/WP.5, 11; A Cassese, *International Law* (OUP 2005) 121; Human Rights Council 'Promotion and Protection of All Human Rights, Civil, Political, Economic, Social and Cultural Rights, Including the Right to Development' Report of the Special Rapporteur on the Human Rights of Migrants, Jorge Bustamante (25 February 2008) UN Doc A/HRC/7/12, para 36; R Cholewinski, 'The Human and Labor Rights of Migrants: Visions of Equality' (2007–2008) 22 Geo Immigr LJ 177, 195; G Cornelisse, *Immigration Detention and Human Rights: Rethinking Territorial Sovereignty* (Brill 2010) 178; International Commission of Jurists, *Migration and International Human Rights Law, Practitioners Guide No 6* (International Commission of Jurists 2011) 138. The Special Rapporteur of the International Law Commission has instead argued that the prohibition of collective expulsion is a general principle of law, see ILC 'Third Report on the Expulsion of Aliens, M Kamto, Special Rapporteur' (19 April 2007) UN Doc A/CN.4/581, 37. Among the rare authors denying the existence of a customary norm prohibiting collective expulsion, see R Perruchoud, 'L'expulsion en masse d'étrangers' (1988) XXXIV AFDI 677, 682.

[333] UNGA, 'Report of the International Law Commission on the work of its fifty-seventh session' Summary record of the 11 Meeting (23 November 2005) UN Doc A/C.6/60/SR.11, see particularly para 54 for China and para 84 for Iran.

[334] See also A de Zayas, 'Collective Expulsion in the Light of International Law' (1977) 24 AWR Bulletin 268; and Henckaerts, *Mass Expulsion* (n 332) 45–47.

The impact of the prohibition of collective expulsion is quite straightforward for states. It requires that each and every expulsion decision be taken on the basis of an individual assessment, irrespective of migration status. This requirement flows from the very definition of collective expulsion which does not depend upon the number of individuals collectively expulsed, but focuses on the absence of an individual examination of the situation of the migrants in the concerned group:[335]

[A]ny measure compelling aliens, as a group, to leave a country, except where such a measure is taken on the basis of a reasonable and objective examination of the particular case of each individual alien of the group. Moreover, the fact that a number of aliens receive similar decisions does not lead to the conclusion that there is a collective expulsion when each person concerned has been given the opportunity to put arguments against his expulsion to the competent authorities on an individual basis.[336]

Furthermore, the prohibition of collective expulsion binds states as soon as migrants fall within their jurisdiction, including in interception cases on the high seas,[337] and applies irrespective of the denomination of the act of removal as long as it consists in 'driv[ing] away from a place'.[338] With such a generic understanding of expulsion, refusal of entry with concomitant collective removal falls within the purview of the prohibition.[339] Likewise, the prohibition of collective expulsion applies even in cases of mass influx.[340] The large number of irregular migrants arriving in a country and any related challenges it may raise for the state have indeed no bearing on states' obligation.[341]

Besides the specific prohibition of collective expulsion, a more controversial issue concerns the right to judicial review of an expulsion order. Guy S Goodwin-Gill argues that such a right is required under general international law even for expulsion

---

[335] See for instance IACtHR, *Nadege Dorzema et al v Dominican Republic* (Judgment) Series C No 251 (IACtHR, 24 October 2012) para 172 citing ECtHR, *Hirsi Jamaa and Others v Italy* ECHR 2012-II 97, para 184.

[336] ECtHR, *Andric v Sweden*, App No 45917/99 (ECtHR, 23 February 1999) para 1. For subsequent reaffirmations of this definition, see most notably: *Conka v Belgium* ECHR 2002-I 93, para 59; *Sultani v France* ECHR 2007-IV 69, para 81; *Georgia v Russia (I)* ECHR 2014-IV 109, para 175; *Sharifi and Others v Italy and Greece*, App No 16643/09 (ECtHR, 21 October 2014) para 210; ECtHR, Grand Chamber, *Khlaifia and Others v Italy* (n 308) para 238; and *ND and NT v Spain*, App nos 86751/15 and 8697/15 (ECtHR, 3 October 2017) paras 98 and 99. For similar definitions coined by other human rights bodies, see: IACtHR, *Report on Terrorism and Human Rights*, OEA/SER.L/V/II.116, Doc 5 rev 1 corr (22 October 2002) para 404; Inter-American Commission of Human Rights, *Andrea Mortlock v United States*, Report No 63/08, Case No 12.534 (25 July 2008) para 78.

[337] ECtHR, *Hirsi Jamaa and Others v Italy* (n 335) paras 169–80.

[338] ibid para 174 referring to the *travaux préparatoires* of art 4 of Protocol No 4.

[339] ECtHR, *Khlaifia and Others v Italy* (n 308) para 243.

[340] See for instance Human Rights Council, 'Principles and Practical Guidance on the Protection of the Human Rights of Migrants in Vulnerable Situations, Report of the United Nations High Commissioner for Human Rights' (7 February 2018) UN Doc A/HRC/37/34/Add.1, Principle 6, Guideline 2; and Institute of International Law, *Mass Migration, Final Resolution* (9 September 2017) art 11; and ILC, 'Draft Articles on the Expulsion of Aliens' (2014) draft art 9.

[341] See for instance ECtHR, *Khlaifia and Others v Italy* (n 308) para 241, where the Grand Chamber noted that 'problems with managing migratory flows or with the reception of asylum-seekers cannot justify recourse to practices which are not compatible with the Convention or the Protocols thereto'; citing ECtHR, *Hirsi Jamaa and Others v Italy* (n 335) para 179. See also ECtHR, *ND and NT v Spain* (n 336) para 101; *Georgia v Russia (I)* (n 336) para 177.

proceedings against undocumented migrants,[342] whereas for Maurice Kamto the right to an individual appeal against an expulsion order only exists under customary law for migrants who are lawfully within the territory of states.[343] By contrast, Richard Plender considers in categorical terms that 'there is no general obligation in international law to afford a judicial review of the merits of a decision to expel an alien'.[344]

The contradictory views of scholars fairly reflect the absence of any clear-cut norm of customary international law in this field. Furthermore, the treaty law-related practice does not provide a uniform pattern for substantiating the existence of a customary right to judicial review of an expulsion order. The applicability of the right to fair trial to the expulsion process has raised diverging interpretations and its impact accordingly varies from one treaty to another. Under both the ACHR and the ACHPR, the right to fair trial has been construed by their respective treaty bodies as applicable to the deportation process of undocumented migrants.[345] Unlike the Inter-American Court and the African Commission, the Human Rights Committee[346] and the ECtHR[347] consider that the right to a fair trial does not apply to decisions on entry, stay, and expulsion of aliens on the disputable ground that they do not concern the determination of civil rights or criminal obligations under the meaning of their respective provisions.

Irrespective of the controversies surrounding the applicability of the right to a fair trial to expulsion, the right to an effective review offers a firmer avenue for ensuring procedural guarantees to undocumented migrants. All human rights treaties, including the ICCPR and the ECHR, acknowledge the right to an effective review.[348]

---

[342] Goodwin-Gill, *International Law* (n 272) 262 and 280.

[343] ILC 'Sixth Report on the Expulsion of Aliens Submitted by Mr. Maurice Kamto Special Rapporteur' (9 July 2010) UN Doc A/CN.4/625/Add.2 and (28 May 2010) UN Doc A/CN.4/625/Add.1, 7 and 15–16.

[344] Plender, *International Migration Law* (n 87) 472. He nevertheless adds that 'there is, however, some support for the proposition that a decision to deport an alien from a territory in which he is lawfully present is arbitrary, save where there are overwhelming considerations of national security to the contrary, unless he is informed of the allegations against him and is afforded an opportunity to advance reasons against his deportation, before some competent authority independent of those proposing to deport him'.

[345] IACtHR, *Juridical Condition and Rights of Undocumented Migrants* (Advisory Opinion) OC-18/03 Series A no 18 (IACtHR, 17 September 2003) paras 124–27; *Vélez Loor v Panama* (n 309) para 146; *Riebe Star and Others v Mexico*, Inter-American Court of Human Rights Report No 49/99 (13 April 1999) para 71. With regard to the interpretation of the African Commission, see in particular *Rencontre africaine pour la défense des droits de l'homme (RADDH) v Zambia* (1996) Communication No 71/92, 60, para 29; *Institute for Human Rights and Development in Africa (IHRDA) v Republic of Angola* (2008) Communication No 292/2004, para 59.

[346] HRC 'General Comment No 32: Article 14: Right to Equality before Courts and Tribunals and to a Fair Trial' (23 August 2007) UN Doc CCPR/C/GC/32, para 17. See also HRC, *Ernst Zundel v Canada* (14 May 2006) Communication No 1341/2005 UN Doc CCPR/C/89/D/1341/2005, paras 6.7 and 6.8.; and HRC, *Mario Esposito v Spain* (30 May 2007) Communication No 1359/2005 UN Doc CCPR/C/89/D/1359/2005, para 7.6.

[347] *Maaouia v France* App no 39652/98 (ECtHR, 5 October 2000) para 40.

[348] Although the right to an effective remedy can only be invoked in conjunction with other protected rights and freedoms under the relevant treaty, it is sometimes alleged as being part of customary international law, see R Pisillo Mazzeschi, 'The Relationship between Human Rights and the Rights of Aliens and Immigrants' in U Fastenrath et al (eds), *From Bilateralism to Community Interest: Essays in Honour of Judge Bruno Simma* (OUP 2011) 562.

According to the prevailing interpretation of these last instruments, migrants are entitled to challenge a refusal of admission and/or removal when there is an arguable claim of violation of their rights under the relevant treaties (including the right to family and private life, as well as the prohibition of torture, or inhuman or degrading treatment or punishment, and the correlative duty of *non-refoulement*).[349]

In sum, although the right to judicial review against an expulsion order is currently not part of customary international law, treaty law offers largely similar guarantees under general human rights instruments.[350] The importance of these procedural guarantees has been notably reaffirmed in the Global Compact for Migration, according to which states 'commit [...] to guarantee due process, individual assessment and effective remedy'.[351]

Enforcement of immigration control and the right to human dignity

In parallel with the rules governing detention and removal of undocumented migrants, general international law retains a residual role for channelling the enforcement of immigration control. The most important norm in this field is clearly the prohibition of torture or inhuman or degrading treatment or punishment. States' obligation to carry out refusals of admission and forced removals with due regard to the human dignity of migrants has been further reiterated in a substantial number of international instruments and case-law.[352] In some exceptional circumstances, forced removal and refusal of admission may also constitute a degrading treatment per se. This may notably happen because of the severe medical condition of the immigrant and the lack of appropriate treatment upon removal.[353] Similarly,

---

[349] See, for instance, HRC, *Maksudov and others v Kyrgyzstan* (16 July 2008) Communication No 1461 UN Doc CCPR/C/93/D/1461, 1462, 1476 and 1477/2006, para 12.7; HRC, *Al Zery v Sweden* (10 November 2006) Communication No 1416/2005 UN Doc CCPR/C/88/D/1416/2005, para 11.8; and ECtHR, *GHH and others v Turkey* ECHR 2000-VIII 317, paras 34 and 36.

[350] One should further add that the right to an effective remedy is also guaranteed by EU law. See in particular Council Directive 2001/40/EC of 28 May 2001 on the mutual recognition of decisions on the expulsion of third country nationals [2001] OJ L 149/34, art 4; Council Directive 2003/109/EC of 25 November 2003 concerning the status of third-country nationals who are long-term residents [2004] OJ L 16-44 art 12(4); and Directive 2008/115/EC of the European Parliament and of the Council of 16 December 2008 on common standards and procedures in Member States for returning illegally staying third-country nationals [2008] OJ L 348/98-348/107, art 13.

[351] Global Compact for Safe, Orderly and Regular Migration (n 253) para 37. See also: ibid para 27(c).

[352] See for instance Convention on International Civil Aviation (adopted 7 December 1944, entered into force 4 April 1947) 15 UNTS 295 (Chicago Convention), and especially Annex 9 to International Civil Aviation Organization (ICAO) 'International Standards and Recommended Practices' (12th edn, 2005) para 5.2.1; Council of Europe (n 331) Guideline 17; EU Return Directive (n 128) art 8(3); and Regulation (EU) 2016/399 the European Parliament and the Council of 9 March 2016 on a Union Code on the rules governing the movement of persons across borders (Schengen Borders Code) (n 129). With regard to the numerous arbitral cases, see also *Bofolo Case* (Netherlands-Venezuela) (1903) Mixed Claims Commission, 10 RIAA (1903), and *Maal Case* in ibid 730.

[353] See in particular Committee against Torture, *GRB v Sweden* (15 May 1998) Communication No 93/1997 UN Doc CAT/C/20/D/83/1997, para 6.7; *D v The United Kingdom* ECHR 1997-III 805, para 54; and *Paposhvili v Belgium* App no 41738/10 (ECtHR, 13 December 2016) paras 181–93.

[T]he repeated expulsion of an individual, whose identity was impossible to establish, to a country where his admission is not guaranteed, may raise an issue under Article 3 of the [European] Convention […]. Such an issue may arise, *a fortiori*, if an alien is, over a long period of time, deported repeatedly from one country to another without any country taking measures to regularise his situation.[354]

The refusal of admission based on racial grounds also constitutes a degrading treatment in violation of international law.[355] One should further underline in this regard that the prohibition of racial discrimination is part of general international law.[356] As a result of this fundamental norm, immigration control cannot be carried out in such a way as to target only persons with specific physical or ethnic characteristics.

The right to life constitutes another well-established norm of customary international law[357] which sadly retains its relevance in the field of migration. The most obvious instance relies on the time-honoured customary duty to rescue persons in distress at sea, as notably codified in Article 98 of the 1982 Convention of the Law of the Sea.[358] More generally, due respect for the right to life requires that coercive measures to carry out forced removals of undocumented migrants be used as a last resort and be strictly proportionate to the resistance of the returnees.[359] States are

---

[354] *Harabi v the Netherlands* App no 10798/84 (ECtHR, 1986) 112. See also in this sense African Commission on Human and Peoples' Rights, *John K Modise v Bostwana* Communication No 97/9 3(6 November 2000) 97/93_14AR, para 91.

[355] See especially the well-known case of the European Commission on Human Rights, *East African Asians v United Kingdom* App nos 4403/70–4419/79, 4422/70, 4423/70, 4416/70, 4417/70, 4418/70 (10 October 1970) reprinted in 3 EHRR 76 (1973) DR 78-B, 62. See also, with regard to discrimination based on sex, HRC, *Aumeeruddy-Cziffra and 19 other Mauritian women v Mauritius* (9 April 1981) Communication No 35/1978 UN Doc CCPR/C/12/D/35/1978.

[356] The legal nature of this principle is detailed in section 2.3 of this chapter.

[357] The prohibition of arbitrary deprivation of life is frequently asserted as a norm of *jus cogens*. See for instance HRC 'General Comment No 24' (n 298) para 10; IACtHR, *Case of the 'Street Children' (Villagrán-Morales et al) v Guatemala* (Merits, Reparations, and Costs) Series C No 63 (IACtHR, 19 November 1999), see particularly the opinion of Judges Cançado Trindade and Abreu-Burelli, para 2; IAComHR, *Victims of the Tugboat '13 de Marzo' v Cuba,* Report No 47/96 Case 11.436 (IAComHR, 16 October 1996) para 79; and *Youssef Nada v State Secretariat for Economic Affairs, Federal Department of Economic Affairs* (14 November 2007) ILDC 361 (CH 2007) (Swiss Federal Supreme Court, First Public Law Chamber).

[358] Article 98(a) and (b) of the Convention on the Law of the Sea (adopted 10 December 1982, entered into force 16 November 1994) 1833 UNTS 3 (168 States Parties). See also Article 1.3.2 International Convention on Maritime Search and Rescue (adopted 27 April 1979, entered into force, 25 March 1980) 405 UNTS 97 (as amended by IMO, Resolution MSC.70 (69), Amendments to the International Convention on maritime search and rescue of 27 April 1979, 18 May 1998) (SAR Convention) (112 States Parties); Chapter V, International Convention for the Safety of Life at Sea (adopted 1 November 1974, entered force, 25 May 1980) 1184 UNTS 3 (as amended by IMO Resolution MSC. 153(78), Amendments to the SOLAS Convention, 20 May 2004) (SOLAS Convention) (164 States Parties). Among many other acknowledgements of the customary nature of this basic obligation, see, inter alia, UN Commission on International Law, 'Commentary on Draft Article 12 of the United Nations Convention on the High Seas' (1956) UN Doc. A/3179; International Maritime Organization (IMO), 'Resolution MSC.167(78), Guidelines on the Treatment of Persons Rescued at Sea' (20 May 2004) para 6; UNHCR, 'Mapping Disembarkation Options: Towards Strengthening Cooperation in Managing Irregular Movements by Sea' Background Paper (4 March 2014).

[359] These well-established obligations deriving from the right to life have been restated in the specific context of forced return by several instruments. See for instance, Council of Europe (n 331)

further bound to open an independent and impartial inquiry on any excessive use of force, as well as to prosecute and punish the perpetrators and offer compensation to the victim's family.[360]

Whether grounded on treaty law or customary law, the rights of migrants are inherent in the universality of human rights and they shall be respected accordingly. As restated by the Global Compact for Migration, 'respect for the rule of law, due process and access to justice are fundamental to all aspects of migration governance. This means that the State, public and private institutions and entities, as well as persons themselves are accountable to laws that are publicly promulgated, equally enforced and independently adjudicated, and which are consistent with international law.'[361]

2.3 The Sojourn of Migrants

Although customary international law is far from being indifferent to the limits imposed on states in carrying out immigration control, its most substantial impact concerns the sojourn of migrants in their host states. As a result of a longstanding evolution described in Chapter 1, human rights law has become the primary source for protecting non-citizens. This extensive body of law has substantially eroded the traditional *summa divisio* based on the distinction between nationals and nonnationals. This evolution is congenital to human rights which are by definition inherent in human dignity and they accordingly apply to all persons as human beings.

The Universal Declaration of Human Rights and the two UN Covenants proclaim in the first recital of their preamble that human rights derive from the 'recognition of the inherent dignity and of the equal and inalienable rights of all members of the human family'. Similarly, the preamble of the American Convention on Human Rights recalls in more explicit terms that, 'the essential rights of man are not derived from one's being a national of a certain state, but are based upon attributes of the human personality'.[362] This philosophical and normative underpinning is reinforced by the principle of non-discrimination which is solidly anchored in general international law (section 2.3.1), although its impact on non-nationals requires further scrutiny (section 2.3.2).

Guideline 19; EU Return Directive (n 128) art 8(4); and International Air Transport Association and Control Authorities Working Group, 'Guidelines on Deportation and Escort' in 'ECAC Policy Statement in the field of Civil Aviation Facilitation' (9th edn, 2003) ECAC.CEAC Doc No 30, part I, annex D, para 8.

[360] For a restatement of these basic obligations in connection to the death of a Nigerian citizen, when he was being forcibly repatriated by air from Switzerland, see Committee against Torture, 'Concluding Observations: Switzerland' (25 May 2010) UN Doc CAT/C/CHE/CO/6, para 16.

[361] Global Compact for Safe, Orderly and Regular Migration (n 253) para 15.

[362] ACHR (n 49) preamble para 2.

2.3.1 The principle of non-discrimination in customary international law

The principle of non-discrimination is the cornerstone upon which the whole edifice of human rights protection is built. It permeates human rights law as a founding—if not existential—axiom. As David Weissbrodt recalls, 'the architecture of international human rights law is built on the premise that all persons, by virtue of their essential humanity, should equally enjoy all human rights'.[363] The prohibition of discrimination is the only human right specifically mentioned in the UN Charter, thereby binding every Member State. As proclaimed in its Article 1(3), one major purpose of the UN consists 'in promoting and encouraging respect for human rights and for fundamental freedoms for all without distinction as to race, sex, language, or religion'.[364] The Universal Declaration of Human Rights recalls in its Article 2 that: 'Everyone is entitled to all the rights and freedoms set forth in this Declaration, without distinction of any kind, such as race, colour, sex, language, religion, political or other opinion, national or social origin, property, birth or other status.'

Its Article 7 further restates that 'All are equal before the law and are entitled without any discrimination to equal protection of the law.' The notions of 'equality' and 'non-discrimination' are frequently described as the positive and negative statement of the same principle: the former requires that equals be treated equally, whereas the latter prohibits difference of treatment based on specific grounds.[365] Despite their apparent overlapping, their respective scope slightly diverges since equality before the law is an autonomous guarantee, whereas non-discrimination relates to the enjoyment of internationally recognized human rights.

Whether associated or not with equality before the law,[366] the principle of non-discrimination is embodied in all human rights treaties, be they concluded at the

---

[363] D Weissbrodt, *The Human Rights of Non-Citizens* (OUP 2008) 34. For further studies on the principle of non-discrimination, see CFJ Doebbler, *The Principle of Non-Discrimination in International Law* (CD Publishing 2007); N Lerner, *Group Rights and Discrimination in International Law* (2nd edn, Martinus Nijhoff 2003); W McKean, *Equality and Discrimination under International Law* (Clarendon Press 1983); M Bossuyt, *L'interdiction de la discrimination dans le droit international des droits de l'homme* (Bruylant 1976); EW Vierdag, *The Concept of Discrimination in International Law* (Martinus Nijhoff 1973).

[364] This is restated in several other key provisions of the UN Charter: Articles 13(1), 55, and 76.

[365] IACtHR, *Proposed Amendments to the Naturalization Provisions of the Constitution of Costa Rica* (Advisory Opinion) OC-4/84 Series A No 4 (IACtHR, 19 January 1984), see especially the separate opinion of Rodolfo E Piza (J) para 10, 'it appears clear that the concepts of equality and non-discrimination are reciprocal, like the two faces of one same institution. Equality is the positive face of non-discrimination. Discrimination is the negative face of equality.' For further developments on the two notions see D Moeckli, 'Equality and Non-Discrimination' in D Moeckli, S Shah, and S Sivakumaran (eds), *International Human Rights Law* (2nd edn, OUP 2013) 157–73; J Clifford, 'Equality' in D Shelton (ed), *The Oxford Handbook of International Human Rights Law* (OUP 2013) 420–45; M Craven, 'Non-Discrimination and Equality' in M Craven (ed), *The International Covenant on Economic, Social and Cultural Rights: A Perspective on Its Development* (Clarendon Press 1995) 153–93; AF Bayefsky, 'The Principle of Equality or Non-discrimination in International Law' (1990) 11(2) HRLJ 1–34; BG Ramcharan, 'Equality and Non-discrimination' in L Henkin (ed), *The International Bill of Rights* (n 100) 246–69.

[366] See essentially ICCPR (n 263) article 26; ICRPD (n 39) art 5; ACHR (n 49) art 24; Inter-American Convention Against All Forms of Discrimination and Intolerance (5 June 2013, not yet in force) OAS Treaty Series A No 69, arts 2 and 3; EU Charter (n 48) art 20; Arab Charter (n 52) art 11; CIS Convention (n 51) art 3; Protocol to the African Charter on Human and Peoples' Rights on the

regional level[367] or the universal one, including the widely ratified ICCPR and ICERD.[368] It has been further restated in many interstate declarations as 'a fundamental rule of international human rights law'[369] and 'a generally accepted and recognized principle of international law',[370] whereas violations thereof have been condemned as 'an affront to human dignity and a disavowal of the principles of the Charter of the United Nations'.[371]

Rights of Women in Africa (adopted 1 July 2003, entered into force 25 November 2005) reprinted in 1 Afr Hum Rts LJ 40 (Maputo Protocol) art 8; and African Union Convention for the Protection and Assistance of Internally Displaced Persons in Africa (adopted 23 October 2009, entered into force 6 December 2012) art 3(1)(d) (Kampala Convention) available at <https://au.int/sites/default/files/treaties/7796-treaty-0039_-_kampala_convention_african_union_convention_for_the_protection_and_assistance_of_internally_displaced_persons_in_africa_e.pdf> accessed 9 October 2018.

[367] ACHR (n 49) art 1; Additional Protocol to the American Convention on Human Rights in the Area of Economic, Social and Cultural Rights (adopted 17 November 1988, 16 November 1999) OAS Treaty Series A No 52 (Protocol of San Salvador) art 3; Inter-American Convention on the Prevention, Punishment and Eradication of Violence against Women (adopted 9 June 1994) OAS Treaty Series A No 61 (Convention of Belem Do Para) art 6; Inter-American Convention on the Elimination of All Forms of Discrimination against Person with Disabilities (adopted 8 June 1999, entered into force 14 September 2001) OAS Treaty Series A No 65, art 1(2); Inter-American Convention Against Racism, Racial Discrimination, and Related Forms of Intolerance (adopted 5 June 2013, entered into force 11 November 2017) OAS Treaty Series A No 68, art 1; Inter-American Convention Against All Forms of Discrimination and Intolerance (n 366) art 1; ECHR, as amended by Protocols Nos 11 and 14 (n 264) arts 1 and 14; Protocol No 12 to the European Convention for the Protection of Human Rights and Fundamental Freedoms (adopted 4 November 2000, entered into force 1 April 2005) ETS No 177, art 1; European Social Charter (n 285) art 19; EU Charter (n 48) art 21; ACHPR (n 50) art 2; Arab Charter (n 52) art 2; African Charter on the Rights and Welfare of the Child (n 263) art 3; Protocol to the African Charter on Human and Peoples' Rights on the Rights of Women in Africa (n 366) art 2; Kampala Convention (n 366) arts 3(1)(d), 5(1) and 9; CIS Convention (n 51) art 20(2).

[368] See also ICRPD (n 39) art 3(b); ICESCR (n 263) art 2(2); Convention on the Elimination of All Forms of Discrimination against Women (adopted 18 December 1979, entered into force 3 September 1981) 1249 UNTS 13 art 1; CRC (n 264) art 2; ICRMW (n 298) art 1; Convention relating to the Status of Refugees (n 45) art 3; Convention relating to the Status of Stateless Persons (n 46) art 3; ILO Convention C097: Migration for Employment Convention (Revised) (Convention concerning Migration for Employment (Revised 1949)) (adopted 32nd Conference Session Geneva 1 July 1949, entered into force 22 January 1952) 120 UNTS 71, art 6; ILO Convention C111: Discrimination (Employment and Occupation) Convention (Convention concerning Discrimination in Respect of Employment and Occupation) (adopted 42nd Conference Session Geneva 25 June 1958, entered into force 15 June 1960) 362 UNTS 31, arts 1–3; ILO Convention C143: Migrant Workers (Supplementary Provisions) Convention (Convention concerning Migrations in Abusive Condition and the Promotion of Equality of Opportunity and Treatment of Migrant Workers (adopted 60th Conference Session Geneva 24 June 1975, entered into force 9 December 1978) 1120 UNTS 324, arts 8 and 10; ILO Convention C168: Employment Promotion and Protection against Unemployment Convention (Convention concerning Employment Promotion and Protection against Unemployment (adopted 75th Conference Session Geneva 21 June 1988, entered into force 17 October 1991) 1654 UNTS 67, art 6; and UNESCO Convention against Discrimination in Education (adopted 14 December 1960, entered into force 22 May 1962) in *UNESCO Records of the General Conference* (UNESCO 1961) 119, art 1.

[369] Vienna Declaration and Programme of Action (adopted by the World Conference on Human Rights 14-25 June 1993) UN Doc A/CONF.157/23, I-15.

[370] UNESCO Declaration on Race and Racial Prejudice (adopted 27 November 1978) art 9(1).

[371] See Declaration on the Elimination of All Forms of Intolerance and of Discrimination Based on Religion or Belief in UNGA Res 36/55 (25 November 1981) UN Doc A/RES/36/55, art 3. For other restatements of the principle of non-discrimination in soft law instruments, see notably American Declaration of the Rights and Duties of Man (n 79) art II; Final Act of the International Conference on Human Rights (adopted in Teheran 13 May 1968) UN Doc A/CONF. 32/41 (Proclamation of Teheran) paras 8 and 11; and Cairo Declaration on Human Rights in Islam (n 80) art 1(a). See

Following this trend, the ICJ observed in its well-known Advisory Opinion on Namibia delivered in 1971 that 'to establish […] and to enforce, distinctions, exclusions, restrictions and limitations exclusively based on grounds of race, colour, descent or national or ethnic origin […] constitute[s] a denial of fundamental human rights' and 'is a flagrant violation of the purposes and principles of the Charter'.[372] The International Criminal Tribunal for the Former Yugoslavia has further concurred in acknowledging 'a firmly established principle of international law of equality before the law, which encompasses the requirement that there should be no discrimination in the enforcement or application of the law'.[373] In fact, non-discrimination is not only 'a basic and general principle relating to the protection of human rights' as restated by the Human Rights Committee;[374] it is also a fundamental guarantee of international humanitarian law notably endorsed in Common Article 3 of the four Geneva Conventions,[375] as well as in several other key provisions of Additional Protocols I and II.[376] Even more significantly, the principle of non-discrimination is recognized as a norm of customary international law applicable in both international and non-international armed conflicts.[377]

Quite predictably, the same observation equally applies in times of peace. As acknowledged by many scholars, the principle of non-discrimination is firmly embedded in customary international law.[378] It certainly represents one of the rarest

---

also Declaration on the Rights of Persons Belonging to National or Ethnic, Religious and Linguistic Minorities in UNGA Res 47/135 (18 December 1992) UN Doc A/RES/47/135 art 4(1); ASEAN Human Rights Declaration (n 81) art 2.

[372] *Legal Consequences for States of the Continued Presence of South Africa in Namibia (South West Africa) Notwithstanding Security Council Resolution 276* (Advisory Opinion) General List No 53 [1971], [16]–[54] para 131.

[373] *Prosecutor v Delalic* (Judgment) ICTY-IT-96-21-A (20 February 2001) para 605.

[374] HRC, 'General Comment No 18: Non-discrimination' in 'Compilation of General Comments and General Recommendations Adopted by Human Rights Treaty Bodies' (10 November 1989) UN Doc HRI/GEN/1/Rev.1 (1994) 26, para 1.

[375] See also Geneva Convention Relative to the Treatment of Prisoners of War (adopted 12 August 1949, entered into force 21 October 1950) 75 UNTS 136 (Third Geneva Convention) art 16; and Fourth Geneva Convention (n 40) art 13.

[376] See in particular Protocol I (n 283) art 75(1); and Article 2(1) of Protocol II (n 283).

[377] Henckaerts and Doswald-Beck, *Customary International Humanitarian Law* (n 284) 308.

[378] See among other acknowledgements of its customary law nature B Saul, D Kinley, and J Mowbray, *The International Covenant on Economic, Social and Cultural Rights. Commentary, Cases, And Materials* (OUP 2014) 176; M Weller and K Nobbs, *Political Participation of Minorities: A Commentary on International Standards and Practice* (OUP 2010) 98–99; D Shelton, 'Prohibited Discrimination in International Human Rights Law' in A Constantinides and N Zaiko (eds), *The Diversity of International Law: Essays in Honour of Professor Kalliopi K. Koufa*, (Martinus Nijhoff 2009) 273; D Moeckli, *Human Rights and Non-Discrimination in the War on Terror* (OUP 2008) 59; CFJ Doebbler, *The Principle of Non-Discrimination* (n 363) 11; S Besson, 'The Principle of Non-Discrimination in the Convention on the Rights of the Child' (2005) 13 Int'l J Child Rts 433, 440; Commission on Human Rights, 'The Concept and Practice of Affirmative Action, Preliminary Report Submitted by Mr. Marc Bossuyt, Special Rapporteur, in accordance with Sub-Commission Resolution 1998/5. Comprehensive Examination of Thematic Issues Relating to Racial Discrimination' (19 June 2000) UN Doc E/CN.4/Sub.2/2000/11, fn 36; H Hannum, 'The Status of the Universal Declaration of Human Rights in National and International Law' (1996) 25 Ga J Int'l & Comp L 287, 342; Lord Lester of Herne Hill, 'Non-Discrimination in International Human Rights Law' (1993) 19(4) CLB 1653, 1659; A Bayefsky, 'The Principle of Equality' (n 365) 19; Y Dinstein, 'Discrimination and International Human Rights' (1985) 15 Israel Yrbk Hum Rts 11; RB Lillich, 'Civil Rights' in T Meron (ed), *Human Rights in International Law*, vol 1 (OUP 1984) 115–70, see especially page 133; BG Ramcharan, 'Equality and

legal norms which have been unanimously approved by all UN Member States. Besides the vast array of multilateral treaties endorsing it and their widespread ratification, the principle of non-discrimination is commonly considered as a basic precept of any legal system and is thus endorsed in most constitutions in the world.

Furthermore, no state proclaims to have the right to discriminate individuals. They instead claim that this is a lawful difference of treatment which does not equate with an unlawful discrimination. Indeed, the prohibition of discrimination does not include (and preclude) all differences of treatment. According to the prevailing understanding of discrimination, a difference of treatment is not discriminatory when three cumulative conditions are fulfilled: the differentiation is reasonable, objective, and proportionate to achieve a legitimate aim.[379] From this angle, allegations of a lawful difference of treatment must be seen as a confirmation of the customary law prohibition of discrimination in line with the ICJ *dictum* in the well-known *Nicaragua* case quoted in section 2.1.2.

The Inter-American Court of Human Rights has gone one step further in affirming that, '[a]t the existing stage of the development of international law, the fundamental principle of equality and non-discrimination has entered the realm of *jus cogens*', because 'the whole legal structure of national and international public order rests on it and it is a fundamental principle that permeates all laws'.[380] This assertion, however, has raised some varying comments: although some authors acknowledged the peremptory nature of non-discrimination,[381]

Non-discrimination' in L Henkin (ed), *The International Bill of Rights* (n 100) 249; JP Humphrey, 'The Implementation of International Human Rights Law' (1978–1979) 24 NYL Sch L Rev 31, 32; MS McDougal, HD Lasswell, and L Chen, 'The Protection of Respect and Human Rights: Freedom of Choice and World Public Order' (1975) 24 Am UL Rev 919, 1068. More disputably, it has been sometimes argued that it was part of customary international law even before the Universal Declaration of Human Rights, see *Namibia Case* (n 372) 76, on the separate opinion of Ammoun J, 'One right which must certainly be considered a pre-existing binding customary norm which the Universal Declaration of Human Rights codified is the right to equality, which by common consent has ever since the remotest times been deemed inherent in human nature.'

[379] Among many other acknowledgements of this well-established definition, see for instance HRC, 'General Comment No 18' (n 374) para 13; UN Committee on Economic, Social and Cultural Rights (CESCR) 'General Comment No 20: Non-discrimination in Economic, Social and Cultural Rights (art 2, para 2, of the International Covenant on Economic, Social and Cultural Rights)' (2 July 2009) UN Doc E/C.12/GC/20, para 13; UN Committee on the Elimination of Racial Discrimination (CERD) 'General Recommendation XXX on Discrimination Against Non-citizens' (1 October 2002) UN Doc HRI/GEN/1/Rev.7/Add.1 (2004) para 4; *Case Relating to Certain Aspects of the Laws on the Use of Languages in Education in Belgium, European Commission of Human Rights v Belgium* 1 EHRR 252 (ECHR 1968) para 10; IACtHR, *Legal Status and Human Rights of the Child* (Advisory Opinion) OC-17/02 Series A No 17 (IACtHR, 2002) para 47; and IACtHR, *Proposed Amendments to the Naturalization Provisions of the Constitution of Costa Rica* (Advisory Opinion) OC-4/84 Series A No 4 (IACtHR, 1984) para 57.

[380] IACtHR, *Juridical Condition and Rights of Undocumented Migrants* (Advisory Opinion) OC-18/03 Series A No 18 (IACtHR, 17 September 2003) 99, para 101. For a comment of this important advisory opinion, see especially Dembour, *When Humans Become Migrants: Study of the European Court of Human Rights with an Inter-American Counterpoint* (n 310) 296–312; B Lyon, 'The Inter-American Court of Human Rights Defines Unauthorized Migrant Workers Rights for the Hemisphere: A Comment on Advisory Opinion 18' (2003–2004) 28 NYU Rev L & Soc Change 547.

[381] VD Degan, *Sources of International Law* (Martinus Nijhoff 1997) 232; T Einarsen, 'Discrimination and Consequences for the Position of Aliens' (1995) 64 Nord J Int'l L 429, 430; L Hannikainen,

others have been more sceptical of the statement of the Inter-American Court.[382]

This lack of consensus calls for one substantial caveat. At the current stage of international law, the fundamental principle of non-discrimination is part of *jus cogens* in the matter of race. Indeed, as notably acknowledged by the ILC,[383] the CERD,[384] and several UN Rapporteurs,[385] the prohibition of racial discrimination is a peremptory norm of general international law. This has been confirmed, implicitly at least, by the ICJ in its well-known *Barcelona Traction* Judgment of 1970:

When a State admits into its territory [...] foreign nationals, whether natural or juristic persons, it is bound to extend to them the protection of the law and assumes obligations concerning the treatment to be afforded them. These obligations, however, are neither absolute nor unqualified. In particular, an essential distinction should be drawn between the obligations of a State towards the international community as a whole, and those arising vis-à-vis another State in the field of diplomatic protection. By their very nature the former are the concern of all States. In view of the importance of the rights involved, all States can

Peremptory Norms (Jus Cogens) in International Law: Historical Development, Criteria, Present Status (Finnish Lawyers' Publishing Company 1988) 482; McKean, *Equality and Discrimination* (n 363) 283. See also OHCHR Regional Office for Europe, 'The European Union and International Human Rights Law' 24 available at <https://europe.ohchr.org/Documents/Publications/EU_and_International_Law.pdf> accessed 9 October 2018.

[382] See in particular S Sivakumaran, 'The Rights of Migrant Workers One Year on: Transformation or Consolidation?' (2004) 36 Geo J Int'l L 113, 136; A Bianchi, 'Human Rights and the Magic of Jus Cogens' (2008) 19(3) EJIL 491, 506–07; P Weckel, 'Chronique de la jurisprudence internationale. Court interaméricaine des droits de l'homme' (2004) 108 RGDIP 215, 236–37; C Laly-Chevalier, F Da Poïan, and H Tigroudja, 'Chronique de la jurisprudence de la Cour interaméricaine des droits de l'homme (2002–2004)' (2005) 62 RTDH 459, 464–68.

[383] See ILC, 'Fragmentation of International Law: Difficulties Arising from the Diversification and Expansion of International Law. Report of the Study Group of the International Law Commission' (18 July 2006) UN Doc A/CN.4/L.702, para 33; and ILC, 'Report of the International Law Commission on the Work of its Fifty-third Session' (2001) UNGAOR 56th session Supp No 10 UN Doc A/56/10, 112.

[384] UNGA 'Statement on Racial Discrimination and Measures to Combat Terrorism' in 'Report of the Committee on the Elimination of Racial Discrimination' Sixtieth session (4–22 March 2002) Sixty-first session (5–23 August 2002) UN Doc Supp No 18 (A/57/18) 107. This has been reaffirmed by members of the CERD on several occasions. See for instance, CERD 'Seventh to Ninth Periodic Reports of Switzerland: Consideration of Reports, Comments and Information submitted by States Parties under Article 9 of the Convention' in 'Summary Record of the 2283rd Meeting on 14 February 2014' (3 June 2014) UN Doc CERD/C/SR.2283, para 12 (Mr Diaconu); see also Mr Van Boven in CERD 'Fourteenth Periodic Report of the United Kingdom of Great Britain and Northern Ireland: Consideration of Reports, Comments and Information Submitted by States Parties under Article 9 of the Convention' in 'Summary Record of the 1186th Meeting on 3 March 1997' (6 March 1997) UN Doc CERD/C/SR.1186, para 47.

[385] See, for example, ECOSOC Permanent Forum on Indigenous Issues 'Study on the Impacts of the Doctrine of Discovery on Indigenous Peoples, Including Mechanisms, Processes and Instruments of Redress. Note by the Secretariat' (20 February 2014) UN Doc E/C.19/2014/3, para 4; Human Rights Council, 'Report of the Special Rapporteur on the Promotion and Protection of Human Rights and Fundamental Freedoms while Countering Terrorism, Martin Scheinin' (29 January 2007) UN Doc A/HRC/4/26, para 41. See also Commission on Human Rights, Sub-Commission on Prevention of Discrimination and Protection of Minorities, 'Globalization in the Context of Increased Incidents of Racism, Racial Discrimination and Xenophobia. Working paper submitted by J Oloka-Onyango in Accordance with Sub-Commission Decision 1998/104' (22 June 1999) UN Doc E/CN.4/Sub.2/1999/8, para 32.

be held to have a legal interest in their protection; they are obligations *erga omnes*. [...] Such obligations derive, for example, in contemporary international law, from the outlawing of acts of aggression, and of genocide, as also from the principles and rules concerning the basic rights of the human person, including protection from slavery and racial discrimination.[386]

Despite the obvious nuances between *erga omnes* obligations and norms of *jus cogens*,[387] racial discrimination is tellingly mentioned among other well-established peremptory norms, such as the prohibition of aggression and genocide.[388] Unsurprisingly, many scholars—including eminent authorities such as Brownlie,[389] Cassese,[390] and Dugard[391]—have observed that the prohibition of racial discrimination is a norm of *jus cogens*.[392] Among other states' acknowledgements,[393] as early as in 1978, the World Conference to Combat Racism and Racial Discrimination endorsed it as 'an imperative norm of the international community'[394] before the Durban Declaration reaffirmed in 2001 that 'no derogation from the prohibition of racial discrimination [...] is permitted'.[395]

The consequences of its *jus cogens* nature are quite straightforward: any rule that is contrary to the prohibition of racial discrimination is void *ab initio*, whether it is grounded on a treaty, a custom, or arguably a unilateral act of the state.[396] In addition to the usual consequences under the law of state responsibility, a serious

---

[386] *Case Concerning the Barcelona Traction, Light and Power Company, Limited (Belgium v Spain)* (Judgment) [1970] ICJ Rep 3 [32] paras 33–34.

[387] *Erga omnes* obligations overlap but do not automatically equate with norms of *jus cogens*. All peremptory norms are *erga omnes* but the reverse is not true: *erga omnes* obligations can also be based on treaty law and customary law.

[388] See also in this sense *Case Concerning Armed Activities on the Territory of the Congo (Democratic Republic of the Congo v Rwanda)* Jurisdiction and Admissibility (Judgment) [2006] ICJ Rep 6, para 78; *Application of the International Convention on the Elimination of All Forms of Racial Discrimination (Georgia v Russian Federation)* [2011] ICJ Rep 70, Dissenting Opinion by Judge Cancado Trindade, para 180.

[389] I Brownlie, *Principles of Public International Law* (7th edn, OUP 2008) 511.

[390] A Cassese, *International Law* (OUP 2005) 65.

[391] J Dugard, *International Law: A South African Perspective* (Juta 2011) 39.

[392] See also, among others, T Weatherall, *Jus Cogens: International Law and Social Contract* (CUP 2015) 240–41; De Schutter, *International Human Rights Law* (n 18) 65; A Aust, *Handbook of International Law* (2nd edn, CUP 2010) 10; Moeckli, *Human Rights and Non-Discrimination* (n 378) 67; J Rehman, *The Weaknesses in the International Protection of Minority Rights* (Martinus Nijhoff 2000) 104; TA Johnson 'A Violation of Jus Cogens Norms as an Implicit Waiver of Immunity under the Federal Sovereign Immunities Act' (1995) 19(2) Maryland Journal of International Law 259, 260.

[393] See, for instance, *South West Africa Case (Ethiopia v South Africa)* [1966] 4 ICJ Pleadings 493; UN Conference on the Law of treaties 'Summary of Records of the Plenary Meetings and of the Meetings of the Committee of the Whole' First session, 26 March–24 May 1968 in Vienna (1969) UN Doc A/CONF.39/11, 301–03; *Sarei v Rio Tinto*, PLC, 487 F 3d, 1193, 1202 (9th Cir 2007).

[394] UNGA 'Report of the World Conference to Combat Racism and Racial Discrimination' Geneva, 14-25 August 1978 (1979) UN Doc A/CONF.92/40, para 13, annex IC.

[395] UNGA 'Report of the World Conference against Racism, Racial Discrimination, Xenophobia and Related Intolerance' Durban, 31 August–8 September 2001 (2002) UN Doc A/CONF.189/12, see Declaration page 7.

[396] For further developments on the effects of *jus cogens*, see notably R Kolb, *Peremptory International Law—Jus Cogens: A General Inventory* (Bloomsbury Publishing 2015) 185–88; U Linderfalk, 'The Effect of Jus Cogens Norms: Whoever Opened Pandora's Box, Did You Ever Think About the Consequences?' (2007) 18(5) EJIL 853–71; C Focarelli, 'Promotional Jus Cogens: A Critical Appraisal of Jus Cogens' Legal Effects' (2008) 77 Nord J Int'l L 429–59; Cassese, *International Law* (n 390) 205–08.

breach of a peremptory norm triggers three specific effects: a duty of non-assistance in maintaining the situation created by the breach, a duty of non-recognition of the lawfulness of such a situation, and a duty of cooperation to bring to an end, through lawful means, the breach of the peremptory norm.[397]

2.3.2 Nationality, immigration status, and the principle of non-discrimination

As ICJ Judge Tanaka noted in the *West Africa Case* of 1966, 'although the existence of this principle [of non-discrimination] is universally recognized […], its precise content is not very clear'.[398] Its application to non-nationals is no exception. In contrast to several specialized treaties,[399] general human rights conventions do not explicitly mention nationality among the prohibited grounds of discrimination. They refer instead to 'national origin'. Although common sense would include nationality within the scope of national origin, the drafting history of the Universal Declaration suggests that 'the words "national origin" should be interpreted […] not in the sense of citizen of a state, but in the sense of national characteristics'.[400] This ground of non-discrimination was thus primarily conceived to prohibit discrimination between nationals who were born in the country and those who had become naturalized citizens.[401]

Yet, the absence of an explicit ground referring to nationality shall not be viewed as permitting discrimination between nationals and non-nationals in the enjoyment of human rights. According to both the drafting history and the wording of human

[397] ILC 'Article 41 of the Draft Articles on Responsibility of States for Internationally Wrongful Acts' in A/56/10 (n 383) 113; *Legal Consequences of the Construction of a Wall in the Occupied Palestinian Territory* (Advisory Opinion) [2004] ICJ Rep 136, para 159.

[398] *South West Africa Case* (n 393) 6. This is not peculiar to non-discrimination. The same observation can be done for many other well-established norms of general international law, such as the prohibition of the use of armed force and the longstanding debates on the exact content of 'armed attack' and 'self-defence'.

[399] See in particular, ICRMW (n 298) art 1; Inter-American Convention against All Forms of Discrimination and Intolerance (n 366) art 1; and UNESCO Convention (n 368) art 3(e). See also Convention Relating to the Status of Refugees (n 45) art 3 which refers to 'the country of origin' and thus, includes nationality as a prohibited ground. Some other treaties prohibit any form of discrimination without regard to a particular ground, for instance, ICRPD (n 39) art 3(b); African Union Convention for the Protection and Assistance of Internally Displaced Persons in Africa (n 366) arts 3(1) and (d); and Inter-American Convention on the Prevention, Punishment and Eradication of Violence against Women (n 367) art 6.

[400] Commission on Human Rights, Sub-Commission on the Prevention of Discrimination and the Protection of Minorities, 'Report Submitted to the Commission on Human Rights' First Session (6 December 1947) UN Doc E/CN.4/52, 5.

[401] See Commission on Human Rights, Sub-Commission on Prevention of Discrimination and Protection of Minorities, 'Summary Records of the Fifth Meeting' First Session (27 November 1947) UN Doc E/CN.4/SUB.2/SR.5 (1947) 9. Contrary to other representatives, the Australian delegate considered, however, that the notion of 'national origin' 'was synonymous with nationality, but […] it might also have a wider meaning', see ibid 7. This opinion was isolated and the drafting history of the Covenants confirmed the prevailing understanding of 'national origin'. See for instance UNGA Third Committee, 'Agenda Item 28. Draft International Covenants on Human Rights' (9 November 1955) UN Doc A/C.3/SR.657, paras 16 and 24.

rights treaties (with the terms 'such as' and 'or other status'), the prohibited grounds of discrimination are not exhaustive but merely illustrative.[402] As notably confirmed by the Human Rights Committee, it is clear that the ground of nationality falls under the rubric of 'other status' and is accordingly prohibited.[403] The European Court of Human Rights has further stressed that 'very weighty reasons would have to be put forward before the Court could regard a difference of treatment based exclusively on the ground of nationality as compatible with the Convention'.[404] In fact, virtually all treaty bodies have acknowledged nationality as a prohibited ground of discrimination.[405] This reflects today's common understanding of the principle of non-discrimination when applied to non-nationals.

Nonetheless, this well-established interpretation suffers from one important exception: according to Article 1(2) of the ICERD, '[t]his Convention shall not apply to distinctions, exclusions, restrictions or preferences made by a State Party to this Convention between citizens and non-citizens'.[406] The exact implications of this provision are unclear, since Articles 5 and 6 of the same Convention explicitly apply to 'everyone', whereas other provisions prohibit 'racial discrimination in all its forms' (Articles 2(1) & 4).[407] It has been argued that '[a]lthough the Article [1(2)] literally operates as a restriction on the Convention, it has not in practice operated as a limitation with great force'.[408] This has been confirmed by the interpretation of the CERD. Given the uncertainties surrounding this provision, the CERD adopted the General Recommendation XXX on Discrimination Against Non-Citizens in 2002 with a view to clarifying the responsibilities of States Parties. While referring to the human rights listed in Article 5 of the ICERD, the Committee observed that:

---

[402] See, for instance, Commission on Human Rights, E/CN.4/52 (n 400) 4; MJ Bossuyt, *Guide to the 'Travaux Préparatoires' of the International Covenant on Civil and Political Rights* (Martinus Nijhoff 1987) 486.

[403] HRC, *Ibrahima Gueye et al v France* (1989) Communication No 196/1985 UN Doc CCPR/C/35/D/196/1985, para 9.4. This observation has been done with regard to Article 26 but the same applies to Article 2. See also HRC, *Simunek v Czech Republic* (1995) Communication No 516/1992 UN Doc CCPR/C/54/D/516/1992; and HRC, *Adam v Czech Republic* (23 July 1996) Communication No 586/1994 UN Doc CCPR/C/57/D/586/1994.

[404] *Gaygusuz v Austria* ECHR 1996-IV para 42.

[405] See notably *International Federation for Human Rights, Inter-African Union for Human Rights, African Rencontre for Human Rights, National Organisation of Human Rights in Senegal and Malian Association of Human Rights v Angola*, Communication no 159/96 (African Commission on Human and People's Rights, 11 November 1997), para 18 as well as the other references from UN treaty bodies and the Inter-American Court of Human Rights quoted infra in this section.

[406] Article 1(3) also adds that 'Nothing in this Convention may be interpreted as affecting in any way the legal provisions of States Parties concerning nationality, citizenship or naturalization, provided that such provisions do not discriminate against any particular nationality.'

[407] The preamble of the Convention further acknowledges that 'all human beings are equal before the law and are entitled to equal protection of the law against any discrimination and against any in-citement to discrimination'. The ambiguity of Article 1(2) is exacerbated by the fact that, despite this provision, four States Parties felt obliged to express a reservation with regard to the treatment of aliens under the Convention. Monaco, Singapore, and Switzerland entered a specific reservation regarding the admission of foreigners to the labour market, whereas the UK considered that the Commonwealth Immigrants Acts of 1962 and 1968 or their application did not involve any racial discrimination under the definition given by Article 1(1).

[408] D Mahalic and JG Mahalic, 'The Limitation Provisions of the International Convention on the Elimination of All Forms of Racial Discrimination' (1987) 9(1) HRQ 74, 79.

Although some of these rights, such as the right to participate in elections, to vote and to stand for election, may be confined to citizens, human rights are, in principle, to be enjoyed by all persons. States parties are under an obligation to guarantee equality between citizens and non-citizens in the enjoyment of these rights to the extent recognized under international law.[409]

The CERD accordingly concludes that '[u]nder the Convention, differential treatment based on citizenship or immigration status will constitute discrimination if the criteria for such differentiation, judged in the light of the objectives and purposes of the Convention, are not applied pursuant to a legitimate aim, and are not proportional to the achievement of this aim'.[410] This interpretation did not raise major objections from States Parties and most of them routinely include non-citizens in their reports on the implementation of the ICERD. Thus, most of the practical effects of Article 1(2) have been largely neutralized by subsequent interpretation.[411]

As underlined by the CERD, such a narrow understanding of Article 1(2) flows from the premise that this provision must be construed so as to avoid undermining the basic prohibition of discrimination as recognized by international law.[412] Hence 'it should not be interpreted to detract in any way from the rights and freedoms recognized and enunciated in particular in the Universal Declaration of Human Rights, the International Covenant on Economic, Social and Cultural Rights and the International Covenant on Civil and Political Rights'.[413] Accordingly, although the exact meaning of Article 1(2) is still difficult to grasp with certainty, the general principle of non-discrimination incorporated in other human rights instruments remains unchanged and plainly applicable.

The impact of the principle of non-discrimination on the human rights of migrants

From the perspective of the ICCPR, the impact of non-discrimination is particularly straightforward when applied to non-citizens. Interpreting Article 2(1) of the Covenant, the Human Rights Committee underlined in its General Comment No 15 on the Position of Aliens under the Covenant that '[i]n general, the rights set forth in the Covenant apply to everyone, irrespective of reciprocity, and irrespective

[409] CERD 'General Recommendation XXX' (n 379) para 3.   [410] ibid para 4.
[411] Such an ambiguous provision has been rarely reiterated in subsequent instruments. On the contrary, the Inter-American Convention against All Forms of Discrimination and Intolerance makes clear in Article 1(1) that prohibited 'discrimination may be based on nationality [...]; migrant, refugee, repatriate, stateless or internally displaced status' among other grounds. Only the EU Racial Equality Directive Council Directive asserts in its Article 3(2) that 'this Directive does not cover difference of treatment based on nationality', see Council Directive 2000/43/EC of 29 June 2000 implementing the principle of equal treatment between persons irrespective of racial or ethnic origin [2000] OJ L 180, 22–26. However, a lawful difference of treatment based on nationality does not constitute an unlawful discrimination based on the same ground.
[412] CERD, 'General Recommendation XXX' (n 379) para 2.
[413] ibid. This is in line with the literal meaning of Article 1(2): by affirming that this specific convention does not apply to distinctions between citizens and non-citizens, it presupposes that this question is governed by other instruments.

of his or her nationality or statelessness. [...] Thus, the general rule is that each one of the rights of the Covenant must be guaranteed without discrimination between citizens and aliens.'[414]

The Human Rights Committee further delineated the rights of non-nationals deriving from the ICCPR. The list enumerated in its General Comment No 15 proves to be extensive:

Aliens thus have an inherent right to life, protected by law, and may not be arbitrarily deprived of life. They must not be subjected to torture or to cruel, inhuman or degrading treatment or punishment; nor may they be held in slavery or servitude. Aliens have the full right to liberty and security of the person. If lawfully deprived of their liberty, they shall be treated with humanity and with respect for the inherent dignity of their person. Aliens may not be imprisoned for failure to fulfil a contractual obligation. They have the right to liberty of movement and free choice of residence; they shall be free to leave the country. Aliens shall be equal before the courts and tribunals, and shall be entitled to a fair and public hearing by a competent, independent and impartial tribunal established by law in the determination of any criminal charge or of rights and obligations in a suit at law. Aliens shall not be subjected to retrospective penal legislation, and are entitled to recognition before the law. They may not be subjected to arbitrary or unlawful interference with their privacy, family, home or correspondence. They have the right to freedom of thought, conscience and religion, and the right to hold opinions and to express them. Aliens receive the benefit of the right of peaceful assembly and of freedom of association. They may marry when at marriageable age. Their children are entitled to those measures of protection required by their status as minors. In those cases where aliens constitute a minority within the meaning of Article 27, they shall not be denied the right, in community with other members of their group, to enjoy their own culture, to profess and practise their own religion and to use their own language. Aliens are entitled to equal protection by the law. There shall be no discrimination between aliens and citizens in the application of these rights. These rights of aliens may be qualified only by such limitations as may be lawfully imposed under the Covenant.[415]

The fundamental rights listed therein are not only applicable to non-citizens, many of them are considered as being part of customary international law.[416] Hence, the

---

[414] HRC 'General Comment No 15' (n 266) paras 1–2.

[415] ibid para 7. Needless to say that all the rights under the ICCPR have been reaffirmed by many other human rights treaties at both the regional and universal level.

[416] There is no room here for a detailed analysis of the customary law nature of the civil and political rights referred therein. Nonetheless, the HCR asserted the customary law nature of the prohibitions of slavery and of torture, cruel, inhuman, or degrading treatment or punishment, the right to life, the prohibition of arbitrarily arrest and detention, freedom of thought, conscience, and religion, the prohibition of national, racial, or religious hatred, the right to marry, or the right of minorities to enjoy their own culture, profess their own religion, or use their own language. See HRC 'General Comment No 24' (n 298) para 8. See also *Mary and Carrie Dann v United States Case 11.140* Report No 75/02 Doc 5 Rev 1 at 860 (IACtHR, 27 December 2002) para 163. See particularly, concurring opinion of Judge Malinverni in *Nada v Switzerland* ECHR 2012-V 115, para 20; American Institute, *Restatement (Third) of the Foreign Relations Law of the United States* (American Law Institute Publishers 1987). In addition to the numerous materials and references already mentioned in the previous sections, see notably RB Lillich, 'The Growing Importance of Customary International Human Rights Law' (1995–1996) 25 Ga J Int'l & Comp L 1, 25; H Hannum, 'The Status of the Universal Declaration of Human Rights in National and International Law' (1995) 6 Ga J Int'l & Comp L 287–397; L Henkin, *The Age of Rights* (Columbia University Press 1990) 19; MS McDougal, H Lasswell, and L-C Chen, *Human Rights and World Public Order* (Yale University Press 1980) 272; LB Sohn, 'The Human Rights Law of the Charter' (1977) 129 Tex Int'l LJ 129, 133.

general applicability of human rights to non-citizens, combined with the customary law nature of these rights, has the side effect of anchoring migrants' rights in customary international law. Thus, migrants' rights are universal and must be respected as such because migrants' rights are human rights.

However, this does not mean that all human rights automatically apply to migrants on the same footing as nationals. Some rights are limited to citizens only or at least to any persons—including non-citizens—who are lawfully within the territory of the state. While such rights are very few in numbers, their impact is both significant and representative of the stance of non-citizens under international law. The rights reserved to citizens concern primarily the right to vote and to be elected. This exclusion, in turn, highlights the structural vulnerability of non-citizens to the political power of host states. Likewise, although only two rights guaranteed by the ICCPR require a lawful presence within the territory, the two rights in question markedly govern the movement of persons within and across borders: a lawful presence is required for exercising the right to liberty of movement and freedom to choose one's residence within the territory (Article 12(1)), as well as for benefiting from due process guarantees governing expulsion from the territory (Article 13).[417]

The combination of these two provisions graphically exhibits the specificities and the limits of the legal status of migrants under contemporary international law: a non-citizen must be lawfully present within the territory of a state to be able to benefit from the right to liberty of movement and the freedom to choose residence; but, even if lawfully within the territory, he/she may still be deported from that territory provided that some basic conditions and procedural guarantees are fulfilled. This signals the ultimate feature of alienage. That being said, the requirement of a lawful presence highlights both the limits of human rights law concerning the right to liberty of movement and its potential with regard to the great majority of the other rights that are not subordinated to such a condition.

Literally speaking at least, all other human rights that do not require a lawful presence are presumably applicable irrespective of immigration status. Besides the very wording of the relevant rights, the general prohibition of discrimination based on 'other status' plainly covers the immigration status and the lack of proper documentation. In the case of *Bah v UK*, the European Court of Human Rights confirmed that immigration status can fall within the ambit of 'other status' as a prohibited ground of discrimination.[418] Although this specific case focused on a particular type of UK immigration status, the same conclusion should equally apply to the absence of proper documentation.[419] This is indeed the prevailing interpretation of human rights treaty bodies. For instance, the Committee on the Rights of the Child reasserted in its *General Comment No. 6* that 'the enjoyment of rights stipulated in

---

[417] A similar pattern can be found in other general human rights treaties concluded at the regional level.

[418] *Bah v the United Kingdom* ECHR 2011-VI 1, paras 45–46.

[419] This is implicit in *Ponomaryovi v Bulgaria* ECHR 2011-III 365, paras 59–63. The ECtHR also acknowledged that a difference of treatment between documented and undocumented migrants can fall under the prohibition of discrimination, see *Anakomba Yula v Belgium* App no 45413/07 (ECtHR, 10 March 2009) para 37.

the Convention is not limited to children who are citizens of a State party and must therefore, if not explicitly stated otherwise in the Convention, also be available to all children—including asylum-seeking, refugee, and migrant children—irrespective of their nationality, immigration status, or statelessness'.[420]

The general applicability of human rights irrespective of immigration status has been further restated in a plethoric number of interstate resolutions—such as those of the UN General Assembly—that acknowledge the duty of all states 'to promote and protect effectively the human rights and fundamental freedoms of all migrants, regardless of their migration status'.[421] This well-established principle has been reaffirmed in the Global Compact for Migration, whereby states commit to 'ensure effective respect, protection and fulfilment of the human rights of all migrants, regardless of their migration status, across all stages of the migration cycle'.[422]

Although these endorsements have been articulated in soft law instruments, they reflect the current state of general international law, because in essence human rights 'are a function of a person's status as a human being, not as a citizen of a particular state'.[423] When discussing state responsibility and the treatment of aliens under customary international law, the ILC Special Rapporteur William Riphagen underlined that:

> While a *jus communicationis*, in the sense that a State is obliged to admit aliens, does not exist under customary international law, the rules on the treatment of aliens apply irrespective of any formal act of admission. In other words, the mere presence of the alien within the jurisdiction of another State is considered to give rise to an international situation which entails obligations and rights of the States concerned.[424]

---

[420] CRC Committee, 'General Comment No 6' (n 281) para 12.

[421] See for instance UNGA Res 70/147 (25 February 2016) UN Doc GA/Res/70/147, para 1; UNGA Res 69/167 (12 February 2015) UN Doc GA/RES/69/167; UNGA Res 68/17 (28 January 2014) UN Doc GA/RES/68/17, para 1; UNGA Res 67/172 (3 April 2013) UN Doc GA/RES/67/172, para 1; UNGA Res 66/172 (29 March 2012) UN Doc GA/RES/66/172, para 1; UNGA Res 65/212 (1 April 2011) UN Doc GA/RES/65/212, para 1; UNGA Res 64/166 (19 March 2010) UN Doc GA/RES/64/166, para 1; UNGA Res 63/184 (17 March 2009) UN Doc GA/RES/63/184, para 1; UNGA Res 62/156 (7 March 2008) UN Doc GA/RES/62/156, para 1; UNGA Res 61/165 (23 February 2007) UN Doc GA/RES/61/165, para 1; and UNGA Res 60/169 (7 March 2006) UN Doc GA/RES/60/169, para 5. See also, among many other similar instances ILO, *Multilateral Framework on Labour Migration: Non-binding Principles and Guidelines for a Rights-based Approach to Labour Migration* (ILO 2006); 'Programme of Action' in 'Report of the World Conference against Racism, Racial Discrimination, Xenophobia and Related Intolerance' (Durban, 31 August–8 September 2001) UN Doc A/CONF.189/12 (25 January 2002), para 27.

[422] Global Compact for Safe, Orderly and Regular Migration (n 253) para 15. See also ibid paras 11, 23(b), 27, 29(h), and 31.

[423] TA Aleinikoff, 'International Legal Norms and Migration: A Report' in TA Aleinikoff and V Chetail (eds), *Migration and International Legal Norms* (TMC Asser Press 2003) 1–8. For similar acknowledgements, see among others R Cholewinski, 'The Rights of Migrant Workers' in Cholewinski, Perruchoud, MacDonald (eds), *International Migration Law* (n 210) 255–64.

[424] ILC, 'Third Report on the Content, Forms and Degrees of International Responsibility (Part Two of the Draft Articles) by Mr Willem Riphagen, Special Rapporteur' Thirty-fourth session, Geneva (1982) UN Doc A/CN.4/354 Corr 1 Add.1 & 2, para 48.

The scope and content of the principle of non-discrimination with regard to economic and social rights of migrants

As mentioned above, according to the principle of non-discrimination, a difference of treatment remains permissible as long as the criteria for such differentiation are reasonable, objective, and proportionate to pursue a legitimate aim. Drawing the line between unlawful discrimination and lawful difference of treatment is not always straightforward in practice. Such an exercise can be particularly perilous when it comes to the economic and social rights of non-citizens. From a purely legal perspective, this may be surprising, since in contrast to the ICCPR, none of the rights enshrined in the ICESCR are contingent upon nationality or the immigration status of their beneficiaries.

Furthermore, the principle of non-discrimination endorsed in Article 2(2) ICESCR is well acknowledged as a fundamental guarantee which 'is neither subject to progressive implementation nor dependent on available resources'[425] (as this is the case for most rights enshrined in the ICESCR).[426] Its treaty body logically inferred from the duty of non-discrimination that '[t]he Covenant rights apply to everyone including non-nationals, such as refugees, asylum-seekers, stateless persons, migrant workers and victims of international trafficking, regardless of legal status and documentation'.[427] Interestingly, out of the 169 States Parties, only seven of them have formulated a reservation related to non-citizens.[428]

Nonetheless, contrary to its ICCPR counterpart, the principle of non-discrimination under the ICESCR is limited by a noteworthy—albeit circumstantiated—exception. According to Article 2(3), 'developing countries, with due regard to human rights and their national economy, may determine to what extent they would guarantee the economic rights recognized in the present Covenant to non-nationals'. As any other exception to a principle, this one should be restrictively interpreted. This is especially the case when the principle at stake is so fundamental and represents one of the founding backbones of the Covenant. Moreover, the wording of this provision is circumscribed by three substantial

---

[425] CESCR, 'General Comment No 18: The Right to Work' (24 November 2005) UN Doc E/C.12/GC/18 (6 February 2006), para 33. See also CESCR, 'General Comment No 3: The Nature of States Parties Obligations (Art 2, Para 1 of the Covenant)' (14 December 1990) UN Doc E/1991/23, para 1; CESCR, 'General Comment No 9: The Domestic Application of the Covenant' (3 December 1998) UN Doc E/C.12/1998/24, para 9; and CESCR, 'General Comment No 20' (n 379) paras 2 and 7. See also Commission on Human Rights, 'Note Verbale Dated 5 December 1986 from the Permanent Mission of the Netherlands to the United Nations Office at Geneva Addressed to the Centre for Human Rights' (8 January 1987) UN Doc E/CN.4/1987/17 ('Limburg Principles on the Implementation of the International Covenant on Economic, Social and Cultural Rights') para 35 and Maastricht Guidelines on Violations of Economic, Social and Cultural Rights, para 11.

[426] As underlined in Article 2(1) of the ICESCR, States Parties undertake 'to take steps, individually and through international assistance and co-operation . . . to the maximum of its available resources, with a view to achieving progressively the full realization of the rights recognized in the present Covenant'.

[427] CESCR 'General Comment No 20' (n 379) para 30.

[428] These are Bahamas, Belgium, China (Hong Kong), France, Kuwait, Monaco, and the UK. The list and content of reservations are available at https://treaties.un.org/pages/ViewDetails. aspx?src=TREATY&mtdsg_no=IV-3&chapter=4&lang=en accessed 10 October 2018.

cumulative conditions regarding respectively the states concerned, the nature of the rights subjected to this exception, and the degree of permissible restrictions thereto.

With regard to the first set of conditions, Article 2(3) is a permissive—not a mandatory—provision, which can be invoked only by 'developing countries'. While the notion of 'developing countries' is a factual rather than a legal one, it is commonly understood as including 'countries which have gained independence and which fall within the appropriate United Nations classifications of developing countries'.[429] Although this kind of qualification referring to developing countries is common in international trade law and other related areas, it remains quite unique in the field of human rights law. This specificity must be understood in light of the historical context which prevailed during the drafting of the UN Covenant.

Article 2(3) is a reminiscence of the traditional law of aliens and its longstanding debates between newly independent states and Western states. The delegate of Indonesia who proposed this provision explained during the drafting that the only purpose of this paragraph was to protect the rights of nationals of former colonies against the abuses deriving from 'the dominant economic position enjoyed by [mostly Western] foreigners as a result of the colonial system'.[430] In summing up the debates between the delegations, the Third Committee further insisted that:

[T]he sole aim of the proposals in question was to rectify situations which frequently existed in the developing countries, particularly those which recently won their independence. In such countries, the influence of non-nationals on the national economy—a heritage of the colonial era—was often such that nationals were not in a position fully to enjoy the economic rights set forth in the draft Covenant.[431]

A small majority of states finally adopted Article 2(3) with forty-one votes to thirty-eight and twelve abstentions.[432]

The second range of conditions governing the scope of Article 2(3) relates to the rights concerned by this exception to the principle of non-discrimination. The provision is exclusively limited to the 'economic rights recognized in the present Covenant'. Although the Covenant does not explicitly define this notion, the ordinary meaning of the terms presupposes that the rights in question primarily consist of the right to work (Article 6) and other related rights, such as the enjoyment of

[429] 'Limburg Principles' (n 425) para 44. Although its assertion remains highly disputable, the UK declared, when it ratified the Covenant, that 'for the purposes of article 2 (3) the British Virgin Islands, the Cayman Islands, the Gilbert Islands, the Pitcairn Islands Group, St. Helena and Dependencies, the Turks and Caicos Islands and Tuvalu are developing countries'.

[430] UNGA, Third Committee, '1185th Meeting' UN GAOR 25th Session (1962) UN Doc A/C.3/SR.1185, para 37. Although the Committee on Economic, Social and Cultural Rights has not yet specified the meaning of this provision, the 'Limburg Principles' (n 425) reassert that 'The purpose of article 2(3) was to end the domination of certain economic groups of non-nationals during colonial times', see para 43.

[431] UNGA, 'Draft International Covenants on Human Rights, Report of the Third Committee' Seventeenth session (17 December 1962) UN Doc A/5365, para 68.

[432] UNGA, Third Committee '1206th Meeting' UN GAOR 17th session UN Doc A/C.3/SR.1206 (1962) paras 42–45.

just and favourable conditions of work (Article 7).[433] This excludes both social and cultural rights for which non-discrimination remains plainly operational.

Thirdly, according to the cautious and restrictive wording of Article 2(3), developing countries are not allowed to suspend but only to 'determine to what extent they would guarantee the economic rights' of non-nationals.[434] They can thus merely envisage restrictions to the exercise of economic rights, which should be determined in any case 'with due regard to human rights and their national economy' as explicitly required by Article 2(3). Possible restrictions on the economic rights of non-nationals are therefore deemed acceptable as long as they do not impair the enjoyment of other human rights. Following this stance, a general prohibition of the right to work imposed on non-citizens would be unjustifiable if no welfare assistance is provided to them instead.[435]

In any event, Article 2(3) cannot justify any breach of economic rights and other related guarantees provided by other treaties, such as the Refugee Convention or the Migrant Workers Conventions. Article 5(2) of the ICESCR ensures that a more favourable treatment granted by any other domestic legislation and treaties remains plainly applicable. This safeguard clause has further far-reaching effects with regard to the more favourable treatment enshrined in regional human rights treaties. Indeed, both the 1981 African Charter on Human and Peoples' Rights and the 1988 Additional Protocol to the American Convention on Human Rights in the Area of Economic, Social and Cultural Rights[436] guarantee economic rights without any discrimination. In such cases, Article 2(3) is literally neutralized.

In addition to due respect for other human rights and more favourable treatment, restrictions on the economic rights of non-citizens are conditional upon the 'national economy' of the developing countries. Although these states retain a substantial margin of appreciation, some commentators have advanced that Article 2(3) can be triggered 'only when the state of the economy of the nation as a whole so warrants'.[437] In sum, despite the apparent vagueness of its wording, Article 2(3) represents a limited and balanced exception to the principle of non-discrimination.

---

[433] See also EVO Dankwa, 'Working Paper on Article 2(3) of the International Covenant on Economic, Social and Cultural Rights' (1987) HRQ 230, 240; R Cholewinski, *Migrant Workers in International Human Rights Law: Their Protection in Countries of Employment* (OUP 1997) 59; M Sepulveda, *The Nature of the Obligations under the International Covenant on Economic, Social and Cultural Rights* (Intersentia 2003) 415.

[434] During the drafting of Article 2(3), the delegate of Indonesia underlined that this provision 'recognised the principle that non-nationals were entitled to enjoy the same economic rights as the nationals of a state; it was only the extent of such enjoyment that could be limited by the State'. See UNGA 'Agenda Item 43. Draft International Covenants on Human Rights' Seventeenth Session (6 December 1962) UN Doc A/C.3/SR.1204, para 2.

[435] For a similar account, see notably A Edwards, 'Human Rights, Refugees, and the Right "to Enjoy" Asylum' (2005) 17(2) IJRL 293, 325.

[436] Additional Protocol to the American Convention on Human Rights in the Area of Economic, Social and Cultural Rights (adopted 17 November 1988, entered into force 16 November 1999) OAS Treaty Series No 69.

[437] Dankwa, 'Working Paper' (n 433) 242.

More fundamentally, this provision remains—for the moment at least—a rather virtual exception because 'no developing State has sought to invoke it'.[438] Save for a possible future invocation of Article 2(3), the principle of non-discrimination thus constitutes an 'immediate and cross-cutting obligation'[439] binding all States Parties. Given the absence of any practice related to Article 2(3), this provision is undoubtedly not part of customary international law. While retaining its validity as a treaty provision, it does not affect the stance of the general principle of non-discrimination under customary international law.

From this broader stance, although states remain anxious with regard to economic and social rights, there is a growing consensus to guarantee undocumented migrants equal access to a minimum core set of rights.[440] The CESCR has notably endorsed equal access to the core content of economic and social rights, stating that 'all persons, irrespective of their nationality, residency or immigration status, are entitled to primary and emergency medical care'.[441] This trend is not confined to the core content obligations under the ICESCR. It is arguably part of a growing customary law process. According to the CESCR, 'basic economic, social and cultural rights as part of the minimum standards of human rights are guaranteed under customary international law and are also prescribed by international humanitarian law'.[442]

This assertion finds additional support in a well-established norm of general international law: the absolute prohibition of degrading and inhuman treatment. Indeed, violating a minimum of subsistence rights can cross the threshold of degrading treatment.[443] The interdependent and interrelated nature of human rights is

---

[438] Sepulveda, *The Nature of the Obligations* (n 433) 415; M Craven, 'The International Covenant on Economic, Social and Cultural Rights' in R Hanski and M Suksi (eds), *An Introduction to the International Protection of Human Rights: A Textbook* (Institute for Human Rights 1999) 111; B Saul, D Kinley, and J Mowbray, *The International Covenant on Economic, Social and Cultural Rights. Commentary, Cases and Materials* (OUP 2014) 214.

[439] CESCR, 'General Comment No 20' (n 379) para 7.

[440] See also S da Lomba, 'Immigration Status and Basic Social Rights: A Comparative Study of Irregular Migrants' Right to Health Care in France, the UK and Canada' (2010) 28 NQHR 6, 17; R Cholewinski, *Study on Obstacles to Effective Access of Irregular Migrants to Minimum Social Rights* (Council of Europe 2005) 27–28.

[441] CESCR 'General Comment No 19, The Right to Social Security (art 9)' Thirty-ninth session (4 February 2008) UN Doc E/C.12/GC/19, para 37. See also CESCR, 'General Comment No 14: The Right to the Highest Attainable Standard of Health (Art 12)' Twenty-second session (11 August 2000) UN Doc E/C.12/2000/4, para 34; and CESCR, 'Concluding Observations of the Committee on Economic, Social and Cultural Rights: Spain' Thirty-second session (7 June 2004) UN Doc E/C.12/1/Add.99, para 7.

[442] CESCR, 'Report of the Twenty-fifth, Twenty-sixth and Twenty-seventh Sessions (23 April–11 May 2001, 13–31 August 2001, 12–30 November 2001)' ESCOR (2002) Supp No 2 UN Doc E/C.12/2001/17, para 703.

[443] This interpretation has been notably confirmed by the European Court in the case *MSS v Belgium and Greece* (n 326). Although it recalls, in line with its previous jurisprudence, that Article 3 does not 'entail any general obligation to give refugees financial assistance to enable them to maintain a certain standard of living' (see *Müslim v Turkey* App No 53566/99 (ECtHR, 26 April 2005) para 85), the court acknowledges the particular vulnerability of asylum-seekers: 'the Court attaches considerable importance to the applicant's status as an asylum seeker and, as such, a member of a particularly underprivileged and vulnerable population group in need of special protection. It notes the existence of a broad consensus at the international and European level concerning this need for special protection, as evidenced by the Geneva Convention, the remit and the activities of the UNHCR and the standards set out in the European Union Reception Directive.' See *MSS v Belgium and Greece* (n 326) para 251.

reinforced by the principle of equality before the law that applies to all matters regulated and protected by public authorities, including economic and social rights.[444]

A similar pattern is observable with regard to some of the core labour rights reaffirmed in several widely ratified ILO treaties.[445] In addition to the widespread and representative participation in these treaties, the customary law nature of the core norms enshrined therein might be inferred from the *ILO Declaration on Fundamental Principles and Rights at Work*:

All Members, even if they have not ratified the Conventions in question, have an obligation arising from the very fact of membership in the Organization to respect, to promote and to realize, in good faith and in accordance with the Constitution, the principles concerning the fundamental rights which are the subject of those Conventions, namely:

(a) freedom of association and the effective recognition of the right to collective bargaining;
(b) the elimination of all forms of forced or compulsory labour;
(c) the effective abolition of child labour; and
(d) the elimination of discrimination in respect of employment and occupation.[446]

While referring to the complementary obligation to provide decent material conditions under the EU Reception Directive, the court concludes that 'the situation in which he has found himself for several months, living in the street, with no resources or access to sanitary facilities, and without any means of providing for his essential needs . . . have attained the level of severity required to fall within the scope of Article 3 of the Convention'. ibid para 263.

[444] See, for instance, HRC, *F H Zwaan-de Vries v the Netherlands* (1990) Communication No 182/1984 UN Doc CCPR/C/OP/2, paras 12.3-15; HRC, *Kríž v Czech Republic* (18 November 2005) Communication No 1054/2002 UN Doc CCPR/C/85/D/1054/2000, para 7.3.

[445] ILO Convention C029: Forced Labour Convention (Convention concerning Forced or Compulsory Labour) (14th Conference Session 28 June 1930, entered into force 1 May 1932) 39 UNTS 55, 178 Contracting States; ILO Convention C087: Freedom of Association and Protection of the Right to Organise Convention (Convention concerning Freedom of Association and Protection of the Right to Organise) (31st Conference Session 9 July 1948, entered into force 4 July 1950) 68 UNTS 17, 155 Contracting States; ILO Convention C098: Right to Organise and Collective Bargaining Convention (Convention concerning the Application of the Principles of the Right to Organise and to Bargain Collectively) (32nd Conference Session 1 July 1949, entered into force 18 July 1951) 96 UNTS 257, 166 Contracting States; ILO Convention C100: Equal Remuneration Convention (34th Conference Session 29 June 1951, entered into force 23 May 1953) 165 UNTS 303, 173 Contracting States; ILO Convention C105: Abolition of Forced Labour Convention (Convention concerning the Abolition of Forced Labour) (40th Conference Session 25 June 1957, entered into force 17 Jan. 1959) 320 UNTS 291, 173 Contracting States; ILO Convention C111: Discrimination (Employment and Occupation) (Convention concerning Discrimination in Respect of Employment and Occupation) (42nd Conference Session 25 June 1958, entered into force 15 June 1960) 362 UNTS 31, 175 Contracting States; ILO Convention C138: Minimum Age Convention (Convention concerning Minimum Age for Admission to Employment) (58th Conference Session 26 June 1973, entered into force 19 June 1976) 1015 UNTS 297, 171 Contracting States; and ILO Convention C182: Worst Forms of Child Labour Convention (Convention concerning the Prohibition and Immediate Action for the Elimination of the Worst Forms of Child Labour) (87th Conference Session 17 June 1999, entered into force 19 November 2000) 2133 UNTS 161, 182 Contracting States.

[446] International Labour Conference (86th Session) 'Declaration on Fundamental Principles and Rights at Work' (Geneva June 1998). For further discussion about the customary law nature of the core rights reaffirmed in the ILO Declaration see notably F Maupain, 'Revitalization not Retreat: The Real Potential of the 1998 ILO Declaration for the Universal Protection of Workers' Rights' (2005) 16(3) EJIL 439, 458; P Alston, 'Core Labour Standards and the Transformation of International Labour Rights Regime' (2004) 15(3) EJIL 457, 493; J Wouters and B de Meester 'The Role of International Law in Protecting Public Goods: Regional and Global Challenges' (2003) Working Paper No 1, Leuven Interdisciplinary Research Group on International Agreements and Development, 21;

The clear applicability of these rights to migrants—whether documented or not—has been further confirmed in 2004 at the 92nd International Labour Conference: 'The fundamental principles and rights at work are universal and applicable to all people in all States, regardless of the level of economic development. They thus apply to all migrant workers without distinction, whether they are temporary or permanent migrant workers, or whether they are regular migrants or migrants in an irregular situation.'[447]

At the regional level, the Inter-American Court of Human Rights reached a similar conclusion in its Advisory Opinion on Juridical Condition and Rights of the Undocumented Migrants. It deduced from the principle of non-discrimination and equality before the law some far-reaching consequences regarding labour rights of undocumented migrant workers:

A person who enters a State and assumes an employment relationship, acquires his labor human rights in the State of employment, irrespective of his migratory status, because respect and guarantee of the enjoyment and exercise of those rights must be made without any discrimination. In this way, the migratory status of a person can never be a justification for depriving him of the enjoyment and exercise of his human rights, including those related to employment.[448]

Such a general assertion calls for an important caveat: although most human rights (whether civil, political, economic, social, or cultural) are presumably applicable irrespective of nationality or immigration status, this presumption is rebuttable when a difference of treatment is reasonable, objective, and proportionate to pursue a legitimate aim.[449] Under the current state of international law, one can fairly say

---

Y Daudet, 'Preface' in L Dubin, *La protection des normes sociales dans les échanges internationaux* (Presses Universitaires d'Aix-Marseilles 2003) 3; J Bellace, 'The ILO Declaration of Fundamental Principles and Rights at Work' (2001) 17(3) IJCCLIR 269, 272–73; F Lenzerini, 'International Trade and Child Labour Standards' in F Francioni (ed), *Environment, Human Rights and International Trade* (Hart Publishing 2001) 308; JF Hellwig, 'The Retreat of the State? The Massachusetts Burma Law and Local Empowerment in the Context of Globalization(s)' (2000) 18 Wis Int'l L J 477, 505; J Gross, *Workers' Rights as Human Rights* (Cornell University Press 2003) 123.

[447] International Labour Conference (92nd Session) Report VI: Toward a Fair Deal for Migrant Workers in the Global Economy (Geneva June 2004) 82, para 229.

[448] *Juridical Condition and Rights of Undocumented Migrants* (Advisory Opinion) OC-18/03 Series A No 18 (IACtHR, 17 September 2003) para 101. The rights in question notably include the prohibition of forced labour and child labour, freedom of association and to organize and join a trade union, fair wages, and social security. For other regional restatements of non-discrimination in relation to economic and social rights of migrants, see for instance: Council of Europe, Parliamentary Assembly, 'Resolution 1509 on the Human Rights of Irregular Migrants' (27 June 2006) Doc 10924, para 13.5; Council of Europe, Committee of Social Rights, 'Complaint No 14/2003, *International Federation of Human Rights Leagues (FIDH) v France*' (2004) paras 30–32; and African Commission on Human and People's Rights, *Institute for Human Rights and Development in Africa (IHRDA) v Republic of Angola* (n 345) para 80.

[449] As recalled by the CESCR in line with all the other treaty bodies, '[d]ifferential treatment based on prohibited grounds will be viewed as discriminatory unless the justification for differentiation is reasonable and objective. This will include an assessment as to whether the aim and effects of the measures or omissions are legitimate, compatible with the nature of the Covenant rights and solely for the purpose of promoting the general welfare in a democratic society. In addition, there must be a clear and reasonable relationship of proportionality between the aim sought to be realised and the measures or omissions and their effects', see CESCR, 'General Comment No 20' (n 379) para 13.

that all migrants—whether documented or not—benefit on an equal footing as nationals from a core content of economic, labour, and social rights, including most notably primary and emergency health care, prohibition of forced labour and child labour, primary education, equal remuneration, freedom of association, and the right to collective bargaining.[450] By contrast, it is conventionally contended that access to employment and social security can be subjected to lawful restrictions based on nationality or immigration status.[451] These restrictions closely depend on the concrete circumstances of each particular situation as well as on the type and content of the relevant rights and benefits. As a result, drawing the line between a lawful difference of treatment and an unlawful discrimination requires a subtle case-by-case assessment which offers states a relatively broad margin of appreciation.

Against this framework, while the fundamental principle of non-discrimination is not contested as such, the concrete implications flowing therefrom for non-citizens are not always clear and may be difficult to grasp with certainty. This highlights the schizophrenic nature of an international legal system which is grounded on two contradictory driving forces. On the one hand, due respect for non-discrimination is primarily ensured by a decentralized scheme of implementation entrusted to states. On the other hand, the 'universal respect for, and observance of, human rights and fundamental freedoms for all without distinction' is acknowledged as one of the founding principles of the international legal order instituted by the UN Charter. But much more remains to be done for drawing all the normative and practical consequences for those who are not nationals of the country in which they live.

To conclude on the founding principles governing the departure, admission, and sojourn of migrants, one cannot help but notice that the movement of persons between states is framed by international law. This has always been the case even if the trivialization of immigration control has muddied the role of international norms. Beyond the great diversity of instruments and issues associated with migration, customary international law is instrumental in identifying and highlighting the key concepts at stake and their applicable norms. This foundational source of public international law frames and structures international migration law, and, by doing so, unveils its internal logic. International migration law is grounded on three existential features: departure, admission, and sojourn. Each of its core components is governed by several customary and conventional norms which interact and overlap within the migration cycle. Table 2.2 captures in schematic terms some of the most important customary law foundations of international migration law.

---

[450] In addition to the primary sources quoted above, see also Global Compact for Safe, Orderly and Regular Migration, (n 253) paras 15, 22(e)–(i), 23(b) and (d), and 31.

[451] Out of the seven reservations formulated to the ICESCR concerning non-citizens, five of them focus on access to employment and social security. The same pattern can be observed with regard to other human rights treaties for which the great majority of reservations related to non-citizens concern these two sensitive issues. Despite this restrictive trend, one should add however that, in the Global Compact, states explicitly 'commit to assist migrant workers at all skills levels to have access to social protection in countries of destination and profit from the portability of applicable social security entitlements and earned benefits in their countries of origin or when they decide to take up work in another country'. Global Compact for Safe, Orderly and Regular Migration (n 253) para 38.

Table 2.2 The customary law foundations of international migration law

Departure	Admission	Sojourn
• Right to leave any country, except when restrictions are provided by law, necessary to protect public order, and consistent with other fundamental rights	• Right to return to one's own country • Principle of *non-refoulement* • Family reunion of children • Prohibition of arbitrary detention and arbitrary deprivation of life • Access to consular protection • Prohibition of collective expulsion	• Principle of non-discrimination • Prohibition of slavery, forced labour, and child labour • Right to a fair trial in civil and criminal matters • Freedom of conscience, of expression, and of association, except when restrictions are provided by law, necessary to protect public order, and consistent with other fundamental rights

From a systemic perspective, the main interest of customary international law is twofold: it provides the global picture of international migration law, and it anchors this discrete field in the heart of general international law. When compared to treaty law, customary international law further provides two main added values: it is the only vehicle for creating universal rules binding all states and, in a substantial number of them, it is also directly applicable before domestic courts.[452] Despite this potential, its impact and content shall not be overestimated. It is strong on principles, but rather weak in providing a detailed and comprehensive account of the field. In practice, customary international law cannot be dissociated from its broader legal environment in which treaty law and domestic legislation are still influential.

---

[452] See, for instance, on this last point M Shaw, *International Law* (6th edn CUP 2008) 128–79; L Henkin, 'International Law as Law in the United States' (1984) 82 Mich L Rev 1555; V Nanda, 'Application of Customary International Law by Domestic Courts: Some Observations' (1966) 12(2) NYL Forum 187; DF Klein, 'A Theory for the Application of the Customary International Law of Human Rights by Domestic Courts' (1988) 13 Yale J Int'l L 332.

PART II

THE TREATY REGIMES OF INTERNATIONAL MIGRATION LAW

Introduction to Part II

'Nous pensons tous l'immigration [...] comme l'État nous demande de la penser et, en fin de compte, comme il la pense lui-même.'

Abdelmalek Sayad[1]

The general principles of customary international law governing the departure, admission, and sojourn of migrants are supplemented, reinforced, and detailed by a complex set of conventional regimes focusing on more specific issues. Although commentators often lament the lack of a comprehensive treaty governing all aspects of migration, this situation does not differ from that of many other branches of international law. To mention a few, international humanitarian law, human rights law, labour law, and environmental law are all grounded on a broad variety of multilateral treaties addressing specific situations. International migration law thus constitutes no exception. The plurality of international instruments is even necessary in such a complex and multi-dimensional field.

At the universal level, multilateral treaties specifically adopted in this multifaceted area follow a segmented approach focusing on three distinctive categories of migrants. First, refugees are primarily governed by the 1951 Convention relating to the Status of Refugees, as amended by its 1967 Protocol.[2] Second, migrant workers are dealt with in three multilateral treaties: the 1949 Convention Concerning Migration for Employment (Revised) (No 97);[3] the 1975 Convention Concerning Migrations in Abusive Conditions and the Promotion of Equality of Opportunity and Treatment of Migrant Workers (No 143);[4] and the 1990 International Convention on the Protection of the Rights of All Migrant Workers

---

[1] A Sayad, 'Immigration et "pensée d'Etat"' (1999) 129 Actes de la recherche en sciences sociales 5, 7.

[2] Convention relating to the Status of Refugees (adopted 28 July 1951, entered into force 22 April 1954) 189 UNTS 137 and Protocol relating to the Status of Refugees (adopted 31 January 1967, entered into force 4 October 1967) 606 UNTS 267.

[3] ILO Convention C097: Migration for Employment Convention (Revised) (Convention concerning Migration for Employment (Revised 1949)) (adopted 32nd Conference Session Geneva 1 July 1949, entered into force 22 January 1952) 120 UNTS 71.

[4] ILO Convention C143: Migrant Workers (Supplementary Provisions) Convention (Convention concerning Migrations in Abusive Condition and the Promotion of Equality of Opportunity and Treatment of Migrant Workers) (adopted 60th Conference Session Geneva 24 June 1975, entered into force 9 December 1978) 1120 UNTS 324.

and Members of Their Families (ICRMW).[5] Third, smuggled and trafficked migrants have emerged in 2000 as a new category of international concern which prompted the adoption of the Protocol against the Smuggling of Migrants by Land, Sea and Air, and the Protocol to Prevent, Suppress and Punish Trafficking in Persons, Especially Women and Children, Supplementing the United Nations Convention against Transnational Organized Crime.[6]

These seven multilateral instruments establish particularly detailed conventional regimes and represent the core specialized treaties of international migration law. The juxtaposition of these UN instruments creates a complex mosaic of rules that highlights both the limits and the potential of international law. These specialized treaty regimes may be viewed in two opposite ways depending on whether they are approached in isolation from one another or from a holistic perspective.

On the one hand, the compartmentalized approach of these specialized treaty regimes mirrors the categorization scheme of international migration law that captures migrants through distinctive labels: refugees, migrant workers, smuggled and trafficked migrants. The focus on these specific categories says much more about the dominant discourse of governments and their enduring misperceptions than it does about the fluid reality of migration that defies easy categorization. While reflecting the concerns and priorities of states, these specialized treaty regimes provide a highly fragmented legal framework when they are taken individually.

This fragmentation is exacerbated by the uneven number of ratifications among international instruments. The UN conventions governing refugee protection, trafficking, and smuggling have been ratified by an impressive number of states gathering respectively 147, 173, and 147 countries across the world. By contrast, ninety states have ratified at least one of the three UN conventions on migrant workers. Although this ratification record remains significant and has been too frequently ignored, there are important variations from one treaty to another: the ICRMW is ratified by fifty-four states, while the ILO Conventions No 97 and No 143 respectively gather forty-nine and twenty-three States Parties.

On the other hand, focusing too much on the specialized treaty regimes provides a distorted vision that fails to capture the reach and significance of international law. The UN conventions devoted to migration are not self-contained regimes. They are an integral part of the broader ecosystem of international law. Two main lessons shall be drawn from this holistic perspective.

First, in addition to the customary law principles governing the departure, admission, and stay of migrants, migration is governed by a vast network of general conventions that remain plainly relevant. Their continuing applicability underpins, enriches, and shapes the more specific conventional regimes. From this systemic

---

[5] International Convention on the Protection of the Rights of All Migrant Workers and Members of Their Families (adopted 18 December 1990, entered into force 1 July 2003) 2220 UNTS 3 (ICRMW).
[6] Protocol against the Smuggling of Migrants by Land, Sea and Air (adopted 15 November 2000, entered into force 28 January 2004) 2241 UNTS 507 (Smuggling Protocol); Protocol to Prevent, Suppress and Punish Trafficking in Persons, Especially Women and Children, Supplementing the United Nations Convention against Transnational Organized Crime (adopted 15 November 2000, entered into force 25 December 2003) 2237 UNTS 319 (Trafficking Protocol).

angle, general treaties adopted in the broader field of human rights provide a common legal framework that is applicable to all migrants regardless of their categorization. The normative relations between general and specific UN instruments are twofold. Specialized treaty regimes refine and detail the general ones, whereas the latter have considerably shaped the meaning of the former and compensated for the limited reach of their scope. To give an obvious illustration, the rights of migrant workers cannot be understood without taking into account the vast number of general treaties adopted under the auspices of ILO that apply to both nationals and non-nationals.

Second, this integrated approach of international law sheds new light on the interactions among specialized treaty regimes themselves. Although they have been adopted through a compartmentalized approach, they make sense only when understood in relation to one another. Their respective scope and content are closely interrelated and provide an incremental protection. Indeed, the specific categories of migrants addressed by the UN conventions considerably overlap both in law and in practice. The same person may fit in several legal categories, either simultaneously or consecutively. Depending on the relevant instruments, a refugee can fall within the legal definition of migrant worker and *vice-versa*. Likewise, an undocumented migrant may be protected as an asylum-seeker, a migrant worker, and a victim of trafficking at the same time. When taken together, the specialized treaty regimes are thus not exclusive but mutually reinforcing alongside a complex normative continuum.

Acknowledging the fluidity of legal categories is more consonant with the changing reality of migration. It also offers a more nuanced and dynamic account which discloses the unity and diversity of international migration law. From the perspective of treaty law, international migration law follows a dual pattern of both independent and interdependent specialized conventions. This Part accordingly focuses on each category of migrants under their relevant UN instruments: refugees (Chapter 3), migrant workers (Chapter 4), as well as trafficked and smuggled migrants (Chapter 5). The specific characteristics of each treaty regime will be assessed through their respective legal norms and basic notions. The very content of these specialized UN instruments will be also analyzed in light of their broader normative context to better appraise their interactions with one another as well as the overarching influence of general human rights treaties.

3

Refugees

The universal treaty regime of refugee protection is primarily governed by two specific instruments: the UN Convention Relating to the Status of Refugees of 28 July 1951 and its 1967 Protocol. Currently ratified by 147 states across the world, they establish a sophisticated body of international rules based on three parameters: the refugee definition (section 3.1), the refugee status (section 3.2), and the principle of *non-refoulement* (section 3.3). Each of them discloses a subtle balancing act between the competence of the state to control access to its territory and the protection of victims of human rights' violations. This foundational tension represents the existential dilemma of refugee protection which underlies the design of the Geneva Convention as adopted after the Second World War and the subsequent development of international law.

3.1 The Refugee Definition

From the perspective of general international law, identifying foreigners who deserve protection is the normative corollary to the absence of a generalized freedom of movement. It is not by coincidence that the emergence of modern refugee law occurred with the generalization of migration controls during the interwar period. International refugee law constitutes an exception to the migration control paradigm and, as such, the former legitimates the latter within a self-referential logic.[1] Hence, defining who is a refugee not only identifies persons in need of protection, but also determines the correlative extent of states' international obligations under the Geneva Convention. This duality informs the very structure of the refugee definition (section 3.1.1) and reveals some of its most obvious limits (section 3.1.2).

3.1.1 The structure and rationale of the refugee definition

The refugee definition has always been considered the 'crux of the entire matter'[2] and 'the cornerstone on which the entire edifice of the Convention

---

[1] JC Hathaway, *The Law of Refugee Status* (1st edn, Butterworths 1991) 231.
[2] See the statement of Mr Leslie of Canada in UN ECOSOC 'Ad Hoc Committee on Statelessness and Related Problems: Summary Record of the Second Meeting' (17 January 1950) First Session (1950) UN Doc E/AC.32/SR/2, 6.

rested'.[3] At the same time, during the 1951 Conference of Plenipotentiaries, state representatives stressed that they 'could not sign a blank cheque and assume unlimited and indefinite commitments in respect of all refugees'.[4] Given such anxiety, 'the Convention definition was tailored to fit an approximately foreseeable number of prospective beneficiaries who fell within acceptable categories'.[5] This reflects the original premise of refugee protection. As Jaqueline Bhabha observes, 'from the outset, the refugee protection regime was intended to be restrictive and partial, a compromise between unfettered state sovereignty over the admission of aliens, and an open door for non-citizen victims of serious human rights violations. It was always clear that only a subset of forced transnational migrant persecutees were intended beneficiaries.'[6]

The selectivity of the refugee definition is inherent in its very structure, which is composed of three different layers of requirements, commonly labelled as the inclusion, exclusion, and cessation clauses.[7] Article 1(A)(2) of the Geneva Convention spells out the inclusion criteria on the basis of four cumulative conditions: first, a refugee is outside his/her country of origin; second, he/she is unable or unwilling to avail himself/herself of the protection of his/her country; third, such inability or unwillingness is attributable to a well-founded fear of persecution; and fourth, persecution or the lack of protection therefrom is linked to at least one of five limitative grounds (race, religion, nationality, membership of particular social group, or political opinion).

The exclusion clauses further reinforce the selectiveness of the refugee definition in line with the typical concerns of states. Even if a person duly satisfies all

---

[3] See the statement of Mr Giraldo-Jamarillo of Colombia in UNGA 'Conference of Plenipotentiaries on the Status of Refugees and Stateless Persons: Summary Record of the Twenty-first Meeting' (26 November 1951) UN Doc A/CONF.2/SR/21, 8.

[4] See Mr Mostafa of Egypt referring to the statement of the French representative in UNGA 'Conference of Plenipotentiaries on the Status of Refugees and Stateless Persons: Summary Record of the Twentieth Meeting' (26 November 1951) UN Doc A/CONF.2/SR/20, 5. More generally, see K Bem, 'The Coming of a "Blank Cheque"—Europe, the 1951 Convention, and the 1967 Protocol' (2004) 16(4) IJRL 609.

[5] J Sztucki, 'Who Is a Refugee? The Convention Definition: Universal or Obsolete?' in F Nicholson and P Twomey (eds), *Refugee Rights and Realities: Evolving International Concepts and Regimes* (CUP 1999) 55–57.

[6] J Bhabha, 'Internationalist Gatekeepers? The Tension between Asylum Advocacy and Human Rights' (2002) 15 Harv Hum Rts J 151, 155, 167. States' concern is also evidenced by the fact that the refugee definition was originally limited to persons fleeing events occurring before January 1951 and States Parties were able to further restrict its scope to events occurring in Europe. These temporal and geographical limitations were removed by the 1967 Protocol, thereby giving the Geneva Convention a universal coverage.

[7] For an in-depth analysis of the refugee definition as applied in state practice, see especially JC Hathaway and M Foster, *The Law of Refugee Status* (2nd edn, CUP 2014); A Zimmermann and C Mahler, 'Article 1A, para 2 (Definition of the Term "Refugee")' in A Zimmermann (ed), *The 1951 Convention Relating to the Status of Refugees and its 1967 Protocol: A Commentary* (OUP 2011) 281–465; GS Goodwin-Gill and J McAdam, *The Refugee in International Law* (3rd edn, OUP 2007) 63–197; J-Y Carlier, 'Droit d'asile et des réfugiés: De la protection aux droit' (2007) 332 Collected Courses of the Hague Academy of International Law 9, 190–247; D Alland and C Teitgen-Colly, *Traité du droit de l'asile* (Presses universitaires de France 2002) 343–479; N Sitaropoulos, *Judicial Interpretation of Refugee Status: In Search of a Principled Methodology Based on a Critical Comparative Analysis with Special Reference to Contemporary British, French and German Jurisprudence* (Ant N Sakkoulas 1999).

the conditions spelt out in Article 1(A)(2), he or she is excluded from the Geneva Convention under two different sets of circumstances. First, a person cannot enjoy the surrogate protection offered by the refugee status if he or she already benefits from some form of international or national protection, be it UN protection (Article 1(D)) or the rights and obligations attached to the possession of nationality in the country of residence (Article 1(E)). Second, Article 1(F) additionally excludes those who have committed particularly serious crimes. According to the French delegate during the 1951 Conference, this provision was introduced for the very purpose 'of separating the wheat from the chaff'.[8] As acknowledged by subsequent state practice, 'the rationale... is that those who are responsible for the persecution which creates refugees should not enjoy the benefits of a Convention designed to protect those refugees'.[9] Their exclusion is nevertheless limited to the most severe crimes that are exhaustively enumerated in Article 1(F), namely crimes against peace, war crimes, crimes against humanity, serious non-political crimes, and acts contrary to the purposes and principles of the United Nations.

The cessation clauses enumerated in Article 1(C) further underline the temporary nature of the protection granted by the Refugee Convention. The refugee status is terminated as soon as the need thereof is no longer justified. The Geneva Convention thus sets out the criteria for considering that a person has ceased to be a refugee, either because of voluntary acts on the part of the concerned individual[10] or due to a fundamental change in circumstances in the country of origin.[11]

As epitomized by the three layers of requirements governing inclusion, exclusion, and cessation of the refugee status, the Geneva Convention was not conceived as a comprehensive instrument aimed at protecting all persons who are forcibly displaced from their own country. This restrictive stance permeates all the components of the definition adopted in 1951. Nonetheless, the subsequent development of international law has considerably shaped its meaning and rationale. As with any other conventional rules, the Geneva Convention must be construed and applied within the normative context prevailing at the time of its interpretation, including, therefore, in light of the human rights treaties adopted since its entry into force.[12] Such an *evolutive interpretation* has proved to be essential to adapt the 1951

---

[8] For the statement of Mr Rochefort of France, see UNGA 'Conference of Plenipotentiaries on the Status of Refugees and Stateless Persons: Summary Record of the Nineteenth Meeting' (26 November 1951) UN Doc A/CONF.2/SR/19, 5.

[9] *Pushpanathan v Canada (Minister of Citizenship and Immigration)* [1998] 1 SCR 982, para 63.

[10] The circumstances exhaustively enumerated in Article 1C(1)-(4) include voluntary re-availment of the protection of the country of origin, voluntary reacquisition of nationality, acquisition of a new nationality, and voluntary re-establishment in the country of origin.

[11] According to Article 1C(5), the Convention shall cease to apply if a refugee 'can no longer, because the circumstances in connexion with which he has been recognized as a refugee have ceased to exist, continue to refuse to avail himself of the protection of the country of his nationality'.

[12] As restated by the International Court of Justice, 'an international instrument has to be interpreted and applied within the framework of the entire legal system prevailing at the time of the interpretation': ICJ, *Legal Consequences for States of the Continued Presence of South Africa in Namibia* (1971) ICJ Rep 16, 31. Furthermore, human rights treaties constitute 'any relevant rules of international law applicable in the relations between the parties' under Article 31(1)(c) of the Vienna Convention on the Law of Treaties (adopted 23 May 1969, entered into force 27 January 1980, 1155 UNTS 331). Their relevance is confirmed by the very object and purpose of the Refugee Convention as underlined in its

Convention to the ever-changing reality of forced migration. Human rights law also provides a universal and uniform set of standards which constitutes a persuasive device for harmonizing the unilateral and frequently diverging interpretations of States Parties to the Refugee Convention.

As acknowledged by domestic courts, the term 'refugee' is 'to be understood as written against the background of international human rights law, including as reflected or expressed in the Universal Declaration of Human Rights ... and the International Covenant on Civil and Political Rights'.[13] The five limitative grounds of persecution provide an obvious illustration: the grounds of religion and political opinion are clearly based on freedoms of thought, opinion, and expression, while the other ones—race, nationality, and membership in a particular social group—are anchored in the principle of non-discrimination. Although gender is not explicitly listed among the grounds of persecution, human rights law has played a crucial role in developing a gender-sensitive approach to the refugee definition.[14] More generally, the very notion of persecution is nowadays conventionally defined as a serious violation of human rights. To give one instance among many others, the EU Qualification Directive defines persecution as acts which must '(a) be sufficiently serious by their nature or repetition as to constitute a severe violation of basic human rights'; or '(b) be an accumulation of various measures, including violations of human rights which is sufficiently severe as to affect an individual in a similar manner as mentioned in (a)'.[15]

Human rights law has thus become the ultimate benchmark for determining who is a refugee. It has been instrumental in instilling a common and dynamic understanding of the refugee definition more consonant with, and loyal to, the evolution

preamble: 'the Charter of the United Nations and the Universal Declaration of Human Rights approved on 10 December 1948 by the General Assembly have affirmed the principle that human beings shall enjoy fundamental rights and freedoms without discrimination'.

[13] *Applicant A v Minister for Immigration and Multicultural Affairs* (1997) 190 CLR 225, 296–97 (Kirby J). See also: *Pushpanathan v Canada (Minister of Citizenship and Immigration and Multicultural Affairs)* (1998) 1 SCR 982, 1024 (Bastarache J).

[14] For further discussion about this topical issue, see notably: DE Anker, 'Refugee Law, Gender, and the Human Rights Paradigm' (2002) 15 Harv Hum Rts L J 133; W Kälin, 'Gender-Related Persecution' in V Chetail and V Gowlland-Debbas (eds), *Switzerland and the International Protection of Refugees* (Brill 2002) 111; R Haines QC, 'Gender-Related Persecution' in E Feller, V Türk, and F Nicholson (eds), *Refugee Protection in International Law, UNHCR's Global Consultations on International Protection* (CUP 2003) 319; H Crawley, *Refugees and Gender: Law and Process* (Jordan Publishing Limited 2001); K Daley and N Kelley, 'Particular Social Group: A Human Rights Based Approach in Canadian Jurisprudence' (2000) 12 IJRL 148.

[15] Article 9 of the Directive 2011/95/EU of the European Parliament and of the Council of 13 December 2011 on standards for the qualification of third-country nationals or stateless persons as beneficiaries of international protection, for a uniform status for refugees or for persons eligible for subsidiary protection, and for the content of the protection granted (recast) [2011] OJ L 337. Article 9(2) also provides an illustrative list of human rights violations amounting to persecution, such as 'acts of physical or mental violence, including acts of sexual violence' and 'legal, administrative, police, and/or judicial measures which are in themselves discriminatory or which are implemented in a discriminatory manner'. Although these violations are traditionally framed by reference to civil and political rights, other serious breaches of economic, social, and cultural rights (including discriminatory treatments in the benefit of those rights) can be considered persecution. For further discussion, see the comprehensive and stimulating book of M Foster, *International Refugee Law and Socio-Economic Rights* (CUP 2009).

of international law and the changing realities of forced migration. This human rights-based approach to the refugee definition has also informed the whole rationale of the Geneva Convention. Its primary function is to provide a protection of substitution when the state of origin fails to fulfil its duty of protection towards its own citizens. The UK Supreme Court observed in the landmark case of *Horvath* that 'the general purpose of the convention is to enable the person who no longer has the benefit of protection against persecution for a convention reason in his own country to turn for protection to the international community'.[16] It further underlined that:

What [the Geneva Convention] seeks to achieve is the preservation of those rights and freedoms for individuals where they are denied them in their own state. Another state is to provide a surrogate protection where protection is not available in the home state. The convention assumes that every state has the obligation to protect its own nationals. But it recognises that circumstances may occur where that protection may be inadequate. The purpose of the convention is to secure that a refugee may in the surrogate state enjoy the rights and freedoms to which all are entitled without discrimination and which he cannot enjoy in his own state.[17]

From this stance, international refugee law cogently constitutes a right to have rights, when victims of human rights' violations have no other option than to leave their own country and ask for the substitute protection of another state. As asserted by James Hathaway and Michelle Foster, 'refugee law may be the world's most powerful international human rights mechanism'.[18] However, the systemic function assigned to refugee protection still collides with the specific ethos of the Geneva Convention and the limits inherent in its definition.

3.1.2 The limits of the refugee definition

Even though human rights law has expanded its interpretation and shaped its rationale, the refugee definition is far from covering all types of forced migration. The most obvious instance of its restrictive stance is provided by the prerequisite condition to be outside the country of origin. This requirement excludes the vast number of forcibly displaced persons within the territory of their own states despite their manifold similarities with refugees. The exclusion of those who were called 'internal refugees' was primarily due to historical reasons. During the drafting of the 1951 Convention, the treatment of nationals within the territory of their own country was deemed to fall under the sovereignty of each state because at the time no human rights treaty had been adopted by the UN to protect them from abuses by their own governments. The French delegate stressed at the Geneva Conference that:

Whatever formula might ultimately be chosen [to define the term 'refugee'], it would not and could not in any event apply to internal refugees who were citizens of a particular country and enjoyed the protection of the government of that country. There was no general definition

---

[16] *Horvath v Secretary of State for the Home Department* [2001] 1 AC 489, 497 (Lord Hope of Craighead).
[17] ibid 508 (Lord Clyde).   [18] Hathaway and Foster, *The Law of Refugee Status* (n 7) 1.

covering such refugees, since any such definition would involve an infringement of national sovereignty.[19]

Albeit not covered by the Geneva Convention, internally displaced persons are protected under contemporary international law by one specific regional treaty, the African Union Convention for the Protection and Assistance of Internally Displaced Persons in Africa concluded in 2012. They are also covered by the general normative framework established by international human rights law and international humanitarian law, as notably restated in the UN Guiding Principles on Internal Displacement adopted in 1998.[20]

Furthermore, even for those who manage to cross an international border, the refugee definition and its focus on persecution exclude many other typical drivers of forced migration, such as natural disaster, famine, extreme poverty, or pandemic. Clearly, the Geneva Convention was not conceived to obviate any failure of protection from the state of origin.[21] The Canadian Supreme Court observed in the famous *Ward* case that:

The international role was qualified by built-in limitations. These restricting mechanisms reflect the fact that the international community did not intend to offer a haven for all suffering individuals. The need for 'persecution' in order to warrant international protection, for example, results in the exclusion of such pleas as those of economic migrants, i.e., individuals in search of better living conditions, and those of victims of natural disasters, even when the

---

[19] See the statement of Mr Rochefort in UN ECOSOC 'Summary Record of the 172nd meeting held at the Palais des Nations, Geneva, on Saturday, 12 August 1950' (24 August 1950) UN Doc E/AC.7/SR/172, 4. The US delegate, Mrs Roosevelt, also explained that 'internal refugee[s] [...] were separate problems of a different character, in which no question of protection of the persons concerned was involved. All credit was due to the Governments which bore the heavy burdens of those movements of people unilaterally, but those problems should not be confused with the problem before the General Assembly, namely, the provision of protection for those outside their own countries, who lacked the protection of a Government and who required asylum and status in order that they might rebuild lives of self-dependence and dignity' in UNGA, Third Committee, 'UN General Assembly Official Records' Fourth Session, Summary Records (2 December 1949) 473.

[20] According to the UN Guiding Principles, internally displaced persons are defined as 'persons or groups of persons who have been forced or obliged to flee or to leave their homes or places of habitual residence, in particular as a result of or in order to avoid the effects of armed conflict, situations of generalized violence, violations of human rights or natural or human-made disasters, and who have not crossed an internationally recognized State border'. For further developments concerning the applicable legal framework, see especially W Kälin, 'The Guiding Principles on Internal Displacement and the Search for a Universal Framework of Protection for Internally Displaced Persons' in V Chetail and C Bauloz (eds), *The Research Handbook on International Law and Migration* (Edward Elgar Publishing 2014) 612–33; M Duchatellier and C Phuong, 'The African Contribution to the Protection of Internally Displaced Persons: A Commentary on the 2009 Kampala Convention' in V Chetail and C Bauloz (eds), *The Research Handbook on International Law and Migration* (Edward Elgar Publishing 2014) 650–68; W Kälin, 'Guiding Principles on Internal Displacement: Annotations' (2008) 38 Stud Transnat'l Legal Pol'y 1; E Mooney, 'The Concept of Internal Displacement and the Case for Internally Displaced Persons as a Category of Concern' (2005) 24(3) RSQ 9, 26; S Bagshaw, *Developing a Normative Framework for the Protection of Internally Displaced Person* (Transnational Publishers 2005); C Phuong, *The International Protection of Internally Displaced Persons* (CUP 2004); N Geissler, 'The International Protection of Internally Displaced Persons' (1999) 11(3) IJRL 451–78.

[21] See, for instance, *Anor v Minister for Immigration and Ethnic Affairs* [1997] 2 BHRC 143, 160 (Dawson J); and *Minister for Immigration and Multicultural Affairs v Respondents S152/2003* [2004] HCA 18, 73 (McHugh J).

home state is unable to provide assistance, although both of these cases might seem deserving of international sanctuary.[22]

This restrictive stance of the Geneva Convention was thus premeditated. Even apart from persons fleeing natural disasters and extreme poverty, states were well aware that the narrow definition would only include a subset of refugees. Accordingly, the Conference of Plenipotentiaries recommended in its Final Act that States Parties should apply the Geneva Convention beyond 'its contractual scope' to other refugees 'who would not be covered by the terms of the Convention'. This call for a broadening of the refugee definition spurred the subsequent adoption of regional instruments in Africa, Latin America, and Europe.

However, the regionalization of the refugee definition has witnessed two diametrically opposed approaches that mirror the emblematic divide between the Global South and the Global North. In the Global South, a pioneering regional instrument was adopted quite early, in 1969, by the then Organization of African Unity. Article 1(2) of the Convention governing the Specific Aspects of Refugee Problems in Africa considerably expands the scope of the universal definition:

The term refugee shall also apply to every person who, owing to external aggression, occupation, foreign domination, or events seriously disturbing public order in either part or the whole of his country of nationality, is compelled to leave his place of habitual residence in order to seek refuge in another place outside of his country of origin or nationality.[23]

Beyond the explicit inclusion of refugees from armed conflicts,[24] the main added value of this enlarged definition relies on the very notion of 'events seriously disturbing public order'. This broad and objective understanding of the term 'refugee' has the potential to capture the great diversity of drivers underpinning forced migration. Indeed, the main contemporary causes of forced displacement, whether triggered by natural disaster, extreme poverty, or pandemic, seriously disturb public order either in part of or in the whole country of origin. This enlarged and updated definition of refugees has been endorsed in Latin America by the Cartagena Declaration on Refugees adopted in 1984. This regional instrument includes among refugees 'persons who have fled their country because their lives, safety or freedom have been threatened by generalized violence, foreign aggression, internal conflicts, massive violations of human rights or other circumstances which have seriously disturbed

---

[22] *Canada v Ward* [1993] 103 DLR (4th) 1, 67–68.

[23] Convention governing the Specific Aspects of Refugee Problems in Africa (adopted 10 September 1969, entered into force 20 June 1974) 1001 UNTS 45.

[24] The protection of refugees who have fled armed conflicts is not as such an added value of the OAU Convention as the refugee definition set out in the Geneva Convention is also fully capable of covering refugees having fled armed conflicts (see UNHCR, *Guidelines on International Protection No 12: Claims for Refugee Status Related to Situations of Armed Conflict and Violence under Article 1A(2) of the 1951 Convention and/or 1967 Protocol Relating to the Status of Refugees and the Regional Refugee Definitions* (2 December 2016) UN Doc HCR/GIP/16/12). However, in practice, a restrictive interpretation of the Geneva Convention has often been made to exclude those fleeing indiscriminate/generalized violence. For further discussion see notably H Storey, 'Armed Conflict in Asylum Law: The "War-Flaw" ' (2012) 31(2) RSQ 1.

public order'.[25] A similar definition was also adopted in 2001 by the Asian-African Legal Consultative Organization (AALCO) through the 1966 Bangkok Principles on Status and Treatment of Refugees.[26] However, compared to the Cartagena Declaration, this expanded definition has not been as well received by states as testified by the reservations some have made to the concerned provision.[27]

The extensive and protective definition adopted in Africa and Latin America starkly contrasts with the minimalist approach followed by the EU. The EU Qualification Directive simply restates the refugee definition of the Geneva Convention, while clarifying, nonetheless, its close relationship with international human rights law.[28] Rather than broadening the refugee definition, the Directive extends protection to other forcibly displaced persons through the creation of a new status of subsidiary protection. Subsidiary protection is circumscribed to three specific and rather narrow situations. They consist of '(a) the death penalty or execution; or (b) torture or inhuman or degrading treatment or punishment of an applicant in the country of origin; or (c) serious and individual threat to a civilian's life or person by reason of indiscriminate violence in situations of international or internal armed conflict'.[29] The reach of subsidiary protection is not only limited when assessed with reference to the contemporary forms of forced migration across the world. It also overlaps to a great extent with the refugee definition under the 1951 Convention. This has raised

[25] Conclusion No 3 of the Cartagena Declaration. Cartagena Declaration on Refugees, Colloquium on the International Protection of Refugees in Central America, Mexico and Panama (adopted 22 November 1984) Annual Report of the Inter-American Commission on Human Rights, OAS Doc. OEA/Ser.L/V/II.66/doc.10, rev.1, at 190–93 (1984–1985). Though the Cartagena Declaration is not formally binding, it has been endorsed in the domestic law of several states and is considered as a primary instrument of protection in the region. For further discussion about the OAU Convention and the Cartagena Declaration, see G Okoth-Obbo, 'Thirty Years On: A Legal Review of the 1969 OAU Convention Governing the Specific Aspects of Refugee Problems in Africa' (2001) 20(1) RSQ 79–138; E Arboleda, 'Refugee Definition in Africa and Latin America: The Lessons of Pragmatism' (1991) 3 IJRL 185–207; P Nobel, 'Refugee, Law, and Development in Africa' (1982) 3 Michigan YB Int'l Leg Stud 255–88.

[26] See Article 1(2) of the Bangkok Principles on the Status and Treatment of Refugees, adopted at the Asian-African Legal Consultative Organization's (AALCO) 40th Session (31 December 1966) in New Delhi. The first and third paragraphs of Article 1 build otherwise on the refugee definition of the Geneva Convention, although the former expands the five reasons for persecution by including colour, ethnic origin, and gender. However, rather than constituting a broadening of the refugee definition, these additions confirm the evolutive interpretation of the Geneva Convention made in light of the development of international human rights law. See above section 3.1.1. A similar definition is also endorsed in Article 1 of the Arab Convention on Regulating the Status of Refugees in the Arab Countries, providing that the refugee definition extends to '[a]ny person who unwillingly takes refuge in a country other than his country of origin or his habitual place of residence because of sustained aggression against, occupation and foreign domination of such country or because of the occurrence of natural disasters or grave events resulting in major disruption of public order in the whole country of any part thereof'. While adopted by the League of Arab States in 1994, the Convention is still, however, not into force.

[27] See the notes, comments, and reservations made by states on Article 1(2) of the Bangkok Principles, and more particularly by Bahrain, Singapore, and India.

[28] See especially the definitions of persecution and reasons of persecution respectively provided in Articles 9 and 10 of Directive 2011/95/EU of the European Parliament and of the Council of 13 December 2011 (n 15).

[29] Article 15 of Directive 2011/95/EU of the European Parliament and of the Council of 13 December 2011 (n 15).

longstanding controversies whether the EU subsidiary protection is supplementary to, or concurrent with, the universal definition.[30]

3.2 The Refugee Status

The very purpose of the refugee definition adopted in 1951 is to identify the beneficiaries of the legal status detailed in the Geneva Convention. Contrary to human rights treaties adopted later on, this Convention does not simply enumerate rights without distinction as to their beneficiaries. Moreover, the vast majority of its provisions are framed as states' duties instead of individual rights. Such normative digression was inevitable in light of the historical context in which the Geneva Convention was drafted. In 1951, individuals did not have human rights conventionally binding at the universal level.[31] One would have to wait 15 years after the adoption of the Geneva Convention for the UN Covenants to give a conventional basis to the rights proclaimed in the Universal Declaration of Human Rights. Furthermore, any attempt to draft a true Bill of Rights for refugees would have impinged upon the ongoing negotiations of the forthcoming UN Covenants. This particular normative context explains the byzantine complexity of the refugee status, when it comes to its content and rationale.

3.2.1 The content of the refugee status

The refugee status can be compared to a mathematic equation based on two variables. With some exceptions, the content of refugee status is subordinated to the superposition of two cumulative conditions. The first governs the criteria of entitlement (the

---

[30] For further discussion see notably: C Bauloz and G Ruiz, 'Refugee Status and Subsidiary Protection: Towards a Uniform Content of International Protection?' in V Chetail, P De Bruycker, and F Maiani (eds), *Reforming the Common European Asylum System: The New European Refugee Law* (Brill Nijhoff 2016); LH Storgaard, 'Enhancing and Diluting the Legal Status of Subsidiary Protection Beneficiaries under Union Law. The CJEU Judgment in Alo and Osso' (EU Law Analysis, 9 March 2016) available at <http://eulawanalysis.blogspot.com/2016/03/enhancing-and-diluting-legal-status-of.html> accessed 17 October 2018; C Bauloz, 'The (Mis)Use of International Humanitarian Law under Article 15(c) of the EU Qualification Directive' in J-F Durieux and D Cantor (eds), *Refuge from Inhumanity: Enriching Refugee Protection Standards Through Recourse to International Humanitarian Law* (Martinus Nijhoff 2013); H Battjes, 'Subsidiary Protection and Other Alternative Forms of Protection' in V Chetail and C Bauloz (eds), *Research Handbook on Migration and International Law* (n 26); J McAdam, *Complementary Protection in International Refugee Law* (OUP 2007); R Piotrowicz and C Van Eck, 'Subsidiary Protection and Primary Rights' (2004) 53 ICLQ 107–38.

[31] At this time, the Charter of the United Nations was the only one to have proclaimed in its Article 1 the 'respect for human rights and for fundamental freedoms for all without distinction as to race, sex, language, or religion', without identifying the rights and freedoms in question. The 1948 Universal Declaration of Human Rights was adopted as a non-binding resolution of the General Assembly and only specific treaties focusing on some particular aspects were adopted at the time, mainly under the auspices of the ILO and with regard, for instance, to the prohibition of forced labour. At the regional level, only one regional human rights instrument was adopted in 1950, but it entered into force in 1953 after the adoption of the Geneva Convention. See Convention for the Protection of Human Rights and Fundamental Freedoms (European Convention on Human Rights, as amended by Protocols 11 and 14) (adopted 4 November 1950, entered into force 3 September 1953) 213 UNTS 222 (ECHR).

applicability of the norm) and the second relates to the standard of treatment (the content of the norm).[32]

As far as the first set of conditions is concerned, the entitlement criteria are determined in reference to three distinct levels of applicability. The first level refers to the term 'refugee' without any further qualification. This concerns a core set of basic guarantees which includes the prohibition of discrimination (Article 3), the acquisition of movable and immovable property (Article 13), free access to domestic courts (Article 16(1)), rationing (Article 20), primary education (Article 22(1)), fiscal equality (Article 29), and the protection against *refoulement* (Article 33(1)).

While all refugees benefit from these core guarantees, additional entitlements are determined by the existence of a territorial bond with the asylum state, whose degree of intensity varies from one right to another. The two other levels of applicability respectively require the presence or residence of the refugee, further depending on its physical or lawful nature. Concerning the second level, on the one hand, mere *physical presence* within the territory entails the benefit of freedom of religion (Article 4), the delivery of identity papers (Article 27), and the prohibition of penalties on account of illegal entry (Article 31(1)). A *lawful presence* is further required for other sets of rights such as to engage in self-employment (Article 18), to freely move within the host territory (Article 26), and to be protected against expulsion (Article 32).

As for the third level of applicability, the Convention envisions an additional subdivision based on the nature of residence, the latter breaking down into three variants: physical, lawful, and habitual residence or stay. *Physical residence* entitles refugees to administrative assistance for civil status documents (Article 25). A *lawful residence or stay* on the territory of the asylum state grants the right of association and trade unions (Article 15), wage-earning employment (Article 17), liberal professions (Article 19), housing (Article 21), public relief (Article 23), labour legislation and social security (Article 24), as well as travel documents (Article 28). Finally, *habitual residence* allows refugees to access legal assistance (Article 16(2)), as well as artistic rights and industrial property (Article 14). As a result of this progressive entitlement regime, the Geneva Convention provides an incremental continuum of protection that depends on the intensity of the territorial bond between a refugee and his or her state of asylum. In sum, the longer the refugee remains in the territory of a State Party, the broader becomes the range of entitlements.

Once these entitlement criteria are fulfilled, the precise content of applicable norms is determined according to the traditional distinction between nationals and non-nationals since, at the time of the Convention's drafting, no

---

[32] For other possible classifications, see Carlier, 'Droit d'asile et des réfugiés' (n 7) 271–98; Goodwin-Gill and McAdam, *The Refugee in International Law* (n 7) 506–27; JC Hathaway, *The Rights of Refugees under International Law* (CUP 2005) 154–200.

other normative framework of reference existed. Accordingly, the content of the benefits attached to the refugee status hinges upon three standards of treatment: nationals of the asylum state, most-favoured foreigners, and ordinary aliens. First, refugees benefit from the *same treatment accorded to nationals* regarding freedom of religion (Article 4), artistic and industrial property (Article 14), legal assistance (Article 16(2)), rationing (Article 20), elementary education (Article 22(1)), public relief (Article 23), labour legislation and social security (Article 24), and fiscal charges (Article 29). Second, refugees benefit from the *most favourable treatment accorded to nationals of a foreign country in the same circumstances* concerning the right of association (Article 15) and wage-earning employment (Article 17). Third, the Convention grants a *treatment not less favourable than that accorded to aliens generally in the same circumstances* regarding movable and immovable property (Article 13), self-employment (Article 18), liberal professions (Article 19), housing (Article 21), education other than elementary education (Article 22(2)), and freedom of movement within the asylum state (Article 26).

The superposition of various entitlement criteria with different standards of treatment is subject to one notable exception. A core content of specific guarantees is not contingent upon one of the three standards of treatment, but it applies as soon as the entitlement criteria are fulfilled (refugee, presence, residence). This concerns non-discrimination between and among refugees (Article 3), their personal status in host states (Article 12), access to courts (Article 16(1)), administrative assistance (Article 25), the issuance of identity papers (Article 27) and travel documents (Article 28), the transfer of assets in event of resettlement (Article 30), the prohibition of penalties for illegal entry or presence (Article 31), the protection from expulsion (Article 32), and from *non-refoulement* (Article 33), as well as the facilitation of their naturalization by asylum states (Article 34). The fact that these provisions do not depend upon a particular standard of treatment unveils two fundamental characteristics: these guarantees are specific to refugees, which, in turn, highlights the unique nature of 'refugeehood'.[33] At the same time, they also benefit from an autonomous content that is not contingent upon the treatment accorded by States Parties to nationals or aliens.

The overall picture of the refugee status remains overwhelmingly complex if not puzzling. Table 3.1 intends to bring some clarity to the complicated scheme of refugee rights inherited from the Geneva Convention. The rows identify the entitlement criteria (ie refugee, presence, residence), whereas the columns specify the relevant content which may be either autonomous or relative (ie depending on whether or not it is contingent upon a particular standard of treatment).

---

[33] Hathaway, *The Rights of Refugees under International Law* (n 32) 237.

Table 3.1 Gradual protection of refugees under the Geneva Convention

Entitlement criteria		Autonomous content (specific guarantees)	Contingent standards of treatment		
			Nationals	Most-favoured aliens	Ordinary aliens
Refugee		Non-discrimination (art 3) Personal status (art 12) Transfer of assets (art 30) *Non-refoulement* (art 33) Naturalization (art 34)	Rationing (art 20) Primary education (art 22(1)) Fiscal charges (art 29)		Movable and immovable property (art 13) Education (other than elementary education— art 22(2))
Presence	Physical	Access to courts (art 16(1)) Identity papers (art 27) Prohibition of penalties for illegal entry or presence (art 31)	Freedom of religion (art 4)		
	Lawful	Expulsion (art 32)	Freedom of movement (art 26)		Self-employment (art 18)
Residence/ Stay	Physical	Administrative assistance (art 25)			
	Lawful	Travel documents (art 28)	Public relief (art 23) Labour legislation and social security (art 24)	Right of association (art 15) Wage-earning employment (art 17)	Liberal profession (art 19) Housing (art 21)
	Habitual		Artistic rights and industrial property (art 14) Legal assistance (art 16(2))		

3.2.2 The *ratio legis* of the refugee status

The refugee status with its various entitlement criteria and different standards of treatment remains extremely complex.[34] The rationale underlying such a patchwork of standards is all but obvious and one can surely raise doubts about the practical interest of this sophisticated differentiation. A possible way to conceptualize the *ratio legis* of the gradual protection granted by the Geneva Convention is to equate the refugee status with an 'assimilative path' as elaborated by James C Hathaway in his seminal book on *The Rights of Refugees under International Law*.[35] Following this assimilative approach, the progressive entitlement to rights and benefits encapsulates and determines the applicable law at the three essential stages of refugees' life cycle.

At the outset of this incremental protection regime, the declaratory nature of the refugee status presupposes that asylum-seekers are entitled at a minimum to the core benefits applicable to all refugees without further territorial qualification, as well as, depending on the circumstances, those that are contingent on the physical and lawful presence in the state territory. As underlined by the UNHCR, 'the gradations of treatment allowed by the Convention ... serve as a useful yardstick in the context of defining reception standards for asylum-seekers'.[36] From this angle, the limited range of benefits is grounded in the assumption that the presence of asylum-seekers is bound to be a temporary one for the sole purpose of examining their claims. At the second stage, once a refugee is formally recognized as such, an additional range of entitlements will be granted to then facilitate his or her progressive integration in the new country of residence. At the end of this assimilative process, Article 34—the last provision devoted to the refugee status—encourages States Parties to naturalize refugees. Accordingly, naturalization ensures the full range of rights entitled to nationals and, by the same token, marks the end of the interim protection provided by the refugee status.

Albeit attractive, this conceptualization of the refugee status as an assimilative process remains an *a posteriori* and essentially doctrinal reconstruction.[37] Although some support can be found in the drafting history of the Geneva Convention, the position of plenipotentiaries was neither clear nor unanimous.[38] Besides the limited utility of the

---

[34] This has been exacerbated by a substantial number of reservations formulated by States Parties. See further A Pellet, 'Article 42 of the 1951 Convention/Article VII of the 1967 Protocol' in A Zimmermann (ed), *The 1951 Convention Relating to the Status of Refugees and its 1967 Protocol* (n 7) 1615; Goodwin-Gill and McAdam, *The Refugee in International Law* (n 7) 509–12, Hathaway, *The Rights of Refugees under International Law* (n 32) 95–96; S Blay and M Tsamenyi, 'Reservations and Declarations under the 1951 Convention and the 1967 Protocol Relating to the Status of Refugees' (1990) 2 IJRL 527; A Collella, 'Les réserves à la Convention de Genève (28 juillet 1951) et au Protocole de New York (31 janvier 1967) sur le statut des réfugiés' (1989) 35 AFDI 446.

[35] Hathaway, *The Rights of Refugees under International Law* (n 32) 156.

[36] UNHCR 'Global Consultations on International Protection/Third Track: Reception of Asylum-Seekers, Including Standards of Treatment in the Context of Individual Asylum Systems' (4 September 2001) UN Doc EC/GC/17, para 3.

[37] In this sense, see also Carlier, 'Droit d'asile et des réfugiés' (n 7) 288–89.

[38] For discussion between delegations, see UN ECOSOC 'Ad Hoc Committee on Statelessness and Related Problems: Summary Record of the Fifteenth Meeting' (27 January 1950) First Session (6 February 1950) UN Doc E/AC/32/SR.15; and UN ECOSOC 'Ad Hoc Committee on Statelessness and Related Problems: Summary Record of the Forty-Second Meeting' (24 August 1950) Second Session (28 September 1950) UN Doc E/AC.32/SR.42.

travaux préparatoires, the actual practice barely reflects such an assimilative approach as states remain reluctant to acknowledge the plain applicability of the refugee status to asylum-seekers beyond Articles 31 and 33.[39] More importantly, even for those who have been officially recognized as refugees, the assimilative approach fails to capture the whole picture of the refugee status. Indeed, while this approach remains useful for explaining the first parameter regarding the territorial bond with the asylum state, it says nothing about the second one concerning the relevant standards of treatment.

Furthermore, if the assimilative approach constituted the *ratio legis* of the refugee status, one would expect a causal relation between the criteria of entitlement (refugee, presence, or residence) and the standards of treatment (ordinary aliens, most favoured aliens, or nationals). In other words, the longer a refugee remains in the territory of the State Party, the more protective ought to be the standard of treatment he or she should be able to enjoy. As such, the same treatment accorded to nationals should be equally applicable to a refugee residing lawfully or habitually within the country, whereas the mere presence of the refugee in the territory of States Parties should have triggered the same treatment as for ordinary aliens. This is, however, not the case for there is no correlation between the entitlement criteria and the standards of treatment. Even worse, the two parameters of the refugee status may be different for the same right or subject-matter, such as, for instance, in the field of employment. A lawful stay is required for both wage-earning employment (Article 17) and liberal profession (Article 19), while self-employment activities only depend on a lawful presence (Article 19). In any case, there is no causal link between the entitlement criteria and the standards of treatment since refugees are assimilated to most-favoured aliens for the purpose of wage-earning employment, whereas self-employment and liberal profession are determined in reference to the minimum treatment accorded to ordinary aliens.

Against such a background, one should concede that the content of the refugee status does not result from a deliberate nor coherent design of its drafters.[40] Beyond any possible conceptualization of the rationale underlying the refugee status, the historical normative context prevailing at the time of the drafting of the Geneva Convention played a decisive role in framing the refugee rights regime. This explains both the complexity and specificity of the refugee status. From such a retrospective viewpoint, the refugee status appears as a hybrid legal creation caught in-between the traditional law of aliens and the emerging law of human rights.

While the objective proclaimed by the preamble of the Geneva Convention is 'to assure refugees the widest possible exercise of ... fundamental rights and freedoms', most of the legal categories underlying the 1951 Convention have been borrowed from the law of aliens. Indeed, the two variables of the refugee status are directly inspired by the legislation on aliens, the conventions of establishment, and other related bilateral agreements adopted during the first half of the 20th century.[41] The analogy

---

[39] See, for instance, *R v Secretary of State for the Home Department, ex parte Jammeh* [1998] INLR 701 (CA) 710-711; *Krishnapillai v Canada (Minister of Citizenship and Immigration)* [2002] 3(1) FC 74, para 25.

[40] In this sense, see also Carlier, 'Droit d'asile et des réfugiés' (n 7) 288–89.

[41] For further discussion, see V Chetail, 'Les relations entre droit international privé et droit international des réfugiés: Histoire d'une brève rencontre' (2014) 141(2) JDI 447–75. Historically speaking,

with the law of aliens is obvious with regard to the first parameter of the refugee status, since the notions of presence and residence are the traditional entitlement criteria to define the legal status of aliens.[42] Likewise, the standards of treatment are typically determined with reference to the categories of nationals, most favoured foreigners, and ordinary aliens, in line with the conventions of establishment at the time.[43]

The refugee status has thus been forged on the basis of the legal categories inherited from the law of aliens which were refined and adapted to the specific situation of refugees.[44] This explains why a core content of specific guarantees applies to refugees regardless of any standard of treatment as soon as the entitlement criteria are fulfilled. These guarantees are specific to refugees and they did not have any exact equivalent under the law of aliens because refugees are by definition unprotected by their own states.[45]

Likewise, the need to adapt the law of aliens is further required by the notion of reciprocity, another traditional principle governing the status of foreigners. While acknowledging that reciprocity 'is at the root of the idea of the juridical status of foreigners', the Ad-Hoc Committee underlined that '[s]ince a refugee is not protected by any State the requirement of reciprocity loses its *raison d'être*'.[46] After longstanding discussions between state representatives, however, the final version of Article 7 does not entirely exclude reciprocity. Its second paragraph provides an exemption from legislative reciprocity after a relatively substantial residence period of three years. In order to mitigate this last condition, Article 7(4) recommends States Parties to consider favourably the possibility of extending this exemption to refugees who do not fulfil the requirement of a three-year residence.

Among other instances, the filiation between the law of aliens and refugee law is particularly apparent in Article 7(1), according to which 'except where this Convention contains more favourable provisions, a Contracting State shall accord to refugees the same treatment as is accorded to aliens generally'. Article 7(1), in this sense, functions as a safeguard securing a minimum standard which cannot fall below the treatment accorded to other aliens. As noted by the US representative

the Refugee Conventions concluded in 1933 and 1938 were influenced by the law of aliens, before the same technique was used for the drafting of the 1951 Geneva Convention.

[42] See, for instance, Convention of Establishment between Iraq and Turkey (signed 9 January 1932) 139 LNTS 263; Convention of Establishment between Luxemburg and the Netherlands (signed 1 April 1933) 179 LNTS 11; Convention of Establishment between Belgium and Siam (signed 5 November 1937) 190 LNTS 163.

[43] ibid. See also Treaty of Commerce between Japan and the Czechoslovak Republic (signed 30 October 1925) 58 LNTS 263; Treaty of Friendship, Commerce and Navigation between the United States of America and Siam (signed 13 November 1937) 192 LNTS 247.

[44] See, for instance, art 6 of the 1951 Convention relating to the Status of Refugees.

[45] The Ad-Hoc Committee in charge of preparing the first draft of the Geneva Convention explained that 'Refugees do not enjoy the protection and assistance of the authorities of their country of origin. Consequently, even if the Government of the country of asylum grants the refugee a status which ensures him treatment equivalent to or better than that enjoyed by aliens, he may not in some countries be in a position to enjoy the rights granted him.' See UN ECOSOC 'Report of the Ad Hoc Committee on Statelessness and Related Problems (Corrigendum)' (2 April 1950) UN Doc E/AC.32/5, 53.

[46] ibid 41. See also, the statement of the US representative in UN ECOSOC 'Ad Hoc Committee on Statelessness and Related Problems: Summary Record of the Twenty-Third Meeting' (3 February 1950) First Session (10 February 1950) UN Doc E/AC.32/SR.23, 2.

during the drafting of the Geneva Convention, one can still argue that 'when the Convention gave refugees the same privileges as aliens in general, it was not giving them very much'.[47] Nevertheless, Article 7(1) retains its relevance by restating that refugees cannot be excluded from the rights and benefits granted to other aliens under domestic and international law. This general referral can be traced back to the law of aliens and the normative context prevailing at the time of the drafting of the Geneva Convention. In 1951, the law of aliens provided a normative framework of reference as there was no other equivalent until the subsequent development of human rights law, which profoundly reshaped the basic tenets of the refugee status.

3.2.3 The enlargement of the refugee status by human rights law

Since the adoption of the Geneva Convention, human rights law has become a crucial source of refugee rights.[48] Its added value has been instrumental at four main levels. First, human rights law extends the personal scope of international protection beyond the category of refugees to cover all individuals, including asylum-seekers and other migrants who might face risks of human rights' violation in their own country. As notably acknowledged by the Human Rights Committee[49] and the Committee on Economic, Social and Cultural Rights,[50] the two UN Covenants clearly apply to asylum-seekers. They provide an essential source of protection for this category of persons who are excluded from the Geneva Convention due to States Parties' restrictive and disputable interpretation of its provisions. The impact of human rights law, however, stretches far beyond the legal status of asylum seekers.

Second, even for formally recognized refugees, human rights law has considerably enriched the material scope of international protection by granting a broad range of supplementary rights. For instance, although the Refugee Convention is not indifferent to civil and political rights, it contains a fairly limited range of these fundamental

[47] UN ECOSOC 'Ad Hoc Committee on Refugees and Stateless Persons: Summary Record of the Thirty-Seventh Meeting' (16 August 1950) Second Session (26 September 1950) UN Doc E/AC.32/SR.37, 7.

[48] For further discussion about the impact of human rights law on refugee law, see among other publications V Chetail, 'Are Refugee Rights Human Rights? An Unorthodox Questioning of the Relations between Refugee Law and Human Rights Law' (2014) in R Rubio-Marin (ed), *Human Rights and Immigration* (OUP 2014) 19, 72; Hathaway, *The Rights of Refugees under International Law* (n 32) 1–14; Bhabha, 'Internationalist Gatekeepers?' (n 6) 155; J-F Flauss, 'Les droits de l'homme et la Convention de Genève du 28 juillet 1951 relative au statut des réfugiés' in V Chetail and J-F Flauss (eds), *La Convention de Genève du 28 juillet 1951 relative au statut des réfugiés 50 ans après: Bilan et perspectives* (Bruylant 2001) 91; B Gorlick, 'Human Rights and Refugees: Enhancing Protection through International Human Rights Law' (2000) 69(2) NJIL 117–77; T Clark and F Crépeau, 'Mainstreaming Refugee Rights: The 1951 Refugee Convention and International Human Rights Law' (1999) 17(4) NQHR 389–410.

[49] HRC 'General Comment 31(80): The Nature of the General Legal Obligation Imposed on States Parties to the Covenant' (29 March 2004) Eighteenth Session (26 May 2004) UN Doc CCPR/C/21/Rev.1/Add.13, para 10.

[50] See UN Committee on Economic, Social and Cultural Rights (CESCR), 'General Comment No 20: Non-Discrimination in Economic, Social and Cultural Rights (art 2, para 2, of the International Covenant on Economic, Social and Cultural Rights)' (4–22 May 2009) Forty-second Session (2 July 2009) UN Doc E/C.12/GC/20, para 30, 'The Covenant rights apply to everyone including non-nationals, such as refugees, asylum-seekers, stateless persons, migrant workers and victims of international trafficking, regardless of legal status and documentation.'

rights, covering non-discrimination, freedom of religion, freedom of association, access to court, freedom of movement, and due process guarantees governing expulsion. At the outset, the drafters of the Geneva Convention were aware of this apparent lacuna. During the *travaux préparatoires*, the Belgian delegation proposed an explicit reference to Articles 18 and 19 of the UDHR (devoted to freedoms of thought and expression respectively) in the text of the Geneva Convention. This proposal was finally withdrawn after the UK representative explained that 'a Convention relating to refugees could not include an outline of all the articles of the UDHR; furthermore, by its universal character, the Declaration applied to all human groups without exception, and it was pointless to specify that its provisions applied also to refugees'.[51]

The continuing applicability of human rights law is thus essential to ensure an additional set of crucial rights that are not guaranteed by the Geneva Convention. As far as the ICCPR is concerned, it includes the right to an effective remedy for any violations of the rights recognized in the Covenant (Article 2(3)), the equal right of men and women to the enjoyment of all civil and political rights set forth in the Covenant (Article 3), the right to life (Article 6), the prohibition of torture and cruel, inhuman or degrading treatment or punishment (Article 7), freedom from slavery and forced labour (Article 8), the right of all persons deprived of their liberty to be treated with humanity (Article 10), the prohibition of detention on the ground of inability to fulfil a contractual obligation (Article 11), the right to return to one's own country (Article 12(4)), the right to a fair trial (Article 14), the prohibition of retroactive application of criminal law (Article 15), the right to recognition as a person before the law (Article 16), the right to private and family life (Article 17), the right to hold opinions and freedom of expression (Article 19), the right of peaceful assembly (Article 21), the protection of children (Article 24), the right to equality before the law (Article 26), and the cultural rights of persons belonging to ethnic, religious or linguistic minorities (Article 27).

Third, human rights law is not only broader than refugee law with regard to its personal and material scope, but more fundamentally, the former supplants the latter even when their respective norms overlap on the same subject matter. This is notably exemplified by the prohibition of discrimination under Article 3 of the Geneva Convention which is limited by three substantial qualifications: 1) this provision only prohibits discrimination between and among refugees (thereby excluding any other discrimination between refugees and other foreigners or nationals); 2) the prohibited grounds of discrimination are restricted to 'race, religion or country of origin'; and 3) the scope of Article 3 is circumscribed to the application of the provisions of the Geneva Convention.

By contrast, the principle of equality before the law, as notably enshrined in Article 26 of the ICCPR, provides a free-standing and autonomous protection against discrimination which extends beyond the rights provided by the ICCPR. It further enumerates a non-exhaustive list of prohibited discriminatory grounds that covers both forms of discrimination between refugees and those between refugees

---

[51] UN ECOSOC 'Ad Hoc Committee on Statelessness and Related Problems: Summary Record of the Eleventh Meeting' (1 February 1950) UN Doc E/AC.32/SR1, 8.

and nationals. As such, Article 3 of the Geneva Convention has for the most part—if not totally—been neutralized by Article 26 of the Covenant.[52] The same observation can be made with regard to many other overlapping norms governed by both human rights treaties and the Geneva Convention, such as detention and freedom of association, among others.[53] The fact that human rights law prevails over refugee law is still in line with the Geneva Convention itself, since its Article 5 ensures that 'nothing in this Convention shall be deemed to impair any rights and benefits granted by a Contracting State to refugees apart from this Convention'.

Fourth and finally, human rights law provides a vital source of protection for all refugees and asylum-seekers who are living in states which have not ratified the Geneva Convention or its Protocol. Forty-three UN Member States have neither signed nor ratified either of them. Although refugee lawyers frequently overlook this basic fact, some of these non-parties are among the largest countries of asylum. According to UN estimates, they notably include Jordan (2.9 million refugees), Lebanon (1.6 million), and Pakistan (1.4 million).[54]

3.3 The Principle of *Non-refoulement*

The functional link between the definition and the status of refugees as conferred by the Geneva Convention is ensured by the principle of *non-refoulement*. According to Article 33(1), 'no Contracting State shall expel or return ('refouler') a refugee in any manner whatsoever to the frontiers of territories where his life or freedom would be threatened on account of his race, religion, nationality, membership of a particular social group or political opinion'. This principle is commonly hailed as 'the cornerstone of international refugee law'.[55] Article 42 further endorses the cardinal importance of such an elementary rule by prohibiting any reservation to Article 33.

3.3.1 The scope and content of the principle of *non-refoulement*: an overview

The scope of the *non-refoulement* duty is conceived by the Geneva Convention in relatively broad terms. As further confirmed by subsequent state practice, the inclusive language of Article 33—through the generic expression 'in any manner whatsoever'—clearly acknowledges that the prohibition of *refoulement* applies to any act of forcible removal or rejection that puts the person concerned at risk of persecution. According to the drafters of the Geneva Convention, it means in pith and substance

---

[52] See Hathaway *The Law of Refugee Status* (n 1) 258–59.

[53] For further discussion, see Chetail, 'Are Refugee Rights Human Rights?' (n 48).

[54] UNDESA, Population Division, *International Migration Report 2017: Highlights* (United Nations 2017) ST/ESA/SER.A/403, 7.

[55] San Remo Declaration on the Principle of Non-Refoulement (September 2001), available at <https://www.peacepalacelibrary.nl/ebooks/files/IIHL1_en.pdf> accessed 8 October 2018; UNHCR 'Note on the Principle of Non-Refoulement' (November 1997), available at <http://www.refworld.org/docid/438c6d972.html> accessed 17 October 2018.

that 'refugees fleeing from persecution ... should not be pushed back into the arms of their persecutors'.[56] The legal nature of the act is therefore not relevant, whether it is labelled deportation, extradition, non-admission at the border, maritime interception, transfer, or rendition.[57] The decisive consideration for the purposes of Article 33 is the consequence of this act, namely whether one's life or liberty would be threatened on account of a Convention reason.

Following this stance, the prohibition of *refoulement* applies to both asylum-seekers and recognized refugees, provided that they are within the jurisdiction of a State Party. The primary function of this principle is twofold. On the one hand, Article 33 ensures asylum-seekers access to protection in order to assess whether they fulfil the refugee definition under Article 1(A)(2). On the other hand, it guarantees the stability of the refugee status for those who have been formally recognized as refugees. The applicability of Article 33 to asylum-seekers is firmly based on two main grounds: the declaratory nature of the refugee status and the basic principles governing interpretation of treaties. As acknowledged by the UNHCR Handbook on Procedures:

A person is a refugee within the meaning of the 1951 Convention as soon as he fulfils the criteria contained in the definition. This would necessarily occur prior to the time at which his refugee status is formally determined. Recognition of his refugee status does not therefore make him a refugee but declares him to be one. He does not become a refugee because of recognition, but is recognized because he is a refugee.[58]

Because of the declaratory nature of the refugee status, Article 33 applies to refugees who have not been formally recognized but are claiming protection. UNHCR rightly stresses that:

[56] UN ECOSOC 'Ad Hoc Committee on Refugees and Stateless Persons, Statement of the Chairman, Mr Chance of Canada' (2 February 1950) UN Doc E/AC.32/SR.21, 7, para. 26. See also UN ECOSOC, 'Ad Hoc Committee on Refugees and Stateless Persons, Memorandum by the Secretary General' (3 January 1950) UN Doc E/AC.32/2, Comments on Article 24 of the preliminary draft, para 3.
[57] For further discussion about the material scope of the non-refoulement duty, see especially W Kälin, M Caroni, and L Heim, 'Article 33, para 1 Prohibition of Expulsion or Return ("Refoulement")/ Défense d'expulsion et de refoulement)' in A Zimmermann (ed), *The 1951 Convention Relating to the Status of Refugees and its 1967 Protocol* (n 7) 1327–95; CW Wouters, *International Legal Standards for the Protection from Refoulement* (Intersentia 2009); Carlier, 'Droit d'asile et des réfugiés' (n 7) 332; Goodwin-Gill and McAdam, *The Refugee in International Law* (n 7) 201–84; Hathaway, *The Rights of Refugees under International Law* (n 32) 278–369; E Lauterpacht and D Bethlehem, 'The Scope and Content of the Principle of Non-Refoulement: Opinion' in E Feller, V Türk, and F Nicholson (eds), *Refugee Protection in International Law* (n 14) 87; V Chetail, 'Le principe de non refoulement et le statut de réfugié en droit international' in V Chetail and J-F Flauss (eds), *La Convention de Genève du 28 juillet 1951 relative au statut des réfugiés 50 ans après* (n 48) 3.
[58] UNHCR 'Handbook and Guidelines on Procedures and Criteria for Determining Refugee Status under the 1951 Convention and the 1967 Protocol Relating to the Status of Refugees' (2011) UN Doc HCR/1P/4/ENG/REV.3, para 38. Among many other acknowledgements of the declaratory nature of the refugee status, see notably art 31 of European Parliament and Council Directive 2011/95/EU of 13 December 2011 (n 15); *Mileva v Canada (Minister of Employment and Immigration)* [1991] FCA 27 ACWS 3d 480, art 45; *Khaboka v Secretary of State for the Home Department* [1993] Imm AR 484 (CA), 489 (Nolan LJ).

Every refugee is, initially, also an asylum-seeker; therefore, to protect refugees, asylum-seekers must be treated on the assumption that they may be refugees until their status has been determined. Otherwise, the principle of non-refoulement would not provide effective protection for refugees, because applicants might be rejected at borders or otherwise returned to persecution on the grounds that their claim had not been established.[59]

This well-established understanding is confirmed by the principle of effectiveness (*effet utile*), which constitutes 'one of the fundamental principles of interpretation of treaties'.[60] According to this basic notion, amongst several possible interpretations, the one that best guarantees the practical effect of the relevant provision shall prevail. Any other interpretation that excludes asylum-seekers from *non-refoulement* would defeat the very object and purpose of the Geneva Convention as a whole in blatant contradiction with the basic principles of interpretation codified in Article 31 of the Vienna Convention on the Law of Treaties. The plain applicability of Article 33 to asylum-seekers has been further acknowledged by States Parties in their subsequent interpretation of the Convention.[61]

The impact of its application to asylum-seekers is particularly straightforward for the mere act of asking for protection triggers the benefit of *non-refoulement* in order to assess whether the applicant actually corresponds to the definition of refugees. Furthermore, contrary to many other provisions of the Geneva Convention, Article 33 is not dependent on the presence—whether regular or irregular—of asylum-seekers. It thus applies as soon as asylum seekers are within the territorial or extraterritorial jurisdiction of States Parties. The notion of extraterritorial jurisdiction is traditionally understood in international law as extending to 'anyone within the power or effective control of that State Party, even if not situated within the territory of the State Party',[62] such as in the case of maritime

---

[59] UNCHR 'Note on International Protection: Submitted by the High Commissioner' (31 August 1993) UN Doc A/AC.96/815, 5. See also, among others, UNHCR EXCOM Conclusion No 6 (XXVIII) 'Non-Refoulement' (1977) UN Doc A/32/12/Add.1, para e; UNHCR EXCOM Conclusion No 79 (XLVII) 'General Conclusion on International Protection' (1996) UN Doc A/AC.96/878 and A/51/12/Add.1, para j.

[60] *Case Concerning the Territorial Dispute (Libyan Arab Jamahiriya/Chad)* (Judgment) [1994] ICJ Rep 6, para 51.

[61] See, among many other similar acknowledgements, UNGA Res 44/137 (15 December 1989) UN Doc A/RES/44/137, para 3; UNGA Res 45/140 (14 December 1991) UN Doc A/RES/45/140, para 4; UNGA Res 46/106 (16 December 1991) UN Doc A/RES/46/106, para 4; UNGA Res 51/75 (12 December 1996) UN Doc A/RES/51/75, preamble; UNGA Res 52/103 (12 December 1997) UN Doc A/RES/52/103, para 5; UNGA Res 52/132 (12 December 1997) UN Doc A/RES/52/132, para 16; UNGA Res 53/125 (9 December 1998) UN Doc A/RES/53/125, para 5; UNGA Res 54/146 (17 December 1999) UN Doc A/RES/54/146, para 6; UNGA Res 55/74 (4 December 2000) UN Doc A/RES/55/74, para 6; UNGA Res 59/170 (20 December 2004) UN Doc A/RES/59/170, para 14; UNGA Res 59/172 (20 December 2004) UN Doc A/RES/59/172, para 13. At the regional level, see also, EU Qualification Directive (n 21), art 21 and Bangkok Principles on the Status and Treatment of Refugees, adopted at the Asian-African Legal Consultative Organization's (AALCO) 40th Session (31 December 1966) art III(3); Parliamentary Assembly of the Council of Europe, Recommendation 293 on the Right of Asylum (29 September 1961) art 1(3). See also among other domestic restatements: *R v Secretary of State for the Home Department, ex parte Adan & Aitseguer* [2001] 1 All ER 593 (HL), 603 (Lord Steyn).

[62] HRC 'General Comment No 31-Nature of the General Legal Obligation Imposed on States Parties to the Covenant' (26 May 2004) UN Doc CCPR/C/21/Rev.1/Add.13, para 10, as confirmed by

interception.[63] This explains the powerful attraction exercised by the principle of *non-refoulement* over the traditional competence of states in carrying out migration controls, whether outside or within their borders.[64]

The extensive scope of this duty of *non-refoulement* is, however, qualified by two exceptions spelt out in Article 33(2) of the Refugee Convention. According to this provision, the principle of *non-refoulement* cannot be claimed by a refugee or an asylum-seeker 'whom there are reasonable grounds for regarding as a danger to the security of the country in which he is, or who, having been convicted by a final judgement of a particularly serious crime, constitutes a danger to the community of that country'. Each exception follows its own rationale and purpose: the first is aimed at safeguarding the security of the state and its institutions, while the second one focuses on the protection of the host society against criminality.

As with any exception to a principle (especially when fundamental rights are at stake), 'it is clear that Article 33(2) exception must be interpreted restrictively'.[65] While states retain a substantial margin of appreciation, the threshold of these two exceptions remains relatively high. Regarding the first one, '[t]he wording of the provision ... requires the person him or herself to constitute a danger to national security'.[66] That a person be able to threaten the security of a whole country confines such a hypothesis to highly exceptional circumstances, mainly limited to terrorism, military operations, espionage, and other related activities aimed at overthrowing its institutions. In any event, 'the threat must be "serious", in the sense that it must be grounded on objectively reasonable suspicion based on evidence and in the sense that the threatened harm must be substantial rather than negligible'.[67]

The second exception is also quite restrictive as exemplified by the cautious wording of Article 33(2). It is circumscribed by three cumulative conditions: first,

the ICJ, Advisory Opinion, *Legal Consequences of the Construction of a Wall in the Occupied Palestinian Territory* [2004] ICJ 136, paras 108–11.

[63] Among many other confirmations, see for instance: IAComHR, *The Haitian Centre for Human Rights et al v United States*, Case No 10.675, Report No 51/96 (IAComHR13 March 1997) Doc OEA/Ser.L/V/II.95 Doc 7 Rev, paras 156–57; ECtHR, *Hirsi Jamma and others v Italy* ECHR 2012-II 97, paras 70–77. For further analysis, see T De Boer, 'Closing Legal Black Holes: The Role of Extraterritorial Jurisdiction in Refugee Rights Protection' (2014) 28(1) JRS 118–34; S Trevisanut, 'The Principle of *Non-Refoulement* and the De-Territorialization of Border Control at Sea' (2014) 27 LJIL 661–75; GS Goodwin-Gill, 'The Right to Seek Asylum: Interception at Sea and the Principle of *Non-Refoulement*' (2011) 23 IJRL 443; B Ryan and V Mitsilegas (eds), *Extraterritorial Immigration Control: Legal Challenges* (Martinus Nijhoff 2010); A Fischer-Lescano, T Löhr, and T Tohidipur, 'Border Controls at Sea: Requirements under International Human Rights and Refugee Law' (2009) 21(2) IJRL 256–96; R Barnes, 'Refugee Law at Sea' (2004) 53(1) ICLQ 47–77.

[64] See the next section for further discussion about the interaction between *non-refoulement* and asylum.

[65] *Attorney General v Zaoui* (2004) Dec No CA20/04, at para 136. Whether this should amount to a proportionality test between the threat to national security and the risk of persecution is more controversial in state practice. Compare for instance: *Attorney General v Zaoui and others* (2005) NZSC 38, paras 19–42 and *Secretary of State for the Home Department v Rehman* (2001) UKHL 47, at para 16 (Lord Slynn) and para 56 (Lord Hoffmann).

[66] *Attorney General v Zaoui* (2004) (n 65) para 148.

[67] *Suresh v Canada (Minister of Citizenship and Immigration)* (2002) 1 SCR 3, para 90. See also: *Attorney General v Zaoui* (2004) (n 65) paras 133 and 140; *NSH v Secretary of State for the Home Department* (1988) Imm AR 410.

the refugee must have been 'convicted by a final judgement', presupposing thus the exhaustion of all judicial remedies; second, this conviction has been pronounced for 'a particularly serious crime', thereby requiring a case-by-case assessment of the nature of the crime, the gravity of the inflicted harm and the circumstances surrounding its perpetration; and third, because of his/her criminal record and the risk of subsequent offence, the refugee represents him or herself 'a danger to the community' as a whole.[68]

As exemplified by these exceptions, the principle of *non-refoulement* operates as a pragmatic attempt to reconcile two competing values. It preserves a subtle—and sometimes insecure—compromise between the inescapable competence of states to control access to their territory and the imperious protection of refugees threatened in their life and liberty. This balancing act explains in turn the complex interaction between *non-refoulement* and asylum.

3.3.2 The relations between asylum and *non-refoulement*

Although its scope and content are well settled, the principle of *non-refoulement* retains some ambiguous relations with the very notion of asylum. From both a conceptual and legal perspective, *non-refoulement* must be distinguished from asylum. At the conceptual level, *non-refoulement* is a negative notion, prohibiting states from sending any person back to a country of persecution. As underlined during the drafting of the Geneva Convention, '[i]t imposed a negative duty forbidding the expulsion of any refugee to certain territories but did not impose the obligation to allow a refugee to take up residence'.[69] By contrast, asylum is a positive concept, which entails the admission to a new residence and a long-lasting protection against the jurisdiction of another state.[70] This conceptual distinction between asylum and

---

[68] See in particular: *A v Minister for Immigration and Multicultural Affairs* (1999) FCA 227, para 42. For further analysis of Article 33(2), see notably: A Zimmermann and P Wennholz, 'Article 33, para. 2', in A Zimmermann (ed), *The 1951 Convention Relating to the Status of Refugees and its 1967 Protocol* (n 7) 1397; Goodwin-Gill and McAdam, *The Refugee in International Law* (n 7) 234–44; Hathaway, *The Rights of Refugees under International Law* (n 32) 342–54; Lauterpacht and Bethlehem 'The Scope and Content of the Principle of Non-Refoulement' (n 57) 128–40; Chetail, 'Le principe de non refoulement' (n 57) 12–15 and 39–46.

[69] See the statement of Mr Weis of the International Refugee Organization in UN ECOSOC 'Ad Hoc Committee on Refugees and Stateless Persons: Summary Record of the Fortieth Meeting' (22 August 1950) Second Session (27 September 1950) UN Doc E/AC.32/SR40, 33. For a more recent acknowledgement, see *M38/2002 v Minister for Immigration and Multicultural and Indigenous Affairs* [2003] FCAGC 131, para 39.

[70] More generally, the notion of asylum is much broader than the one of refugee protection under the Geneva Convention since the former includes all types of protection, whether discretionary or not, granted by states under domestic or international law. According to the generic definition adopted in 1950 by the Institute of International Law, asylum means 'the protection that a state grants on its territory or in other place subject to certain of its organs to an individual who comes to seek it' (translation from the author). See Institut de droit international, Session de Bath, *L'asile en droit international public (à l'exclusion de l'asile neutre)* (1950) art 1. For further discussion, see notably M-T Gil-Bazo, 'Asylum as a General Principle of International Law' (2015) 27(1) IJRL 3–28; R Boed, 'The State of the Right of Asylum in International Law' (1994) 5 Duke J Comp & Int'l L 1–33; G Gilbert, 'Right of Asylum: A Change of Direction,' (1983) 32 ICLQ 633, 637; A Grahl-Madsen, *Territorial Asylum* (Almqvist & Wiksell International 1980); SP Sinha, *Asylum and International Law* (Martinus Nijhoff 1971).

non-refoulement is further grounded on their respective legal nature: *non-refoulement* is an obligation of states, whereas asylum is a right of states. As stressed by several domestic courts, 'it has long been recognised that, according to customary international law, the right of asylum is a right of States, not of the individual'.[71]

As a result of this normative disjuncture, and although the content of the refugee status is spelt out in considerable details, the Geneva Convention does not contain any provision on asylum.[72] The silence on this crucial issue may be surprising for 'to speak of refugees is to speak of asylum, the very condition of their existence'.[73] Such normative hiatus between the right of asylum and the obligation of *non-refoulement* was, however, intentional. The Geneva Convention was carefully drafted to make sure that no obligation to grant asylum was explicitly imposed on States Parties. The UK delegate made clear at the 1951 Conference that '[t]he right of asylum ... was only a right, belonging to the State, to grant or refuse asylum not a right belonging to the individual and entitling him to insist on its being extended to him'.[74] Nevertheless, he admitted that 'the only article which had any bearing on that aspect of the matter was the article [33] prohibiting the expulsion of a refugee to a country where his life or freedom would be in danger'.[75]

The principle of *non-refoulement* plays indeed a pivotal role in the absence of a human right to asylum. The Universal Declaration of Human Rights has failed to enshrine an individual right to be granted asylum. Its Article 14 refers instead to a vague and permissive proclamation without any correlative obligation of admission. It declares in minimalist terms that '[e]veryone has *the right to seek and to enjoy* in other countries asylum from persecution'.[76] Lauterpacht described this formula as 'artificial to the point of flippancy', for 'there was no intention to assume even a moral obligation to grant asylum' and, accordingly, 'no declaration would be necessary to give an individual the right to seek asylum without an assurance of receiving

---

[71] *Minister for Immigration and Multicultural Affairs v Khawar* [2002] HCA 14, para 42 (McHugh and Gummow JJ). See also, among many other similar judicial statements, *R v Immigration Officer at Prague Airport and another ex parte Roma Rights Centre and others* [2004] UKHL 55, paras 11–17 (Lord Bingham of Cornhill).

[72] The only explicit reference to asylum can be found in the preamble of the Geneva Convention in rather pejorative terms, 'considering that the grant of asylum may place unduly heavy burdens on certain countries, and that a satisfactory solution of a problem of which the United Nations has recognized the international scope and nature cannot therefore be achieved without international co-operation'.

[73] S Aga Khan, 'Legal Problems Relating to Refugees and Displaced Persons' (1976) 149(I) Collected Courses of the Hague Academy of International Law 287, 316.

[74] UNGA 'Conference of Plenipotentiaries on the Status of Refugees and Stateless Persons: Summary Record of the Thirteenth Meeting' (22 November 1951) UN Doc A/CONF.2/SR/13, 13.

[75] UNGA 'Conference of Plenipotentiaries on the Status of Refugees and Stateless Persons: Summary Record of the Nineteenth Meeting' (26 November 1951) UN Doc A/CONF.2/SR/19, 18.

[76] Universal Declaration of Human Rights (adopted 10 December 1948) UNGA Res 217 A(III) (UDHR) (emphasis added). Even formulated in such evasive terms, the right to seek and to enjoy asylum is further restricted by the traditional exception based on criminal behaviour and other related acts. According to art 14(2), '[t]his right may not be invoked in the case of prosecutions genuinely arising from non-political crimes or from acts contrary to the purposes and principles of the United Nations'. On this last provision, see S Kapferer, 'Article 14(2) of the Universal Declaration and Human Rights and Exclusion from International Refugee Protection' (2008) 27(3) RSQ 53–75.

it'.[77] In fact, the right of asylum shares the same fate as the right to property, being the only rights proclaimed in the Universal Declaration that were not restated in the UN Covenants.[78]

The traditional distinction between the state obligation of *non-refoulement* and its sovereign right to grant or refuse asylum does not reflect, however, their close intermingling for the former frames and constrains the latter. In other words, the right for a state to grant or refuse asylum shall be exercised in accordance with its duty of *non-refoulement*. From this angle, the distinction between *non-refoulement* and asylum appears highly artificial in practice.[79] Although *non-refoulement* is primarily an obligation of result, asylum is generally the only practical means to respect and ensure respect for Article 33. Indeed, how can a state remove an asylum-seeker without first and foremost assessing whether his or her life or liberty is threatened in the country of destination? Such a constructive ambiguity was the price to pay for preserving the appearance of state sovereignty with due regard to the most essential right of refugees.

In practice, states have two options for complying with their duty of *non-refoulement*: granting temporary asylum in order to examine whether the asylum-seeker is a refugee under the Geneva Convention, or sending him or her to a different country where there is no risk of persecution.[80] Even in the latter case, the removal to a safe third country requires some form of temporary admission to assess that the third country is not a country of persecution and provides effective protection against any subsequent *refoulement* in breach of Article 33.[81] It further presupposes

---

[77] H Lauterpacht, 'The Universal Declaration of Human Rights' (1948) 25 BYIL 354. The 1967 Declaration on Territorial Asylum restates in the same vein as the Universal Declaration that '[a]sylum granted by a State, in the exercise of its sovereignty, to persons entitled to invoke article 14 of the Universal Declaration of Human Rights, including persons struggling against colonialism, shall be respected by all other States' (art 1(1)), and '[i]t shall rest with the State granting asylum to evaluate the grounds for the grant of asylum' (art 1(3)).

[78] At the regional level, however, the American Convention on Human Rights ((adopted 22 November 1969, entered into force 18 July 1978) 1144 UNTS 123) and the African Charter on Human and Peoples' Rights ((adopted 27 June 1981, entered into force 21 October 1986) 1520 UNTS 217) have explicitly endorsed 'the right to seek and be granted asylum'. This straightforward endorsement is still mitigated by the requirement to be exercised 'in accordance with the [domestic] legislation of the state'. See art 22 (7) of the American Convention and art 12(3) of the African Charter.

[79] Referring to the interaction between asylum and *non-refoulement*, the UK Supreme Court has acknowledged that 'although a refugee has no direct right to insist on asylum, there are certain statutory restrictions on the Secretary of State's freedom of choice as to the destination to which a person refused permission to remain may be sent, which may in practice achieve the same result'. See *T v Secretary of State for the Home Department* [1996] AC 742, 754 (Lord Mustill).

[80] These two alternatives are acknowledged in state practice and they may be inferred from Article 31(2) of the Geneva Convention, which provides that 'restrictions [to the movement of refugees] shall only be applied until their status in the country is regularized or they obtain admission into another country'.

[81] The very notion of safe third country remains however a highly debatable and ambiguous practice. Under international law, the Geneva Convention neither explicitly authorizes nor formally prohibits the contested notion of safe third country. On the one hand, no provision of the Geneva Convention requires asylum seekers to ask for protection in the first safe country they have reached. On the other hand, removal toward safe third countries is not prohibited by the principle of *non-refoulement* (Article 33), while asylum seekers coming from third states are not immune from penalty on account of their illegal entry (Article 31). The notion of safe third country is accordingly built on the silence of the Geneva Convention for the very purpose of refusing any assessment of asylum claims and deflecting

that the asylum-seeker would be admissible in the safe third country. This requirement is hardly satisfied in the absence of readmission agreements or other related schemes for allocating the responsibility of examining the asylum request (such as the Dublin Regulation for European Union Member States and Associated States).[82] In sum, whatever option taken by states to implement Article 33, due respect for the principle of *non-refoulement* implicitly requires 'a de facto duty to admit the refugee' whether formally recognized or not.[83] This obligation is, however, not absolute and may be refused in accordance with the exceptions contained in Article 33(2).

Despite its qualified and implicit nature, the duty to grant temporary admission to asylum-seekers finds additional support in Article 31(1) of the Geneva Convention, which prohibits the imposition of penalties for irregular entry or stay in the territory of States Parties.[84] This provision is specifically aimed at exempting asylum-seekers from the entry requirements generally imposed on immigrants. The drafters of the Geneva Convention were indeed plainly aware that:

A refugee whose departure from his country of origin is usually a flight, is rarely in a position to comply with the requirements for legal entry (possession of national passport and visa) into the country of refuge. It would be in keeping with the notion of asylum to exempt from penalties a refugee, escaping from persecution, who after crossing the frontier clandestinely presents himself as soon as possible to the authorities of the country of asylum and is recognized as a *bona fide* refugee.[85]

As confirmed by domestic courts afterwards, the purpose of Article 31 is 'to provide immunity for genuine refugees whose quest for asylum reasonably involved them in breaching the law' of States Parties.[86] The principle of *non-refoulement*,

---

such responsibility onto other states. For further discussion see: V Moreno-Lax, 'The Legality of the Safe Third Country Notion Contested: Insights from the Law of Treaties' in GS Goodwin-Gill and P Weckel (eds), *Migration and Refugee Protection in the 21st Century: International Legal Aspects* (Martinus Nijhoff 2015) 665–721; M-T Gil-Bazo, 'The Practice of Mediterranean States in the Context of the European Union's Justice and Home Affairs External Dimension: The Safe Third Country Concept Revisited' (2006) 18(3-4) IJRL 571–600; M Foster, 'Responsibility Sharing or Shifting? 'Safe' Third Countries and International Law' (2008) 25(2) Refuge 64–78; Chetail, 'Le principe de non-refoulement' (n 57) 25–34.

[82] Regulation (EU) No 604/2013 of the European Parliament and of the Council of 26 June 2013 establishing the criteria and mechanisms for determining the Member States responsible for examining an application for international protection lodged in one of the Member States by a third-country national or a stateless person (recast) [2013] OJ L 180, 31–59.

[83] Hathaway, *The Rights of Refugees under International Law* (n 32) 301. See also among many others: Carlier 'Droit d'asile et des réfugiés' (n 7) 85; Goodwin-Gill and McAdam *The Refugee in International Law* (n 7) 384.

[84] 'The Contracting States shall not impose penalties, on account of their illegal entry or presence, on refugees who, coming directly from a territory where their life or freedom was threatened in the sense of article 1, enter or are present in their territory without authorization, provided they present themselves without delay to the authorities and show good cause for their illegal entry or presence.'

[85] Memorandum by the Secretary General (n 56) Comments on Article 24 of the preliminary draft, para 3.

[86] *R v Uxbridge Magistrates' Court ex parte Adimi* (1999) 4 All ER 520, at 527 (Simon Brown LJ). It also confirmed that 'Article 31 extends not merely to those ultimately accorded refugee status but also to those claiming asylum in good faith (presumptive refugees) is not in doubt. Nor is it disputed that Article 31's protection can apply equally to those using false documents as to those … who enter a country clandestinely.'

combined with the duty of non-penalization, considerably challenge the traditional prerogative of states in the field of migration control.[87] The Australian High Court acknowledges in this sense that 'the Convention represents a significant but quali-fied limitation upon the absolute right of the member States to admit those whom they choose'.[88]

As a result of the twofold obligation of *non-refoulement* and non-penalization, states are committed to grant temporary admission in order to assess the claims for protection submitted by any persons at risk of persecution. They still retain, at the domestic level, a particularly broad margin of appreciation in assessing asylum requests, because the Geneva Convention is silent on the procedures for recognizing refugee status. In prac-tice, domestic asylum procedures have increasingly become a stand-alone migration control tool rather than a proper means for identifying persons in need of international protection.[89] States accordingly recapture at the implementation level a portion of the sovereignty they have alienated at the normative level by agreeing to a detailed regime of refugee protection.

3.3.3 The principle of *non-refoulement* under human rights law

Similarly to the refugee status examined above, the normative development of human rights law has considerably reinforced and consolidated the principle of *non-refoulement* as a fundamental tool of protection. At the universal level, this basic principle has been expressly endorsed in the 1984 UN Convention against Torture (Article 3)[90] and the 2006 UN International Convention for the Protection of All

---

[87] One should stress that, while irregular entry is utterly irrelevant for benefiting from the prin-ciple of *non-refoulement*, the prohibition of penalties is much more limited in scope. It does not apply to all asylum-seekers but only to those who satisfy the three following conditions: they come dir-ectly from a country of persecution; they present themselves without delay to the national author-ities; and show good cause for their illegal entry or presence. See on the scope and content of Article 31(1): G Noll, 'Article 31 (Refugees Unlawfully in the Country of Refuge)' in A Zimmermann (ed), *The 1951 Convention relating to the Status of Refugees and Its 1967 Protocol* (n 7) 1243; Hathaway, *The Rights of Refugees under International Law* (n 32) 385–412; GS Goodwin-Gill, 'Article 31 of the 1951 Convention Relating to the Status of Refugees: Non-Penalization, Detention and Protection' in E Feller, V Türk, and F Nicholson (eds), *Refugee Protection in International Law* (n 14) 185; R Dunstan, 'United Kingdom: Breaches of Article 31 of the 1951 Refugee Convention' (1998) 10 IJRL 205.

[88] *Minister for Immigration and Multicultural Affairs v Khawar* (2002) HCA 14, para 68 (McHugh and Gummow JJ).

[89] The EU directive governing asylum procedures did not change this basic pattern, as it mainly endorses restrictive national practices. For instance, the accelerated asylum procedure leaves a consid-erable margin of appreciation to Member States. Although this kind of procedural devices is not *stricto sensu* incompatible with international law, the discretion left to decision-makers can increase the risk of *refoulement* in breach of the Refugee Convention. Such a risk is all but virtual, given the subjectivity inherent in the grounds justifying an accelerated procedure. See art 31 of the Directive 2013/32/EU of the European Parliament and of the Council of 26 June 2013 on common procedures for granting and withdrawing international protection (recast) [2013] OJ L 180, 60–95.

[90] '1. No State Party shall expel, return ("refouler") or extradite a person to another State where there are substantial grounds for believing that he would be in danger of being subjected to torture. 2. For the purpose of determining whether there are such grounds, the competent authorities shall take into account all relevant considerations including, where applicable, the existence in the State con-cerned of a consistent pattern of gross, flagrant or mass violations of human rights.' Convention against

Persons from Enforced Disappearance (Article 16).[91] At the regional level, numerous conventions have similarly done so, most notably in the 1969 American Convention on Human Rights (Article 22(8)),[92] the 1985 Inter-American Convention to Prevent and Punish Torture (Article 13(4)),[93] the 2000 Charter of Fundamental Rights of the European Union (Article 19(2)),[94] and—to some extent—the 2004 Arab Charter on Human Rights (Article 28).[95]

Besides these explicit endorsements, most general human rights treaties have been construed by their respective monitoring bodies as inferring an implicit prohibition of *refoulement*. As early as 1961, the European Commission of Human Rights considered that the removal of foreigners may raise an issue under the general prohibition of torture, inhuman, and degrading treatment.[96] This purposive interpretation was notably endorsed in 1965 by the Parliamentary Assembly of the Council of Europe,[97] before being finally confirmed in 1989 by the European Court of Human Rights in the landmark *Soering* case.[98] Since then, this implied duty of *non-refoulement* has been endorsed by the Human Rights Committee,[99] the Committee on the Rights of the Child,[100] the Committee on the Elimination

Torture and Other Cruel, Inhuman or Degrading Treatment or Punishment (adopted 10 December 1984, entered into force 26 June 1987) 1465 UNTS 85 (CAT).

[91] '1. No State Party shall expel, return ("refouler"), surrender or extradite a person to another State where there are substantial grounds for believing that he or she would be in danger of being subjected to enforced disappearance. 2. For the purpose of determining whether there are such grounds, the competent authorities shall take into account all relevant considerations, including, where applicable, the existence in the State concerned of a consistent pattern of gross, flagrant or mass violations of human rights or of serious violations of international humanitarian law.' International Convention for the Protection of All Persons from Enforced Disappearance (adopted 20 December 2006, entered into force 23 December 2010) 2716 UNTS 3.

[92] 'In no case may an alien be deported or returned to a country, regardless of whether or not it is his country of origin, if in that country his right to life or personal freedom is in danger of being violated because of his race, nationality, religion, social status, or political opinions.' American Convention on Human Rights (n 78).

[93] 'Extradition shall not be granted nor shall the person sought be returned when there are grounds to believe that his life is in danger, that he will be subjected to torture or to cruel, inhuman or degrading treatment, or that he will be tried by special or ad hoc courts in the requesting State.' Inter-American Convention to Prevent and Punish Torture (adopted 9 December 1985, entered into force 28 February 1987) OAS Treaty Series No 67.

[94] 'No one may be removed, expelled or extradited to a State where there is a serious risk that he or she would be subjected to the death penalty, torture or other inhuman or degrading treatment or punishment.' Charter of Fundamental Rights of the European Union (18 December 2000, entered into force 1 December 2009) OJ C 326.

[95] Article 28 refers to the prohibition of extradition instead of the more generic term of *refoulement*: 'Political refugees may not be extradited.'

[96] *X v Belgium* (1961) 6 CD 39.

[97] Parliamentary Assembly of the Council of Europe 'Recommendation 434 on the Granting of Asylum to European Refugees' (1 October 1965) paras 3–4.

[98] *Soering v the United Kingdom* (1989) 11 EHRR 439, paras 87–88.

[99] HRC, 'General Comment No 20: Article 7 (Prohibition of Prohibition of Torture and Cruel Treatment or Punishment)' in 'Note by the Secretariat, Compilation of General Comments and General Recommendations adopted by Human Rights Treaty Bodies' (2008) UN Doc HRI/GEN/1/Rev.9 Vol I, para 9.

[100] UN Committee on the Rights of the Child (CRC Committee) 'General Comment No 6 (2005): Treatment of Unaccompanied and Separated Children Outside their Country of Origin' (1 September 2005) UN Doc CRC/GC/2005/6, para 27.

of Discrimination against Women,[101] the Inter-American Commission of Human Rights,[102] and the African Commission on Human and Peoples' Rights.[103]

Even though treaty bodies have remained surprisingly evasive about the exact basis of their praetorian construction, this implicit duty of *non-refoulement* is anchored in the theory of positive obligations. States not only have the negative obligation to refrain from violating human rights; they also have the positive obligation to prevent violations so as to ensure the effective enjoyment of the basic rights at stake.[104] This obligation of prevention is applicable to virtually all human rights provided that there is a real risk of serious violation in the receiving state. The implied duty of *non-refoulement* has been notably acknowledged by the Human Rights Committee with regard to any right under the Covenant.[105] The European Court is, however, more hesitant and obviously embarrassed by any further enlargement besides the prohibition of torture, inhuman or degrading treatment, the right to life, freedom from slavery and arbitrary detention, and the right to a fair trial.[106] In any case, identifying the specific human rights triggering the principle of *non-refoulement* largely remains an academic and arguably sterile exercise. Serious violations of any human rights would prompt the correlative prohibition of *refoulement*, as soon as the gravity of the prospective violation amounts to degrading treatment.

Following that stance, the human rights principle of *non-refoulement* coincides in substance with its refugee law counterpart. While the notions of degrading treatment and of persecution retain their own autonomous meanings, defining them by

---

[101] UN Committee on the Elimination of Discrimination Against Women (CEDAW) 'Communication No 33/2011 concerning MNN v Denmark' in 'Decision adopted by the Committee at its fifty-fifth session 8–26 July 2013' (15 August 2013) UN Doc CEDAW/C/D/33/2011, para 8.10.

[102] *The Haitian Centre for Human Rights et al v United States*, Case No 10.675, Report No 51/96 (IAComHR 13 March 1997) Doc OEA/Ser.L/V/II.95 Doc 7 Rev, para 167; *John K Modise v Botswana*, Decision on Merits, Comm No 97/93, IHRL 223 (AComHPR 2000) para 91.

[103] African Commission on Human and Peoples' Rights (AComHPR) 'Resolution on Guidelines and Measures for the Prohibition and Prevention of Torture, Cruel, Inhuman or Degrading Treatment or Punishment in Africa (Robben Island Guidelines)' (2nd edn, Addis Ababa 2008) part I (D).

[104] V Chetail, 'Le droit des réfugiés à l'épreuve des droits de l'homme' (2004) 37(1) RBDI 155, especially 160–70. For further discussion about the possible rationale underlying the implicit duty of *non-refoulement*, see also: H Battjes, 'The *Soering* Threshold: Why Only Fundamental Values Prohibit Refoulement in ECHR Case Law' (2009) 11 EJML 205; M Foster, 'Non-Refoulement on the Basis of Socio-Economic Deprivation' (2009) NZLRev 257, 265–79; M Den Heijer, 'Whose Rights and Which Rights? The Continuing Story of Non-Refoulement under the European Convention on Human Rights' (2008) 10 EJML 277; W Kälin, 'Limits to Expulsion under the International Covenant on Civil and Political Rights' in F Salerno (ed), *Diritti Dell'Uomo, Estradizione ed Espulsione* (CEDAM 2003) 143; G Noll, *Negotiating Asylum: The EU Acquis, Extraterritorial Protection and the Common Market of Deflection* (Kluwer 2000), at 453–74; S Zühlke and J-C Pastille, 'Extradition and the European Convention—Soering Revisited' (1999) 59 ZAÖRV 749.

[105] See, for instance: HRC, *Kindler v Canada* (1993) CCPR/C/48/D/470/1991, para 13.2; *GT v Australia*, (1997) CCPR/C/61/D/706/1996, paras 8.1–8.7; 'General Comment No. 31: The Nature of the General Legal Obligation Imposed on States Parties to the Covenant' (2004) CCPR/C/21/Rev.1/ add.13, para 12.

[106] See in particular: *Omar Othman (Abu Qatada) v the United Kingdom* ECHR 2012-I 249; *Al Saadoon and Mufdhi v The United Kingdom* ECHR 2010-II 61; *Z and T v the United Kingdom*, App No 27034/05 (ECtHR, 28 February 2006); *Tomic v the United Kingdom*, App No 17387/03 (ECtHR, 14 October 2003); *Ould Barar v Sweden*, Admissibility Decision, App No 42367/98 (ECtHR, 19 January 1999).

reference to a serious violation of human rights significantly erodes their distinctive character. Already in 1984, the European Commission acknowledged that:

Although the risk of political persecution, as such, cannot be equated to torture, inhuman or degrading treatment, … it may, in a particular case, raise an issue under Art. 3 if it brings about a prejudice for the individual concerned which reaches such level of severity as to bring it within the scope of this provision e.g. an arbitrary sentence … or inhuman detention conditions.[107]

Conversely, from the perspective of the Geneva Convention, a degrading treatment equates with a persecution under the refugee definition.[108] The same material convergence may be observed with regard to the assessment of the risk. Whether it is phrased as 'a well-founded fear of being persecuted' or 'a real risk of being subjected to torture, inhuman or degrading treatment', both are prospective in nature. Although the different formula used by treaty bodies and refugee status decision-makers have raised disproportionate attention among commentators, the difference of wording is largely semantic. The reality of the risk under the Refugee Convention and the human rights treaties requires a case-by-case assessment grounded on two prognostic factors: the personal circumstances of the applicant as well as the general situation prevailing in the country of origin. In both cases, assessing the alleged risk is by essence a hypothetical projection to predict what might happen if the applicant is returned to his or her country of origin.

Notwithstanding this substantial convergence between the two variants of the *non-refoulement* obligation, human rights law provides a broader protection than refugee law in three significant regards. First, the human rights principle of *non-refoulement* is not subordinated to the five grounds of persecution required by the refugee definition under the Geneva Convention. However, this divergence should not be overestimated, for it can be counterbalanced by a cogent interpretation of the grounds of persecution with due regard to the object and purpose of the Geneva Convention. The second distinctive feature is more straightforward: whereas the refugee definition exclusively applies to a person who is 'outside the country of his nationality',[109] no such geographical limitation is required under human rights law.

---

[107] *C v Netherlands* (1984) DR 38, 224. Besides the specific examples mentioned by the Commission, assessing whether the level of severity amounts to a degrading treatment requires an *in concreto* examination of all the circumstances of each case. According to a well-established jurisprudence, 'ill-treatment must attain a minimum level of severity if it is to fall within the scope of Article 3. The assessment of this minimum is, in the nature of things, relative; it depends on all the circumstances of the case, such as the duration of the treatment, its physical or mental effects and, in some cases, the sex, age and state of health of the victim, etc.' *Ireland v the United Kingdom*, ECHR (1978) Series A No 25, para 162. Moreover, an accumulation of human rights violations may cross the threshold under Article 3. Such a conclusion flows from the common understanding of degrading treatment defined as an ill-treatment which 'humiliates or debases an individual, showing a lack of respect for, or diminishing, his or her human dignity, or arouses feelings of fear, anguish or inferiority capable of breaking an individual's moral and physical resistance'. *MSS v Belgium and Greece* ECHR 2011-I 255, para 220; *Pretty v the United Kingdom* ECHR 2002-III 155, para 52; *Ireland v the United Kingdom* ECHR (1978) Series A No 25, para 167.

[108] Among an abundant case-law, see for instance: *Cheung v Canada (Minister of Employment and Immigration)* (1993) 1 CF 314, 324; *SZ and JM (Iran CG) v The Secretary of State for the Home Department* (2008) UKAIT 00082, paras 168–69.

[109] Art 1(A)(2) of the Geneva Convention; *R v Immigration Officer at Prague Airport and another ex parte Roma Rights Centre and others* (2004) UKHL 55, paras 16–18 (Lord Bingham of Cornhill).

As a result, the human rights principle of *non-refoulement* still applies to any person who is in a diplomatic mission, in an area controlled by peacekeeping and occupying forces, or is otherwise under the effective control of another state within the territory of his or her own country.[110]

The third and most well-known characteristic relies on the absolute nature of the *refoulement* prohibition in a state where there is a real risk of torture, inhuman, or degrading treatment. It thus applies to asylum-seekers and refugees who have been excluded from the protection of the Geneva Convention under the exclusion clauses of the refugee definition or in application of Article 33(2).[111] This last feature has retained most of the attention from both states and commentators in a context largely dominated by the fight against terrorism.[112] In practice, though, one should observe that this feature appears more symbolic than real, for it concerns a very marginal number of persons compared to the total population of refugees and other persons in need of protection.[113] It remains, however, emblematic of the impact of human rights law on refugee law. Indeed, the archetypal balance between state sovereignty and human rights has reached its breaking point in favour of the latter. This reveals in turn the distinctive rationale underlying each branch of law: whereas refugee law is bound to grant protection only to those who deserve it, human rights law is universal and inclusive in essence.

Following this stance, the human rights principle of *non-refoulement* stands out as a practical and powerful means to ensure the effective respect for fundamental rights. It is an integral part of the broader enforcement device of human rights law. William Schabas rightly observes in this sense that '[i]t may be better to see it as a piece in the international struggle for the enforcement of fundamental rights. Approached in this way, States should not expel persons to a place where they may

---

[110] Despite its far-reaching effects, this last characteristic has not yet given rise to a substantial practice of treaty bodies. See however: ECtHR, *Al-Saadoon v United Kingdom* ECHR 2010-II 61, paras 141–44, where the European Court held that the transfer carried out by the UK forces to the Iraqi police within the territory of Iraq was a violation of Article 3. For further discussion, see also: Wouters, *International Legal Standards* (n 57) 217–21, 375–76, and 533; G Noll, 'Seeking Asylum at Embassies: A Right to Entry under International Law?' (2005) 17 IJRL 542.

[111] See most notably *Saadi v Italy* ECHR 2008-II 207, paras 138–41; *Chahal v United Kingdom* (1996) 23 EHRR 413, para 80; CAT, *Tapia Paez v Sweden*, CAT/C/18/D/39/1996 (1996), para 14.5.

[112] Among a plethoric literature see: A Farmer, 'Non-Refoulement and Jus Cogens: Limiting Anti-Terror Measures that Threaten Refugee Protection' (2008) 23 Geo Immigr L J 1; R Haines, 'National Security and Non-Refoulement in New Zealand: Commentary on Zaoui v. Attorney-General (N°2)' in J McAdam (ed), *Forced Migration, Human Rights and Security* (Hart Publishing 2008) 63; D Weissbrodt and A Bergquist, 'Extraordinary Rendition and the Torture Convention' (2006) 46 Va J of Int'l L 585; J Fitzpatrick, 'Rendition and Transfer in the War against Terrorism: Guantanamo and Beyond' (2003) 25 Loyola Int'l & Comp L Rev 457; S Bourgon, 'The Impact of Terrorism on the Principle of 'Non-Refoulement' of Refugees: The Suresh Case Before the Supreme Court of Canada' (2003) 1 JICJ 169; R Bruin and K Wouters, 'Terrorism and the Non-Derogability of *Non-Refoulement*' (2003) 15 IJRL 5; O Chinedu Okafor and P Lekuwuwa Okoronkwo, 'Re-Configuring *Non-Refoulement*? The *Suresh* Decision, "Security Relativism" and the International Human Rights Perspective' (2003) 15 IJRL 30.

[113] In France, for instance, exclusion from refugee status only represents around 0.25 per cent of the judicial decisions delivered each year on the basis of Article 1 of the Geneva Convention: Alland and Teitgen-Colly, *Traité du droit* (n 7) 520.

be threatened with torture, or the death penalty, or other serious abuses, because this is a method of promoting global observance of human rights.'[114]

Even though the duty of *non-refoulement* is well acknowledged by human rights law, states have not yet drawn all the consequences of this principle as a vehicle of refugee protection. This ambiguity is well reflected by the Global Compact for Migration. On the one hand, states have reaffirmed in clear and broad terms the prohibition 'of returning migrants when there is a real and foreseeable risk of death, torture, and other cruel, inhuman, and degrading treatment or punishment, or other irreparable harm, in accordance with our obligations under international human rights law'.[115] On the other hand, this principle is acknowledged merely as an obstacle to removal and not as a ground of international protection on its own.[116] The confinement of the human rights principle of *non-refoulement* is further exacerbated by the Global Compact on Refugees in which it is not referred to. Although human rights law has considerably shaped and refined refugee law, it is not yet fully taken into account by states for updating and reinforcing refugee protection.

---

[114] WA Schabas, 'Non-Refoulement' in Office for Democratic Institutions and Human Rights (ODIHR), Office of the High Commissioner for Human Rights (OHCHR), Principality of Liechtenstein, 'Expert Workshop on Human Rights and International Co-operation in Counter-Terrorism' (21 February 2007) ODIHR.GAL/14/07, 47.

[115] Global Compact for Safe, Orderly and Regular Migration, para 37 available at https://refugeesmigrants.un.org/sites/default/files/180713_agreed_outcome_global_compact_for_migration.pdf accessed 12 October 2018.

[116] The principle of *non-refoulement* is only mentioned in the objective of the Compact that is dedicated to return, but not in the other relevant objectives related to pathways for regular migration, the vulnerability of migrants, and border management.

4

Migrant Workers

While constituting the most important portion of migrants across the world, migrant workers are governed by three specialized treaties at the universal plane. Two of them have been concluded under the auspices of the International Labour Organization (ILO) in 1949 and 1975, whereas the most recent and comprehensive one, the International Convention on the Protection of the Rights of All Migrant Workers and Members of Their Families (ICRMW), was adopted within the UN in 1990. Although each of them has been conceived as a distinct treaty, their respective content provides a complementary and mutually reinforcing legal framework.

When taken together, the two ILO conventions and the ICRMW can be viewed as establishing an international charter of migrant workers that lays down a comprehensive normative framework on a broad variety of issues, including, most notably, the definition and rights of migrant workers as well as inter-state cooperation on labour migration. In order to better appraise their specific characteristics and common features, the ILO conventions and the ICRMW are analysed separately in this chapter through the same basic structure addressing respectively: the definition of migrant workers, the regulation of labour migration, the rights of migrant workers, as well as the difficulties raised by their ratification.

4.1 The ILO's Conventions on Migrant Workers

The ILO has been involved in the protection of migrant workers since its foundation in 1919. Today, besides the general labour conventions that apply to both nationals and non-nationals, there exist two specialized treaties: the Migration for Employment Convention (Revised), 1949 No 97[1] and the Migrant Workers (Supplementary Provisions) Convention, 1975 (No 143).[2] These two specialized treaties contain a common legal definition of migrant workers (section 4.1.1), and

---

[1] ILO Convention C097: Migration for Employment Convention (Revised) (Convention concerning Migration for Employment (Revised 1949)) (adopted 32nd Conference Session Geneva 1 July 1949, entered into force 22 January 1952) 120 UNTS 71.
[2] ILO Convention C143: Migrant Workers (Supplementary Provisions) Convention (Convention concerning Migrations in Abusive Condition and the Promotion of Equality of Opportunity and Treatment of Migrant Workers (adopted 60th Conference Session Geneva 24 June 1975, entered into force 9 December 1978) 2220 UNTS 3.

regulate labour migration by providing a flexible framework of inter-state cooperation (section 4.1.2) and protecting the rights of migrant workers (section 4.1.3).

4.1.1 The definition of migrant workers

Convention No 97 is the first multilateral treaty to provide a legal definition of migrant workers. The same definition was then restated in Convention No 143. According to Article 11(1) of the two instruments, 'the term *migrant for employment* means a person who migrates from one country to another with a view to being employed otherwise than on his own account and includes any person regularly admitted as a migrant for employment'.

This definition is broad and narrow at the same time. On the one hand, it is broad because of its prospective nature which includes the vast majority of migrants who are leaving their own countries in order to find a job abroad. Indeed, as evidenced by the wording of common Article 11(1), the prospect of being employed—and not the fact of already having been recruited before departure—represents the triggering factor of this definition. As further confirmed by the ILO supervisory body (the Committee of Experts on the Application of Conventions and Recommendations, hereinafter CEACR), such a definition encompasses both spontaneous and organized forms of labour migration, comprising 'government-sponsored and privately arranged recruitment as well as workers who migrate outside such programmes in the search for employment'.[3]

Likewise, the length of the stay in the state of employment is not relevant. The definition of migrant workers equally applies to workers who have migrated for permanent residence as well as those who have migrated for short-term or even seasonal work.[4] It also includes any type of employment, be it skilled or unskilled. The CEACR has notably recalled that managers, executive staff, enterprise administrators, and highly qualified technicians are migrant workers within the meaning of Article 11(1).[5] Furthermore, both the drafting history of Convention No 97 and the subsequent interpretation of CEACR confirm that the definition of migrant workers includes refugees in so far as they are working outside their country of nationality.[6] This highlights the porous nature of the traditional distinction between

---

[3] International Labour Conference (87th Session) Report III (1B) Migrant Workers: General Survey on the Reports of the Migration for Employment Convention (Revised) (No 97), and Recommendation (Revised) (No 86), 1949, and the Migrant Workers (Supplementary Provisions) Convention (No 143), and Recommendation (No 151), 1975 (Geneva June 1999) ILC.87/III(1B), 47. See also International Labour Conference (105th Session) Report III (1B) Promoting Fair Migration: General Survey concerning the Migrant Workers Instruments (Geneva 22 January 2016) ILC.105/III(1B), 32.

[4] International Labour Conference, 'Migrant Workers' (n 3) 43; International Labour Conference, 'Promoting Fair Migration' (n 3) 36–37. Despite several attempts to exclude seasonal workers, the drafters decided that they will be covered by the two conventions: International Labour Conference (32nd Session) Record of Proceedings (Geneva 1949) app XIII, 590–91; and International Labour Conference (60th session) Record of Proceedings (Geneva 1975) 646; International Labour Conference (60th Session) Record of Proceedings: Report V (2) (Geneva 1975) 19.

[5] International Labour Conference, 'Migrant Workers' (n 3) 47.

[6] International Labour Conference (32nd Session) Record of Proceedings (Geneva 1949) 285; International Labour Conference, 'Migrant Workers' (n 3) 41; International Labour Conference,

refugees and migrant workers: instead of one excluding the other, both categories are governed by overlapping and mutually reinforcing international treaties.[7]

On the other hand, and despite its broad scope, the legal definition of migrant workers is restricted by three substantial qualifications. First, Article 11(1) is limited to 'any person regularly admitted as a migrant for employment', thus excluding undocumented migrant workers.[8] Second, self-employed migrant workers are left out of this provision as they have to be employed 'otherwise than on [their] own account'. Third, Article 11(2) of Convention No 97 excludes three specific categories of workers from the scope of its provisions: frontier workers; members of the liberal professions and artists who entered on a short-term basis; and seamen.

While confirming these last exceptions, Convention No 143 adds two other categories of persons excluded from the definition of migrant workers: those coming specifically for the purpose of training or education, as well as employees who have been admitted temporarily at the request of their employer to undertake specific tasks for a limited and defined period of time, and who are required to leave that country upon completion of their duty. According to both the preparatory work of Convention No 143 and the interpretation of the CEACR, this last exception does not concern all fixed-term workers but mainly applies to workers who have specialized skills to undertake specific short-term and technical assignments.[9] In any event, the new exceptions added by Convention No 143 only concern Part II of this treaty and thus neither extend to its Part I nor to Convention No 97 as a whole.

4.1.2 The regulation of labour migration: an open-ended framework of inter-state cooperation

In contrast to the Refugee Convention, ILO treaties do not contain—even indirectly—a duty of admission of migrant workers. The sovereign competence of the state to allow or refuse entry of foreigners into its territory is accordingly taken

'Promoting Fair Migration' (n 3) 37–38. See also, ILO Convention C097 (n 1) art 11 of Annex II; ILO, Model Agreement on Temporary and Permanent Migration for Employment, including Migration of Refugees and Displaced Persons, annexed to ILO Recommendation R086: Migration for Employment Recommendation (Revised) (Recommendation concerning Migration for Employment) (32nd Conference Session Geneva 1 July 1949); and *Montenegro* (2013) Direct Request (CEACR) on the application of Migrant Workers (Supplementary Provisions) Convention (No 143), 1975 (adopted 2012, published 102nd ILC session 2013).

[7] The Model Agreement on Temporary and Permanent Migration for Employment adopted by ILO acknowledged the principle of *non-refoulement* two years before its recognition in the 1951 Refugee Convention. According to its art 25(2), 'The Government of the territory of immigration undertakes not to send refugees and displaced persons or migrants who do not wish to return to their country of origin for political reasons back to their territory of origin as distinct from the territory from which they were recruited, unless they formally express this desire by a request in writing addressed both to the competent authority of the territory of immigration and the representative of the body set up in accordance with the provisions of an international instrument which may be responsible for the protection of refugees and displaced persons who do not benefit from the protection of any Government.'

[8] Part I of ILO Convention C143 (n 2), however, applies to irregular migration.

[9] International Labour Conference, Record of Proceedings: Report V (2) (n 4) 19–20; International Labour Conference, 'Migrant Workers' (n 3) 46.

for granted. This does not mean that ILO treaties have no role to play in the admission of migrant workers. While providing some limited encroachments on state sovereignty in the field of admission, the two ILO conventions provide a flexible framework of cooperation with the twofold purpose of managing regular migration and fighting irregular migration.

Inter-state cooperation on regular migration

Convention No 97 establishes a general framework of dialogue between sending and receiving states in order to better manage and organize regular migration of workers. Inter-state cooperation can take several forms. The first is that of mutual exchange of information about domestic legislation and policies governing emigration, immigration, and the legal status of migrant workers, as well as bilateral or multilateral agreements on these matters (Article 1).[10] Article 7 further requires States Parties to cooperate through their employment and migration related services. According to Article 10, States Parties shall also, 'whenever necessary or desirable', conclude agreements for regulating matters of common interest when the number of migrants going from one state to another is significant.

Articles 1, 7, and 10 establish the core minimum framework of inter-state cooperation which is supplemented by three annexes detailing the recruitment, placement, and working conditions of migrant workers who are not (Annex I) or who are (Annex II) recruited on the basis of arrangements made under government control, as well as the importation of migrant workers' personal effects, tools, and equipment (Annex III). States may exclude all or any of the annexes from ratification, but they may also accept them at a later date (Article 14). Convention No 97 is further supplemented and detailed by the non-binding Migration for Employment Recommendation (Revised), 1949 (No 86) which most notably includes a 'Model Agreement on temporary and permanent migration for employment, including migration of refugees and displaced persons.' States Parties may take it into account in framing bilateral agreements on labour migration regarding a wide range of issues (such as administrative formalities and contracts of employment, conditions of migration and selection of migrant workers, their transport, return, as well as living and working conditions).

In sum, Convention No 97 establishes a flexible framework of inter-state cooperation based on three incremental layers of binding, optional, and recommendatory provisions. This *à la carte* regime aims at facilitating dialogue between sending and receiving countries while preserving state sovereignty in the management of labour migration. However, Convention No 97 also provides two specific restrictions to states' competence in controlling immigration. The first one prohibits the removal of migrant workers and members of their family in the event of incapacity to work (Article 8(1)).[11] While this might appear as a significant encroachment upon state

---

[10] This information has to be made available upon request to other ratifying states and to the International Labour Office.

[11] 'A migrant for employment who has been admitted on a permanent basis and the members of his family who have been authorised to accompany or join him shall not be returned to their territory of

sovereignty, such a restriction is limited to those who have been admitted lawfully on a permanent basis (thus excluding undocumented workers, as well as temporary and fixed term workers who are documented). Furthermore, the incapacity to work must be due to an illness contracted or an injury sustained subsequent to entry.[12] The CEACR underlines that:

> Article 8 does not concern the admission or entry of workers […] but the maintenance of the right of migrant workers who have already been admitted on a permanent basis to continue to reside in the country in the event of incapacity for work. It wishes to point out that security of residence of permanent workers is one of the most important provisions of the Convention. Where this right is not effectively applied, permanent resident migrants find themselves living under the constant threat of repatriation.[13]

When assessing the UK report, the CEACR specified that, under Article 8 of Convention No 97, 'permanent or indefinite residency permits should not be revoked if the individual becomes a burden on public funds or if it appears that the holder is not able to maintain himself or herself or his or her dependents'.[14] The Committee further admitted that this represents the main difficulty for States Parties and constitutes a barrier to ratification by receiving states because 'in many states residency permits can be revoked when migrant becomes a burden on public funds, regardless of their residency status'.[15]

The second restriction to state sovereignty in deciding on the admission of migrant workers is more indirect than the first. It stems from CEACR's interpretation of Article 5 which demands appropriate medical services at the time of departure, during the journey, and upon arrival in the territory of destination. While acknowledging that 'medical testing and the prohibition of entry of persons on the ground that they may constitute a grave risk to public health is likely to be a routine and a responsible precaution prior to permitting entry of non-nationals', CEACR considers that refusal of entry or removal on a medical ground which has no effect on the task for which the worker has been recruited, constitutes 'an unacceptable form of discrimination'.[16] Following this stance, the 2010 ILO Recommendation concerning

origin or the territory from which they emigrated because the migrant is unable to follow his occupation by reason of illness contracted or injury sustained subsequent to entry, unless the person concerned so desires or an international agreement to which the Member is a party so provides.' Paragraph 2 of the same article specifies that, in the case of migrants admitted on a permanent basis upon arrival in the country of immigration, paragraph 1 shall take effect only after a reasonable period which shall in no case exceed five years from the date of admission.

[12] Article 8(1) further provides two exceptions to this prohibition of removing documented migrant workers: when an international agreement ratified by a State Party provides for such a removal or when the person concerned gives his or her consent to be returned to the country of origin.
[13] *Trinidad and Tobago* (2009) Direct Request (CEACR) on the application of the Migration for Employment Convention (Revised) (No 97), 1949 (adopted 2008, published 98th ILC session 2009).
[14] *United Kingdom* (2009) Direct Request (CEACR) on the application of the Migration for Employment Convention (Revised) (No 97), 1949 (adopted 2008, published 98th ILC session 2009).
[15] International Labour Conference, 'Migrant Workers' (n 3) 225. See also ibid 226–27.
[16] *Belize* (2014) Direct Request (CEACR) on the application of the Migration for Employment Convention (Revised) (No 97), 1949 (adopted 2013, published 103rd ILC session 2014); *Trinidad and Tobago* (2014) Direct Request (CEACR) on the application of the Migration for Employment Convention (Revised) (No 97), 1949 (adopted 2013, published 103rd ILC session 2014); *Guyana*

HIV and AIDS and the World of Work (No 200) underlines that 'migrant workers, or those seeking to migrate for employment, should not be excluded from migration by the countries of origin, of transit or of destination on the basis of their real or perceived HIV status'.[17] Furthermore, migrant workers should not be required to undergo HIV testing or disclose HIV-related information.[18]

Inter-state cooperation on irregular migration

To complement the general framework provided in Convention No 97, Convention No 143 focuses on the fight against irregular migration through the threefold objective of detection, suppression, and repression. The duty of detection is conceived in particularly strong and broad terms. According to Article 2, each State Party 'shall systematically seek to determine whether there are illegally employed migrant workers on its territory'. While the concrete measures to do so are left to each state, Article 6 requires the adoption of domestic legislation or regulation in order to ensure 'effective detection' of migrant workers' illegal employment. In practice, CEACR has observed that the measures adopted by the large majority of states to implement the duty of detection follow two main trends: 'first, police checks have been stepped up considerably, both at borders and spot-checks within the country's borders, and second, transport companies (including airlines and land and sea transport) are increasingly held responsible for verifying passengers' travel documents and residence permits'.[19]

Besides the duty of detection, Article 3 of Convention No 143 requires each State Party to adopt 'all necessary and appropriate measures [...] to suppress clandestine movements of migrants for employment and illegal employment of migrants, and [...] against the organisers of illicit or clandestine movements of migrants for employment [...] and against those who employ workers who have immigrated in illegal conditions'. The measures to be taken to achieve these objectives shall include: systematic contact and exchange of information between states (Article 4); the prosecution of migrant workers' traffickers irrespective of the country from which they exercise their activities (Article 5); and the application of administrative, civil, and penal sanctions (which include imprisonment) in case of illegal employment of migrant workers, the organization of irregular movement of labour migration,

(2013) Direct Request (CEACR) on the application of the Migration for Employment Convention (Revised), 1949 (No 97) (adopted 2012, published 102nd ILC session 2013); *United Kingdom* (n 14). See also, International Labour Conference, 'Migrant Workers' (n 3) 83.

[17] ILO Recommendation R200: Recommendation concerning HIV and AIDS and the World of Work (99th Conference Session Geneva 17 June 2010) para 28.

[18] ibid paras 25–26. For further discussion, see notably A Devillard, 'The Principle of Non-Discrimination and Entry, Stay and Expulsion of Foreigners Living with HIV/AIDS' (2009) 11(2) IJMS 91, 102; GS Goodwin-Gill, 'AIDS and HIV, Migrants and Refugees: International Legal and Human Rights Dimensions' in M Haour-Knipe and R Rector (eds), *Crossing Border: Migration, Ethnicity and AIDS* (Taylor & Francis 1996) 50–69.

[19] International Labour Conference, 'Migrant Workers' (n 3) 121.

and assistance thereto whether for profit or otherwise (Article 6).[20] Furthermore, as observed by the CEACR, most countries require the authorization of the employment service or ministry of labour before any employment contract can begin, albeit with some exceptions (in particular for nationals of States Parties to free movement agreements).[21]

As it is apparent, the various measures provided by Convention No 143 against irregular migration target the demand of clandestine labour rather than the supply.[22] Hence, the duty of prosecuting and/or imposing sanctions does not apply to undocumented migrants themselves but rather to employers and those who organize or assist irregular migration.[23] Imposing sanctions on migrants for their irregular entry/stay is accordingly governed by domestic law in accordance with the relevant rules of international law notably endorsed in the Refugee Convention, the UN Protocols on smuggling and trafficking, and other applicable human rights treaties.[24]

The removal of undocumented migrant workers similarly falls beyond the scope of Convention No 143. While the Migrant Workers Recommendation No 151 provides for a suspensive right of appeal before an administrative or judicial instance (para 33), this instrument is not formally binding as such. Convention No 143 only makes a limited reference to removal in Article 9(3), which merely requires that the cost of expulsion shall not be borne by migrant workers or their families. According to CEACR, this prohibition does not refer to the return travel expenses but only to the costs of expulsion per se (ie the costs incurred by a state in ensuring that undocumented workers leave the country such as administrative or judicial procedures involved in issuing an expulsion order or in implementing the order, including escort and surveillance costs).[25] Notwithstanding the foregoing, States Parties are free

---

[20] Although focusing on documented migrant workers, ILO Convention C097 (n 1) also provides that 'any person who promotes clandestine or illegal immigration shall be subject to appropriate penalties'. See in particular art 8 of Annex I and art 13 of Annex II.

[21] International Labour Conference, 'Migrant Workers' (n 3) 125.   [22] ibid 130.

[23] ibid 130.

[24] One should add that the CEACR expressed its concern that the Italian Legislative Decree No 286/1998 introducing the offence of illegal entry or residence would 'marginalize and stigmatize migrant workers in an irregular situation, and increase their vulnerability to exploitation and violation of their basic human rights': in International Labour Conference (101st Session), Report III (Part 1A) Report of the Committee of Experts on the Application of Conventions and Recommendations (Geneva 2012) ILC.101/III1A, 909. See also, International Labour Conference (99th Session) Report III (Part 1A) Report of the Committee of Experts on the Application of Conventions and Recommendations (Geneva 2010) ILC.99/III1A, 727.

[25] International Labour Conference, 'Migrant Workers' (n 3) 113. See also *Serbia* (2014) Direct Request (CEACR) on the application of Migration for Employment Convention (Revised) (No 97), 1949 (adopted 2013, published 103rd ILC session 2014); *Norway* (1995) Direct Request (CEACR) on the application of Migration for Employment Convention (Revised) (No 97), 1949 (adopted 1995, published 82nd ILC session 1995); *Norway* (1993) Direct Request (CEACR) on the application of Migration for Employment Convention (Revised) (No 97), 1949 (adopted 1993, published 80th ILC session 1993). However, return costs, including transport expenses, should not fall upon the migrant worker when his or her irregular situation cannot be attributed to him or her (such as redundancy before the expected end of contract or when the employer failed to fulfil the necessary formalities to engage a foreign worker): see International Labour Conference, 'Migrant Workers' (n 3) 121. See also *Norway* (2014) Direct Request (CEACR) on the application of Migration for Employment Convention (Revised) (No 97), 1949 (adopted 2013, published 103rd ILC session 2014); *Bosnia and Herzegovina*

to regularize the situation of undocumented workers. As recalled by Article 9(4) of Convention No 143, 'nothing in this Convention shall prevent Members from giving persons who are illegally residing or working within the country the right to stay and to take up legal employment.' Neither Convention No 143 nor the Migrant Workers Recommendation No. 151 specify the criteria of regularization which are left to the discretion of States Parties.[26]

Likewise, the admission of migrant workers within the territory of States Parties is not governed by Convention No 143. The CEACR emphasizes that this Convention 'does not in any way affect the sovereign right of each member State to allow or refuse to allow a foreigner to enter its territory and that it leaves it to each State to determine the manner in which it intends to organize the potential entry of migrant workers or the refusal of their entry'.[27] Nevertheless, Article 8(1) provides a non-trivial exception to states' competence in controlling immigration. Similarly to Convention No 97, it does not concern the entry of migrant workers as such but the removal of those who are documented. According to this provision, the loss of employment shall not result in the withdrawal of residence or work permit. Hence, migrant workers shall not be regarded as in an irregular situation after loss of employment and they cannot be deported on this ground. Such a safeguard, however, is explicitly circumscribed to migrants who have 'resided legally in the territory for the purpose of employment'. The overall objective of this provision is 'to prevent exploitation by employers, who, by terminating the employment of migrant workers, might also effectively determine their stay in the host country'.[28] When lawful residents lose their job, Article 8(2) further requires that they shall enjoy equality of treatment with nationals regarding security of employment, alternative employment, and relief work.

These two paragraphs have raised difficulties of application as well as misunderstandings among states. In order to dispel these concerns, CEACR clarified the scope of this provision in two ways. First, it pointed out that Article 8(1) refers exclusively to migrant workers who lose their employment, as opposed to those whose employment comes to an end as foreseen in their contract.[29] Accordingly, returning migrants to their home countries at the end of a time-bound contract is

(2013) Direct Request (CEACR) on the application of Migration for Employment Convention (Revised) (No 97), 1949 (adopted 2012, published 102nd ILC session 2013); *Albania* (2010) Direct Request (CEACR) on the application of Migration for Employment Convention (Revised) (No 97), 1949 (adopted 2010, published 100th ILC session 2011); *Macedonia* (2013) Direct Request (CEACR) on the application of Migration for Employment Convention (Revised) (No 97), 1949 (adopted 2013, published 102nd ILC session 2013).

[26] ILO Recommendation R151: Migrant Workers Recommendation (Recommendation concerning Migrant Workers) (60th Conference Session Geneva 24 June 1975) para 8(1)–(2) simply adds that a decision on regularization should be taken as soon as possible and migrant workers whose position has been regularized should benefit from all the rights accorded to migrant workers lawfully within the territory.

[27] International Labour Conference, 'Migrant Workers' (n 3) 107.

[28] R Cholewinski, *Migrant Workers in International Human Rights Law* (OUP 1997) 130; International Labour Conference (59th Session) Report VII (1): Migrant Workers (Geneva 1974) 51–52.

[29] International Labour Conference, 'Migrant Workers' (n 3) 219; International Labour Conference, 'Promoting Fair Migration' (n 3) 137–38.

not a violation of this provision.[30] Second, Article 8(2) does not require a state to extend residence permits in case of loss of employment, but refers only to equality of treatment with national workers for the remainder of the validity of that permit.[31]

4.1.3 The international protection of migrant workers

As it is the case with the prevailing domestic practice of states, the protection of migrant workers under ILO treaties varies depending on their legal status: a core content of basic rights applies to all migrant workers, including undocumented ones, whereas more specific guarantees are reserved for documented workers only.

The basic human rights of all migrant workers

Convention No 143 is the first treaty which specifically addresses the rights of undocumented migrant workers. According to its Article 1, 'each Member for which this Convention is in force undertakes to respect the basic human rights of all migrant workers'.[32] The personal scope of this provision is particularly broad and inclusive. It applies to all migrant workers irrespective of their legal status in host states (whether destination or transit countries). As confirmed by the drafting history of Convention No 143 and the CEACR, the primary objective of this provision is to affirm—without challenging states' competence in migration control—the right of migrant workers to be protected, whether or not they entered the country on a regular basis.[33] The basic restatement contained in Article 1 further covers all migrant workers, be they permanent or temporary, and regardless of the type of residence or work permit.[34] The CEACR has confirmed that it also applies to refugees and trafficked persons, in so far as they are employed outside their home country.[35]

---

[30] International Labour Conference, 'Migrant Workers' (n 3) 219; International Labour Conference, 'Promoting Fair Migration' (n 3) 137–38.

[31] International Labour Conference, 'Migrant Workers' (n 3) 223; International Labour Conference 'Promoting Fair Migration' (n 3) 142–43.

[32] See also the specific rights arising out of past employment contained in ILO Convention C143 (n 2) art 9(1).

[33] ibid 39; International Labour Conference (60th Session) Record of proceedings (Geneva 1975) 641.

[34] *Sweden* (2013) Direct Request (CEACR) on the application of Migrant Workers (Supplementary Provisions) Convention (No 143), 1975 (adopted 2012, published 102nd ILC session 2013). See also the observation of CEACR on Albania's report on ILO Convention C143 in International Labour Conference (103rd Session) Report III (Part 1A) Report of the Committee of Experts on the Application of Conventions and Recommendations' (Geneva 2014) 539.

[35] *Serbia* (2014) Direct Request (CEACR) on the application of Migrant Workers (Supplementary Provisions) Convention (No 143), 1975 (adopted 2013, published 103rd ILC session 2014); *Montenegro* (2013) Direct Request (CEACR) on the application of Migrant Workers (Supplementary Provisions) Convention (No 143), 1975 (adopted 2012, published 102nd ILC session 2013); *Bosnia and Herzegovina* (2013) Direct Request (CEACR) on the application of Migrant Workers (Supplementary Provisions) Convention (No 143), 1975 (adopted 2012, published 98th ILC session 2013); *Bosnia and Herzegovina* (2009) Direct Request (CEACR) on the application of Migrant Workers (Supplementary Provisions) Convention (No 143), 1975 (adopted 2008, published 98th ILC session 2009); *Serbia* (2008) Direct Request (CEACR) on the application of Migrant Workers (Supplementary Provisions) Convention (No 143), 1975 (adopted 2007, published 97th ILC session 2008); *Serbia*

Regarding its material scope, the duty restated in Article 1 relates to the 'basic human rights' of migrant workers, though the drafting history never identified what such 'basic rights' actually are. Article 1 was introduced upon request of the government delegates of Algeria and Mexico at the last session of the International Labour Conference. While their original amendment referred to 'the human rights and labour guarantees', the workers' delegates proposed to replace it with a generic expression of basic human rights 'in order to emphasise what was essential'.[36] This new wording was finally adopted unanimously by delegates without further specifying the very notion of 'basic rights'. The supervisory body of ILO acknowledges that it primarily covers 'the fundamental rights contained in the international instruments adopted by the UN in this domain', such as the International Covenant on Civil and Political Rights and the International Covenant on Economic, Social and Cultural Rights.[37] It also comprises more specialized instruments, including the ICRMW[38] and ILO treaties governing, for instance, freedom of association, the right to collective bargaining, the elimination of forced labour and child labour, as well as the elimination of discrimination in respect of employment and occupation.[39]

Thus, Article 1 does not create new rights but confirms the plain applicability of general ILO and human rights instruments to all migrant workers. Nevertheless, mere ratification of the relevant treaties is not enough to guarantee due respect for these rights, as they must be 'ensured both in law and practice'.[40] States Parties are

---

(2005) Direct Request (CEACR) on the application of Migrant Workers (Supplementary Provisions) Convention (No 143), 1975 (adopted 2004, published 93rd ILC session 2005).

[36] International Labour Conference (60th session) Record of proceedings (Geneva 1975) 641.

[37] International Labour Conference, 'Migrant Workers' (n 3) 108; *Albania* (2011) Direct Request (CEACR) on the application of Migrant Workers (Supplementary Provisions) Convention (No 143), 1975 (adopted 2010, published 100th ILC session 2011). One should add that the broad interpretation on the part of CEACR is notably confirmed by the French version of ILO Convention C143 (n 2) which refers to 'droits fondamentaux' and not to 'droits élémentaires' in the sense of a restrictive set of basic rights.

[38] International Labour Conference, 'Promoting Fair Migration' (n 3) 90.

[39] See, for instance, with regard to freedom of association and trade union rights, *Tajikistan* (2015) Direct Request (CEACR) on the application of Freedom of Association and Protection of the Right to Organise Convention (No 87), 1948 (adopted 2014, published 104th ILC session 2015). See also the observation of CEACR on Albania in International Labour Conference (103rd Session) Report III (Part 1A) Report of the Committee of Experts on the Application of Conventions and Recommendations (Geneva 2014); *Philippines* (2013) Direct Request (CEACR) on the application of Freedom of Association and Protection of the Right to Organise Convention (No 87), 1948 (adopted 2012, published 102nd ILC session 2013).

[40] See notably *Burkina Faso* (2013) Direct Request (CEACR) on the application of Migrant Workers (Supplementary provisions) Convention (No 143), 1975 (adopted 2012, published 102nd ILC session 2013) 1. Besides applicable treaties, the general duty to respect the basic rights of all migrant workers should arguably include the rights enshrined in customary international law. Although the CEACR has not referred explicitly to customary international law, it has acknowledged that the Universal Declaration of Human Rights and the ILO Declaration on Fundamental Principles and Rights at Work are relevant instruments for identifying the basic rights under art 1 of Convention No 143: see International Labour Conference, 'Migrant Workers' (n 3) 108. However, it is dubious that the general restatement of art 1 of Convention C143 does create on its own an obligation for States Parties to apply non-binding resolutions. The only way to reconcile this, in line with the interpretation of the CEACR, is to presume that, according to the ILO monitoring body, both declarations are part of customary international law and thus binding upon States Parties to Convention C143.

accordingly bound to adopt legislative and administrative measures in order to ensure full respect for the basic rights of all migrant workers.[41] Although states retain a substantial margin of appreciation, the CEACR emphasizes that they must guarantee the 'effective application of this provision'.[42] Hence, the main added value of Article 1 is twofold: it explicitly acknowledges the applicability of human rights to migrant workers and the correlative duty to ensure their effective implementation both in law and practice. These 'minimum standards of protection'[43]—as labelled by the CEACR—are far from being trivial, given migrant workers' vulnerability to exploitation and violation of their rights, especially when they are in an irregular situation.

The rights of migrant workers in a regular situation

In comparison to undocumented migrant workers, those who are lawfully within the territory of States Parties benefit from a broader and more detailed set of rights, mainly related to equality of treatment with nationals.[44] According to Article 6(1) of Convention No 97, documented migrant workers shall benefit from no less favourable treatment than the one applicable to nationals in respect of working and living conditions (such as remuneration, membership of trade unions, and enjoyment of benefits of collective bargaining as well as accommodation), social security (including employment injury, maternity, sickness, invalidity, death, unemployment, and family responsibilities), employment taxes, and access to justice. As confirmed by the ILO monitoring body, equality of treatment shall apply to both permanent and temporary migrant workers.[45] Accordingly, the imposition of residency requirements is not contrary to the Convention if and only if the same condition also applies to nationals.[46] Furthermore, Article 6(1) refers to any 'immigrants lawfully within [the] territory', thus including the family members of migrant workers.

---

[41] See, for instance, *Cameroon* (2013) Direct Request (CEACR) on the application of Migrant Workers (Supplementary provisions) Convention (No 143), 1975 (adopted 2012, published 102nd ILC session 2013).

[42] *Norway* (2009) Direct Request (CEACR) on the application of Migrant Workers (Supplementary provisions) Convention (No 143), 1975 (adopted 2008, published 98th ILC session 2009) 1. The CEACR also underlines that states 'must ensure that the measures adopted to address the current economic and financial crises do not hamper the enjoyment of migrant workers' human rights'. See *Portugal* (2014) Direct Request (CEACR) on the application of Migrant Workers (Supplementary provisions) Convention (No 143), 1975 (adopted 2013, published 103rd ILC session 2014).

[43] *Italy* (2012) Observation (CEACR) on the application of Migrant Workers (Supplementary provisions) Convention (No 143), 1975 (adopted 2011, published 101st ILC session 2012).

[44] Beyond equality of treatment, ILO Convention C097 (n 1) art 9 requires States Parties to ensure free transfer of earnings and savings within the limits allowed by national law concerning export and import of currency. ILO Convention C143 (n 2) also contains two provisions respectively devoted to family reunification and free choice of employment. However, the relevant provisions, arts 13 and 14, are worded in permissive, rather than mandatory terms.

[45] *The Former Yugoslav Republic of Macedonia* (2013) Direct Request (CEACR) on the application of Migration for Employment Convention (Revised) (No 97), 1949 (adopted 2012, published 102nd ILC session 2013); *Malaysia* (2011) Observation (CEACR) on the application of Right to Organise and Collective Bargaining Convention (No 98), 1949 (adopted 2010, published 100th ILC session 2011).

[46] *Serbia* (2008) (n 35); *New Zealand* (2002) Direct Request (CEACR) on the application of Migration for Employment Convention (Revised) (No 97), 1949 (adopted 2001, published 90th ILC

Despite its broad scope, CEACR has emphasized that the wording of Article 6(1) according to which states shall apply a 'treatment no less favourable than that which it applies to its own nationals' 'allows the application of treatment which, although not identical, would be equivalent in its effects to that enjoyed by nationals'.[47] The ILO Committee of Experts has not specified what such equality of treatment actually entails, thus leaving States Parties a broad margin of appreciation. At the minimum, however, Article 6(1) prohibits any form of discrimination based on nationality, race, religion, or sex.[48]

From this angle, Convention No 143 is more demanding than Convention No 97. It does not only require repealing any discriminatory legislation or administrative practice, but also adopting positive actions in order to promote equality of treatment and opportunity. According to its Article 10,

Each Member for which the Convention is in force undertakes to declare and pursue a national policy designed to promote and to guarantee [...] equality of opportunity and treatment in respect of employment and occupation, of social security, of trade union and cultural rights and of individual and collective freedoms for persons who as migrant workers or as members of their families are lawfully within its territory.

Article 10 does not specify whether equality of treatment is to be sought with nationals. Nevertheless, the interpretation of this provision by the CEACR,[49] as well as Article 12(e) of Convention No 143, and paragraph 2 of Recommendation No 151, make clear that this shall be the case.

States Parties still enjoy considerable freedom in choosing the methods to carry out this policy of equality. Article 10 merely acknowledges that these methods must be 'appropriate to national conditions and practice', while Article 12 specifies that they shall include educational programmes, the repeal of any contradictory legislation or administrative practice, and shall seek the cooperation of employers and

---

session 2002) 2. Article 6(1)(b) still allows two limitations to the principle of equality of treatment in the field of social security: first, when there are appropriate arrangements for the maintenance of acquired rights and rights in course of acquisition or, second, when national legislation prescribes special arrangements concerning benefits which are payable wholly out of public funds and concerning allowances paid to persons who do not fulfil the contribution conditions prescribed for the award of a normal pension. The CEACR recalls, however, that these arrangements cannot be interpreted as providing a legal basis for permitting the automatic exclusion of a category of migrant workers from qualifying for social security benefits. The main purpose of these exceptions is to prevent possible abuses and to safeguard the financial balance of non-contributory schemes rather than depriving some migrant workers of the rights guaranteed by the Convention. See International Labour Conference, 'Migrant Workers' (n 3) 172; *New Zealand* (2008) Observation (CEACR) on the application of Migration for Employment Convention (Revised) (No 97), 1949 (adopted 2007, published 97th ILC session 2008) para 2.

[47] International Labour Conference, 'Migrant Workers' (n 3) 145–46. See also, International Labour Conference, 'Promoting Fair Migration' (n 3) 111; *Algeria* (2014) Direct Request (CEACR) on the application of Migration for Employment Convention (Revised) (No 97), 1949 (adopted 2013, published 103rd ILC session 2014).

[48] One should add that the CEACR is not always consistent with its own notion of equivalent treatment as it is used to assume that art 6 requires equality of treatment *tout court* (and not an equivalent one). See, for instance, *United Kingdom* (n 14).

[49] See, for instance, *San Marino* (2015) Direct Request (CEACR) on the application of Migrant Workers (Supplementary provisions) Convention (No 143), 1975 (adopted 2014, published 104th ILC session 2015).

workers' organizations and other appropriate bodies. In addition, CEACR restates that the mere existence of a legislation which prohibits discrimination is insufficient to ensure equality of opportunity and treatment in actual practice.[50] According to the ILO monitoring body, Article 10 further requires states 'to take an active policy to secure acceptance and observance of the principle of non-discrimination by society in general and to assist migrant workers and their families to make use of the equal opportunities offered to them'.[51]

The acceptance and observance of non-discrimination by host societies is further reinforced by Article 4 of Convention No 97 according to which States Parties shall 'take all appropriate steps against misleading propaganda relating to emigration and immigration'. In line with the broad wording of this provision, CEACR observes that states are bound to prevent false information not only about nationals leaving the country (emigration), but also regarding non-nationals arriving in the country (immigration).[52] As the ILO monitoring body reminded France, New Zealand, and the United Kingdom, Article 4 prohibits propaganda targeting the non-national population, such as the circulation of spurious stereotypes of migrants as being more susceptible to crime, violence, drug abuses, or regarding their educational and employment abilities.[53]

4.1.4 The quest for ratifications and the parallel application of general labour conventions

Both Conventions Nos 97 and 143 offer a flexible framework for the twofold purpose of managing labour migration and protecting the rights of migrant workers. They further provide a balanced approach, with due respect for the sovereignty of states, regarding the admission of migrant workers and their traditional concerns about irregular migration. In spite of this, the two specialized treaties of the ILO still suffer from low ratification rates in comparison to the Refugee Convention and the Protocol against the Smuggling of Migrants, which are each ratified by 147 states. By contrast, Convention No 97 is ratified by forty-nine states, whereas Convention No 143 counts only twenty-three States Parties.

Against this background, one could be tempted to assert, together with Kees Groenendijk, that '[t]he existing ILO rules are clear. It is the readiness to

---

[50] *Bosnia and Herzegovina* (2009) (n 35).

[51] *Armenia* (2012) Direct Request (CEACR) on the application of Migrant Workers (Supplementary provisions) Convention (No 143), 1975 (adopted 2011, published 101st ILC session 2012) 3. See also, among others, *Slovenia* (2009) Observation (CEACR) on the application of Migrant Workers (Supplementary provisions) Convention (No 143), 1975 (adopted 2008, published 98th ILC session 2009).

[52] International Labour Conference, 'Migrant Workers' (n 3) 82.

[53] *United Kingdom* (2015) Direct Request (CEACR) on the application of Migration for Employment Convention (Revised) (No 97), 1949 (adopted 2014, published 104th ILC session 2015); *New Zealand* (2014) Direct Request (CEACR) on the application of Migration for Employment Convention (Revised) (No 97), 1949 (adopted 2013, published 103rd ILC session 2014); *France* (2013) Direct Request (CEACR) on the application of Migration for Employment Convention (Revised) (No 97), 1949 (adopted 2012, published 102nd ILC session 2013).

understand, subscribe and apply those rules which is lacking'.[54] Nonetheless, as Ryszard Cholewinski rightly underlines, 'it would be incorrect to conclude that the adoption of international labour standards relating specifically to migrant workers has had little or no impact in practice'.[55] In particular, the diversity of States Parties ranges from various regions across the world (mainly Africa, Asia, Europe, and Latin America) and includes both countries of origin and destination (comprising, among the latter, France, Germany, Italy, New Zealand, Norway, and the United Kingdom as far as Convention No 97 is concerned).[56]

The legal obstacles to ratification

According to the survey carried out in 1999 by CEACR, the main barrier to ratification relates to the prohibition of removing documented migrant workers in the event of incapacity to work and loss of employment as endorsed in Article 8 of Conventions Nos 97 and 143.[57] Although this kind of difficulty could be easily resolved by formulating a reservation to the relevant provision,[58] obstacles to ratification are exacerbated by the fact that reservations to ILO Conventions are prohibited. Curiously enough, such a prohibition is not based on any explicit legal provision of the ILO Constitution, the Conference Standing Orders, or the Conventions themselves. The main grounds for this longstanding institutional practice relate to the

[54] K Groenendijk, 'The Metamorphosis of Migrant Labour: Will New Rules Help Migrant Workers?' (1999) 1(2) EJML 173, 175.

[55] R Cholewinski, 'International Labour Migration' in B Opeskin, R Perruchoud, and J Redpath-Cross (eds), *Foundations of International Migration Law* (CUP 2012) 290. The author recalls that, while being applicable to a diverse range of countries, the two ILO treaties provided inspiration for the adoption of the ICRMW and they have had a broad impact on national law of ILO Member States and on the development of regional standards.

[56] However, out of the forty-nine States Parties to Convention C97, twenty-seven have excluded one or several annexes, as allowed by art 14, governing recruitment, placing and condition of labour, as well as personal effects of migrant workers. Furthermore, among the Western countries of immigration mentioned above, only Italy and Norway have also ratified Convention C143. At the time of writing, States Parties to the two ILO conventions are Albania, Armenia, Bosnia and Herzegovina, Burkina Faso, Cameroon, Cyprus, Italy, Kenya, Norway, Serbia, Slovenia, and Tajikistan. Further information about the ratification of the ILO treaties are available at: http://www.ilo.org/dyn/normlex/en/f?p=1000:11001:0::NO accessed 17 October 2018.

[57] International Labour Conference, 'Migrant Workers' (n 3) 225–32. Article 14 of Convention C143 on free choice of employment is also a major issue for receiving states. The CEACR further observes that 'the need to ensure equality of *treatment* between migrant workers and national workers as regards conditions of work, social security and access to social services does not raise any difficulties in principle', but 'the same cannot be said for the promotion of equality of *opportunity* and treatment in the areas covered by Convention No. 143 and Recommendation No. 151', because 'the provisions of these instruments offer a higher degree of protection that afforded by national legislation'. ibid 242. See also, International Labour Conference, 'Promoting Fair Migration' (n 3) 175.

[58] According to the definition given by the Vienna Convention on the Law of Treaties (adopted 23 May 1969, entered into force 27 January 1980) 1155 UNTS 331, art 2(1)(d), a reservation means 'a unilateral statement, however phrased or named, made by a State, when signing, ratifying, accepting, approving or acceding to a treaty, whereby it purports to exclude or to modify the legal effect of certain provisions of the treaty in their application to that State'.

specificity of labour conventions and ILO's tripartite structure which includes representatives of workers, employers, and governments.[59]

While acknowledging the 'respectable tradition' of prohibiting reservations to ILO treaties, the International Law Commission has argued that its rationale 'is somewhat less than convincing', mainly because the participation of non-governmental representatives in the adoption of ILO Conventions does not alter their legal nature as inter-state treaties.[60] The UN Commission has further highlighted that the position of ILO, which distinguishes prohibited reservations from permitted opting-out clauses, represents 'a restrictive view of the concept of reservations which is not reflected in the Vienna Conventions nor in the [...] Guide to Practice [on Reservations to Treaties] adopted by the International Law Commission in 2011'.[61]

Indeed, notwithstanding the prohibition of formulating reservations to ILO treaties, most labour conventions permit the exclusion of a part of them from ratification. However, Convention No 97 limits such possibility to its Annexes that do not contain the contested Article 8. Furthermore, while Convention No 143 permits the exclusion of either Part I or Part II from ratification, the relevant Article 8 is in Part I devoted to irregular migration. Excluding Part I as a whole can prevent states from ratifying a convention that would accordingly be limited to Part II governing equality of treatment between documented migrant workers and nationals without its counterpart on irregular migration.

The continuing application of general labour conventions

The poor ratification record of the two specialized ILO treaties does not reflect the reach of the legal protection granted by international law to migrant workers. Aside from other applicable bilateral agreements and human rights treaties, migrant workers are protected by two additional sets of international labour standards. First, several ILO conventions have been adopted with the specific purpose of ensuring equality of treatment between nationals and non-nationals in the field of social security. They include the Equality of Treatment (Accident Compensation) Convention No 19 (1925), the Maintenance of Migrants' Pension Rights Convention No 48 (1935), the Equality of Treatment (Social Security) Convention No 118 (1962), and the Maintenance of Social Security Rights Convention No 157 (1982).[62]

---

[59] For further discussion, see G Raimondi, 'Réserves et conventions internationales du travail' in J-C Javillier and B Gernigon (eds), *Les normes internationales du travail: Un patrimoine pour l'avenir, Mélanges en l'honneur de Nicolas Valticos* (International Labour Office 2004) 527–39; WP Gormley, 'The Modification of Multilateral Conventions by Means of "Negotiated Reservations" and Other "Alternatives": A Comparative Study of the ILO and Council of Europe' (October 1970–March 1971) 39 Fordham L Rev 413. See also the memorandum submitted by the ILO to the International Court of Justice in the Genocide Case, ILO, *Official Bulletin*, vol XXXIV (International Labour Office 1951) 274–312.

[60] International Law Conference, 'Report of the International Law Commission on its 63rd Session' (26 April–3 June and 4 July–12 August 2011) UN Doc A/66/10/Add.1, 58.

[61] ibid 59.

[62] Furthermore, more general social security conventions frequently include specific provisions on equality of treatment between nationals and non-nationals. See especially ILO Convention C102: Social Security (Minimum Standards) Convention (adopted 28 June 1952, entered into force 27 April 1955;

Although they are ratified by an uneven number of states (respectively 121, 8, 37, and 4), States Parties include both countries of origin and destination. This is essential for the protection of the rights of migrant workers because, in contrast to Conventions Nos 97 and 143, social security conventions are subjected to the principle of reciprocity (ie each State Party is bound to apply the relevant treaty only to nationals of states which have ratified it). Interestingly, both Convention No 118 and Convention No 157 extend their scope of application to refugees and stateless persons, as defined by the 1951 Geneva Convention and the Convention relating to the Status of Stateless Persons of 28 September 1954.[63] For obvious reasons, refugees and stateless persons are exempted from the requirement of reciprocity.[64]

Second and more importantly, migrant workers remain protected by the vast majority of general labour conventions.[65] Most ILO treaties apply to all 'workers' or 'persons' in general, without any qualification based on nationality or migration status, thereby including migrant workers but also, when relevant, refugees, stateless persons, or trafficked and smuggled migrants. These general labour conventions concern a wide range of issues encompassing, for instance, equal remuneration,[66] protection of wages and minimum wage,[67] holidays with pay,[68] weekly rest,[69] occupational safety and health,[70] collective

55 States Parties) 210 UNTS 131, art 68; ILO Convention C121: Employment Injury Benefits Convention (adopted 8 July 1964, entered into force 28 July 1967; 24 States Parties) 602 UNTS 259, art 27; and ILO Convention C130: Medical Care and Sickness Benefits Convention (adopted 25 June 1969, entered into force 27 May 1972; 16 States Parties) 826 UNTS 3, art 32.

[63] ILO Convention C118: Equality of Treatment (Social Security) Convention (adopted 28 June 1962, entered into force 25 April 1964; 37 States Parties) 494 UNTS 271, art 1(g)–(h); ILO Convention C157: Maintenance of Social Security Rights Convention (adopted 21 June 1982, entered into force 11 September 1986; 4 States Parties) 1932 UNTS 29, art 1(e)–(f).

[64] ILO Convention C118 (n 63) Art 10(1); ILO Convention No C157 (n 63) Art 9.

[65] International Labour Conference, 'Migrant Workers' (n 3) 19–20; ILO, *ILO Multilateral Framework on Labour Migration: Non-binding Principles and Guidelines for a Rights-based Approach to Labour Migration* (International Labour Office 2006) principle 9(a), 'all international labour standards apply to migrant workers, unless otherwise stated'. For similar acknowledgements, see, among many others, Cholewinski, *Migrant Workers* (n 28) 98; RB Lillich, *The Human Rights of Aliens in Contemporary International Law* (Manchester University Press 1984) 70; N Valticos, *International Labour Law* (Springer 1979) 211.

[66] ILO Convention C100: Equal Remuneration Convention (adopted 29 June 1951, entered into force 23 May 1953; 173 States Parties) 165 UNTS 303.

[67] ILO Convention C26: Minimum Wage-Fixing Machinery Convention (adopted 16 June 1928, entered into force 14 June 1930; 104 States Parties) 39 UNTS 3; ILO Convention C095: Protection of Wages Convention (adopted 1 July 1949, entered into force 24 September 1952; 97 States Parties) 138 UNTS 225; ILO Convention C131: Minimum Wage Fixing Convention (adopted 22 June 1970, entered into force 29 April 1972; 54 States Parties) 825 UNTS 77.

[68] ILO Convention C132: Holidays with Pay Convention (Revised) (adopted 24 June 1970, entered into force 30 June 1973; 37 States Parties) 883 UNTS 97.

[69] ILO Convention C014: Weekly Rest (Industry) Convention (adopted 17 November 1921, entered into force 19 June 1923; 120 States Parties) 38 UNTS 187; ILO Convention C106: Weekly Rest (Commerce and Offices) Convention (adopted 26 June 1957, entered into force 4 March 1959; 63 States Parties) 325 UNTS 279.

[70] ILO Convention C155: Occupational Safety and Health Convention (adopted 22 June 1981, entered into force 11 August 1983; 67 States Parties) 1331 UNTS 279. See also ILO Convention C152: Occupational Safety and Health (Dock Work) Convention (adopted 25 June 1979, entered into force 5 December 1981; 27 States Parties) 1260 UNTS 3; ILO Convention C167: Safety and Health in Construction Convention (adopted 20 June 1988, entered into force 11 January 1991;

bargaining,[71] or nursing personnel.[72] Some other ILO conventions explicitly recall

31 States Parties) 1592 UNTS 13; ILO Convention C176: Safety and Health in Mines Convention (adopted 22 June 1995, entered into force 5 June 1998; 33 States Parties) 2029 UNTS 207; ILO Convention C184: Safety and Health in Agriculture Convention (adopted 21 June 2001, entered into force 20 September 2003; 16 States Parties) 2227 UNTS 241; ILO Convention C187: Promotional Framework for Occupational Safety and Health Convention (adopted 20 February 2006, entered into force 20 February 2009; 46 States Parties) 2564 UNTS 291; ILO Protocol P155: Protocol of 2002 to the Occupational Safety and Health Convention, 1981 (adopted 20 June 2002, entered into force 9 February 2005; 12 States Parties) 2308 UNTS 112.

[71] ILO Convention C098: Right to Organise and Collective Bargaining Convention (adopted 1 July 1949, entered into force 18 July 1951; 165 States Parties) 96 UNTS 257; ILO Convention C154: Collective Bargaining Convention (adopted 3 June 1981, entered into force 11 August 1983; 48 States Parties) 1331 UNTS 267.

[72] ILO Convention C149: Nursing Personnel Convention (adopted 21 June 1977, entered into force 11 July 1979; 41 States Parties) 1141 UNTS 123. Other ILO conventions that are applicable to migrant workers in general include: ILO Convention C029: Forced Labour Convention (adopted 28 June 1930, entered into force 1 May 1932; 178 States Parties) 39 UNTS 55; ILO Convention C077: Medical Examination of Young Persons (Industry) Convention (adopted 9 October 1946, entered into force 29 December 1950; 43 States Parties) 78 UNTS 197; ILO Convention C078: Medical Examination of Young Persons (Non-Industrial Occupations) Convention (adopted 9 October 1946, entered into force 29 December 1950; 39 States Parties) 78 UNTS 213; ILO Convention C081: Labour Inspection Convention (adopted 11 July 1947, entered into force 7 April 1950; 146 States Parties) 54 UNTS 3; ILO Convention C094: Labour Clauses (Public Contracts) Convention (adopted 29 June 1949, entered into force 20 September 1952; 62 States Parties) 138 UNTS 207; ILO Convention C105: Abolition of Forced Labour Convention (adopted 25 June 1957, entered into force 17 January 1959; 173 States Parties) 320 UNTS 291; ILO Convention C115: Radiation Protection Convention (adopted 22 June 1960, entered into force 17 June 1962; 50 States Parties) 431 UNTS 41; ILO Convention C120: Hygiene (Commerce and Offices) Convention (adopted 8 July 1964, entered into force 29 March 1966; 51 States Parties) 560 UNTS 201; ILO Convention C124: Medical Examination of Young Persons (Underground Work) Convention (adopted 23 June 1965, entered into force 13 December 1967; 41 States Parties) 614 UNTS 239; ILO Convention C128: Invalidity, Old-Age and Survivors' Benefits Convention (adopted 29 June 1967, entered into force 1 November 1969; 17 States Parties) 699 UNTS 185; ILO Convention C129: Labour Inspection (Agriculture) Convention (adopted 25 June 1969, entered into force 19 January 1972; 53 States Parties) 812 UNTS 87; ILO Convention C135: Workers' Representatives Convention (adopted 23 June 1971, entered into force 30 June 1973; 85 States Parties) 883 UNTS 111; ILO Convention C138: Minimum Age Convention (adopted 26 June 1973, entered into force 19 June 1976; 171 States Parties) 1015 UNTS 297; ILO Convention C139: Occupational Cancer Convention (adopted 24 June 1974, entered into force 10 June 1976; 41 States Parties) 1010 UNTS 5; ILO Convention C141: Rural Workers' Organisations Convention (adopted 23 June 1975, entered into force 24 November 1977; 41 States Parties) 1060 UNTS 263; ILO Convention C142: Human Resources Development Convention (adopted 23 June 1975, entered into force 19 July 1977; 68 States Parties) 1050 UNTS 9; ILO Convention C145: Continuity of Employment (Seafarers) Convention (adopted 28 October 1976, entered into force 3 May 1979; 5 States Parties) 1136 UNTS 91; ILO Convention C146: Seafarers' Annual Leave with Pay Convention (adopted 29 October 1976, entered into force 13 June 1979; 4 States Parties) 1138 UNTS 205; ILO Conference C147: Merchant Shipping (Minimum Standards) Convention (adopted 29 October 1976, entered into force 28 November 1981; 14 States Parties) 1259 UNTS 336; ILO Convention C148: Working Environment (Air Pollution, Noise and Vibration) Convention (adopted 20 June 1977, entered into force 11 July 1979; 46 States Parties) 1141 UNTS 106; ILO Convention C150: Labour Administration Convention (adopted 26 June 1978, entered into force 11 October 1980; 76 States Parties) 1201 UNTS 179; ILO Convention C151: Labour Relations (Public Service) Convention (adopted 27 June 1978, entered into force 25 February 1981; 55 States Parties) 1218 UNTS 87; ILO Convention C159: Vocational Rehabilitation and Employment (Disabled Persons) Convention (adopted 20 June 1983, entered into force 20 June 1985; 83 States Parties) 1401 UNTS 235; ILO Convention C161: Occupational Health Services Convention (adopted 25 June 1985, entered into force 17 February 1988; 33 States Parties) 1498 UNTS 19; ILO Convention C162: Asbestos Convention (adopted 24 June 1986, entered into force 16 June 1989; 35 States Parties) 1539 UNTS 315; ILO Convention C164: Health Protection and

that they apply 'without distinction whatsoever'[73] or 'irrespective of nationality, race, colour, sex, religion, political opinion or social origin'[74] in various areas, such as freedom of association, maternity protection, or paid educational leave.[75]

Furthermore, although they have been adopted for a broader purpose, several general labour conventions contain more specific provisions devoted to migrant workers. The following five treaties are particularly relevant:[76]

- The Plantations Convention, 1958 (No 110) applies to 'all plantation workers without distinction as to race, colour, sex, religion, political opinion, nationality, social origin, tribe or trade union membership'.[77] Moreover, its Part II

Medical Care (Seafarers) Convention (adopted 8 October 1987, entered into force 11 January 1991; 4 States Parties) 1592 UNTS 13; ILO Convention C166: Repatriation of Seafarers Convention (Revised) (adopted 9 October 1987, entered into force 3 July 1991; 5 States Parties) 1644 UNTS 311; ILO Convention C171: Night Work Convention (adopted 26 June 1990, entered into force 4 January 1995; 17 States Parties) 1855 UNTS 305; ILO Convention C172: Working Conditions (Hotels and Restaurants) Convention (adopted 25 June 1991, entered into force 7 July 1994; 16 States Parties) 1820 UNTS 445; ILO Convention C173: Protection of Workers' Claims (Employer's Insolvency) Convention (adopted 23 June 1992, entered into force 8 June 1995; 21 States Parties) 1886 UNTS 3; ILO Convention C174: Prevention of Major Industrial Accidents Convention (adopted 22 June 1993, entered into force 3 January 1997; 18 States Parties) 1967 UNTS 232; ILO Convention C175: Part-Time Work Convention (adopted 24 June 1994, entered into force 28 February 1998; 17 States Parties) 2010 UNTS 51; ILO Convention C177: Home Work Convention (adopted 20 June 1996, entered into force 22 April 2000; 10 States Parties) 2108 UNTS 161; ILO Convention C178: Labour Inspection (Seafarers) Convention (adopted 22 October 1996, entered into force 22 April 2000; 2 States Parties) 2108 UNTS 173; ILO Convention C182: Worst Forms of Child Labour Convention (adopted 17 June 1999, entered into force 19 November 2000; 182 States Parties) 2133 UNTS 161; ILO Maritime Labour Convention, 2006 (adopted 23 February 2006, entered into force 20 August 2013; 88 States Parties) 2952 UNTS; ILO Protocol P081: Protocol of 1995 to the Labour Inspection Convention (22 June 1995, entered into force 9 June 1998; 12 States Parties) 1985 UNTS 527; ILO Protocol P089: Protocol of 1990 to the Night Work (Women) Convention (Revised) (adopted 26 June 1990, entered into force 26 June 1990; 3 States Parties) 1846 UNTS 418; ILO Protocol P110: Protocol of 1982 to the Plantations Convention 1958 (adopted 18 June 1982, entered into force 18 June 1982; 2 States Parties) 1413 UNTS 428.

[73] ILO Convention C087: Freedom of Association and Protection of the Right to Organise Convention (adopted 9 July 1948, entered into force 4 July 1950; 155 States Parties) 68 UNTS 17, art 2. See also ILO Convention C183: Maternity Protection Convention (adopted 15 June 2000, entered into force 7 February 2002; 34 States Parties) 2181 UNTS 253, which applies to any woman and any child 'without discrimination whatsoever' (art 1).

[74] ILO Convention C163: Seafarers' Welfare Convention (adopted 8 October 1987, entered into force 3 October 1990; 5 States Parties) 1580 UNTS 161, art 3(1). See also ILO Convention C103: Maternity Protection Convention (Revised) (adopted 28 June 1952, entered into force 7 September 1955; 24 States Parties) 214 UNTS 321, art 2 defines a woman as 'any female person, irrespective of age, nationality, race, or creed.' Other conventions replace the term 'nationality' by 'national extraction', see, for instance, ILO Convention C111: Discrimination (Employment and Occupation) Convention (adopted 25 June 1958, entered into force 15 June 1960; 175 States Parties) 362 UNTS 31, art 1; ILO Convention C140: Paid Educational Leave Convention (adopted 24 June 1974, entered into force 23 September 1976; 35 States Parties) 1023 UNTS 243, art 8; ILO Convention C158: Termination of Employment Convention (adopted 22 June 1982, entered into force 23 November 1985; 35 States Parties) 1412 UNTS 159, art 5.

[75] See the relevant treaties quoted in the two previous footnotes.

[76] When relevant, they presumably apply to refugees, stateless persons, as well trafficked and smuggled migrants in so far as they are working in a foreign country.

[77] ILO Convention C110: Plantations Convention (adopted 24 June 1958, entered into force 22 January 1960; 10 States Parties) 348 UNTS 275, art 2.

details the engagement and recruitment of migrant workers (Articles 5 to 19). It is currently ratified by ten states from the Global South (including Cuba, Côte d'Ivoire, Guatemala, Mexico, and the Philippines).

- The Employment Promotion and Protection against Unemployment Convention, 1988 (No 168) ensures 'equality of treatment for all persons protected, without discrimination on the basis of race, colour, sex, religion, political opinion, national extraction, nationality, ethnic or social origin, disability or age'.[78] According to Article 8(1), 'migrant workers lawfully resident in the country' are among the categories of disadvantaged persons who shall benefit from special programmes to promote job opportunities and employment assistance. Article 26(1) further requires that 'migrant workers on return to their home country' shall receive social benefits, except in so far as they have acquired rights under the legislation of the country where they last worked. This Convention, however, has so far only been ratified by eight states (mainly European ones).

- The Private Employment Agencies Convention, 1997 (No 181) is ratified by thirty-three states from various regions across the world.[79] It requires States Parties to ensure that private employment agencies treat workers without discrimination (Article 5(1)). Article 8(1) further requires Member States 'to provide adequate protection for and prevent abuses of migrant workers recruited or placed in its territory by private employment agencies.' Paragraph 2 of Article 8 also encourages the conclusion of bilateral agreements to prevent abuses and fraudulent practices in recruitment, placement, and employment.

- The Domestic Workers Convention, 2011 (No 189) is applicable to 'all domestic workers', including foreigners, and requires more specifically that migrant domestic workers receive a written job offer or contract of employment, addressing the terms, and conditions of employment prior to crossing national borders.[80] According to Article 8(4), each State Party shall also specify in its domestic law the conditions under which migrant domestic workers are entitled to repatriation upon the expiry or termination of employment contract. Article 15 further details the duty of Member States to effectively protect migrant domestic workers against abusive practices of private employment agencies. This Convention is currently ratified by twenty-seven states, including both countries of origin and of destination (such as the Philippines and Germany).

- The Protocol of 2014 to the Forced Labour Convention, 130 (No 29) calls on Member States to take measures in protecting migrant workers from abusive

[78] ILO Convention C168: Employment Promotion and Protection against Unemployment Convention (adopted 21 June 1988, entered into force 17 October 1991; 8 States Parties) 1654 UNTS 67, art 6(1).
[79] ILO Convention C181: Private Employment Agencies Convention (adopted 19 June 1997, entered into force 10 May 2000; 33 States Parties) 2115 UNTS 249.
[80] ILO Convention C189: Domestic Workers Convention (adopted 16 June 2011, entered into force 5 September 2013; 27 States Parties) 2995 UNTS, arts 2(1) and 8(1) respectively.

and fraudulent practices during the recruitment and placement process.[81] Article 4(1) also restates that 'all victims of forced or compulsory labour, irrespective of their presence or legal status in the national territory, have access to appropriate and effective remedies, such as compensation'. Even though it is the most recent ILO Protocol, it has already been ratified by twenty-eight states, including both countries of origin and of destination.[82]

4.2 The International Convention on the Protection of the Rights of All Migrant Workers and Members of Their Families

The detailed set of labour standards adopted within the ILO framework is supplemented and reinforced by the ICRMW. As observed by the CEACR, 'the UN Convention on Migrant Workers and the ILO instruments on labour migration are complementary and mutually reinforcing'.[83] Despite its close interaction and overlap with ILO conventions, the ICRMW constitutes the most comprehensive treaty in the field of labour migration. As acknowledged in its preamble, the *raison d'être* of the ICRMW is that of 'reaffirming and establishing basic norms in a comprehensive convention which could be applied universally'. Following the same pattern as the other specialized ILO conventions, the ICRMW contains and details three sets of provisions governing the definition of migrant workers (section 4.2.1), the inter-state regulation of labour migration (section 4.2.2), as well as the rights of migrant workers (section 4.2.3).

4.2.1 The definition of migrant workers

Compared to any other international treaties, the ICRMW provides the most comprehensive definition of migrant workers.[84] Its drafters intended to adopt 'a broader concept of migrant workers for the purpose of including certain categories of workers that have not been covered by ILO Conventions'.[85] According to Article

---

[81] ILO Protocol P029: Protocol of 2014 to the Forced Labour Convention, 1930 (adopted 11 June 2014, entered into force 9 November 2016; 28 States Parties), art 2(d).

[82] Argentina, Bosnia and Herzegovina, Cyprus, Czech Republic, Denmark, Djibouti, Estonia, Finland, France, Iceland, Israel, Jamaica, Latvia, Mali, Mauritania, Mozambique, Namibia, the Netherlands, Niger, Norway, Panama, Poland, the Russian Federation, Spain, Sweden, Switzerland, Thailand, and the UK.

[83] International Labour Conference, 'Promoting Fair Migration' (n 3) 90.

[84] For a similar account and further comments, see especially Cholewinski, *Migrant Workers* (n 28) 149–54.

[85] See the statement by the representative of Finland in UNGA 'Report of the Open-ended Working Group on the Elaboration of an International Convention on the Protection of the Rights of All Migrant Workers and Their Families on its inter-sessional meetings from 10 to 21 May 1982' (11 June 1982) UN Doc A/C.3/37/1, para 67. See also the statement of the representative of Sweden in UNGA 'Report of the Open-ended Working Group on the Elaboration of an International Convention on the Protection of the Rights of All Migrant Workers and Their Families' (October 1983) UN Doc A/C.3/38/5, para 75. The statements of the representatives of Norway and Greece can be found in UNGA 'Report of the Open-ended Working Group on the Elaboration of an International Convention on the

2(1), 'the term "migrant worker" refers to a person who is to be engaged, is engaged or has been engaged in a remunerated activity in a State of which he or she is not a national'.

The scope of the UN definition of migrant workers

The concise and factual definition of 'migrant worker' under the ICRMW is much more comprehensive than the ones laid down in the ILO Conventions Nos 97 and 143 on four critical counts. First, in contrast to the ILO definition, Article 2(1) of the ICRMW includes both documented and undocumented migrant workers.[86] Despite the reluctance of the US and Germany,[87] the protection of migrant workers in an irregular situation was considered by most states' representatives as 'the main purpose of the new Convention'[88] with a view to adopting 'a global legal instrument'.[89]

As epitomized in the preamble of the UN Convention, the rationale of such inclusion follows the twofold objective of protection and prevention. On the one hand, the vulnerability of undocumented migrant workers calls for protection because of 'the human problems' raised by irregular migration (recital 13), including the fact that undocumented migrant workers 'are frequently employed under less favourable conditions of work than other workers' (recital 14). On the other hand, from a preventive perspective, 'recourse to the employment of migrant workers who are in irregular situation will be discouraged if the fundamental human rights of all migrant workers are more widely recognized' (recital 15). Following this dual approach, the protection of undocumented migrant workers is supposed to work in tandem with the prevention of irregular migration on the ground that granting them rights would diminish the incentives of some employers to recruit them and exploit their vulnerability.

Protection of the Rights of All Migrant Workers and Their Families' (June 1985) UN Doc A/C.3/40/1, paras 29 and 38.

[86] International Convention on the Protection of the Rights of All Migrant Workers and Members of their Families (adopted 18 December 1990, entered into force 1 July 2003) 2220 UNTS 3 (ICRMW) art 5 defines undocumented migrant workers in opposition to documented ones as including those who are not authorized to enter, stay, and engage in a remunerated activity in the state of employment pursuant to the law of that state and international agreements to which that state is a party. By contrast, and as mentioned in the previous section, the ILO definition of migrant workers is explicitly limited to 'any person regularly admitted as a migrant for employment', although ILO Convention C143 (n 2) contains several provisions about irregular migration.

[87] UNGA 'Report of the Open-ended Working Group on the Elaboration of an International Convention on the Protection of the Rights of All Migrant Workers and Their Families' (June 1984) UN Doc A/C.3/39/1, para 103; UNGA 'Report of the Open-ended Working Group on the Elaboration of an International Convention on the Protection of the Rights of All Migrant Workers and Their Families' (June 1985) para 61.

[88] See the statement of the representative of Mexico in UNGA 'Report of the Open-ended Working Group' (June 1985) (n 87) para 48.

[89] See also the statement of the representative of Denmark in ibid, para 30. Among other instances, see also the statements by the representatives of Argentina, the Dominican Republic, Ghana, and Yugoslavia in UNGA, 'Report of the Open-ended Working Group' (June 1984) (n 87), paras 104 and 106.

Defining migrant workers irrespective of their documentation status further reflects the reality of labour migration and the need for a truly comprehensive instrument encapsulating a broad variety of situations. The inclusion of undocumented migrant workers represents the key added value of the ICRMW, which has been praised by commentators as 'a major accomplishment',[90] 'a considerable step forward in the international protection of this vulnerable group,'[91] and 'the most ambitious statement to date of international concern for the problematic condition of undocumented migrants.'[92] However, undocumented migrant workers are not entitled to the full range of rights enshrined in the ICRMW. As discussed below, the UN Convention cautiously distinguishes the basic rights of undocumented migrant workers from the rights granted to those who are in a regular situation in order to satisfy concerns raised by destination states.

The second enlargement of the definition of migrant workers, as endorsed by the ICRMW, relates to its inclusion of all foreigners engaged in a remunerated activity, thereby extending beyond the definition in ILO Conventions Nos 97 and 143 which is limited to those who migrated for the very purpose of employment. The personal scope of the ICRMW thus covers all migrants who came on a ground other than that of employment (such as family reunion or tourism) and non-citizens who were born in the host state, as soon as they are engaged in a remunerated activity.

At the same time, the inclusion of all foreign workers does not imply that the ICRMW only focuses on states of employment. The ICRMW addresses all States Parties whether they are countries of destination, transit, or origin. Although the same observation is applicable to many provisions of the two ILO Conventions, the treaty body of the ICRMW has been particularly proactive in stressing the responsibility of states of origin towards their nationals working abroad. The CMW has notably insisted on the duty of sending countries to provide effective consular protection,[93] to facilitate transfer of remittances in their own economy,[94] and to

---

[90] S Hune, 'Drafting an International Convention on the Protection of the Rights of All Migrant Workers and Their Families' (1985) 19(3) International Migration Review 570, 573.

[91] Cholewinski, *Migrant Workers* (n 28) 190.

[92] LS Bosniak, 'Human Rights, State Sovereignty and the Protection of Undocumented Migrants under the International Migrant Workers Convention' (1991) 25(4) International Migration Review 737, 740.

[93] UN Committee on the Protection of the Rights of All Migrant Workers and Members of Their Families (CMW), 'Concluding observations on the initial report of Guinea' (8 October 2015) UN Doc CMW/C/GIN/CO/1, para 26; CMW, 'Concluding observations on the initial report of Cabo Verde' (October 2015) UN Doc CMW/C/CPB/CO/1, para 35; CMW, 'Concluding observations on the second periodic report of the Philippines' (2 May 2014) UN Doc CMW/C/PHL/CO/2, para 31; CMW, 'Concluding observations of the Committee on the second periodic report of Mali' (May 2014) UN Doc CMW/C/MLI/CO/2, para 27; CMW, 'Concluding observations on the initial report of El Salvador' (May 2014) UN Doc CMW/C/SL/CO/2, para 27; CMW, 'Concluding observations on the second periodic report of the Plurinational State of Bolivia, adopted at its eighteenth session (15–26 April 2013)' (15 May 2013) UN Doc CMW/C/BOL/CO/2, para 31; CMW, 'Concluding observations: Egypt' (25 May 2007) UN Doc CMW/C/EGY/CO/1, para 47.

[94] CMW, 'Concluding observations on the initial report of Ghana' (26 September 2014) UN Doc CMW/C/GHA/CO/1, para 31; CMW, 'Concluding observations: Sri Lanka' (October 2009) UN Doc CMW/C/LKA/CO/1, paras 35–36.

guarantee the right of nationals abroad to vote in elections of their home states,[95] as well the right to leave and to return to their own country (including the facilitation of durable reintegration for those who came back to their state of nationality).[96]

The third area where the ICRMW significantly supplements its ILO counterparts concerns the type of professional occupations. The ICRMW refers to any 'remunerated activities' in general,[97] whereas the ILO definition is limited to workers who are 'employed otherwise than on [their] own account'. Contrary to the ILO Conventions, the ICRMW extends to both employees and self-employed workers.[98] This represents another significant addition to the definition, given the importance of self-employed migrants in the informal economy of many states. Following the same inclusive logic, several other categories of workers who are excluded from the ILO Conventions Nos 97 and 143 are specifically covered by the ICRMW, most notably frontier workers, itinerant workers, as well as project-tied and specified-employment workers hired for a defined period.[99]

[95] CMW, 'Concluding observations on the initial report of Cabo Verde' (n 93) para 45; CMW, 'Concluding observations on the initial report of the Morocco, adopted by the Committee at its nineteenth session (9–13 September 2013)' (8 October 2009) UN Doc CMW/C/MAR/CO/1, para 42; CMW, 'Concluding observations on the second periodic report of the Plurinational State of Bolivia, adopted at its eighteenth session (15–26 April 2013)' (n 93) para 37; CMW, 'Concluding observations on the initial report of Burkina Faso, adopted by the Committee at its nineteenth session (9–13 September 2013)' (8 October 2013) UN Doc CMW/C/BFA/CO/1, para 33; CMW, 'Concluding observations: Paraguay' (16 May 2012) UN Doc CMW/C/PRY/CO/1, para 39; CMW, 'Concluding observations: Chile' (19 October 2011) UN Doc CMW/C/CHL/CO/1, para 49; CMW, 'Concluding observations on the initial report of Ghana' (n 94) para 31; CMW, 'Concluding observations: Sri Lanka' (n 94) para 34.

[96] On the right to leave one's own country, see especially the following concluding observations, CMW, 'Concluding observations on the initial report of Morocco' (n 95) para 24; CMW, 'Concluding observations: Tajikistan' (16 May 2012) UN Doc CMW/C/TJK/CO/1, para 26; CMW, 'Concluding observations: Ecuador' (5 December 2007) UN Doc CMW/C/ECU/CO/1, para 22. Regarding return and reintegration of nationals, see also CMW, 'Concluding observations on the initial report of El Salvador' (n 93), para 41; CMW, 'Concluding observations of the Committee on the second periodic report of Mali' (n 93), paras 43–45; CMW, 'Concluding observations on the second periodic report of Colombia, adopted by the Committee at its eighteenth session (15–26 April 2013)' (27 May 2013) UN Doc CMW/C/COL/CO/2 para 35; CMW, 'Concluding observations: Chile' (n 95), para 51. The CMW frequently recommends that states of origin conclude international agreements with countries of destination and transit in order to better protect the rights of their nationals working abroad. See, for instance, CMW, 'Concluding observations on the initial report of Ghana' (n 94), para 41; CMW, 'Concluding observations on the second periodic report of the Philippines' (n 93) para 33; and CMW, 'Concluding observations: Sri Lanka' (n 94) para 40.

[97] The term 'remunerated activity' is not defined by the ICRMW, but state delegates agreed that 'activities contrary to the rules of *ordre public* in the State in which they took place were out of the scope of the Convention', see UNGA, 'Report of the Open-ended Working Group' (June 1985) (n 87) para 174.

[98] ICRMW (n 86) art 2(2)(h) defines the term 'self-employed workers' as including 'a migrant worker who is engaged in a remunerated activity otherwise than under a contract of employment and who earns his or her living through this activity normally working alone or together with members of his or her family, and to any other migrant worker recognized as self-employed by applicable legislation of the State of employment or bilateral or multilateral agreements'.

[99] All these categories are defined by ICRMW (n 86) art 2(2). Part V further details to what extent the rights granted to all migrant workers must be adapted to and compatible with the duration and specificities of their economic activities. Seasonal workers are also covered by the ICRMW but, as discussed before, they are as well implicitly covered by the ILO Conventions.

The fourth difference relates to the timeline of the relevant professional activity, which is slightly broader in the ICRMW. While covering both prospective and current economic activities, in line with the ILO Conventions, the ICRMW additionally includes past remunerative activities. The expression 'has been engaged' in Article 2(1) was understood by the drafters as referring to 'a person who had left the country where he worked as a migrant worker and who, for certain rights provided for under the Convention, he or she still continued to be considered as a migrant worker.'[100] Article 1(2) confirms the ICRMW's broader personal scope by underlying that the Convention shall apply 'during the entire migration process', including upon preparation to migrate, departure, transit, stay, and return.

The application of the ICRMW to prospective migrant workers who are still in their country of origin raised some discussions during the drafting of the Convention. The term 'seek to engage' was replaced by 'is to be engaged', so that the Convention would not be applicable to 'persons having the mere intent to migrate'.[101] Nonetheless, the definition of migrant workers finally retained by the ICRMW is broad enough to comprise prospective workers in their own country. While interpreting the expression 'is to be engaged' under Article 2(1), the Chairman of the working group in charge of drafting the Convention made clear that 'a work contract with an employer or a similar document would constitute the starting point for the recognition of a person as a migrant worker, even before that person left his country of origin or normal residence'.[102]

Family members of migrant workers

The broad coverage of the ICRMW is not limited to the definition of migrant workers. The personal scope of the Convention extends to their families with a view to providing a truly comprehensive instrument. This broad scope represents another key added value of the ICRMW compared to other specialized treaties of international migration law. ILO Conventions Nos 97 and 143 contain very few provisions on family, whereas the Refugee Convention remains silent in this respect. On the contrary, the rationale of the ICRMW is to approach the migrant worker as both an economic and social entity.

The inclusion of family members was accordingly taken for granted and did not raise major objections during the drafting of the Convention. Most discussions focused instead on the definition of family. While Western states proposed restricting its definition to the nuclear family, developing states were in favour of a broader

---

[100] See the statement of Mexico as the Chairman of the Working Group in UNGA, 'Report of the Open-ended Working Group' (June 1985) (n 87) para 168. The Chairman mentioned, as other possible examples, persons who have contracted an occupational disease which only manifests itself after the departure from the country of employment, unemployed migrant workers seeking re-employment, victims of a work accident who have to stay in the country of employment for the purpose of invalidity benefits or those who are on temporary leave from the host country. ibid para 169.

[101] UNGA, 'Report of the Open-ended Working Group' (June 1985) (n 87) para 141.

[102] ibid para 168.

definition encompassing the extended family.[103] The definition finally retained by Article 4 is broad and flexible enough to encompass any partner in a marital or non-marital relationship, children, as well as other dependents who are considered members of the family by applicable legislation or treaties.[104]

Refugees, stateless persons, and the definition of migrant workers

Despite its particularly broad and inclusive scope, the definition of migrant workers under the ICRMW is more restrictive than the one of the ILO Conventions regarding two significant categories of migrants. In stark contrast with Conventions Nos 97 and 143, refugees and stateless persons are excluded from the scope of the ICRMW, unless domestic legislation or an international instrument provides for such application (Article 3(d)).[105] However, this exclusion does not reflect the subtle yet substantial impact of the ICRMW on stateless persons and refugees.

As far as stateless persons are concerned, the ICRMW draws an implicit distinction between migrant workers and their children. On the one hand, stateless migrant workers are excluded from the benefits of the Convention (unless provided otherwise by international or national instruments). They are thus primarily governed by the 1954 Convention relating to the Status of Stateless Persons and the 1961 Convention on the Reduction of Statelessness, in addition to general human rights treaties. On the other hand, children who are stateless in their host country are included within the scope of the ICRMW. According to Article 29, each child of a migrant worker—whether documented or not—shall have the right to a nationality. As confirmed by the CMW, States Parties must accordingly ensure that their domestic legislation would not create stateless children.[106] The resulting distinction between migrant workers and their children appears somewhat formal and rigid. Although the *travaux préparatoires* provide no clear hints about the motivation behind such a distinction, the absence of any provision on nationality for migrant workers probably echoes the anxiety of states towards their naturalization and permanent settlement.

---

[103] UNGA 'Report of the Open-ended Working Group on the Elaboration of an International Convention on the Protection of the Rights of All Migrant Workers and Their Families' (10 October 1986) UN Doc A/C.3/41/3, paras 29–51.

[104] 'For the purposes of the present Convention the term "members of the family" refers to persons married to migrant workers or having with them a relationship that, according to applicable law, produces effects equivalent to marriage, as well as their dependent children and other dependent persons who are recognized as members of the family by applicable legislation or applicable bilateral or multilateral agreements between the States concerned.' Although the case was not envisaged during the drafting process, same-sex relationships can fall within this definition provided that they produce effects equivalent to marriage under the applicable law of the State Party.

[105] Foreign investors are also excluded from the ICRMW (n 86) but not from the ILO Conventions. The other cases of exclusion enumerated in Article 3 of the ICRMW largely coincide with the ones of the ILO Conventions. They concern, most notably, students and trainees, persons sent or employed by international organizations as well as those sent or employed by a state outside its territory to perform official functions or to participate in development or cooperation programmes.

[106] See, for instance, CMW, 'Concluding observations: Chile' (n 95) para 33; CMW, 'Concluding observations: Colombia' (22 May 2009) UN Doc CMW/C/COL/CO/1 para 29.

The situation is more complex and arguably confusing with regards to refugees. During the drafting of the Convention, most delegates agreed on the exclusion of refugees 'because those persons had a specific international status' governed by the Geneva Convention as amended by its Protocol.[107] Their exclusion from the ICRMW differs from the scope of other relevant specialized treaties and accordingly creates a hiatus in their continuing application: refugees are covered by the ILO definition of migrant workers, and, inversely, migrant workers can fall within the refugee definition under Article 1(A)(2) of the Geneva Convention. In this case, however, refugees no longer benefit from the protection of the ICRMW. This complex articulation between the specialized treaties of international migration law calls for a particularly substantial caveat. Indeed, the subsequent interpretation provided by the monitoring body of the ICRMW has considerably circumscribed and mitigated the exclusion of refugees from the definition of migrant workers.

Although the Committee did not explicitly elaborate the rationale of its inclusive approach, its unexpected activism in the field of refugee protection can still be reconciled with the text of the ICRMW. The term 'refugee' under Article 3(d) of the ICRMW may be construed in a literal and restrictive sense as referring to refugees formally recognized as such by States Parties in application of the Geneva Convention relating to the Status of Refugees. As a result of this interpretation, asylum-seekers and other persons in need of protection (including beneficiaries of complementary protection to the refugee status) fall within the scope of the ICRMW, provided that they are engaged in a remunerated activity following the broad definition of migrant workers under Article 2(1).[108]

This seems to be the prevailing understanding of the CMW when it comes to persons in need of protection who are not formally recognized as refugees under the Geneva Convention. For instance, in its Concluding Observations on Syria adopted in 2008, the Committee assumed that Iraqi nationals who have fled violence in their country after 2003 (and remained in Syria) fall within the definition of migrant workers.[109] Another illustration of this inclusive interpretation can be found in the Concluding Observations on Ecuador. The Committee expressed its concern that 'there is in the State party a high number of persons in need of international protection, notably Colombians, who do not apply for asylum for a number of reasons (including the fear of being deported and stringent documentation requirements) and remain in a very vulnerable and marginalized situation'.[110] It further

---

[107] UNGA, 'Report of the Open-ended Working Group on the Elaboration of an International Convention on the Protection of the Rights of All Migrant Workers and Their Families' (15 October 1985) UN Doc A/C.3/40/6, para 112.

[108] Following this interpretation, the ICRMW is also applicable to those who have been excluded from the refugee status but cannot be returned to their own country because of the risk of torture, inhuman, or degrading treatment prevailing therein.

[109] CMW, 'Concluding observations: Syrian Arab Republic' (2 May 2008) UN Doc CMW/C/SYR/CO/1, paras 29–30. Unfortunately, the Committee came to this conclusion without further elaborating its reasoning. It merely took note that Iraqi nationals are not considered as refugees by Syria and, thus, not excluded by Article 3(d). Curiously enough, the Committee did not mention that Syria never ratified the UN Convention relating to the Status of Refugees.

[110] CMW, 'Concluding observations: Ecuador' (n 96) para 28.

recommended in particularly strong terms that 'the State Party [shall] ensure that migration control measures do not undermine the safeguards granted by either the 1951 Geneva Convention relating to the Status of Refugees, where applicable, or the present Convention, in order to guarantee that no vulnerable group is left without adequate protection'.[111]

Similarly, the application of the ICRMW to asylum-seekers was acknowledged by the CMW in its Concluding Observations on Mexico,[112] Turkey,[113] and Burkina Faso,[114] where it stressed the need to provide access to asylum procedures for migrant workers willing to do so.[115] Following the same logic, its General comment No 2 on the rights of migrant workers in an irregular situation and members of their families underlines that all undocumented migrant workers held in detention shall be informed of their right to request asylum.[116] Furthermore, General comment No 2 acknowledges, in line with other human rights treaty bodies, an implicit duty of *non-refoulement* deriving from the general prohibition of torture, inhuman, or degrading treatment, and the right to life. While referring to the relevant Articles 9 and 10 of the ICRMW, the Committee considers that 'this principle [of *non-refoulement*] covers the risk of torture and cruel, inhuman or degrading treatment or punishment, including inhumane and degrading conditions of detention for migrants or lack of necessary medical treatment in the country of return, as well as the risk to the right to life'.[117]

Overall, and although the piecemeal approach followed by the Committee is not always crystal clear, its broad interpretation unveils the huge potential of the ICRMW to fill the gaps of the Geneva Convention relating to the Status of Refugees. While the ICRMW excludes refugees formally recognized under the 1951 Convention, it provides, at the same time, some form of protection to both asylum-seekers and other beneficiaries of complementary protection which is not otherwise granted by the Geneva Convention. The normative and practical consequences of such a cross-cutting application are straightforward: asylum-seekers and persons in need of protection who are not officially recognized as refugees are entitled to the rights of the ICRMW as soon as they are engaged in a remunerated activity. Moreover, the ICRMW can even protect those who are not involved in any economic activity as family members of migrant workers, while they remain, in any event, under the ambit of general human rights instruments.

---

[111] ibid para 29.

[112] CMW, 'Concluding observations: Mexico' (May 2011) UN Doc CMW/C/MEX/CO/2, para 41.

[113] CMW, 'Concluding observations on the initial report of Turkey' (May 2016) UN Doc CMW/C/TUR/CO/1, paras 41(d)–(e).

[114] CMW, 'Concluding observations on the initial report of Burkina Faso' (n 95) para 39(d).

[115] One should add that the application of the ICRMW to asylum-seekers was acknowledged in the legal doctrine long before its endorsement by the CMW. See R Bohning, 'The ILO and the New UN Convention on Migrant Workers: The Past and Future' (1991) 25(4) International Migration Review 698, 707, 708; Cholewinski, *Migrant Workers* (n 28) 153.

[116] CMW, 'General comment No 2 on the rights of migrant workers in an irregular situation and members of their families' (28 August 2013) UN Doc CMW/C/GC/2, para 34.

[117] ibid para 50.

Exploiting the potentialities of the ICRMW further calls for a more systematic and principled approach of the CMW to complement the Geneva Convention and compensate for its limited protective reach for asylum-seekers and beneficiaries of complementary protection to the refugee status. Addressing the specific vulnerabilities of these categories of persons would, in turn, provide a crucial source of protection in ICRMW States Parties where there is a significant number of asylum-seekers (eg Morocco and Turkey) or in those that did not ratify the Geneva Convention relating to the Status of Refugees (eg Lebanon and Libya).

4.2.2 The regulation of labour migration under the ICRMW: between cooperation and constraint

Similarly to its ILO counterparts, the ICRMW does not create any duty of admission to the benefit of migrant workers. On the contrary, the whole Convention pays tribute to state sovereignty, echoing the traditional concern of destination countries. Such a deference is evidenced by the distinction between the rights of undocumented migrant workers and those of workers in a regular situation. Article 79 also makes clear that 'nothing in the present Convention shall affect the right of each state party to establish the criteria governing admission of migrant workers and members of their families'.[118] As stressed by the US representative during the drafting of the Convention, this provision aims to reaffirm 'the well-recognized principle that all states have the sovereign right to adopt and enforce their own immigration policies'.[119] Accordingly, the ICRMW preserves the sovereignty of States Parties in deciding whether to admit migrant workers within their territory.

Nevertheless, the ICRMW does not give states a blank cheque in the field of admission. Like ILO Conventions Nos 97 and 143, it provides some guidance to States Parties in designing and implementing their immigration policy through two primary means. On the one hand, it offers a flexible framework of inter-state cooperation in order to better manage regular migration and fight irregular migration. On the other hand, the rights of migrant workers enshrined in the ICRMW constitute another set of indirect restrictions on the implementation of immigration control.

---

[118] The same concern transpires from Article 35 according to which, 'Nothing in the present part [III] of the Convention [on the rights of all migrant workers] shall be interpreted as implying the regularization of the situation of migrant workers or members of their families who are non-documented or in an irregular situation or any right to such regularization of their situation, nor shall it prejudice the measures intended to ensure sound and equitable-conditions for international migration as provided in part VI of the present Convention.'

[119] UNGA, 'Report of the Open-ended Working Group on the Elaboration of an International Convention on the Protection of the Rights of All Migrant Workers and Their Families' (20 June 1988) UN Doc A/C.3/43/1, para 13. The US, supported by Canada, proposed a broad interpretation of the term 'admission' encompassing 'all terms and conditions pursuant to which migrant workers and members of their families may enter and remain in the United States, as well as those conditions which would result in their expulsion.' This interpretation is disputable and hardly in line with Article 79 given that the ordinary meaning of this provision is limited to 'the criteria governing admission'. By contrast, other matters (such as expulsion or residence permits) are explicitly covered by several provisions of the Convention as detailed below.

The multilateral framework of inter-state cooperation

The guidance provided by the ICRMW in promoting inter-state cooperation is quite general and arguably minimalist. Nonetheless, the strength of this collaborative framework relies on its flexibility in facilitating dialogue among states. Part VI of the ICRMW enshrines a duty of cooperation between States Parties for achieving three complementary objectives. The first aim of such inter-state cooperation is to promote 'sound, equitable and humane conditions' of migration for workers and members of their families (Article 64(1)). To do so, States Parties shall pay regard not only to labour needs and resources, but also to the needs of migrant workers as well as the consequences of migration for the communities concerned (Article 64(2)).

The implicit premise underlying this duty of inter-state cooperation is to promote lawful migration in a balanced and transparent way. However, the concrete measures to pursue this ambitious objective are left to States Parties. Unsurprisingly, the few indications given by the ICRMW are kept to a minimum. According to Article 65, States Parties shall maintain 'appropriate services' to cooperate with the competent authorities of other states, to formulate and implement their own migration policies, and to provide information to employers and migrant workers regarding the laws and regulations governing migration and employment. The ICRMW also requires States Parties to supervise the recruitment of migrant workers with a view to enabling lawful migration in sound, equitable, and humane conditions. Although the Convention neglects to detail the content of such supervision, the 'right to undertake operations with the view to the recruitment of workers for employment in another State' is restricted to specific authorities, namely public services of the state of origin, public services of the state of employment on the basis of an agreement between the states concerned, a body established by virtue of an international agreement, or private agencies provided that they are authorized, approved, and supervised by the public authorities of the state concerned (Article 66).[120]

The second objective to be pursued through inter-state cooperation concerns the 'orderly return' of migrant workers and their families to their country of origin (Article 67(1)). As explained during the drafting of the Convention, the term 'orderly' implies that return shall be 'in accordance with the law and in a manner not affecting the fundamental rights of migrant workers'.[121] Article 67(2) further prescribes that inter-state cooperation shall promote adequate economic conditions and facilitate their durable reintegration in the country of origin. Once again, States Parties enjoy a broad margin of appreciation in defining what cooperation entails

---

[120] While restating the obligation of States Parties to effectively regulate and monitor recruitment, the CMW has provided some useful guidance in its General Comment No 1 on migrant domestic workers, where it recommends the adoption of a licensing system for recruitment agencies with a monitoring and reporting mechanism able to sanction abuses. See CMW, 'General Comment No 1 on migrant domestic workers' (23 February 2011) UN Doc CMW/C/GC/1, paras 33–36. See also, CMW, 'Concluding observations on the initial report of the Philippines' (22 May 2009) UN Doc CMW/C/PHL/CO/1, para 41.

[121] UNGA 'Report of the Open-ended Working Group on the Elaboration of an International Convention on the Protection of the Rights of All Migrant Workers and Their Families' (October 1983) (n 85) para 18 (Mexico as the chairman).

when it concerns return and reintegration. While the conclusion of readmission agreements between countries of origin and employment represents a typical tool of inter-state cooperation, the CMW recalled that these treaties shall include 'appropriate procedural guarantees'[122] for migrant workers and members of their families in line with the Convention.

The third objective, which is by far the most substantial and demanding one, focuses on the prevention and elimination of irregular migration. States Parties, including transit ones, are not only bound to cooperate in order to combat irregular migration, they are also committed to adopt specific measures within their jurisdiction (Article 68(1)). These measures include countering the dissemination of misleading information relating to emigration and immigration, the detection and suppression of clandestine movements of migrant workers, as well as the adoption of effective sanctions against those who organize such unlawful movements or use violence and intimidation against undocumented migrant workers. States of employment are further bound to take effective measures to eliminate the employment of undocumented migrant workers, notably by imposing sanctions on employers (Article 68(2)). As underlined by Cholewinski, this wide range of duties 'dispels the myth that the ICRMW somehow promotes irregular migration'.[123] On the contrary, several state delegates made clear during the drafting history of the convention that 'illegal migration had to be fought and should not be tolerated in any way'.[124]

Fighting irregular migration is, however, not an end in itself. It must equally combine measures of prevention, including, most notably, regular opportunities of labour migration based on actual demand. Indeed, promoting lawful migration and fighting irregular migration are two faces of the same coin. The CMW has underlined in this regard that, 'by making regular channels of migration available, states parties also contribute to the aim of preventing and eliminating illegal or clandestine movements and employment of migrant workers in an irregular situation (Article 68)'.[125] Article 69(1) of the ICRMW further exemplifies this interface between regular and irregular forms of migration. According to this provision, when undocumented migrant workers are within their territory, States Parties are bound to 'take appropriate measures to ensure that such a situation does not persist'. The exact content and implications of such a vague provision remain unclear. Quite tellingly, however, the only specific means envisaged by Article 69(2) to end such irregular

---

[122]   See, for instance, the following concluding observations CMW, 'Concluding observations on the initial report of Azerbaijan' (May 2013) UN Doc CMW/C/AZE/CO/2, para 25; CMW, 'Concluding observations on the initial report of Bosnia and Herzegovina' (September 2012) UN Doc CMW/C/BIH/CO/2, para 24; CMW, 'Concluding observations on the initial report of Albania' (December 2010) UN Doc CMW/C/ALB/CO/1, para 36.

[123]   R Cholewinski, 'The Rights of Migrant Workers' in R Cholewinski, R Perruchoud, and E MacDonald (eds), *International Migration Law: Developing Paradigms and Key Challenges* (TMC Asser Press 2007) 259.

[124]   See the statement of Finland, supported by Italy and Denmark, in UNGA 'Report of the Open-ended Working Group on the Elaboration of an International Convention on the Protection of the Rights of All Migrant Workers and Their Families' (October 1988) UN Doc A/C.3/43/7, para 116.

[125]   CMW, 'General Comment No 2' (n 116) para 17. See also, CMW, 'General Comment No 1' (n 120) para 51.

situation relies on the possibility of regularizing undocumented workers and members of their families.

As underlined by the CMW, although 'states parties have no obligation to regularize the situation of migrant workers or members of their families',[126] 'regularization is the most effective measure to address the extreme vulnerability of migrant workers and members of their families in an irregular situation'.[127] Whenever States Parties consider the possibility of regularization, Article 69(2) of the ICRMW requires them to take into account 'the circumstances of their entry, the duration of their stay [...] and other relevant considerations, in particular those relating to their family situation'. The CMW has further stressed that access to such procedures must be 'non-discriminatory and effective'.[128] It has also expressed concerns that 'long delays, failure to meet procedural deadlines and the cost of procedures, hinder the regularization of migrant workers and may discourage them from pursuing the procedure for regularization, hence perpetuating their illegal or irregular situation'.[129]

The rights of migrant workers as a limit to migration control

Besides the general guidance provided in Part VI for promoting sound and equitable labour migration policies, some specific—albeit indirect—restrictions to immigration control stem from the rights of migrant workers enshrined in the ICRMW. The CMW has observed, in line with commentators,[130] that:

The Convention strikes a balance between the sovereign power of states parties to control their borders and to regulate the entry and stay of migrants workers and members of their families, on the one hand, and the protection of the rights, under Part III of the Convention, of all migrant workers and members of their families, including those in an irregular situation, on the other.[131]

As a result of this balancing act, the right to enter under Article 8(2) is typically circumscribed to the states of origin only. Notwithstanding this traditional account, several other general provisions may have an impact on migrant workers' entry into foreign states. In particular, the principle of non-discrimination restated in Article 7 prohibits entry requirements exclusively applicable to one specific nationality. For instance, the CMW considered the legislative requirement imposed by Ecuador on

---

[126] CMW, 'General Comment No 2' (n 116) para 15.   [127] ibid para 16.
[128] ibid para 15.
[129] CMW, 'Concluding Observations: Bolivia' (2 May 2008) UN Doc CMW/C/BOL/CO/1, para 31.
[130] Cholewinski, *Migrant Workers* (n 28) 192. LS Bosniak also underlines that 'the Convention accommodates the competing concerns about sovereignty and human rights by substantially incorporating them both. It counterposes rights narrowed by state immigration interests against state immigration interests curtailed—though only minimally—by rights. This scrupulous balancing is an effort to provide full assurance to states that their sovereign powers are not in jeopardy without frustrating the ultimate objective of the instrument, which is human rights for migrants.' See Bosniak, 'Human Rights, State Sovereignty' (n 92) 758.
[131] CMW, 'General Comment No 2' (n 116) para 13.

Colombian migrants to provide a certificate of criminal record to be a form of unlawful discrimination and had to accordingly be revoked.[132]

Furthermore, as mentioned before, due respect for the right to life and the prohibition of torture or cruel, inhuman, or degrading treatment under Articles 9 and 10 has been construed by the CMW as implying a duty of *non-refoulement*.[133] Likewise, as restated by the CMW alongside many other treaty bodies, forced removal may be prohibited when it constitutes an arbitrary interference with the right to family and private life under Article 14.[134]

More generally, immigration control must be carried out and enforced with due respect for the rights of migrant workers contained in the Convention. When assessing state reports on the implementation of the Convention, the CMW has recalled some basic principles:

(a) migration controls and inspections are conducted with respect for the right to integrity of the person;

(b) the personnel who conduct these inspections are trained in the application of the rules and standards regulating the use of force; and

(c) inspections are carried out only by authorities expressly authorized to do so. The State Party is encouraged to conduct serious investigations into incidents in which there have been complaints of excessive use, and abuse, of force by officials, and to punish those responsible.[135]

These guarantees cogently derive from the duty to ensure due respect for the right to life and the prohibition of torture, and inhuman or degrading treatment. Article 16(2) further restates that migrant workers and members of their families are 'entitled to effective protection by the state against violence, physical injury, threats and intimidation, whether by public officials or by private individuals, groups or institutions'.[136]

Article 16 also details the rules governing detention of undocumented migrant workers, including most notably the prohibition of arbitrary arrest or detention (Article 16(4)), the right to communicate with consular authorities (Article 16(7)), and the right to contest the lawfulness of detention before a court (Article 16(8)). As recalled by the CMW, alongside other treaty bodies, each deprivation of liberty must be 'exceptional and always based on a detailed and individualized assessment'.[137]

---

[132] CMW, 'Concluding observations: Ecuador' (15 December 2010) UN Doc CMW/C/ECU/CO/2, para 26. The CMW also urged Belize to repeal all discriminatory provisions in its domestic legislation allowing refusal of entry on medical grounds irrespective of whether or not there is a risk to public health: see, CMW, 'Concluding observations on Belize in the absence of a report' (26 September 2014) UN Doc CMW/C/BLZ/CO/1, paras 18–19.

[133] CMW, 'General Comment No 2' (n 116) para 50.　　　[134] ibid.

[135] CMW, 'Concluding Observations: Mexico' (n 112) para 32. See also, CMW, 'Concluding observations on the second periodic report of Colombia, adopted by the Committee at its eighteenth session (15–26 April 2013)' (27 May 2013) UN Doc CMW/C/COL/CO/2, para 22.

[136] Article 16(3) adds that '[a]ny verification by law enforcement officials of the identity of migrant workers or members of their families shall be carried out in accordance with procedure established by law'.

[137] CMW, 'General Comment No 2' (n 116) para 26.

The principle of proportionality further requires States Parties to detain migrant workers 'only as a last resort' and to give 'preference to less coercive measures', especially non-custodial ones.[138]

Following this stance, the CMW has made clear that domestic legislation must not criminalize migrant workers based on their irregular situation.[139] In line with the Special Rapporteur on the human rights of migrants,[140] its General Comment No. 2 underlines that:

Crossing the border of a country in an unauthorized manner or without proper documentation, or overstaying a permit of stay does not constitute a crime. Criminalizing irregular entry into a country exceeds the legitimate interest of States parties to control and regulate irregular migration, and leads to unnecessary detention. While irregular entry and stay may constitute administrative offences, they are not crimes per se against persons, property or national security.[141]

Another significant constraint governing the enforcement of immigration control concerns expulsion from the territory of States Parties. Article 22 of the ICRMW prohibits collective expulsion and provides procedural safeguards in individual expulsion proceedings with respect to both regular and irregular migrant workers and members of their families. While Article 22 primarily regulates the procedure (and not the substantive grounds of expulsion), its main purpose is to prevent arbitrary expulsions.[142] According to this provision, any decision of expulsion shall be taken by the competent authority in accordance with the law and it shall be communicated to migrant workers in a language they understand (with the reasons for the decision, save in exceptional circumstances related to national security). The person in question has the right to have his or her case reviewed by a competent authority, unless compelling reasons of national security require otherwise.

While these basic guarantees do not fundamentally differ from those already enshrined in many other human rights conventions, the ICRMW offers a broader scope of protection in two significant ways. Article 22 applies to both documented and undocumented migrant workers, whereas other human right treaties are expressly limited to foreigners who are 'lawfully in the territory of a state party'.[143] Furthermore, the ICRMW explicitly provides some additional procedural guarantees, such as the right to seek to stay during the review process (Article 22(4)), the possibility to seek entry into a state other than the one of origin (Article 22(7)), and

---

[138] ibid.

[139] See notably, the following concluding observations, CMW, 'Concluding observations: Algeria' (19 May 2010) UN Doc CMW/C/DZA/CO/1, para 11; CMW, 'Concluding observations of the Committee on the initial periodic report of Rwanda, adopted at its seventeenth session (10–14 September 2012)' (10 October 2012) UN Doc CMW/C/RWA/CO/1, para 22; CMW, 'Concluding observations on the initial report of Guinea' (n 93) para 22(b).

[140] See HRC 'Report of the Special Rapporteur on the human rights of migrants, François Crépeau' (2 April 2012) UN Doc A/HRC/20/24, para 13.

[141] CMW, 'General Comment No 2' (n 116) para 24.

[142] ibid para 49. The CMW also acknowledges that 'Article 22 applies to all procedures aimed at the obligatory departure of migrant workers whether described in national law as expulsion or otherwise.'

[143] See for instance, International Covenant on Civil and Political Rights (adopted 16 December 1966, entered into force 23 March 1976) 999 UNTS 171 (ICCPR) art 13.

the preservation of acquired rights regarding wages and other related entitlements (Article 22(9)). Article 20(2) further adds that no migrant worker nor member of his or her family shall be deprived of his or her authorization of residence or work permit or expelled merely on the ground of failure to fulfil an obligation arising out of a work contract (unless fulfilment of that obligation constitutes a condition for such authorization or permit).[144]

Regarding migrant workers in a regular situation, the grant and withdrawal of residence permits are also subject to some basic standards in order to harmonize domestic legislation. According to Article 49, the duration of the residence permit must be the same as the authorization to work. Hence, the termination of a remunerated activity prior to the expiration of the work authorization cannot be a ground for withdrawing the residence permit.[145] Moreover, residence permits cannot be withdrawn for a minimum period during which migrant workers are entitled to unemployment benefits. Article 50 further specifies that, in case of death or dissolution of marriage, states of employment shall favourably consider granting family members an authorization to stay. As exemplified by this last provision, States Parties retain substantial autonomy in designing their own immigration policies.

Following the same rationale, the benefit of family reunification is limited to migrant workers who are in a regular situation and the relevant provision of the ICRMW is flexible enough to accommodate the great diversity of domestic legislations. Article 44(2) provides that:

States Parties shall take measures that they deem appropriate and that fall within their competence to facilitate the reunification of migrant workers with their spouses or persons who have with the migrant worker a relationship that, according to applicable law, produces effects equivalent to marriage, as well as with their minor dependent unmarried children.

The cautious wording of this provision is the result of lengthy discussions during the drafting of the Convention. Several delegates reaffirmed that 'family reunion was a basic human right',[146] whereas others insisted on the fact that 'the sovereign right of states to establish their own immigration policies had to be protected'.[147] The resulting compromise retained in Article 44(2) has been criticized in the legal doctrine as 'a significant step backwards' that would allow States Parties 'to control and restrict at will the entry of migrant workers' families'.[148] While it is undeniable that States Parties benefit from a broad margin of discretion to decide upon family reunification of migrant workers, the text of this provision is more balanced than a blatant endorsement of states' freedom.

[144] See also, ICRMW (n 86) art 56.   [145] ibid art 51.

[146] See the statement by the representative of Greece in UNGA, 'Report of the Open-ended Working Group' (June 1985) (n 87) para 38. See also, statements by the representatives of Morocco and Tunisia in UNGA, 'Report of the Open-ended Working Group on the Elaboration of an International Convention on the Protection of the Rights of All Migrant Workers and Their Families' (October 1987) UN Doc A/C.3/42/6, para 205.

[147] See the statements by the representatives of the US, Norway, and France, respectively in UNGA, 'Report of the Open-ended Working Group' (October 1987) (n 146) paras 216, 219, and 222.

[148] Cholewinski, *Migrant Workers* (n 28) 173.

Although the Convention does not expressly refer to a duty to grant family re-unification, States Parties are committed to adopting appropriate measures aimed at its facilitation. By asserting that States Parties 'shall take measures' for this pur-pose, Article 44(2) thus endorses a qualified duty to facilitate reunification.[149] Nonetheless, the appropriate means to achieve this objective are left entirely to States Parties and, as acknowledged during the *travaux préparatoires*, domestic legis-lation can subordinate the enjoyment of family reunification to several conditions in terms of duration of stay, housing, and resources.[150] Furthermore, as confirmed by the CMW, Article 44(2) requires, as a minimum, the adoption of clear provi-sions on family reunification in domestic legislation in order to protect the unity of migrant workers' families.[151] Such legislation cannot be limited to spouses only[152] or to migrant workers with a permanent residence permit.[153] Domestic law must accordingly include all documented migrant workers as well as all members of their families as defined in Articles 4 and 44(2) of the ICRMW.

4.2.3 The international protection of migrant workers

The international protection of migrant workers under the ICRMW attempts to reconcile the universality of human rights with the concerns of states regarding ir-regular migration. This internal tension is at the heart of the whole Convention. On the one hand, the ICRMW represents the most comprehensive treaty specifically devoted to the rights of migrant workers. On the other hand, the scope of their protection is still contingent on their immigration status and accordingly depends on whether migrant workers are documented. Following this dual approach, Part III of the ICRMW restates a broad range of civil, social, and labour rights for all migrant workers and members of their families (including undocumented ones), whereas Part IV identifies additional rights that are granted only to those in a regular situation. As Cholewinski observes, 'this division is the clearest illustration of the schism between the protection of migrants' rights and the principle of state sover-eignty underlying the whole text'.[154]

However, this ongoing tension between human rights and immigration status is not unique to the ICRMW. It is a defining feature of many other specialized treaties

---

[149] The proposal to replace 'shall' with 'may' in Article 44(2) was rejected during the drafting of this provision. This clearly contradicts the view of the delegate of Norway who argued that Article 44(2) would be understood 'as a statement of guidance only, and not as imposing any obligations on the State of employment'. See the statement of Norway in UNGA, 'Report of the Open-ended Working Group' (October 1987) (n 146) para 219.

[150] See the statement of the French delegate in ibid para 222.

[151] CMW, 'Concluding observations on the initial report of Azerbaijan' (n 122) para 39. On the duty to adopt legislation on family reunification in line with the ICRMW see also CMW, 'Concluding Observations: Peru' (May 2015) UN Doc CMW/C/PER/CO/1, para 44; CMW, 'Concluding obser-vations: Chile' (n 95) para 39.

[152] CMW, 'Concluding Observations: Algeria' (n 139) para 32.

[153] CMW, 'Concluding observations on the initial report of Timor-Leste' (8 October 2015) UN Doc CMW/C/TLS/CO/1, paras 45–46.

[154] Cholewinski, *Migrant Workers* (n 28) 138.

of international migration law, including the ILO Conventions Nos 97 and 143, as well as the Geneva Convention relating to the Status of Refugees, where the allocation of rights is largely conditioned by the distinction based on the regular or irregular status of their beneficiaries. The same distinction was accordingly taken for granted during the drafting of the ICRMW. In fact, the main controversy raised during the negotiation process concerned the overlap between the rights contained in the ICRMW and those already endorsed in international human rights law. Several state representatives (including Senegal, Morocco, the Soviet Union, Algeria, and India) asserted that the provisions of the ICRMW on fundamental human rights constituted a codification of customary international law.[155] The US and German representatives disagreed, arguing that the Convention would only bind States Parties that have ratified it.[156]

Whatever its standing under customary international law, the ICRMW has been heavily influenced by pre-existing conventions devoted to the protection of fundamental rights. During the drafting of the Convention, most of its provisions were drawn from general human rights treaties, most notably the two UN Covenants.[157] The resulting overlap between this specialized treaty and general human rights instruments has raised some diverging opinions among commentators on the question of whether the ICRMW creates new rights or merely reaffirms basic human rights under other existing treaties.[158]

The normative commonalities between the ICRMW and general human rights conventions

When compared to general human rights treaties adopted at the universal and regional levels, the provisions of the ICRMW can be classified into four main categories.

First, the vast majority of the rights acknowledged in the ICRMW are reiterating existing rights. This unsurprisingly concerns the most basic rights applicable to all migrant workers and members of their families, including undocumented ones. As observed by the CMW, '[m]ost of the rights protected in Part III are common to a host of international human rights treaties'.[159] This set of overlapping rights includes, for instance, the right to life (Article 9), the prohibition of torture, cruel,

---

[155] UNGA, 'Report of the Open-ended Working Group on the Elaboration of an International Convention on the Drafting of an International Convention on the Protection of the Rights of All Migrant Workers and Their Families' (22 June 1987) UN Doc A/C.3/42/1, paras 328, 330, and 331.

[156] ibid paras 326 and 329.

[157] Among many other instances, see notably ibid paras 23–24, 51, 79, 219, 238, and 244; UNGA, 'Working paper prepared by the Chairman of the Working group' (October 1980) UN Doc A/C.3/35/WG.1/CRP.3, para 2.

[158] Compare, for instance, D Weissbrodt, 'The Protection of Non-citizens in International Human Rights Law' in R Cholewinski, R Perruchoud, and E MacDonald (eds), *International Migration Law* (n 123) 226 with B Ryan, 'In the Defence of the Migrant Workers Convention: Standard Setting for Contemporary Migration' in J Satvinder (ed), *The Ashgate Research Companion to Migration Law, Theory and Policy* (Ashgate 2013) 493.

[159] CMW, 'General Comment No 2' (n 116) para 6.

inhuman, or degrading treatment (Article 10), the prohibition of slavery and forced labour (Article 11), freedom of thought, conscience, and religion (Article 12), the right to hold opinions and freedom of expression (Article 13), the right to family and private life (Article 14), the right to property (Article 15),[160] equal access to courts and due process guarantees (Article 18), the prohibition of retroactive criminal law (Article 19), the prohibition of collective expulsion (Article 22(1)), the right to recognition as a person before the law (Article 24), the right to join trade unions, to seek their assistance, and to take part in their activities (Article 26), the rights of children to a name, registration of birth, and nationality (Article 29), and the right of children to education (Article 30). This normative commonality between the ICRMW and other general human rights treaties can also be observed in Part IV which details several additional rights granted to migrant workers in a regular situation. Such rights comprise the right to liberty of movement and residence within the territory of States Parties (Article 39) and the right to vote and to be elected in the state of origin (Article 41).

Second, another category of provisions relates to existing rights that are contextualized and specified by the ICRMW in order to take into account the particular situation of migrant workers. They notably comprise some procedural safeguards in individual expulsion proceedings, as discussed in the previous section. Likewise, the right of any person deprived of their liberty to be treated with humanity has been restated and refined in Article 17 of the ICRMW by underlining that migrant workers who are detained for violating domestic migration law shall be held, in so far as practicable, separately from convicted persons. A similar contextualization of existing rights is also evident in the principle of non-discrimination in Article 7. This provision contains a more extensive list of prohibited grounds that explicitly includes nationality, economic position, age, and marital status. While these additions serve as a useful clarification, one should not overestimate their added value since the prohibited grounds of discrimination are by definition not exhaustive. Furthermore, the ICRMW's specific additions to such grounds are implicitly covered by general human rights treaties through the generic ground of 'other status'.[161] Article 7 of the ICRMW further confirms in this sense that the prohibition of discrimination restated in this provision is 'in accordance with the international instruments concerning human rights'.

Third, in contrast to the numerous provisions of the ICRMW restating and refining existing rights under general instruments, very few rights are truly specific to the Convention. They primarily refer to the protection against unauthorized confiscation and destruction of identity documents (Article 21) and the right to be informed of the conditions of admission and the rights arising out of the Convention (Article 33). The CMW has also argued that the right to have recourse to consular or diplomatic protection and assistance (Article 23), the right to respect for cultural

---

[160] Although the right to property is not mentioned in the two UN Covenants as a result of the Cold War's antagonisms at the time of their drafting, such a right is acknowledged in all general human rights treaties adopted at the regional level.

[161] See the discussion on the ground of nationality in Chapter 2, section 2.3.2.

identity of migrant workers (Article 31), and the right to transfer their earnings and savings (Article 32) are 'Convention-specific'.[162] It is true that access to consular or diplomatic protection is not mentioned in general human rights treaties, but it is guaranteed, in any event, by the widely-ratified Vienna Convention on Consular Relations (Article 36). The specific nature of the two other rights listed by the CMW is more debatable on a normative plane. When compared to other human rights treaties, they are more a specification of existing rights than an enactment of new rights. Indeed, the right to respect the cultural identity of migrant workers mainly reinforces and details the right of persons belonging to minorities to enjoy their own culture, to practice their own religion, or to use their own language, as notably recognized in Article 27 of the ICCPR.[163] Similarly, the right to transfer earnings and savings can be viewed as a positive obligation deriving from the right to property. This understanding was acknowledged during the drafting of the ICRMW when state representatives stressed that the right to transfer earnings and savings is 'a basic human right' and 'in the case of migrant workers this right constitutes the effective exercise of the right to property'.[164]

Fourth and lastly, several other provisions of the ICRMW arguably fall below the standards of protection established by general human rights treaties. According to the CMW, 'most of the economic, social and cultural rights in Part III of the Convention have a narrower scope than their counterparts in the Covenant [on Economic, Social and Cultural Rights]'.[165] The right to health is the most obvious example. Migrant workers in a regular situation have access to any health service on an equal footing with nationals (Article 43), whereas those who are undocumented can only benefit from urgent medical care for the preservation of their life or avoidance of irreparable harm (Article 28). Excluding undocumented migrant workers from all non-urgent health services is in contradiction with the core content of the right to health under Article 12 of the ICESCR, which comprises primary health care, as well as preventive, curative, and palliative health services.[166] The same incompatibility between the ICRMW and general human rights treaties can also be found in the right to form trade unions. Such a right is granted by Article 40 of the ICRMW to documented migrant workers only, whereas a number of treaties—Article 8 of the ICESCR, Article 22 of the ICCPR, and Article 2 of ILO Convention No 87 (1948) concerning Freedom of Association and Protection of the Rights to Organise—recognize the right to form trade unions for everyone regardless of immigration status.[167]

---

[162] CMW, 'General Comment No 2' (n 116) para 6.

[163] The HRC has confirmed that Article 27 is not limited to citizens but it also applies to migrant workers. See, HRC 'General Comment No 23: Article 27 (Rights of Minorities)' (8 April 1994) UN Doc CCPR/C/21/Rev.1/Add.5, para 5.2.

[164] UNGA 'Report of the Open-ended Working Group' (June 1982) (n 85) para 47.

[165] CMW, 'General comment No 2' (n 116) para 10.

[166] ibid para 72; UN Committee on Economic, Social and Cultural Rights (CESCR), 'General Comment No 14: The Right to the Highest Attainable Standard of Health' (11 August 2000) UN Doc E/C.12/2000/4, para 34.

[167] CMW, 'General Comment No 2' (n 116) para 65.

The fact that general human rights treaties may be more protective than specialized ones is not specific to the ICRMW since similar observations can be made with regard to other conventions, such as the Geneva Convention relating to the Status of Refugees. Both the ICRMW and the Refugee Convention have endorsed the principle of the most favourable treatment in order to resolve potential conflicts of norms. Article 81(1) of the ICRMW makes clear that nothing in this Convention shall affect more favourable rights granted by domestic law of States Parties or international treaties ratified by them. In turn, Article 81(1) highlights the vital importance of an integrated approach to articulate in a coherent and comprehensive way the great diversity of rules applicable to migrants. While endorsing this approach, the CMW underlined that 'a State's obligation under the Convention must be read with respect to the core human rights treaties and other relevant international instruments to which it is a party. Although separate and freestanding, these treaties are complementary and mutually reinforcing.'[168]

The mutually reinforcing relationship between this specialized treaty and the general ones is essential. As detailed above, most of ICRMW's provisions restate or specify rights already enshrined in other instruments, whereas only a few are truly specific to this Convention. Against this background, one can fairly agree with the argument of Sandesh Sivakumaran that:

The novel nature of the Convention is difficult to ascertain. However, this in itself shows the value of the Convention at the very least as a clarifying instrument. Thus, not only is the Migrant Workers Convention useful as an instrument in its own right, but it also clarifies the pre-existing international instruments regarding their applicability to migrant workers.[169]

Indeed, the normative commonality between the ICRMW and other existing treaties does not diminish the importance of the former. After all, many other specialized human rights treaties often duplicate and contextualize existing rights, such as those adopted by the UN to protect children and disabled persons, among many other obvious examples. Migrant workers are not an exception to this general pattern. As exemplified above, the ICRMW contributes to the protection of migrant workers by contextualizing a broad range of existing human rights to the specific situation of migrant workers. Like many other specialized treaties, this characteristic constitutes the main strength of the ICRMW.

4.2.4 The ratification of the ICRMW and the long road to universality

The synergies between the ICRWM and other existing treaties create a powerful incentive for ratification. Nevertheless, the ICRMW suffers from a low level of ratifications compared to the other core UN human rights treaties. It is currently ratified by fifty-four States Parties, though the count has steadily increased by thirty-one

---

[168] ibid para 7.
[169] S Sivakumaran, 'The Rights of Migrant Workers one Year on: Transformation or Consolidation?' (2004) 36 Geo J Int'l L 113.

States Parties since it entered into force on 1 July 2003.[170] Furthermore, no major receiving countries from the Global North have ratified it yet. In fact, only two States Parties are European (Albania, and Bosnia and Herzegovina), whereas all the others are in the Global South, including twenty-four African states (Algeria, Benin, Burkina Faso, Cabo Verde, Congo, Egypt, Ghana, Gambia, Guinea, Guinea-Bissau, Lesotho, Libya, Madagascar, Mali, Mauritania, Morocco, Mozambique, Niger, Nigeria, Rwanda, Sao Tome and Principe, Senegal, Seychelles, and Uganda), eighteen Latin American and Caribbean states (Argentina, Belize, Bolivia, Chile, Colombia, Ecuador, El Salvador, Guatemala, Guyana, Honduras, Jamaica, Mexico, Nicaragua, Paraguay, Peru, Saint Vincent and the Grenadines, Uruguay, and Venezuela), and ten Asian states (Azerbaijan, Bangladesh, Indonesia, Kyrgyzstan, the Philippines, Sri Lanka, Syria, Tajikistan, Timor-Leste, and Turkey).

However, the current composition of States Parties does not diminish the practical and normative value of the Convention. On the contrary, the ICRMW remains particularly relevant given that a significant portion of migration movements in the world is taking place in the Global South: in 2015, South-South migration exceeded South-North migration and represented 37 per cent of the total international migrant stock.[171] Moreover, contrary to the common belief, the vast majority of current States Parties are both countries of emigration and immigration. Out of the thirty-three states examined in the reporting procedure between May 2006 and December 2016, the CMW only recognized four of them as 'mainly a country of origin',[172] whereas most of the others were considered as both countries of destination and origin.[173]

---

[170] See, ICRMW's status of ratification, available at: http://indicators.ohchr.org/ (interactive dashboard) and https://treaties.un.org/Pages/ViewDetails.aspx?src=IND&mtdsg_no=IV-13&chapter=4&clang=_en accessed 23 October 2018. One should add that ICRMW is signed by an additional fifteen states. Although signatory states are not formally bound by the Convention, signature still has some legal effects under the law of treaties. According to Article 18 of the Vienna Convention on the Law of Treaties, any signatory state is obliged to refrain from acts which would defeat the object and purpose of the treaty until it shall have made its clear intention not to become a party thereto.

[171] IOM, '2015 Global Migration Trends: Factsheets' (February 2017) 7.

[172] This concerns Paraguay, the Philippines, Sri Lanka, and the Syrian Arab Republic. See the following: CMW, 'Concluding observations: Paraguay' (n 95) para 3; CMW, 'Concluding observations: the Philippines' (22 May 2009) UN Doc CMW/C/PHL/CO/1, para 3; CMW, 'Concluding observations: Sri Lanka' (n 94) para 3; CMW, 'Concluding observations: Syrian Arab Republic' (n 109) para 3.

[173] This concerns Albania, Algeria, Azerbaijan, Bolivia, Bosnia and Herzegovina, Cabo Verde, Colombia, Ecuador, Egypt, El Salvador, Guatemala, Honduras, Mexico, Nicaragua, Niger, Peru, Senegal, Sri Lanka, and Turkey. See: CMW, 'Concluding observations on the initial report of Albania' (n 122) para 3; CMW, 'Concluding observations: Algeria' (n 139) para 3; CMW, 'Concluding observations: Azerbaijan' (19 May 2009) UN Doc CMW/C/AZE/CO/1, para 3, 1; CMW, 'Concluding observations: Bolivia' (n 129) para 3; CMW, 'Concluding observations: Bosnia and Herzegovina' (3 June 2009) UN Doc CMW/C/BIH/CO/1, para 3; CMW, 'Concluding observations on Cabo Verde in the absence of a report' (8 October 2015) UN Doc CMW/C/CPV/CO/1 (8 October 2015), para 5; CMW, 'Concluding observations: Colombia' (n 106) para 3; CMW, 'Concluding observations: Ecuador' (n 132) para 3; CMW, 'Concluding observations: Egypt' (n 93) para 3; CMW, 'Concluding observations: El Salvador' (4 February 2009) UN Doc CMW/C/SLV/CO/1, para 3; CMW, 'Concluding observations: Guatemala' (18 October 2011) UN Doc CMW/C/GTM/CO/1, para 3; CMW, 'Concluding observations on the initial report of Honduras' (3 October 2016) UN Doc CMW/C/HND/CO/1, para 5; CMW, 'Concluding observations: Mexico' (20 December 2006) UN Doc CMW/C/MEX/CO/1, para 3; CMW, 'Concluding observations on the initial report of Nicaragua' (11 October 2016) UN

The obstacles to ratification

The lack of ratification by Western states remains troubling, to say the least. Such persisting reluctance toward this Convention starkly contrasts with their wide ratification of the other UN human rights treaties and the influential role they played in the drafting of the ICRMW during its long negotiation process. The real or perceived obstacles to the ICRMW's ratification have triggered a vast literature which identifies four types of obstacles: the prevailing misconceptions about the content of the Convention, the financial and administrative costs of its application, its (in)compatibility with domestic law, and the lack of political will.[174] All authors acknowledge, in line with Kristina Touzenis and Alice Sironi, that 'there are no insurmountable barriers to ratification and that the decision on ratification is largely driven by political choice rather than by an objective legal scrutiny'.[175]

Indeed, with regard to the first obstacle to ratification, misconceptions of what the provisions of the Convention actually entail can be easily defeated by a superficial reading of the ICRMW. States refusing to take part in the ICRMW frequently claim that its ratification would result in a loss of sovereignty on admission policies or that it would encourage irregular migration. However, as previously explained, Article 79 of the ICRMW preserves the sovereign right of States Parties to decide upon admission of migrant workers and members of their families.[176] Article 35 restates in the same vein that ICRMW shall not imply the regularization of migrant workers or members of their families who are in an irregular situation. Likewise, the

Doc CMW/C/NIC/CO/1, para 5; CMW, 'Concluding observations on the initial report of Niger' (11 October 2016) UN Doc CMW/C/NER/CO/1, para 3; CMW, 'Concluding observations on the initial report of Peru' (13 May 2015) UN Doc CMW/C/PER/CO/1, para 4; CMW, 'Concluding observations: Senegal' (10 December 2010) UN Doc CMW/C/SEN/CO/1, para 3; CMW, 'Concluding observations on the combined second and third periodic reports of Senegal' (20 May 2016) UN Doc CMW/C/SEN/CO/2-3, para 3; CMW, 'Concluding observations on the initial report of Turkey' (n 113) para 4; CMW, 'Concluding observations on the second periodic report of Sri Lanka' (11 October 2016) UN Doc CMW/C/LKA/CO/2 para 3. One should add that Argentina, Chile, and Morocco are also both countries of origin and countries of destination.

[174] See, most notably, K Touzenis and A Sironi, *Current Challenges in the Implementation of the UN international Convention on the Protection of the Rights of All Migrant Workers and Members of their Families* (European Union 2013); S Gonzalez del Pino, *Rights of Migrant Workers in Europe* (OHCHR Regional Office for Europe 2011); R Plaetevoet and M Sidoti, *Ratification of the UN Migrant Workers Convention in the European Union: Survey on the Positions of Governments and Civil Society Actors* (EPMWR 2010); P de Guchteneire, A Pécoud, and R Cholewinski (eds), *Migration and Human Rights: The United Nations Convention on Migrant Workers' Rights* (UNESCO/CUP 2009); E MacDonald and R Cholewinski, *The Migrant Workers Convention in Europe, Obstacles to the Ratification of the International Convention on the Protection of the Rights of All Migrants and Members of their Families: EU/EEA Perspectives* (UNESCO 2007); B Lyon, 'The Unsigned United Nations Migrant Worker Rights Convention: An Overlooked Opportunity to Change the "Brown Collar" Migration Paradigm' (2010) 42(2) NYU J Int'l Law & Pol 389–500; D Vanheule and others, 'The Significance of the UN Migrant Workers' Convention of 18 December 1990 in the Event of Ratification by Belgium' (2004) 6(4) EJML 285–322; P Taran, 'Status and Prospects for the UN Convention on Migrants' Rights' (2000) 2(1) EJML 85–100; S Hune and J Niessen, 'Ratifying the UN Migrant Workers Convention: Current Difficulties and Prospects' (1994) 12(4) NQHR 393–404.

[175] Touzenis and Sironi, *Current Challenges* (n 174) 1.

[176] Likewise, the provision contained in Article 44(2) leaves States Parties a broad margin of discretion to decide upon family reunification of migrant workers.

basic rights granted to undocumented migrant workers in Part III of the ICRMW can hardly be seen as encouraging irregular migration because most of them overlap in any case with existing rights under general human rights treaties. Furthermore, Part VI of the Convention lists a broad range of straightforward duties for States Parties in order to prevent and eliminate irregular movements of migrant workers.

The fanciful misunderstanding about the exact content and implications of the ICRMW is partially due to a lack of awareness of the Convention. Despite routine calls by the UN General Assembly to ratify it 'as a matter of priority',[177] the ICRMW remained the 'best-kept secret of the United Nations'[178] for a while. It took six years after its adoption by the General Assembly before the Office of the High Commissioner for Human Rights (OHCHR) actually produced a booklet publicizing the text of this core human rights instrument, and it was only in 2005 that an internal task force on migration was created at the Office. Since then, however, the High Commissioner for Human Rights has been more active in promoting the ratification of the ICRMW.[179] Accordingly, it is dubious to argue that its late ownership within the UN and the correlative lack of awareness are the main reasons behind its poor ratification rate today. Thus, the question remains whether these persisting misconceptions are really due to the ignorance of the governing elite or are merely an excuse for refusing ratification.

A more plausible obstacle, at least for developing states, relates to the administrative and financial costs entailed by the Convention's implementation.[180] It is undeniable that protecting and enforcing rights always imply costs for a broad range of state agents (including the judiciary, the government, and law enforcement authorities). It is also true that the ICRMW is the longest UN core human rights

---

[177] See, for example, UNGA Res 45/158 (18 December 1990) UN Doc A/RES/45/158, para 3; UNGA Res 60/169 (7 March 2006) UN DOC A/RES/60/169, para 7; UNGA Res 62/156 (7 March 2008) UN Doc A/RES/62/156, para 4; UNGA Res 63/184 (17 March 2009) UN Doc A/RES/63/184, para 3; UNGA Res 65/212 (1 April 2011) UN Doc A/RES/65/212, para 3(d); UNGA Res 69/167 (12 February 2015) UN Doc A/RES/69/167, para 3(e).

[178] Oral statement at the founding meeting of the International Migrants Rights Watch Committee during the UN International Conference on Population and Development in Cairo, 1994, quoted in M Grange and M D'Auchamp, 'Role of Civil Society in Campaigning for and Using the ICRMW' in R Cholewinski, P de Guchteneire, and A Pécoud (eds), *Migration and Human Rights: The United Nations Convention on Migrant Workers' Rights* (CUP 2009) 76.

[179] See the High Commissioner's statement at the 99th Session of the IOM Council on 1 December 2010, 8, available at: http://www.ohchr.org/Documents/Issues/MHR/HC_Statement_99SessionIOMCouncil.pdf; Opening Statement by Mr Zeid Ra'ad Al Hussein, United Nations High Commissioner for Human Rights, to mark the 25th Anniversary of the Adoption of the Convention on the Protection of the Rights of All Migrant Workers and Members of their Families (8 September 2015) is also available at: http://www.ohchr.org/en/NewsEvents/Pages/DisplayNews.aspx?NewsID=16397&LangID=E accessed 3 October 2018.

[180] This argument is rarely invoked by Western states. See, notably, Touzenis and Sironi, *Current Challenges* (n 174) 28; MacDonald and Cholewinski, *The Migrant Workers Convention* (n 174) 58. France seems to be an exception. The duty to 'take appropriate measures to facilitate [...] transfers' of remittances under Article 47 has been viewed by the Ministry of Finance as an obstacle to ratification due to the banking practice of charging high fees for such transfers and because of the fear that facilitating such transfers could result in significant financial outflows for the French economy. See H Oger, 'The French Political Refusal on Europe's Behalf' in P de Guchteneire, A Pécoud, and R Cholewinski (eds), *Migration and Human Rights* (n 174) 316–17.

treaty[181] and its complexity mirrors the cross-cutting nature of labour migration. The ICRMW accordingly addresses a large variety of issues that demands a solid infrastructure and thorough coordination between several state organs. However, this does not fundamentally diverge from other specialized human rights treaties. When compared with other widely-ratified UN treaties—namely, the Convention on the Rights of the Child or the Convention on the Rights of Persons with Disabilities—it would be difficult to assert that the ICRMW bears more substantial costs for its implementation.

One thing that is sure is that the administrative and financial costs prove to be higher for the implementation of the Refugee Convention, as it presupposes the establishment of asylum procedures, the benefit of reception conditions for asylum-seekers as well as the granting of a quite complex and detailed status for those who are recognized as refugees. Overall, the amount of resources needed to apply the ICRMW is thus eminently relative and does not constitute an insurmountable barrier to ratification. This is eloquently exemplified by the fact that one-quarter of its States Parties are among the least developed countries in the world.[182]

The third obstacle to ratification relates to domestic legislation. This common ground for refusing to take part in the ICRMW moves in two opposite directions. On the one hand, the incompatibility of national legislation with the Convention is viewed by some states—notably in Asia—as hindering its ratification.[183] On the other hand, the conformity of domestic law with the provisions of the ICRMW is invoked by Western states to claim that the Convention is superfluous and unnecessary.[184] Sometimes, these two lines of arguments are advanced together by the same states. For instance, Canada, France, and the UK have contended that migrant workers are already well protected under their domestic law, while highlighting, at the same time, few specific provisions thereof which contradict the ICRMW.[185]

None of these arguments are really convincing. The incompatibility of domestic law with an international treaty is usually overcome, either by modifying relevant

---

[181] The ICRMW is comprised of ninety-three articles whereas, among the other core UN treaties, the longest one is the Convention on the Rights of the Child with fifty-four articles.

[182] Seventeen States Parties are listed by the UN among the least developed countries as of September 2018. These are: Bangladesh, Benin, Burkina Faso, Gambia, Guinea, Guinea-Bissau, Lesotho, Madagascar, Mali, Mauritania, Mozambique, Niger, Rwanda, Sao Tome and Principe, Senegal, Timor-Leste, and Uganda.

[183] N Piper, 'Obstacles to, and Opportunities for, Ratification of the ICRMW in Asia' in P de Guchteneire, A Pécoud, and R Cholewinski (eds), *Migration and Human Rights* (n 174) 171–92.

[184] Another variation of this argument is that the rights of migrant workers are already protected by other ratified human rights treaties. However, like all the other specialized human rights treaties, the key added value of the ICRMW lies in its specification and contextualization of existing rights in order to better take into account the particular situation of migrant workers and members of their families. Furthermore, the whole Part VI of the ICRMW devoted to inter-state collaboration on migration has no equivalence in other human rights treaties (with the only exception of the ILO Conventions Nos 97 and 143 that are nonetheless still less comprehensive than the ICRMW).

[185] For further discussion, see especially V Piché, E Depatie-Pelletier, and D Epale, 'Obstacles to Ratification of the ICRMW in Canada' in P de Guchteneire, A Pécoud, and R Cholewinski (eds), *Migrant and Human Rights* (n 174) 193–218; B Ryan, 'Policy on the ICRMW in the United Kingdom' in P de Guchteneire, A Pécoud, and R Cholewinski (eds), *Migration and Human Rights* (n 174) 278–94; Oger, 'The French Political Refusal' (n 180) 295–322.

provisions of the national legislation or by making reservations to the treaty in question. Contrary to ILO treaties, the ICRMW allows states to formulate reservations at the time of ratification. Such a possibility is even acknowledged by the Convention with very few restrictions. As restated by its Article 91(2) in line with the Vienna Convention of the Law of Treaties, any reservation must be compatible with the object and purpose of the Convention. Besides this traditional and basic requirement, Article 88 of the ICRMW only prohibits reservations that exclude a whole part of the Convention or a particular category of migrant workers covered therein. States Parties thus enjoy a broad margin of appreciation to formulate reservations when domestic law appears to be in conflict with the Convention. Inversely, if domestic law is in accordance with the ICRMW, this rather represents a stronger incentive for its ratification. Arguing the contrary would mean that Western states should have refrained from ratifying the vast majority of the other human rights treaties that were already in line with their own legislation.

The contradictions in the reasons raised against the ICRMW ratification are graphically illustrated by the position of the EU Commission on this issue. While the EU Parliament has consistently urged Member States to ratify the ICRMW since 1998,[186] the position of the Commission has changed over the years towards a more reluctant posture. As early as 1994, it encouraged Member States to be part thereof,[187] but then fell short of calling for ratification. In 2013, the Commission justified its new approach on the incongruous grounds that:

The insufficient distinction in the 1990 UN International Convention on the Protection of the Rights of All Migrant Workers and Members of Their Families between the economic and social rights of regular and irregular migrant workers is not in line with national and EU policies; and that the already existing EU instruments provide far-reaching protection for both regular and irregular migrants, and safeguards that are often broader than those provided by the Convention.[188]

The inconsistency of such an argumentation is perhaps too obvious to be missed: how can the ICRMW's distinction between the economic and social rights of regular

---

[186] European Parliament Resolution A4-0034/98 on respect for human rights in the European Union [1998] OJ C80/43, para 10; European Parliament resolution on the EU's priorities and recommendations for the 61st Session of the UN Commission on Human Rights in Geneva (14 March to 22 April 2005) [2005] P6_TA-PROV(2005)0051, para 22; European Parliament resolution on development and migration [2006] INI/2005/2244, para 80; European Parliament resolution on women's immigration: the role and place of immigrant women in the European Union (2006/2010(INI)) [2006] OJ E313/118 P6_TA-PROV(2006)0437, para 8; European Parliament resolution of 14 January 2009 on the situation of fundamental rights in the European Union 2004–2008 (2007/2145(INI)) [2009] P6_TA(2009)0019, point 158. See also European Economic and Social Committee, 'Opinion on the 'International Convention on Migrants' in 'Office Journal of the European Union' (7 December 2004) 2004/C302/12. Within the Council of Europe, see, among other instances, Parliamentary Assembly of the Council of Europe, Recommendation 1737 (2006) on new trends and challenges for Euro-Mediterranean migration policies, point 12.

[187] Commission, 'Communication to the Council and the European Parliament on immigration and asylum policies' COM (1994) 29, paras 109–10.

[188] Commission, 'Maximising the Development Impact of Migration: The EU contribution for the UN High-level Dialogue and next steps towards broadening the development-migration nexus' COM (2013) 292 final, 6.

and irregular migrant workers contradict national and EU policies if, as mentioned by the EU Commission, existing instruments already provide 'far-reaching' and 'broader' protection for both regular and irregular migrant workers? More importantly, the alleged 'insufficient distinction' between documented and undocumented migrant workers pertaining to their economic and social rights is incorrect. As explained before, the ICRMW establishes a very clear distinction between the basic rights of undocumented migrant workers and the additional ones granted to those in a regular situation. Many additional rights reserved to documented migrant workers are economic and social in nature, including access to housing, social and health services, and vocational training (Articles 43 and 45), access to remunerated activity (Articles 51 and 52), as well as protection against dismissal and unemployment benefits (Article 54). Furthermore, as previously mentioned, the ICRMW provides less extensive protection to undocumented migrant workers (precisely in the field of economic and social rights) than other general human rights treaties, such as the ICESCR, which has been ratified by all EU Member States.

The politicization of non-ratification

None of the obstacles to ratification discussed above are insurmountable and each of them can be easily mitigated through a better understanding of the ICRMW and the use of reservations by ratifying states. The various reasons raised by Western governments not to ratify appear more as an excuse than a sound and rational justification. This unveils the key reason behind their rhetoric, that is, the lack of political will which is heavily influenced by the domestic context prevailing in many states. Put crudely, for many politicians, ratifying a treaty devoted to the protection of migrant workers would put them at risk of losing votes in the politically sensitive context surrounding migration. In 2006, Antoine Pécoud and Paul de Guchteneire had already observed that:

Migration is often strongly present in the public opinion, but in a negative way, and ratifying the ICRMW then appears as a political risk. Several states, in Europe and the Asia Pacific notably, have witnessed the emergence of political populism, which relies heavily on migration issues in order to exploit citizens' frustration and fears of 'invasion' by foreigners.[189]

More than one decade after this account, the politically toxic context surrounding migration has worsened. Populism and its anti-migrants rhetoric have never been so

---

[189] A Pécoud and P de Guchteneire, 'Migration, Human Rights and the United Nations: An Investigation into the Obstacles to the UN Convention on Migrant Workers' Rights' (2006) 24 Windsor YB Access Just 241, 260. Besides all the doctrinal references already quoted above, see also for a similar account P Taran, 'Clashing Worlds: Imperative for a Rights-based Approach to Labour Migration in the Age of Globalization' in V Chetail (ed), *Mondialisation, migration et droits de l'homme: le droit international en question/Globalization, Migration and Human Rights: International Law under Review* (Bruylant 2007) 414–15.

visibly potent since the inter-war period. As a result of this xenophobic atmosphere, for many governments, ratifying the ICRWM is seen as a political non-starter.

The resilience of domestic politics is further exacerbated by the traditional inter-state structure of international law. As a result of the consensual basis of treaty law-making, ratification remains a discretionary decision of any state, that is, inherent to its very sovereignty. In other words, no state is bound to ratify a treaty. As acknowledged by the Permanent Court of International Justice in the well-known *Wimbledon* case of 1923, 'the right of entering into international engagements is an attribute of State sovereignty'.[190] Such a sovereign discretion to ratify a treaty (or not) is obviously more acute when it comes to migration. Although the ICRMW preserves the sovereignty of States Parties in deciding whether to admit migrant workers, much remains to be done in order to dispel the prevailing myths surrounding the content and impact of this Convention.

The recurrent misperceptions surrounding migration say more about the lack of ratification by Western states than any other rational explanation. Their disinclination towards the ICRMW cannot be attributed to a denial of migrant workers' basic rights, simply because they are already protected by all human rights conventions in addition to several other specialized treaties concluded at the bilateral and regional levels. Above all, denying the human rights of migrant workers is incompatible with the very premise of human rights as inalienable and universal to all human beings. The most decisive reason behind the lack of ratification by Western states is subtler than a mere denial of rights. It relies on their reluctance to recognize migrant workers as a vulnerable group of persons entitled as such to a specific form of protection.

Apart from—and also because of—the political manoeuvring and resentment against foreigners, there is a widespread perception among decision-makers, public opinion, and the mass media that migrant workers are not as vulnerable as other groups, such as children, women, or disabled persons, whose protection has triggered specialized and widely ratified UN treaties. Following this belief, children, women, and disabled persons are considered vulnerable by simply being a child, a woman, or a disabled person, irrespective of their own will and agency. In contrast, migrant workers are often held responsible for their own choice to migrate, following a traditional and simplistic understanding of labour migration as voluntary in nature. MacDonald and Cholewinski observe in this sense that:

Such beliefs, although prevalent in the general public and frequently both engendered and encouraged by a hostile media, display an almost complete lack of understanding not only of the complex phenomenon of migration, and the contribution that migrants, both regular and irregular, make to the host society's economy, but also of the nature and function of human rights, as currently conceived.[191]

---

[190] *Case of the SS Wimbledon (UK v Japan)* PCIJ Rep Series A No 1, para 35.
[191] MacDonald and Cholewinski, *The Migrant Workers Convention* (n 174) 64. Following this account, one should add that the international community has moved away from the notion of

In addition to the persistent misperceptions about migrant workers, another possible reason behind the reluctance of Western states to ratify the ICRMW could be found in their unwillingness to have their human rights record scrutinized at the international plane by the Convention's monitoring body composed of independent experts (namely the CMW). This supervision would inevitably make human rights abuses against migrant workers more visible, while providing an international arena to question their domestic policies. The relevance of this argument, however, is doubtful and it cannot be considered as a key political barrier to ratification. Such an international supervision is already carried out by regional courts and UN treaty bodies under general human rights treaties, and most of them are increasingly involved in migration matters. Furthermore, by choosing not to ratify the ICRMW, Western states are losing the opportunity to participate in its monitoring mechanism and to influence its interpretation of the Convention (most notably through the adoption of general comments by the CMW).[192]

As illustrated, the governing elite of the West neglects the costs of remaining outside of the ICRMW. Among many other instances, ratifying the ICRMW could provide the opportunity to shift the political climate towards a more rational and efficient policy on labour migration.[193] At the global level, the most obvious cost relates to the legitimacy and reputation of Western states in the field of human rights. Their refusal to ratify one of the core UN human rights treaties casts doubts on their legitimacy in promoting due respect for human rights. Hence, it

vulnerable group to embrace that of migrants in vulnerable situations. This last concept is based on a broad variety of factors, including prejudice, marginalization, and human rights abuses which are particularly relevant for considering that migrant workers might also find themselves in vulnerable situations. For different, albeit similar, definitions of migrants in vulnerable situations, see, most notably, United Nations High Commissioner for Human Rights (OHCHR) and Global Migration Group (GMG), 'Principles and Guidelines, Supported by Practical Guidance, on the Human Rights Protection of Migrants in Vulnerable Situations' (2017), available at: https://www.ohchr.org/en/issues/migration/pages/vulnerablesituations.aspx accessed 17 October 2018; IOM, 'Protection of the Human Rights and Fundamental Freedoms of Migrants and the Specific Needs of Migrants in Vulnerable Situations' (2017), available at https://www.iom.int/sites/default/files/our_work/ODG/GCM/IOM-Thematic-Paper-Protection-of-Human-Rights-and-Vulnerable-Migrants.pdf accessed 17 October 2018; UNHCR, ' "Migrants in Vulnerable Situation" UNHCR Perspective' (June 2017), available at: http://www.refworld.org/docid/596787174.html accessed 17 October 2018.

[192] For further discussion about the role and functions of the CMW, see V Chetail, 'The Committee on the Protection of the Rights of All Migrant Workers and Members of Their Families' in P Alston and F Mégret (eds), *The United Nations and Human Rights: A Critical Appraisal* (2nd edn, OUP 2019).

[193] For further discussion about the benefits to be part of the ICRMW in the particular context of the US, see Lyon, 'The Unsigned United Nations' (n 174) 389–500. The author observes, alongside other similar studies dedicated to European states, that a significant portion of the Convention overlaps with existing US international commitments, whereas the few provisions that are incompatible with US domestic law can be overcome through the formulation of reservations. She then demonstrates that ICRMW ratification would be beneficial to the US in five main areas. First, it would enable policy reform by shifting the political climate; second, it would improve the situation of migrant workers; third, it would encourage identification and examination of best practices in labour migration; fourth, it would advance foreign policy goals (by improving its leadership vis-à-vis the Global South, encouraging additional ratifications, and enabling the US to shape the interpretation of the Convention); and, fifth, it would benefit the US civil society.

creates a double standard: while Western states are eager to disseminate lessons on human rights abroad, they are unable to practice at home what they preach when it comes to migrant workers. More generally, demanding states from the Global South to respect human rights while refusing to protect their nationals working in the Global North is not only a major paradox of Western democracies, it also undermines any constructive dialogue on migration between sending and receiving countries.

By failing to ratify the Convention, Western states are missing the opportunity to develop sound and comprehensive cooperation between states. The ICRMW is much more than a human rights treaty. Its Part VI establishes a flexible framework of intergovernmental dialogue and consultation to better manage labour migration and to fight irregular movements of migrant workers. As detailed before, this encompasses a wide range of issues in line with the typical concerns of Western states (most notably concerning the return of migrant workers and members of their families to their countries of origin, as well as the criminal sanctions against traffickers and employers of undocumented migrant workers).

Looking beyond Western politics of non-ratification

The continued reluctance of Western states to ratify the ICRMW represents a consequential impediment to developing a comprehensive and cogent legal framework on labour migration at the universal plane. However, to argue that the Convention is insignificant because of the lack of ratifications among states in the Global North denotes a Western-centric bias that is fundamentally flawed. While morally questionable, such a Western tropism obscures the practical and legal value of the ICRMW for many other states. It also betrays a lack of understanding about labour migration that is far from being confined to South-North movements of workers. In fact, labour migration is a truly global phenomenon affecting virtually all states, most of them being simultaneously countries of origin, transit, and destination. Regardless of the prospect of ratifications among Western nations, the number of States Parties will continue to grow in other regions of the world.

Furthermore, the ICRMW should not be seen in isolation from other applicable instruments. When taken together, the three specialized treaties adopted by the UN and ILO have attracted a significant number of ratifications. As listed in Table 4.1 below, no less than ninety States Parties have ratified one or more of the three universal treaties devoted to migrant workers.

As Table 4.1 illustrates, the geographical spread of ratifications embraces all continents as well as both countries of immigration and emigration. States Parties to this 'international charter of migrant workers' include thirty-one states from Africa, twenty-six from Latin America and the Caribbean, twenty from Europe, and thirteen from Asia and the Pacific region. Although this basic account is frequently ignored by scholars and decision-makers, the very fact that ninety States Parties have ratified at least one of these three specialized treaties provides a much more nuanced and substantial picture to take stock of the current binding commitments agreed on by states and their potential for future developments.

Table 4.1 States Parties to the three universal treaties devoted to migrant workers

States	Ratification ILO C-97	Ratification ILO C-143	Ratification or accession ICRMW
Albania	2 Mar 2005	12 Sep 2006	5 Jun 2007
Algeria	19 Oct 1962		21 Apr 2005
Argentina			23 Feb 2007
Armenia	27 Jan 2006	27 Jan 2006	
Azerbaijan			11 Jan 1999
Bahamas	25 May 1976		
Bangladesh			24 Aug 2011
Barbados	8 May 1967		
Belgium	27 Jul 1953		
Belize	15 Dec 1983		14 Nov 2001
Benin		11 Jun 1980	6 Jul 2018
Bolivia			16 Oct 2000
Bosnia &-Herzegovina	2 Jun 1993	2 Jun 1993	13 Dec 1996
Brazil	18 Jun 1965		
Burkina Faso	9 Jun 1961	9 Dec 1977	26 Nov 2003
Cameroon	3 Sep 1962	4 Jul 1978	
Cabo Verde			16 Sep 1997
Chile			21 Mar 2005
Colombia			24 May 1995
Congo			31 Mar 2017
Cuba	29 Apr 1952		
Cyprus	23 Sep 1960	28 Jun 1977	
Dominica	28 Feb 1983		
Ecuador	5 Apr 1978		5 Feb 2002
Egypt			19 Feb 1993
El Salvador			14 Mar 2003
France	29 Mar 1954		
Gambia			28 Sep 2018
Germany	22 Jun 1959		
Ghana			7 Sep 2000
Grenada	9 Jul 1979		
Guatemala	13 Feb 1952		14 Mar 2003
Guinea		5 Jun 1978	7 Sep 2000
Guinea-Bissau			22 Oct 2018
Guyana	8 Jun 1966		7 Jul 2010
Honduras			9 Aug 2005

Table 4.1 Continued

States	Ratification ILO C-97	Ratification ILO C-143	Ratification or accession ICRMW
Indonesia			31 May 2012
Israel	30 Mar 1953		
Italy	22 Oct 1952	23 Jun 1981	
Jamaica	26 Dec 1962		25 Sep 2008
Kenya	30 Nov 1965	9 Apr 1979	
Kyrgyzstan	10 Sep 2008		29 Sep 2003
Lesotho			16 Sep 2005
Libyan Arab Jamahiriya			18 Jun 2004
The FYR of Macedonia	7 Nov 1991	17 Nov 1991	
Madagascar	14 Jun 2001		13 May 2015
Malawi	22 Mar 1965		
Malaysia (Sabah)	3 Mar 1964		
Mali			5 Jun 2003
Mauritania			22 Jan 2007
Mauritius	2 Dec 1969		
Mexico			8 Mar. 1999
Moldova	12 Dec 2005		
Montenegro	3 Jun 2006	3 Jun 2006	
Morocco			21 Jun 1993
Mozambique			19 Aug 2013
Netherlands	20 May 1952		
New Zealand	10 Nov 1950		
Nicaragua			26 Oct 2005
Niger			18 Mar 2009
Nigeria	17 Oct 1960		27 Jul 2009
Norway	17 Feb 1955	24 Jan 1979	
Paraguay			23 Sep 2008
Peru			14 Sep 2005
Philippines	21 Apr 2009	14 Sep 2006	5 Jul 1995
Portugal	12 Dec 1978	12 Dec 1978	
Rwanda			15 Dec 2008
Saint Lucia	14 May 1980		
San Marino		23 May 1985	
Saint Vincent and the Grenadines			29 Oct 2010

(*continued*)

Table 4.1 Continued

States	Ratification ILO C-97	Ratification ILO C-143	Ratification or accession ICRMW
Sao Tome and Principe			10 Jan 2017
Senegal			9 Jun 1999
Serbia	24 Nov 2000	24 Nov. 2000	
Seychelles			15 Dec 1994
Slovenia	29 May 1992	29 May 1992	
Spain	21 Mar 1967		
Sri Lanka			11 Mar 1996
Sweden		28 Dec 1982	
Syria			2 Jun 2005
Tajikistan	10 Apr 2007	10 Apr 2007	8 Jan 2002
Tanzania (Zanzibar)	22 Jun 1964		
Trinidad & Tobago	24 May 1963		
Timor Leste			30 Jan 2004
Togo		08 Nov 1983	
Turkey			27 Sep 2004
Uganda		31 Mar 1978	14 Nov 1995
United Kingdom	22 Jan 1951		
Uruguay	18 Mar 1954		15 Feb 2001
Venezuela	9 Jun 1983	17 Aug 1983	25 Oct 2016
Zambia	2 Dec 1964		

*China notified 1 July 1997 regarding continued application of ILO Convention 97 in Hong Kong Special Administrative Region.

Sources: for the ratifications of ILO Convention C97, see the website of the ILO: http://www.ilo.org/dyn/normlex/en/f?p=1000:11300:0::NO:11300:P11300_INSTRUMENT_ID:312242 accessed 17 October 2018; for the ratifications of ILO Convention C143 , see the website of the ILO: http://www.ilo.ch/dyn/normlex/en/f?p=NORMLEXPUB:11300:0::NO::P11300_INSTRUMENT_ID:312288 accessed 17 October 2018; ratifications of ICRMW are available at: https://treaties.un.org/Pages/ViewDetails.aspx?src=IND&mtdsg_no=IV-13&chapter=4&clang=_en accessed 23 October 2018.

Furthermore, similar to many other fields of international law, the legal framework of labour migration cannot only be limited to the specific treaties adopted at the universal level. As discussed in Chapters 1 and 2, labour migration is still governed by two additional sets of applicable treaties, including a broad range of general conventions on various relevant issues (such as human rights, labour standards, and trade), as well as a substantial number of bilateral and regional agreements specifically devoted to migrant workers. Labour migration is accordingly framed by a vast network of universal, regional, and bilateral treaties that shows both the significance and the complexity of treaty law as a source of international migration law.

5

Trafficked and Smuggled Migrants

In addition to the traditional categories of migrant workers and refugees, new legal classifications of migrants emerged in 2000 with the adoption of the UN Protocol against the Smuggling of Migrants by Land, Sea and Air, and the UN Protocol to Prevent, Suppress and Punish Trafficking in Persons, Especially Women and Children, Supplementing the United Nations Convention against Transnational Organized Crime.[1]

Entered into force in 2004 and 2003 respectively, these two Protocols follow an entirely different pattern compared to the other specialized treaties of international migration law adopted so far. They have been conceived as instruments of criminal law to supplement the UN Convention against Transnational Organized Crime, in stark contrast with the logic of protection that prevails under the other specialist treaties devoted to refugees and migrant workers. This crime and control approach probably explains the broad number of ratifications gathered by the Smuggling and Trafficking Protocols with 147 and 173 States Parties respectively.[2] While reflecting

---

[1] Protocol against the Smuggling of Migrants by Land, Sea and Air (adopted 15 November 2000, entered into force 28 January 2004) 2241 UNTS 507 (Smuggling Protocol); Protocol to Prevent, Supress and Punish Trafficking in Persons, Especially Women and Children, supplementing the UN Convention against Transnational Organized Crime (adopted 15 November 2000, entered into force 25 December 2003) 2237 UNTS 319 (Trafficking Protocol). The Trafficking Protocol is broader in scope as it does not only concern migrants, but more generally victims of trafficking.

[2] Information regarding the ratification, acceptance, approval, accession, and succession of the Trafficking Protocol is available at: https://treaties.un.org/Pages/ViewDetails.aspx?src=IND&mtdsg_no=XVIII-12-a&chapter=18&lang=en; the same set of information concerning the Smuggling Protocol is available at: https://treaties.un.org/pages/ViewDetails.aspx?src=IND&mtdsg_no=XVIII-12-b&chapter=18&clang=_en accessed 17 October 2018. This enthusiastic reception by states has also prompted the adoption of a broad range of regional treaties and soft law instruments mainly focusing on trafficking in persons. See, most notably, among regional conventions, ASEAN Convention against Trafficking in Persons, especially Women and Children (adopted 21 November 2015, entered into force 8 March 2017) (ACTIP), available at http://asean.org/storage/2012/05/ACTIP-2015.pdf accessed 17 October 2018; Council of Europe Convention on Action against Trafficking in Human Beings (adopted 16 May 2005, entered into force 1 February 2008) CETS No 197; Directive 2011/36/EU of the European Parliament and of the Council of 5 April 2011 on preventing and combating trafficking in human beings and protecting its victims [2011] OJ L101/1; Joint ECOWAS/ECCAS Regional Plan of Action to Combat Trafficking in Persons, especially Women and Children (2006-2008) (adopted 6 July 2006), available at: https://www.ilo.org/dyn/natlex/docs/ELECTRONIC/79461/110989/F-1992279795/ORG-79461.pdf accessed 17 October 2018; SAARC Convention on Preventing and Combating Trafficking in Women and Children for Prostitution (adopted 5 January 2002, entered into force 15 November 2005), available at: http://www.jus.uio.no/english/services/library/treaties/02/2-04/saarc-traff-women-children.xml accessed 17 October 2018. See also, among other soft law instruments adopted at the regional level: Bali Declaration on People Smuggling, Trafficking in Persons, and Related Transnational Crime, adopted at the Sixth Ministerial Conference

the trend toward the securitization of migration, these UN Protocols raise more questions than answers when it comes to the definition of trafficking and smuggling (section 5.1), the duties of States Parties in the fight against these crimes (section 5.2), as well as the protection of trafficked persons and smuggled migrants (section 5.3).

5.1 The Definitions of Trafficking and Smuggling

The legal regime established by the Palermo Protocols relies on two definitions supposedly capturing the characteristics and differences between trafficking in persons (section 5.1.1) and smuggling of migrants (section 5.1.2), even if their respective scope and content considerably overlap both in law and practice (section 5.1.3).

5.1.1 The constitutive elements of trafficking in persons

The fight against human trafficking has been a longstanding concern in international law, which has triggered the adoption of a broad range of conventions since the beginning of the 20th century.[3] Nevertheless, the Palermo Protocol is the first treaty

on People Smuggling, Trafficking in Persons and Related Transnational Crime (23 March 2016), available at: http://www.refworld.org/docid/5799ef3c4.html accessed 17 October 2018; Inter-American Declaration against Trafficking in Persons (Declaration of Brasilia), adopted at the third plenary session (5 December 2014) OEA/Ser.K/XXXIX.4 RTP-IV/doc.5/14 rev.1; The Comprehensive Arab Strategy for Combating Trafficking in Human Beings, adopted by the Council of Arab Ministers of Justice Resolution (15 February 2012) No 879-27-15/2/2012 (CASCTHB); Parliamentary Assembly of the Council of Europe, Recommendation 2011 on the trafficking of migrant workers for forced labour (25 January 2013) (9th Sitting); Ouagadougou Action Plan to Combat Trafficking in Human Beings, Especially Women and Children, adopted by the Ministerial Conference on Migration and Development (Tripoli 22–23 November 2006), available at: https://ec.europa.eu/anti-trafficking/sites/antitrafficking/files/ouagadougou_action_plan_to_combat_trafficking_en_1.pdf accessed 17 October 2018; ASEAN Declaration Against Trafficking in Persons Particularly Women and Children (adopted 29 November 2004), available at http://asean.org/asean-declaration-against-trafficking-in-persons-particularly-women-and-children-4/ accessed 17 October 2018; OSCE Declaration on Trafficking in Human Beings, adopted at the tenth meeting of the Ministerial Council (Porto 6–7 December 2002) MC.DOC/1/02 (7 December 2002), 11; ASEM Action Plan to Combat Trafficking in Persons, especially Women and Children, adopted by the ASEM Foreign Ministers Meeting (Beijing 24–25 May 2001) available at: https://childhub.org/en/system/tdf/library/attachments/asem_action_plan_3.pdf?file=1&type=node&id=17249 accessed 17 October 2018; ECOWAS Declaration on the Fight against Trafficking in Persons, adopted at the 25th Ordinary Session of Authority of Heads of State and Government (Dakar 20–21 December 2001) A/DC12/12/01.

[3] See, for instance, International Agreement for the Suppression of the 'White Slave Traffic' (18 May 1904, entered into force 18 July 1905) 1 LNTS 83, amended by Protocol Amending the International Agreement for the Suppression of the White Slave Traffic, and Amending the International Convention for the Suppression of the White Slave Traffic (adopted 4 May 1949, entered into force 21 June 1951) 30 UNTS 23; International Convention for the Suppression of the White Slave Traffic (adopted 4 May 1910, entered into force 8 August 1912) 3 LNTS 278, amended by Protocol Amending the International Agreement for the Suppression of the White Slave Traffic, and Amending the International Convention for the Suppression of the White Slave Traffic (adopted 4 May 1949, entered into force 21 June 1951) 30 UNTS 23 (1910 White Slavery Convention) art 2; International Convention for the Suppression of Traffic in Women and Children (adopted 30 September 1921, entered into force 15 June 1922) 9 LNTS 415, amended by Protocol to Amend the Convention for the Suppression of the Traffic in Women and

to provide a definition of the term 'trafficking in persons'. After lengthy discussions and vivid controversies during the negotiation process,[4] Article 3(a) defines human trafficking as:

The recruitment, transportation, transfer, harbouring or receipt of persons, by means of the threat or use of force or other forms of coercion, of abduction, of fraud, of deception, of the abuse of power or of a position of vulnerability or of the giving or receiving of payments or benefits to achieve the consent of a person having control over another person, for the purpose of exploitation.

This definition is both complex and comprehensive. It comprises three cumulative components: an action (recruitment, transportation, transfer, harbouring, or receipt of persons); a means (threat or use of force or other forms of coercion, abduction, fraud, deception, abuse of power, abuse of a position of vulnerability, or the giving or receiving of payments or benefits to achieve the consent of a person having control over another person); and a specific purpose (exploitation).[5]

However, none of these key terms are defined by the Protocol, thereby leaving uncertainty about the exact scope of this definition. Article 3 merely acknowledges that the consent of the victim is irrelevant, and the same provision further exemplifies the notion of exploitation as including 'at a minimum, the exploitation of the prostitution of others or other forms of sexual exploitation, forced labour or services, slavery or practices similar to slavery, servitude or the removal of organs'. Nevertheless, once again, the Protocol does not define any of these forms of exploitation. While some of them—such as forced labour,[6] slavery, and similar practices[7]—are defined

Children and the Convention for the Suppression of the Traffic in Women of Full Age (adopted 20 October 1947, entered into force 12 November 1947) 53 UNTS 13; International Convention for the Suppression of the Traffic in Women of Full Age (adopted 11 October 1933, entered into force 24 August 1934) 150 LNTS 431, amended by Protocol to Amend the Convention for the Suppression of the Traffic in Women and Children and the Convention for the Suppression of the Traffic in Women of Full Age (adopted 20 October 1947, entered into force 12 November 1947) 53 UNTS 13; Convention on the Elimination of All Forms of Discrimination against Women (adopted 18 December 1979, entered into force 3 September 1981) 1249 UNTS 13 art 6; Convention on the Rights of the Child (20 November 1989, entered into force 2 September 1990) 28 ILM 1448 arts 32, 34–35; Optional Protocol on the Sale of Children, Child Prostitution and Child Pornography (adopted 25 May 2000, entered into force 18 January 2002) 39 ILM 1290 art 3.

[4] For an overview of the drafting history regarding the definition of trafficking, see UN Office on Drugs and Crime (UNODC), *Travaux Préparatoires of the Negotiations for the Elaboration of the United Nations Convention against Transnational Organized Crime and the Protocols thereto* (United Nations Publication 2006) 339–48; D McClean, *Transnational Organized Crime: A Commentary on the UN Convention and its Protocols* (OUP 2007) 315–30.

[5] According to Article 3(c) of the Protocol, the second component of this definition is not required when the victim of trafficking is a child provided that the two other conditions are fulfilled.

[6] ILO Convention C029: Forced Labour Convention (Convention concerning Forced or Compulsory Labour) (adopted 14th Conference Session Geneva 28 June 1930, entered into force 1 May 1932) 39 UNTS 55 art 2(1) defines forced labour as referring to 'all work or service which is exacted from any person under the menace of any penalty and for which the said person has not offered himself voluntarily'.

[7] The term 'slavery' is defined in art 1(1) of the Slavery Convention (adopted 25 September 1926, entered into force 1926) 60 LNTS 253 as 'the status or condition of a person over whom any or all of the powers attaching to the right of ownership are exercised'. The broader notion of 'practices similar to slavery' is defined in art 1 of the Supplementary Convention on the Abolition of Slavery, the Slave Trade, and Institutions and Practices Similar to Slavery (adopted 7 September 1956, entered into force 30 April

by other UN treaties that are supposed to be incorporated by the relevant States Parties, the definitions of prostitution and sexual exploitation are entirely left to each Contracting State.

Furthermore, States Parties are free to add other types of exploitation in their domestic laws because the Protocol only mentions some forms of exploitation 'at a minimum'. This *à la carte* definition remains unfortunate: although exploitation captures the very essence of trafficking, its exact scope and meaning may vary from one state to another. It may in turn destabilize the principle of legality under international and national criminal law which first and foremost requires clear definitions of crimes.

Overall, the vagueness of the Palermo definition and the broad discretion of states to specify its key components significantly undermine its common meaning and effective implementation. The UN Model Law against Trafficking in Persons, prepared in 2009 by the United Nations Office on Drugs and Crime (UNODC) provides interpretative guidance about some of the constitutive elements of the Palermo definition. However, this endeavour is neither comprehensive nor binding, and preserves states' margin of appreciation in interpreting the key terms of the Palermo definition in their national legislation.[8]

Because of the great variance in its domestic incorporation by States Parties, several scholars have argued that 'no effective trafficking definition exists'.[9] It is true

1957) 226 UNTS 3, as including: '(a) Debt bondage, that is to say, the status or condition arising from a pledge by a debtor of his personal services or of those of a person under his control as security for a debt, if the value of those services as reasonably assessed is not applied toward the liquidation of the debt or the length and nature of those services are not respectively limited and defined; (b) Serfdom, that is to say, the condition or status of a tenant who is by law, custom or agreement bound to live and labour on land belonging to another person and to render some determinate service to such other person, whether for reward or not, and is not free to change his status; (c) Any institution or practice whereby: (i) A woman, without the right to refuse, is promised or given in marriage on payment of a consideration in money or in kind to her parents, guardian, family or any other person or group; or (ii) The husband of a woman, his family, or his clan, has the right to transfer her to another person for value received or otherwise; or (iii) A woman on the death of her husband is liable to be inherited by another person; (d) Any institution or practice whereby a child or young person under the age of 18 years, is delivered by either or both of his natural parents or by his guardian to another person, whether for reward or not, with a view to the exploitation of the child or young person or of his labour.'

[8] With respect to, for instance, the crucial notion of exploitation, the commentary of the UN Model merely observes that the term 'is not defined in the Protocol. However, it is generally associated with particularly harsh and abusive conditions of work, or "conditions of work inconsistent with human dignity" [as notably acknowledged in the Penal Codes of Belgium and France].' While preserving the broad margin of appreciation of States, the UN Model further underlines, in rather permissive terms, that the other forms of exploitation that States can add in their domestic legislation 'should be well defined. Other forms of exploitation that, for example, may be included are: (a) Forced or servile marriage; (b) Forced or coerced begging; (c) The use in illicit or criminal activities [including the trafficking or production of drugs]; (d) The use in armed conflict; (e) Ritual or customary servitude [any form of forced labour related to customary ritual] [exploitative and abusive religious or cultural practices that dehumanize, degrade or cause physical or psychological harm]; (f) The use of women as surrogate mothers; (g) Forced pregnancy; (h) Illicit conduct of biomedical research on a person.' See UN Office on Drugs and Crime (UNODC), 'Model Law against Trafficking in Persons' (5 August 2009) V.09-81990 (E), 35–36.

[9] J Allain, 'No Effective Trafficking Definition Exists: Domestic Implementation of the Palermo Protocol' (2014) 7 Alb Govt L Rev 111–42. See also, among others, V Stoyanova, 'The Crisis of a Definition: Human Trafficking in Bulgarian Law' (2013) 5 Amsterdam LF 64–79; G Noll, 'The

that, from the standpoint of domestic law, there are as many definitions of trafficking as States Parties to the UN Protocol because of their broad margin of appreciation. Nonetheless, from the perspective of international law, the Palermo definition exhibits a core content of trafficking that is now widely accepted by states at the universal level. Its parameters still need to be refined through a uniform and authoritative framework of interpretation. The UN Model Law against Trafficking in Persons still has to be improved before being able to fully provide a more straightforward and detailed guidance. Alternatively, the International Court of Justice may play a role in case of a dispute between two or more States Parties concerning the interpretation or application of the Protocol since, under Article 15, any of them may refer a dispute to the Court.[10]

5.1.2 The constitutive elements of the smuggling of migrants

In contrast to trafficking in persons, the smuggling of migrants is a new term within the lexicon of international law. The term was never mentioned in any convention before the adoption of the Smuggling Protocol in 2000. Article 3 (a) defines 'smuggling of migrants' as 'the procurement, in order to obtain, directly or indirectly, a financial or other material benefit, of the illegal entry of a person into a State Party of which the person is not a national or a permanent resident.' This definition is based on two cumulative components: an action (the procurement of illegal entry) and a

---

Insecurity of Trafficking in International Law' in V Chetail (ed), *Globalization, Migration and Human Rights: International Law under Review/Mondialisation, migration et droits de l'homme: le droit international en question* (Bruylant 2007) 343–61.

[10] Likewise, the International Criminal Court could provide some interpretative guidance in the future. Although trafficking in persons is not a crime on its own under the Rome Statute, the material element of crimes against humanity includes 'enslavement', 'sexual exploitation', and 'enforced prostitution'. Interestingly, trafficking in persons is explicitly mentioned in the definition of enslavement under art 7(2)(c) of the Rome Statute as the 'the exercise of any or all of the powers attaching to the right of ownership over a person and includes the exercise of such power in the course of trafficking in persons, in particular women and children'. Although trafficking must amount to slavery to fall under the competence of the International Criminal Court, there are some interesting parallels with the Palermo definition. The Rome Statute's Elements of Crimes specify that exercising 'any or all powers attaching to the right of ownership over one or more persons' includes, but is not limited to, 'purchasing, selling, lending or bartering such a person or persons, or by imposing on them a similar deprivation of liberty'. It further adds that 'deprivations of liberty may, in some circumstances, include exacting forced labour or otherwise reducing a person to a servile status as defined in the Supplementary Convention on the Abolition of Slavery, the Slave Trade, and Institutions and Practices Similar to Slavery of 1956. It is also understood that the conduct described in this element includes trafficking in persons, in particular women and children.' A similar parallel between the Palermo definition and the notion of slavery has been noted by the International Criminal Tribunal for the Former Yugoslavia, stating that 'indications of enslavement include elements of control and ownership; the restriction or control of an individual's autonomy, freedom of choice or freedom of movement; and, often, the accruing of some gain to the perpetrator. The consent or free will of the victim is absent. It is often rendered impossible or irrelevant by, for example, the threat or use of force or other forms of coercion; the fear of violence, deception or false promises; the abuse of power; the victim's position of vulnerability; detention or captivity, psychological oppression or socio-economic conditions. Further indications of enslavement include exploitation; the exaction of forced or compulsory labour or service, often without remuneration and often, though not necessarily, involving physical hardship; sex; prostitution; and human trafficking.' See *Prosecutor v Kunarac* (Judgment) IT-96-23-T (22 February 2001) paras 537 and 542.

purpose (to obtain a benefit). The apparent simplicity of this definition, however, is not free from ambiguities.

Regarding its first component, the key notion of 'procurement' is curiously not defined by the Protocol nor by the UN Model Law against the Smuggling of Migrants.[11] The absence of any clear-cut definition creates considerable uncertainty about the exact scope entailed by the 'smuggling of migrants'. It has also raised controversies as to whether the term 'procurement' is only limited to the action of illegal entry[12] or encompasses other acts of facilitation more broadly.[13] The first interpretation is more in line with the general principle of criminal law according to which any crime must be interpreted restrictively. It is further confirmed by the context of the Smuggling Protocol as exemplified by other relevant provisions referring to the facilitation of illegal entry.

Unlike the crime of trafficking in persons, Article 6(1)(a) requires the smuggling of migrants to be criminalized as a stand-alone offence. Hence, other specific offences that may be committed to facilitate illegal entry (such as the act of producing, procuring, or providing a fraudulent travel or identity document,[14] the act of participating as an accomplice, as well as that of organizing or directing other persons)[15] are addressed separately from the crime of smuggling. As a result, although the definition of smuggling does not explicitly comprise the facilitation of illegal entry, States Parties are still required to criminalize it in their domestic legislation as a distinct offence.

Contrary to the term 'procurement', 'illegal entry' is defined by the Protocol as any 'crossing borders without complying with the necessary requirements for legal entry into the receiving State' (Article 3 (b)). This definition is particularly extensive, given that it covers all 'necessary requirements' including even minor and purely administrative ones (such as completing the proper forms on arrival),[16] and it refers to any 'receiving State' that is not necessarily a State Party nor the state in which prosecution might be carried out.[17] Despite this particularly broad scope, Article 3(a) limits its definition of smuggling to persons who are neither nationals nor permanent residents, thereby not extending to permanent residents' illegal entry.

---

[11] The commentary of the Model Law merely provides some vague suggestions based on English dictionaries with 'procurement' meaning 'to obtain something or to cause a result by effort'. See UN Office on Drugs and Crime (UNODC), *Model Law against the Smuggling of Migrants* (United Nations Publishing and Library Section, Vienna 2010) 31. The drafting history of the Protocol is equally unhelpful to define this term.

[12] See especially, in this sense, A Aljehani, 'The Legal Definition of the Smuggling of Migrants in Light of the Provisions of the Migrant Smuggling Protocol' (2015) 79(2) JCL 122, 123, 126; V Muntarbhorn, 'Combating Migrant Smuggling and Trafficking in Persons, Especially Women: The Normative Framework Re-appraised' in TA Aleinikoff and V Chetail (eds), *Migration and International Legal Norms* (TMC Asser Press 2003) 151.

[13] See notably AT Gallagher and F David, *The International Law of Migrant Smuggling* (CUP 2014) 364–65; A Schloenhardt and JE Dale, 'Twelve Years On: Revisiting the UN Protocol against the Smuggling of Migrants by Land, Sea and Air' (2012) 67 JPL 129, 135.

[14] Smuggling Protocol (n 1) art 6(1)(b).   [15] ibid art 6(2)(b) and (c).

[16] Gallagher and David, *The International Law of Migrant Smuggling* (n 13) 365.

[17] McClean, *Transnational Organized Crime* (n 4) 384.

Likewise, the definition of smuggling exclusively focuses on entry and, in turn, excludes the 'procurement' of illegal residence. However, similarly to the notion of 'facilitation' discussed above, this nuance must not be overestimated. Although the facilitation of illegal residence is not a part of the smuggling definition, Article 6(1)(c) still requires States Parties to criminalize it in their domestic legislation as a distinct offence. The overall logic of the Protocol thus remains confusing and undermines the relevance of the smuggling definition, which must be read in conjunction with other provisions criminalizing additional offences that are closely related to smuggling.

In any event, procuring illegal entry is not a crime on its own under the Palermo Protocol. To be considered as a crime, it must have been committed with the specific intention of obtaining 'directly or indirectly, a financial or other material benefit'. According to this definitional requirement, the procurement of illegal entry without the intention to make a profit is not smuggling of migrants and shall not be criminalized. As specified by the *travaux préparatoires* of the Protocol, the reference to 'a financial or other material benefit' is aimed at excluding the activities of family members or non-governmental organizations from the definition of smuggling.[18] The same exclusion shall apply *a fortiori* to other individuals or entities (such as a state or an international organization) who assist a migrant in crossing a border without obtaining a particular benefit. As underlined during the negotiation process, the key objective of the Smuggling Protocol is to focus on the activities of organized criminal groups acting for profit.[19] The Legislative Guides prepared by UNODC to implement the Protocol further exhibit that 'the intention of the drafters was to require legislatures to create criminal offences that would apply to those who smuggle others for gain, but not those who procure only their own illegal entry or who procure the illegal entry of others for reasons other than gain'.[20]

The purpose of obtaining a benefit is thus critical to draw the line between what is prohibited and what is not. Despite its crucial importance, the term 'financial or other material benefit' is left undefined by the Protocol. Nevertheless, the same expression can be found in the definition of an 'organised criminal group' under Article 2(a) of the Organized Crime Convention with the Interpretative Note attached thereto proposing the following broad interpretation:

The words 'in order to obtain, directly or indirectly, a financial or other material benefit' should be understood broadly, to include, for example, crimes in which the predominant motivation may be sexual gratification, such as the receipt or trade of materials by members of child pornography rings, the trading of children by members of paedophile rings or cost-sharing among ring members.[21]

While endorsing this extensive interpretation, the UN Model Law against the Smuggling of Migrants defines 'financial or other material benefit' as including 'any

[18] UNODC, *Travaux Préparatoires* (n 4) 469.   [19] ibid.
[20] UN Office on Drugs and Crime (UNODC), *Legislative Guides for the Implementation of the United Nations Convention against Transnational Organized Crime and the Protocol thereto* (United Nations Publication 2004) 341.
[21] ibid 17.

type of financial or non-financial inducement, payment, bribe, reward, advantage, privilege or service (including sexual or other services)'.[22] Its Commentary further underlines that 'payment or profit arising from smuggling of migrants can include non-financial inducements, such as a free train or airplane ticket, or property, such as a car. Thus, it is important to ensure that the definition of "financial or other material benefit" is as broad and inclusive as possible.'[23] This extensive meaning of the term 'benefit' raises the question of the overlap between smuggling and trafficking as both crimes are perpetrated to make a profit.

5.1.3 The overlap between the trafficking in persons and the smuggling of migrants

Distinguishing smuggling from trafficking constitutes the most challenging and controversial issue, which has triggered plenty of critiques.[24] The distinction between the two notions is frequently portrayed as 'unclear',[25] 'blurred',[26] if not 'artificial and unhelpful',[27] or even 'dangerous.'[28] Legally speaking, smuggling and trafficking are two different offences governed by separate instruments. Although the constitutive elements of the two offences differ, they were drafted in a vague and open-ended manner that inevitably creates an overlap between the two.

As exemplified above, the definitions of trafficking and smuggling raise more questions than answers. This generates a considerable amount of confusion and uncertainty regarding their respective scope and specificity. Furthermore, as the distinction between trafficking and smuggling was taken for granted from the very beginning of the negotiation process, no serious effort was made to think and question its rationale and relevance. As a result of this lack of concern, and despite the request of UN agencies,[29] the Protocols fail to provide any guidance on

---

[22] UNODC, *Model Law against the Smuggling of Migrants* (n 11) 13.   [23] ibid.

[24] Among the copious literature criticizing this distinction, see especially Aljehani, 'The Legal Definition' (n 12) 122–137; T Baird, 'Defining Human Smuggling in Migration Research: An Appraisal and Critique' (2016) EUI Working Papers RSCAS 2016/30; J Bhabha and M Zard, 'Smuggled or Trafficked?' (2006) 25 Forced Migration Review 6–8; BS Buckland, 'Human Trafficking and Smuggling: Crossover and Overlap' in C Friesendorf (ed), *Strategies Against Human Trafficking: The Role of the Security Sector* (National Defence Academy, Austrian Ministry of Defence and Sports, and Geneva Centre for the Democratic Control of Armed Forces 2009) 137–65; L Butterly, 'Trafficking v Smuggling; Coercion v Consent: Conceptual Problems with the Transnational Anti-Trafficking Regime' (2014) 2 UKSLR 45, 46; M McAdam, 'What's in a Name? Victim Naming and Blaming in Rights-based Distinctions between Human Trafficking and Migrant Smuggling' (2015) 4 International Human Rights Law Review 1–32; J Elliott, *The Role of Consent in Human Trafficking* (Routledge 2015) 22–24 and 143–46.

[25] International Council on Human Rights Policy, *Irregular Migration, Migrant Smuggling and Human Rights: Towards Coherence* (ICHRP 2010) 79.

[26] R Skeldon, 'Trafficking: A Perspective from Asia' (2000) 38(3) International Migration 7, 9.

[27] M Lee, 'Human Trade and the Criminalization of Irregular Migration' (2005) 33 Int'l J Soc L 1, 7.

[28] W Chapkis, 'Trafficking, Migration and the Law: Protecting Innocents, Punishing Immigrants' (2003) 17(6) Gender & Society 923, 931.

[29] UNGA 'Note by the Office of the United Nations High Commissioner for Human Rights, the Office of the United Nations High Commissioner for Refugees, the United Nations Children's

the procedure to be followed in order to identify trafficked persons and smuggled migrants.[30]

More importantly, the binary opposition between trafficking and smuggling oversimplifies a fluid and multifaceted reality. In practice, while there are certainly pure cases of trafficking and smuggling, most situations fall along a continuum of abuses that defies easy categorization. As observed by the OHCHR, 'trafficking and migrant smuggling are *processes*—often interrelated and almost always involving shifts, flows, overlaps and transitions. An individual can be smuggled one day and trafficked the next.'[31] UNODC also concedes that, '[t]he distinctions between smuggling and trafficking are often very subtle and they sometimes overlap. Identifying whether a case is one of trafficking in persons or smuggling of migrants can be very difficult [...].'[32] Despite this acknowledgement, UNODC opines that the difference between smuggling and trafficking lies in three distinctive characteristics: transnationality, exploitation, and consent.[33] A closer review of each defining feature, however, paints a much more nuanced picture that considerably blurs the distinction between smuggling and trafficking.

Regarding the first distinguishing feature, it is true that the transnational element of smuggling is inherent in its very definition, whereas trafficking may occur across borders or within a single country. This clear-cut distinctive character is mitigated by Article 4 of the Trafficking Protocol, according to which the Protocol shall apply, except as otherwise stated, where the offences are 'transnational in nature and involve an organized criminal group'.[34] This provision has raised contradictory comments among scholars as to whether the offence of trafficking shall be transnational[35] or not.[36] The discrepancy between Articles 3 and 4 of the Protocol could still be reconciled in the following terms: States Parties are only bound to prosecute transnational

---

Fund and the International Organization for Migration on the Draft Protocols Concerning Migrant Smuggling and Trafficking in Persons' (8 February 2000) UN Doc A/AC.254/27 para 2.

[30] For further discussion about the importance of an identification process, see especially AT Gallagher, *The International Law of Human Trafficking* (CUP 2010) 278–83; J Elliott, '(Mis) Identification of Victims of Human Trafficking: The Case of *R v O*' (2009) 21 IJRL 727–41.

[31] Office of the United Nations High Commissioner for Human Rights (OHCHR), *Commentary on the Recommended Principles and Guidelines on Human Rights and Human Trafficking* (United Nations Publication 2010) HR/PUB/10/2, 34–35.

[32] UN Office on Drugs and Crime (UNODC), *Toolkit to Combat Smuggling of Migrants: Understanding the Smuggling of Migrants* (United Nations Publishing and Library Section, Vienna 2010) 38.

[33] ibid 39.

[34] According to art 3(2), an offence is transnational if: '(a) It is committed in more than one State; (b) It is committed in one State but a substantial part of its preparation, planning, direction or control takes place in another State; (c) It is committed in one State but involves an organized criminal group that engages in criminal activities in more than one State; or (d) It is committed in one State but has substantial effects in another State.' Art 2(a) further defines an 'organized criminal group' as meaning 'a structured group of three or more persons, existing for a period of time and acting in concert with the aim of committing one or more serious crimes or offences established in accordance with this Convention, in order to obtain, directly or indirectly, a financial or other material benefit.'

[35] See, for instance, JC Hathaway, 'The Human Rights Quagmire of "Human Trafficking"' (2008) 49 Va J Int'l L 1, 10, 11.

[36] See notably AT Gallagher, 'Human Rights and Human Trafficking: Quagmire or Firm Ground? A Response to James Hathaway' (2009) 49(4) Va J Int'l L 789, 817.

trafficking while they still have the possibility—but not the duty—to criminalize national trafficking in their domestic legislation.

However, both the Legislative Guides and the Model Law against Trafficking propose a wide-ranging interpretation of states' duty to establish trafficking as a criminal offence irrespective of its transnational nature.[37] Both documents put forward reasons that are neither entirely clear nor very convincing.[38] Even assuming that this extensive interpretation is correct, it does not resolve the overlap between trafficking and smuggling. Even worse, it exacerbates the prevailing confusion between the two because Article 4 of the Smuggling Protocol contains the same qualifications as the Trafficking Protocol. Both the Legislative Guides and the Model Law against Smuggling deduce from this provision that '[i]n the case of smuggling of migrants, domestic offences should apply even where transnationality and the involvement of organized criminal groups does not exist or cannot be proved'.[39] One should accordingly admit that transnationality is not a distinguishing feature between smuggling and trafficking. The difference is much subtler and more circumscribed: smuggling requires illegal entry, whereas trafficking can occur even when entry is legal.

The two other distinctive characteristics—exploitation and consent—reveal similar shortfalls in distinguishing trafficking from smuggling. While exploitation is inherent in trafficking, its differentiation from the notion of benefit under the definition of smuggling is not obvious since both involve the same purpose of making an illicit profit. As acknowledged by the Legislative Guides, 'in many cases, smuggled migrants and victims of trafficking are both moved from one place to another by organized criminal groups for the purpose of generating illicit profits'.[40]

Even if the source of profit-making differs, one additional difficulty is linked to the legal nature of their constitutive elements. The two notions of 'exploitation' and 'benefit' refer to the mental element of the offences. Distinguishing trafficking from smuggling, thus, requires a complex inquiry into the real intentions of the perpetrators. Assessing such an intent can turn into a particularly perilous exercise given the vague and open-ended definitions of exploitation and benefit under the Palermo Protocols. Establishing the specific *mens rea* of the two offences is further complicated by their material elements that substantially overlap and consequently blur their specificities. On the one hand, receiving a benefit is explicitly listed among the prohibited means within the definition of trafficking. On the other

---

[37] UNODC, *Legislative Guides* (n 20) 258–59; UNODC, 'Model Law against Trafficking' (n 8) 7.

[38] ibid. It is first contended that the requirements contained in art 4 are not part of the definition of the offence of trafficking and should be discarded. One can still argue the contrary: the scope of the Protocol being qualified by art 4, such a limitation is supposed to apply to all its provisions (including the one devoted to the definition of trafficking). Second, it is further observed that art 4 of the Protocol has to be read together with art 34(2) of the Organized Crime Convention, according to which 'The offences established in accordance with articles 5, 6, 8 and 23 of this Convention shall be established in the domestic law of each State party independently of the transnational nature or the involvement of an organized criminal group [. . .].' However, this provision is only limited to the offences set out under arts 5, 6, 8, and 23 of this Convention and it says nothing about the offence of trafficking under the Protocol.

[39] UNODC, *Legislative Guides* (n 20) 334; UNODC, *Model Law against the Smuggling of Migrants* (n 11) 7.

[40] UNODC, *Legislative Guides* (n 20) 340.

hand, exploitation is an aggravating circumstance of the offence of smuggling under Article 6(3) of the Smuggling Protocol. In short, although exploitation and benefit are supposed to be two distinct notions that draw the line between the two offences, trafficking may include a benefit and smuggling may involve exploitation.

The role of consent further exacerbates the porous and unstable distinction between smuggling and trafficking. Although the definition of the Smuggling Protocol does not explicitly include an element of consent, smuggling is assumed to be voluntary because it has been conceived as a consensual transaction between the smuggler and the migrant who both agree to circumvent immigration controls. By contrast, Article 3 of the Trafficking Protocol states that the consent of a victim of trafficking in persons is irrelevant once it is demonstrated that deception, coercion, force, or other prohibited means have been used.

However, this sharp distinction between consent and coercion proves to be more complex as the two are not mutually exclusive. Even if smuggled migrants are well-informed and not misled, their initial consent could be withdrawn at a later stage when, for instance, they become victims of human rights abuses or when the conditions of transportation become too dangerous. As Bhabha and Zard rightly observed, whether they are categorized as smuggled or trafficked persons, 'most transported undocumented migrants appear to consent in some way to an initial proposition to travel but frequently en route or on arrival in the destination country, circumstances change'.[41]

Furthermore, trafficking can occur without any use of coercion. The prohibited means listed in the definition of trafficking are not limited to the threat or use of force. They also include 'abduction', 'fraud', 'deception', and 'the abuse of power or of a position of vulnerability' that may equally apply to smuggled migrants. While the Trafficking Protocol does not define any of these notions, an Interpretative Note on Article 3 explains that 'reference to the abuse of a position of vulnerability is understood to refer to any situation in which the person involved has no real and acceptable alternative but to submit to the abuse involved'.[42] This working definition can encompass a broad range of situations, including destitution, persecution, violence, and extreme poverty, which are plainly applicable to smuggled migrants too. While endorsing the definition of the Interpretative Note, the Model Law against Trafficking also acknowledges that the position of vulnerability may be inferred from 'the economic situation of the victim or of dependency on any substance, as well as [...] the objective situation or on the situation as perceived by the victim'.[43]

---

[41] Bhabha and Zard, 'Smuggled or Trafficked?' (n 24) 7.
[42] UNODC, *Travaux Préparatoires* (n 4) 347.
[43] UNODC, 'Model Law against Trafficking in Persons' (n 8) 9–10. The Explanatory Report of the 2005 Council of Europe Trafficking Convention highlights in the same sense that 'the vulnerability may be of any kind, whether physical, psychological, emotional, family-related, social or economic. The situation might, for example, involve insecurity or illegality of the victim's immigration status, economic dependence or fragile health.' See Council of Europe, 'Explanatory Report to the Council of Europe Convention on Action Against Trafficking in Human Beings' (2005) para 83 of CM(83)32 addendum 2 Final of 3 May 2005.

Against such a background, one can reasonably conclude that the element of consent is inadequate in drawing a clear-cut distinction between trafficking and smuggling.

Despite its dubious relevance, the dichotomy between coerced trafficking and consensual smuggling has been instrumental in drawing the line between victims and complicit actors. Following a self-referential logic, trafficked persons are victims because they are coerced, whereas smuggled migrants are complicit because they consented to it.[44] Accordingly, the former deserve protection, but not the latter. This rationale does not only fail to capture the complex reality of migration and the overlap between the definitions of trafficking and smuggling, but such a Manichean divide also unveils a bias against smuggled migrants. They 'are considered less deserving of protection and support because of their original motive—the decision to choose to migrate illegally'.[45]

5.2 The Fight against Trafficking and Smuggling

Despite the alleged differences between smuggling and trafficking, the two Protocols follow the same pattern when it comes to their respective content. Both instruments focus on two central devices—criminalization and immigration control—which are supposed to be mutually reinforcing, alongside a typical law and order approach.

5.2.1 The criminalization of trafficking and smuggling

The *raison d'être* of the Palermo Protocols is to criminalize trafficking and smuggling. Both Protocols require States Parties to establish these criminal offences in their domestic law in accordance with the definitions contained therein, provided that trafficking and smuggling are committed intentionally.[46] The two Protocols further oblige Contracting States to criminalize the attempt to commit such offences, the participation as an accomplice, and the organization or direction of others to commit these offences.[47] This extensive duty of criminalization is supplemented by the Organized Crime Convention which establishes corruption[48] and

---

[44] UNODC, *Legislative Guides* (n 20) 340; UNODC, *Model Law against Smuggling* (n 11) 19.

[45] Bhabha and Zard, 'Smuggled or Trafficked?' (n 24) 6. See also, among others, Chapkis, 'Trafficking, Migration and the Law' (n 28) 923–37; Buckland, 'Human Trafficking and Smuggling' (n 24) 152–62. The distinction between consensual smuggling and coerced trafficking has been also criticized as perpetuating gendered stereotypes, 'consent is an issue in the Trafficking Protocol because it is largely seen as an instrument to protect the stereotypical "trafficked woman." Conversely, consent is a non-issue in the Smuggling Protocol because the stereotypical "smuggled person" is perceived, even if incorrectly, as a male economic migrant who has weighed his options and chosen to migrate for better economic opportunities, which he can seek himself because he is not under the control of traffickers once he reaches his destination', see K Abramson, 'Beyond Consent, Towards Safeguarding Human Rights: Implementing the United Nations Trafficking Protocol' (2003) 44 Harv Int'l L J 473, 479. See also I van Liempt, 'Different Geographies and Experiences of "Assisted" Types of Migration: A Gendered Critique on the Distinction between Trafficking and Smuggling' (2011) 18(2) Gender, Place, and Culture 179, 193.

[46] Trafficking Protocol (n 1) art 5(1); Smuggling Protocol (n 1) art 6(1).

[47] Trafficking Protocol (n 1) art 5(2); Smuggling Protocol (n 1) art 6(2).

[48] United Nations Convention against Transnational Organized Crime (adopted 8 January, entered into force 29 September 2003) (Organized Crime Convention) 2225 UNTS 209 art 8.

the laundering of the proceeds of smuggling and trafficking as criminal offences.[49] All States Parties are also required to ensure the liability of legal persons[50] and to co-operate with one another in the investigation, prosecution, and judicial proceedings through joint investigations,[51] mutual legal assistance,[52] and extradition.[53]

Despite this common pattern, the duty of criminalization is broader in the Smuggling than in the Trafficking Protocol. While the latter only criminalizes trafficking in persons as such, the former further requires the criminalization of additional offences related to smuggling. They include the acts of producing, procuring, providing, or possessing a fraudulent travel or identity document for the purpose of enabling the smuggling of migrants, as well as the conduct of 'enabling a person who is not a national or a permanent resident to remain in the state concerned without complying with the necessary requirements for legally remaining in the state by [illegal] means [...]'.[54] Furthermore, contrary to the Trafficking Protocol, each State Party to the Smuggling Protocol is required to establish aggravating circumstances to the crime of smuggling and other related offences. They include any conduct that is likely to, or does, endanger the lives and safety of the concerned migrants as well as any inhuman or degrading treatment, including exploitation.[55]

In order to compensate for the broad repressive scope of the Smuggling Protocol, Article 5 underlines that 'migrants shall not become liable to criminal prosecution under this Protocol for the fact of having been the object of conduct set forth in article 6 of this Protocol.' Thus, the duty of criminalization enshrined in the Smuggling Protocol focuses on smugglers, not migrants themselves. Article 5 further clarifies that illegal entry does not constitute a criminal offence on its own and that, even if it falls within the scope of smuggling, migrants are exempted from prosecution for all the offences listed in Article 6.[56] The Legislative Guides acknowledge that:

> [It was] the intention of the drafters that the sanctions established in accordance with the Protocol should apply to the smuggling of migrants by organized criminal groups and not to mere migration or migrants, even in cases where it involves entry or residence that is illegal under the laws of the State concerned [...]. Mere illegal entry may be a crime in some countries, but it is not recognized as a form of organized crime and is hence beyond the scope of the Convention and its Protocols.[57]

The resulting distinction between smuggling and irregular migration however remains very subtle and highly relative. Article 5 does not grant blanket immunity to smuggled migrants as they may be prosecuted for another offence under domestic law. Indeed, Article 6(4) of the Smuggling Protocol preserves the margin of

---

[49] ibid art 6.   [50] ibid art 10.   [51] ibid art 19.   [52] ibid art 18.
[53] ibid art 16.   [54] Smuggling Protocol (n 1) arts 6(1)(b) and (c).
[55] ibid art 6(3). Though not required by the Trafficking Protocol, the Model Law against Trafficking in Persons recommends an optional provision in domestic law on aggravating circumstances when, for instance, trafficking involves serious injury or death of the victim or when the victim is particularly vulnerable. See UNODC, 'Model Law against Trafficking' (n 8) 38–39.
[56] Likewise, and as confirmed by an Interpretative Note, a migrant who possessed a fraudulent document to enable his or her own smuggling falls outside the scope of art 6. See UNODC, *Travaux Préparatoires* (n 4) 489.
[57] UNODC, *Legislative Guides* (n 20) 340.

appreciation of states, by stressing that 'nothing in this Protocol shall prevent a State Party from taking measures against a person whose conduct constitutes an offence under its domestic law'. The Legislative Guides confirm in this sense that:

The Protocol itself takes a neutral position on whether those who migrate illegally should be the subject of any offences: article 5 ensures that nothing in the Protocol itself can be interpreted as requiring the criminalization of mere migrants or of conduct likely to be engaged in by mere migrants as opposed to members of or those linked to organized criminal groups. At the same time, article 6, paragraph 4, ensures that nothing in the Protocol limits the existing rights of each State party to take measures against persons whose conduct constitutes an offence under its domestic law.[58]

In short, while States Parties are prohibited from prosecuting migrants for offences established by the Protocol, they still retain the possibility to do so for other offences under domestic law, such as irregular entry. Even assuming that this literal interpretation of the Smuggling Protocol is correct, states are bound by other applicable rules of international law, including the prohibition of penalty for irregular entry as endorsed in the Refugee Convention. Although Article 5 of the Smuggling Protocol and Article 31 of the Refugee Convention are mutually supportive and overlap to some extent, their respective scope are not the same. On the one hand, the former is broader than the latter for two reasons. Article 5 applies to any smuggled migrants, not only refugees or asylum seekers. Furthermore, Article 5 is not qualified by the three cumulative conditions of its refugee law counterpart, including the requirement to come directly from a country of persecution.[59] On the other hand, the prohibition contained in Article 31 of the Refugee Convention extends to any penalty for irregular entry, even when it constitutes an offence under domestic law.

Strangely enough, the Trafficking Protocol does not contain any similar provision to Article 5 of the Smuggling Protocol. Non-criminalization of trafficked persons is nonetheless inherent in their status of victims as inferred from Articles 6 to 9 of the Protocol. This finds additional support in the very purpose of the Protocol 'to protect and assist the victims of such trafficking, with full respect for their human rights' (Article 2(b)), as well as in the subsequent interpretation of many stakeholders. Alongside the views of the Working Group on Trafficking in Persons (established by the Conference of States Parties),[60] the Model Law against Trafficking in Persons endorses the principle of non-criminalization for offences committed as a direct consequence of their situation as trafficked persons and for immigration offences under domestic law.[61] A similar interpretation has been acknowledged in a broad range

[58] ibid 347.
[59] For further discussion, see notably JC Hathaway, 'Prosecuting a Refugee for "Smuggling" Himself' (2014) University of Michigan Public Law Research Paper No 429; A Schloenhardt and H Hickson, 'Non-Criminalization of Smuggled Migrants: Rights, Obligations, and Australian Practice under Article 5 of the Protocol against the Smuggling of Migrants by Land, Sea, and Air' (2013) 25(1) IJRIL 39–64.
[60] UN Conference of the Parties to the United Nations Convention against Transnational Organized Crime, Working Group on Trafficking in Persons, 'Non-Punishment and Non-Prosecution of Victims of Trafficking in Persons: Administrative and Judicial Approaches to Offences Committed in the Process of Such Trafficking' (9 December 2009) UN Doc CTOC/COP/WG.4/2010/4, paras 10–11.
[61] UNODC, 'Model Law against Trafficking in Persons' (n 8) 42.

of soft law instruments, including many General Assembly resolutions[62] and the OHCHR Recommended Principles and Guidelines on Human Rights and Human Trafficking.[63]

Scholars diverge on whether non-criminalization of trafficked persons has become 'a widely accepted normative standard'[64] or if 'it is premature to speak of an established principle'.[65] The former view is more in line with the general principles of interpretation codified in the Vienna Convention on the Law of Treaties. Non-criminalization of trafficked persons naturally stems from a good faith interpretation of the Protocol in accordance with its objective and context as confirmed by subsequent instruments. This interpretation has been recently endorsed by the Global Compact for Migration, where states commit to 'strengthen legislation to … avoid criminalization of migrants who are victims of trafficking in persons for trafficking-related offences'.[66]

In any case, the non-criminalization of trafficked persons remains an explicit duty for States Parties to the ILO Protocol to the Forced Labour Convention,[67] the Council of Europe Convention on Action against Trafficking in Human Beings,[68] and Directive 2011/36/EU of the European Parliament and of the Council of 5

---

[62] See, among other instances, Trafficking in women and girls, UNGA Res 63/156 (30 January 2009) UN Doc A/RES/63/156, para 12; Trafficking in women and girls, UNGA Res 65/190 (21 December 2010) UN Doc A/RES/65/190, para 17; Further Actions and Initiatives to Implement the Beijing Declaration and Platform for Action, UNGA Res S-23/3 (16 November 2000) UN Doc A/RES/S-23/3, para 70(c); Trafficking in women and girls, UNGA Res 67/145 (20 December 2012) UN Doc A/RES/67/145, para 20; Trafficking in women and girls, UNGA Res 69/149 (18 December 2014) UN Doc A/RES/69/149, para 25.

[63] See especially principle 7, 'Trafficked persons shall not be detained, charged or prosecuted for the illegality of their entry into or residence in countries of transit and destination, or for their involvement in unlawful activities to the extent that such involvement is a direct consequence of their situation as trafficked persons.' Among many other soft law instruments adopted at the regional level, see, for example, OSCE Action Plan to Combat Trafficking in Human Beings (2 December 2003) MC.DEC/2/03, recommendation 1.8; Conclusions and Recommendations of the Meeting of National Authorities on Trafficking in Persons, adopted at the 1st meeting by the Permanent Council of the Organisation of American States (26 April 2006) OEA/Ser.K/XXXIX, section IV(7); Brussels Declaration on Preventing and Combating Trafficking in Human Beings, adopted by the European Conference on Preventing and Combating Trafficking in Human Beings (20 September 2002) 10, para 13; Ouagadougou Action Plan to Combat Trafficking in Human Beings, Especially Women and Children, adopted at the Ministerial Conference on Migration and Development by the European Union and African States (22–23 November 2006) (Ouagadougou Action Plan) 4.

[64] Gallagher, *The International Law of Human Trafficking* (n 30) 285.

[65] A Schloenhardt and R Markey-Towler, 'Non-Criminalisation of Victims of Trafficking in Persons: Principles, Promises, and Perspectives' (2016) 4(1) Groningen Journal of International Law 10, 37.

[66] Global Compact for Safe, Orderly and Regular Migration (13 July 2018) para 26(g) available at https://refugeesmigrants.un.org/sites/default/files/180713_agreed_outcome_global_compact_for_migration.pdf accessed 12 October 2018.

[67] According to its art 4(2), 'each Member shall, in accordance with the basic principles of its legal system, take the necessary measures to ensure that competent authorities are entitled not to prosecute or impose penalties on victims of forced or compulsory labour for their involvement in unlawful activities which they have been compelled to commit as a direct consequence of being subjected to forced or compulsory labour'.

[68] Art 26 acknowledges that 'each Party shall, in accordance with the basic principles of its legal system, provide for the possibility of not imposing penalties on victims for their involvement in unlawful activities, to the extent that they have been compelled to do so'.

April 2011 on preventing and combating trafficking in human beings and protecting its victims.[69] While these treaty provisions express a broad acceptance of
non-criminalization, none explicitly refers to immigration offences under domestic
law. The silence of both Protocols on this last issue unveils another key objective of
the fight against trafficking and smuggling: the criminalization of smuggling and
trafficking works in tandem with the strengthening of immigration control.

5.2.2 The reinforcement of immigration control

The Palermo Protocols rely on the preconceived idea that tighter border controls
can prevent migrants from being smuggled or trafficked. This simplistic assumption remains highly debatable because restrictive immigration laws are more likely
to exacerbate the smuggling and trafficking of migrants than the contrary. Anne
Gallagher observes in this sense that:

> Many governments ignore the fact that irregular migration (including trafficking and mi-
> grant smuggling) happens because of the enormous difference between the number of people
> who wish (or are forced) to migrate and the legal opportunities for them to do so. There is a
> growing body of evidence that severely restrictive immigration policies are more likely to fuel
> organised, irregular migration than to stop it.[70]

The same opinion is shared by many stakeholders, including, for instance, the
Special Rapporteur on Trafficking in Persons, who notes that:

> There is a strong causal link between restrictive immigration policies and trafficking. [...]
> While a number of States have deployed immigration control and border security measures
> in response to the smuggling of and trafficking in persons, such measures are often counter-
> productive, as many prospective migrants are not deterred by them and would rely on inter-
> mediaries to facilitate their entry to destination countries through informal and clandestine
> channels.[71]

Despite this well-known evidence, the Palermo Protocols refrain from promoting
safe and legal pathways to migrate as an effective means to combat irregular migration. Instead, the measures adopted in the Protocols to prevent irregular migration closely follow a control-oriented approach. They include, for example, a public

---

[69] 'Article 8—Non-prosecution or non-application of penalties to the victim Member States shall,
in accordance with the basic principles of their legal systems, take the necessary measures to ensure that
competent national authorities are entitled not to prosecute or impose penalties on victims of trafficking
in human beings for their involvement in criminal activities which they have been compelled to commit
as a direct consequence of being subjected to any of the acts referred to in Article 2.'

[70] AT Gallagher, 'Trafficking, Smuggling and Human Rights: Tricks and Treaties' (2002) 12 Forced
Migration Review 25, 28. Among many other similar accounts, see, for instance, A Zalewski, 'Migrants
for Sale: The International Failure to Address Contemporary Human Trafficking' (2005) 29 Suffolk
Transnat'l L Rev 113, 135; JM Chacon, 'Tensions and Trade-offs: Protecting Trafficking Victims in
the Era of Immigration Enforcement' (2010) 158(6) U Pa L Rev 1609, 1653; J Doomernik, 'Migrant
Smuggling between Two Logics: Migration Dynamics and State Policies' (2013) 48(3) The International
Spectator 113–29.

[71] UNGA 'Trafficking in Persons, Especially Women and Children: A Note by the Secretary General'
(9 August 2010) UN Doc A/65/288, 8.

campaign to prevent potential migrants from becoming smuggled and development programmes aiming at combating the root causes of migration, such as poverty.[72] As noted by several commentators, these provisions are 'largely aspirational'[73] and 'it is difficult to discern, from those texts, any sense of legal obligation on the part of States to take such measures'.[74]

This begs the question whether the Palermo Protocols are nothing else than a pretext to export the immigration control agenda of Western states, as frequently advanced by scholars.[75] After all, the Protocols are the only universal treaties providing such a particularly broad and detailed set of duties to carry out and reinforce immigration control. This comprehensive regime typically focuses on three types of measures: border control, identity and travel documents, and return.

Regarding the first set of measures, Article 11(1) of the two Protocols requires all States Parties to 'strengthen [...] such border controls as may be necessary to prevent and detect the smuggling of migrants' and 'trafficking in persons'. The insertion of this provision was requested by the US and Argentina with the support of Australia and Canada.[76] Its final version establishes a far-reaching obligation for States Parties across the world, although its content remains broad and evasive. Contrary to many other provisions, its scope has not been refined by the Legislative Guides or the Model Laws against the Smuggling of Migrants and Trafficking in Persons. Article 11(1) provides only two qualifications, albeit vague and limited, thus leaving States Parties with a significant margin of appreciation. The first qualification requires strengthened border controls 'to the extent possible' in order to take into account the varying means and resources available to each state, as well as the practical difficulties relating to the nature of borders which may raise further challenges in such controls.[77] Second, it requires the reinforcement of border controls 'without prejudice to international commitments in relation to the free movement of people'.

This last caveat is unduly limited to free movement agreements and fails to consider many other relevant rules of international law that restrict the competence of states to carry out border controls. During the drafting process, several UN agencies rightly expressed their concern about the need to ensure that border control measures 'do not impinge upon the human rights of individuals as set out in the major international instruments, including the International Covenant on Civil and Political Rights, the Convention relating to the Status of Refugees of 1951 and the Convention on the Rights of the Child.'[78] This omission was ultimately resolved through the insertion of saving clauses in both Protocols, acknowledging that they

---

[72] Smuggling Protocol (n 1) art 15(2)–(3); Trafficking Protocol (n 1) art 9(2)–(4).

[73] McClean, *Transnational Organized Crime* (n 4) 425.

[74] Gallagher and David, *The International Law of Migrant Smuggling* (n 13) 502.

[75] See, among many others, Hathaway, 'The Human Rights Quagmire' (n 35) 25–26; Chacon, 'Tensions and Trade-offs' (n 70) 1619 and 1642; M Lee, 'Human Trafficking and Border Control in the Global South' in K Franko Aas and M Bosworth (eds), *The Borders of Punishment: Migration, Citizenship and Social Exclusion* (OUP 2013) 128–45.

[76] UNODC, *Travaux Préparatoires* (n 4) 403.

[77] McClean, *Transnational Organized Crime* (n 4) 358.

[78] UNGA 'Note by OHCHR, UNICEF and IOM' (n 29) 4.

shall not affect any other obligation of states under international law.[79] Despite this general acknowledgement, the limited qualification of Article 11(1) exemplifies the enduring misperceptions surrounding the role of international law when it comes to border controls.

While being astonishingly vague about the limitations imposed by international law, the other provisions contained in Article 11 prove to be more explicit concerning the measures to be taken to strengthen border controls. They typically include the denial of entry or revocation of visas of persons implicated in the commission of the offences established by the Protocols (Article 11(5)), as well as strengthening the co-operation among border control agencies of States Parties by, inter alia, establishing and maintaining direct channels of communication (Article 11(6)).[80] Furthermore, following the practice of Western countries since the 1980s, all States Parties shall commit commercial carriers to ascertain that all passengers are in possession of re-quired travel documents for entry (Article 11(3)). As underlined by the relevant Interpretative Note, this provision 'requires States Parties to impose an obligation on commercial carriers only to ascertain whether or not passengers have the neces-sary documents in their possession and not to make any judgement or assessment of the validity or authenticity of the documents'.[81]

Despite this last caveat, the personal scope of this obligation remains extensive and goes well beyond the ambit of the Palermo Protocol as it concerns all passengers and not only those who are trafficked or smuggled. The Interpretative Note further recalls that the obligation imposed upon commercial carriers 'does not unduly limit the discretion of States parties not to hold carriers liable for transporting undocu-mented refugees'.[82] Such a discretion is not mandatory, as further confirmed by the Legislative Guides,[83] which further begs the question of its compatibility with the duty enshrined in Article 31 of the Refugee Convention.

Alongside border measures imposed by both Protocols, specific attention is also paid to the smuggling of migrants by sea. Articles 7 to 9 of the Smuggling Protocol establish a detailed regime of cooperation and law enforcement which does not fundamentally depart from the existing rules already provided under the law of the sea.[84] The novelty of the Smuggling Protocol, however, cannot be underestimated. For the first time in international law, states are authorized to intercept certain ves-sels suspected of carrying smuggled migrants. By contrast, the UN Convention on the Law of the Sea only permits such interceptions on the high seas for the crimes of slavery, piracy, illicit traffic in psychotropic substances, and unauthorized

---

[79] Smuggling Protocol (n 1) art 19; Trafficking Protocol (n 1) art 14.
[80] Exchange of information between States Parties is further detailed in both Protocols, (n 79) art 10.
[81] UNODC, *Travaux Préparatoires* (n 4) 521.   [82] ibid.
[83] UNODC, *Legislative Guides* (n 20) 298 and 374.
[84] For further discussion about the content of these rules, see especially: V Moreno-Lax and E Papastavridis (eds), *'Boat Refugees' and Migrants at Sea: A Comprehensive Approach. Integrating Maritime Security with Human Rights* (Brill 2017); I Mann, *Humanity at Sea: Maritime Migration and the Foundations of International Law* (CUP 2016); P Mallia, *Migrant Smuggling by Sea: Combatting a Current Threat to Maritime Security Through the Creation of a Cooperative Framework* (Martinus Nijhoff 2010); Gallagher and David, *The International Law of Migrant Smuggling* (n 13) 403–89.

broadcasting therefrom.[85] The new ground of interception at sea, combined with the duties mentioned above to control borders by land and air, establish a unique and comprehensive treaty law regime reflecting the concerns of destination states.

The strengthening of immigration control is supplemented by a second set of measures that focuses on travel and identity documents. The overall logic remains the same: the two Protocols commit all States Parties to ensure the integrity and security of travel or identity documents in order to make immigration control more efficient. According to their common Article 12(a), '[e]ach State Party shall take such measures as may be necessary [...] to ensure that travel and identity documents [...] are of such quality that they cannot easily be misused and cannot readily be falsified, or unlawfully altered, replicated or issued'. This obligation is quite extensive and comprises a broad range of situations. According to the relevant Interpretative Note, it includes not only the creation of false documents, but also the alteration of legitimate documents, the completion of blank documents, and the use of valid documents by a person other than the lawful holder.[86] Article 13 of both Protocols further obliges States Parties, when requested by another State Party, to 'verify within a reasonable time the legitimacy and validity of travel or identity documents issued or purported to have been issued in its name [...]'.

The third and last battery of measures focuses on the return of smuggled migrants and the repatriation of trafficked persons. Whether labelled repatriation or return, the two Protocols largely follow the same pattern. The key provision introduced at the initiative of the US[87] establishes a duty of readmission for countries of origin. According to Article 18(1) of the Smuggling Protocol and Article 8(1) of its Trafficking counterpart, each State Party agrees to facilitate and accept, without undue or unreasonable delay, the return of smuggled migrants and trafficked persons who are its nationals. Such a straightforward duty reflects a major concern and demand of Western states in order to facilitate the enforcement of removals toward countries of origin. Though adopted with some reluctance,[88] the importance and novelty of this duty should not be underestimated. The Palermo Protocols are indeed the only treaties concluded at the universal level that provide a duty of readmission.

This duty is conceived in particularly broad terms, as it is not only limited to nationals but also includes permanent residents.[89] This last category of persons slightly diverges from one instrument to the other regarding the time-frame of those eligible

---

[85] See Convention on the Law of the Sea (adopted 10 December 1982, entered into force 16 November 1994) 1833 UNTS 3 arts 99–109 and 110.

[86] UNODC, *Travaux Préparatoires* (n 4) 525.   [87] ibid 547.

[88] During the drafting process, 'some delegations expressed the view that making provision for the return of migrants was necessary as a means of deterring migrants and organized criminal groups and also to ensure the right of the migrants themselves to return to their place of origin. Other delegations proposed either deletion or modification on the basis that the provision was beyond the mandate given to the Ad Hoc Committee by the General Assembly and that it unfairly placed the burden on the migrants themselves.' ibid 548.

[89] According to the relevant Interpretative Notes, the term 'permanent residence' is understood 'as meaning long-term, but not necessarily indefinite residence', and is without prejudice to any domestic legislation regarding both the granting of the right of residence and the duration of residence. See UNODC, *Travaux Préparatoires* (n 4) 388 and 552.

to permanent residence. The Trafficking Protocol embraces any person who 'had the right of permanent residence at the time of entry into the territory of the receiving State', whereas the Smuggling Protocol only refers to a person who 'has the right of permanent residence in its territory at the time of return'. States Parties to the Smuggling Protocol still have the possibility—but not the duty—to readmit those who had the right of permanent residence at the time of entry (Article 18(2)). Though it seems more accidental than deliberate,[90] this variation in the scope of the two Protocols makes their implementation unduly complicated. Furthermore, as a result of this hiatus, trafficked persons may be in a more precarious position than smuggled migrants. As noted by the Legislative Guides, 'a person who had residency status on entering the country of destination but who has subsequently lost it could be repatriated if he or she is also a victim of trafficking but not if he or she is a smuggled migrant or illegal resident'.[91]

More fundamentally, returning trafficked persons is at odds with their very status of victims as recognized by the Protocol. One can hardly contest that '[t]here is something offensive in the notion that a victim, compelled by illicit force to move to another State, should then be compelled, albeit by legitimate force, to move once again'.[92] It is true that, in contrast to the Smuggling Protocol, the return of trafficked persons 'shall preferably be voluntary', according to Article 8(2) of the Trafficking Protocol. Yet, this preference for voluntary return is neutralized by an Interpretative Note highlighting that it does not create any obligation on the State Party returning the victims.[93] The resulting convergence between the two Protocols regarding the forced removal of trafficked persons and smuggled migrants does not only undermine the alleged difference between trafficking and smuggling. It also unveils a prevalent feature of the Palermo Protocols: they are conceived less as instruments of criminal justice than as vehicles of migration control.

Although none of the Protocols explicitly endorses a duty of forced removal, both instruments have been primarily conceived as a way to facilitate it. The duty of readmission has been specifically established against the background of forced removals. Indeed, there was no need for such a legal basis concerning voluntary return, as it is already enshrined in the right to enter one's own country under human rights law treaties. Furthermore, the alternative to forced or voluntary return, namely the grant of a residence permit, is not envisaged by the Smuggling Protocol. The Trafficking Protocol provides this possibility, but its Article 7 remains very permissive for States Parties and fails to establish any clear-cut obligation to grant a residence permit to victims of trafficking.[94]

---

[90] According to the Legislative Guides, '[t]his difference arises from positions taken by delegations during the negotiations and the fact that the language of the provisions was developed at separate times, but it does not arise from any particular policy objective of the Ad Hoc Committee as a whole, which negotiated both instruments'. UNODC, *Legislative Guides* (n 20) 312.

[91] ibid 311.   [92] McClean, *Transnational Organized Crime* (n 4) 347–48.

[93] UNODC, *Travaux Préparatoires* (n 4) 388.

[94] According to art 7 'each State Party shall consider adopting legislative or other appropriate measures that permit victims of trafficking in persons to remain in its territory, temporarily or permanently, in appropriate cases'.

By contrast, the Palermo Protocols create a clear incentive for States Parties to carry out forced removals of smuggled and trafficked migrants. The far-reaching duty of readmission contained therein is reinforced by two additional obligations addressed to countries of origin. At the request of a receiving State Party, any State Party must verify whether the person is one of its nationals or permanent residents and, in such a case, the State Party shall issue any travel documents or other authorizations needed to permit his or her return.[95] This robust regime aimed at facilitating removals is only qualified by very few and vague constraints. The Protocols merely require taking into account the safety of the person who is returned,[96] while recalling that their provisions are without prejudice to any right afforded by domestic and international law.[97]

5.3   The International Protection of Trafficked Persons and Smuggled Migrants

The protection of trafficked persons and smuggled migrants constitutes the weakest point of the Palermo Protocols. Their strong focus on crime and immigration control has relegated the issue of protection to a marginal consideration, even if protecting human rights of trafficked persons and smuggled migrants is explicitly listed as an objective of the two Protocols.[98]

5.3.1   The limits of protection in the Palermo Protocols

The initial drafts of the Smuggling Protocol did not contain any specific provision on protection.[99] The inclusion of such a provision resulted from the intervention of several UN agencies urging the drafters to do so.[100] The final version of Article 16 still reflects the reluctance of states to protect smuggled migrants in a comprehensive and robust way. Article 16 of the Smuggling Protocol does not only fail to establish any new duties for States Parties, it is also couched in such vague and

---

[95]   Trafficking Protocol (n 1) art 8(3)–(4); Smuggling Protocol (n 1) art 18(3)–(4).

[96]   Trafficking Protocol (n 1) art 8(1)–(2); Smuggling Protocol (n 1) art 18(4).

[97]   Trafficking Protocol (n 1) art 8(5)–(6); Smuggling Protocol (n 1) art 18(7)–(8).

[98]   For a similar account, see, for instance, T Obokata, 'Human Trafficking' in N Boister and RJ Currie, *Routledge Handbook of Transnational Criminal Law* (Routledge 2015) 178; A Schloenhardt and KL Stacey, 'Assistance and Protection of Smuggled Migrants: International Law and Australian Practice' (2013) 35 Syd LR 53, 64; Zalewski, 'Migrants for Sale' (n 70) 130.

[99]   UNGA, Ad Hoc Committee on the Elaboration of a Convention against Transnational Organized Crime, 'Draft Elements for an International Legal Instrument against Illegal Trafficking and Transport of Migrants' (15 December 1998) UN Doc A/AC.254/4/Add.l; UNGA, Ad Hoc Committee on the Elaboration of a Convention against Transnational Organised Crime, 'Revised Draft Protocol against the Smuggling of Migrants by Land, Air and Sea, supplementing the United Nations Convention against Transnational Organized Crime' (23 November 1999) UN Doc A/AC.254/4/Add.1/Rev.4.

[100]   See especially UNGA, Ad Hoc Committee on the Elaboration of a Convention against Transnational Organized Crime, 'Informal Note by the United Nations High Commissioner for Human Rights' (1 June 1999) UN Doc A/AC.254/16; UNGA, 'Note by OHCHR, UNICEF and IOM' (n 29).

permissive terms that it might even pose the risk of undermining existing obligations of international law.

Article 16(1) of the Smuggling Protocol merely underlines that States Parties shall take 'all appropriate measures, including legislation if necessary, to preserve and protect the rights [of smuggled migrants] as accorded under applicable international law, in particular the right to life and the right not to be subjected to torture or other cruel, inhuman or degrading treatment or punishment'. This basic restatement adds nothing to what is already provided under existing human rights law, and does not specify the type and content of the relevant 'appropriate measures' to be adopted by states. As underlined by the relevant Interpretative Note, 'this paragraph should not be understood as imposing any new or additional obligations on States parties to this protocol beyond those contained in existing international instruments and customary international law'.[101]

The same Interpretative Note further observes that the explicit reference to the right to life and freedom from torture and related mistreatments in Article 16(1) shall be without prejudice to any other applicable right that is not listed therein.[102] Although both the Legislative Guides and the UN Model Law fail to provide a comprehensive list of rights,[103] all human rights are presumably applicable to smuggled migrants except for the very few rights that are conditional upon nationality or lawful presence (eg freedom of movement within the territory of a state). The same observation shall apply to the relevant ILO instruments, whether they are general in scope or specific to migration.

The other provisions of Article 16 embrace the same vague language. Its second and third paragraphs call for States Parties to protect smuggled migrants from violence and assist those whose life or safety is in danger for being the object of smuggling. None of these provisions contains specific guidance about the nature and type of protection. This broad margin of appreciation is exacerbated by the loose wording of Article 16(2) and (3): States Parties are only required to provide protection when considered 'appropriate'. The Legislative Guides are silent on what should be considered 'appropriate' to protect smuggled migrants, and the Model Law concurs by acknowledging that:

> The Protocol does not provide guidance on what is meant by 'appropriate measures' of protection. This will need to be decided at the national level, bearing in mind the types of violence likely to be inflicted on smuggled migrants, the situations where violence may arise, the communities and individuals that may be affected, and the resources that are available to respond to these issues.[104]

The only two provisions of Article 16 that do not refer to this imprecise notion of 'appropriate assistance' are still very general and equivocal. The fourth paragraph merely restates that the provisions of Article 16 shall be implemented taking into

---

[101] UNODC, *Travaux Préparatoires* (n 4) 541.   [102] ibid.
[103] The UN Model Law only refers, as a possible example, to access to emergency medical care deriving from the right to life. See UNODC, *Model Law against Smuggling of Migrants* (n 11) 65–66.
[104] ibid 67.

account the special needs of women and children, while the fifth paragraph allows States Parties to detain smuggled migrants as long as they are afforded consular access in accordance with the 1963 Vienna Convention on Consular Relations. The more robust and detailed obligations governing detention under human rights law are astonishingly not mentioned, although they remain plainly applicable as confirmed by the saving clause of Article 19.

The provisions of the Trafficking Protocol devoted to protection and assistance are more detailed and specific than those of the Smuggling Protocol. They suffer, however, from the same weakness: the provisions contained in Article 6 of the Trafficking Protocol are either optional or heavily qualified. For instance, while listing a broad range of protective measures (including housing, counselling, medical assistance, employment, and education opportunities), Article 6(3) is discretionary as States Parties are only supposed to 'consider implementing [such] measures'. Article 6(5) stipulates in the same vein that States Parties shall 'endeavour to provide' for the physical safety of trafficked persons. Even when the wording of other provisions appears to be mandatory, it remains carefully qualified by several expressions that considerably undermine its binding force. This is notably exemplified by Article 6(1): 'In appropriate cases and to the extent possible under its domestic law, each State Party shall protect the privacy and identity of victims of trafficking in persons.'

5.3.2 The saving clauses of the Palermo Protocols: a case for an integrated approach to international migration law

Against this weak framework of protection, the main source of rights and entitlements for smuggled and trafficked migrants must be found elsewhere than in the Palermo Protocols, that is, in the other applicable rules of international law. This highlights the need for a systemic and integrated approach to articulate and supplement the Palermo Protocols with the other duties of States Parties under international law.[105] This approach finds its legal basis in the Protocols themselves. The saving clauses contained in Article 14(1) of the Trafficking Protocol and Article 19(1) of the Smuggling Protocol underline that:

---

[105] For a similar account, see especially C Thomas, 'Convergences and Divergences in International Legal Norms on Migrant Labor' (2011) 32 Comp Lab L & Pol'y J 405, 441; A Edwards, 'Traffic in Human Being: At the Intersection of Criminal Justice, Human Rights, Asylum/Migration and Labor' (2008) 36 Denv J Int'l L & Pol'y 9–53; J Fitzpatrick, 'Trafficking as a Human Rights Violation: The Complex Intersection of Legal Frameworks for Conceptualizing and Combating Trafficking' (2003) 24 Mich J Int'l L 1143–67. For further discussion about the role and importance of international human rights law in the context of trafficking and smuggling, see also, among a vast literature, R Piotrowicz, 'States' Obligations under Human Rights Law towards Victims of Trafficking in Human Beings: Positive Developments in Positive Obligations' (2012) 24 IJRL 181–201; Gallagher, *The International Law of Human Trafficking* (n 30) 144–217; Gallagher and David, *The International Law of Migrant Smuggling* (n 13) 125–201; T Obokata, *Trafficking of Human Beings from a Human Rights Perspective: towards a Holistic Approach* (Martinus Nijhoff 2006); T Obokata, 'Smuggling of Human Beings from a Human Rights Perspective: Obligations of Non-State and State Actors under International Human Rights Law' (2005) 17 IJRL 394–415.

Nothing in this Protocol shall affect the rights, obligations and responsibilities of States and individuals under international law, including international humanitarian law and international human rights law and, in particular, where applicable, the 1951 Convention and the 1967 Protocol relating to the Status of Refugees and the principle of *non-refoulement* as contained therein.[106]

The significance of this clause should not be underestimated. Restating the plain applicability of the other relevant rules of international law does not only fill the protection gap of the two Protocols. The very existence of this saving clause also establishes an order of priority in case of conflict between these other applicable rules and the Protocols. According to the customary law principle notably endorsed in Article 30(2) of the Vienna Convention on the Law of Treaties,[107] these other applicable rules of international law shall prevail over those established in the Palermo Protocols. Thus, for instance, the Palermo Protocols can be neither invoked nor implemented to unduly restrict or compromise the right to leave any country, the prohibition of collective expulsion and arbitrary detention, as well as the principle of *non-refoulement*.

More generally, both smuggled migrants and trafficked persons are plainly entitled to the whole panoply of human rights and other related guarantees recognized by international law (except for the few rules that require citizenship or lawful status). The duty of states to protect them under general human rights instruments has been regularly restated by UN treaty bodies.[108] The Model Law against the Smuggling of Migrants also acknowledges in this sense that:

Regardless of their immigration status, smuggled migrants have certain inalienable rights arising from international law. These rights are defined in key international treaties, including the International Covenant on Civil and Political Rights, the International Covenant on

[106] The second paragraph further restates that the Protocol shall be interpreted and applied in a way that is not discriminatory. The relevant Interpretative Notes highlight that 'any State that becomes a party to this protocol but is not a party to another international instrument referred to in [the saving clause of] the protocol would not become subject to any right, obligation or responsibility under that instrument'. In practice, however, the vast majority of States Parties have ratified several treaties of human rights law, humanitarian law, and/or refugee law. Furthermore, customary international law clearly falls within the scope of the saving clause and remains plainly binding for all States Parties to the Palermo Protocols.

[107] Vienna Convention on the Law of Treaties (adopted 23 May 1969, entered into force 27 January 1980) 1155 UNTS 331 art 30(2) provides that 'when a treaty specifies that it is subject to, or that it is not to be considered as incompatible with, an earlier or later treaty, the provisions of that other treaty prevail'.

[108] HRC 'Concluding observations on the sixth periodic report of Chile' (13 August 2014) UN Doc CCPR/C/CHL/CO/6, para 20; HRC, 'Concluding Observations: Belgium' (12 August 2004) UN Doc CCPR/CO/81/BEL, para 15; UN Committee on the Elimination of Discrimination against Women (CEDAW Committee), 'Concluding observations on the fourth and fifth periodic reports of Eritrea' (12 March 2015) UN Doc CEDAW/C/ERI/CO/5, paras 8 and 2; CEDAW Committee, 'Concluding observations: Argentina' (12–13 July 2010) UN Doc CEDAW/C/ARG/CO/6, para 46; UN Committee on the Rights of the Child (CRC Committee), 'Concluding observations: Costa Rica' (2 May 2007) UN Doc CRC/C/OPSC/CRI/CO/1, para 21; CMW, 'Concluding observations: Mexico' (3 May 2011) UN Doc CMW/C/MEX/CO/2 paras 41 and 50. See also, among others, CESCR, 'General Comment No 20, Non Discrimination in economic, social and cultural rights' (2 July 2009) UN Doc E/C.12/GC/20 para 30.

Economic, Social and Cultural Rights, the Convention against Torture and Other Cruel, Inhuman or Degrading Treatment or Punishment, the Convention on the Elimination of All Forms of Discrimination against Women, the International Convention on the Elimination of All Forms of Racial Discrimination and customary international law. More specific protections relating to the standards of treatment of persons outside their country of origin are provided in the Convention relating to the Status of Refugees and the 1967 Protocol Relating to the Status of Refugees, the Convention on the Rights of the Child and the International Convention on the Protection of the Rights of All Migrant Workers and Members of Their Families. As recognized in the Protocol, States parties have agreed to ensure that these rights are not compromised in any way by the implementation of anti-smuggling measures.[109]

The same observation applies *mutatis mutandis* to victims of trafficking, as notably restated by the Recommended Guidelines on Human Rights and Human Trafficking adopted by the OHCHR in 2002.[110]

Furthermore, as explicitly recognized by the saving clauses of the two Protocols, both trafficked persons and smuggled migrants may fall within the refugee definition under the 1951 Convention. This is especially the case when there is a risk of retaliation, re-trafficking, or other serious violations of human rights that typically amount to an act of persecution in their own country.[111] Inversely, an asylum seeker may be trafficked or smuggled irrespective of his or her eligibility for refugee status.[112] Moreover, those who are not recognized as refugees under the 1951 Convention still benefit from the principle of *non-refoulement* under human rights law when there is a real risk of torture, inhuman, or degrading treatment, or of other severe violations of human rights in the country of origin.

Trafficked and smuggled migrants might also fall within the definition of a migrant worker. Similar to eligibility for refugee status, there is no automaticity. Their

---

[109] UNODC, *Model Law against Smuggling of Migrants* (n 11) 8 (footnotes omitted). This list of treaties identified above is not exhaustive. It also includes the ILO conventions and regional human rights conventions among others applicable treaties.

[110] 'Anti-trafficking measures should not adversely affect the human rights and dignity of persons and, in particular, the rights of those who have been trafficked, migrants, internally displaced persons, refugees and asylum-seekers', see UN ECOSOC 'Recommended Principles and Guidelines on Human Rights and Human Trafficking' in 'Report of the United Nations High Commissioner for Human Rights to the Economic and Social Council' (20 May 2002) UN Doc E/2002/68/Add.1, 3. See also, among many other instances, UNGA Res 61/180 (8 March 2007) UN Doc A/RES/61/180, para 9; UNGA Res 61/144 (1 February 2007) UN Doc A/RES/61/144, paras 15 and 17; UNGA Res 59/166 (10 February 2005) UN Doc A/RES/59/166, paras 13 and 15; UNGA Res 58/137 (4 February 2004) UN Doc A/RES/58/137, para 6.

[111] See, for instance, UNHCR 'Guidelines on International Protection No 7: The Application of Article lA(2) of the 1951 Convention and/or 1967 Protocol Relating to the Status of Refugees to Victims of Trafficking and Persons at Risk of being trafficked' (7 April 2006) HCR/GIP/06/07; *In re X* [1999] Decision No T98-06186 CRDD 1, 4, and 7 (Canada); *A*, Immigration Appellate Tribunal Appeal No CC/63673/2002, 18 February 2003 (UK).

[112] For further discussion about the applicability of the refugee definition in the context of trafficking, see most notably I Atak and JC Simeon, 'Human Trafficking: Mapping the Legal Boundaries of International Refugee Law and Criminal Justice' (2014) 12 JICJ 1019, 1038; H Simon, 'Human Trafficking from an International Protection Perspective: Probing the Meaning of Anti-Trafficking Measures for the Protection of Trafficking Victims, with Special Regard to the United Kingdom' (2009) 28 Penn St Int'l L Rev 633–73; K Saito, 'International Protection for Trafficked Persons and those who Fear Being Trafficked' (2007) UNHCR Research Paper No 149; R Piotrowicz, 'Victims of People Trafficking and Entitlement to International Protection' (2005) 24 Aust YBIL 159–79.

inclusion in the definition of a migrant worker depends on the individual circumstances of the migrant and the specific requirements of the relevant instruments. The 1949 Migration for Employment Convention No 97 is bound to play a limited role. It is mainly confined to trafficked migrants who entered lawfully in a foreign country, because its Article 11(1) is circumscribed to migrants regularly admitted in the territory. Although smuggled migrants and undocumented trafficked persons are left out by this definition, they are still protected by the relevant provisions of the ILO Convention No 143 and the ICRMW.

According to Article 2(1) of the ICRMW, a smuggled or trafficked migrant falls within the definition of a migrant worker as soon as he or she is, has been or is to be engaged in a remunerated activity. Despite the comprehensive scope of this definition which includes both documented and undocumented workers, the requirement of a remunerated activity is at odds with the reality of many migrants who are exploited or forced to work by their traffickers or smugglers. Nonetheless, many trafficked and smuggled migrants fall within the scope of the ICRMW if the definition of migrant worker is interpreted in accordance with the object and purpose of the Convention.

As explicitly acknowledged in its preamble, one of the key objectives pursued by the ICRMW is 'to prevent and eliminate clandestine movements and trafficking in migrant workers, while at the same time assuring the protection of their fundamental human rights'. The inclusion of smuggled and trafficked migrants is further confirmed by several provisions of the ICRMW. According to Article 1, the ICRMW applies to all migrant workers without distinction of any kind (thus irrespective of whether they are smuggled or trafficked). Among other instances of overlap between this Convention and the Palermo Protocols, Article 11 of the ICRMW prohibits forced labour, slavery, and servitude.[113]

Against this background, smuggled and trafficked migrants are covered by the definition of a migrant worker on two main grounds. First, the expression 'remunerated activity' and the ordinary meaning to be given to these terms are broad enough to comprise a wide variety of financial and other material benefits, advantages, or services. From this angle, a typical case of non-financial benefit involves the

---

[113] One should acknowledge that the drafting history of the ICRMW has raised some confusion about the application of this Convention to trafficked and smuggled migrants. The Working Group, indeed, considered that 'activities contrary to the rules of *ordre public* in the State in which they took place were out of the scope of the Convention': UNGA, 'Report of the Open-ended Working Group on the Elaboration of an International Convention on the Protection of the Rights of All Migrant Workers and Their Families, A/C.3/40/1 (June 1985) para 174. This general and vague statement might be seen as excluding trafficking from the scope of the Convention when it entails the commission, by the trafficked victims, of activities which are contrary to the rules of *ordre public*. This interpretation, however, is contradicted by the very text of art 2(1): the definition of migrant worker finally retained by the drafters is not qualified by any rules of *ordre public* nor by the unlawful nature of the relevant activity. The only requirement is to be remunerated for the said activity. In short, the text of the treaty is clear and categorical enough to prevail over any possible qualification deriving from the drafting history. According to the Vienna Convention on the Law of Treaties (n 107), the *travaux préparatoires* can only be used as a supplementary means of interpretation in very specific circumstances that are not fulfilled in the present case, that is, when the ordinary meaning of the treaty is 'ambiguous' or leads to a 'manifestly absurd or unreasonable' result.

procurement or facilitation of irregular entry in exchange for work, as frequently happens in practice. Second, smuggled and trafficked migrants must be considered as migrant workers even if they are not actually remunerated as initially promised by their traffickers or smugglers. Indeed, according to the wording of Article 2(1), the mere prospect of being engaged in a remunerated activity is enough to trigger the definition of migrant worker, notwithstanding any deception or subsequent coercion by the employer.

As exemplified above and in the previous chapters, the legal categories established by the specialized treaty regimes of international migration law are much more porous and fluid than it is frequently assumed by lawyers and decision-makers. When assessed from a systemic and integrated approach, the categories of 'refugee', 'migrant worker', and 'smuggled migrant' overlap to a significant extent. Their interaction provides, in turn, a more nuanced account of the role and impact of international law that is more consonant with the reality of migration.

PART III

SOFT LAW AND GLOBAL MIGRATION GOVERNANCE

Introduction to Part III

What men, what monsters, what inhuman race,
What laws, what barbarous customs of the place,
Shut up a desert shore to drowning men,
And drive us to the cruel seas again?

                                                               Virgil[1]

While international migration law is anchored in a rather dense and eclectic network of legal norms grounded in customary international law and treaty law, it
is also profoundly shaped by soft law through a vast number of non-binding instruments adopted by states and international organizations. The proliferation of
soft law instruments on migration is all but new and was already witnessed during
the inter-war period.[2] Nonetheless, it has experienced an unprecedented development over the last decades and has become, today, a defining feature of international
migration law.

   This trend is not specific to the field of migration. It reflects a broader evolution
of the international legal system, whereby the law-making process becomes increasingly informal and fluid to adapt to the changing needs and new concerns of the
international community. Although soft law has been regularly questioned by several positivist lawyers,[3] its intensive resort by states and international organizations
constitutes an inescapable reality which cannot be ignored. In a growing number
of areas, contemporary international law is often the product of a subtle and dynamic interplay between binding and non-binding instruments. As observed by
many scholars, 'soft law should not be considered a "normative sickness" but rather
a symbol of contemporary times and a product of necessity'.[4] Resorting to soft law is

---

[1] Virgil, *Aenid I,* 539–40, Dryden's translation 1 (760–63), quoted in H Grotius, *Mare Liberum
1609* (edited and annotated by R Feenstra, Brill 2009) 11.
[2] See Chapter 1.
[3] See most notably P Weil, 'Towards Relative Normativity in International Law?' (1983) 77 AJIL
413–42; J Klabbers, 'The Undesirability of Soft Law' (1998) Nord J Int'l L 381–91; J d'Aspremont,
'Softness in International Law: A Self-Serving Quest for New Legal Materials' (2008) 19(5) EJIL
1075–93.
[4] P-M Dupuy, 'Soft Law and the International Law of the Environment' (1991) 12(2) Mich J Int'l
L 420, 422. Among many other acknowledgements of the increasing influence of soft law in public
international law, see D Thürer, 'Soft Law' in *Max Planck Encyclopedia of Public International Law*
(OUP 2015); C Castañeda, 'A Call for Rethinking the Sources of International Law: Soft Law and the
Other Side of the Coin' (2013) 13 Anuario Mexicano de Derecho Internaciónal 355–403; J Pauwelyn,

no longer confined to new or emerging topics of international concern, but extends as well to many traditional fields of international law, such as trade or investment.[5]

Despite its obvious proliferation and influence, the expanded use of soft law remains a truly ambivalent phenomenon which may either reinforce or weaken binding rules of law. Its ambiguity is even more palpable when it is associated with the managerial concept of governance. Although the very notion of governance is as vague and disputable as the one of soft law, the two have become closely imbricated. The term governance has been defined in a very broad sense by the UN Commission on Global Governance as 'a continuing process through which conflicting or diverse interests may be accommodated and cooperative action may be taken. It includes formal institutions and regimes empowered to enforce compliance, as well as informal arrangements that people and institutions either have agreed to or perceive to be in their interest.'[6]

Against this background, global migration governance is a generic and descriptive term aimed at capturing the sum of formal and informal policies and processes, as well as social norms and legal rules that regulate the conducts and relations among states, international organizations, and non-state actors. As acknowledged by the Global Commission on International Migration, '[i]n the domain of international migration, governance assumes a variety of forms, including the migration policies and programmes of individual countries, inter-state discussions and agreements, multilateral fora and consultative processes, the activities of international organizations, as well as the laws and norms'.[7]

The interactions between soft law and global governance are manifold, complex, and ambiguous. On the one hand, soft law reflects the reluctance of states to commit to a binding form of global governance. From this stance, the extensive resort to soft law may be viewed as a strategy of evasion to avoid the adoption of legally binding instruments and to dilute the authority of international law with a view to preserving states' sovereignty. On the other hand, one cannot deny that the spread of non-binding instruments and consultative processes has been instrumental in fostering international cooperation and consolidating global migration governance. This renewed interest and commitment towards multilateralism have

RA Wessel, and J Wouters (eds), *Informal International Lawmaking* (OUP 2012); A Boyle, 'Soft Law in International Law-Making' in M Evans (ed), *International Law* (OUP 2010) 118–36; AT Guzman and T Meyer, 'International Soft Law' (2010) 2(1) J Legal Anal 171–225; AE Boyle and C Chinkin, *The Making of International Law* (OUP 2007); D Shelton (ed), *Commitment and Compliance: The Role of Non-binding Norms in the International Legal System* (OUP 2000); G Abi-Saab, 'Cours général de droit international public' (1987) 207 Collected Course of the Hague Academy of International Law 9, 205–13; C Chinkin, 'The Challenge of Soft Law: Development and Change in International Law' (1989) 38(4) ICLQ 850–66; T Gruchalla-Wesierski, 'A Framework for Understanding "Soft Law"' (1984–1985) 30(1) McGill LJ 37–88; R Baxter, 'International Law in "Her Infinite Variety"' (1980) 29(4) ICLQ 549–66.

[5] See, for instance, AK Bjorklund and A Reinisch (eds), *International Investment Law and Soft Law* (Edward Elgar 2012); ME Footer, 'The (Re)turn to "Soft Law" in Reconciling the Antinomies in WTO Law' (2010) 11(2) Melb J Int'l L 241–76.

[6] UN Commission on Global Governance, *Our Global Neighbourhood* (OUP 1995), 2.

[7] Global Commission on International Migration (GCIM), *Migration in an Interconnected World: New Directions for Action* (GCIM 2005), 65.

recently materialized in the 2016 New York Declaration for Refugees and Migrants[8] and were reaffirmed with the adoption, in 2018, of the Global Compact for Safe, Orderly and Regular Migration and the Global Compact on Refugees.[9]

Despite the enduring ambivalence of its long and turbulent evolution, global migration governance has reached a new turning point that was hardly imaginable a few years ago. Although it is premature to predict the actual impact of the New York Declaration and the two UN Compacts into the real world, soft law and global governance are clearly bound to continue working in tandem for the years to come. In order to bring some clarity on their imbrication and influence, Chapter 6 exposes the functions of soft law in the context of international migration law, as well as its evolution and impact on inter-state cooperation. Chapter 7 then draws the resulting architecture of global migration governance at the multilateral level.

---

[8] UNGA Res 71/1 (19 September 2016) UN Doc A/RES/71/1.

[9] Global Compact for Safe, Orderly and Regular Migration (13 July 2018) available at https:// refugeesmigrants.un.org/sites/default/files/180713_agreed_outcome_global_compact_for_migration.pdf accessed 18 October 2018; and Global Compact on Refugees (Report of the United Nations High Commissioner for Refugees—Part II, Global compact on Refugees) (2 August 2018, reissued 13 September 2018) UN Doc A/73/12.

6

The Functions and Evolution of Soft Law in Global Migration Governance

Global migration governance represents a paradigmatic case for unveiling both the potential and the limits of soft law under public international law. The lack of binding force that characterizes soft law inevitably questions its role and added value within the international legal order. For international lawyers, 'it is easy to be too condescending toward soft law, even if firm law would be preferable'.[1]

This chapter accordingly starts by investigating the main functions of soft law in international migration law (section 6.1). The interactions between hard law and soft law are indeed much more complex and nuanced than the binary opposition based on their binding or non-binding nature. Their relations are not always mutually exclusive; they are frequently intermingled in an incremental process of consolidation and cross-fertilization. From this angle, soft law fulfils a variety of legal and para-legal functions to reinforce and supplement hard law. This evolution constitutes neither a progress, nor a retreat of legally binding rules of law. It simply reflects the reality of our times, as grounded in the practice of states and intergovernmental organizations, to inform and capture an increasingly fluid and dynamic international law-making process.

Despite its interplay with binding rules of law, the most influential role of soft law remains fundamentally political and social: it works as a vehicle of consensus and convergence in a decentralized society composed of multiple actors with diverging interests. From this perspective, soft law has become a powerful catalyst of global migration governance to promote inter-state dialogue and international cooperation on a traditionally divisive issue. The rapid growth of multilateralism in an area that has long been associated with domestic jurisdiction has been possible through the proliferation of non-binding instruments and consultative processes during the last three decades.

The second section of this chapter (section 6.2) consequently traces the long evolution of global migration governance that has been shaped and developed by soft law. Although its influence is not free from ambiguities, the unprecedented expansion of soft law has been decisive in building confidence and creating a routine of intergovernmental dialogue. By doing so, it has forged a common language and a

---

[1] J Gold, 'Strengthening the Soft International Law of Exchange Arrangements' (1983) 77 AJIL 443, 443.

growing consensus among states that unveil the role of multilateralism as a counter-narrative to populism and unilateralism.

6.1 The Functions of Soft Law in International Migration Law

The ambiguity inherent in the term 'soft law' and the longstanding controversies among scholars and practitioners call for some preliminary clarifications about the notion itself by distinguishing the form of non-binding instruments from their substance (section 6.1.1). This distinction between the form and the substance underlines the two main functions of soft law in international law: it may either constitute a support to hard law (section 6.1.2) or an alternative thereto (section 6.1.3). This duality further highlights both the potential and the limits of soft law that are particularly visible in the field of migration (section 6.1.4).

6.1.1 Definition of soft law

While 'soft law means different things to different people',[2] most misunderstandings derive from the confusion between form and substance. With such a distinction in mind, soft law shall be taken for what it is, that is, a convenient description to encapsulate a variety of non-binding instruments adopted by states and international organizations.[3] This working definition accordingly focuses on the form (*instrumentum*), in opposition to its very substance (*negotium*). Such a distinction is crucial to assess whether a given instrument may be legally relevant or not. It is true that, in many cases, both the form and substance are devoid of legal value because the resort to soft law is particularly prone to foster mere hortatory language, aspirational pleas, and other related diplomatic verbiage.

However, in other circumstances, the non-binding form of an instrument does not necessarily prejudice its binding content and *vice-versa*. It is well known that a treaty can fail to entail any sense of legal duty when its provisions are too vague, or merely contemplate a total freedom of action for States Parties. The specialized treaties of international migration law provide several illustrations, even though such weak provisions are less common than one would expect. Quite predictably, most of them concern migrant workers[4] and focus on specific issues, such as

---

[2] G Handl and others, 'A Hard Look at Soft Law' (1988) 82 ASIL Proc 371.

[3] Although the increasing number of non-binding instruments adopted by non-state actors could be added to this definition, this chapter focuses exclusively on those emanating from states and international organizations. This does not mean that initiatives by non-state actors are not of interest or do not have an impact. In fact, many of them have been adopted by scholars and the civil society in the field of migration. However, their function within international migration law is primarily promotional and/or pedagogical. In the absence of any endorsement by states and international organizations, the legal value of such endeavours is close to null, even if the political, promotional, and social impact of these initiatives is undisputable.

[4] See, however, in the context of the smuggling of migrants, Protocol against the Smuggling of Migrants by Land, Sea and Air (adopted 15 November 2000, entered into force 28 January 2004) 2241 UNTS 507 art 18(6): 'States Parties may cooperate with relevant international organizations in the implementation of this article [governing the return of smuggled migrants].'

education schemes in the mother tongue of migrant workers' children (Article 45(4) of the ICRMW),[5] political rights in the state of employment (Article 42(3) of the ICRMW),[6] recognition of occupational activities and diplomas acquired abroad, as well as restrictions concerning the access to some limited categories of employment (Article 14 of ILO Convention No 143).[7]

More frequently, specialized treaties of international migration law endorse an obligation of conduct that is legally binding, but hardly enforceable before a court, because of its lack of precision or its promotional purpose. This type of provision mainly concerns the duty to facilitate the naturalization of refugees (Article 34 of the Refugee Convention),[8] the obligation to promote development programmes with a view to combating the socio-economic causes of migrants' smuggling (Article 15(3) of the Smuggling Protocol),[9] or the commitment to adopt measures aimed at ensuring the integrity and security of travel or identity documents (Article 12 of the Smuggling Protocol).[10] In an even more evasive formulation, Article 7 of the Trafficking Protocol commits each State Party to 'consider adopting legislative or other appropriate measures that permit victims of trafficking in persons to remain in its territory of the state, temporarily or permanently, in appropriate cases'.

Inversely, distinguishing the *instrumentum* from the *negotium* highlights the dual nature of soft law instruments adopted by states and international organizations. These instruments are by definition formally non-binding, but they may be mandatory in substance when their content exhibits, reinforces, or clarifies a binding rule of international law endorsed in a formal source of international law. When assessed in light of their very substance, soft law and hard law are far from being mutually exclusive but prove to be complementary in many important respects. The former supplements the latter in two different ways: soft law is either an integral component of hard law or an alternative thereto. Each of these functions depends on the very

---

[5] 'States of employment may provide special schemes of education in the mother tongue of children of migrant workers, if necessary in collaboration with the States of origin.' International Convention on the Protection of the Rights of All Migrant Workers and Members of their Families (adopted 18 December 1990, entered into force 1 July 2003) 2220 UNTS 3 (ICRMW).

[6] 'Migrant workers may enjoy political rights in the State of employment if that State, in the exercise of its sovereignty, grants them such rights.'

[7] 'A Member may [...] after appropriate consultation with the representative organisations of employers and workers, make regulations concerning recognition of occupational qualifications acquired outside its territory, including certificates and diplomas; [and] restrict access to limited categories of employment or functions where this is necessary in the interests of the State.'

[8] 'The Contracting States shall as far as possible facilitate the assimilation and naturalization of refugees.'

[9] 'Each State Party shall promote or strengthen, as appropriate, development programmes and cooperation at the national, regional and international levels, taking into account the socio-economic realities of migration and paying special attention to economically and socially depressed areas, in order to combat the root socio-economic causes of the smuggling of migrants, such as poverty and underdevelopment.'

[10] 'Each State Party shall take such measures as may be necessary, within available means: (a) To ensure that travel or identity documents issued by it are of such quality that they cannot easily be misused and cannot readily be falsified or unlawfully altered, replicated or issued; and (b) To ensure the integrity and security of travel or identity documents issued by or on behalf of the State Party and to prevent their unlawful creation, issuance and use.'

substance of the *instrumentum* and, accordingly, deserves careful consideration to apprehend the potential and the limits of soft law.

6.1.2 Soft law as a support to hard law

The first systemic function of soft law is to support hard law in reinforcing its legal standing and meaning within the international legal system. In such a complex and subtle law-making process, soft law and hard law are sometimes so intermingled that a non-binding instrument may be mandatory as a result of its amalgamation with customary law or treaty law. Indeed, soft law has become an influential catalyst of international customary law. The revival and dynamism of international customs since the second half of the 20th century are largely attributable to states' extensive resort to non-binding instruments with a view to developing a more formalized and predictable customary law-making process.[11] As acknowledged by the ICJ in longstanding jurisprudence, inter-state declarations and resolutions of intergovernmental organizations, such as those of the General Assembly of the United Nations (UNGA), have been influential in providing evidence of state practice or expressing their conviction to be bound by a custom.[12]

From this angle, soft law interacts with customary law in three main ways: 1) it can codify a pre-existing custom in a written form, which in turn, provides greater precision to its content; 2) it can consolidate a customary law process and crystallize the formation of a given rule by providing the final impetus for its endorsement; 3) it can constitute the starting point of a customary law process that might ultimately generate a new binding rule. In all these three scenarios, soft law does not operate in isolation. Instead, it is an integral part of a broader normative process that influences and channels states' behaviours. The right to leave any country provides a telling illustration: while its recognition in the Universal Declaration of Human Rights was the starting point of a customary law process, it has finally matured into a custom through an incremental and widespread process of endorsement and emulation in a vast number of subsequent treaties, domestic constitutions, and other related states' declarations.[13]

Likewise, most soft law instruments usually contain a variety of provisions that may be viewed either as a codification or a progressive development of international law. This is well exemplified by the New York Declaration for Refugees and Migrants, through which all UN Member States agreed on a rather broad number

---

[11] For further discussion, see notably AE Boyle and C Chinkin, *The Making of International Law* (OUP 2007) 225–30; JI Charney, 'Universal International Law' (1993) 87 AJIL 529, 543–50; G Abi-Saab, 'Cours général de droit international public' (1987) 207 Collected Course of the Hague Academy of International Law 9, 154–78.

[12] See especially *Military and Paramilitary Activities in and against Nicaragua (Nicaragua v United States)* (Merits) [1986] ICJ Rep 14, para 188; *Legality of the Threat or Use of Nuclear Weapons* (Advisory Opinion) [1996] ICJ Rep 226 [77]. The relevant extracts are quoted in Chapter 2. As already mentioned, to be relevant, the non-binding resolutions must be formulated in prescriptive terms and adopted by consensus or, at least, by a broad and representative majority of states.

[13] For further discussion see Chapter 2.

of commitments. On the one hand, the New York Declaration restates several pre-existing rules of international customary law that consolidate, reinforce, and shape the current normative framework governing migration. From this perspective, the UN Declaration underpins the two driving forces of international migration law, following a typical balancing act between state sovereignty and individual rights. UN Member States 'reaffirm and will fully protect the human rights of all refugees and migrants, regardless of status' and they 'recall at the same time that each State has a sovereign right to determine whom to admit to its territory, subject to that State's international obligations'.[14] While confirming the plain validity of these two founding principles of international migration law, the Declaration further refers to other well-established customary norms, such as the right to leave any country and to return to one's own country, the principle of *non-refoulement* and the right to seek asylum, as well as the prohibitions of discrimination and arbitrary detention.[15]

As a result of these restatements, UN Member States make clear that their sovereign competence to decide upon admission of non-nationals shall be carried out in due accordance with existing obligations of international law: 'Recognizing that States have rights and responsibilities to manage and control their borders, we will implement border control procedures in conformity with applicable obligations under international law, including international human rights law and international refugee law.'[16] On the other hand, the New York Declaration contains many statements that are not related to or do not reflect the current state of international law. Some provisions are merely aspirational, such as those related to the root causes of migration,[17] whereas others are aimed at stimulating the subsequent development of law, for instance, to address the vulnerabilities of migrants[18] or to expand regular pathways for migration and resettlement programmes for refugees.[19]

Similarly to customary law, a soft law instrument may be the first step towards the negotiation and conclusion of a multilateral treaty, by facilitating awareness and consensus among states to produce a binding instrument. Although this has not always been the case for the specialized treaties of international migration law, all recent general human rights conventions that are applicable to migrants have been preceded by the adoption of non-binding declarations.

Besides its role of precursor, soft law complements treaty law in two important ways: non-binding instruments may elaborate practical standards to detail specific issues and to fill gaps of a given convention or, as it happens more frequently, they may provide an authoritative interpretation of treaty provisions. The archetype of non-binding standards aimed at complementing a binding treaty is provided by International labour Organization (ILO) Conventions Nos 97 and 143.[20] Like

---

[14] New York Declaration for Refugees and Migrants, UNGA Res 71/1 (19 September 2016) UN Doc A/RES/71/1 paras 5 and 42.
[15] ibid paras 13–14, 24, 26–27, 29, 31, 33, 39, 42, 58, and 67.   [16] ibid para 24.
[17] ibid paras 12, 17, 37, and 64.   [18] ibid paras 23, 29, 30, 52, and 60.
[19] ibid paras 57, 77–79.
[20] To give another example among others, the International Maritime Organization has adopted a detailed set of operational standards to address the difficulties arising in implementing the treaty-law duty of providing assistance to migrants in distress at sea, under the 1974 International Convention for the Safety of Life at Sea, the 1979 International Convention on Maritime Search and Rescue, and the

many other ILO conventions, these two specialized treaties on migrant workers are supplemented by particularly detailed recommendations to provide a common line of action for States Parties on several substantive provisions contained in these treaties. Interestingly, although States Parties are free not to follow them, they are bound to submit the recommendations to their national authorities for consideration and to report on the measures taken on the matters. This twofold obligation of conduct is endorsed in Article 19(6) ILO Constitution and works as an incentive for compliance with the recommendations, even though they are not formally binding for States Parties.

The most influential function of soft law in relation to treaty law is to interpret the general provisions of a given convention. When adopted by States Parties, the interpretation endorsed in a non-binding instrument may amount to a 'subsequent agreement between the parties regarding the interpretation of the treaty or the application of its provisions', under the customary rules of interpretation codified in Article 31(3)(a) of the Vienna Convention on the Law of Treaties.[21] By giving a concrete content to a conventional rule, the interpretation agreed on by States Parties in a soft law instrument is hardly dissociable from the binding support of the interpreted legal norm and may become mandatory for the purpose of specifying the meaning of the treaty provisions. As acknowledged by both the ILC and the ICJ, 'an agreement as to the interpretation of a provision reached after the conclusion of the treaty represents an authentic interpretation by the parties which must be read into the treaty for purposes of its interpretation'.[22] In such a situation, as notably acknowledged by Christine Chinkin, 'the hard and soft law are inter-dependent and [...] the latter derives authority from, and extends the meaning of, the former'.[23]

Yet, the same conclusion cannot be drawn when a soft law instrument is adopted by an international body in charge of supervising a treaty. In such a case, States Parties do not formally agree on the interpretation elaborated by the treaty body. This kind of interpretative guidance nevertheless retains a persuasive role to frame the meaning of a binding convention, as it emanates from the organ specifically established by the treaty to interpret its provisions and monitor its application. As

---

1982 Convention on the Law of the Sea. These standards are contained in Guidelines on the Allocation of Responsibilities to Seek the Successful Resolution of Stowaways Cases in International Maritime Organization (IMO) Resolution A.871(20) (adopted 27 November 1997) FAL.2/Circ.43; Interim Measures for Combating Unsafe Practices Associated with the Trafficking or Transport of Migrants by Sea (Revised 12 June 2001) MSC/Circ.896/Rev.1; and Guidelines on the Treatment of Persons Rescued at Sea in IMO Resolution MCS.167(78) Annex 34 (adopted 20 May 2004) MSC 78/26/Add.2. As underlined in paragraph 1.2 of this last document, the Guidelines 'are intended to help Governments and masters better understand their obligations under international law and provide helpful guidance with regard to carrying out these obligations'.

   [21] See notably in this sense *Kasikili/Sedudu Island (Botswana/Namibia)* (Judgment) [1999] ICJ Rep 1045, paras 48–52; Boyle and Chinkin, *The Making of International Law* (n 11) 216–17; T Gruchalla-Wesierski, 'A Framework for Understanding "Soft Law"' (1984–1985) 30(1) McGill LJ 25.

   [22] ILC, *Yearbook of the International Law Commission* Vol II (United Nations 1966) UN Doc A/CN.4/SER.A/1996/Add.1, 221, para 14; *Kasikili/Sedudu Island* (n 21) paras 48–49.

   [23] C Chinkin, 'Normative Development in the International Legal System' in D Shelton (ed), *Commitment and Compliance: The Role of Non-binding Norms in the International Legal System* (OUP 2000) 30.

already discussed in the previous chapters, general comments of UN treaty bodies have been influential in specifying the meaning of general human rights conventions in the particular context of migration, while the interpretative guidelines adopted by the UN High Commissioner for Refugees (UNHCR) and the Committee of Experts on the Application of Conventions and Recommendations (CEACR) of ILO have clarified the scope and content of the specialized conventions on refugees and migrant workers. Although not formally binding, such a guidance may turn into an authoritative interpretation when it is not objected by States Parties or when it is incorporated into their own legislation and domestic practice or endorsed by national and international courts.[24]

Furthermore, although this may come as a surprise for some, soft law may be binding even without any direct relation to treaty law and customary law. This exceptional situation can happen in two specific circumstances. First, a soft law instrument may become legally binding through the general principle of estoppel. According to this well-acknowledged principle of international law, a state may be bound by a recommendation when its conduct gives rise to reasonable expectations of compliance on the part of other states that have acted upon these expectations.[25] This occurs notably when a state has publicly declared to be committed by a soft law instrument. Although estoppel has so far not been invoked in the field of migration, this might change in the future as a side effect of the commitments agreed upon by UN Member States in the New York Declaration and the Global Compact for Migration. Second, a recommendation adopted by an international organization is legally binding upon its subsidiary organs (but not on its Member States).[26] For instance, UNHCR is bound by the resolutions of the UNGA

[24] Furthermore, the acquiescence or support of States Parties vis-à-vis the interpretation of a treaty body may be viewed as a subsequent practice under the rules of interpretation codified in Vienna Convention on the Law of Treaties (adopted 23 May 1969, entered into force 27 January 1980) 1155 UNTS 331 art 31(3)(b). For further discussion about the interpretative guidance of treaty bodies, see notably G Weeks, *Soft Law and Public Authorities: Remedies and Reform* (Hart Publishing 2016); KL McCall-Smith, 'Interpreting International Human Rights Standards: Treaty Body General Comments as Chisel or a Hammer' in S Lagoutte, T Gammeltoft-Hansen, and J Cerone (eds), *Tracing the Roles of Soft Law in Human Rights* (OUP 2016) 27–46; H Keller and L Grover, 'General Comments of the Human Rights Committee and their Legitimacy' in H Keller and G Ulfstein (eds), *UN Human Rights Treaty Bodies: Law and Legitimacy* (CUP 2012) 116–98; C Blake, 'Normative Instruments in International Human Rights Law: Locating the General Comment' (2008) NYU Law Center for Human Rights and Global Justice Working Paper Series 17/2008; ILA, Committee on International Human Rights Law and Practice, 'Final Report on the Impact of the Findings of the United Nations Human Rights Treaty Bodies' (Berlin Conference, 2004).

[25] See among other acknowledgements CF Amerasinghe, *Principles of the Institutional Law of International Organizations* (2nd edn, CUP 2005) 215; FB Sloan, *United Nations General Assembly Resolutions in our Changing World* (Brill 1991) 34 and 65; A Aust, 'The Theory and Practice of Informal International Instruments' (1986) 35 ICLQ 787, 810–12; Institute of International Law, 'International Texts of Legal Import in the Mutual Relations of their Authors and Texts Devoid of Such Import' (Session of Cambridge 1983) paras 6 and 9; M Virally, 'La distinction entre textes internationaux ayant une portée juridique dans les relations mutuelles entre leur auteurs et les textes juridiques qui en sont dépourvus' (1983) 60(1) AIDI 166, 343–44; Gruchalla-Wesierski, 'A Framework for Understanding "Soft Law"' (n 21) 62–63; O Schachter, 'The Crisis of Legitimation in the United Nations' (1981) 50 Nordisk Tidskrift for International Ret: Acta Scandinavica juris gentium 3, 16.

[26] See notably in this sense Amerasinghe, *Principles of the Institutional Law of International Organizations* (n 25) 175–81; Sloan, *United Nations General Assembly Resolutions in our Changing*

addressed thereto as a subsidiary organ of the latter, whereas the resolutions of the International Organization for Migration (IOM) Council are mandatory for the whole organization.[27]

To sum up, soft law fulfils a variety of functions to supplement hard law as a precursor, a catalyst, or an integral component thereof. Both interact in a mutually supportive way to such an extent that the distinction between binding and non-binding instruments is much more porous than it is assumed by hard-core positivists. Whether one likes it or not, soft law has become influential and supportive of hard law through a complex and subtle cross-fertilization process. In a highly decentralized society, states extensively resort to soft law, simply because it corresponds to their needs and expectations of a more formalized and predictable law-making process.

6.1.3 Soft law as an alternative to hard law

Soft law plays another important role as an alternative to hard law when the former follows its own stand-alone function without any connection to the latter. In fact, the vast majority of non-binding instruments adopted by states and international organizations are neither related to nor aimed at developing legally binding rules. This is as true for migration as for many other areas of transnational concern, such as environment or sustainable development. This does not mean that such instruments are devoid of any normative significance. Any society is governed by norms of a different nature that are either legal or social. The international society does not make an exception to this basic pattern. In such a decentralized society, non-binding instruments are increasingly used as an essential receptacle of social norms. Dinah Shelton observes that:

The considerable recourse to and compliance with non-binding norms may represent a maturing of the international system. The on-going relationships among States and other actors, deepening and changing with globalization, create a climate that may diminish the felt need to include all expectations between States in formal legal instruments. Not all arrangements in business, neighborhoods, or in families are formalized, but are often governed by informal social norms and voluntary, non-contractual arrangements. Non-binding norms or informal social norms can be effective and offer a flexible and efficient way to order responses to common problems. They are not law and they do not need to be in order to influence conduct in the desired manner.[28]

World (n 25) 32; Gruchalla-Wesierski, 'A Framework for Understanding "Soft Law"' (n 21) 52–53; I Seidl-Hohenveldern, 'International Economic "Soft Law"' (1979) 163 Collected Courses of the Hague Academy of International Law 165, 173, 175; M Virally, 'La valeur juridique des recommandations des organisations internationales' (1956) 2(1) AFDI 66–96.

[27] For further discussion, see Chapter 7.

[28] D Shelton, 'International Law and Relative Normativity' in M Evans (ed), *International Law* (OUP 2010) 163. Among other similar assessments, see M Bothe, 'Legal and Non-legal Norms: A Meaningful Distinction in International Relations?' (1980) XI NYIL 65, 93 (footnotes omitted): 'there is an important body of rules which regulate state behaviour in international relations, and which do not fall within the category of legal rules. Being social rules, they have many features in common with legal rules, but there are also important differences. Both kinds of rules formulate community expectations.

Soft law thus works as a coordinating device to frame the relations among a plurality of actors by providing flexible and informal guidance that is mutually agreed, albeit not legally binding. This explains why soft law has become a new mode of governance in so many areas of international law at both the universal and regional levels.[29] One can indeed hardly deny that 'the turn to soft law in international governance has been one of the signature developments in the field over the past forty years'.[30] Its intensive use as a promoter of governance unveils two important functions: first, soft law is a vehicle of socialization that promotes a collective approach among a broad variety of actors; and, second, it is a factor of stabilization which makes behaviours more predictable and convergent.

This twofold function has been particularly influential in fostering international cooperation on new or sensitive topics of global concern. In such cases, the alternative is not between a binding instrument and a non-binding instrument, but between a non-binding instrument and no instrument at all.[31] In this sense, Anne Peters underlines that:

Soft regulation is therefore often the means of escape from a no-go situation, not a deliberate 'alternative' to hard law. Soft law—especially in international law—may be an alternative to anarchy. A soft solution can overcome deadlocks in the relations between states when efforts at firmer solutions have failed. Powerful states may favour soft solutions which allow them to retain their liberty of action while at the same time displaying a cooperative attitude. Weak states might promote a soft law instrument on matters of concern to themselves as the best they can politically achieve.[32]

Hence, soft law is not always a deliberate choice but more frequently a product of necessity to bypass the limits inherent in the rigidity and formalism of a state-centric

---

They provide some stability in international relations by making state behaviour more predictable, but non-legal rules do so to a lesser extent.'

[29] Among an abundant literature devoted to the role of soft law in global governance, see especially JA Ocampo and JA Alonso (eds), *Global Governance and Rules for the Post-2015 Era: Addressing Emerging Issues in the Global Environment* (Bloomsbury Academic 2015); J Friedriech, *International Environmental 'Soft Law': The Functions and Limits of Nonbinding Instruments in International Environmental Governance and Law* (Springer 2013); C Bailliet (ed), *Non-State Actors, Soft Law and Protection Regimes* (CUP 2012); G Shaffer and M Pollack, 'Hard vs Soft: Alternatives, Complements, and Antagonists in International Governance' (2010) 94 Minn L Rev 706–99; F Sindico, 'Soft Law and the Elusive Quest for Sustainable Global Governance' (2006) 19 LJIL 829–46; K Abbott and D Snidal, 'Hard and Soft Law in International Governance' (2000) 54 International Organization 421–56; U Mörth, *Soft Law in Governance and Regulation: An Interdisciplinary Analysis* (Edward Elgar 2004); J Kirton and MJ Trebilcock, *Hard Choices, Soft Law: Voluntary Standards in Global Trade, Environment, and Social Governance* (Routledge 2004). The use of soft law to foster governance is however far from being confined to the universal plane. It may be also observed within more centralized legal environments, such as in the EU. See in particular A Peters, 'Soft Law as a New Mode of Governance' in U Diedrichs, W Reiners, and W Wessels (eds), *The Dynamics of Change in EU Governance* (Edward Elgar 2011) 21–51; A Héritier and M Rhodes (eds), *New Modes of Governance in Europe: Governing in the Shadow of Hierarchy* (Macmillan 2010); DM Trubek, P Cottrell, and M Nance, ' "Soft Law", "Hard Law", and European Integration: Toward a Theory of Hybridity' (2005) NYU School of Law Jean Monnet Working Paper No 2; S Borrás and K Jacobsson, 'The Open Method of Co-ordination and New Governance Patterns in the EU' (2004) 11(2) JEPP 185–208.

[30] J Galbraith and D Zaring, 'Soft Law as Foreign Relations Law' (2014) 99 Cornell L Rev 735, 745.

[31] See also among others Shelton, 'International Law and Relative Normativity' (n 28) 163.

[32] Peters, 'Soft Law as a New Mode of Governance' (n 29) 37.

legal system. For international organizations, this is even their only option, since most of them lack any general law-making competence to adopt binding rules. For states, soft law enables them to explore areas that they would be reluctant to address in a binding form.

Against this background, one should not be surprised that global migration governance constitutes a paradigmatic illustration of the multifaceted functions of soft law as an alternative to hard law. In a field so closely associated with national sovereignty as migration is perceived to be, states are reluctant to accept additional legal duties. They privilege non-binding instruments to preserve their margin of appreciation, while agreeing on common guidance in their mutual relations. Soft law accordingly operates as a pragmatic—if not opportunistic—compromise between autonomy and heteronomy, sovereignty and order. It has become the privileged avenue to foster global migration governance because its flexibility and lack of binding force reassure states and encourage them to go beyond the black letter of hard law with a view to developing a common line of conduct.

Clearly, confidence-building represents the main reason for the proliferation of non-binding instruments in the field of migration. As exemplified in the second section of this chapter, soft law typically exerts its influence through a three-stage process: it first creates a space for dialogue to explore new or contentious issues of common interest; it then deepens mutual trust and initiates a learning process among states; and, finally, it facilitates compromises and, thus, mutually beneficial cooperation between states with diverging interests alongside the traditional divide between countries of origin and destination. However, the virtuous cycle of soft law shall not be taken for granted in any circumstances, as it can equally degenerate into a vicious one.

6.1.4 Soft law as a double-edged sword

As a truly ambiguous notion, soft law remains a double-edged sword for the whole international legal system. The perils and promises of soft law are inherent in its ambivalent standing in international law, but they are particularly visible in the field of migration.

The perils of soft law

When soft law is used as an alternative to hard law, the most obvious risk is to undermine binding rules of international law and further weaken the international legal system. Such a risk can materialize at five different levels.

First, non-binding instruments may be an easy excuse for not adopting binding ones. Soft law may be an obstacle to hard law for a variety of reasons. Sometimes, this is merely 'the consequence of a lack of consensus and of the reluctance to give up authority and control, which prevents the adoption of hard regulation'.[33] Hence,

---

[33] ibid 44.

'[t]he use of soft norms may mask the absence of any true agreement, and therefore create illusory expectations on compliance. This state of affairs has been witnessed more than once in the context of the natural environment, even if the relevant norms were not all deprived of effect.'[34] In other instances, promoting non-binding instruments may be a deliberate strategy to avoid any binding commitment. Indeed, 'soft law may also serve as a strategy to a few powerful states to strengthen their position and undermine the will of the remainder i.e. whenever a few powerful states do not agree with the will of the rest; they may seek "non-binding soft law" as a refuge'.[35]

Against this background, one should remember that, in the field of migration, the proliferation of soft law started in the 1990s, that is, just after the adoption of the ICRMW. Instead of ratifying a convention elaborated after a long and intense negotiation process, many states, especially Western countries of destination, have preferred instead to promote non-binding instruments reflecting their own interests. This probably explains why the sovereignty of states in the field of migration is more frequently restated in soft law instruments than in all the other binding treaties of international migration law.

Second, soft law may undermine existing rules of international law that are legally binding for states. Positivist scholars of international law have criticized soft law for diluting the binding nature and effectiveness of international law. By blurring the border between law and politics, critics argue that soft law 'becomes nothing else but a fig leaf for power'.[36] Although international law scholars frequently overestimate this risk, it is a real concern. The extensive resort to non-binding instruments can easily weaken the authority of established legal norms. States may water down their binding commitments through several means. This strategy of evasion can be done either in a frontal way, by formulating soft norms that are contrary to legally binding norms, or in a subtler manner, by circumventing legally binding norms through the endorsement of concurrent non-binding norms or with the adoption of an alternative interpretation of binding ones. Too frequently, 'soft rhetoric [. . .] masks hard practices'.[37]

From this perspective, it is difficult not to observe that the propagation of soft law instruments in the field of migration starkly contrasts with the poor record of compliance with hard law. States are increasingly, and sometimes openly, violating binding rules of international migration law. This raises in turn the question of whether soft law is a smokescreen, if not a masquerade, for the patent violations of

---

[34] R Kolb, *Theory of International Law* (Hart Publishing 2016) 155.
[35] IA Olsson, 'Four Competing Approaches to International Soft Law' (2013) 58 Sc St L 177, 194. Among other acknowledgements, see for instances M Reisman, 'The Concept and Functions of Soft Law in International Politics' in EG Bello and BA Ajibola (eds), *Essays in Honour of Judge Taslim Olawale Elias*, vol I (Martinus Nijhoff Publishers 1992) 142: 'The elites who compose the politically relevant strata of the international system, for all their diversity, share a consuming interest in maintaining their own power. That is a potential basis for agreement, co-operation and accommodation. [. . .] This factor may account for the proliferation of normative formulations which are produced in international arenas despite the fact that their proponents are well aware or expect that they have little or no chance of effectuation.'
[36] J Klabbers, 'The Undesirability of Soft Law' (1998) 67(4) Nord J Int'l L 381–91.
[37] A Di Robilant, 'Genealogies of Soft Law' (2006) 54 Am J Comp L 499, 508.

existing rules: why do states devote so much energy to adopting non-binding instruments instead of complying with binding ones?

Third, the typical shortcoming of soft law is the lack of accountability under international law. Soft law is, by definition, non-binding and a violation thereof thus does not trigger the responsibility of states under international law.

Fourth, the proliferation of soft law instruments may exacerbate the fragmentation of existing rules. This risk is well exemplified by the numerous non-binding instruments adopted by international organizations and UN agencies to defend their own mandate and advance their institutional interest to the detriment of a more coherent articulation among existing institutions and rules.[38]

Fifth, the lack of transparency and democratic control of soft law is frequently underlined by scholars. Contrary to treaties, non-binding instruments are usually drafted through a closed process, without any public record about the negotiation process. Once adopted, these instruments do not have to be made public, unlike treaties under Article 102(1) of the UN Charter. Such a risk is however more pronounced for bilateral instruments than for universal ones that are adopted through an open and transparent process, as exemplified by the Global Compact for Migration. In the absence of any duty of publication, the numerous bilateral memoranda of understanding concluded in different areas of migration are simply unknown and escape the reach of public scrutiny. In addition, opting for a soft instrument allows states to avoid parliamentary control, which is required for the ratification of any convention.

The promises of soft law

If the risks associated with soft law are numerous and real, its potentials are equally enormous. From a positive viewpoint, soft law may have the important impact of domesticating the conduct of states. Indeed, the fact that a given instrument has no binding force does not mean that it has no legal effect, even if many lawyers often confuse the two. Depending on its wording and conditions of adoption, a soft law instrument adopted by states may have three main legal effects that are particularly significant and well acknowledged: the internationalization of the subject matter addressed in the given instrument, the duty of states to give due consideration thereto, as well as an expectation of compliance.

The first immediate and fundamental legal effect of a soft law instrument is to internationalize a subject matter by removing it from the domestic jurisdiction of states.[39] In other words, once a particular issue has been dealt with in a soft law instrument, states that have adopted it can no longer claim that this issue falls

---

[38] For an overview of the vast number of soft law instruments and guidelines adopted by UN agencies and other related international organizations, see section 6.2 of this chapter.

[39] See notably Abi-Saab, 'Cours général de droit international public' (n 11) 210; Gruchalla-Wesierski, 'A Framework for Understanding "Soft Law" ' (n 21) 58–59; Institute of International Law, 'International Texts of Legal Import' (n 25) para 6; Virally, 'La distinction entre textes internationaux' (n 25) 347; RR Baxter, 'International Law in "Her Infinite Variety" ' (1980) 29(4) ICLQ 549, 565.

within their *domaine réservé*. From this angle, although the rights of migrants are anchored in a significant number of legally binding rules, other aspects of migration governance are not regulated in binding instruments and have been internationalized through, most notably, the New York Declaration, the Global Compact on Refugees, and the Global Compact for Migration. The importance of such a shift shall not be underestimated in a field that has been traditionally viewed as an integral part of domestic jurisdiction. The New York Declaration acknowledges in this sense that the movement of refugees and migrants 'are global phenomena that call for global approaches and global solutions. No one State can manage such movements on its own.'[40]

The internationalization of migration governance explains *a contrario* the rationale underlying the sudden withdrawal of the US from the negotiations of the Global Compact for Migration on the official—albeit disputable—ground that 'the global approach in the New York Declaration is simply not compatible with U.S. sovereignty'.[41] According to the US Secretary of State, '[w]e simply cannot in good faith support a process that could undermine the sovereign right of the United States to enforce our immigration laws and secure our borders'.[42] While the US missed an opportunity to influence its content, the Global Compact for Migration is the only soft law instrument on migration that has been adopted within the UN without the participation of the US in the last three decades.

The second legal effect of soft law relates to the duty of states to consider it in good faith. As acknowledged by the legal doctrine, states are bound to give soft law instruments due consideration and, if they decide otherwise, they have to give reasons for their departure from the line of conduct agreed on in the relevant instrument.[43] This twofold duty is an obligation of means, not of result. However, it remains a legal duty on its own, grounded in the general principle of good faith as reinforced by Article 2(2) of the UN Charter, as well as Member States' duties inherent in UN

---

[40] New York Declaration (n 14) para 7.

[41] United States Mission to the United Nations (USUN), 'United States Ends Participation in Global Compact on Migration' (*USUN*, 2 December 2017) <https://usun.state.gov/remarks/8197> accessed 18 October 2018. This line of argument is, however, at odds with the very fact that the US was actively involved in the drafting of the New York Declaration. Among the typical concerns of the US endorsed by the New York Declaration, it explicitly acknowledged 'border control and management as an important element of security for States, including issues relating to battling transnational organized crime, terrorism and illicit trade'. Its withdrawal was relatively unexpected given the enthusiastic support of the US expressed a few months before its retraction, when its representative declared at the UNGA in April 2017 that 'the United States [...] looks forward to engaging actively during the preparatory process, the negotiation of the compact and the intergovernmental conference in 2018': see UNGA 'Follow-up to the outcome of the Millennium Summit' UNGAOR 71st Session (6 April 2017) UN Doc A/71/PV.74 (2017), 2.

[42] RW Tillerston, Secretary of State, Press Statement, US Ends Participation in the Global Compact on Migration, <https://www.state.gov/secretary/20172018tillerson/remarks/2017/12/276190.htm> accessed 18 October 2018.

[43] Among other well-known acknowledgements of this twofold duty, see Amerasinghe, *Principles of the Institutional Law of International Organizations* (n 25) 177–78; Sloan, *United Nations General Assembly Resolutions in our Changing World* (n 25) 28–29; J Gold, 'Strengthening the Soft International Law of Exchange Arrangements' (1983) 77 AJIL 443; Virally, 'La valeur juridique des recommandations' (n 26) 86–91.

membership.[44] As confirmed by the ICJ, 'the very fact of [...] membership of the Organization entails certain mutual obligations of co-operation and good faith incumbent upon [Member States] and upon the Organization'.[45] They include, at a minimum, the duty of Member States to consider non-binding instruments adopted by the organization. When discussing the legal value of the UNGA resolutions, Judge Lauterpacht explained in the *Voting Procedure case* of the ICJ:

> It is one thing, to affirm the somewhat obvious principle that the recommendations of the General Assembly [...] addressed to the Members of the United Nations are not legally binding upon them in the sense that full effect must be given to them. It is another thing to give currency to the view that they have no force at all whether legal or other and that therefore they cannot be regarded as forming in any sense part of a legal system of supervision. [...] A Resolution recommending [...] a specific course of action creates *some* legal obligation which, however rudimentary, elastic and imperfect, is nevertheless a legal obligation [...]. The State in question, while not bound to accept the recommendation, is bound to give it due consideration in good faith. If [...] it decides to disregard it, it is bound to explain the reasons for its decision.[46]

As a result of this obligation of means, the third legal effect of soft law is to raise an expectation of compliance, unless the state concerned clearly expresses its intention not to follow it. Put differently, states are expected to do what they have agreed on and declared to do in a soft law instrument. Joseph Gold well summarizes this subtle—albeit frequently misunderstood—effect of a non-binding instrument: 'the essential ingredient of soft law is an expectation that the states accepting these instruments will take their content seriously and will give them some measure of respect', because 'a common intent is implicit in the soft law as formulated, and it is this common intent, when elucidated, that is to be respected'.[47] This expectation of

---

[44] 'Although there is no automatic obligation to accept fully a particular recommendation or series of recommendations, there is a legal obligation to act in good faith in accordance with the principles of the Charter [...]. An administering State may not be acting illegally by declining to act upon a recommendation or series of recommendations on the same subject. But in doing so it acts at its peril when a point is reached when the cumulative effect of the persistent disregard of the articulate opinion of the Organization is such as to foster the conviction that the State in question has become guilty of disloyalty to the Principles and Purposes of the Charter. Thus an administering State which consistently sets itself above the solemnly and repeatedly expressed judgment of the Organization, in particular in proportion as that judgment approximates to unanimity, may find that it has overstepped the imperceptible line between impropriety and illegality, between discretion and arbitrariness, between the exercise of the legal right to disregard the recommendation and the abuse of that right, and that it has exposed itself to consequences legitimately following as a legal sanction.' See Separate Opinion of Judge Lauterpacht in *South-West Africa—Voting Procedure Case* [1955] ICJ Rep 67, 120. For a more recent restatement, see Amerasinghe, *Principles of the Institutional law of International Organizations* (n 25) 178–79.

[45] *Interpretation of the Agreement of 25 March 1951 between the WHO and Egypt* [1980] ICJ Rep 73, 93.

[46] *South-West Africa—Voting Procedure* (Advisory Opinion) 1955 ICJ Rep 67 Separate Opinion of Judge Lauterpacht in ibid 118–19. Judge Klaestad expressed a similar view in his individual opinion in the same case, ibid 88.

[47] Gold, 'Strengthening the Soft International Law' (n 43) 43. In addition to the doctrine quoted below, see also in this sense T Meyer, 'Soft Law as Delegation' (2009) 32(3) Fordham Int'l LJ 888, 889, 890.

compliance does not concern all soft law instruments, but only those exhibiting a clear commitment that has been agreed on by states.

After all, a commitment which is not legally binding remains a commitment. States are supposed to comply with it, even if it is not legally enforceable. This is exemplified in many different fields of international law, where it is recognized that 'compliance with non-binding norms and instruments is extremely good and probably would not have been better if the norms were contained in a binding text'.[48] It has even been asserted that 'soft law [. . .] seems to have equal and sometimes higher compliance rates than hard law'.[49] As early as 1980, Bothe observed that:

It appears from the international practice that obligations which are clearly non-legal are still taken seriously by states. Documents which do not create legal obligations nevertheless formulate community or shared expectations of state behaviour. It may be that policy declarations or joint statements of intent are, in certain cases, propaganda, but a certain *favor seriositatis* should be granted to states. It should not lightly be presumed that states did not mean what they said. It is hard to assume that the European States would have adopted the CSCE Final Act in the solemn form which they did if they had had no intention to do what the Act required. It has also been shown that the implementation record of binding resolutions is only marginally better than that of non-binding ones. The practice of providing implementation procedures for resolutions which are not formally binding lends additional weight to the submission that there is a serious expectation of compliance.[50]

Of course, an expectation of compliance must not be confused with a legal duty of compliance. Such an expectation is unable on its own to transform a political commitment into a legally binding one. This possibility is truly exceptional and remains confined to the very specific context of estoppel, as discussed above. Nevertheless, the Institute of International Law has gone one step further in arguing that a violation of a political commitment may be submitted to a procedure of peaceful settlement. Its resolution adopted in 1983 at a session in Cambridge asserts that:

The violation of a purely political commitment justifies the aggrieved party in resorting to all means within its power in order to put an end to, or compensate for, its harmful consequences or drawbacks, in so far as such means are not prohibited by international law.

Disputes arising from such violations may be submitted to all appropriate means of peaceful settlement and must be submitted to peaceful settlement procedures in the circumstances specified in Article 33, para 1, of the Charter of the United Nations [including through negotiation, enquiry, mediation, arbitration, judicial settlement, or other peaceful means of their own choice].[51]

---

[48] Shelton, 'International Law and Relative Normativity' (n 28) 163.

[49] J Pauwelyn, 'Is It International Law or Not and Does it Even Matter?' in J Pauwelyn, RA Wessel, and J Wouters (eds), *Informal International Lawmaking* (OUP 2012) 151. See also, among others, D Thürer, 'Soft Law' in *Max Planck Encyclopedia of Public International Law* (OUP 2015) para 6: 'it must be noted that a high level of compliance is not a distinctive quality of hard law: the compliance pull, and as a consequence compliance itself, of a specific soft law norm can be significantly higher than the one of hard law norms'.

[50] Bothe, 'Legal and Non-legal Norms' (n 28) 85. See also Abi-Saab, 'Cours général de droit international public' (n 11) 160–69.

[51] Institute of International Law, 'International Texts of Legal Import' (n 25) para 5.

This assertion remains dubious and does not fairly reflect the state of positive international law, for only a violation of a legally binding commitment triggers the responsibility of states under international law. Hence, the breach of a purely political commitment cannot be considered an internationally wrongful act of a state that can be submitted to judicial settlement.[52] Indeed, this represents the inescapable dividing line between legally and non-legally binding commitments: 'the essence of any soft law rule is that it is not enforceable'.[53] Hence, 'soft law may be thought of as a naked norm, whereas hard law is a norm clothed in a penalty'.[54]

The lack of enforceability inherent in soft law still calls for two main caveats that mitigate its practical variance from hard law. On the one hand, the violation of a political commitment may trigger political sanctions that are usually more persuasive and effective than legal ones. On the other hand, the violation of a legally binding commitment is rarely followed by a legal sanction because, in stark contrast with domestic law, the enforcement regime of international law remains decentralized and primarily depends on the reaction of the injured states. As acknowledged by the ICJ, 'in the international field, the existence of obligations that cannot in the last resort be enforced by any legal process, has always been the rule rather than the exception'.[55] As a matter of principle, the jurisdiction of international courts to settle inter-state disputes remains purely optional and consensual. In practice, only a marginal portion of internationally wrongful acts committed by states is submitted to international courts. Inversely, the decisions of most supervisory mechanisms of conventions duly ratified by States Parties are not formally binding, as exemplified by the UN human rights treaty bodies.

Hence, although soft law is not legally enforceable by nature, most violations of hard law do not give rise to legal sanctions either. This unveils the specificity of the international legal system. Under public international law, compliance with hard law is rarely triggered by coercion. It relies instead on a broad variety of incentives that are legal and non-legal. It is well-known that:

[I]f 'hard' international law is normally observed and applied, it is hardly because of the fear of eventual enforcement measures. Observance owes more to its general acceptance, to the recognition that the existing legal rules reflect the shared values and interests of the members of the international community and are, therefore, legitimate. [...] In other words: States have a shared interest in the maintenance of predictable behavior patterns and this reciprocal interest contributes more to the performance of obligations than the possibility of sanctions.[56]

---

[52] As codified by art 2 of the ILC Draft articles on the responsibility of states for internationally wrongful acts, 'there is an internationally wrongful act of a State when conduct consisting of an action or omission: (a) is attributable to the State under international law; and, (b) constitutes a breach of an international obligation of the State'.

[53] A D'Amato, 'Softness in International Law: A Self-Serving Quest for New Legal Materials: A Reply to Jean d'Aspremont' (2009) 20 EJIL 897, 899.

[54] ibid 902.

[55] *South West Africa Cases (Ethiopia v South Africa; Liberia v South Africa) Second Phase* (Judgment of 18 July 1966) [1966] ICJ Report 6 para 86.

[56] K Zemanek, 'Is the Term 'Soft Law' Convenient?' in G Hafner et al (eds), *Liber Amicorum: Professor Ignaz Seidl-Hohenveldern in Honour of his 80th Birthday* (Kluwer Law International 1998) 856.

This is as true for hard law as it is for soft law. As highlighted by Dinah Shelton, compliance with non-legally binding rules depends on several parameters, including the content of the norm, the legitimacy of the process by which it is adopted, the international context, and, more importantly, the institutional follow-up process.[57] She concludes that:

The growing complexity of the international legal system is reflected in the increasing variety of forms of commitment adopted to regulate State and non-State behaviour in regard to an ever-growing number of transnational problems. The various international actors create and implement a range of international commitments, some of which are in legal form, others of which are contained in non-binding instruments. The lack of a binding form may reduce the options for enforcement in the short term (i.e. no litigation), but this does not deny that there can exist sincere and deeply held expectations of compliance with the norms contained in the non-binding form.[58]

This expectation of compliance explains why soft law instruments are drafted by states with considerable care, as vividly exemplified by the negotiating process of the New York Declaration and the Global Compact for Migration. The wording and consequences of their provisions have been so intensely debated and meticulously drafted by states that the overall process resembles the negotiation of a real treaty to a large extent.

Although the New York Declaration and the Global Compact for Migration are not formally binding, the expectation of compliance remains particularly high for three main reasons. First, the very rationale of these two instruments is to officially endorse a long list of commitments agreed upon by UN Member States. According to the New York Declaration, 'we [Member States] have endorsed today a set of commitments that apply to both refugees and migrants, as well as separate sets of commitments for refugees and migrants'.[59] While reaffirming the commitments of the New Declaration, the Global Compact for Migration has further identified twenty-three objectives and 'each objective contains a commitment, followed by a range of actions considered to be relevant policy instruments and best practices'.[60]

Second, compliance with these commitments is presumed because states have repeatedly expressed their determination to implement the Global Compact into practice. In stark contrast with previous soft law instruments adopted in this field, the Global Compact has been adopted with a view to 'ensuring that the words in this document translate into concrete actions for the benefit of millions of people in every region of the world'.[61] While underlining their commitment to ensure the 'effective implementation of the Global Compact', Member States have devoted a whole section to its implementation.[62]

[57] D Shelton, *Commitment and Compliance: The Role of Non-Binding Norms in the International Legal System* (1st ed, OUP 2000) 556.
[58] Shelton, 'International Law and Relative Normativity' (n 28) 163.
[59] New York Declaration (n 14) para 21.
[60] Global Compact for Safe, Orderly and Regular Migration (13 July 2018) available at https://refugeesmigrants.un.org/sites/default/files/180713_agreed_outcome_global_compact_for_migration.pdf accessed 18 October 2018 para 16.
[61] ibid para 14.   [62] ibid paras 39 c) and 40–47.

Third, states' compliance with the commitments they agreed on in the Global Compact is further reinforced by the establishment of a periodic follow-up procedure to 'review the progress made at local, national, regional and global levels in implementing the Global Compact'.[63] This specific mechanism, referred to as the 'International Migration Review Forum', will be organized by the General Assembly every four years.

Against such a background, the least we can say is that states are strongly expected to comply with the commitments they have agreed on. Although it is obviously too early to draw any conclusion about the effective implementation of the Global Compact, the very fact that states have agreed on a broad range of commitments to be implemented and reviewed represents an achievement of its own.

6.2 Soft Law as a Catalyst of Global Migration Governance: The Long Road towards a Comprehensive and Balanced Approach

The adoption of the Global Compact for Migration is the culmination of a long evolution towards a more comprehensive and balanced approach which underlines the incremental albeit persuasive role played by soft law. During the last three decades, soft law has become an influential catalyst of global migration governance through the intensive use of non-binding instruments and other related consultative processes to promote and inform international cooperation.

The rapid development of global migration governance has been characterized by three successive phases that highlight the profound influence of soft law. A first cycle of intensive experimentation and expansion of informal state consultations has been developed from 1994 to 2005. A second cycle, from 2006 to 2015, then witnessed the revival of the UN through the migration-development nexus, before the launch of a new turn in 2016 with the New York Declaration for Refugees and Migrants as well as the subsequent negotiation and adoption of the Global Compacts.

6.2.1 Experimentation and expansion of informal dialogue and inter-state cooperation: 1994–2005

One of the first attempts to discuss migration in a global forum dates back to the International Conference on Population and Development organized in Cairo from 5 to 13 September 1994 by the United Nations Population Fund (UNFPA) and the United Nations Department for Economic and Social Affairs (UNDESA). After intense negotiations, 179 States' representatives endorsed a 20-year Programme of Action which contained a whole chapter devoted to migration. Although this question of common interest was already discussed in the previous UN Conferences on Population in 1974 and 1984,[64] the 1994 Programme of Action represents the first

---

[63] ibid para 48.
[64] *Report of the United Nations World Population Conference* (Bucharest, 19–30 August 1974) (United Nations Publication 1975) Sales No E.75.XIII.3 UN Doc E/CONF. 60/19; *Report of the International*

comprehensive soft law instrument adopted within the UN on the multifaceted issues related to migration. It formulates 24 recommendations grouped around four themes: migration and development; documented migrants; undocumented migrants; refugees, asylum seekers, and displaced persons.[65]

The overall rationale is to promote a balanced and consensual approach in order to reconcile the diverging interests between countries of origin and countries of destination alongside the North-South divide. Following this stance, the Cairo Programme of Action has been a pioneer in providing a comprehensive blueprint on the multiple linkages between migration and development. The UN Programme emphasizes that the long-term priority is 'to make the option of remaining in one's country viable for all people', while acknowledging the 'positive impacts [of migration] on both the communities of origin and the communities of destination, providing the former with remittances and the latter with needed human resources'.[66] This balanced approach to the migration-development nexus is based on three complementary objectives:

(a) To address the root causes of migration, especially those related to poverty;

(b) To encourage more cooperation and dialogue between countries of origin and countries of destination in order to maximize the benefits of migration to those concerned and increase the likelihood that migration has positive consequences for the development of both sending and receiving countries; and

(c) To facilitate the reintegration process of returning migrants.[67]

While acknowledging the need to promote inter-state cooperation to achieve these ambitious objectives, the Programme of Action also underlines that 'the role of international organizations with mandates in the area of migration should be strengthened so that they can deliver adequate technical support to developing countries, advise in the management of international migration flows and promote intergovernmental cooperation through, *inter alia*, bilateral and multilateral negotiations, as appropriate'.[68]

Overall, and although most recommendations are quite general and largely aspirational, the UN Programme of Action has been instrumental in developing a common language among states on a broad variety of issues. They include: the facilitation of remittances and temporary migration, due respect for the human rights of all migrants, protection against racism and discrimination, social and economic integration of documented migrants, return and reintegration of undocumented migrants, the fight against trafficking and exploitation as well as access to fair and expeditious asylum procedures, voluntary repatriation of refugees, and due respect for the principle of *non-refoulement*. By outlining a broad set of common understandings, the Programme of Action has constituted an influential source of inspiration

---

Conference on Population (Mexico City, 6–14 August 1984) (United Nations Publication 1984) Sales No E.84.XIII.8 UN Doc E/CONF.76/19.

[65] *Report of the International Conference on Population and Development* (Cairo, 5–13 September 1994) (United Nations Publication 1995) UN Doc A/CONF.171/13, Ch X.

[66] ibid para 10.1.   [67] ibid para 10.2.   [68] ibid para 10.8.

for many subsequent initiatives aimed at fostering international cooperation on migration. At the time of its adoption, however, its wide-ranging and far-reaching approach was premature and failed to deliver on its promises. The UN Programme of Action thus largely remained a dead letter in practice during the following decade.

Meanwhile, from 1993 to 2003, the proposal to convene a UN conference on migration was regularly discussed within the UN General Assembly, yet systematically postponed because of the reluctance of Western states, as well as the indifference of many other UN Member States.[69] In fact, the UN Population Division carried out no less than four surveys in 1995, 1997, 1999, and 2003 to collect the views of Member States about the opportunity of convening a UN conference on migration. Yet, a majority of UN Member States—54 per cent—never responded to any of the four inquiries.[70] The eighty-nine countries that replied to at least one of the four surveys mainly replicated the traditional division between countries of origin and countries of destination: the sixty Member States in favour of a UN Conference were from Africa, Asia, Latin America, and Eastern Europe, whereas the twenty-nine states opposed thereto were Western states and other migrant-receiving countries (including Saudi Arabia, Singapore, and the United Arab Emirates).[71]

The rise of mini-multilateralism and inter-state dialogue outside the UN

The lack of consensus to convene a UN conference on migration did not halt the need for closer cooperation at the international level. On the contrary, a number of intergovernmental initiatives sprang up outside the UN to continue and deepen the dialogue among states. Because and in spite of the deadlock within the UN to provide a forum of discussion, a new but softer and less inclusive form of inter-state dialogue was experimented with and expanded through several coalitions of willing states that were keen to pursue intergovernmental consultations at a smaller and less formal level than the universal one. Although largely improvised and experimental at that time, this phenomenon is now commonly labelled 'minilateralism', 'whereby small groups of interested States work together to develop and implement new ideas that can then be debated, and perhaps adopted, in more formal settings.'[72]

---

[69]   UNGA Res 48/113 (1993) UN Doc A/RES/48/113, para 2; UNGA Res 49/127 (1994) UN Doc A/RES/49/127, para 2; UNGA Res 50/123 (1995) UN Doc A/RES/50/123, para 8; UNGA Res 52/189 (1997) UN Doc A/RES/52/189, para 7; UNGA Res 54/212 (1999) UN Doc A/RES/54/212, para 9; UNGA Res 56/203 (2001) UN Doc A/RES/56/203, para 5; UNGA Res 58/208 (2003) UN Doc A/RES/58/208, para 9.

[70]   J Chamie and B Mirkin, 'Who's Afraid of International Migration in the United Nations' in R Koslowski (ed), *Global Mobility Regimes* (Springer 2011) 248.

[71]   ibid.

[72]   UNGA 'Report of the Special Representative of the Secretary-General on Migration' (2017) UN Doc A/71/728, 30. The term has been first coined outside the field of migration by Moses Naim to develop a 'more targeted approach [that] should bring to the table the smallest possible number of countries needed to have the largest possible impact on solving a particular problem', see M Naim, 'Minilateralism' (Foreign Policy, 21 June 2009) <http://foreignpolicy.com/2009/06/21/minilateralism> accessed 18 October 2018.

This new trend in global migration governance emerged during the 1990s and culminated at the turn of the millennium with four main platforms presented above: the regional consultative processes that have considerably expanded since the 1990s, the Berne Initiative and the International Agenda for Migration Management (2001–2004), the International Dialogue on Migration launched in 2001, and the Global Commission on International Migration (2003–2005). Despite their great diversity, these initiatives followed a similar pattern: they were developed on an ad-hoc basis outside the UN as an informal, non-binding, and state-driven forum of dialogue.

First, a rather atypical form of inter-state dialogue has been developed through the so-called 'regional consultative processes'. These processes are usually not associated with regional organizations. They are instead state-owned processes—comprising countries from the same region or like-minded countries from different regions—to share their respective positions and priorities on migration. Regional consultative processes provide a regular yet informal dialogue focusing on information-sharing, good practices, and capacity building. The first one has been established in 1985 by sixteen Western countries of destination[73] and serves as a model for subsequent expansion to other regions alongside the main routes of migration. Since the mid-1990s, regional consultative processes have proliferated, now covering almost all regions of the world.[74]

Many of these ad hoc processes focus on immigration control and the fight against irregular migration and trafficking, even though they increasingly address a broader

---

[73] Intergovernmental Consultations on Asylum, Refugee and Migration Policies in Europe, North America and Australia.

[74] They include, in the chronological order of their creation: the *Budapest Process*, founded in 1991; the *Regional Conference on Migration*, RCM (Puebla Process), founded in 1996; the *Pacific Immigration Directors' Conference* (PIDC), created in 1996; the *South American Conference on Migration* (SACM), founded in 2000; the *Migration Dialogue for Southern Africa* (MIDSA), established in 2000; the *Migration Dialogue for West Africa* (MIDWA), founded in 2001; the *Regional Ministerial Conference on Migration in the Western Mediterranean* (5+5 Dialogue), created in 2002; the *Bali Process on People Smuggling, Trafficking in Persons and Related Transnational Crime* (Bali Process), established in 2002; the *Mediterranean Transit Migration Dialogue* (MTM), founded in 2003; *Ministerial Consultation on Overseas Employment and Contractual Labour for Countries of Origin in Asia* (Colombo Process), established in 2003; the *Intergovernmental Authority on Development—Regional Consultative Process on Migration* (IGAD-RCP), founded in 2008; the *Ministerial Consultation on Overseas Employment and Contractual Labour for Countries of Origin and Destination in Asia* (Abu Dhabi Dialogue), created in 2008; the *Prague Process,* established in 2009; the *Eastern Partnership Panel on Migration and Asylum* (EaPPMA), founded in 2011; the *Migration Dialogue from the Common Market for Eastern and Southern Africa Member States* (MIDCOM), founded in 2013; the *Almaty Process on Refugee Protection and International Migration* (Almaty Process) established in 2013; the *Migration Dialogue for Central African States* (MIDCAS), endorsed by the ECCAS Council of Ministers in 2014; the *Arab Regional Consultative Process on Migration and Refugees Affairs* (ARCP), created in 2015 and the *Caribbean Migration Consultations* (CMC), founded in 2016. For further description see notably C Harns, *Regional Inter-State Consultation Mechanisms on Migration: Approaches, Recent Activities and Implications for Global Governance of Migration* (IOM Migration Research Series (MRS) No 45, IOM 2013); C Thouez and F Channac, 'Shaping International Migration Policy: The Role of Regional Consultative Processes' (2006) 29(2) W Eur Pol 370–87; M Klein Solomon, 'International Migration Management through Inter-State Consultation Mechanisms' (2005) Paper prepared for United Nations Expert Group Meeting on International Migration and Development; A Klekowski von Koppenfels, *The Role of Regional Consultative Processes in Managing International Migration* (IOM 2001).

range of issues (such as labour migration, migration and development, or human rights of migrants). Regional consultative processes are also frequently criticized by scholars for their lack of transparency and accountability, as well as the strong influence of Western countries that fund most of them with the support of IOM.[75] The development of these consultative processes remains an ambivalent phenomenon: while facilitating dialogue and confidence-building among states, they have also served as a means to disseminate the agenda and practices of Western countries in the Global South.

The second platform for inter-state dialogue has been developed through the Berne Initiative as a way to expand at the global level the methods and strategies initiated within regional consultative processes. Launched in June 2001 by the Swiss government with the support of IOM, the Berne Initiative was 'a state-owned consultative process with the goal of obtaining better management of migration at the national, regional and global levels through cooperation between States'.[76] After broad consultation involving many governments from different regions, its main outcome was the adoption of the International Agenda for Migration Management in 2004. While this Agenda was 'not aimed at creating new migration law', its self-declared objective was 'to assist government migration practitioners and policy makers in developing effective mechanisms for inter-state cooperation on migration, fully respecting their sovereignty in this field'.[77] This focus on sovereignty reasonably reflects the overall tone and objective pursued by the International Agenda for Migration Management.

This non-binding and practice-oriented document consists of two components: the first set of twenty 'common understandings for the management of international migration' typically reaffirms the prime responsibility of each state in developing national migration policies and the correlative need for cooperation and dialogue among all stakeholders, while the second list of twenty 'effective practices for a planned, balanced and comprehensive approach to management of migration' addresses a broad range of issues in a rather systematic way.[78] The International

---

[75] F Crépeau and I Atak, 'Global Migration Governance: Avoiding Commitments on Human Rights, yet Tracing a Course for Cooperation' (2016) 34(2) NQHR 140, 142; S Lavenex and others 'Regional Migration Governance' in TA Börzel and T Risse (eds), *The Oxford Handbook of Comparative Regionalism* (OUP 2016) 457–85; J Köhler, 'What Government Networks Do in the Field of Migration: An Analysis of Selected Regional Consultative Processes' in R Kunz, S Lavenex, and M Panizzon (eds), *Multilayered Migration Governance* (Routledge 2011) 67–93; A Betts, *Global Migration Governance* (OUP 2012) 17–18; V Giraudon and G Lahav, 'Comparative Perspectives on Border Control: Away from the Border and Outside the State' in P Andreas and T Snyder (eds), *The Wall Around the West: State Borders and Immigration Control in North America and Europe* (Rowman and Littlefield Publishers 2000) 55–77.

[76] The Berne Initiative, *International Agenda for Migration Management* (FOM/IOM 2005) 16.

[77] ibid 17.

[78] These 'effective practices' focus on: international cooperation, national migration policy, entry and stay (including visa requirement and border control), regular migration (whether temporary or permanent), labour migration, irregular migration, human rights of migrants, asylum and international protection of refugees, integration, naturalization and nationality, return, capacity building, migration and its relations with development, trade, health, environment and security, public information, as well as research and data.

Agenda for Migration Management was thus conceived as 'a common reference document mapping out the constituent elements of a comprehensive migration policy strategy'.[79] However, like the regional consultative processes, its main motivation was to influence and frame the ongoing discussions at the international level by providing a tool-kit for interested states in elaborating national policies and enhancing their capacities to control migration.

In parallel with this state-led initiative, the third platform of policy dialogue has been institutionalized within IOM on the occasion of its 50th anniversary. Established in November 2001, the International Dialogue on Migration officially aspires 'to contribute to a better understanding of migration and to strengthen cooperative mechanisms between governments to comprehensively and effectively address migration issues'.[80] Its main activity takes the form of an annual conference, where a broad range of stakeholders discuss and exchange their views on a specific topic related to international cooperation and migration governance.[81] Like the regional consultative processes and the Berne Initiative, it is an informal and non-binding forum of dialogue and exchanges. The International Dialogue on Migration is nonetheless more inclusive: it is open to all IOM Member and Observer States, thereby including both countries of destination and origin, while representatives of other international organizations, non-governmental organizations, the private sector and academia are regularly invited to participate and present their views.

A fourth global initiative was launched outside the UN with the creation of the Global Commission on International Migration (2003–2005). This new commission was initiated by the UN Secretary-General with the support of Brazil, Morocco, the Philippines, Sweden, and Switzerland. This independent body of nineteen commissioners from different parts of the world was mandated to provide 'the framework for the formulation of a coherent, comprehensive and global response to the issue of international migration'. The final report delivered in October 2005 elaborates six 'principles for action' and thirty-three related recommendations to be used as 'a guide to the formulation of comprehensive, coherent and effective migration

---

[79] Berne Initiative, 'Chairman's Summary' in 'Managing Migration through International Cooperation: The International Agenda for Migration Management' (Berne II Conference, Berne 16–17 December 2004), 6 <www.iom.int/berne-initiative> accessed 18 October 2018.

[80] Klein Solomon, 'International Migration Management' (n 74) 12.

[81] The themes of the previous annual conferences were: Inclusive and Innovative Partnerships for Effective Global Governance of Migration (2018); Strengthening International Cooperation on and Governance of Migration Towards the Adoption of a Global Compact on Migration in 2018 (2017); Follow-up and Review of Migration in the Sustainable Development Goals (2016); Conference on Migrants and Cities (2015); Human Mobility and Development: Emerging Trends and New Opportunities for Partnerships (2014); Diaspora Ministerial Conference (2013); Managing Migration in Crisis Situations (2012); The Future of Migration: Building Capacities for Change (2011); Migration and Social Change (2010); Human Rights and Migration: Working Together for Safe, Dignified and Secure Migration (2009); Return Migration: Challenges and Opportunities (2008); Migration Management in the Evolving Global Economy (2007); Partnerships in Migration (2006); Towards Policy Coherence on Migration (2005); Valuing Migration (2004); Migration in a Globalized World (2003); Selected Policy Challenges (2002); Migration Challenges in the 21st Century (2001). For further information see <www.iom.int/idm> accessed 18 October 2018.

policies' at the national, regional, and global levels.[82] Both its form and content largely echo the ones of the International Agenda for Migration Management and have raised mixed comments from scholars for their lack of originality and ambition.[83] Similarly to the previous state-led initiatives, the report of the Global Commission on International Migration mainly called for 'improved coherence and strengthened capacity at the national level; greater consultation and cooperation between states at the regional level, and more effective dialogue and cooperation among governments and between international organizations at the global level'.[84]

While it reproduced many recommendations elaborated within regional consultative processes and the Berne Initiative, the report of the Global Commission still appears 'less state-centric'[85] than the previous initiatives. In particular, it was slightly more focused on the human rights of migrants and the institutional architecture of migration. The Commission notably acknowledged that 'the main obstacle to the protection of migrant rights is not the absence of law, but the failure of states to respect those conventions, agreements and declarations that they have freely accepted'.[86] Hence, 'the establishment of a coherent approach to migration requires states to demonstrate a greater respect for the provisions of the legal and normative framework affecting international migrants, especially the seven core UN human rights treaties'.[87]

Regarding the institutional framework of migration at the global level, the Global Commission on International Migration further noted 'the lack of inter-agency cooperation' and the 'overlaps within the current institutional architecture that at times undermine an integrated, coherent and effective response to the opportunities and challenges presented by international migration'.[88] Against this background, the report acknowledged that 'in the longer term a more fundamental overhaul of the current institutional architecture relating to international migration will be required [...] to bring together the disparate migration-related functions of existing UN and other agencies within a single organization'.[89] It identified three main options: creating a new agency, possibly by merging IOM and UNHCR; designating a 'lead agency' among existing agencies, such as UNHCR or ILO; or bringing IOM into the UN system to take the lead on issues related to voluntary migration.[90]

The Commission, however, abstained from taking any position among these three different scenarios. It preferred instead to consider them as long-term options

---

[82] Global Commission on International Migration (GCIM), *Migration in an Interconnected World: New Directions for Action* (GCIM 2005) 3.

[83] See, for instance, J Chamie and MG Powers (eds), *International Migration and the Global Community: A Forum on the Report of the Global Commission on International Migration* (Center for Migration Studies New York 2006); TA Aleinikoff, 'International Legal Norms on Migration: Substance without Architecture' in R Cholewinski, R Perruchoud, and E Macdonald, *International Migration Law: Developing Paradigms and Key Challenges* (TMC Asser Press 2007) 476; Crépeau and Atak, 'Global Migration Governance' (n 75) 129.

[84] GCIM, *Migration in an Interconnected World: New Directions for Action* (n 82) 82.

[85] A Pecoud, *Depoliticising Migration: Global Governance and International Migration Narratives* (Palgrave Macmillan 2015) 32.

[86] GCIM, *Migration in an interconnected world: New Directions for Action* (n 82) 54.

[87] ibid 2.   [88] ibid 73.   [89] ibid 75.   [90] ibid.

to be discussed at a later stage in the broader context of the ongoing reform of the UN, on the ground that 'there is currently no consensus concerning the introduction of a formal global governance system for international migration, involving the establishment of new international legal instruments or agencies'.[91] The only concrete and short-term action recommended by the Commission was to transform the Geneva Migration Group—established in 2003 to bring together the heads of IOM, ILO, UNHCR, UNCTAD, and UNODC—into a more inclusive and formal structure aimed at reinforcing inter-agency coordination. This limited and practical proposal was eventually endorsed by the UN Secretary General a few months later with the creation of the Global Migration Group.

The increased involvement of UN specialized institutions

Overall, and despite their limits and ambiguities, the various state-led initiatives carried out from 1995 to 2005 were instrumental in bypassing the deadlock of the UN through the development of alternative spaces of dialogue and consultation. Although the UN disappeared from the radar as an inter-state forum of dialogue, its organs and specialized agencies were increasingly active in two main directions. On the one hand, some important institutional changes were initiated by the UN Commission on Human Rights and the United Nations Population Division. In 1999, the former created the mandate of Special Rapporteur on the human rights of migrants 'to examine ways and means to overcome the obstacles existing to the full and effective protection of the human rights of this vulnerable group'.[92] In 2002, the latter launched the Annual Coordination Meetings on International Migration to discuss the collection and exchange of information on migration and to facilitate coordination of activities within the UN system and among other relevant organizations.[93]

On the other hand, in parallel to these institutional developments, UNHCR and ILO adopted several soft law standards within their respective mandates. From 2000 to 2002, UNHCR launched the Global Consultations on International Protection, a broad consultative process involving states, international and non-governmental organizations, and refugee experts in order to 'revitalize the 1951 Convention framework and to equip States better to address the challenges in a spirit of dialogue and cooperation'.[94] Its key outcome was the adoption of the Agenda for Protection,

---

[91] ibid 3.
[92] Commission on Human Rights Res 44 (1999) UN Doc E/CN.4/RES/1999/44, para 3. The functions of this new mandate are: '(a) To request and receive information from all relevant sources, including migrants themselves, on violations of the human rights of migrants and their families; (b) To formulate appropriate recommendations to prevent and remedy violations of the human rights of migrants, wherever they may occur; (c) To promote the effective application of relevant international norms and standards on the issue; (d) To recommend actions and measures applicable at the national, regional and international levels to eliminate violations of the human rights of migrants.'
[93] UNDESA, 'Coordination Meeting on International Migration New York, 11–12 July' (UN, 2002) available at <www.un.org/en/development/desa/population/migration/events/coordination/1/index.shtml?A2011> accessed 18 October 2018.
[94] UNGA 'Agenda for Protection' (26 June 2002) UN Doc A/AC.96/965/Add.1, 1.

consisting of two parts: a Declaration of States Parties to the 1951 Convention and its 1967 Protocol, adopted in December 2001, reaffirming their commitments to implement these binding instruments; and a Programme of Action. The latter focused on six goals: strengthening implementation of the 1951 Convention and its 1967 Protocol; protecting refugees within broader migration movements; sharing burdens and responsibilities more equitably and building capacities to receive and protect refugees; addressing security-related concerns more effectively; redoubling the search for durable solutions for refugees; and meeting the protection needs of refugee women and children.[95] Shortly after the adoption of the Agenda for Protection, UNHCR embarked on a new consultative process from 2003 to 2005 called 'the Convention Plus initiative'. This new endeavour, however, failed to meet its own objectives of adopting special agreements between UNHCR and governments on three areas that are inadequately covered by the 1951 Convention, namely resettlement, irregular secondary movements, and development assistance.[96]

ILO was equally proactive in developing soft law guidance on labour migration with more tangible results than UNHCR. According to the ILO Declaration on Fundamental Principles and Rights at Work adopted in 1998, all ILO Members States are bound, without regard to their ratification status, by a core content of four basic labour rights (freedom of association, elimination of forced labour, abolition of child labour, and elimination of discrimination in respect of employment and occupation).[97] While this Declaration was adopted in a much broader context than labour migration, its preamble acknowledged the special needs of migrant workers. In addition, in 2004, the 92nd International Labour Conference reaffirmed the plain applicability of this Declaration to all migrant workers (including undocumented ones).[98] At the same 92nd session, the International Labour Conference also adopted an ILO Plan of Action for Migrant Workers to develop 'a rights-based approach, in accordance with existing international labour standards and ILO principles, which recognizes labour market needs and the sovereign right of all nations to determine their own migration policies'.[99]

---

[95] ibid 2–23. For further comments and discussion, see T Clark and J Simeon, 'UNHCR International Protection Policies 2000–2013: From Cross-Road to Gaps and Responses' (2014) 33 RSQ 1–33.

[96] The Convention Plus initiative was terminated in November 2005 without adopting any of these purported agreements, even if a basic and consensual *Framework of Understandings on Resettlement* was reached in 2004. See UNHCR, High Commissioner's Forum, 'Multilateral Framework of Understandings on Resettlement' (2004) Forum/2004/6; UNHCR, High Commissioner's Forum, 'Progress Report: Convention Plus' (2005) Forum/2005/6. See also M Zieck, 'Doomed to Fail from the Outset? UNHCR's Convention Plus Initiative Revisited' (2009) 21 IJRL 387–420; A Betts and JF Durieux, 'Convention Plus as a Norm-Setting Exercise' (2007) 20 JRS 509–35.

[97] International Labour Conference (86th Session) Declaration on Fundamental Principles and Rights at Work (Geneva June 1998).

[98] International Labour Conference (92nd Session) Provisional record, Sixth item on the agenda: Migrant workers, Conclusions concerning a fair deal for migrant workers in a global economy (Geneva 2004) 58, para 12. See also International Labour Conference (92nd Session) Report VI: Toward a Fair Deal for Migrant Workers in the Global Economy (Geneva 2004) 72, para 229.

[99] International Labour Conference (92nd Session) Provisional Record (n 98) 60, para 20.

Following this initiative, the ILO Multilateral Framework on Labour Migration: Non-binding Principles and Guidelines for a Rights-based Approach to Labour Migration was adopted in November 2005 at the ILO Tripartite Meeting of Experts, which was subsequently endorsed by its Governing Body a few months later.[100] When compared to the other international initiatives adopted within and outside the UN, the ILO Multilateral Framework constitutes the most comprehensive and detailed soft law instrument specifically devoted to labour migration. It comprises fifteen general principles, each supported and detailed by practical guidelines, and a compendium of best practices.

This set of principles and guidelines focuses on nine areas encompassing a broad range of issues: decent work; international cooperation; global knowledge base; effective management of labour migration; protection of migrant workers; prevention of and protection against abusive practices; migration process; social integration and inclusion, as well as migration, and development.[101] Moreover, the ILO Multilateral Framework presents two other added values. First, it is not only addressed to states but also to employers' and workers' organizations. Second, it also provides a follow-up mechanism through the ILO Governing Body, which shall periodically review progress made in the implementation of the Multilateral Framework.

To sum up, from 1994 to 2005, global migration governance became an increasing concern of the international community. Despite the false start of the Cairo Programme of Action and the failure to convene a UN conference on migration, this intense period of experimentation and expansion of dialogue and consultation has resulted in three main outcomes and lessons learned.

First and more importantly, the proliferation of international initiatives on migration has created habits of cooperation among states on this particularly divisive and sensitive issue. The spread and dissemination of consultative processes and fora of dialogue have been crucial in building confidence and developing a common language among states with diverging interests, alongside the traditional divide between countries of origin and destination. This turn toward intergovernmental cooperation represents an important progress on its own: while the very notion of global migration governance was considered an intrusion in national sovereignty for a long period of time, it turned, from then on, into a truly international issue. Migration has thus become a matter of international cooperation which can no longer fall within the domestic jurisdiction of states.

Second, despite their great variety and some noticeable divergences, these multiple international initiatives have exhibited a substantial degree of convergence on

---

[100] ILO, *ILO Multilateral Framework on Labour Migration: Non-binding Principles and Guidelines for a Rights-based Approach to Labour Migration* (ILO 2006).

[101] For further comments on the ILO Framework, see G Goodwin-Gill, 'Migrant Rights and "Managed Migration"' in V Chetail (ed), *Globalization, Migration and Human Rights: International Law under Review* (Bruylant 2007) 178–85; R Cholewinski, 'Labour Migration Management and the Rights of Migrant Workers' in A Edwards and C Ferstman (eds), *Human Security and Non-Citizens: Law, Policy and International Affairs* (CUP 2010) 296–97; J Fudge, 'The Precarious Migrant Status and Precarious Employment: The Paradox of International Rights for Migrant Workers' (2011) Metropolis British Columbia Centre of Excellence for Research on Immigration and Diversity Working Paper No 11-15, 40–42.

three basic common understandings: 1) minimizing the negative aspects of migration by addressing the root causes of forced and irregular migration (such as poverty, human rights violations, and armed conflicts); 2) strengthening the positive effects of migration on the economic development of both countries of origin and destination (through the use of fair recruitment practices, the facilitation of remittances and of temporary labour migration to satisfy the needs of the labour markets, as well as the promotion of voluntary return and reintegration of migrants); and 3) protecting the human rights of migrants (most notably through combating discrimination, racism, and xenophobia, securing migrant workers' rights and labour standards, and protecting migrants from abuses, exploitation, and human trafficking).[102] This convergence of views is neither spectacular nor trivial; yet it displays a better understanding and a growing consensus among states concerning the multifaceted dimensions of migration.

Third, the spread of international initiatives aimed at fostering dialogue and cooperation on migration has created momentum. Kathleen Newland observed in 2005 that 'for most of the decade of the 1990s, international migration [...] was all but invisible on the global policy agenda. [...] All this changed quite suddenly around the turn of the millennium. Suddenly, migration was everywhere one looked in the UN system and beyond.'[103] This wave of international mobilization has paved the way for a new turn in global migration governance and eventually prepared the ground for the next phase of its development: the revival of the UN and the move toward a more consensual approach under the banner of the migration-development nexus.

6.2.2 The revival of the UN and the migration-development nexus: 2006–2015

After an intensive period of experimentation and expansion, global migration governance entered a new phase of acceleration from 2006 to 2015, which witnessed the revitalization of the UN under the auspices of the migration-development nexus. Approaching migration from the broader and less divisive aegis of development has provided the UN with an entry point to become a forum of dialogue after two decades of tergiversation. The renewed interest in the migration-development nexus has not only been a pragmatic way to promote the UN as a new platform of intergovernmental discussion. It has also generated an atmosphere propitious to constructive dialogue based on the mutual interests of both states of origin and destination. Since 2006, the migration-development nexus has thus been rediscovered

---

[102] See also C Bauloz, *A Comparative Thematic Mapping of Global Migration Initiatives: Lessons Learned towards a Global Compact for Safe, Orderly and Regular Migration* (IOM Migration Research Leaders' Syndicate 2017).

[103] K Newland, 'The Governance of International Migration: Mechanisms, Processes and Institutions' (2005) Paper prepared for the Policy Analysis and Research Programme of the Global Commission on International Migration, 1.

as the new mantra of inter-state cooperation in an attempt to reshape the North-South divide into a more comprehensive and balanced approach.

In his lengthy report on migration and development published in May 2006, the UN Secretary-General celebrated 'one of migration's most promising aspects: its relationship to development', by emphasizing that 'there is an emerging consensus that countries can cooperate to create triple wins, for migrants, for their countries of origin and for the societies that receive them'.[104] Building on the lessons learned from the regional consultative processes, the Berne Initiative, and the Global Commission on International Migration, Kofi Annan stressed that:

Member States now share a core set of migration-related goals that include: enhancing the development impact of international migration; ensuring that migration occurs mainly through legal channels; ensuring the protection of the rights of migrants; preventing the exploitation of migrants, especially those in vulnerable situations; and combating the crimes of smuggling of migrants and trafficking in persons. Governments should recommit to these goals and develop a strategy based on co-development to reach them. [...] At the international level, a framework based on co-development goals could lead to novel initiatives to promote the beneficial effects of international migration, in particular through: facilitating, reducing the costs of and leveraging remittances; strengthening the knowledge, trade and investment links between the societies of origin and their expatriate communities; and promoting return migration and circulation.[105]

In the wake of this growing optimism, the UN Secretary-General initiated two institutional changes that have strongly framed the multilateral framework of migration governance. In January 2006, he created the UN Special Representative of the Secretary-General for International Migration to promote the UN agenda on migration and, a few months after, in April 2006, the Global Migration Group to improve inter-agency cooperation.[106] Beyond the impetus triggered by the UN Secretary-General, the most spectacular development has been the dawn of the General Assembly as a forum of inter-state dialogue.

The rise of the General Assembly as a forum of inter-state dialogue

Since 2006, the General Assembly has become the catalyst of global migration governance in initiating several important markers under the broader and relatively uncontroversial auspices of the migration-development nexus. In less than ten years, it organized the first High-level Dialogue on International Migration and Development in 2006 which resulted in the creation of the Global Forum on Migration Development. In 2013, it also held a second High-level Dialogue that produced the very first declaration on migration and development agreed on by all UN Member States, before further mainstreaming migration within the 2030 Agenda for Sustainable Development adopted in 2015.

---

[104] UNGA 'International Migration and Development' in 'Report of the Secretary-General' (2006) UN Doc A/60/871, 5.
[105] ibid 16.   [106] For further discussion, see Chapter 7.

The revival of the UN has triggered an important shift in the evolution of global migration governance. At the same time, however, this change in the institutional framework of dialogue has mainly transposed at the universal plane the methods of the previous state-led initiatives launched outside the UN. This was particularly evident during the first High-Level Dialogue on International Migration and Development organized by the General Assembly on 14 and 15 September 2006. The decision to convene this intergovernmental meeting was clearly a strategy to resolve the lack of consensus between countries of origin and destination to convene a UN conference on migration. The High-level Dialogue thus replicated within the General Assembly the same approach which was experimented outside the UN by state-led informal processes carried out over the preceding decade. Its main purpose was to provide a forum of discussion among Member States in order 'to identify ways and means to maximize the developmental benefits of international migration and to reduce its negative impacts'.[107] It gathered 162 states' representatives around four roundtables, focusing respectively on: 1) the effects of migration on development; 2) measures to ensure respect for, and protection of, the human rights of all migrants, and to prevent and combat smuggling of migrants and trafficking in persons; 3) the multidimensional aspects of international migration and development, including remittances; and 4) the building of partnerships, capacity-building, and the sharing of best practices at the bilateral, regional, and global levels.[108]

Although this first High-level Dialogue fell short of producing any declaration, the very fact that states discussed migration within the UN system was viewed as an accomplishment. Instead of exacerbating the North-South polarization, it produced a broad consensus to continue and deepen inter-state dialogue at the global level. Despite the reticence of the US and Australia,[109] the first High-level Dialogue generated widespread support for the proposal of the Secretary-General to create the Global Forum on Migration and Development.[110] This new framework of inter-state dialogue was to become a major component of global migration governance. Contrary to the Secretary-General's proposal, however, it has been established outside the UN as a process driven by states. It is thus largely modelled on the regional consultative processes as a voluntary, non-binding, and informal mechanism. The Global Forum on Migration and Development has met annually since 2007 and has eventually become a unique platform of multilateral dialogue on migration and development.[111]

One year after the first meeting of the Global Forum on Migration and Development, the General Assembly convened a second High-level Dialogue on Migration and Development which took place in October 2013 with the

---

[107] UNGA 'Summary of the High-level Dialogue on International Migration and Development' in 'Note by the President of the General Assembly' (2006) UN Doc A/61/515, 2.

[108] ibid 1.

[109] P Martin, S Martin, and S Cross, 'High-Level Dialogue on Migration and Development' (2007) 45 International Migration 7, 21.

[110] UNGA 'Summary of the High-level Dialogue on International Migration and Development' (n 107) 5.

[111] For further discussion, see Chapter 7.

self-declared objective of 'identifying concrete measures to strengthen coherence and cooperation'.[112] While perpetuating the same model of informal discussion among states' representatives, the second High-level Dialogue featured a major difference compared to the first one: UN Member States unanimously adopted a Declaration of the High-level Dialogue on International Migration and Development. The significance of this outcome should not be underestimated. For the first time since 1985,[113] the General Assembly was able to produce a negotiated and formal declaration on migration that was accepted by all Member States. Its adoption signals a growing convergence among UN Member States 'to work towards an effective and inclusive agenda on international migration that integrates development and respects human rights'.[114]

Even though the content of the Declaration remains very consensual and not fundamentally new, it exemplifies two subtle shifts in the way the migration-development nexus is understood by Member States. First, the traditional root-causes approach to migration is not mentioned but rather replaced with a more positive and collaborative assertion of migration as a tool for the development of all states. While acknowledging the 'important contribution made by migrants and migration to development in countries of origin, transit and destination',[115] the Declaration recognizes 'human mobility' as 'a key factor for sustainable development',[116] and 'encourage[s] Member States to cooperate on mobility programmes that facilitate safe, orderly and regular migration'.[117]

Second, the Declaration strongly emphasizes human and labour rights. While reaffirming 'the need to protect the human rights of all migrants, regardless of their migration status',[118] the Declaration pays specific attention to migrant workers by underlining 'the need to respect and promote international labour standards' and 'the rights of migrants in their workplaces'.[119] It further notes 'the contribution of [the ICRMW] to the international system for the protection of migrants' and 'strongly condemn[s] the acts, manifestations and expressions of racism, racial discrimination, xenophobia and related intolerance against migrants'.[120] The 2013 Declaration has arguably paved the way for a new turn toward a more balanced and comprehensive approach to migration. As notably acknowledged by ILO at the International Labour Conference of 2014, the UNGA Declaration has been 'widely regarded as a landmark in the multilateral system's approach to migration'.[121]

Following the impetus initiated by the second High-level Dialogue, the General Assembly mainstreamed migration into the 2030 Agenda for Sustainable Development adopted in September 2015. The Declaration of the 2030 Agenda

---

[112] UNGA Res 63/225 (2008) UN Doc A/RES/63/225, para 16; UNGA Res 67/219 (2012) UN Doc A/RES/67/219, para 3.
[113] Declaration on the Human Rights of Individuals Who Are Not Nationals of the Country in Which They Live In, UNGA Res 40/144 (13 December 1985) UN Doc A/RES/40/144.
[114] Declaration of the High-level Dialogue on International Migration and Development, UNGA Res 68/4 (2013) UN Doc A/RES/68/4, para 3.
[115] ibid para 2.   [116] ibid para 8.   [117] ibid para 18.   [118] ibid para 10.
[119] ibid para 14.   [120] ibid paras 15–16.
[121] International Labour Conference (103rd Session) Report of the Director-General: Report I(B): Fair Migration: Setting an ILO Agenda (Geneva 2014) 17.

reaffirms 'the positive contribution of migrants for inclusive growth and sustainable development' and acknowledges that all Member States 'will cooperate internationally to ensure safe, orderly and regular migration involving full respect for human rights and the humane treatment of migrants regardless of migration status, of refugees and of displaced persons'.[122]

The 2030 Agenda for Sustainable Development further integrates migration in ten of the 169 targets of the sustainable development goals (SDGs) to cover some of the common issues associated with the migration-development nexus, such as the facilitation of remittances (target 10.c), the protection of labour rights of migrant workers (target 8.8), and the facilitation of orderly, safe, and regular migration (target 10.7).[123] Although migration-related targets are still far from providing comprehensive and detailed coverage, for the first time, through the SDGs, migration has been incorporated into the global development framework. As such, this represents a progress compared to the previous Millennium Development Goals which failed to address migration.[124]

Despite the explicit acknowledgment of migration, the Agenda for Sustainable Development has been criticized on the ground that the SDGs, as a whole, promote 'a sedentary perspective of development', whereby migration is primarily conceived as a binary and linear process with a view to addressing its root causes.[125] These criticisms are neither new nor specific to the SDGs. They reflect instead the ambiguity inherent in the migration-development nexus that replicates but also reframes, within a broader context, the traditional tension between controlling and facilitating migration. Despite the apparent convergence of interests between developing and developed countries, the migration-development nexus is at the junction of two conflicting paradigms: the root causes approach follows a control-oriented paradigm devised to alleviate migration pressure from countries of origin through

---

[122] UNGA Res 70/1 (2015) UN Doc A/RES/70/1, para 29.

[123] The other related-migration targets include the retention of the health workforce in developing countries to prevent the brain drain phenomenon (target 3.c), the increase of scholarships available in developing countries for study abroad (target 4.b), the eradication of human trafficking (targets 5.2, 8.7, and 16.2), the provision of legal identity for all, including birth registration (target 16.9) and the increase of data disaggregated by migratory status (target 17.18). For further discussion, see notably UNESCAP 'International Migration, the 2030 Agenda for Sustainable Development and the Global Compact for Safe, Orderly and Regular Migration' in 'Note by the Secretariat' (2017) UN Doc E/ESCAP/GCM/PREP/2; Overseas Development Institute (ODI), *Migration and the 2030 Agenda for Sustainable Development* (ODI 2017).

[124] The Millennium Development Goals made no mention of migration as a positive force for development. The only reference to migration was made in a negative way, highlighting the violations of migrants' rights and the potential for migration to spread epidemic disease. See: UNGA 'Road Map towards the Implementation of the United Nations Millennium Declaration' in 'Report of the Secretary-General' (2001) UN Doc A/56/326, paras 104 and 214.

[125] G Nijenhuis and M Leung, 'Rethinking Migration in the 2030 Agenda: Towards a De-Territorialized Conceptualization of Development' (2017) 44(1) Forum for Development Studies 51. For further critical accounts, see S Suliman, 'Migration and Development after 2015' (2017) 14(3) Globalizations 415; K Preibisch, W Dodd, and Y Su, 'Pursuing the Capabilities Approach within the Migration-Development Nexus' (2016) 42(13) Journal of Ethnic and Migration Studies 2111; K Sexsmith and P McMichael, 'Formulating the SDGs: Reproducing or Reimagining State-Centered Development?' (2015) 12(4) Globalizations 581.

development assistance, whereas a more positive viewpoint of migration focuses on its potential for the development in both countries of origin and destination.[126] While these two contradictory driving forces still coexist to a large extent, the constructive ambiguity of the migration-development nexus has been instrumental in facilitating dialogue among states of destination and origin.

Although it provides a pragmatic venue for North-South dialogue, the ambivalent nature of the migration-development nexus represents its main limit as exemplified by the controversial EU policy over the past few decades.[127] Many scholars have repeatedly asserted that the real objective pursued by European states is more likely to curb immigration than to contribute to the development of sending countries.[128] In other words, the 'contamination of the development agenda'[129] is nothing more than a 'camouflage'[130] for justifying a 'policy of containment'.[131] From this stance, development appears to be the continuation by other means of the migration control policy promoted by EU Member States. This is evidently illustrated by the recurrent temptation of the EU to subordinate development assistance to the externalization of migration control in and by countries of origin and transit.[132] This

---

[126] For further discussion on the evolving pattern of the migration-development nexus, see V Chetail, 'Paradigm and Paradox of the Migration-Development Nexus: The New Border for North-South Dialogue' (2008) 51 Germ Yrbk Int'l L 183–215.

[127] ibid. For a more recent account, see also in this sense, among many other publications, M Funk et al, 'Tackling Irregular Migration through Development—A Flawed Approach?' (2017) EPC Discussion Paper; L Zanfrini, 'Migration and Development: Old and New Ambivalences of the European Approach' (2015) ISMU Paper; J Crush, 'The EU-ACP Migration and Development Relationship' (2015) 4(1) Migration and Development 39.

[128] See among many others: S Lavenex and R Kunz, 'The Migration-Development Nexus in EU External Relations' (2008) 30(3) J Europ Integration 439–57; F Pastore, 'Europe, Migration and Development: Critical Remarks on an Emerging Policy Field' (2007) 50(4) Development 56–62; H de Hass, 'Turning the Tide? Why "Development instead of Migration" Policies Are Bound to Fail' (2006) International Migration Institute (IMI) University of Oxford Working Paper No 2, 18; K Newland, 'Migration as a Factor in Development and Poverty Reduction' (Migration Policy Institute, 1 June 2003) available at<www.migrationpolicy.org/article/migration-factor-development-and-poverty-reduction> accessed 18 October 2018; S Stanton Russell, 'Migration and Development: Reframing the International Policy Agenda' (Migration Policy Institute, 1 June 2003) available at<www.migrationinformation.org/Feature/display.cfm?ID=126> accessed 18 October 2018; S Gent, 'The Root Causes of Migration: Criticizing the Approach and Finding a Way Forward' (2002) Sussex Migration Working Paper No 11, 15.

[129] B Hayes and T Bunyan, 'Migration, Development and the EU Security Agenda' in *Europe in the World: Essays on EU Foreign, Security and Development Policies* (British Overseas NGOs for Development (BOND) 2003) 71.

[130] P Weil, 'Towards a Coherent Policy of Co-Development' (2002) 40(3) International Migration 41, 42.

[131] C Lindstrom, 'Addressing the Root Causes of Forced Migration: A European Union Policy of Containment?' (2003) Refugee Studies Centre University of Oxford Working Paper No 11 available at <www.rsc.ox.ac.uk/publications/addressing-the-root-causes-of-forced-migration-a-european-union-policy-of-containment > accessed 18 October 2018. See also C Boswell, 'The External Dimension of EU Immigration and Asylum Policy' (2003) 79(3) International Affairs 619–38; D Bouteillet-Paquet, 'Passing the Buck: A Critical Analysis of the Readmission Policy Implemented by the European Union and Its Member States' (2003) 5 European Journal of Migration and Law 359, 360.

[132] For a recent illustration see Commission, 'Communication from the Commission to the European Parliament, the European Council, the Council and the European Investment Bank on establishing a new Partnership Framework with third countries under the European Agenda on Migration' COM (2016) 385 final (7 June 2016), 7 and 17: '[It] is important to ensure that development assistance helps partner countries manage migration more effectively, and also incentivises them to effectively cooperate

strategy of intimidation and persuasion is, however, bound to be counterproductive because it exacerbates the tensions with third states and relies on a flawed perception of the migration-development nexus.

The relations between migration and development are, indeed, much more subtle and complex than it is commonly assumed by diplomats and policymakers. A large body of evidence has shown that their interactions are far from being negatively correlated processes. While the two intersect at their margins, development is not an answer to migration and *vice-versa*. On the one hand, contrary to the simplistic assumption of the root-causes approach, development initially leads to an increase rather than a decrease in migration, in so far as economic growth of developing countries raises new opportunities and encouragements to find a better life abroad.[133] In the short run, 'international migration does not stem from a lack of economic development, but from development itself'.[134] This phenomenon—called the 'migration hump'—tends to disappear in the long run, when the level of development in the country of origin reaches a more stable stage.

On the other hand, notwithstanding the common assertion that 'migration is the oldest action against poverty',[135] international migration remains a selective process, simply because 'the poorest of the poor, that is the 1.2 billion people living on less than US$1 a day, do not have the connections and resources needed to engage in inter-continental migration'.[136] The survival migration of the poorest is thus

on readmission of irregular migrants. Positive and negative incentives should be integrated in the EU's development policy, rewarding those countries that fulfil their international obligation to readmit their own nationals, and those that cooperate in managing the flows of irregular migrants from third countries, as well as those taking action to adequately host persons fleeing conflict and persecution. Equally, there must be consequences for those who do not cooperate on readmission and return. The same should be true of trade policy, notably where the EU gives preferential treatment to its partners. [...] All EU policies including education, research, climate change, energy, environment, agriculture, should in principle be part of a package, bringing maximum leverage to the discussion. [...] This means, for each partner country, the development of a mix of positive and negative incentives, the use of which should be governed by a clear understanding that the overall relationship between the EU and that country will be guided in particular by the ability and willingness of the country to cooperate on migration management.' For previous failed attempts aimed at conditioning development assistance to migration control, see European Council, 'Presidency Conclusions' (Seville, 21–22 June 2002) 13463/02 POLGEN 52, paras 35–36; Austrian Presidency of the European Union, 'Strategy Paper on Immigration and Asylum' (1 July 1998) 9809/98 LIMITE CK 4 27 ASIM 170, para 59.

[133] See among an abundant literature: R Black and others, 'Migration and Development: Causes and Consequences' in R Penninx, M Berger, and K Kraal (eds), *The Dynamics of International Migration and Settlement in Europe: A State of the Art* (Amsterdam University Press 2006) 41; D Ellerman, 'Policy Research on Migration and Development' (2003) World Bank Policy Research Working Paper No 3117; PL Martin and JE Taylor, 'The Anatomy of a Migration Hump' in JE Taylor (ed), *Development Strategy, Employment, and Migration: Insights from Model* (OECD Publishing 1996) 43.

[134] DS Massey et al, *Worlds in Motion: Understanding International Migration at the End of the Millennium* (OUP 1998) 227.

[135] JK Galbraith, *The Nature of Mass Poverty* (Harvard University Press 1979) 7.

[136] N Nyberg-Sørensen, N Van Hear, and P Engberg-Pedersen, 'The Migration-Development Nexus: Evidence and Policy Options' (2002) 40(5) International Migration 49, 51. See also among others R Skeldon, 'Migration and Poverty' (2002) 17 Asia-Pacific Population Journal 67; U Kothari, 'Migration and Chronic Poverty' (2002) University of Manchester Working Paper No 16; A de Haan, 'Livelihoods and Poverty: The Role of Migration: A Critical Review of the Migration Literature' (1999) 36 J Dev Stud 1.

primarily within their country of origin (generally from rural to urban areas). From that angle, development cannot be a substitute for international migration but rather an objective in its own right, conducted for the purpose of poverty reduction. Otherwise, a development policy targeted to reduce migration pressure carries the risk of diverting international aid from non-sending countries, which include the poorest regions of the world.[137]

Despite its limits and ambiguities, the migration-development nexus has been a persuasive tool for fostering and consolidating habits of collaboration on the universal plane. The internationalization of dialogues within the UN has appeased—albeit not dissipated—the tensions inherent in the conflicting agendas pursued by states. By becoming the main forum of intergovernmental dialogue, the General Assembly has steadily reframed the terms of the discussion. Both literally and metaphorically, it has made room for a more balanced and less confrontational approach, whereby all UN Member States are able to present and exchange their views with their counterparts on an equal footing. Member States have progressively learned to collaborate and build consensus beyond the traditional North-South divide. As a result of this ongoing process, the General Assembly has been able to channel and eventually take stock of this growing convergence: the two High-level Dialogues and the Agenda for Sustainable Development have concurred in acknowledging the benefit of migration for the development of both countries of origin and destination, while maintaining the focus of the broader development agenda on the reduction of poverty as an objective of its own.

The progressive enlargement of the international agenda beyond the migration-development nexus

While the migration-development nexus has served as a unifying theme for the General Assembly, new issues of common concern have progressively emerged in the international agenda. The need to expand the multilateral dialogue beyond the traditional migration-development nexus has been driven by the growing anxiety, whether real or perceived, about the impact of climate change and natural disasters on migration. This new field of inter-state cooperation has prompted the adoption of a significant number of soft law initiatives within various intergovernmental fora.[138]

The nexus between climate change and migration was addressed for the first time by the United Nations Framework Convention on Climate Change (UNFCCC) in 2010, which resulted in the adoption of the Cancún Adaptation Framework,

---

[137] See also in this sense LT Katseli, REB Lucas, and T Xenogiani, 'Policies for Migration and Development: A European Perspective' in *Gaining from Migration* (EC/OECD 2006) 29; C Boswell and J Crisp, 'Poverty, International Migration and Asylum' (2004) UNU World Institute for Development Economics Research (UNU-WIDER) Policy Brief No 8, 19.

[138] For a general overview, see especially E Ferris and J Bergmann, 'Soft Law, Migration and Climate Change Governance' (2017) 8 JHRE 6; B Mayer and F Crépeau (eds), *Research Handbook on Climate Change, Migration and the Law* (Edward Elgar Publishing 2017); SL Nash, 'From Cancun to Paris: An Era of Policy Making on Climate Change and Migration' (2018) 9(1) Global Policy 53–63.

inviting states to take 'measures to enhance understanding, coordination and co-operation with regard to climate change induced displacement, migration and planned relocation, where appropriate, at the national, regional and international levels'.[139] Two years later, at the Doha Conference, UNFCCC emphasized the need for 'further work to advance the understanding of […] how impacts of climate change are affecting patterns of migration, displacement and human mobility'.[140]

Despite this growing concern, the Paris Agreement of 2015 failed to adopt any binding provision on migration. Its preamble only acknowledges that 'Parties should, when taking action to address climate change, respect, promote and consider their re-spective obligations on human rights, the right of […] migrants, […] and people in vulnerable situations.'[141] Although the preamble is not legally binding per se, it is still relevant to interpret the operative part of the Agreement and it represents, after all, the first recognition of migration in the text of a treaty devoted to climate change. The re-port accompanying the Agreement further calls for the establishment of a task force 'to develop recommendations for integrated approaches to avert, minimize and address displacement related to the adverse impacts of climate change'.[142]

In parallel with the modest but ongoing developments within the UNFCCC, several soft law instruments have been adopted both within and outside the UN in the broader context of disasters. In 2015, the Sendai Framework on Disaster Risk Reduction 2015–2030 was adopted by UN Member States at the Third World Conference on Disaster Risk Reduction and endorsed by the UN General Assembly.[143] While acknowledging the consequences of disasters on displacement,[144]

---

[139] UNFCCC 'Decision 1/CP.16: The Cancun Agreements: Outcome of the Work of the Ad Hoc Working Group on Long-term Cooperation Action under the Convention' (10–11 December 2010) contained in Report of the Conference of the Parties on its Sixteenth Session FCCC/CP/2010/7/Add.1, para 14(f). For further comments see K Warner, 'Human Migration and Displacement in the Context of Adaptation to Climate Change: The Cancun Adaptation Framework and Potential for Future Action' (2012) 30 Environment and Planning C: Government and Policy 1061.

[140] UNFCCC 'Decision 3/CP.18 Approaches to Address Loss and Damage Associated with Climate Change Impact in Developing Countries That Are Particularly Vulnerable to the Adverse Effects of Climate Change to Enhance Adaptive Capacity' (8 December 2012) contained in Report of the Conference of the Parties on its Eighteenth Session FCCC/CP/2012/8/Add.1, para 7(vi).

[141] UNFCCC 'Decision 1/CP.21 Adoption of the Paris Agreement' (12 December 2015) contained in Report of the Conference of the Parties on its Twenty-First Session FCCC/CP/2015/10/Add.1, Annex, 21.

[142] ibid 8. This task force is integrated within the Warsaw International Mechanism for Loss and Damage Associated with Climate Change Impacts which was created in 2013 'to address loss and damage associated with impacts of climate change, including extreme events and slow onset events, in developing countries that are particularly vulnerable to the adverse effects of climate change', see UNFCCC, 'Decision 2/CP.19: Warsaw International Mechanism for Loss and Damage Associated with Climate Change Impacts' (31 January 2014) UN Doc FCCC/CP/2013/10/Add.1, para 1. For further discussion about the Paris Agreement in connection with migration, see DR Klein (ed), *The Paris Agreement on Climate Change: Analysis and Commentary* (OUP 2017); B Mayer, 'Migration in the UNFCCC Workstream on Loss and Damage: An Assessment of Alternative Framings and Conceivable Responses' (2017) 6 Transnational Environmental Law 107; O Serdeczny, *What Does it Mean to 'Address Displacement' Under the UNFCCC?: An Analysis of the Negotiations Process and the Role of Research* (Deutsches Institut für Entwicklungspolitik 2017).

[143] Sendai Framework on Disaster Risk Reduction 2015–2030, Annex II in UNGA Res 69/283 (2015) UN Doc A/RES/69/283.

[144] ibid para 4.

the Sendai Framework calls for national and local authorities to include migrants in disaster risk reduction,[145] and to ensure rapid and effective response to disaster-related displacement, including access to safe shelter and relief supplies.[146] Outside the UN, two other initiatives have been carried out as state-owned consultative processes to elaborate non-binding guidelines and best practices, namely the Nansen Initiative and the Migrants in Countries in Crisis (MICIC) Initiative.

The Nansen Initiative was launched in 2012 by Norway and Switzerland as a follow-up to the UNHCR Ministerial Conference organized in 2011 to commemorate the 60th anniversary of the Refugee Convention and the 50th anniversary of the Convention on the reduction of statelessness. It led to the adoption of the Agenda for the Protection of Cross-Border Displaced Persons in the Context of Disasters and Climate Change. Endorsed by 109 governmental delegations in 2015, the Agenda conceptualizes a 'comprehensive approach to disaster displacement' and compiles a broad set of 'effective practices' on admission, stay, and non-return from and in countries of destination, as well as vulnerability, resilience, and planned relocation in countries of origin.[147] In 2016, the Platform on Disaster Displacement was established as another state-led process to follow up on the work initiated by the Nansen Initiative and to implement the recommendation of its Agenda.[148]

In parallel with this endeavour, the MICIC Initiative was launched in 2014 by the US and the Philippines at the Global Forum on Migration and Development, following a call for action during the 2013 UN General Assembly High-level Dialogue. Its main outcome was the adoption of the Guidelines to Protect Migrants in Countries Experiencing Conflict or Natural Disaster in 2016, which identifies ten principles further detailed by fifteen guidelines and related best practices focusing on three main areas: crisis preparedness, emergency response, and post-crisis action.[149]

---

[145] ibid paras 7, 27(h) and 36 (a)(vi).
[146] ibid para 33(h). For further comments, see K Sudmeier-Rieux et al (eds), *Identifying Emerging Issues in Disaster Risk Reduction, Migration, Climate Change and Sustainable Development* (Springer International Publishing 2017); L Guadagno, 'Human Mobility in the Sendai Framework for Disaster Risk Reduction' (2016) 7(1) International Journal of Disaster Risk Science 30; W Kälin, 'Sendai Framework: An Important Step Forward for People Displaced by Disasters' (*Brookings*, 20 March 2015) available at <www.brookings.edu/blog/up-front/2015/03/20/sendai-framework-an-important-step-forward-for-people-displaced-by-disasters> accessed 24 November 2017.
[147] Nansen Initiative, *Agenda for the Protection of Cross-Border Displaced Persons in the Context of Disasters and Climate Change* (The Nansen Initiative 2015). For further discussion, see J McAdam, 'From the Nansen Initiative to the Platform on Disaster Displacement: Shaping International Approaches to Climate Change, Disasters and Displacement' (2016) 39(4) UNSW Law Journal 1518; W Kälin, 'The Nansen Initiative: Building Consensus on Displacement in Disaster Contexts' (2015) 49 Forced Migration Review 5.
[148] Platform on Disaster Displacement, 'Addressing the Protection Needs of People Displaced across Borders in the Context of Disasters and Climate Change' (May 2016). The four strategic priorities of this new platform are to 1) address knowledge and data gaps, 2) enhance the use of identified effective practices and strengthen cooperation among relevant actors, 3) promote policy coherence and mainstreaming of human mobility challenges in, and across, relevant policy and action areas, and 4) promote policy and normative development in gap areas.
[149] Migrants in Countries in Crisis (MICIC) Initiative, *Guidelines to Protect Migrants in Countries Experiencing Conflict or Natural Disaster* (MICIC Initiative 2016).

As exemplified by these two recent initiatives, the rise of 'mini-multilateralism' has become a defining feature of global migration governance, building confidence and consensus among states and developing non-binding standards on emerging issues. When compared to the state-led consultative processes carried out over the preceding decade, the Nansen and MICIC initiatives present two main differences regarding their scope and origin. Instead of discussing migration in general, they focus on a more targeted and narrower topic of international concern (namely the protection of migrants from disasters and conflicts) and, contrary to the previous ones, these two informal processes found their roots within the UN before continuing outside through a coalition of willing states. The Nansen and MICIC initiatives share, however, the same limits and ambiguities as the preceding endeavours: they do not enjoy an endorsement as universal and authoritative as the UN could offer; they are primarily led and financed by Western states; they do not create new international legal rules; and they might exacerbate fragmentation through the development of overlapping initiatives on similar issues. Nonetheless, the Nansen and MICIC initiatives have pioneered the mainstreaming of migration into the context of disaster and crisis. At the same time, they may also provide an incentive for further discussion and involvement within the UN system.

From a systemic perspective, the spread of intergovernmental initiatives addressing the impact of climate change, disaster, and crisis epitomizes a broader shift of global migration governance towards a more comprehensive approach which is no longer confined to the migration-development nexus. The enlargement of the international agenda on migration has been further consolidated by UN agencies and other related institutions. They have adopted a significant number of soft law initiatives primarily addressed to states on a broad range of issues associated with border control and migration governance.

Among the most prominent initiatives, UNHCR launched the Dialogue on Protection Challenges in 2007, an annual informal forum of discussion between states, non-governmental and intergovernmental organizations, the academic community, and other stakeholders.[150] While claiming that 'UNHCR is not a migration organization and does not consider its role activities to fall within the function that is commonly described as "migration management"',[151] in the same year, the UN Refugee Agency adopted the 10-Point Plan of Action on Refugee Protection

---

[150] Like the International Dialogue on Migration launched by IOM in 2001, the UNHCR Dialogue focuses each year on a specific topic: Protection and Solutions in Urban Settings: Engaging with Cities (2018); Toward a Global Compact on Refugees (2017); Children on the Move (2016); Understanding and Addressing Root Causes of Displacement (2015); Protection at Sea (2014); Protecting the Internally Displaced (2013); Faith and Protection (2012); Climate Change and Displacement (2011); Protection Gaps and Responses (2010); Humanitarian Challenges in the Context of Urbanization (2009); Protracted Refugee Situations (2008); Refugee Protection and Durable Solutions in the Context of International Migration (2007). For further information see UNHCR, 'High Commissioner's Dialogue' (*UNHCR*) available at<www.unhcr.org/high-commissioners-dialogue.html> accessed 18 October 2018; Clark and Simeon, 'UNHCR International Protection Policies 2000–2013' (n 95) 25–31.

[151] UNHCR, 'Refugee Protection and Durable Solutions in the Context of International Migration' Discussion Paper (19 November 2007) UNHCR/DPC/2007/Doc.02, para 11.

and Mixed Migration to assist States in developing and implementing protection-sensitive migration strategies alongside the specific needs of refugees.[152]

Following a similar endeavour, in 2014 OHCHR adopted the Recommended Principles and Guidelines on Human Rights at International Borders in order to translate human rights law into practical measures on border governance.[153] The same year, ILO launched its Fair Migration Agenda[154] and within this broader agenda, the Fair Recruitment Initiative, a multi-stakeholder process that resulted in the adoption of the ILO General Principles and Operational Guidelines for Fair Recruitment.[155] Furthermore, despite its longstanding reluctance toward this kind of endeavour, IOM has recently multiplied non-binding frameworks to guide and inform the organization and its Member States on the most salient aspects of its mandate. In 2012, it adopted the Migration Crisis Operational Framework,[156]

---

[152] The UNHCR Plan consists of ten action points addressing, in general and sometimes vague terms, the following items: 1) Cooperation among key partners; 2) Data collection and analysis; 3) Protection-sensitive entry systems; 4) Reception arrangements; 5) Mechanisms for profiling and referral; 6) Differentiated processes and procedures; 7) Solutions for refugees; 8) Addressing secondary movements; 9) Return arrangements for non-refugees and alternative migration options; 10) Information strategy. See UNHCR, 'Refugee Protection and Mixed Migration: A 10-Point Plan of Action' (January 2007).

[153] OHCHR, 'Recommended Principles and Guidelines on Human Rights at International Borders' (23 July 2014) UN Doc A/69/CRP.1. This document identifies three principles and ten guidelines to assist states in practical ways to address the following key items: promotion and protection of human rights, legal and policy framework, building human rights capacity, ensuring human rights in rescue and interception, human rights in the context of immediate assistance, screening and interviewing, identification and referral, avoiding detention, human rights-based return or removal, cooperation and coordination. The General Assembly has taken note of these recommended principles and guidelines in its resolution on the protection of migrants adopted without a vote in UNGA Res 69/167 (2014) UN Doc A/RES/69/167, para 16.

[154] International Labour Conference (103rd Session) Report I(B) of the Director-General: Fair Migration: Setting an ILO Agenda (Geneva June 2014). The tenets of this agenda are: making migration a choice by creating decent work opportunities in countries of origin; respecting the human rights, including labour rights, of all migrants; ensuring fair recruitment and equal treatment of migrant workers; forging stronger linkages between employment and labour migration policies; involving Ministries of labour, trade unions, and employers' organizations in migration policy making; and fostering genuine cooperation between countries and within regions.

[155] ILO, 'Fourth Supplementary Report: Outcome of the Meeting of Experts on Fair Recruitment' (Geneva, 5–7 September 2016) GB.328/INS/17/4 (12 October 2016), 3–13: 'Appendix: General Principles and Operational Guidelines for Fair Recruitment'. The objective of these non-binding general principles and operational guidelines is to inform the work of the ILO and of other organizations, national legislatures, and the social partners on promoting and ensuring fair recruitment. There are thirteen general principles to orient implementation at all levels and thirty-one operational guidelines identifying the responsibilities of key actors in the recruitment process and containing possible interventions and policy tools.

[156] IOM Resolution No 1243 (CI) 101st Session (27 November 2012). The IOM Migration Crisis Operational Framework is organised around two pillars that focus on the three phases of crisis (namely pre-crisis prevention of forced migration, emergency response to a migration crisis and recovery initiatives) and fifteen sectors of assistance (camp management and displacement tracking; shelter and non-food items; transport assistance for affected populations; health support; psychosocial support; (re)integration assistance; activities to support community stabilisation and transition; disaster risk reduction and resilience building; land and property support; counter-trafficking and protection of vulnerable migrants; technical assistance for humanitarian border management; emergency consular assistance; diaspora and human resource mobilisation; migration policy and legislation support; and humanitarian communications).

and in 2015, the Migration Governance Framework,[157] and the Principles for Humanitarian Action,[158] as well as the Progressive Resolution of Displacement Situations Framework in 2016.[159]

Global migration governance has thus significantly grown in a relatively short period of ten years. The UN has become a leading actor thanks to the unifying theme of the migration-development nexus. This strategic and pragmatic entry point has enabled the General Assembly to channel and pacify the traditional North-South divide through a more balanced and consensual approach. While becoming the centre of gravity for intergovernmental dialogue on migration, the General Assembly has initiated several normative and institutional markers (such as the Global Forum on International Migration and Development, the Declaration of the High-level Dialogue on International Migration and Development and the Agenda for Sustainable Development). Since then, multilateral dialogue on migration and development has become routine, while the international agenda has been progressively enlarged to address other issues of common concern within the diverse contexts of disaster, crisis, and border management. This gradual move toward a more comprehensive and integrated approach has culminated in a new decisive phase of global migration governance.

6.2.3 The New York Declaration and the UN Global Compacts: 2016–2018

From 2016 to 2018, migration has been more prominent than ever on the UN agenda. After one decade of intensive dialogue and consolidation, migration is now addressed as a topic of international concern on its own, without any connections or interferences with development, climate change, and other overlapping fields. The year 2016 witnessed a new wave of international mobilization mainly triggered

---

[157] IOM Resolution No 1310 (CI) 106th Session (24 November 2015). The IOM Migration Governance Framework sets out the essential elements to support planned and well-managed migration alongside the view and the mandate of the organization. It identifies the following three basic principles: 'Good migration governance would require adherence to international standards and the fulfilment of migrants' rights'; 'Migration and related policies are best formulated using evidence and whole-of-government approaches'; and 'Good migration governance relies on strong partnerships', as well as three related objectives: 'Good migration governance and related policy should seek to advance the socioeconomic well-being of migrants and society'; 'Good migration governance is based on effective responses to the mobility dimensions of crises'; and 'Migration should take place in a safe, orderly and dignified manner.'

[158] IOM, 'IOM's Humanitarian Policy: Principles for Humanitarian Action' (2015) C/106/CRP/20. The Principles for Humanitarian Action define IOM's responsibilities vis-à-vis internationally agreed core humanitarian principles and clarify its role at all levels. They highlight the most relevant aspects of its mandate, the basic principles informing its work (humanity, impartiality, neutrality, independence, and its main activities related to protection.

[159] IOM, *The Progressive Resolution of Displacement Situation Framework* (IOM 2016). This Framework is intended to guide IOM's approach to the progressive resolution of displacement situations and focuses on three strategic objectives: identifying and strengthening coping capacities weakened as a result of displacement situations; fostering self-reliance by responding to the longer-term consequences of displacement; creating conducive environments by addressing the root causes of crisis and displacement. See also IOM, *Framework for Addressing Internal Displacement* (IOM 2017).

by the plight of refugees from Syria and the so-called refugee crisis in Europe. Following several plenary meetings discussing the situation of Syrian refugees, the UN General Assembly decided on 22 December 2015 to convene a High-Level Plenary Meeting on Addressing Large Movements of Refugees and Migrants on 19 September 2016.[160]

In the wake of the new impulse triggered by the UNGA, many other international initiatives were launched to address the situation in Syria. They included, most notably, the Supporting Syria and the Region Conference held in London in February 2016 and co-hosted by the UN Secretary-General and the governments of Germany, Kuwait, Norway, and the UK,[161] the High-Level Meeting on Global Responsibility Sharing through Pathways for Admission of Syrian Refugees organized in Geneva under the auspices of UNHCR in March 2016,[162] and the Forum on New Approaches to Protracted Forced Displacement co-hosted by the World Bank, UNHCR, and the UK in London in April 2016.[163]

This new momentum culminated with the UN summit of 19 September 2016.[164] For the first time, a UNGA meeting was entirely devoted to migration without the broader and reassuring patronage of development. The High-Level Plenary Meeting on Addressing Large Movements of Refugees and Migrants constitutes a landmark in the long and turbulent history of global migration governance: it has not only adopted a wide-ranging declaration addressing both migration and refugee protection, but it has also endorsed the entry of IOM into the UN system and launched an ambitious process with a view to adopting two UN Global Compacts.

The New York Declaration for Refugees and Migrants

The New York Declaration for Refugees and Migrants[165] is the most comprehensive soft law instrument endorsed by all UN Member States to address both migration and refugee protection. For this reason, it represents a milestone in its own right. Nonetheless, soon after its adoption, the New York Declaration raised very polarized

---

[160] UNGA Res 70/290 (2015) UN Doc A/RES/70/290.

[161] 'Supporting Syria and the Region' (National Archive, 1 June 2018) available at<www.supportingsyria2016.com/about> accessed 18 October 2018.

[162] 'Pathways for Admission of Syrian Refugees' (UNHCR) available at www.unhcr.org/pathways-for-admission-of-syrian-refugees.html accessed 18 October 2018.

[163] 'Event: Forum on New Approaches to Protracted Forced Displacement (WP1461)' (Wilton Park, 2016) available at <https://www.wiltonpark.org.uk/event/wp1461/> accessed 18 October 2018. See also the World Humanitarian Summit (WGS) organized at Istanbul in May 2016 at 'World Humanitarian Summit' (*Agenda for Humanity*, 2016) available at www.agendaforhumanity.org/summit accessed 18 October 2018.

[164] In addition, on the margins of the General Assembly, the US President Obama co-hosted on 20 September 2016 the Leaders' Summit on Refugees, with Canada, Ethiopia, Germany, Jordan, Mexico, and Sweden. Participating states' representatives pledged to boost multilateral humanitarian assistance by approximately $4.5 billion over 2015 levels and to increase lawful admission of refugees via UNHCR resettlement programmes, the provision of humanitarian and family reunification visas and educational scholarships. See UNHCR 'Summary Overview Document Leader's Summit on Refugees' (UNHCR, 2016) available at www.unhcr.org/events/conferences/58526bb24/overview-leaders-summit-on-refugees.html accessed 18 October 2018.

[165] UNGA Res 71/1 (2016) UN Doc A/RES/71/1.

comments: it was portrayed either as 'a miracle' by UNHCR[166] or an 'abject failure' by Amnesty International.[167] Some scholars also criticized the Declaration as a missed opportunity,[168] whereas, for others, it offered reasons 'for both disappointment and hope'.[169] Expectations were indeed high. From this perspective, the summit failed to endorse the UN Secretary-General's proposal to resettle ten per cent of the global refugee population annually.[170] The main opposition to the Secretary-General's proposal went beyond the traditional North-South divide. It came from a heteroclite club of sovereignty-conscious states that included Australia, China, Egypt, EU Member States, India, Russia, and Pakistan.[171] Besides this controversy on the resettlement of refugees, the whole negotiation process also appeared to be more intense and fierce than usual: every sentence was argued and negotiated like a treaty, despite the fact that the New York Declaration is not formally binding.

Although the resulting compromise achieved by states inevitably pervades the whole Declaration, it remains a significant step forwards when compared to the previous UNGA Declaration adopted in 2013. The tone and the content of the New York Declaration are much more compelling and demanding than the preceding one, with a clear focus on the duties of states and a long list of agreed-upon commitments. The very term 'commitments' might signal a stronger sense of engagement from UN Member States, even if it is fairly difficult to assess whether this new element of language is purely semantic or not.

The commitments identified by the New York Declaration are, nonetheless, quite numerous and very specific. While detailing further what was agreed on three years before in the previous UNGA Declaration, the New York Declaration is much broader and more inclusive. It provides a comprehensive approach that includes not only migrants, but refugees as well. The first set of commitments applies to both of them, and two other separate sets of commitments distinctively focus on refugees and migrants. While detailing specific commitments for each category, the

---

[166] V Türk, 'Once-in-a-Lifetime Opportunity to Enhance Refugee Protection' (UNSW Sydney, Andrew and Renata Kaldor Centre for International Refugee Law, 11 October 2016) available at <www.kaldorcentre.unsw.edu.au/news/new-york-declaration-once-lifetime-opportunity-enhance-refugee-protection> accessed 18 October 2018.

[167] 'UN Refugee Summit Talks End in Abject Failure' (Amnesty International, 3 August 2016) available at <www.amnesty.org/en/latest/news/2016/08/un-refugee-summit-talks-end-in-abject-failure> accessed 17 October 2018.

[168] A Betts, 'UN Summit on Refugees Fails to Offer Solutions' (The Irish Times, 20 September 2016) available at <www.irishtimes.com/opinion/un-summit-on-refugees-fails-to-offer-solutions-1.2797049> accessed 18 October 2018.

[169] DG Papademetriou and S Fratzke, 'Global Refugee Summits Offer Reasons for Both Disappointment and Hope' (Migration Policy Institute, September 2016) available at <www.migrationpolicy.org/print/15709#.WYhrizN0B-U> accessed 18 October 2018. For a balanced account see also E Ferris, 'In Search of Commitments: The 2016 Refugee Summits' (2016) Kaldor Centre for International Refugee Law Policy Brief No 3.

[170] UNGA 'In Safety and Dignity: Addressing Large Movements of Refugees and Migrants' in 'Report of the Secretary-General' (2016) UN Doc A/70/59, 25.

[171] J Crisp, 'Minor Miracle or Historic Failure? Assessing the UN's Refugee Summit' (UNSW Sydney Andrew and Renata Kaldor Centre for International Refugee Law, 5 August 2016) available at <http://www.kaldorcentre.unsw.edu.au/publication/minor-miracle-or-historic-failure-assessing-un's-refugee-summit> accessed 18 October 2018.

New York Declaration underlines in clear-cut terms that both migrants and refugees are 'rights holders': '[t]hough their treatment is governed by separate legal frameworks, refugees and migrants have the same universal human rights and fundamental freedoms'.[172]

Despite this inclusive approach, the ambiguity of the New York Declaration is exemplified by the ongoing tension between two opposite poles. On the one hand, the New York Declaration reaffirms on many occasions the commitments of UN Member States to protect the human rights of all migrants and refugees regardless of their migratory status[173] and to facilitate orderly, safe, regular, and responsible migration in accordance with the 2030 Agenda.[174] On the other hand, however, the New York Declaration is more control-oriented than the previous Declaration of 2013. This shift is evidenced by a new and strong emphasis on two typical concerns of destination states: addressing the root causes of large movements of refugees and migrants[175] and facilitating the removal and readmission of undocumented migrants.[176] This reorientation of the international discourse is further reinforced by the determination expressed in the Declaration 'to promote international cooperation on border control and management as an important element of security for States'.[177]

The real significance of the New York Declaration, however, lies less in what it says than in the ambitious and momentous process it has initiated. The Declaration has resulted in two major institutional and normative outcomes that will durably frame global migration governance: it endorsed the entry of IOM into the UN system and launched a vast standard-setting process of two UN Global Compacts respectively devoted to migration and refugees.

The entry of IOM into the UN system

At the institutional level, the most significant and concrete outcome of the UN summit is the incorporation of IOM into the UN family. Although it was almost unnoticed outside the circle of specialists, this institutional change was long overdue following over a decade of discussions and hesitations within IOM and the UN, despite their well-established relations of cooperation.[178] In July 2016, the

---

[172] New York Declaration for Refugees and Migrations (n 14) paras 5–6. Concerning the specific commitments on refugees, apart from reaffirming the obligations contained in the 1951 Refugee Convention, the New York Declaration contains a commitment 'to a more equitable sharing of the burden and responsibility for hosting and supporting the world's refugees, while taking account of existing contributions and the differing capacities and resources among States' (ibid para 68). Among other salient issues, it also commits to 'providing humanitarian assistance to refugees' (ibid para 80), while acknowledging that 'refugee camps should be the exception and, to the extent possible, a temporary measure in response to an emergency' (ibid para 73).

[173] ibid paras 5–6, 11, 13, 22, 24, 26, 31, 32–33, 41–43, 48, 58–59, and 66.

[174] ibid para 16; see also ibid paras 4, 16–17, 43, 46, 54, and 88.

[175] ibid paras 12, 17, 37, 43–44, 64, and 72.   [176] ibid paras 41–42, 58, and 75.

[177] ibid para 24.

[178] In 1992, IOM became a permanent observer in the General Assembly and signed in 1996 a cooperation agreement with the UN that was updated in 2013 through a memorandum of understanding. Since 2003, its relations with the UN have been also extensively discussed within IOM. See notably: IOM, 'IOM-UN Relationship: Preliminary Report' (2003) WG/IOM-UN/1; IOM, IOM-UN

General Assembly adopted a resolution approving the Agreement concerning the Relationship between the United Nations and the International Organization for Migration[179] that was eventually signed during the UN summit of September 2016 and endorsed in the New York Declaration with an explicit view 'to strengthening global governance of migration'.[180]

The main consequence of this new development is to transform IOM into 'a related organization' of the UN. While this UN-related status represents an important step forward on its own, the mandate and governing structure of IOM remain unaffected. Article 2(3) of the 2016 Agreement overtly confirms IOM as 'an independent, autonomous and non-normative international organization'.[181] This *status quo* has raised strong criticisms from commentators who consider its relations with the UN as an 'unfinished business'[182] or a 'missed opportunity'.[183] Although partially justified, these critics do not do justice to the importance of the 2016 agreement in the long, complex, and sometimes discordant relations between IOM and the UN. In fact, the entry of IOM into the UN system was inconceivable to both IOM and the UN until very recently.

Against this background, the hybrid status of IOM as a related organization is clearly the result of a compromise that reflected the longstanding hesitations from both the UN and IOM about their respective roles and the overall design of global migration governance. This hesitation was also exacerbated by the fierce competition among the numerous UN agencies and other related organizations working in the field of migration. This sense of mutual doubt and suspicion between the UN and IOM is evidently illustrated by the convoluted provision contained in Article 2(1) of the Agreement. The UN recognizes IOM 'as an organization with *a* global leading role in the field of migration', whereas IOM Member States regard it as '*the* global lead agency on migration'.[184] This specious and calculated wording says a lot about the parochial attitude of both sides. The last sentence of Article 2(1) reiterates in the same vein that 'The foregoing shall be without prejudice to the mandates and activities of the United Nations, its Offices, Funds and Programmes in the field of migration.'[185] In a metaphoric sense, the two partners were thus willing to conclude a civil partnership but not ready—or confident enough—to be married.

Relationship (2006) MC/INF/285; IOM, 'Options for the IOM-UN Relationship: Additional Analysis of Costs and Benefits' (2007) MC/INF/290. For an overview on the long relations between IOM and the UN, see especially S Martin, *International Migration: Evolving Trends from the Early Twentieth Century to the Present* (CUP 2014).

[179] UNGA Res 70/296 (2016) UN Doc A/RES/70/296.

[180] New York Declaration for Refugees and Migrations (n 14) para 49.

[181] For further discussion about the mandate and governance structure of IOM, see Chapter 7.

[182] E Guild, S Grant, and K Groenendijk, 'IOM and the UN: Unfinished Business' (2017) Queen Mary School of Law Legal Studies Research Paper No 255/2017.

[183] NR Micinski and TG Weiss, 'International Organization for Migration and the UN System: A Missed Opportunity' (2016) Future United Nations Development System Briefing 42, 4.

[184] Emphasis added.

[185] The sixth and final paragraph of Article 2 further restates that 'the United Nations and the International Organization for Migration will cooperate and conduct their activities without prejudice to the rights and responsibilities of one another under their respective constituent instruments'.

They still have to learn to live under the same roof before deciding on any further commitments.

As a result of its status as a related organization, IOM enjoys greater independence than any other UN institutions in the field of migration. In particular, contrary to specialized agencies as well as UN Funds and Programmes, IOM does not have any obligation to report to ECOSOC or the UNGA. Instead, according to Article 4 of the Agreement with the UN, IOM '*may, if it decides it to be appropriate*, submit reports on its activities to the General Assembly through the Secretary-General' (emphasis added). The absence of such a duty, however, is not unique to IOM when compared to other related organizations working on different fields than migration. Four of them are not bound by a duty of reporting to the UN: the WTO,[186] the International Criminal Court,[187] the Preparatory Commission for the Comprehensive Nuclear-Test-Ban Treaty Organization,[188] and the International Tribunal for the Law of the Sea,[189] whereas the other related organizations are explicitly committed to doing so (including, most notably, the International Atomic Energy Agency,[190] and the Organization for the Prohibition of Chemical Weapons).[191]

Following this comparative standpoint, the content of the agreement concluded with IOM is much more robust and detailed than the one with WTO, but largely similar to and modelled upon the agreements concluded with other existing related organizations. It establishes a strong duty of cooperation between the UN and IOM, which typically covers the exchange of information and documents (Article 7), mutual consultation on matters within their respective competence (Article 3(3) and (4)), administrative cooperation regarding their staff, facilities, and secretariats (Articles 8 to 11), as well as reciprocal representation of the Secretary-General in the sessions of the IOM Council and of the IOM Director-General in the meeting of the UNGA (Article 5), and a reciprocal possibility to propose agenda items for consideration (Article 6). Besides this common pattern and contrary to most of the other related organizations (with the exceptions of WTO and IAEA), IOM participates in and cooperates with the UN System Chief Executive Board for Coordination and other relevant UN bodies established to improve the coordination within the UN system (Article 3(2)).

---

[186] Arrangements for Effective Cooperation with other Intergovernmental Organizations-Relations between the WTO and the United Nations (3 November 1995) WT/GC/W/10 available at https://docs.wto.org/dol2fe/Pages/SS/directdoc.aspx?filename=q:/WT/GC/W10.pdf accessed 18 October 2018.
[187] Negotiated Relationship Agreement between the United Nations and the International Criminal Court (adopted 22 July 2004) 2283 UNTS 195 art 6.
[188] See art 4 of the Agreement to regulate the relationship between the United Nations and the Preparatory Commission for the Comprehensive Nuclear-Test-Ban Treaty Organization (2000) UN Doc A/RES/54/280.
[189] See art 5 of the Agreement on Cooperation and Relationship between the United Nations and the International Tribunal for the Law of the Sea in UNGA Res 52/251 (15 September 1998) UN Doc A/RES/52/251.
[190] See art 10 of the Agreement Governing the Relationship Between the United Nations and the International Atomic Energy Agency in UNGA Res 1145 (XII) (1957).
[191] See art 4 of the Cooperation Agreement between the United Nations and the Organization for the Prohibition of Chemical Weapons in UNGA Res 51/230 (1997) UN Doc A/RES/51/230.

Overall, the technical niceties of its new status as a related organization should not undermine the significance of its incorporation within the UN system. After sixty-five years outside the UN system, its rapprochement represents a milestone in the institutional landscape of migration and opens a new era of cooperation. As a result of the 2016 Agreement, IOM is explicitly committed to conducting its activities in accordance with the UN Charter, the policies and instruments of the UN in the fields of migration, refugee, and human rights (Article 2(5)). As exemplified by the recent proposal of the UN Secretary-General to transform IOM into a specialized agency, the agreement concluded in 2016 should be viewed as the first step of many others to strengthen the role of IOM within the UN system.[192]

The drafting process of the UN Global Compacts for Migration and Refugees

The New York Declaration for Refugees and Migrants set in motion an ambitious standards-setting process with a view to adopting two UN Compacts: the Global Compact for Safe, Orderly and Regular Migration and the Global Compact on Refugees. UN Member States decided to develop two separate Compacts, despite their acknowledgement in the New York Declaration that both refugees and migrants have 'the same universal human rights', 'similar vulnerabilities', and 'many common challenges'.[193]

During the UN summit of September 2016, the distinction between the two Compacts was primarily pushed by several European states and UNHCR for very different reasons. For the former, having two separate Compacts reinforces the distinction between refugees and migrants in line with their own migration and border control policies. Along with Eastern European states, the UK Prime Minister stressed the concerns that 'refugees and economic migrants must be better differentiated [...] [to] ensure that countries had a right to control their borders'.[194] For UNHCR, distinguishing the two Compacts was a way to acknowledge the specific legal regime on refugee protection, while retaining control over the drafting of the Global Compact on Refugees due to the fear of reopening intergovernmental negotiations on the Geneva Convention.[195] Although the resulting distinction between

---

[192] For further discussion about the Secretary General proposal and the role of IOM within the UN, see Chapter 7, section 7.3.

[193] New York Declaration for Refugees and Migrants (n 14) para 6.

[194] The Minister for Foreign Affairs of the Czech Republic argued in the same vein that 'Europe's need to maintain security and democracy meant that it must protect itself and its values and legal frameworks must be respected by all migrants. To regulate the volume of migration, countries had no choice but to prioritize, distinguishing between refugees and economic migrants, with full respect to the human rights of all migrants.' The President of Bulgaria further concurred by asserting that 'the effectiveness of border controls is of utmost importance in order to combat irregular migration. [...] However, there must be a clear distinction between refugees and economic migrants, he said, noting that the latter group was not eligible for refugee status.' See also the declaration of the President of Poland. All these official declarations are available at <http://www.un.org/press/en/2016/ga11820.doc.htm> accessed 18 October 2018.

[195] 'The New York Declaration specifically provides for two compacts. This is in recognition of the fact that, for refugees, there is a specific legal regime already in place, and a framework that is elaborated in the New York Declaration for addressing large refugee movements. [...] In contrast, there is no specialized comprehensive legal regime concerning migrants, and no agreed framework for addressing

the two overlapping Compacts might perpetuate the prevailing gaps and undermine the comprehensive and coherent nature of the whole endeavour, the UNGA has strongly reaffirmed in its resolution of April 2017 that 'the two processes are separate, distinct and independent'.[196]

As a result of this strict division, the two UN Compacts significantly diverge both on their respective adoption process and outcomes. The Global Compact for Safe, Orderly and Regular Migration has been conceived by the UNGA as 'an intergovernmentally negotiated and agreed outcome'[197] which has accordingly been elaborated through a process of inter-state negotiations. UN Member States were indeed keen to control both its process and content. By contrast, the development of the Global Compact on Refugees has been led by UNHCR, albeit through a multi-stakeholder approach, and its final draft is part of the UNHCR annual report to the UNGA during its seventy-third session in 2018.[198] These different drafting processes and outcomes inevitably impact on the respective legal nature of the two Compacts. Although neither of them is formally binding, the very fact that the Global Compact for Safe, Orderly and Regular Migration has been negotiated and agreed by UN Members States confers considerable authority and legitimacy, whereas the Global Compact on Refugees is primarily a product of UNHCR.

Although the drafting processes of the two Compacts have taken place at the same time, the time-line to achieve this ambitious objective was particularly short. The UN was supposed to accomplish in two years what it did not manage to achieve in two decades. According to the UNGA resolution detailing the modalities for its adoption, the preparatory process of the Global Compact for Safe, Orderly and Regular Migration was to proceed in three phases: (i) consultations (April to November 2017), (ii) stocktaking (November 2017 to January 2018), and (iii) intergovernmental negotiations (February to July 2018).[199] Mexico and Switzerland were appointed by the President of the UNGA to be the co-facilitators for the whole negotiation process, while the new UN Special Representative of the Secretary-General on International Migration—Louise Arbour—acted as Secretary-General of the intergovernmental conference and focal point of the UN system. Quite ironically, despite its so-called non-normative mandate, IOM jointly facilitated the negotiations and drafting process with the UN Special Representative by providing technical and policy expertise.[200] The Global Compact was adopted in December 2018 at an intergovernmental conference in Morocco and then endorsed by the UNGA with 152 votes in favour, twelve abstentions and five votes against (i.e. the Czech Republic, Hungary, Israel, Poland, and the US).

---

large movements of migrants. So, the starting point for achieving greater predictability and responsibility sharing for refugees is different than for enhancing the global governance of migration.' See UNHCR, 'New York Declaration: Frequently Asked Questions' available at <http://www.unhcr.org/584689257.pdf> para 17, accessed 18 October 2018.

[196] UNGA Res 71/280 (17 April 2017) UN Doc A/RES/71/280, first preambular paragraph.
[197] ibid para 1c.
[198] Annex I of the New York Declaration for Refugees and Migrants (n 14) para 19.
[199] UNGA Res 71/280 (n 196) paras 14–31.   [200] ibid para 11.

Though not an intergovernmental process, the timeframe for the development of the Global Compact on Refugees was modelled on the one for the Global Compact for Safe, Orderly and Regular Migration. According to the roadmap elaborated by UNHCR, its drafting process was structured in three phases: informal thematic discussions (January–November 2017), stocktaking (December 2017), and consultations with Member States and other stakeholders (February–July 2018) based on the draft prepared by UNHCR.[201] Then, as mentioned above, it has been incorporated into UNHCR annual report to the UNGA. Besides their drafting process and format, the contents of the two Compacts diverge significantly, not only in terms of substance and coverage, but also with regard to their rationale and objective.

The Global Compact for Safe, Orderly, and Regular Migration

The Global Compact for Migration is basically 'a non-legally binding cooperative framework' which is purported 'to make an important contribution to enhanced cooperation on international migration in all its dimensions'.[202] It presents itself as 'a milestone in the history of international cooperation on migration' and 'the product of an unprecedented review of evidence and data gathered during an open, transparent and inclusive process'.[203] Although there is some exaggeration in this self-congratulation, the Compact is the culmination of a long process of mobilization and awareness initiated in 1994 by the Cairo Conference. In comparison with previous soft law initiatives, the Global Compact for Migration constitutes the most comprehensive multilateral instrument specifically devoted to migration.

The comprehensiveness of this intergovernmental instrument is inherent in its very rationale. As underlined by UN Member States, 'this Global Compact offers a 360-degree vision of international migration and recognizes that a comprehensive approach is needed to optimize the overall benefits of migration, while addressing risks and challenges for individuals and communities in countries of origin, transit and destination'.[204] This all-encompassing approach is built on the premise that 'no country can address the challenges and opportunities of this global phenomenon on its own'.[205] UN Member States 'acknowledge our shared responsibilities to one another as Member States of the United Nations',[206] because 'we are all countries of origin, transit and destination'.[207]

When compared to previous soft law instruments, the main added value of the Compact relies on its wide scope regarding both its addressees and thematic coverage. It is not only addressed to states, but, in contrast to previous UN initiatives on migration, its scope is also enlarged in order to encompass non-state actors. By adopting a 'whole-of-society approach' and 'broad multi-stakeholder partnerships', the Compact extends most remarkably to migrants themselves, local

---

[201] UNHCR, 'Towards a Global Compact on Refugees: A Roadmap' (16 April 2018).
[202] Global Compact for Safe, Orderly and Regular Migration (n 60) Introductive chapeau and para 15
[203] ibid paras 6 and 10   [204] ibid para 11.   [205] ibid para 11.   [206] ibid.
[207] ibid para 39.

communities and civil society, as well as the private sector, trade unions, and the media.[208] Furthermore, the implementation of the Compact is supposed to be mainstreamed within the whole UN system through the establishment of three new mechanisms: a capacity-building mechanism to support UN Member States in their implementation,[209] an International Review Forum to review their progress within the UNGA,[210] and an UN network on migration gathering UN agencies and related organizations on migration to ensure a system-wide support to implementation.[211]

In parallel with this multi-stakeholders approach, the inclusive scope of the Compact is further reflected by its broad thematic coverage which addresses a vast number of topical issues throughout the migration cycle, be it upon departure from the country of origin, during migrants' journey (including in transit countries), upon arrival and stay in the country of destination or upon return to the country of origin. The Compact identifies twenty-three objectives, each containing a commitment which is to be achieved through a long set of actions (Box 6.1).

The list of these twenty-three objectives is extensive and the content of the related actions to achieve these commitments is specified in considerable detail. No less than 187 actions have been identified to realize the objectives agreed upon by UN Member States. Such a vast and detailed range of objectives and actions represents a unique endeavour without equivalent among all the other binding and non-binding instruments on migration.

The comprehensiveness of the Compact however entails two important caveats. First, despite their extensive coverage, the twenty-three objectives identified therein are not exhaustive. Besides the noteworthy absence of internal displacement, a significant portion of cross-border movements falls outside the scope of the Compact. In particular, there is no reference to migration for the purpose of education, trade, service, and investment. Second, when the Compact is assessed as a whole, the general picture remains segmented and reveals a piecemeal approach. The Global Compact is strong on the details but weak on the overall design. As underlined by several commentators, it reads as a laundry list of worthwhile objectives and related actions.[212] There is no clear articulation between the objectives and no priority among them. One should however concede that their cross-cutting nature is hardly compatible with any sense of prioritization. Furthermore and more importantly, the Global Compact is not a *menu à la carte*. All the commitments must be taken into account and implemented as a whole in accordance with the very purpose of the Compact that underpins 'the centrality of a comprehensive and integrated approach to facilitate safe, orderly and regular migration'.[213]

---

[208] ibid para 15.   [209] ibid para 43.   [210] ibid para 49.   [211] ibid para 45.
[212] TA Aleinikoff and S Martin, 'Making the Global Compacts Work: What Future for Refugees and Migrants?' (2018) The Andrew & Renata Kaldor Centre for International Refugee Law and The Zolberg Institute on Migration and Mobility Policy Brief No 6, 21.
[213] Global Compact for Safe, Orderly and Regular Migration (n 60) para 39. See also ibid paras 11–15.

Box 6.1 Objectives for safe, orderly, and regular migration

1) Collect and utilize accurate and disaggregated data as a basis for evidence-based policies
2) Minimize the adverse drivers and structural factors that compel people to leave their country of origin
3) Provide accurate and timely information at all stages of migration
4) Ensure that all migrants have proof of legal identity and adequate documentation
5) Enhance availability and flexibility of pathways for regular migration
6) Facilitate fair and ethical recruitment and safeguard conditions that ensure decent work
7) Address and reduce vulnerabilities in migration
8) Save lives and establish coordinated international efforts on missing migrants
9) Strengthen the transnational response to smuggling of migrants
10) Prevent, combat and eradicate trafficking in persons in the context of international migration
11) Manage borders in an integrated, secure and coordinated manner
12) Strengthen certainty and predictability in migration procedures for appropriate screening, assessment and referral
13) Use migration detention only as a measure of last resort and work towards alternatives
14) Enhance consular protection, assistance and cooperation throughout the migration cycle
15) Provide access to basic services for migrants
16) Empower migrants and societies to realize full inclusion and social cohesion
17) Eliminate all forms of discrimination and promote evidence-based public discourse to shape perceptions of migration
18) Invest in skills development and facilitate mutual recognition of skills, qualifications and competences
19) Create conditions for migrants and diasporas to fully contribute to sustainable development in all countries
20) Promote faster, safer and cheaper transfer of remittances and foster financial inclusion of migrants
21) Cooperate in facilitating safe and dignified return and readmission, as well as sustainable reintegration
22) Establish mechanisms for the portability of social security entitlements and earned benefits
23) Strengthen international cooperation and global partnerships for safe, orderly and regular migration

What is still missing is an overall design that unifies this disparate assemblage of twenty-three objectives within a coherent and integrated approach. From this stance, the numerous objectives may be gathered into five clusters:

- Addressing the drivers of migration and investing in sustainable development (objectives 2, 19, and 20);
- Managing borders for facilitating safe and regular cross-border movements, while preventing irregular migration (objectives 4, 5, 9, 10, 11, 12, and 21);
- Protecting the human rights of migrants and promoting their inclusion in host countries (objectives 6, 7, 8, 13, 14, 15, 16, 17, 18, and 22);
- Strengthening international cooperation and global partnerships (objective 23);
- Improving data and information (objectives 1 and 3).

Despite the cross-cutting and overlapping nature of the twenty-three objectives, these thematic clusters unveil both the overall design of the Compact and the competing interests at stake. From this broader perspective, the Compact may be better appraised as a consolidated document that restates and refines the outcomes of and the lessons learned from the vast number of soft law instruments adopted during the last decades within and outside the UN.

This exercise of consolidation and its consensual nature explain, in turn, that none of the objectives agreed upon by states is fundamentally new. Nonetheless, the Compact places more emphasis on some thematic areas that were previously addressed in a rather oblique and limited way. They include, most notably, the collection and use of accurate and disaggregated data (objective 1), the cooperation to save lives and prevent the deaths of migrant at sea (objective 8), and the strengthening of legal certainty and predictability in migration procedures (objective 12).

Furthermore, although the twenty-three objectives are by definition prospective and thus aspirational, the related actions to realize them are much more detailed and specific than in many other non-binding instruments adopted by the UN. Interestingly, these actions are not only aimed at improving bilateral, regional, and international cooperation. In contrast to many previous soft law instruments, the Compact also addresses a broad range of national measures to be taken by individual states. Some of these domestic actions are legal and call for the review and amendment of existing domestic legislation in line with the objectives of the Compact. Many others are purely operational and include, for instance, information sharing, awareness-raising campaigns, and training of states' civil servants.

Overall, the main achievement of the Global Compact is to sanction and crystallize the consensus of the international community on the most topical issues associated with migration. While expressing the collective commitments of states to improve cooperation, the Compact paves the way for a counter-narrative to the populist rhetoric through a balanced, consensual, and inclusive approach. This narrative is well captured by the following extract from the Global Compact:

Migration has been part of the human experience throughout history, and we recognize that it is a source of prosperity, innovation and sustainable development in our globalized world, and that these positive impacts can be optimized by improving migration govern-ance. The majority of migrants around the world today travel, live and work in a safe, orderly and regular manner. Nonetheless, migration undeniably affects our countries, communities, migrants and their families in very different and sometimes unpredictable ways. It is cru-cial that the challenges and opportunities of international migration unite us, rather than divide us.[214]

This common vision is thus aimed at 'dispelling misleading narratives that generate negative perceptions of migrants',[215] while 'addressing risks and challenges for in-dividuals and communities in countries of origin, transit and destination'.[216] As apparent from this ambitious endeavour, the Global Compact is not an end in itself but a new critical step of an ongoing process which is political by nature. Hence, it must not be seen as a final product but as a road map to frame the international agenda through three basic means: evidence-based information, inclusive dialogue, and the rule of law.

International law is obviously part of the picture, but it is conceived as one means among others towards a broader political end. The Compact reaffirms in clear and strong terms that 'respect for the rule of law, due process and access to justice are fundamental to all aspects of migration governance'.[217] As further highlighted in its preamble, the Compact rests on the UN Charter, the Universal Declaration of Human Rights, the core international human rights conventions, as well as a broad list of other specific treaties.[218] The commitment of states to international law per-meates the whole Compact: due respect for international law in general and for human rights law in particular is reaffirmed fifty-six times across the thirty-four-page document.

The Compact thus reinforces existing international legal norms to underpin the centrality of the rule of law in the context of migration. However, it does not create new rules. Alongside the New York Declaration, the Compact reaffirms the typical balancing act of international migration law between 'the sovereign right of States to determine their national migration policy'[219] and the 'overarching obligation to respect, protect and fulfil the human rights of all migrants, regardless of their migra-tion status'.[220] Against this normative background, the most salient binding rules of international migration law are restated by the Global Compact to distil the rule

---

[214] ibid paras 8–9.   [215] ibid para 10.   [216] ibid para 11.   [217] ibid para 15.
[218] ibid paras 1–2. Besides the UN human rights treaties, the preamble explicitly refers to the UN Convention against Transnational Organized Crime; the Protocol to Prevent, Suppress and Punish Trafficking in Persons Especially Women and Children and the Protocol against the Smuggling of Migrants by Land, Sea and Air; the Slavery Convention and the Supplementary Convention on the Abolition of Slavery, the Slave Trade, and Institutions and Practices Similar to Slavery; the United Nations Framework Convention on Climate Change; the United Nations Convention to Combat Desertification; the Paris Agreement; Migration for Employment Convention of 1949 (No 97); Migrant Workers Convention of 1975 (No 143); Equality of Treatment Convention of 1962 (No 118); and Convention on Decent Work for Domestic Workers of 2011 (No 189).
[219] Global Compact for Safe, Orderly and Regular Migration (n 60) para 15
[220] ibid para 11.

of law. Their reaffirmation underlines the continuing validity of international law to frame migration governance.

Although dispersed across the document, the international legal norms that are restated by the Compact focus on two central issues. A first set of international rules is directly aimed at governing migration control. The most relevant ones include the prohibition of arbitrary detention,[221] the prohibition of collective expulsion,[222] the principle of *non-refoulement* when there is a real and foreseeable risk of death, torture, and other cruel, inhuman, and degrading treatment or punishment, or other irreparable harm,[223] as well as the duty to prevent and penalize the smuggling of migrants and trafficking in persons, while avoiding criminalization of migrants who are smuggled or trafficked.[224] Likewise, due process guarantees, individual assessment and effective remedy,[225] consular protection,[226] and the best interest of the child[227] are restated and mainstreamed throughout the migration cycle.

This body of legally binding norms is significant, but states were not ready to go beyond this restatement. Several important issues related to undocumented migration have been watered down in the final version.[228] Furthermore, despite its potential to frame the future development of international law with regard to labour migration,[229] objective 5 devoted to regular migration does not break new grounds. In particular, humanitarian admission due to sudden-onset natural disasters and family reunification are mentioned in a very general and oblique way.[230]

A second set of legally binding rules focuses on the human rights of migrants during their stay in states' territory. They refer to the elimination of all forms of discrimination and racism,[231] the prohibition of slavery and forced labour,[232] access to basic services regardless of migration status,[233] access to social protection and portability of social security entitlements and earned benefits, as well as equal treatment with nationals with regard to labour rights (including the rights to just and favourable conditions of work, to equal pay for work of equal value, to freedom of peaceful assembly and association, and to the highest attainable standard of physical and mental health).[234]

---

[221] ibid para 29.   [222] ibid paras 24 a) and 37.   [223] ibid para 37.
[224] ibid paras 25 and 26.   [225] ibid paras 24 a), 27 c) and f), and 37.
[226] ibid paras 19 c), 23 e) and j), 24 c), and 30.
[227] ibid paras 15, 21 i), 23, 27 c) and 29 h), and 37 g).
[228] For instance, while the first draft considered irregular entry 'as an administrative, not a criminal offence', the final version merely proposes to review and revise domestic laws 'to determine whether sanctions are appropriate to address irregular entry or stay and, if so, to ensure that they are proportionate, equitable, non-discriminatory, and fully consistent with due process and other obligations under international law' (ibid para 27 f)). Likewise, the firm commitment to ending detention of undocumented children, as contained in the initial draft, has been replaced by the vaguer formulation of 'working to end the practice of child detention.' (ibid para 29 h).
[229] For further discussion see the conclusion of this textbook.
[230] See Global Compact for Safe, Orderly and Regular Migration (n 60) para 21 g) and i).
[231] ibid paras 15, 27 b), 32 i), and 33.   [232] ibid para 22 c) and f),
[233] ibid paras 20, f), 31, and 32 e)   [234] ibid para 22 i).

The Global Compact on Refugees

The comprehensive approach of the Global Compact for Migration contrasts with the one of the Global Compact on Refugees which is much more specific and less inclusive. Contrary to the former, it is not conceived to develop a wide-ranging approach addressing the multifaceted dimensions and challenges of refugee protection. The thrust of the Global Compact on Refugees is to operationalize the principles of burden- and responsibility-sharing alongside the recommendations of the New York Declaration.[235] Its main rationale is to mobilize the political will of states by providing an operational framework on four interdependent objectives: '(i) ease pressures on host countries; (ii) enhance refugee self-reliance; (iii) expand access to third country solutions; and (iv) support conditions in countries of origin for return in safety and dignity'.[236] The political nature of the whole endeavour and the fear of reopening the debate about the relevance of the Refugee Convention have heavily impacted on the overall design and content of the Compact.

In both pith and substance, the Global Compact on Refugees is a political declaration of intent; it is not a soft law instrument aimed at restating and reinforcing international legal norms. Instead, it exposes 'the political will and ambition of the international community as a whole for strengthened cooperation and solidarity with refugees and affected host countries'.[237] As a result of its political nature, the Global Compact on Refugees merely takes note, in its introduction, that it is 'grounded in the international refugee protection regime', as established by the 1951 Convention and its 1967 Protocol, and 'guided' by other relevant instruments on human rights law, humanitarian law, and criminal law.[238] Besides this vague reference, international law has been largely removed from the picture. Even the term 'international refugee law' appears nowhere in the whole Compact on Refugees, whereas—ironically enough—this field of international law is explicitly acknowledged by the Global Compact for Migration to highlight its complementarity with its refugee counterpart.[239]

The marginalization of international law in the Global Compact on Refugees has raised two types of criticisms. On the one hand, by taking for granted the limited definition of refugee under the 1951 Convention, the resulting 'framework is too narrow because it does not reflect the complex realities of forced displacement. For example, internally displaced persons and those fleeing natural disasters are not sufficiently taken into account'.[240] Indeed, both are merely mentioned in passing

---

[235] Annex I of the New York Declaration for Refugees and Migrations (n 14).

[236] Global Compact on Refugees (Report of the United Nations High Commissioner for Refugees—Part II, Global Compact on Refugees) (2 August 2018, reissued 13 September 2018) UN Doc A/73/12 para 7.

[237] ibid para 4.   [238] ibid para 5.

[239] Global Compact for Safe, Orderly and Regular Migration (n 60) para 4. While recalling that 'refugees and migrants are entitled to the same universal human rights and fundamental freedoms', the Compact for Migration underlines in a candid truism that 'only refugees are entitled to the specific international protection as defined by international refugee law'. One should further note that the Global Compact on Refugees does not contain any explicit reference to its migration counterpart.

[240] S Angenendt and N Biehler, 'On the Way to a Global Compact on Refugees: The "Zero Draft"—A Positive, but not yet Sufficient Step' (2018) SWP Comments 18, 2.

to highlight the composite character of large-scale movements and the need to prevent them by addressing their root causes.[241] On the other hand, the Global Compact remains extremely evasive even for the basic rights of refugees under the 1951 Convention.[242] Among the very few references to the rights of refugees, the principle of *non-refoulement* is mentioned only twice in the 20-page long document, whereas the right to seek asylum is relegated to a footnote on the Universal Declaration of Human Rights.[243]

Although the Global Compact on Refugees is bound to have a marginal role with respect to international law, its focus on responsibility and burden-sharing still represents a crucial supplement to the Refugee Convention and its Protocol. Indeed, these two legally binding instruments identify the obligations of host countries, without addressing the collective responsibility of States Parties and its consequences in terms of international cooperation.[244] However, despite its potential to supplement the current international legal framework, the political nature of the Global Compact on Refugees and the resulting compromises pervade its whole content. Its main value is to provide a tool box for states which still heavily depends on their good will and voluntary contributions. The content of the Compact consists of two components: (i) the comprehensive refugee response framework (CRRF), agreed by UN Member States in 2016 and contained in Annex I to the New York Declaration; and (ii) a programme of action prepared by UNHCR to implement and operationalize the CRRF.

The CRRF relies on four pillars that reflect the different stages of refugee movements: admission and reception; support for immediate and ongoing needs of refugees; support for host countries and communities; and durable solutions. However, the content of the CRRF remains very general, conservative, and disappointing, given the numerous challenges surrounding refugee protection. The first pillar, supposedly devoted to admission and reception, says nothing about admission per se and remains quite general about the reception conditions of refugees in host countries. It largely focuses on the identification and registration of asylum-seekers as well as the return and readmission of those who do not qualify for refugee status.[245] The two other pillars related to support for refugees and host countries mainly concentrate on the need to provide adequate resources and access to humanitarian assistance.[246]

The last pillar on durable solutions typically emphasizes voluntary repatriation as the preferred option of host countries, with a rather detailed battery of measures to be adopted by countries of origin to facilitate return and sustainable reintegration.[247]

---

[241] See Global Compact on Refugees (n 236) paras 8, 12, and 53.

[242] TA Aleinikoff and S Martin, *Making the Global Compacts Work: What Future for Refugees and Migrants?* (n 212) 27.

[243] Global Compact on Refugees (n 236) paras 5 and 87.

[244] As mentioned in Chapter 3, the preamble only mentions in passing that 'the grant of asylum may place unduly heavy burdens on certain countries, and that a satisfactory solution of a problem of which the United Nations has recognized the international scope and nature cannot therefore be achieved without international co-operation'.

[245] Global Compact on Refugees (n 236) para 5(a), (d), and (i).   [246] ibid paras 6–8.

[247] These measures include the obligation to receive back their nationals and to provide identification and travel documents, as well as the need to facilitate the socio-economic reintegration of returnees and to foster reconciliation and dialogue. All states and UN agencies are also requested to 'ensure that

By contrast, the other durable solutions, namely local integration and resettlement, are worded in a much vaguer and more cautious language: host states 'would [...] provide legal stay to those seeking and in need of international protection as refugees, recognizing that any decision regarding permanent settlement in any form, including possible naturalization, rests with the host country', whereas third countries 'would consider making available or expanding, including by encouraging private sector engagement and action as a supplementary measure, resettlement opportunities and complementary pathways for admission of refugees'.[248] Overall, as underlined by Aleinikoff and Martin, 'the CRRF breaks little new ground'; 'it essentially calls for an operational model that humanitarian and development agencies had already largely adopted'.[249]

The second component of the Global Compact on Refugees, that is, the programme of action drafted by UNHCR to implement the CRRF, inevitably embodies the same limits. This programme remains largely aspirational with few concrete measures to be taken on the ground. Instead, it details the background for future actions and the general strategy to be developed by states and other stakeholders to foster international cooperation on burden- and responsibility-sharing. From this angle, the programme of action resembles a tool-kit for decision-makers: it endorses a common understanding and methodology that are primarily based on inter-state dialogue, multi-stakeholder partnerships, and complementarity between humanitarian and development actors.[250]

In fact, the added value of the Global Compact on Refugees lays less in its content than in the institutional framework it has established. Its chief achievement is to create two new mechanisms in order to move this ongoing process of cooperation towards a more equitable and predictable burden- and responsibility-sharing. The first and most important innovation is the creation of a Global Refugee Forum. It will gather, every four years, all UN Member States and other stakeholders to announce concrete pledges relating to the objectives of the Compact (including financial, material and technical assistance, resettlement places, and other pathways for admission).[251] This new Forum will also provide an important vehicle to exchange best practices and take stock of the progress toward the achievement of the Compact's objectives.[252]

The second institutional innovation is the establishment of a Global Support Platform to be activated by concerned states in order to deal with more specific situations. This Platform is supposed to be used in emergency situations to mobilize the support of the international community when a host country is overwhelmed by a large-scale movement or needs additional support to address a protracted refugee

national development planning incorporates the specific needs of returnees [...], as a measure to prevent future displacement', ibid para 12(f).

[248] ibid paras 13(a) and 14(a).
[249] TA Aleinikoff and S Martin, *Making the Global Compacts Work: What Future for Refugees and Migrants?* (n 212) 7.
[250] See especially Global Compact on Refugees (n 236) paras 32–44 and 64–67.
[251] ibid paras 17–18.
[252] ibid para 103. Furthermore, biannual high-level officials' meetings on the Global Compact will take place between Forums for mid-term review: ibid, para 104.

situation.[253] It could take the form of a 'solidarity conference' to generate support of the international community.[254] The functions of this Platform are to be understood broadly. They include 'galvanizing political commitment and advocacy for prevention, protection, response and solutions'; 'mobilizing financial, material and technical assistance, as well as resettlement and complementary pathways for admission'; 'facilitating coherent humanitarian and development responses'; and 'supporting comprehensive policy initiatives to ease pressure on host countries'.[255]

Although these new institutional arrangements may be viewed as a diplomatic way to postpone any concrete actions, their importance shall not be underestimated. The Global Refugee Forum and the Global Support Platform fill an important gap in the international architecture of refugee protection. Indeed, 'for the first time since adoption of the 1951 Refugee Convention, international structures would be established to bring States together on a regular basis with the express goal of enhancing international responsibility-sharing'.[256] By providing an institutional framework for cooperation on a long-neglected issue, the Global Refugee Forum and the Global Support Platform have the potential to mobilize states for a more equitable and predictable responsibility-sharing. This is especially important for the Global South, where 82.5 per cent of all refugees in the world are hosted.[257]

To conclude, the main virtue of the two UN Global Compacts on Migration and Refugees is essentially political. Both Compacts are intended to provide a new impetus for multilateralism as a counter-system to unilateralism and populism. They lay down the grounds for a new narrative based on dialogue, trust, and responsibility. Although their legal relevance remains limited and uneven from one Compact to the other, their adoption represents an achievement on its own in the current political context. After a long and tortuous process of maturation initiated in 1994, migration is eventually endorsed as a matter of international cooperation on its own.

The use of soft law instruments has been instrumental in fostering inter-state dialogue and confidence-building on an issue traditionally associated with states' sovereignty. Migration is now acknowledged as a question of shared responsibilities which calls for a global approach. With the two Compacts, the UN and its Member States have a common framework to shape their future actions in line with a broad range of commitments. Because the commitments agreed on by states are prospective by nature, it is obviously premature to assess whether the Global Compacts will deliver on their promise for a more balanced and integrated approach to migration governance. Both Compacts have the potential to improve the lives of migrants and the cooperation among states. Whether that potential is realized will largely depend on their application by states.

---

[253] ibid para 24.   [254] ibid para 27.

[255] ibid para 23. One should add that UNHCR will also establish an Asylum Capacity Support Group. This group could be activated upon request of a concerned state to provide support to relevant national authorities with a view to strengthening their asylum system and procedures. This group could also provide guidance on other protection and humanitarian challenges, including for those forcibly displaced by natural disasters. See ibid paras 62–63.

[256] TA Aleinikoff and S Martin, *Making the Global Compacts Work: What Future for Refugees and Migrants?* (n 212) 10

[257] UNDESA, *International Migration Report 2017: Highlights* (United Nations 2017) ST/ESA/ SER.A/404, 7.

7

The Architecture of Global
Migration Governance

Global migration governance has grown in a relatively short period of time to reach a degree of sophistication that was hardly conceivable a few decades ago. It has now entered a new phase of transition which requires concerted efforts at states' level to honour and implement their numerous commitments and, within the whole UN system, to ensure an effective and coherent institutional framework. Despite the considerable progress accomplished so far, the quest for a more integrated and comprehensive approach still remains a work in progress. This raises the question whether the use of soft law as an alternative to hard law has reached its limit to achieve such an ambitious objective.

As a truly ambivalent phenomenon, the proliferation of soft law is both a catalyst and a symptom of global migration governance. On the one hand, the multiplication of non-binding instruments and consultative processes has been instrumental in creating a routine of inter-state dialogue and in establishing the UN as the leading actor after a long period of marginalization. As a result of an incremental process of learning and confidence-building, migration is now acknowledged as a public good which calls for global solutions at the multilateral level. The renewed commitment in multilateralism represents, by far, the most decisive contribution of the New York Declaration for Refugees and Migrants,[1] the Global Compact for Safe, Orderly and Regular Migration,[2] and the Global Compact on Refugees.[3]

On the other hand, soft law has become a mode of governance on its own which entails its own drawbacks. The *softistication*, or softness, of global migration governance is characterized by a heteroclite network of informal and non-binding co-operative frameworks that are poorly articulated and highly decentralized. Such a proliferation of soft law instruments and consultative processes is more prone to exacerbate fragmentation than to provide a coherent and effective multilateral

---

[1] New York Declaration for Refugees and Migrants, UNGA Res 71/1 (19 September 2016) UN Doc A/RES/71/1.
[2] Global Compact for Safe, Orderly and Regular Migration (13 July 2018) available at<https://refugeesmigrants.un.org/sites/default/files/180713_agreed_outcome_global_compact_for_migration.pdf> accessed 3 October 2018.
[3] Global Compact on Refugees (Report of the United Nations High Commissioner for Refugees—Part II, Global Compact on Refugees) (2 August 2018, reissued 13 September 2018) UN Doc A/73/12.

framework. This does not necessarily mean that there is no overall architecture under-pinning the multiples initiatives launched by states and international organizations.

Global migration governance is now solidly anchored in the UN system, through its political organs, specialized agencies, and affiliated organizations. However, the vast number and great variety of its modules resemble a deconstructivist architec-ture, which unveils its main features as a multi-level form of governance and the way to redress its most obvious shortcomings. This chapter accordingly draws the overall institutional design of global migration governance (section 7.1), before analysing the main pillars (section 7.2) and building blocks (section 7.3) of this multifaceted, if not convoluted, architecture.

7.1 The Institutional Design of Global Migration Governance

The institutional scheme of global migration governance has raised longstanding debates among scholars. Its overall design has been described by Aleinikoff as 'sub-stance without architecture', insofar as the development of legal norms is not correl-ated with a formal institutional structure.[4] Hence, 'the sites and topics of governance may simply be too diffuse to permit a single edifice to be established, particularly at the international level'.[5] This diagnosis was clearly relevant when this assertion was made for, in 2007, the UN General Assembly was still struggling to find its role and the Global Forum on Migration and Development had just been created, while IOM was outside the UN system and led by a US Director-General for decades.

Since then, the rapid and rather unexpected growth of global migration gov-ernance has considerably transformed and shaped its overall design. The resulting scheme is still characterized by the enduring lack of a World Migration Organization (section 7.1) and resembles, instead, a deconstructivist edifice grounded on a com-plex assemblage of multiple institutions and processes that are both multi-layered and imbricated (section 7.2).

7.1.1 The quest for a world migration organization

Most controversies related to the institutional framework of global migration gov-ernance are closely associated with the lack of one single centralized international organization dedicated to migration. To address this institutional shortcoming, sev-eral economists, lawyers, and political scientists have regularly called for the cre-ation of a World Migration Organization. Jagdish Bhagwati advocated for such a worldwide organization as early as 1992.[6] He pointed out that 'the world badly

---

[4] TA Aleinikoff, 'International Legal Norms on Migration: Substance without Architecture' in R Cholewinski, R Perruchoud, and E MacDonald (eds), *International Migration Law: Developing Paradigms and Key Challenges* (TMC Asser Press 2007) 467.
[5] ibid 479.
[6] J Bhagwati, 'A Champion for Migrating Peoples' (The Christian Science Monitor, 28 February 1992) available at<http://www.csmonitor.com/1992/0228/28181.html> accessed 3 October 2018.

needs enlightened immigration policies and best practices to be spread and codified. A World Migration Organization would begin to do that by juxtaposing each
nation's entry, exit, and residence policies toward migrants, whether legal or illegal,
economic or political, skilled or unskilled.'[7] For the eminent economist, a World
Migration Organization should be entrusted with three cardinal tasks: to carry out
periodic country reviews, to establish burden-sharing indices, and to codify the
rights and obligations of migrants.[8] Bimal Gosh has also advanced the need for
establishing a new international regime for the orderly movement of people. For
him, 'the new regime must be based on three central pillars: (1) establishment of a set
of shared objectives; (2) development of an agreed and internationally harmonized
normative framework to ensure coherence of action at national, regional and global
levels; and (3) the setting-up of a coordinated institutional arrangement, including
a monitoring mechanism'.[9]

Among international lawyers, Arthur Helton argued in 2003 for the establishment of a World Migration Organization 'to make and arbitrate global migration
policy, which should be more effective, generous and humane than is currently the
case'.[10] Joel P Trachtman made a similar claim for such an organization in his book
The International Law of Economic Migration published in 2009. The international
trade lawyer proposes to model it upon the World Trade Organization, with a strong
secretariat and a broad set of competences in law making, intergovernmental negotiation, and dispute settlement.[11] The potentialities of such an analogy with WTO
has been further explored by Christopher Rudolph on the assumption that 'given
the expansiveness of its scope, the breadth of its membership, the degree of delegation afforded to it by member countries, the precision of its rules and procedures, and the sophistication of its dispute resolution mechanisms, the World Trade
Organization (WTO) clearly represents a model form for a migration regime to
emulate'.[12] He concludes, however, that 'while there are strong reasons to believe
that a similar institution is necessary to achieve the stated aims of a global mobility
regime, it is highly unlikely that a comprehensive, highly institutionalized regime
similar to the WTO will be established anytime soon'.[13]

Although it might be attractive for some, having a clone of WTO in the field
of migration seems too simple to be true. The so-called model of WTO cannot be

[7] J Bhagwati, 'Borders Beyond Control' (Foreign Affairs, January–February 2003) 98 available at <https://www.foreignaffairs.com/articles/2003-01-01/borders-beyond-control> accessed 3
October 2018.
[8] Bhagwati, 'A Champion for Migrating Peoples' (n 6).
[9] B Gosh, 'New International Regime for Orderly Movement of People: What Will it Look Like?' in
B Gosh (ed), *Managing Migration: Time for a New International Regime?* (OUP 2000) 227.
[10] A Helton, 'People Movement: The Need for a World Migration Organization' (openDemocracy,
1 May 2003) 4 available at <www.opendemocracy.net/people-migrationeurope/article_1192.jsp> accessed 3 October 2018.
[11] JP Trachtman, *The International Law of Economic Migration: Toward a Fourth Freedom* (WE
Upjohn Institute Press 2009) 324–29. See contra: TJ Hatton, 'Should We Have a WTO for International
Migration?' (2007) 22(50) Economic Policy 339–83.
[12] C Rudolph, 'Prospects and Prescriptions for a Global Mobility Regime: Five Lessons from the
WTO' in B Koslowski (ed), *Global Mobility Regimes* (Palgrave Macmillan 2011) 184.
[13] ibid.

transposed *mutatis mutandis* in this area for the mere fact that, unlike goods, people are not commodities that can be exchanged and negotiated at will. This does not mean that WTO has no role to play in the field of migration. On the contrary, as discussed in Chapter 2, its Mode 4 has the potential to become a substantive source of international migration law. However, WTO law has so far failed to deliver on its promises because of the very limited commitments made by its Member States to liberalize the movement of service providers. Furthermore, from a broader perspective, WTO is one particular form of institutional governance among many others. It does not provide a one-size-fits-all approach to be replicated in all fields of transnational nature. In contrast to trade, many other areas of international concern are multidimensional and cross-cutting by essence. They do not only include migration, but also development or environment to quote some obvious examples where the institutional framework of governance is characterized by a plurality of intergovernmental organizations, instead of a single centralized one.

This does not mean that a World Migration Organization would not have any added value. On the contrary, no one contests that the current *status quo* is not a viable option to deal with the multifaceted challenges surrounding migration governance. The Global Commission on International Migration underlined in 2005 that 'in the longer term a more fundamental overhaul of the current institutional architecture relating to international migration will be required, both to bring together the disparate migration-related functions of existing UN and other agencies within a single organization and to respond to the new and complex realities of international migration'.[14]

Even though this view was not endorsed by the UN, its Member States are more aware than ever of the limits of the current institutional framework. This is notably exemplified by the UNGA Declaration on International Migration and Development of 2013, where Member States call upon all relevant UN bodies and other related intergovernmental organizations 'to adopt a coherent, comprehensive and coordinated approach'.[15] They have further 'commit[ted] to strengthening global governance of migration' in the New York Declaration for Refugees and Migrants,[16] while the Global Compact for Migration reaffirms 'the centrality of a comprehensive and integrated approach' and dedicates a specific objective to strengthening international cooperation and global partnerships.[17] These calls however remain conspicuously vague about the concrete modalities and the overall institutional design to be established.

Whether this unprecedented awareness will result in effective action to improve the overall institutional framework is impossible to predict. The least we can say is that establishing *ex nihilo* a World Migration Organization remains a remote option

---

[14] Global Commission on International Migration (GCIM), *Migration in an Interconnected World: New Directions for Action* (GCIM 2005) 75.
[15] Declaration of the High-level Dialogue on International Migration and Development, UNGA Res 68/4 (3 October 2013) UN Doc A/RES/68/4, para 31.
[16] New York Declaration (n 1) Objective 23, para 49.
[17] Global Compact for Migration (n 2) para 39.

in the current political climate. The move towards a more coherent and integrated approach to global migration governance is arguably bound to translate into a progressive endeavour through the consolidation and development of existing institutions. In this view, IOM constitutes the most obvious candidate since its adhesion to the UN system in 2016. Its recognition by the UN 'as an organization with a global leading role in the field of migration'[18] provides new impetus for a more ambitious institutional reform.

IOM has the potential to become a truly comprehensive organization provided that its current mandate is consolidated and expanded. Its comparison with WTO poignantly highlights their distinctive characteristics and the long road towards a true World Migration Organization. From this comparative perspective, two obvious parallels between WTO and IOM can be drawn when it comes to their legal stance within the UN system and the specialized nature of their mandates. Like WTO, IOM is a related organization to the UN. In parallel with the specific focus of the former on trade, the latter constitutes the only intergovernmental organization entrusted with a generic and exclusive mandate on migration. However, the similarities between the two international organizations do not go beyond these two basic and superficial points of convergence.

Despite its recent adhesion to the UN system, IOM is still far from becoming the long overdue World Migration Organization due to the limits inherent in its current mandate inherited from its Constitution of 1987.[19] When assessed by reference to their constitutive instruments, IOM is more the anti-thesis of WTO than its counterpart in the area of migration. Contrary to the latter, the former primarily works as a service provider to its Member States with an operational and non-normative mandate. Hence, IOM is not a forum for Member States to negotiate and adopt binding rules, as is the case of WTO. This does not mean that there is no room for evolution under its current mandate. While being a primarily operational organization, the non-normative stance of IOM is more symbolic than real, in both law and practice.[20] Furthermore, its Constitution entrusts the organization to provide a forum to states as well as international and other organizations in relatively broad terms.

According to its Article 1 e), the role of IOM as a forum shall pursue two objectives: 'the exchange of views and experiences', as well as 'the promotion of cooperation and coordination of efforts on international migration issues, including studies on

---

[18] Art 2(1) of the Agreement Concerning the Relationship between the United Nations and the International Organization for Migration, UNGA Res 70/296 (25 July 2016) UN Doc A/RES/70/296.

[19] The original Constitution of 1953 was amended in 1987 and entered into force in 1989. IOM, Constitution of 19 October 1953 of the Intergovernmental Committee for European Migration (adopted 19 October 1953, entered into force 30 November 1954) as amended by Resolution No 724 by the 55th Session of the Council (adopted 20 May 1987, entered into force 14 November 1989) and by Resolution No 997 by the 76th Session of the Council (adopted 24 November 1998, entered into force 21 November 2013).

[20] For more in-depth discussion on this specific question and the overall mandate of IOM see section 7.3 of this chapter. Despite the growing involvement of IOM to promote international migration law, the absence of a supervisory function constitutes a fundamental difference with WTO and its sophisticated mechanism of peaceful settlement of disputes.

such issues in order to develop practical solutions'. As the first purpose highlights, IOM has been conceived as a forum of discussion, not a forum of negotiation. Nonetheless, the second aim of promoting cooperation and coordination may still be construed in a broader sense. Launching studies is obviously one means among many others to develop practical solutions in promoting cooperation and coordination. Much more concrete results could be achieved if IOM becomes a forum for the twofold purpose of discussing best practices on specific issues and, on this basis, negotiating common standards, whether binding or not. This obviously requires the organization and its Member States to be willing to embark on this endeavour.

Although a broad and purposive interpretation of its Constitution offers IOM some margin of manoeuvring to expand its role, its transformation into a truly comprehensive and leading organization can hardly be achieved with its current status. Hence, the recent proposal of the UN Secretary General to transform IOM into a specialized agency represents a new step towards a more integrated and coherent institutional response to migration. He explained in his report of December 2017 entitled 'making migration work for all' that:

> In contrast to refugees, there is still no centralized capacity in the United Nations to deal with migration. The Organization's approach to the issue, unlike its approach to the treatment of refugees, is fragmented. […] There is now an opportunity to develop this relationship further and to better integrate the competences of IOM into the broader United Nations system so as to support the efforts of Member States on migration-related issues.[21]

The UN and its Member States have indeed a lot to gain from upgrading IOM to a specialized agency. Nonetheless, this change in legal status shall not be seen as an end in itself. As discussed below in section 7.3, its transformation into a specialized agency is bound to have a limited impact if it is not accompanied by a more substantial reform of its mandate and a better articulation with that of UNHCR in order to mitigate the prevailing overlaps between the two organizations.[22]

7.1.2 A deconstructivist architecture of global migration governance

Whatever may be the prospects of IOM becoming a true World Migration Organization, the organization is part of a broader ecosystem which can only be understood from a holistic perspective. At the macro level, the overall UN framework is bound to remain decentralized and multi-level given the cross-cutting nature of migration and the vast number of actors involved in this area. Global migration governance is characterized by a complex superposition of nested and parallel

---

[21] UNGA 'Making Migration Work for All: Report of the Secretary-General' (12 December 2017) UN Doc A/72/643, 16–17.

[22] As notably acknowledged in 2017 by the late Special Representative of the Secretary-General on Migration, '[a] strong IOM-UNHCR team is indispensable, especially to steer the United Nations response to mixed migration flows and large, crisis-related movements […] and to co-lead the co-ordination of the work of the United Nations system on migration issues […]': UNGA, 'Report of the Special Representative of the Secretary-General on Migration' (3 February 2017) UN Doc A/71/728, 28.

international institutions that are not hierarchically organized. The fact that the governance of migration is not aligned with that related to trade does not mean that there is no architecture. Like international migration law as a whole,[23] the current institutional framework may be viewed as a deconstructivist architecture, which relies on decentralized and multi-layered governance. In stark contrast with classical architecture based on order and harmony, its institutional design is an iconoclastic construction where complexity, distortion, and contradiction are intrinsic to its very structure.

The overall edifice of global migration governance is accordingly fragile and far from providing an integrated and coherent institutional framework. Its foundations are, however, there to stay. The basement of this deconstructivist architecture relies on multiple building blocks made of two raw material: states and international organizations. As discussed in the previous chapter, the former are more aware than ever of the need for a multilateral approach and the virtue of cooperation beyond the North-South divide between receiving and sending countries. With the adoption of the Global Compact for Migration, States have 'learned that migration is a defining feature of our globalized world, connecting societies within and across all regions, making us all countries of origin, transit and destination'.[24] While this learning process is still ongoing, international organizations have also a major role to play in supporting states' efforts towards a more balanced and collaborative approach.

UN agencies and related organizations have great potential provided that they learn to collaborate and that existing duplication in their work is mitigated within this highly decentralized institutional framework. IOM and UNHCR are clearly the most important building blocks of the UN architecture, even though they are far from being the only ones. The vast majority of UN agencies and departments, as well as related organizations are involved in one way or another in the field of migration due to the transversal and multidimensional nature of the movement of persons across borders.

When assessed by reference to their respective mandates, the broad variety of institutions that are part of the UN system may be classified in three main categories (see Table 7.1). A first group consists of organizations with an exclusive focus on migration, refugee protection and/or mobility that include: IOM, UNHCR, UNRWA, UNWTO, ICAO, and IMO. A second group is composed of those organizations where the movement of persons across borders represents a significant component of their broader mandate. These include ILO, UNODC, OHCHR, WTO, and UNDESA. The third category gathers the many other organizations that are involved in this cross-cutting area as a side effect of their own mandates, that is, when their personal or material scope intersects with the movements of persons across borders. These comprise: UNICEF, UN Women, UNDP, UNESCO, UNCTAD, FAO, WHO, IFAD, UN Regional Commissions, UNEP, UNISDR, OCHA, UNIDO, UNITAR, UNFPA, UNU, the World Bank, WFP, and WMO.

---

[23] V Chetail, 'The Architecture of International Migration Law: A Deconstructivist Design of Complexity and Contradiction' (2017) 111 AJIL Unbound 18.
[24] Global Compact for Migration (n 2) para 10.

Table 7.1 UN agencies, departments, and related organizations involved in migration, refugee protection, and mobility

Institutions with an exclusive mandate on migration, refugee protection, and/or mobility	Institutions with migration, refugee protection, and/or mobility as an integral component of a broader mandate	Institutions with a general mandate that intersects with migration, refugee protection, and mobility
International Organization for Migration (IOM)	International Labour Organization (ILO)	United Nations Children's Fund (UNICEF)
United Nations High Commissioner for Refugees (UNHCR)	United Nations Office on Drugs and Crime (UNODC)	UN Women
United Nations Relief and Works Agency for Palestine Refugees in the Near East (UNRWA)	Office of the United Nations High Commissioner for Human Rights (OHCHR)	United Nations Development Programme (UNDP)
World Tourism Organization (UNWTO)	World Trade Organization (WTO)	United Nations Educational, Scientific and Cultural Organization (UNESCO)
International Civil Aviation Organization (ICAO)	United Nations Department of Economic and Social Affairs (UNDESA)	United Nations Conference on Trade and Development (UNCTAD)
International Maritime Organization (IMO)		Food and Agriculture Organization (FAO)
		World Health Organization (WHO)
		International Fund for Agricultural Development (IFAD)
		UN Regional Commissions
		United Nations Environment Programme (UNEP)
		United Nations Office for Disaster Risk Reduction (UNISDR)
		United Nations Office for the Coordination of Humanitarian Affairs (OCHA)
		United Nations Industrial Development Organization (UNIDO)
		United Nations Institute for Training and Research (UNITAR)
		United Nations Population Fund (UNFPA)
		United Nations University (UNU)
		The World Bank
		World Food Programme (WFP)
		World Meteorological Organization (WMO)
		Joint United Nations Programme on HIV/AIDS (UNAIDS)

In addition to the various building blocks made of Member States and UN institutions, the multilateral architecture of global migration governance relies on three complementary pillars. Each of these pillars have been established to provide a forum of discussion with a view to promoting and informing cooperation among states and other stakeholders.

The most important of these pillars is the UN General Assembly. As detailed in the previous chapter, it has become the most influential catalyst of global migration governance in initiating several decisive markers, including, notably, the holding of three plenary meetings in 2006, 2013, and 2016. Its role is bound to be reinforced through the periodic review on the implementation of the Global Compact for Migration. This new process, called the 'International Migration Review Forum', will be organized by the UNGA every four years to 'serve as the primary intergovernmental global platform for Member States to discuss and share progress on the implementation of all aspects of the Global Compact'.[25] Its first meeting shall take place in 2022 and each edition is supposed to result in an intergovernmental declaration.[26]

In parallel with the generic role entrusted to the UNGA, the two other pillars are more specific and different in both scope and nature. As further detailed in section 7.2, the Global Forum on Migration and Development has been conceived to provide an intergovernmental pillar outside the UN, while the Global Migration Group represents the inter-agency pillar to foster institutional coordination within the UN system.

Similarly to a deconstructivist building, the overall picture of global migration governance is multifarious, intricate, and puzzling. Its overall design reflects the multi-layered and decentralized structure of global migration governance. However, the whole edifice looks like an unfinished building which is still under construction. While multilateralism has grown in this area to an unprecedented degree, global migration governance is clearly witnessing a period of mutation which calls for a more integrated and cogent scheme. The vast number of its building blocks and the uneven nature of its pillars produce an impression of incompleteness and instability which has never been more acute than today. The main challenge for the UN and its Member States is to manage this piecemeal and multi-level array of institutions and processes in order to improve both their efficiency and complementarity.

7.2 The Pillars of Global Migration Governance

The central role played by the UN General Assembly in sustaining and informing global migration governance is supplemented by two specific pillars: an intergovernmental one, through the Global Forum on Migration and Development, and an inter-agency one with the Global Migration Group. At the time of writing, both were experiencing an important reform process which was not yet completed. To

---

[25] ibid para 49.   [26] ibid.

better appraise their potential and limits, the subsequent sections accordingly high-light the main attributions and weaknesses of these two central components.

7.2.1 The intergovernmental pillar of global migration governance: the Global Forum on Migration and Development

The Global Forum on Migration and Development (GFMD) was established in 2006 on a proposal from the UN Secretary-General following the first High-Level Dialogue on International Migration and Development organized by the UN General Assembly. The scope and form of the GFMD were carefully crafted to address the concerns and reticence of Western countries of immigration. It has been accordingly conceived as an informal, non-binding, and voluntary forum of intergovernmental dialogue.[27] Its scope is limited to the reassuring theme of the migration-development nexus from a practical and action-oriented perspective. To secure the acquiescence of destination states, the GFMD is not a decision-making process and, as such, does not produce any negotiated outcomes. Thus, it is nothing more than a multilateral forum of inter-state discussion for governments that are willing to take part therein.

Furthermore, the GFMD was established outside the UN, contrary to the pro-posal of the Secretary-General and despite the views of the Group of 77 and China.[28] Nonetheless, the two entities are closely interdependent. First, GFMD member-ship largely coincides with that of the UN: the former is open to all Member and Observer States of the UN, while UN agencies are invited as observers. Second, the link with the UN is ensured by the attendance of its Secretary-General at the annual meetings of the GFMD and the support provided by the Special Representative of the Secretary-General and the Global Migration Group (GMG) to the Chair of the GFMD.

This forum of intergovernmental dialogue is held on a permanent and regular basis. It is convened every year, which is quite unusual for this kind of worldwide consultation.[29] The official objectives pursued by its annual meetings are:

---

[27] UNGA, 'Summary of the High-level Dialogue on the High-level on International Migration and Development' (13 October 2006) UN Doc A/61/515, 5.

[28] P Martin, S Martin, and S Cross, 'High-Level Dialogue on Migration and Development' (2007) 45(1) International Migration 7, 21.

[29] The meetings of the GFMD take place every year in a different country with a specific overarching theme: First Meeting (Brussels, 9–11 July 2007): Migration and Socio-economic Development; Second Meeting (Manila, 27–30 October 2008): Protecting and Empowering Migrants for Development; Third Meeting (Athens, 2–5 November 2009): Integrating Migration Policies into Development Strategies for the Benefit of All; Fourth Meeting (Puerto Vallarta, 8–11 November 2010): Partnerships for Migration and Human Development; Shared Prosperity, Shared Responsibility; Fifth Meeting (Geneva, 29 November to 2 December 2011): Taking Action on Migration and Development—Coherence, Capacity and Cooperation; Sixth Meeting (Port Louis, 19–22 November 2012): Enhancing the Human Development of Migrants and their Contribution to the Development of Communities and States; Seventh Meeting (Stockholm, 14–16 May 2014): Unlocking the Potential of Migration for Inclusive Development; Eighth Meeting (Istanbul, 14–16 October 2015): Strengthening Partnerships: Human Mobility for Sustainable Development; Ninth Meeting (Dhaka 10–12 December 2016): Migration that Works for Sustainable Development for All: Towards a Transformative Migration Agenda; Tenth

1. To provide a venue for policy-makers and high-level policy practitioners to informally discuss relevant policies and practical challenges and opportunities of the migration-development nexus [...];

2. To exchange good practices and experiences, which can be duplicated or adapted in other circumstances, in order to maximize the development benefits of migration and migration flows;

3. To identify information, policy and institutional gaps necessary to foster synergies and greater policy coherence at national, regional and international levels between the migration and development policy areas;

4. To establish partnerships and cooperation between countries, and between countries and other stakeholders, such as international organizations, diaspora, migrants, academia etc, on migration and development;

5. To structure the international priorities and agenda on migration and development.[30]

Despite the informal nature of the GFMD, its internal organization relies on a rather elaborate institutional structure. No less than five organs with specific functions and memberships have been established to manage and support the GFMD process.[31] They include:

- A Troika, formed by the current Chair in Office as well as by two Co-Chairs represented by the previous and forthcoming Chairs;[32]

- A light Support Unit to assist the Chair-in-Office with its administrative, financial, and logistic needs;[33]

- A Steering Group comprised of governments committed to support to the GFMD process and ensure its continuity;[34]

Meeting (Berlin, 28–30 June 2017): Towards a Global Social Contract on Migration and Development; Eleventh Meeting (Marrakesh, 5–7 December 2018).

[30] GFMD, 'Background' available at <https://gfmd.org/process/background> accessed 3 October 2018.

[31] Contrary to other global initiatives, the GFMD operating modalities were not formalized by the UN General Assembly. The High-Level Dialogue of 2006 merely highlighted some of its basic characteristics as a state-led informal forum of discussion that is unable to produce negotiated outcomes or normative decisions. See UNGA, 'Summary of the High-level Dialogue' (n 27) 5. The GFMD operating modalities were adopted in 2007 at the first meeting in Brussels, see GFMD, 'Operating Modalities' (11 July 2007) available at <https://gfmd.org/process/operating-modalities> accessed 3 October 2018.

[32] The Co-Chairs shall assist the Chair in Office which assumes responsibility for the preparatory process and the implementation of each Forum. In principle, the Chair in Office alternates annually between a developing and a developed country.

[33] See GFMD, 'Support Unit' available at <https://gfmd.org/process/supporting-framework/support-unit> accessed 3 October 2018.

[34] The composition of the Steering Group is in principle regionally balanced and takes into account different migration perspectives, although more than one third of its current members are Western states. The Steering Group is comprised of 30 governments, namely: Argentina, Australia, Bangladesh, Belgium, Canada, Ecuador, Egypt, France, Germany, Ghana, Greece, India, Indonesia, Israel, Kenya, Mauritius, Mexico, Morocco, Netherlands, Philippines, Portugal, Republic of Korea, Spain, Sweden, Switzerland, Thailand, Tunisia, Turkey, United Arab Emirates, and United States. See GFMD, 'Steering Group' available at <https://gfmd.org/process/supporting-framework/steering-group> accessed 3 October 2018.

- A consultative body called the Friends of the Forum, comprising all States Members and Observers of the United Nations;[35]
- A network of National Focal Points, composed of high-level government representatives who ensure the liaison between the GFMD and participating governments.[36]

In its ten years of existence, the GFMD has raised longstanding criticisms from various sides. Both NGOs and scholars have described this 'strange creature',[37] as a ' "talkshop" for governments, which accomplishes little, lacks in transparency and public control and is normatively dubious as it is formally outside of the UN system'.[38] Within the UN, its relations with the Global Migration Group have been tense and sometimes adversarial. The former Special Rapporteur on the human rights of migrants also denounced that:

Owing to its voluntary, informal and non-binding nature, it has so far not led to much substantive change. One of the main objectives of the Global Forum is to exchange good practices and experiences, but, in the absence of a normative framework to guide the discussions, this can turn into an exchange of bad practices or even a race to the bottom in terms of policies.[39]

Crépeau further regretted that 'the Global Forum does not monitor whether or how Governments follow up on its outcomes. It has a lack of institutional memory, as the Chair alternates annually, between developed and developing countries, and despite the existence of a small support unit, it does not have a permanent secretariat.'[40] Among these numerous critical accounts, the lack of any standard-setting attribution has become less relevant since the adoption of the two UN Global Compacts. Furthermore, as an informal consultative process established outside the UN, the GFMD is hardly a space for negotiating agreements at the multilateral level. In principle, such a normative function should be assumed by the UN General Assembly, whether by negotiating UN conventions (like the ICRMW) or adopting soft law standards, most notably through formal declarations (such as the ones adopted in 2013 and 2016).

Regarding the internal organization of the GFMD, the lack of a permanent budget and secretariat represents one of its main weaknesses. This is at odds with

---

[35] The UN, its specialized agencies, and other international organizations may be invited as observers. See GFMD, 'Friends of the Forum—Terms of Reference (2013–14)' available at<https://gfmd.org/process/supporting-framework/friends> accessed 3 October 2018.

[36] See GFMD, 'Focal Points' available at <https://gfmd.org/process/supporting-framework/focal-points> accessed 3 October 2018

[37] S Rother, ' "Inside-Outside" or "Outsiders by Choice?" Civil Society Strategies towards the 2nd Global Forum on Migration and Development in Manila' (2009) 111 Asien: the German Journal on Contemporary Asia 95, 100.

[38] S Kalm and A Uhlin, *Civil Society and the Governance of Development: Opposing Global Institutions* (Palgrave Macmillan 2015) 126. For a more positive account, see S Martin, *International Migration* (CUP 2014) 255–60.

[39] See UNGA 'Report of the Special Rapporteur on the human rights of migrants' in 'Human rights of migrants: Note by the Secretary-General' (7 August 2013) UN Doc A/68/283, 10.

[40] ibid.

the institutional structure that has been put in place to support its process through nine different organs. Its lack of transparency and inclusiveness has also raised recurrent concerns, even though the GFMD has been able to evolve over the years. Despite being initially state-centric in its working methods and neoliberal in its understanding of development, the GFMD has progressively been more open in two main counts. First, the thematic coverage of its agenda has extended beyond its focus on the migration-development nexus to include broader topics, like the human rights of migrants, regular pathways for labour migration, or social inclusion of migrants.[41] Second, despite its intergovernmental nature, the state-led meeting is preceded since 2008 by the Civil Society Days of the GFMD and a statement with recommendations from civil society is presented during the opening of the government meeting.[42] Moreover, in 2015, the GFMD Business Mechanism was created to articulate the priorities of the private sector and to enhance the private-public dialogue on migration and development.[43] This move towards a more inclusive GFMD is still a work in progress, since other important stakeholders are not formally integrated, such as trade unions and local authorities (including cities).

Overall, although its concrete achievements are not striking, the GFMD has been influential in creating a routine of intergovernmental exchanges and building confidence among countries of origin and destination. As a result of this process of interstate ownership, the GFMD has made the multilateralization of migration governance commonplace. By offering a unique space for multilateral dialogue, the GFMD has also shaped the international agenda on migration. For instance, the inclusion of the SDG target 10.7 to facilitate orderly, safe, and regular migration within the 2030 Agenda for Sustainable Development came out of an initiative first discussed within the GFMD under the Swedish Chairmanship of 2013–2014.[44] Furthermore, the New York Declaration of 2016 welcomed 'the valuable contribution of the Global Forum on Migration and Development'[45] and invited it, with other stakeholders, to contribute to the preparatory process of the Global Compact for Migration.[46] The UN Global Compact has been intensively discussed during the tenth GFMD meeting of 2017 under the co-chairmanship of Germany and Morocco.[47] The expertise gathered by the GFMD is indeed particularly relevant, as

[41] For an overview see especially GFMD, *Thematic Recollection 2007–2017, prepared by the Global Forum on Migration and Development for the Global Compact for Safe, Orderly and Regular Migration* (GFMD 2017).

[42] Since 2011, the International Catholic Migration Commission has established and managed a GFMD Civil Society Coordinating Office and, in 2014, the Migration and Development Civil Society (MADE) Network has been created to coordinate GFMD civil society activities.

[43] The GFMD Business Mechanism is coordinated by the International Organization of Employers (IOE) and the World Economic Forum Global Future Council on Migration (WEF GFCM) but no representatives of workers are included within this mechanism.

[44] See GFMD, 'GFMD and the 2030 Agenda' available at < https://gfmd.org/gfmd-and-2030-agenda> accessed 3 October 2018.

[45] New York Declaration for Refugees and Migrants (n 1) para 55.

[46] ibid annex II, para 13; UNGA, 'Modalities for the Intergovernmental Negotiations of the Global Compact for Safe, Orderly and Regular Migration' (6 April 2017) UN Doc A/RES/71/280, para 22(b).

[47] The Summary Reports of the GFMD discussions on the Global Compact are available at: <https://gfmd.org/docs/germany-morocco-2017-2018> accessed 3 October 2018.

most of the themes outlined in the Global Compact have been discussed within the GFMD for almost a decade.[48]

Although the GFMD was a pioneer in leading intergovernmental dialogue at the multilateral level, global migration governance had rapidly evolved during its ten years of existence to an extent hardly ever imagined when the GFMD was created, as exemplified by the two UN Global Compacts and the entry of IOM into the UN system. As a result of this new environment, its current format is increasingly questioned both by the GFMD and the UN. The initiator and fervent promoter of the GFMD, the former UN Special Representative for International Migration, Peter Sutherland, observed in his last report published in March 2017 that '[a]s migration becomes more firmly anchored in the work of the United Nations, the Global Forum on Migration and Development will face inevitable questions regarding its continued purpose and added value'.[49] The need to reform the GFMD has been also endorsed by the co-chairs of its tenth meeting[50] as well as by the UN Secretary-General.[51]

Although the GFMD fulfilled a unique role at the time of its establishment, with few if any counterparts at the universal level, this is no longer the case today. During the last decade, the unprecedented involvement of the UN as a forum of interstate discussion has considerably mitigated the added value of the GFMD. The GFMD is thus at risk of losing its *raison d'être* because its function as an intergovernmental forum duplicates to a significant extent the current role of the UNGA. In addition, many other intergovernmental bodies established under the auspices of the UNGA are regularly involved in leading discussions on migration among states' representatives. To name a few, they notably include the Second and Third Committees of the UNGA, the Human Rights Council, the Economic and Social Council, and its Commission on Population and Development. Furthermore, since the entry of IOM into the UN system, several other consultative processes are now within the ambit of the UN, including the International Dialogue on Migration and the regular meetings of the IOM governing body, alongside the work carried out by this organization in providing the secretariat of most regional consultative processes.

---

[48] GFMD, *Thematic Recollection 2007–2017* (n 41).

[49] UNGA 'Report of the Special Representative of the Secretary-General on Migration' (n 22) 27. He continued by proposing that 'the Global Forum on Migration and Development should consider adopting a multi-year programme of work, equipping itself with a more robust secretariat and strengthening its role as a policy review body that helps States assess and evaluate the effectiveness of their policy choices more systematically. It may also want to consider governance reforms to encourage genuine joint ownership by States, civil society and the private sector.'

[50] The future of the GFMD was also discussed during a specific session of its tenth meeting. The final conclusions of the co-chairs for the 2017–2018 GFMD acknowledged that: 'While upholding the GFMD's relevance and continuity, Member States, however, pointed out that there is a need to revisit the existing modalities, mechanisms and supporting structures of the GFMD, so that it becomes fit for the purpose of serving the objectives of the Global Compact and the continued follow up and implementation of the 2030 Agenda', see GFMD, 'Final Conclusions and Recommendations of the 2017–2018 GFMD-Co-Chairs' available at <https://gfmd.org/docs/germany-morocco-2017-2018> accessed 3 October 2018.

[51] UNGA 'Making Migration Work for All: Report of the Secretary-General' (12 December 2017) UN Doc A/72/643, 18.

The risk of duplication and overlap in such a rapidly changing environment has become even more obvious since the UNGA has been entrusted to be the intergovernmental forum for discussing and sharing progress on the implementation of the Global Compact for Migration. In order to supplement the review process carried out by the UNGA every four years, the UN Compact invites the GFMD 'to provide a space for annual informal exchange on the implementation of the Global Compact, and report the findings, best practices and innovative approaches to the International Migration Review Forum'.[52] This informal function questions, however, the continuing relevance of the GFMD remaining outside the UN. It seems odd that an intergovernmental forum established outside the UN will discuss every year the implementation of the UN Global Compact for Migration. Its inclusion within the UN is further required by the need for a more coherent and integrated approach. If the GFMD wants to subsist within this expanding patchwork of overlapping processes, its reform is more needed than ever, in order to ensure its continuing relevance in the current architecture of global migration governance.

7.2.2 The inter-agency pillar of global migration governance: the Global Migration Group

The Global Migration Group (GMG) is an inter-agency group bringing together heads of agencies to foster coordination on migration within the UN. It was established by the United Nations Secretary-General in early 2006 in response to a recommendation of the Global Commission on International Migration for the establishment of a high-level inter-institutional group of agencies involved in activities related to migration. The GMG was created by building on an existing inter-agency group with a more limited membership, the Geneva Migration Group, which was established in April 2003 and comprised UNHCR, IOM, ILO, OHCHR, UNCTAD, and UNODC.

The GMG is a mechanism for inter-agency coordination and consultation. The mandate of the GMG is as broad as it is ambitious. According to its Terms of Reference, its twofold objective is 'to promote the wider application of all relevant international and regional instruments and norms relating to migration and to provide leadership for the improvement of the overall effectiveness and coherence of normative and operational response by the United Nations system and the international community to the opportunities and challenges presented by international migration'.[53] Within this wide-ranging mandate, the GMG has identified the following key priorities:

---

[52] Global Compact for Migration (n 2) para 51.
[53] Global Migration Group, 'Terms of Reference' available at<http://www.globalmigrationgroup. org/system/files/uploads/documents/Final_GMG_Terms_of_Reference_prioritized.pdf> accessed 3 October 2018.

a) Exchanging information and expertise to improve understanding, inter-agency cooperation, and collaboration so as to promote synergies and avoid duplication;

b) Exchanging results and pooling efforts in regard to research, data collection, and analysis;

c) Establishing a comprehensive and coherent approach in the overall institutional response to international migration;

d) Working to ensure the full respect for the human rights and labour rights of international migrants so as to promote human security and development and, in particular, provide protection to vulnerable migrants, including asylum-seekers, refugees, stranded migrants, and victims of exploitation and trafficking;

e) Contributing to the General Assembly High Level Dialogue on Migration and Development, the follow-up to the recommendations of the Global Commission on International Migration and other major initiatives of the international community and GMG members;

f) Identifying critical issues, opportunities, challenges, weaknesses, gaps, and best practices in relation to international migration and its interrelations with development.[54]

However, the far-reaching mandate of the GMG starkly contrasts with its lack of any decision-making power. The GMG is indeed a consultative organ that is unable to take any binding decisions for its agency members and the UN system. This represents the main structural weakness of the GMG. As observed by several commentators, 'the GMG does not have the authority to identify gaps or duplications of efforts and assign responsibilities to its member agencies'.[55]

Instead of providing a robust mechanism of coordination, the GMG is nothing else than a forum of exchange among UN agencies with regular information sharing being its primary function. Since 2006, its membership has considerably expanded to include twenty-two UN agencies and related organizations today. In addition to the traditional UN organizations working on migration (UNHCR, IOM, ILO, OHCHR, and UNODC), the GMG is composed of an eclectic set of many other institutions for which migration is not a major part of their mandate. They are: the Food and Agriculture Organization of the United Nations (FAO); the International Fund for Agricultural Development (IFAD); the UN Regional Commissions; the United Nations Environment Programme (UNEP); the United Nations Children's Fund (UNICEF); the United Nations Conference on Trade and Development (UNCTAD); the United Nations Department of Economic and Social Affairs (UN-DESA); the United Nations Development Programme (UNDP); the United Nations Educational, Scientific and Cultural Organization (UNESCO); the United Nations Entity for Gender Equality and the Empowerment of Women (UN

---

[54] ibid.   [55] Martin, *International Migration* (n 38) 280.

Women); the United Nations Industrial Development Organization (UNIDO); the United Nations Institute for Training & Research (UNITAR); the United Nations Population Fund (UNFPA); the United Nations University (UNU); the World Bank; the World Food Programme (WFP); and the World Health Organization (WHO).

This extensive albeit heterogeneous membership reflects the transversal nature of migration that concerns almost all UN agencies. Yet, the GMG falls short of offering an inclusive forum gathering all the UN agencies working on migration. Indeed, many other important agencies and related organizations are astonishingly not part of the GMG, although their mandate is much more relevant than the ones of the majority of the existing members. Such UN agencies include, most notably, the United Nations Relief and Works Agency for Palestine Refugees (UNRWA), the International Civilian Aviation Organization (ICAO), the World Trade Organization (WTO), the World Tourism Organization (UNWTO), and the International Maritime Organization (IMO). Their exclusion from the GMG is obviously at odds with the very rationale and objective of this UN mechanism for inter-agency coordination. This undermines the effectiveness and comprehensive nature of its work.

Another drawback of the GMG relates to the lack of collective identity among its members. This issue has prompted longstanding criticism within and outside the UN. A report of the UN System Chief Executives Board for Coordination in 2013 acknowledged that 'the stark contrasts and diversity of mandates, governance structures, funding, operations, capacities and priorities among its members continue to pose challenges to the GMG as a collective'.[56] The former Special Rapporteur on the human rights of migrants also noticed, in line with the viewpoints of several commentators, 'the need for a clearer vision, leadership and policy coherence on the part of the Group'.[57] Likewise, Antoine Pécoud, a former civil servant for UNESCO's programme on international migration, pinpointed 'one of GMG's weaknesses, as chairing members tend to use the group to pursue their own mandate, rather than adapting to—and serving—the GMG's own objectives'.[58] He further observed that

---

[56] See UN System Chief Executives Board for Coordination (CEB), *International Migration and Development: Contributions and Recommendations of the International System* (CEB 2013) 25, coordinated by UNFPA and IOM.

[57] UNGA 'Report of the Special Rapporteur on the Human Rights of Migrants' in 'Human Rights of Migrants: Note by the Secretary-General' (7 August 2013) UN Doc A/68/283, 9. See also, among commentators, I Omelaniuk, 'Global Migration Institutions and Processes' in B Opeskin, R Perruchoud, and J Redpath-Cross (eds), *Foundations of International Migration Law* (CUP 2012) 356, noting that 'the GMG has been variously described, mostly in the GFMD context, as ineffective, paralysed by competition and territorialism, and insufficiently cohesive in its support for the GFMD. Some believe it lacks shared vision and leadership, and that it continues to reflect contradictions'; S Angemendt and A Koch, *Global Migration Governance and Mixed Flows: Implications for Development-centred Policies* (Stiftung Wissenschaft und Politik German Institute for International and Security Affairs 2017) 19: 'One drawback of the GMG is that the issues addressed depend strongly on the chair, which rotates annually regardless of how intensely the respective agency is involved in refugee and migration questions. In recent years the chairing agencies have often set the agenda according to their own needs and interests, rather than to those aspects of greatest importance to the membership as a whole.'

[58] A Pécoud, *'Suddenly, Migration Was Everywhere': The Conception and Future Prospects of the Global Migration Group* (Migration Policy Institute, 5 February 2013) available at <www.migrationpolicy. org/article/suddenly-migration-was-everywhere-conception-and-future-prospects-global-migration-group> accessed 3 October 2018.

'even in the drafting of one- to two-page joint statements, each agency may want its specific focus to be explicitly mentioned and fear that the mandate of other agencies will turn out to be more visible than its own. UNODC will add the words smuggling and trafficking wherever possible; OHCHR will do the same with human rights, UNICEF with children, and so on.'[59]

As a result of these criticisms, in 2013 the GMG undertook an internal reform that led to some administrative and technical improvements, including the adoption of multi-year work plans to make GMG coordination more strategic and impactful, the extension of GMG chairmanships from six to twelve months, the establishment of a small administrative team to support the chair and to facilitate continuity in the work of the GMG, as well as the development of thematic working groups and task forces that bring together interested sub-sets of agencies around shared concerns.[60] While welcomed by the General Assembly,[61] these efforts to enhance its functioning and to promote coherence among its member organizations still remain bureaucratic and fail to address the most glaring flaws of the GMG.

The lack of a GMG budget and the rotating chair among its member agencies, which are naturally tempted to promote their own agenda, are clearly the main sources of these internal tensions and contradictions. If the role of the GMG was taken seriously as it should be, its structural weaknesses could be overcome through a more ambitious reform, including a permanent chair and budget. The recent initiative of the UN Secretary-General clearly goes in this direction, even though at the time of writing no information was yet available about its exact role and content. Nonetheless, the replacement of the GMG by 'a United Nations network on migration to ensure effective and coherent system-wide support' has been acknowledged by the Global Compact for Migration.[62] It further specifies that IOM will serve as the coordinator and secretariat of the network.[63]

The relatively limited achievements of the GMG during the past twelve years further call for a reform to effectively carry out its mandate. So far, its work has been mostly focused on producing normative knowledge through the publication of reports on migration-related issues with a particular interest in development and

[59] ibid.
[60] See IOM and the Global Migration Group (GMG), 'Decisions Adopted by the Global Migration Group on 3 July 2013' (Global Migration Group, 2013) available at<http://www.globalmigrationgroup.org/system/files/uploads/GMG-Reform-consolidated-decisions-3-July-2013.pdf> accessed 3 October 2018. At the time of writing, the GMG has three working groups and two task forces: Working Group on Mainstreaming Migration into National Development Strategies, co-chaired by IOM and UNDP; Working Group on Data and Research, co-chaired by IOM and UNDESA; Working Group on Migration, Human Rights and Gender, co-chaired by OHCHR, UN Women and UNICEF; Task Force on Capacity Development, co-convened by IOM and UNITAR; and Task Force on Migration and Decent Work, co-convened by ILO and IOM. For further details about the GMG activities, see Global Migration Group (GMG), 'Multi-Annual Work Plan 2013–2015' (Global Migration Group, 2013) available at <http://www.globalmigrationgroup.org/system/files/uploads/GMG-Reform-consolidated-decisions-3-July-2013.pdf> accessed 3 October 2018; GMG, 'Multi-Annual Work Plan 2016–2018' (Global Migration Group, 2015) available at<http://www.globalmigrationgroup.org/system/files/GMG_MAWP_2016-2018_%2015Sept16.pdf> accessed 3 October 2018.
[61] UNGA 'Declaration of the High-level Dialogue' (n 15) para 32.
[62] Global Compact for Migration (n 2) para 45.   [63] ibid.

the human rights of migrants.[64] In addition, GMG joint statements are regularly adopted to express common positions and outline policy guidance.[65] The GMG has also provided some limited support to the GFMD, the UN Summit of 2016, and the consultation phase of the Global Compact for Migration.[66]

Overall, the most tangible outcome of the GMG has been the adoption of the Principles and Guidelines on the Human Rights Protection of Migrants in Vulnerable Situations in 2017.[67] This comprehensive and detailed guidance has been prepared by the GMG Working Group on Human Rights and Gender Equality, co-chaired by OHCHR and UN Women, through a broad process of consultation. This soft

---

[64] GMG publications include so far: Paper on Migration, Remittances and Financial Inclusion: Challenges and Opportunities for Women's Economic Empowerment (2017); Report of the GMG Multi-Stakeholder Meetings in Preparation for the High-level Plenary Meeting of the General Assembly on Addressing Large Movements of Refugees and Migrants (2016); Stocktaking Report on Protection-at-Sea (2015); Stocktaking Report on Crisis-Related Migration (2015); Conference Summary Report on Harnessing Migration, Remittances and Diaspora Contributions for Financing Sustainable Development (2015); Discussion Paper on Realizing the Inclusion of Migrants and Migration in the Post-2015 United Nations Development Agenda (2015); Migration and Youth: Opportunities and Challenges (2014); Thematic Paper on the Exploitation and Abuse of International Migrants, particularly those in an Irregular Situation—A Human Rights Approach (2013); Symposium Report on Migration and Youth: Harnessing Opportunities for Development (2011); Mainstreaming Migration into Development Planning: A Handbook for Policy-makers and Practitioners (2010); International Migration and Human Rights: Challenges and Opportunities on the Threshold of the 60th Anniversary of the Universal Declaration of Human Rights (2008).

[65] GMG joint statements that are available on its website include: Statement at the UNGA Second Committee General Discussion on International Migration and Development (2016); Statement at the UN GA High-level Summit Addressing Large Movements of Refugees and Migrants (2016); Statement at the Fifth Ministerial Meeting of the Colombo Process (2016); Statement at the Inaugural Meeting of the 'Friends of Migration' Group (2016); Statement at the 49th Session of the Commission on Population and Development (2016); Statement at the Side Event on Policies Empowering Migrant Women and Girls in the Context of the 2030 Agenda for Sustainable Development Held on the Margins of the 60th Session of the Commission on the Status of Women (2016); Statement at the UN Secretary-General's High-Level Panel on Women's Economic Empowerment during the 60th Session of the Commission on the Status of Women (2016); Statement at the 47th Session of the Statistical Commission (2016); Statement at the 2016 IOM International Dialogue on Migration (IDM): Follow-up and Review of Migration in the SDG (2016); Statement at the 14th Coordination Meeting on International Migration (2016); Statement at the 48th Session of the Commission on Population and Development (2015); Joint Communiqué on 'Realizing the Inclusion of Migrants and Migration in the Post-2015 United Nations Development Agenda' (2014); Statement at the First High-level Meeting of the Global Partnership for Effective Development Co-operation (2014); Statement at the 47th Session of the Commission on Population and Development (2014); Statement at the 45th Session of the Statistical Commission (March 2014); Statement at the 12th Coordination Meeting on International Migration (2014); Statement at UN High-level Dialogue on International Migration and Development (2013); Joint Statement and Position Paper for the 2013 UN High-level Dialogue on International Migration and Development (2013); Joint Position Paper on migration and the post-2015 UN Development Agenda (2013); Statement on the Impact of Climate Change (2011); Statement on the Human Rights of Migrants in Irregular Situation (2010).

[66] The GMG mainly delivered common statements at the GFMD, organized meetings around the UN Summit of 2016, and was requested to assist the Secretary-General to submit issues briefs for each informal thematic session of the consultation phase for the development of the Global Compact. See GMG, *Report of Global Migration Group (GMG) Meetings around the UN Summit for Refugees and Migrants* (UN Women 2016) available at<http://www.globalmigrationgroup.org/system/files/UNW_16020_GMG_Report_finaldesign.pdf> accessed 3 October 2018; UNGA Res 71/280 (n 46) para18.

[67] OHCHR and GMG, 'Principles and Guidelines, Supported by Practical Guidance, on the Human Rights Protection of Migrants in Vulnerable Situations' (2017) available at<https://www.ohchr.org/Documents/Issues/Migration/PrinciplesAndGuidelines.pdf> accessed 3 October 2018.

law instrument identifies twenty principles drawn directly from human rights law and related standards (including labour law, refugee law, criminal law, humanitarian law, and the law of the sea).[68] Each principle is supported by a detailed set of more practical guidelines that elaborate international best practices deriving from authoritative interpretations or recommendations by human rights treaty bodies and special procedure mandate holders of the Human Rights Council.

This recent initiative goes in the right direction and should be carried out in a more systematic way to address other issues of common interest among UN agencies working on migration. The GMG has the potential to become an important forum where common standards among its organization members can be drafted and adopted. This would attenuate and channel the segmented and decentralized approach followed so far by UN agencies in developing their own normative standards. As observed in the previous chapter, the last two decades witnessed the proliferation of soft law standards adopted by each individual organization within their respective mandates (including most notably UNHCR, ILO, OHCHR, and IOM). This development has been achieved, however, in a rather erratic and uncoordinated way, to the detriment of the overall coherence of the UN system. On the contrary, the adoption of common standards by the GMG would allow the UN system to speak with one voice while promoting a more coherent and integrated approach among its member organizations.

Although the GMG has done some valuable work in advocating for a wider application of the relevant instruments and norms relating to migration, the same cannot be said regarding its role as an inter-agency mechanism for coordination. Its concrete impact on the overall institutional coherence and effectiveness of the UN system is meagre, to say the least. It is true that, like states, international organizations must learn to cooperate with each other. From this angle, the GMG has been helpful in deepening mutual confidence and common understanding among its members. This, however, is the very minimum one can expect from specialized agencies and related organizations that are supposed to belong to the same UN system. The need for a more coherent and integrated approach within the UN system requires much more than sharing information and adopting joint statements. After twelve years of existence, it is time to transform the GMG into a robust mechanism of coordination with a permanent chair and budget as well as an extended membership encompassing all concerned organizations of the UN system.

However, reforming the GMG is only one side of the coin. The ongoing difficulties it has encountered are symptoms of a broader syndrome. GMG agencies are often in competition with each other because the division of labour between UN agencies and related organizations working on migration is not clearly demarcated.

---

[68] These twenty principles encompass the following key items: primacy of human rights; non-discrimination; access to justice; rescue and immediate assistance; border governance; human rights-based return; protection from violence and exploitation; ending immigration detention; protecting family unity; migrant children; migrant women and girls; right to health; right to an adequate standard of living; right to work; right to education; right to information; monitoring and accountability; human rights defenders; data collection and protection; migration governance and cooperation.

Despite their specific fields of competence, their mandates still overlap to a significant extent and all of them are competing with one another to secure funding from governments, as exemplified by UNHCR and IOM.

7.3 IOM and UNHCR: The Building Blocks of Global Migration Governance

Within the UN universe, the vast constellation of international organizations working on migration and refugee protection largely gravitates around two pivotal satellites: IOM and UNHCR. These two leading organizations represent the centre of gravity, around which the institutional architecture of migration evolves. They are indeed the only UN organizations with an exclusive and comprehensive mandate on migration and refugee protection. IOM is entrusted with a generic mandate on migration to promote international cooperation and provide services for migrants (including refugees and internally displaced persons),[69] while UNHCR primarily focuses on providing protection and seeking permanent solutions for refugees (through voluntary repatriation, local integration, and resettlement).[70]

These two organizations are also particularly influential actors because of their considerable human and financial resources that supersede all the other UN institutions in this field. In 2017, each of them employed more than 10,000 persons in over 130 countries with a total budget of US $ 7.7 billion for UNHCR and 1.789 billion for IOM.[71] As acknowledged by the previous UN Special Representative for International Migration, these two organizations are 'the natural anchors of the Organization's strategy and institutional architecture on international migration (in all its forms) [...]. Both have vastly more resources, expertise and accumulated experience on these issues than any other entity within the system and should thus be the "centre of gravity" around which consultation and coordination are organized.'[72]

Because of their pivotal role within this institutional architecture, IOM and UNHCR cannot be understood in isolation from one to another. They are bound to work in tandem, even if concurrence has too often prevailed over complementarity. Since their establishment in 1951, the two organizations have evolved in a rather disconnected way, following their own institutional agenda alongside the specificities of their respective mandates and constituent instruments. While the two organizations also have their part of responsibility, the prevailing competition is

---

[69] See art 1 of the IOM Constitution (n 19).

[70] UNHCR 'Statute of the Office of the United Nations High Commissioner for Refugees' Annex to UNGA Res 428(V) of 14 December 1950 (1950) para 1.

[71] See UNHCR '2017 Financials' in 'Global Focus UNHCR Operations Worldwide' (November 2017) available at<http://reporting.unhcr.org/financial#_ga=2.145842557.852070554.152465306 5-1410154397.1500379534> accessed 25 April 2018; UNHCR 'Figures at a Glance: Statistical Yearbooks' (UNHCR, 2017) available at <http://www.unhcr.org/figures-at-a-glance.html> accessed 3 October 2018; IOM (Council 108th Session) 'Summary Update on the Programme and Budget for 2017' (16 October 2017) C/108/15; IOM 'IOM Snapshot 2017' (IOM, 2017) available at <https://www.iom.int/sites/default/files/about-iom/iom_snapshot_a4_en.pdf> accessed 3 October 2018.

[72] UNGA 'Report of the Special Representative' (n 22) 28.

inherent in the current institutional architecture because of three structural factors that will be developed in this section.

First, although both of them are part of the UN system, UNHCR and IOM fundamentally diverge in their relations with the UN: the former is an integral part thereof, whereas the latter retains greater independence from the UN than any other institutions in this field. Second, contrary to the segmented approach opposing migration to refugee protection, the division of labour between the two organizations has been considerably blurred in both law and practice, as a result of the overlap of their mandates. Third, despite the convergence of their activities, the main dividing line between UNHCR and IOM lies in the normative and supervisory functions of the former as opposed to the latter. Comparing UNHCR and IOM thus provides a contrasting, if not confusing, picture that undermines the overall effectiveness and coherence of the UN response. While being the crucial building blocks of the institutional architecture, they reflect the fragility of the whole edifice that is far from providing an integrated approach to global migration governance.

7.3.1 The standing and governing structure of UNHCR and IOM within the UN system

The relations of UNHCR and IOM with the UN unveil the most significant difference between the two organizations, even if their own internal governing structures follow a quite similar pattern. In stark contrast to the status of IOM as a related organization, UNHCR is firmly anchored in the UN as a subsidiary organ of the General Assembly. It is bound by its Statute to 'act [...] under the authority of the General Assembly' and 'to follow policy directives given [...] by the General Assembly or the Economic and Social Council'.[73] Although its founding mandate has been dramatically expanded by subsequent resolutions of the General Assembly, its Statute makes clear that UNHCR can only engage in additional activities, 'as the General Assembly may determine, within the limits of the resources placed at his disposal'.[74] Its dependence towards the General Assembly was reinforced by the fact that it was created as a temporary organization for an initial mandate of only three years.[75] Then, for 50 years, UNHCR had to submit a request to the General Assembly for its continued existence every five years. It was only in December 2003 that the General Assembly finally removed the temporal limitation on the continuation of UNHCR and confirmed the Office as a programme of the UN 'until the refugee problem is solved'.[76]

---

[73] UNHCR, 'Statute of the Office of the United Nations High Commissioner for Refugees' (n 70) paras 1 and 3. Paragraph 2 of its Statue also underlines that 'the work of the High Commissioner shall be of an entirely non-political character; it shall be humanitarian and social and shall relate, as a rule, to groups and categories of refugees', although in practice UNHCR is also involved in the protection of individual refugees and not only as a group.

[74] ibid para 9.   [75] ibid para 5.

[76] UNGA 'Implementing Actions Proposed by the United Nations High Commissioner for Refugees to Strengthen the Capacity of his Office to Carry Out its Mandate' (22 December 2003) UN Doc A/RES/58/123, para 9.

The governance structure of UNHCR further reflects the influence of the GA and the ECOSOC at two different levels. The High Commissioner is 'elected by the General Assembly on the nomination of the Secretary-General' for a term of five years and 'shall report annually to the General Assembly'.[77] In addition, the work of the High Commissioner is supervised by the Executive Committee of the Programme of the United Nations High Commissioner for Refugees (thereafter ExCom). Created in 1955 by ECOSOC at the request of the GA,[78] ExCom is the governing body of UNHCR composed of states' representatives. Initially limited to twenty states, its membership has significantly grown over the years to include today no less than 101 states from all regions across the world.[79] Members of the Executive Committee are elected by the ECOSOC 'on the widest possible geographical basis from those States with a demonstrated interest in and devotion to the solution of refugee problems'.[80]

This intergovernmental body exerts considerable influence over UNHCR through two critical functions, including both decision-making and consultative responsibilities. The first function of ExCom is to supervise the work of the High Commissioner and approve the budget of the whole organization. It shall 'determine the general policies under which the High Commissioner shall plan, develop and administer the programmes', 'review at least annually the use of funds made available to the High Commissioner and the programmes', and 'have authority to make changes in, and give final approval to, the use of funds and the programmes'.[81]

This decision-making function is supplemented by a consultative role 'to advise the High Commissioner, at his request, in the exercise of his functions under the Statute of his Office'.[82] In carrying out this second task, ExCom has developed,

[77] UNHCR, 'Statute of the Office of the United Nations High Commissioner for Refugees' (n 70) para 11. According to its Statute, this reporting duty shall be done 'to the General Assembly through the Economic and Social Council'. UNHCR, however, developed the practice of submitting its annual reports to the GA directly. The GA endorsed and regularized this *contra legem* practice in its above-mentioned resolution of 2003, while additionally requesting the High Commissioner to 'make an annual oral report to the Economic and Social Council to keep it informed of the coordination aspects of the work of the Office'. The same resolution further requests the High Commissioner that, every ten years, the report submitted to the General Assembly shall include 'a strategic review of the global situation of refugees and the role of the Office, prepared in consultation with the Secretary-General and the Executive Committee.' See UNGA Res 58/153 (n 76) para 10. More generally, the 1950 Statute also specifies in its paragraphs 11 and 12 that the High Commissioner is 'entitled to present his views before the General Assembly, the Economic and Social Council and their subsidiary bodies' and 'may invite the cooperation of the various specialized agencies'.
[78] ECOSOC 'International Assistance to Refugees within the Mandate of the United Nations High Commissioner for Refugees' (31 March 1955) UN Doc E/RES/565 (XIX); UNGA Res 832 (IX) (21 October 1954).
[79] New state members requesting admission may be admitted by the ECOSOC upon approval by the General Assembly to enlarge the Executive Committee's membership.
[80] ECOSOC Res 565 (XIX) (n 78) para 2(a). Although Member States of ExCom are supposed to have 'a demonstrated interest in and devotion to the solution of refugee problems', they are not limited to State Parties to the Refugee Convention or its Protocol of 1967 and they do not have to be Member States of the UN.
[81] ECOSOC 'Establishment of the Executive Committee of the Programme of the United Nations High Commissioner for Refugees' Res 672 (XXV) (30 April 1958) para 2.
[82] ECOSOC Res 565 (XIX) (n 78) para 1(B).

through its annual conclusions, a considerable body of non-binding standards related to many aspects of refugee protection.[83] From this angle, it is 'the only specialized multilateral forum at the global level responsible for contributing to the development of international standards relating to refugee protection'.[84] Although ExCom conclusions are not formally binding, the very fact that they are adopted by a majority of UN Member States gives them a significant authority in providing intergovernmental guidance on refugee protection.[85]

The governing body of IOM is a Council with quite similar membership and attributions than the ones of ExCom. According to the Constitution of the organization, the IOM Council is composed of Member States, each of them having one representative and one vote.[86] Initially limited to sixteen Member States, IOM membership has considerably grown during the last two decades. It increased from sixty-seven in 1998 to 172 states in 2018, thus gathering a weighty and representative number of countries from every region of the world.[87] Besides this recent expansion in terms of numbers, its intergovernmental membership strikingly converges with the one of the ExCom: in 2018, no less than ninety-nine states were members of both the IOM Council and UNHCR ExCom. The functions of the IOM Council also coincide to a large extent with those of its UNHCR counterpart. According to Article 6 of the IOM Constitution, its main tasks are 'to determine, examine and review the policies, programmes and activities of the Organization', as well as 'to review and approve [...] the budget' of the organization.[88] Likewise, the IOM Council primarily works as 'a forum [...] for the exchange of views and experiences, and the promotion of co-operation and co-ordination of efforts on international migration issues'.[89]

---

[83] For a thematic collection of the numerous conclusions adopted by ExCom, see UNHCR, *A Thematic Compilation of Executive Committee Conclusions* (7th edn, UNHCR 2014).

[84] G Loescher, 'UNHCR and Forced Migration' in E Fiddian-Qasmiyehn and others (eds), *The Oxford Handbook of Refugee and Forced Migration Studies* (OUP 2014) 221.

[85] This is especially true when ExCom conclusions are adopted by consensus or endorsed by the General Assembly, as is frequently the case. For further discussion about the legal value of ExCom conclusions, see J Sztucki, 'The Conclusions on the International Protection of Refugees Adopted by the Executive Committee of the UNHCR Programme' (1989) 1(3) IJRL 287–318 . The author considered that ExCom conclusions 'fall rather low on the relative scale of *de facto* values of non-legal instruments. Whatever the legal relevance of General Assembly resolutions, the Conclusions are hardly on an equal footing with them', ibid 308. Although their legal value clearly does not equate with those of the resolutions adopted by the General Assembly, one should acknowledge that the author wrote at a time when ExCom membership counted only forty-three states and its conclusions were less influential than today. In contrast to its conclusions adopted in the exercise of its advisory function, the executive function of ExCom is mandatory for UNHCR, as acknowledged by the relevant resolutions of the General Assembly establishing ExCom and further confirmed by the binding nature of the resolutions of the General Assembly on internal matters of the UN.

[86] See art 7 of the IOM, 'Constitution' (n 19).

[87] Membership of IOM is open to any state 'with a demonstrated interest in the principle of free movement of persons which undertake to make a financial contribution at least to the administrative requirements of the Organization, [...] subject to a two-thirds majority vote of the Council and upon acceptance by the State of this Constitution', see art 2(b) of the IOM Constitution (n 19). The Council may also admit non-member states, intergovernmental, and non-governmental organizations as observers (art 8).

[88] IOM, 'Constitution' (n 19) art 6.   [89] ibid art 1(1)(e).

In the last few years, it has also adopted some policy principles and non-binding frameworks on a growing number of topical issues, such as crisis management, migration governance, humanitarian action, and internal displacement.[90] In contrast to UNHCR, this new yet increasing role is not grounded on any particular convention. The guidance provided by IOM frameworks is thus much more policy-oriented and less normative than that of ExCom conclusions on international protection. Contrary to the latter, the IOM Council has an additional and important task of electing the Director General of the organization by a two-thirds majority vote for a renewable term of five years.[91] As further specified in Article 13(2) of the IOM Constitution, the Director General is 'responsible to the Council' and shall 'discharge the administrative and executive functions of the Organization in accordance with this Constitution and the policies and decisions of the Council'. Hence, the IOM Director General does not enjoy the same independence from the Council as the High Commissioner may have with regard to ExCom.

Besides the technical niceties of their governing bodies, the most significant difference between UNHCR and IOM relates to their relations with the UN and their respective stance within the world organization. The former is an integral part of the UN as a subsidiary organ of the GA, whereas the latter is a related organization that is independent from the UN. According to Article 2(3) of the 2016 Agreement concerning the relationship between IOM and the UN, '[t]he United Nations recognizes that the International Organization for Migration, by virtue of its Constitution, shall function as an independent, autonomous and non-normative international organization in the working relationship with the United Nations'. Reciprocally, IOM recognizes the responsibilities of the UN, its organs, and agencies in the field of migration (Article 2(4)). It is also committed to conducting its activities in accordance with the UN Charter, the policies and instruments of the UN (Article 2(5)). Nonetheless, as an independent intergovernmental organization, IOM is not bound to report on its activities to the General Assembly (Article 4).

One might be tempted to infer from this opposition between UNHCR and IOM a correlation between the degree of integration within the UN and the subject-matter of the relevant organization: the most integrated institution in the UN system is devoted to refugee protection and the least integrated one to migration. This institutional distribution of tasks is, however, very formalistic and does not reflect the substantial overlap between their mandates, as detailed in the next section. Moreover, the degree of integration within the UN system fails to capture the whole picture of the multilateral framework governing migration that is spreading among many other important UN institutions with a broad variety of legal statuses and

---

[90] See, as discussed above, the IOM, 'Migration Crisis Operational Framework' Council 101st Session (15 November 2012) MC/2355; IOM, 'Migration Governance Framework: The Essential Elements for Facilitating Orderly, Safe, Regular and Responsible Migration and Mobility of People through Planned and Well-managed Migration Policies' Council 106th Session (4 November 2015) C/106/40; and, IOM, 'Framework for Addressing Internal Displacement' SCPF 20th Session (6 June 2017) S/20/4.

[91] IOM, 'Constitution' (n 19) art 13. According to this provision, the term of office may exceptionally be less than five years if a two-thirds majority of the Council so decides.

standing. To mention some of the most relevant ones, OHCHR is part of the UN Secretariat, whereas UNODC and UNRWA are UN programmes and ILO, ICAO, and IMO are specialized agencies. Against this background, one can reasonably conclude that, similarly to many other fields such as environment or development, the differing legal nature of the numerous UN and related institutions is more accidental than premeditated. In other words, it is less the result of an articulated and cogent vision of global migration governance than a by-product of the historical and political contingencies that prevailed at the time of their establishment.

The legal status of IOM may change in the future, for the Secretary-General proposed in 2017 to transform it into a specialized agency.[92] This upgrade would make the overall institutional framework on migration more coherent and efficient. This would also be more consonant with the law and practice of the UN which primarily distinguish specialized agencies from related organizations on the basis of the subject matter of their respective mandates. According to Article 57 of the UN Charter, specialized agencies are defined as being 'established by intergovernmental agreement and having wide international responsibilities, as defined in their basic instruments, in economic, social, cultural, educational, health, and related fields'. By contrast, related organizations are supposed to work in other fields than those mentioned above, including nuclear energy (International Atomic Energy Agency), arms control (Organization for the Prohibition of Chemical Weapons), and trade (World Trade Organization). Following this distribution of tasks, the field of migration in general and the mandate of IOM in particular are clearly more in line with the status of a specialized agency than the one of a related organization.

Interestingly, the IOM Working Group on Institutional Arrangements acknowledged in 2003 that the status of related organizations 'applies to agencies whose mandate does not fall under the terms of reference of ECOSOC, a situation which is not applicable to migration'.[93] The IOM Working Group concluded:

[S]pecialized agency status would provide many advantages for IOM in its relationship with the United Nations, with other specialized agencies, and with UN funds, programmes and other organizations. These combined would constitute for IOM a solid framework for pursuing its ultimate aim of playing a major role in the establishment of a safe and orderly management of migration in which States understand and protect the rights of migrants, and in which migrants respect national and international laws.[94]

Although in 2015 the IOM Council opted for the status of a related organization, the recent proposal of the UN Secretary-General to become a specialized agency calls for further introspection within the organization. Such an upgrade from a related organization to a specialized agency is not without precedent. A particularly salient and relevant analogy is provided by the rather close, if not overlapping, field

---

[92] UNGA 'Making Migration Work for All: Report of the Secretary-General' (12 December 2017) UN Doc A/72/643, 16–17.

[93] IOM Working Group on Institutional Arrangements, 'IOM-UN Relationship: Preliminary Report' (2003) WG/IOM-UN/1, para 46.

[94] ibid para 64; IOM, 'IOM-UN Relationship' 92nd Session (14 November 2006) MC/INF/285 (2006) para 9.

of tourism. The World Organization of Tourism was initially established as a related organization before becoming a specialized agency of the UN. It is also noteworthy that, since the conclusion of the 2016 Agreement, IOM has repeatedly stated to have become the 'UN migration agency',[95] as further exemplified by the new logo of the organization.[96] While this self-proclamation is legally wrong, it reflects the ambiguity of the Agreement concluded with the UN in 2016, where the term 'related organization' is mentioned nowhere.[97]

Regardless of the political considerations at play in any institutional reform, transforming IOM into a specialized agency would have to be approved by the UNGA and the IOM Council as per Article 15 of the 2016 Agreement. Such an upgrade would not necessarily imply a radical transformation of the organization and its internal structure.[98] Contrary to UN programmes (like UNHCR), specialized agencies retain to a large extent their independence from the UN as well as their specific characteristics.[99] The difference between specialized agencies and related organizations is indeed a question of degree, not of nature. Under international law, the two entities are independent international organizations that possess their own rules, legal personality, membership, organs, and financial resources.[100]

According to UN law and practice, the term 'related organization' shall be understood as 'a default expression, describing organizations whose cooperation agreement with the United Nations has many points in common with that of Specialized Agencies, but does not refer to Article 57 and 63 of the United Nations Charter, relevant to Specialized Agencies'.[101] These two provisions of the UN Charter are very general and mainly procedural. As mentioned above, Article 57 merely defines specialized agencies, while Article 63 indicates that ECOSOC 'may enter into

[95] See, inter alia, IOM, 'Summit on Refugees and Migrants Begins as IOM Joins the United Nations' (IOM, 19 September 2016) available at<www.iom.int/news/summit-refugees-and-migrants-begins-iom-joins-united-nations> accessed 3 October 2018; UN City, 'IOM Becomes the UN Migration Agency' (*UN City Copenhagen*, 11 October 2016) available at <http://un.dk/news-and-media/iom-becomes-the-un-migration-agency> accessed 3 October 2018.

[96] See the IOM logo at the top of its website <www.iom.int> accessed 3 October 2018.

[97] One should add that UNHCR also occasionally presents itself as the UN Refugee Agency in contradiction with its legal status. According to the UN law and terminology, UNHCR is not a specialized agency but a UN Programme like UNRWA is.

[98] However, the procedure would be much more demanding, time-consuming, and politically hazardous if its new status implies a redrafting of its Constitution. According to art 25(2) of IOM Constitution, 'fundamental changes in the Constitution' or 'new obligations for its Member States' shall not only be adopted by a two-thirds majority vote of the Council, but must also be ratified by two-thirds of the Member States in accordance with their respective constitutional processes.

[99] The transformation of IOM into a UN Programme would be much more radical: it implies the dissolution of IOM as an intergovernmental organization, and the creation of a new entity under the authority of the ECOSOC and the General Assembly. According to the IOM Constitution, the dissolution of the organization requires a three-quarter majority vote of its Member States. The subsequent decision to revamp it as a UN Programme shall be made by the General Assembly through a resolution that will determine the attributions and the governance structure of the new entity.

[100] For further discussion about the legal status of UN specialized agencies, see N Sybesma-Knol, *The United Nations* (Kluwer Law International 2012) 158–65; P Sands and P Klein, *Bowett's Law of International Institutions* (5th edn, Sweet Maxwell Limited 2001) 77–86; D Williams, *The Specialized Agencies and the United Nations: The System in Crisis* (St Martin's Press 1987) 17–24.

[101] UN System Chief Executives Board for Coordination, 'Directory of the UN System Organizations' (UNSCEB) available at <www.unsceb.org/directory> accessed 3 October 2018.

agreements with any of the [specialized] agencies' and it 'may co-ordinate the activities of the specialized agencies through consultation with and recommendations to such agencies and through recommendations to the General Assembly and to the Members of the United Nations'. In any event, as legally independent international organizations, both specialized agencies and related organizations shall conclude an agreement defining the terms and conditions of their relations with the UN.

The 2016 Agreement between IOM and the UN already displays a striking convergence with those concluded with specialized agencies on a significant number of provisions. They include mutual consultation on administrative cooperation regarding their staff, facilities, and secretariats, reciprocal representation and proposal of agenda items in the meetings of their respective plenary organs, as well as mutual exchange of information and documents. Despite these common provisions, the status of specialized agency entails four main legal consequences.

First of all, the most important difference is the recognition by the agency of 'the coordinating role, as well as the comprehensive responsibilities in promoting economic and social development, of the General Assembly and the Economic and Social Council under the Charter of the United Nations'.[102] This standard clause is accompanied by the commitment of the agency to ensure effective cooperation and coordination with the UN, its organs, and other agencies under Article 58 of the Charter.[103] Reciprocally, the specialized agency is generally, but not always, entrusted with a 'central coordinating role' in the specific field of its mandate.[104] Second, as a result of these close relations, the specialized agency commits to submit to the UN annual reports on its activities and to refer to its plenary organ any formal recommendation which the UN may make to the agency.[105] Third, while they retain considerable financial autonomy, the administrative budgets of specialized agencies are examined by the General Assembly with a view to making recommendations to the agencies.[106] Fourth, specialized agencies may request advisory opinions of the ICJ on legal questions falling within their mandate, and they agree to furnish any information requested by the ICJ in pursuance of Article 34 of the ICJ Statute.[107]

---

[102] This standard clause is contained in all agreements with specialized agencies. To mention the most recent ones, see the Agreement between the United Nations and the World Tourism Organization, UNGA Res 58/232 (2003) UN Doc A/RES/58/232 art 2; the Agreement between the United Nations and the United Nations Industrial Development Organization, UNGA Res 40/1780 (1985) UN Doc A/40/1780; and the Agreement between the United Nations and the World Intellectual Property Organization, UNGA Res 3346 (XXIX) (1974) UN Doc A/RES/3346(XXIX).

[103] ibid.

[104] See, among other examples, art 2 of the Agreement between the World Tourism Organization and the United Nations Industrial Development Organization UNGA Res 40/180 (1985) UN Doc A/RES/40/180.

[105] See arts 5 and 7 of Agreement with the World Tourism Organization (n 102); arts 5, 6, and 13 of the Agreement with the United Nations Industrial Development Organization (n 102); arts 5 and 6 of the Agreement with the World Intellectual Property Organization (n 102).

[106] Art 17(3) of the UN Charter.

[107] Art 10 of the Agreement between the United Nations and the World Tourism Organization (n 102); art 12 of the Agreement between the United Nations and the United Nations Industrial Development Organization (n 102); art 14 of the Agreement between the United Nations and the World Intellectual Property Organization (n 102).

Besides the legal and technical differences between specialized agencies and related organizations, the transformation of IOM is clearly in the mutual interest of both the organization and the UN at the political and institutional levels. IOM has a lot to gain from the status of a specialized agency. Among other obvious advantages, this would considerably increase its leadership in the field of migration and reinforce its standing within the UN, leading to more visibility, influence, and additional access to funding sources, without renouncing its specific features as an independent international organization with its own membership and governing structure. For the UN, a better integration of IOM would bring its extensive operational capacities on migration and substantially improve the overall coherence and effectiveness of the current institutional architecture. Upgrading IOM is, however, not an end in itself. It is bound to have limited impact if it is not part of a broader and more ambitious reform of the UN migration governance.

Establishing a comprehensive and coherent global migration governance calls for a more holistic reform to promote synergies and avoid duplication within the UN system as a whole. The central challenge is to ensure that complementarity prevails over concurrence among the great diversity of UN institutions working in migration and refugee protection. This does not only presuppose a revamping of the GMG to foster institutional coordination as discussed before. It also requires a better articulation between IOM and UNHCR to obviate—or, at least, to mitigate—the current blurring division of labour between the two that has given rise to the prevailing competition between them.

7.3.2 The blurred division of labour between UNHCR and IOM

Despite their different standing within the UN system, UNHCR and IOM have much more in common than it is conventionally assumed. Contrary to the common perception that UNHCR deals with refugee protection and IOM with migration, their respective mandates substantially overlap in both law and practice. Their own constituent instruments, as well as the subsequent evolution of their activities, have blurred the division of labour between the two organizations. This is especially true with regard to their personal and material competences.

The ratione personae *mandates of UNHCR and IOM*

The *ratione personae* mandates of UNHCR and IOM significantly overlap with regard to a broad number of persons on the move. Refugees, asylum seekers, stateless persons, returnees, and internally displaced persons fall equally within the competence of the two organizations. While the founding mandate of UNHCR was initially confined to refugees *stricto sensu*,[108] over the years it has been drastically expanded by the General Assembly to cover many other persons of concern, including

[108] UNHCR mandate over refugees is not exclusive since the United Nations Relief and Works Agency for Palestine Refugees in the Near East (UNRWA) has been established by UNGA Res 302 (IV) (8 December 1949) to carry out direct relief and works programmes for Palestine refugees. UNRWA has

internally displaced persons since 1972,[109] stateless persons since 1974,[110] asylum seekers since 1981,[111] and returnees since 1985.[112] Furthermore, while UNHCR has long claimed that it 'is not a migration organization',[113] it is increasingly involved in activities related to so-called 'mixed migration'.[114]

Inversely, although IOM presents itself as the migration agency, it was created in 1951 to encompass refugees, asylum seekers, and internally displaced persons.[115]

thus a specific mandate over Palestinian refugees residing in five areas of operation: Gaza, West Bank, Lebanon, Jordan, and Syria.

[109] UNGA Res 2958 (XXVII) (1972) paras 2 and 3. Among many other subsequent confirmations of this enlargement, see for instance, UNGA Res 35/187 (1980) UN Doc A/RES/35/187, para 1; UNGA Res 36/125 (1981) UN Doc A/RES/36/125, paras 1, 3–4, and 14; UNGA Res 41/124 (1986) UN Doc A/RES/41/124, para 16; UNGA Res 42/109 (1987) UN Doc A/RES/42/109, para 15; UNGA Res 44/137 (1989) UN Doc A/RES/44/137, paras 16 and 20; UNGA Res 48/116 (1993) UN Doc A/RES/48/116, para 12; UNGA Res 51/75 (1996) UN Doc A/RES/57/75, paras 5, 6, and 20; UNGA Res 53/125 (1998) UN Doc A/RES/53/125, para 21; UNGA Res 58/153 (2003) UN Doc A/RES/58/153, para 5; UNGA Res 62/124 (2007) UN Doc A/RES/62/124, para 9.

[110] UNGA Res 3274 (XXIX) (1974) para 1. UNHCR's founding mandate initially included stateless persons, provided that they fall within the refugee definition before they were included without connection to the refugee status. For other instances, see, inter alia, UNGA Res 31/36 (1976) UN Doc A/RES/31/36; UNGA Res 49/169 (1994) UN Doc A/RES/49/169, para 20; UNGA Res 50/152 (1995) UN Doc A/RES/50/152, para 14; UNGA Res 57/187 (2003) UN Doc A/RES/57/187, para 5; UNGA Res 58/151 (2004) UN Doc A/RES/58/151, para 4; UNGA Res 61/137 (2006) UN Doc 61/137, para 4; UNGA Res 62/124 (2007) UN Doc A/RES/62/124, para 5; UNGA Res 65/194 (2010) UN Doc A/RES/65/194, para 5; UNGA Res 68/141 (2013) UN Doc A/RES/68/141, para 8; UNGA Res 71/172 (2016) UN Doc A/RES/71/172, para 10; UNGA Res 72/150 (2017) UN Doc A/RES/72/150, para 10.

[111] UNGA Res 36/125 (1981) UN Doc A/RES/36/125, para 5(a). Among other subsequent confirmations of the expansion of UNHCR's mandate, see, inter alia, UNGA Res 40/118 (1985) UN Doc A/RES/40/118, para 5; UNGA Res 41/124 (1986) UN Doc A/RES/41/124, para 6; UNGA Res 46/106 (1991) UN Doc A/RES/46/106, para 17; UNGA Res 47/105 (1992) UN Doc A/RES/47/105, paras 17 and 21; UNGA Res 51/75 (1997) UN Doc A/RES/51/75; UNGA Res 52/103 (1997) UN Doc A/RES/52/103, para 17; UNGA Res 59/172 (2004) UN Doc A/RES/59/172, para 13; UNGA Res 62/125 (2007) UN Doc A/RES/62/125, paras 7, 12, and 19; UNGA Res 67/150 (2012) UN Doc A/RES/67/150, para 19; UNGA Res 71/173 (2016) UN Doc A/RES/71/173, paras 12 and 19; UNGA Res 72/152 (2017) UN Doc A/RES/72/152, paras 20 and 22.

[112] UNGA Res 40/118 (1985) UN Doc A/RES/40/118, para 13. Among other subsequent confirmations of this enlargement, see inter alia UNGA Res 41/124 (1986) UN Doc A/RES/41/124, para 16; UNGA Res 42/109 (1987) UN Doc A/RES/42/109, para 15; UNGA 45/140 (1990) UN Doc A/RES/45/140 para 19; UNGA Res 46/106 (1991) UN Doc A/RES/46/106, para 19; UNGA Res 47/105 (1992) UN Doc A/RES/47/105, para 19; UNGA Res 51/71 (1997) UN Doc A/RES/57/71 para 22; UNGA Res 58/149 (2004) UN Doc A/RES/58/149 para 5; UNGA Res 63/148 (2008) UN Doc A/RES/63/148, para 20; UNGA Res 71/173 (2016) UN Doc A/RES/71/173, paras 6 and 13; UNGA Res 72/152 (2017) UN Doc A/RES/72/152, paras 6 and 15.

[113] UNHCR 'Refugee protection and durable solutions in the context of international migration' Discussion Paper (19 November 2007) UNHCR/DPC/2007/Doc.02 para 11.

[114] See for instance UNHCR 'Refugee Protection and Mixed Migration: A 10-Point Plan of Action' (January 2007) available at<http://www.unhcr.org/protection/migration/4742a30b4/refugee-protection-mixed-migration-10-point-plan-action.html> accessed 3 October 2018.

[115] Its first Constitution explicitly included both migrants and refugees, see Constitution of the Intergovernmental Committee for European Migration (adopted 19 October 1953) 207 UNTS 189 art 1. Furthermore, its mandate has been interpreted from its inception as covering internally displaced persons as well. See, for instance, 'Report on the Migration Conference' (1952) MCB/12, 7; 'The Worldwide Dimensions of ICEM's Activities' (5 November 1979) MC/1278, 4. For further discussion, see R Perruchoud, 'From the Intergovernmental Committee for European Migration to the International Organization for Migration' (1989) 1 IJRL 501–17; M Ducasse-Rogier, *The International Organization for Migration, 1951–2001* (IOM 2001); J Elie, 'The Historical Roots of Cooperation Between the UN

To this day, according to Article 1 of the IOM Constitution, the primary purpose and function of the organization are to work for 'the organized transfers of migrants, [...] refugees, displaced persons and other individuals in need of international migration services'.[116] Given the operational and projectized nature of the work carried out by IOM, its Constitution does not define the different groups of persons falling under its mandate. This, in turn, gives considerable flexibility and discretion to the organization and its donors.

Although refugee specialists have, for the most part, overlooked IOM's role, it is an influential actor in the institutional governance of forced migration.[117] The competence of IOM towards refugees is even broader than that of UNHCR. Because its mandate is not limited by any legal definition of the term 'refugee', IOM has long privileged a *lato sensu* meaning of forced migrants, encompassing any person who has been displaced across an international border or within the territory of his or her state of habitual residence.[118] Its *ratione personae* competence includes most notably the significant number of persons falling outside the scope of the refugee definition, those fleeing natural or man-made disasters, and internally displaced persons.[119]

Following this stance, IOM promotes a factual and extensive definition of the term 'migrant', alongside its broad and evasive mandate:

IOM defines a migrant as any person who is moving or has moved across an international border or within a State away from his/her habitual place of residence, regardless of (1) the

High Commissioner for Refugees and the International Organization for Migration' (2010) 16 Global Governance 345–60.

[116] The preamble of the IOM Constitution further underlines in this sense that 'international migration also includes that of refugees, displaced persons and other individuals compelled to leave their homelands, and who are in need of international migration services'. Likewise, the preamble explicitly refers to any kind of migration, including temporary or long-term, return, and intra-regional migration.

[117] Among the very few authors analysing and acknowledging the role of IOM on forced migration, see M Bradley, 'The International Organization for Migration: Gaining Power in the Forced Migration Regime' (2017) 33 Refuge 97–106.

[118] In addition to the sources already mentioned above, see especially IOM 'Internally Displaced Persons: IOM Policy and Activities' (2002) MC/INF/258; IOM, 'IOM Strategy: Council Resolution No 1150 (XCIII) and Annex' (adopted by the Council at its 481st meeting 7 June 2007) (9 November 2007) MC/INF/287; IOM, 'Irregular Migration and Mixed Flows: IOM's Approach' (2009) MC/INF/297; IOM, 'Review of the IOM Strategy' (2010) MC/INF/302; IOM, 'IOM Migration Crisis Operational Framework' (2012) MC/2355; IOM, *IOM Framework for Addressing Internal Displacement* (IOM 2017).

[119] ibid. Regarding internally displaced persons, even before its entry into the UN system, IOM used to refer to the definition of the UN Guiding Principles on Internal Displacement, see IOM, 'Internally Displaced Persons' (n 118) 1. Interestingly, IOM also proposed a working definition of the term 'environmental migrants' in a discussion note adopted in 2007 that includes any 'persons or groups of persons who, for compelling reasons of sudden or progressive changes in the environment that adversely affect their lives or living conditions, are obliged to leave their habitual homes, or choose to do so, either temporarily or permanently, and who move either within their country or abroad', see, IOM 'Discussion Note: Migration and the Environment' (2007) MC/INF/288 1–2. It thus encompasses people who are displaced by natural disasters as well as those who move because of deteriorating conditions within or outside the territory of their state of residence. According to IOM, the intent of this broad working definition 'is also to offer an alternative definition to "environmental refugees", a term that UNHCR has stressed has no legal grounding in international refugee law', see ibid 2.

person's legal status; (2) whether the movement is voluntary or involuntary; (3) what the causes for the movement are; or (4) what the length of the stay is.[120]

According to this working definition, the mandate of IOM transcends the disputable dichotomy between refugees and migrants to cover any persons on the move without regard to their legal categorization, motivations, and causes of migration. In practice, however, IOM is far from exploiting the full potential of its broad and inclusive mandate on migrants because it primarily works as a service provider for its Member States on specific projects dealing with a wide range of particular issues (such as emergency assistance, human trafficking, assisted voluntary return, and border management).

The ratione materiae *mandates of UNHCR and IOM*

The second and much more significant overlap between the two international organizations relates to the material scope of their respective mandate. When UNHCR and the IOM's predecessor were established in 1951, the division of labour between the two was initially clear-cut and complementary: the former was created as a non-operational organization with a strong focus on legal protection, whereas the latter was intended to be exclusively operational in order to provide the logistics for the transportation of migrants and refugees. This distribution of tasks was not the product of a deliberate intent to build a coherent and complementary articulation between the two international organizations. As discussed in Chapter 1, it resulted more trivially from the political context of the Cold War and the influential role of the US and its allies in advancing their foreign policy priorities.

Since then, however, the initial division of labour between UNHCR and IOM has been blurred by the subsequent evolution of their respective mandates. The original nature of UNHCR has been radically transformed through the continuous enlargement of its mandate by the General Assembly to become the most prominent UN operational agency nowadays when it comes to delivering humanitarian assistance on the ground.[121] Hence, 'the provision of assistance to refugees and other persons of concern has come to dominate UNHCR's programme planning and fund-raising efforts, and it is now firmly established as a major element of its mandate. [...] But the result of these developments is that the humanitarian functions of UNHCR are sometimes seen as eclipsing the organization's protection functions.'[122]

---

[120] See IOM, 'Key Migration Terms' (IOM) available at<https://www.iom.int/key-migration-terms> accessed 3 October 2018. To the author's knowledge, this working definition has not been formally endorsed by the IOM Council. To include internally displaced persons within the definition of migrants is legally dubious because it goes against the ordinary meaning of the term 'migrant' and internally displaced persons are, in any event, already covered by the IOM Constitution as 'displaced persons'.

[121] For an overview of this evolution see especially M Zieck, *UNHCR's Worldwide Presence in the Field: A Legal Analysis of UNHCR's Cooperation Agreement* (Wolf Legal 2006) 38–55.

[122] TA Aleinikoff, 'The Mandate of the Office of the United Nations High Commissioner for Refugees' in V Chetail and C Bauloz (eds), *Research Handbook on International Law and Migration* (Edward Elgar 2014) 13.

Nonetheless, from a more practical perspective, distinguishing legal protection from humanitarian assistance sounds quite formal, because the former reinforces the latter and inversely. The two functions are indeed complementary and not mutually exclusive, provided that they are given the same importance. By contrast, prioritizing humanitarian assistance over legal protection remains highly questionable. This shift has been frequently viewed as 'a triumph of politics over law, implying a capitulation to expediency rather than adherence to legal protection'.[123] Goodwin-Gill has observed with many other commentators that '[p]rotection seems to be fading rapidly from the refugee agenda. UNHCR's embrace of "humanitarian action" and the willing endorsement of this move by many states, has compromised the agency's mandate responsibility: it is no longer identified primarily as a protection agency, but primarily as an assistance provider.'[124]

In parallel with the drastic transformation of UNHCR in becoming the leading humanitarian agency within the UN, IOM has primarily remained an operational organization. Although its founding mandate has been amended several times, the IOM Constitution astonishingly says nothing about the protection of migrants and their human rights.[125] This curious omission has raised longstanding criticisms among scholars and activists who lament that IOM 'lacks a legal protection mandate'.[126] The reality, however, is much subtler than this conventional wisdom. Indeed, the constituent instrument of an international organization is far from being the only source of binding norms.

As subjects of international law, international organizations are equally bound by customary international law as well as any other international agreements to which

---

[123] SA Cunliffe and M Pugh, 'UNHCR as Leader in Humanitarian Assistance: A Triumph of Politics over Law' in F Nicholson and P Twomey (eds), *Refugee Rights and Realities: Evolving International Concepts and Regimes* (CUP 1999) 176.

[124] GS Goodwin-Gill, 'Refugee Identity and Protection's Fading Prospect' in F Nicholson and P Twomey (eds), *Refugee Rights and Realities* (n 123) 246. Among many other similar accounts that the role of UNHCR as a humanitarian relief agency may undermine its core function of protection, see JC Hathaway, 'Who Should Watch over Refugee Law?' (2002) 45(1) Law Quad 54, 55; A Betts, 'Regime Complexity and International Organizations: UNHCR as a Challenged Institution' (2013) 13 Global Governance 69, 77; M Barutciski, 'A Critical View on UNHCR's Mandate Dilemmas' (2002) 14 IJRL 365–81; G Loescher, 'UNHCR and the Erosion of Refugee Protection' (2001) Forced Migration Review 28–30.

[125] The preamble of IOM Constitution only mentions in passing 'the specific situation and needs of the migrant as an individual human being' in relation to the need to promote cooperation for research and consultation on migration issues.

[126] F Crépeau and I Atak, 'Global Migration Governance. Avoiding Commitments on Human Rights, Yet Tracing a Course for Cooperation' (2016) 34(2) NQHR 113, 134. See also AL Hirsch and C Doig, 'Outsourcing Control: The International Organization for Migration in Indonesia' (2018) 22(5) IJHR 681–708; E Guild, S Grant, and K Groenendijk, 'IOM and the UN: Unfinished Business' (2017) Queen Mary School of Law Legal Studies Research Paper No 255/2017, 4; F Georgi, 'For the Benefit of Some: The International Organization for Migration and its Global Migration Management' in M Geiger and A Pécoud (eds), *The Politics of International Migration Management* (Palgrave Macmillan 2012) 47; Amnesty International, 'UK/EU/UNHCR: Unlawful and Unworkable—Amnesty International's Views on Proposals for Extraterritorial Processing of Asylum Claims' (2003) IOR 61/004/2003, 8; 'Statement by Amnesty International & Human Rights Watch, IOM Governing Council' (HRW, 2002) <http://pantheon.hrw.org/legacy/press/2002/12/ai-hrw-statement.htm> accessed 3 October 2018.

they are parties, thus including the one concluded with the UN in 2016.[127] In addition to these traditional sources of international law, international organizations are also bound by their own internal rules, interpretations, and established practice governing their mandate. From this angle, one can plausibly assert that, despite its chiefly operational activities, IOM's mandate has evolved to include the protection of migrants on three main legal bases: the doctrine of implied powers, the constitutional interpretation of its mandate as authoritatively determined by its governing body, as well as the subsequent conclusion of the agreement with the UN in 2016.

First, the protection of migrants is an implied power of IOM in carrying out the tasks assigned by its Constitution to deliver assistance and other related services. Under the law of international organizations, every intergovernmental organization possesses implied powers that are additional to those explicitly granted by its constituent instrument and essential to fulfilling the purposes and functions of the organization. This notion of implied powers has been acknowledged by a well-established jurisprudence of the ICJ, according to which: 'Under international law, the Organization must be deemed to have those powers which, though not expressly provided in the Charter, are conferred upon it by necessary implication as being essential to the performance of its duties.'[128] From this angle, there is no doubt that protecting migrants is inherent in and essential to the activities carried out by IOM in accordance with its Constitution. In fact, IOM has long claimed that 'protection and assistance are inextricably linked. IOM recognizes its responsibility to ensure that, when providing assistance to migrants, its activities must obtain full respect for the rights of the individual'.[129]

Second, the protection of migrants is not only an implied power; above all, it is an explicit duty of IOM deriving from the authoritative interpretation developed by its governing body. Here again, the law of international organizations provides a valuable insight. As codified by the ILC in the Draft Articles on the Responsibility of International Organizations, the binding rules of any international organization derive from a broad range of sources encompassing 'in particular, the constituent instruments, decisions, resolutions and other acts of the international organization

---

[127] 'International organizations are subjects of international law and, as such, are bound by any obligations incumbent upon them under general rules of international law, under their constitutions or under international agreements to which they are parties.' See *Interpretation of the Agreement of 25 March 1951 between the WHO and Egypt* (Advisory Opinion) [1980] ICJ Rep 73 [89]–[90].

[128] *Reparation for Injuries Suffered in the Service of the United Nations* (Advisory Opinion) [1949] ICJ Rep 174 [182]. See also *Legality of Use by a State of Nuclear Weapons in Armed Conflicts* (Advisory Opinion) [1996] ICJ Rep 66 [79]: 'the necessities of international life may point to the need for organizations, in order to achieve their objectives, to possess subsidiary powers which are not expressly provided for in the basic instruments which cover their activities. It is generally accepted that international organizations can exercise such powers, known as "implied" powers.' For previous endorsements of the notion of implied powers, see *Certain Expenses of the United Nations* (Advisory Opinion) 1962 ICJ Rep 151 [168]; *Effect of Awards of Compensation Made by the UN Administrative Tribunal* (Advisory Opinion) [1954] ICJ Rep 47 [57]; *Competence of the ILO to Regulate Incidentally the Personal Work of the Employer* (Advisory Opinion) [1926] PCIJ Rep Series B No 13, 18.

[129] IOM, 'IOM Policy on the Human Rights of Migrants' (2002) MC/INF/259, para 4. See also R Perruchoud, 'Persons Falling under the Mandate of the International Organization for Migration (IOM) and to whom the Organization May Provide Migration Services' (1992) 4 IJRL 205, 211–12.

adopted in accordance with those instruments, and established practice of the organization'.[130] Therefore, an international organization is not only bound by its constituent instrument, but also by its own resolutions and established practice that, in turn, constitute an integral part of its mandate. From this perspective, the subsequent interpretation of the mandate by the IOM Council is binding for the whole organization, as the governing body of IOM determines the policies and activities of the organization under Article 6 of the Constitution.[131]

Since at least the 1990s, the IOM Council has formally acknowledged as one of the self-declared objectives of the organization 'to work towards effective respect of the human dignity and well-being of migrants'.[132] The official 'IOM Strategy' adopted by the Council in 2007 (which is currently in force) is even more straightforward. It explicitly endorses 'the effective respect for the human rights of migrants in accordance with international law' as a priority of the organization in carrying out its activities.[133] Interestingly, effective respect for migrants' rights is ranked second among the twelve priorities of the IOM Strategy, the first one being 'to provide secure, reliable, flexible and cost-effective services for persons who require international migration assistance', as required by its Constitution. As stressed by the IOM Strategy, providing migration services in emergency or post-crisis situations also 'relates to the needs of individuals, thereby contributing to their protection'.[134]

The rationale of this last assertion has been refined in a 2010 background document entitled 'Review of the IOM Strategy': '[w]hile IOM does not have a mandate for the development and setting of norms, the Organization focuses on practical, problem-solving approaches to ensure full respect for the human rights

---

[130] ILC, *Yearbook of the International Law Commission* vol II (United Nations 2011) UN Doc A/CN.4/SER.A/2011, art 2(b) of the Draft Articles on the Responsibility of International Organizations. For previous acknowledgements, see also, Vienna Convention on the Law of Treaties between States and International Organizations and between International Organizations (adopted 21 March 1986) UN Doc A/CONF.129/15, art 2(1)(j); *Reparation for Injuries Suffered* (n 128) 180.

[131] As confirmed by the ICJ, the relevant organ of an international organization is primarily responsible for interpreting its own constitution, see *Certain Expenses of the United Nations (Article 17, paragraph 2, of the Chapter)* [1962] ICJ Rep 151, [168]. The authoritative interpretation of the mandate of an international organization carried out by its governing organ is frequently called in the legal doctrine a 'constitutional interpretation'. See for instance J Alvarez, 'Constitutional Interpretation in International Organizations' in J-M Coicaud and V Heiskanen (eds), *The Legitimacy of International Organizations* (United Nations University Press 2001) 104–54; CF Amerasinghe, *Principles of the Institutional Law of International Organizations* (2nd edn, CUP 2005) 25–33.

[132] IOM, 'Council Resolution No 923 (LXXI) of 29 November 1995' (1995) para 2; IOM, 'IOM Strategic Planning: Toward the Twenty-first Century' (1995) MC/1842 para 27.

[133] IOM, 'Council Resolution No 1150 (XCIII) of 7 June 2007' (2007) para 2 and its Annex.

[134] ibid. This ninth priority identified by the IOM Strategy is however accompanied by an ambiguous footnote: 'although IOM has no legal protection mandate, the fact remains that its activities contribute to protecting human rights, having the effect, or consequence, of protecting persons involved in migration'. This footnote is particularly confusing, for asserting the absence of a legal protection mandate is inconsistent with the second priority of ensuring effective respect for migrants' rights. This last assertion has been arguably refuted by the recent IOM policy, as notably defined in the *IOM Principles for Humanitarian Action* of 2015 that endorses a broader interpretation of its mandate to include protection in accordance with international law as discussed below. See IOM, 'IOM's Humanitarian Policy—Principles for Humanitarian Action' Council 106th Session (12 October 2015) C/106/CRP.20.

of migrants'.[135] IOM has justified this purposive interpretation of its mandate by relying on a broad and pragmatic understanding of the very notion of protection itself:

While certain intergovernmental organizations have a legal protection function based on mandate (such as UNHCR and ICRC), the concept and indeed application of protection is not restricted to legal mandate, but also extends to *de facto* protection, where an organization's activities in effect extend protection to persons benefiting from the services of the organization. In other words, the actual assistance rendered constitutes a form of protection, especially where it protects the life and physical well-being of persons at risk. While protection is not the prime objective of the organization concerned, or even necessarily a formally recognized objective, it is a consequence or effect of the implementation of the main or exclusive purpose of the organization. [...] Directly or indirectly, IOM works towards the respect of human dignity and the protection of the individual in the implementation of its activities, that is, through its action.[136]

Providing protection while carrying out assistance is, however, the very minimum one should expect from an international organization as a subject of international law. The enduring question is whether protection *tout court* is part of the IOM mandate. Although the organization often conflates assistance with protection, a noticeable evolution can be observed from the IOM Principles for Humanitarian Action adopted by its Council in 2015. This policy framework acknowledges protection as an integral component of the role and responsibilities of the organization. It affirms, in quite strong terms, that '[p]rotection is at the centre of IOM's humanitarian action'[137] and endorses the definition of protection provided by the Inter-Agency Standing Committee.[138]

Protection is accordingly defined as encompassing 'all activities aimed at ensuring full respect for the rights of the individual in accordance with the letter and the spirit of the relevant bodies of law'.[139] Hence, protection is not only understood by IOM as a core element of its action and, by extension, its mandate as interpreted by the IOM Council. It is also defined in reference to the full respect of individual rights under international law. Even more significantly, IOM has committed itself to being bound by the relevant bodies of international law governing the protection of migrants. Its Principles for Humanitarian Action formally acknowledge that 'IOM adheres to the applicable provisions of international humanitarian law [and] also adheres to human rights law and refugee law'.[140]

---

[135] IOM, 'Review of the IOM Strategy' 99th Session (12 October 2010) MC/IN/302, para 24.

[136] IOM, International Migration Law and Legal Affairs Department, 'Protection of Persons Involved in Migration: Note on IOM's Role' (2007) paras 5 and 6; IOM, 'The Human Rights of Migrants—IOM Policy and Activities' (2009) MC/INF/298, paras 8 and 9.

[137] IOM, 'IOM's Humanitarian Policy' (n 134) section IV.1.

[138] ibid. See also Inter-Agency Standing Committee (IASC), 'Protection of Internally Displaced Persons' Inter-Agency Standing Committee Policy Paper (December 1999) 4.

[139] ibid. The relevant bodies of law mentioned in the definition of the Inter-Agency Standing Committee include *inter alia* humanitarian law, human rights, and refugee law, while the IOM's Humanitarian Policy adds to this non-exhaustive list that 'for the protection of migrants, other bodies of law may be relevant as well, e.g. labour law, maritime law and consular law'.

[140] ibid section VI.6. See also ibid section II.8: 'In line with the Charter of the United Nations and in the spirit of the humanitarian imperative to save lives and alleviate human suffering, IOM is committed

This evolution was eventually sanctioned by the 2016 agreement concluded with the UN, whereby IOM is acknowledged 'as an essential contributor […] in the protection of migrants' (Article 2(1)). As a contracting party to this agreement, IOM is legally bound to protect migrants and to carry out its activities accordingly. Article 2(5) of the agreement further makes clear that: 'The International Organization for Migration undertakes to conduct its activities in accordance with the Purposes and Principles of the Charter of the United Nations and with due regard to the policies of the United Nations furthering those Purposes and Principles and to other relevant instruments in the international migration, refugee and human rights fields.'

This explicit reference to the UN Charter and other relevant instruments dissipates any doubt about IOM's duty to protect migrants and their human rights without any discrimination. It is indeed well-known that one chief purpose of the UN, listed in Article 1(3) of its Charter, is to 'promot[e] and encourage[e] respect for human rights and for fundamental freedoms for all'. Besides this general duty, IOM more specifically commits with the 2016 agreement to carry out its activities in accordance with the UN 'instruments in the international migration, refugee and human rights fields', including, thus, all general human rights treaties (such as the two UN Covenants and the CRC), as well as more specialized conventions, like the Refugee Convention and the ICRMW.[141]

Although IOM is legally committed to protecting migrants when carrying out its mandate, protection remains a marginal part of its activities which mainly unfolds at the edge of its operational work. Despite the clear-cut legal framework binding IOM, the prevailing gap between its language of human rights and the actual practice on the ground has been frequently deplored by NGOs.[142] A number of scholars

---

to providing humanitarian assistance and protection in accordance with international law and norms, where it is needed and where IOM has an added value.' For previous commitments of IOM to be bound by international law, see also IOM, 'Migration Crisis Operational Framework' (2012) MC/2355, para 12: 'IOM is further bound and committed to the existing legal and institutional frameworks contributing to the effective delivery of assistance and protection and ultimately to the respect and promotion of human rights and humanitarian principles.'

[141] Additionally, the vast majority of IOM Member States are equally bound by these UN treaties. In 2018, all of them (with the well-known exception of the US) have ratified the CRC, while respectively 155 and 152 IOM States Parties have ratified the ICCPR and ICESCR among 172 and 169 States Parties. Likewise, 142 IOM Member States have ratified the Refugee Convention and its Protocol among a total number of 147 States Parties, while most States Parties to the ICRMW are members of IOM with the only exceptions of Indonesia and Syria.

[142] See notably Human Rights Watch, 'Rot Here or Die There: Bleak Choices for Iraqi Refugees in Lebanon' (2007) Human Rights Watch Vol 19 No 8(E) available at <https://www.hrw.org/reports/2007/lebanon1207/lebanon1207web.pdf > accessed 3 October 2018, 43–46 and 64; Human Rights Watch, 'The International Organization for Migration (IOM) and Human Rights Protection in the Field: Current Concerns' (Submitted to the IOM Governing Council Meeting 86th Session 18–21 November 2003 in Geneva) (HRW 2003) available at<http://pantheon.hrw.org/legacy/backgrounder/migrants/iom-submission-1103.htm> accessed 3 October 2018; Statement by Amnesty International & Human Rights Watch to the Governing Council, International Organization for Migration in Geneva (2–4 December 2002) IOR 42/0006/2002; Human Rights Watch, 'By Invitation Only: Australia's Asylum Policy' (2002) Human Rights Watch Vol 14 No 10 (C) available at <https://www.hrw.org/legacy/reports/2002/australia/australia1202.pdf> accessed 3 October 2018; Amnesty International, *Australia-Pacific Offending Human Dignity—The 'Pacific Solution'* (25 August 2002) AI Index ASA 12/009/2002.

have been even more vociferous than activists to contend that '[i]t is called an organisation *for* migration, but does much *against* migration, for example, by returning unwanted migrants to their country or preventing unauthorised migration'.[143] Most criticisms focus on the Assisted Voluntary Return and Reintegration Programs (AVRR) that constitute a core activity of IOM in accordance with its Constitution (Article 1(1)(d)).[144] In practice, the number of migrants and rejected asylum seekers assisted per year has dramatically grown from around 25,000 in 2005 to almost 100,000 in 2016.[145] Meanwhile, the truly voluntary nature of these returns and the safety in the countries of origin have regularly been questioned by NGOs and commentators.[146] This raises the disturbing question of how return can be voluntary when safety is not always guaranteed, and the only alternative is forced removal.[147]

While IOM has attracted the most vivid criticisms, UNHCR is neither immune therefrom. The voluntariness and safety of voluntary repatriation programmes carried out by UNHCR in accordance with its founding mandate have frequently been questioned since the 1990s when the General Assembly established voluntary repatriation as '*the* ideal solution to refugee problems'.[148] For many observers of

---

[143] A Pécoud, 'What Do we Know about the International Organization for Migration?' (2017) 44(2) Journal of Ethnic and Migration Studies 1621, 1622. Among other critical accounts, see especially Hirsch and Doig, 'Outsourcing Control' (n 126) 1–28; Georgi, 'For the Benefit of Some' (n 126) 45–72; I Ashutosh and A Mountz, 'Migration Management for the Benefit of Whom? Interrogating the Work of the International Organization for Migration' (2011) 15(1) Citizenship Studies 21–38; R Andrijasevic and W Walters, 'The International Organization for Migration and the International Government of Borders' (2010) 28 Society and Space 977–99.

[144] The scope of AVRR is broadly understood as applying to any migrants, 'whatever the reason [for their return] may be, including a rejected or withdrawn application for asylum, falling victim to human trafficking, exploitation or extortion, being in an irregular situation, or lacking the means to return'. AVRR is heralded by IOM as 'an indispensable part of a comprehensive approach to migration management. It contributes to achieving safe, orderly and dignified migration, since it safeguards the human rights of migrants, upholds international principles and standards, and contributes to preserving the integrity of regular migration structures and asylum systems.' Accordingly, 'from a State perspective, AVRR is a consensual and cost-effective option that helps strengthen the integrity of asylum systems, while avoiding a systematic and generally costly use of law enforcement'. See IOM, 'Supporting Safe, Orderly and Dignified Migration through Assisted Voluntary Return and Reintegration' (2017) Global Compact Thematic Paper, Assisted Voluntary Return and Reintegration, 1 and 3–4.

[145] The exact IOM figures are 24,696 in 2005 and 98,403 in 2016, but this last figure does not include voluntary returns undertaken by IOM from Libya, see IOM, *Assisted Voluntary Return and Reintegration: 2016 Key Highlights* (IOM 2017) 10. In 2016, 83 per cent of the AVRR 'beneficiaries' returned from Europe, while Germany remained the host country from which most migrants returned to their own countries with a total of 54,000 returns, see ibid 14–16.

[146] In addition to the doctrinal sources and NGO reports already quoted above, see I Lietaert, E Broekaert, and I Derluyn, 'From Social Instrument to Migration Management Tool: Assisted Voluntary Return Programmes—The Case of Belgium' (7 December 2017) 51(7) Social Policy & Administration 961–80; J Brachet, 'Policing the Desert: The IOM in Libya beyond War and Peace' (2016) 48(2) Antipode 272–92; F Webber, 'How Voluntary are Voluntary Returns?' (2011) 52(4) Race & Class 98–107. See contra K Newland, 'Migrant Return and Reintegration Policy: A Key Component of Migration Governance' in M McAuliffe and M Klein Solomon (Conveners), *Migration Research Leaders' Syndicate in Support of the Global Compact on Migration: Ideas to Inform International Cooperation on Safe, Orderly and Regular Migration* (IOM 2017).

[147] In 2016, the main countries of origin for AVRR were tellingly: Albania, Iraq, Afghanistan, Serbia, Kosovo, and Ethiopia, see IOM, *Assisted Voluntary Return and Reintegration* (n 145) 19.

[148] UNGA Res 49/169 (1994) UN Doc A/RES./49/169, para 9 (emphasis added). See among other similar restatements UNGA Res 50/152 (1995) UN Doc A/RES/50/152, para 17; UNGA Res 51/75 (1996) UN Doc A/RES/51/75, para 16; UNGA Res 52/103 (1997) UN Doc A/Res./52/103, para 12.

UNHCR's role in voluntary repatriation, 'return, however, seems to have become a political end, to be achieved by whatever means are available and regardless of principle'.[149] The growing convergence of IOM's and UNHCR's activities in this political agenda has not gone unnoticed. As Anne Koch points out, the two organizations collaborate closely on voluntary returns in a self-referential logic to complement and reinforce their respective mandates.[150] She concludes that, 'taken together, the two international agencies enhance states' control over their immigrant population and thereby contribute to a stabilisation of state sovereignty in the governance of migration'.[151]

Following this critical perspective, voluntary returns carried out by international organizations on behalf of Western states are part and parcel of a broader migration control agenda. The involvement of IOM and UNHCR in returning migrants and refugees works in tandem with a diffuse, albeit influential, strategy of containment, both in countries of origin (through the provision of humanitarian assistance to internally displaced persons) and in neighbouring states of asylum and/or transit in the Global South (with the development and management of refugee camps and detention centres). As frequently pinpointed by critics, it is not by chance that IOM and UNHCR's activities have drastically expanded in these two fields.[152]

The schizophrenic stance of UNHCR and IOM towards states

The structural cause of the evolution described above must be found in their financial dependence on Western states. IOM works as a service provider to its Member States because its budget relies on project-based funding, which, in turn, determines

---

[149] Goodwin-Gill, 'Refugee Identity and Protection's Fading Prospect' (n 124) 243. For a critical account on the practice and standards developed by UNHCR on voluntary repatriation, see also J Crisp and K Long, 'Safe and Voluntary Refugee Repatriation: From Principle to Practice' (2016) 4(3) JMHS 141–47; BS Chimni, 'From Resettlement to Involuntary Repatriation: Towards a Critical History of Durable Solutions to Refugee Problems' (2004) 23 (3) RSQ 55–73; V Chetail, 'Voluntary Repatriation in Public International Law: Concepts and Contents' (2004) 23(3) RSQ 1–32; M Barnett, 'UNHCR and the Ethics of Repatriation' (2001) 10 Forced Migration Review 31–34; M Barutciski, 'Involuntary Repatriation When Refugee Protection Is No Longer Necessary: Moving Forward after the 48th Session of the Executive Committee' (1998) 10 IJRL 236–55; S Takahashi, 'The UNHCR Handbook on Voluntary Repatriation: The Emphasis of Return over Protection' (1997) 9(4) IJRL 593–612; S Bagshaw, 'Benchmarks or Deutschmarks? Determining the Criteria for the Repatriation of Refugees to Bosnia and Herzegovina' (1997) 9 IJRL 566–92; BS Chimni, 'The Meaning of Words and the Role of UNHCR in Voluntary Repatriation' (1993) 5(3) IJRL 442–60; BN Stein and FC Cuny, 'Refugee Repatriation during Conflict: Protection and Post-Return Assistance' (1994) 4(3) Development in Practice 173–87.

[150] A Koch, 'The Politics and Discourse of Migrant Return: The Role of UNHCR and IOM in the Governance of Return' (2014) 40(6) Journal of Ethnic and Migration Studies 905–23.

[151] ibid 919.

[152] In addition to the critical literature already quoted before, see M Geiger and A Pécoud, 'International Organisations and the Politics of Migration' (2014) 40(6) Journal of Ethnic and Migration Studies 865–87; S Scheel and P Ratfisch, 'Refugee Protection Meets Migration management: UNHCR as a Global Police of Populations' (2014) 40(6) Journal of Ethnic and Migration Studies 924–41; BS Chimni, 'The Geopolitics of Refugee Studies: A View from the South' (1998) 11(4) JRS 350–74; M Barutciski, 'The Reinforcement of Non-Admission Policies and the Subversion of UNHCR: Displacement and Internal Assistance in Bosnia-Herzegovina' (1996) 8 IJRL 49–110.

the range of its activities. As a result, its operative budget is inevitably financed by wealthier countries that decide upon the scope and nature of IOM activities according to their own priorities and interests. Although critics of IOM are much more vocal and visible in this area as well, its funding model does not fundamentally diverge from that of UNHCR. Since the establishment of the latter, only a negligible portion of its budget (around 3 per cent) has been financed through the UN budget.[153] All operational activities are instead financed by voluntary contributions.

To give a graphic illustration, in 2016, the voluntary contributions of IOM and UNHCR accounted respectively for 90.5 per cent and 88.5 per cent of their total budget.[154] Among these voluntary contributions, Western states contributed 88.2 per cent for IOM and 85.7 per cent for UNHCR.[155] The most important donors of the two organizations are the US, the EU, and Germany, followed by the UK, Japan, Canada, Sweden, Norway, and Australia.[156] This financial dependence is still far from being specific to UNHCR and IOM. Voluntary contributions are indeed commonplace among many other international organizations working in the broader fields of development, humanitarian assistance, and capacity-building, including, for instance, UNICEF, UNDP, and the World Food Programme (WFP).[157]

Notwithstanding the foregoing, it would be excessive to conclude that UNHCR and IOM are merely the Trojan horses of the Western agenda to implement and spread immigration control. This longstanding criticism does not capture the broader picture and calls for four caveats that are respectively practical, institutional, political, and legal by nature. In practice, one cannot deny that IOM and UNHCR are literally saving lives and protecting human dignity when they carry out humanitarian assistance on the ground. Furthermore, their budget and activities are not decided by Western states alone, but by their own governing bodies (UNHCR ExCom and IOM Council) that are composed of a broad and representative number of states from all regions of the world, including the Global South.

In addition, UNHCR and IOM are not the servile servants of states. Like all international organizations, they follow their own institutional interests and agenda

---

[153] See para 20 of the founding Statute of the Office of the UN High Commissioner for Refugees. For further discussion see notably G Loescher, 'Refugees and Internally Displaced Persons' in JK Cogan, I Hurd, and I Johnstone (eds), *The Oxford Handbook of International Organizations* (OUP 2016) 331, 332, 338, and 339.

[154] This estimate is based on the official figures published in the following documents: IOM Council, 'Financial Report for the Year Ended 31 December 2016' (18 May 2017) C/108/3; UNHCR, *Global Report 2016* (UNHCR 2017); UNHCR, 'Contributions to UNHCR for the Budget Year 2016' (UNHCR, 2017) available at <www.unhcr.org/partners/donors/575e74567/contributions-unhcr-budget-year-2016-30-september-2016.html> accessed 3 October 2018.

[155] ibid.

[156] The US is by far the largest donor of both organizations with a total of USD 2,047,527,218 (USD 533,690,742 to IOM and USD 1,513,836,476 to UNHCR in the 2016 fiscal year). The EU Commission takes the second place, with a total contribution of USD 555,258,700, and Germany the third place with USD 434,707,268. See UNHCR, 'Contributions to UNHCR for the Budget Year 2016' (n 154) 1 and IOM, 'Financial Report for the Year Ended 31 December 2016' (n 154) 72–73.

[157] T Ingadottir, 'Financing International Institutions' in J Klabbers and A Wallendahl (eds), *Research Handbook on the Law of International Organizations* (Edward Elgar 2011) 123.

to gain autonomy and influence.[158] The expansion of the organization may be a prominent objective when accepting to carry out a specific activity.[159] Although their action cannot be reduced to the will of their donors, the rules of the game are still largely determined by states in defining their mandates and financing their activities. Hence, while they are major actors of global migration governance, the two organizations must constantly find a precarious compromise between their two primary functions as the subcontractor and counterweight of the states.[160] More generally, the instrumentalization of international organizations is clearly not specific to migration and refugee protection.[161] UNHCR and IOM typically exemplify the enduring dialectics between humanitarianism and *realpolitik*.[162] In both pith and substance, the two organizations have to navigate the delicate path between the Scylla of their own irrelevance and the Charybdis of states' influence.

From a legal perspective, this ambivalence reflects the fundamental tension inherent in any international organization: they are both a creature of the states and an autonomous entity endowed with a distinct legal personality and the correlative powers, either explicit or implied.[163] This unveils the schizophrenic nature of all international organizations. They are at the same time independent from and dependent on Member States. This well-known duality frames and constrains the influence of international organizations within the international legal order: states have created them to do what they cannot achieve unilaterally, but they establish them in such a way that the creatures will not surpass their creators. This symptom is sometimes referred to in the legal doctrine as the 'Frankenstein problem'. Andrew Guzman explains that:

As if they learned the lessons of Frankenstein too well, states have been reluctant to give IOs the authority necessary to make progress on important global issues. Though there is a

---

[158] A Betts, 'Introduction: Global Migration Governance' in A Betts (ed), *Global Migration Governance* (OUP 2012) 20; Hirsch and Doig, 'Outsourcing Control' (n 126) 5; MN Barnett and M Finnemore, 'The Politics, Power, and Pathologies of International Organizations' (1999) 53 International Organization 699–732.

[159] I Venzke, *How Interpretation Makes International Law: On Semantic Change and Normative Twists* (OUP 2012) 132; G Loescher, A Betts, and J Milner, *The United Nations High Commissioner for Refugees: The Politics and Practice of Refugee Protection into the Twenty-first Century* (Routledge 2008) 129. Like many other bureaucracies, the lack of a critical perspective about their daily work and the purpose of their activities within a broader environment than their own institutional silo may be another factor to be taken into account in their decision-making process.

[160] For further discussion about the influence of the EU on UNHCR and IOM, see also in this sense S Lavenex, 'Multilevelling EU External Governance: The Role of International Organizations in the Diffusion of EU Migration Policies' (2016) 42(4) Journal of Ethnic and Migration Studies 554–70.

[161] Brachet, 'Policing the Desert' (n 146) 273. Among many obvious instances, see R Peet, *Unholy Trinity: The IMF, World Bank and WTO* (2nd edn, Zed Books 2009).

[162] For further discussion about the ambiguity of the humanitarian label of IOM and UNHCR, see respectively Bradley, 'The International Organization for Migration' (n 117) 97–106; M Barnett, 'Humanitarianism with a Sovereign Face: UNHCR in the Global Undertow' (2001) 35 International Migration Review 244–77.

[163] As Jan Klabbers underlines, 'many of the ambiguities that the law of international organizations appears to be so particularly rich in become understandable when examined against the background of the relationship between the organization and its members' see J Klabbers, *An Introduction to International Institutional Law* (2nd edn, CUP 2009) 36.

trade-off between the preservation of state control over the international system and the creation of effective and productive IOs, states have placed far too much weight on the former and not nearly enough on the latter.[164]

Even though this issue has been raised in a more general context, it is particularly relevant to capture the challenging environment of international organizations working in the field of migration and refugee protection, where states are especially cautious to maintain their control.

Indeed, the fact that UNHCR and IOM are primarily operational organizations with different albeit overlapping mandates is not a coincidence. Their lack of financial autonomy further heightens their dependence on states as well as the consequential result that they must compete for funding from the same donors. Clearly, 'what appears as "competition" from the point of view of an IO may indeed be a strategy from governments' standpoint'.[165] One should concede that UNHCR and IOM also have their share of responsibility. They are involved in this competition to pursue their own institutional strategy. In a sort of mimicry of their creators, international organizations tend to be as territorial as states when it comes to their respective mandate. Competition among agencies is a way to reaffirm what they believe to be their identity based on their own vision of their mandates. As the two most influential organizations in this field, UNHCR and IOM unsurprisingly aspire and compete with one another to increase their influence and legitimacy. This inclination is exacerbated by their pretension to be the leading organization. UNHCR proclaims to be '*the* global refugee organization',[166] while IOM presents itself as 'the global lead agency on migration'.[167] Their quest for hegemony is vain as long as competition takes over complementarity. The very idea of being the leading organization is frustrated by the fact that the mandates and activities of UNHCR and IOM largely overlap in both law and in practice. In turn, states regain their influence to arbitrate between the two in this counterproductive albeit calculated competition.

7.3.3 The dividing line between UNHCR and IOM: normative and supervisory functions

Despite the growing convergence of the activities carried out by UNHCR and IOM, their respective mandates exhibit a noteworthy difference with regard to the elaboration and supervision of international legal norms. Since its establishment, UNHCR has been mandated with '[p]romoting the conclusion and ratification

---

[164] A Guzman, 'International Organizations and the Frankenstein Problem' (2013) 24 EJIL 999. See also, ND White, *The Law of International Organizations* (3rd edn, Manchester University Press 2017) 107–19.

[165] Geiger and Pécoud, 'International Organisations and the Politics of Migration' (n 152) 873.

[166] UNHCR, *Note on the Mandate of the High Commissioner for Refugees and His Office* (UNHCR 2013) available at<http://www.unhcr.org/protection/basic/526a22cb6/mandate-high-commissioner-refugees-office.html> accessed 3 October 2018, 5 (original emphasis).

[167] IOM, 'Resolution No 1309: IOM-UN Relations' (adopted 24 November 2015) Council 106th Session (4 December 2015) C/106/RES/1309, para 2(a).

of international conventions for the protection of refugees, [and] supervising their application and proposing amendments thereto'.[168] These two complementary functions are not unique: several other international organizations are mandated to promote the conclusion of treaties and to supervise their application. This concerns, for instance, ILO with regard to workers in general and migrant workers in particular. The normative and supervisory functions of UNHCR still constitute a dividing line to IOM. As demonstrated below, this distinctive feature is well grounded in law, but the evolution of their respective mandate has eroded its practical significance.

UNHCR: a normative and supervisory organization?

The normative and supervisory functions initially assigned to UNHCR by its founding statute provide a rather contrasting picture when they are assessed in light of their subsequent evolution and the current practice of the organization. These two tasks have considerably evolved over the years in reaction to a challenging environment characterized by the reluctance of states to accept more commitments in the field of refugee protection. This is especially true for its function of promoting the adoption and ratification of conventions on refugees.

UNHCR has steadily moved from initiating new treaties to adopting soft law guidance on existing treaties. During the first decades of its existence, UNHCR was very active in initiating the adoption of new conventions, including the 1952 Protocol I of the Universal Copyright Convention,[169] the 1957 Agreement relating to Refugee Seamen,[170] and the 1967 Protocol relating to the Status of Refugees. This last treaty is by far the most vital and the greatest achievement of UNHCR in the field of international refugee law. By removing the temporal and geographical restrictions to the refugee definition adopted in 1951, the New York Protocol has transformed the Geneva Convention into a truly universal instrument applicable to all refugees across the world. The drafting process of the Protocol remarkably differed from the usual procedure governing the negotiation and adoption of an international convention. States indeed played a rather passive role in a process which was primarily driven by UNHCR. Instead of negotiating the Protocol through

---

[168]   Section II(8)(a) of the UNHCR Statute. See also Section II(8)(a)(b) and (f): 'Promoting through special agreements with Governments the execution of any measures calculated to improve the situation of refugees and to reduce the number requiring protection' and 'obtaining from Governments information concerning the number and conditions of refugees in their territories and the laws and regulations concerning them'.

[169]   Protocol 1 annexed to the Universal Copyright Convention concerning the application of that Convention to the works of stateless persons and refugees (adopted 6 September 1952, entered into force 16 September 1955) 216 UNTS 132. According to this Protocol, stateless persons and refugees who have their habitual residence in a State Party shall be assimilated to the nationals of that state for the implementation of Universal Copyright Convention.

[170]   Agreement relating to Refugee Seamen (adopted 23 November 1957, entered into force 27 December 1961) 506 UNTS 125. This agreement details in a more robust and binding form the vague guidance contained in art 11 of the 1951 Refugee Convention to 'give sympathetic consideration' to the establishment on its territory of refugees seamen of a ship flying the flag of a Contracting State.

an intergovernmental conference, the draft was prepared by UNHCR and then amended on the basis of comments from States Parties to the Geneva Convention (including ExCom members), before the text of the Protocol was finally submitted to the General Assembly that merely took note of it and requested the Secretary-General to transmit it to states for ratification.[171]

Since this *tour de force*, however, UNHCR has remained quite passive. After the failure of the UN Conference on Territorial Asylum in 1977, it has not initiated the conclusion of any new conventions on refugees at the universal plane. It has been, of course, involved as an observer by sharing its views and comments during the drafting process of several general treaties (such as the Convention on the Rights of the Child as well as the Smuggling and Trafficking Protocols).[172] Nonetheless, UNHCR has abstained from initiating the adoption of any new specific conventions on refugees, despite the profound changes in the patterns of forced migration (as notably exemplified by climate change and natural disasters among other instances). Instead, UNHCR's contribution to international refugee law has focused on the ratification of existing conventions and the elaboration of soft law standards to improve the implementation of treaties.[173]

The reasons for this shift are more political and cultural than truly legal. The risk of reopening the negotiation of the Refugee Convention in a politically toxic environment is frequently raised in UNHCR's circles.[174] This fear is legitimate, but not necessarily relevant from a legal perspective, as it can be obviated by initiating a new and distinct treaty to address some of the numerous issues which fall outside the scope of the Refugee Convention. Besides the obvious political considerations, UNHCR's reluctance may also be attributed to its institutional culture, which has been shaped by the 1951 Convention for more than six decades. This has undermined its ability to conceive refugee protection beyond this foundational, albeit dated, instrument. As a result of political considerations and its own cultural ethos, UNHCR's motto is 'to better stick to what you have got, i.e., the 1951 Refugee Convention'.[175]

Following this strategy, UNHCR has been particularly active in consolidating the acquis of the Refugee Convention by providing interpretative guidance on its provisions and encouraging a more consistent application by States Parties. UNHCR has

---

[171] For further description of the drafting process, see C Lewis, *UNHCR and International Refugee Law: From Treaties to Innovation* (Routledge 2012) 28–29; P Weis, 'The 1967 Protocol Relating to the Status of Refugees and Some Questions of the Law of Treaties' (1967) 42 British Ybk Int'l L 39–70.

[172] Lewis, *UNHCR and International Refugee Law* (n 171) 30–37. See also V Türk, 'The Role of UNHCR in the Development of International Refugee Law' in F Nicholson and P Twomey (eds), *Refugee Rights and Realities: Evolving International Concepts and Regimes* (CUP 1999) 153-219. UNHCR has also provided comments in the drafting of regional instruments, including the 1969 Convention Governing the Specific Aspects of Refugee Problems in Africa and the numerous EU directives and regulations governing asylum.

[173] Although the adoption of soft law standards was not envisioned in its founding statute, it is clearly an implied power of the organization inherent in its mandate.

[174] See, for instance, JAC Gonzaga, 'The Role of the United Nations High Commissioner for Refugees and the Refugee Definition' in S Kneebone (ed), *The Refugees Convention 50 Years On: Globalization and International Law* (Ashgate 2003) 250.

[175] Venzke, *How Interpretation Makes International Law* (n 159) 114.

even become the most prolific producer of soft law among all the UN agencies and other related organizations involved in the field of migration and refugee protection. While disseminating the position, if not the doctrine, of UNHCR on a wide range of issues, producing its own soft law standards also presents for the organization the distinctive advantage of keeping control over their content.

Besides their great number and variety, UNHCR guidelines can be classified in four main categories. The first group, which represents the vast majority of soft law standards produced by the organization, focuses on the interpretation of the refugee definition under Article 1 of the 1951 Convention. UNHCR published the Handbook on Procedures and Criteria for Determining Refugee Status in 1979, which was re-edited in 1992, reissued in 2011, and has been refined and updated since 2002 by twelve Guidelines on International Protection, developing many facets of the refugee definition in considerable detail.[176] They are supplemented by more practical guidelines addressing specific nationalities of asylum-seekers.[177] The second set of non-binding standards is devoted to cross-cutting issues that are insufficiently addressed by the Refugee Convention, such as the protection of refugee

---

[176] UNHCR, *Handbook on Procedures and Criteria for Determining Refugee Status under the 1951 Convention and the 1967 Protocol Relating to the Status of Refugees* (UNHCR 1979), reedited in 1992 and reissued in 2011; UNHCR, 'Guidelines on International Protection No 1: Gender-related Persecution within the Context of Article 1A(2) of the 1951 Convention and/or its 1967 Protocol Relating to the Status of Refugees' (7 May 2002) HCR/GIP/02/01; UNHCR, 'Guidelines on International Protection No 2: Membership of a Particular Social Group' (7 May 2002) HCR/GIP/02/02; UNHCR, 'Guidelines on International Protection No 3: Cessation of Refugee Status under Article 1C(5) and (6)' (10 February 2003) HCR/GIP/03/03; UNHCR, 'Guidelines on International Protection No 4: Internal Flight or Relocation Alternative' (23 July 2003) HCR/GIP/03/04; UNHCR, 'Guidelines on International Protection No 5: Application of the Exclusion Clauses: Article 1F' (4 September 2003) HCR/GIP/03/05; UNHCR, 'Guidelines on International Protection No 6: Religion-Based Refugee Claims' (28 April 2004) HCR/GIP/04/06; UNHCR, 'Guidelines on International Protection No 7: Victims of Trafficking and Persons at Risk of Being Trafficked' (7 April 2006) HCR/GIP/06/07; UNHCR, 'Guidelines on International Protection No 8: Child Asylum Claims' (22 December 2009) HCR/GIP/09/08; UNHCR, 'Guidelines on International Protection No 9: Sexual Orientation and/or Gender Identity' (23 October 2012) HCR/GIP/12/09; UNHCR, 'Guidelines on International Protection No 10: Military Service' (3 December 2013) HCR/GIP/13/10; UNHCR, 'Guidelines on International Protection No 11: Prima Facie Recognition of Refugee Status' (24 June 2015) HCR/GIP/15/11; UNHCR, 'Guidelines on International Protection No 12: Claims for Refugee Status Related to Situations of Armed Conflict and Violence' (2 December 2016) HCR/GIP/16/12.

[177] See among the most recent ones, UNHCR, 'Eligibility Guidelines for Assessing the International Protection Needs of Asylum-Seekers from: Guatemala' (2018) HCR/EG/GTM/18/01; UNHCR, 'Eligibility Guidelines for Assessing the International Protection Needs of Asylum-Seekers from: Honduras' (2016) HCR/EG/HND/16/03; UNHCR, 'Eligibility Guidelines for Assessing the International Protection Needs of Asylum-Seekers from: Afghanistan' (2018) HCR/EG/AFG/18/02; UNHCR, 'Eligibility Guidelines for Assessing the International Protection Needs of Asylum-Seekers from: El Salvador' (2016) HCR/EG/SLV/16/01; UNHCR, 'Eligibility Guidelines for Assessing the International Protection Needs of Asylum-Seekers from: Colombia' (2015) HCR/EG/COL/15/1; UNHCR, 'Eligibility Guidelines for Assessing the International Protection Needs of Asylum-Seekers from: Sri Lanka' (2012) HCR/EG/LKA/12/04; UNHCR, 'Interim Eligibility Guidelines for Assessing the International Protection Needs of Asylum-Seekers from: Côte d'Ivoire' (2012) HCR/EG/CIV/12/01; UNHCR, 'Eligibility Guidelines for Assessing the International Protection Needs of Asylum-Seekers from: Iraq' (2012) HCR/EG/IRQ/12/03; UNHCR, 'Eligibility Guidelines for Assessing the International Protection Needs of Asylum-Seekers from: Pakistan' (2017) HCR/EG/PAK/17/01; UNHCR, 'Eligibility Guidelines for Assessing the International Protection Needs of Asylum-Seekers from: Eritrea' (2011) HCR/EG/ERT/11/01_Rev.1.

women and children or the detention of asylum-seekers.[178] While they are somewhat marginal in terms of number, the two other categories refer respectively to statelessness[179] and operational guidelines.[180]

The proliferation of these non-binding guidelines has considerably expanded the body of applicable standards. From the perspective of public international law, their legal nature is certainly distinct from ExCom's conclusions on international protection, since, contrary to the latter, the former are not endorsed by states and emanate instead from UNHCR itself. They still exert significant influence, by providing an authoritative interpretative guidance that, in turn, shapes the practice of states in implementing their duties under the Geneva Convention. Like ExCom's conclusions, their authoritative, albeit non-binding, nature is reinforced by the obligation of States Parties to cooperate with UNHCR in the exercise of its functions under Article 35(1) of the Refugee Convention.

This duty of cooperation remains, however, an obligation of means, not of result, which is unable to transform soft law into hard law on its own. As underlined by Walter Kälin, it requires at least that UNHCR guidelines and other related standards 'must not be dismissed as irrelevant but regarded as authoritative statements whose disregard requires justification'.[181] This is indeed the very minimum that is expected from States Parties to the Geneva Convention in fulfilling their legal commitments in good faith. Article 35 arguably requires more than this. Domestic courts have frequently inferred from the duty of cooperation enshrined in this provision that UNHCR guidelines and interpretative standards enjoy 'considerable persuasive authority'[182] and they 'should be accorded considerable weight'[183] by national authorities.

---

[178] See for instance UNHCR, 'Regional Guidelines for Responding to the Rights and Needs of Unaccompanied and Separated Children' (2013); UNHCR, 'Guidelines on the Applicable Criteria and Standards relating to the Detention of Asylum-Seekers and Alternatives to Detention' (2012); UNHCR, 'Guidelines on Determining the Best Interests of the Child' (2008); UNHCR, 'Refugee Children: Guidelines on Protection and Care' (1994); UNHCR, 'Guidelines on the Protection of Refugee Women' (1991).

[179] UNHCR, 'Guidelines on Statelessness No 3: The Status of Stateless Persons at the National Level' (2012) HCR/GS/12/03; UNHCR, 'Guidelines on Statelessness No 4: Child's Right to Acquire a Nationality' (2012) HCR/GS/12/04; UNHCR, 'Guidelines on Statelessness No 2: Procedures for Determining whether an Individual is a Stateless Person' (2012) HCR/GS/12/02; UNHCR, 'Guidelines on Statelessness No 1: The Definition of 'Stateless Person' in Article 1(1) of the 1954 Convention Relating to the Status of Stateless Persons' (2012) HCR/GS/12/01.

[180] See especially UNHCR, 'Operational Guidelines for Cash-Based Interventions in Displacement Settings' (2015) UNHCR/OG/2015/3; UNHCR, *Livelihood Programming in UNHCR: Operational Guidelines* (UNHCR 2012); UNHCR, 'Policy and Procedural Guidelines: Addressing Resettlement Fraud Perpetrated by Refugees' (March 2008); UNHCR, *Operational Guidelines on Maintaining the Civilian and Humanitarian Character of Asylum* (UNHCR 2006).

[181] W Kälin, 'Supervising the 1951 Convention Relating to the Status of Refugees: Article 35 and Beyond' in E Feller, V Türk, and F Nicholson (eds), *Refugee Protection in International Law, UNHCR's Global Consultations on International Protection* (CUP/UNHCR 2003) 627.

[182] *Re SA Refugee Appeal No 1/92* (1992) New Zealand Refugee Status Appeals Authority.

[183] *R v Uxbridge Magistrates' Court and Another, ex p Adimi* [1999] 4 All ER 520. See also among similar acknowledgements *R v Secretary of State for the Home Department, ex p Adan and Aitseguer* [2001] 2 AC 477 (UK) 516, 520; *Secretary of State for the Home Department v Fornah*, House of Lords [2006] UKHL 46.

UNHCR has been particularly influential in framing the interpretation and thus the implementation of the refugee definition at the national level. As regularly acknowledged in domestic case law, the UNHCR Handbook on Procedures and Criteria for Determining Refugee Status as well as the subsequent Guidelines on International Protection 'are all useful and authoritative sources of guidance to decision makers in the asylum process'.[184] Lord Steyn explains in a convincing and straightforward way that 'UNHCR plays a critical role in the application of the Refugee Convention' and 'contracting states are obliged to co-operate with UNHCR. It is not surprising therefore that the UNHCR Handbook, although not binding on states, has a highly persuasive authority and is much relied on by domestic courts and tribunals.'[185] Lord Woolf further observes that '[t]here is no international court charged with the interpretation and implementation of the Convention, and for this reason the Handbook on Procedures and Criteria for Determining Refugee Status [. . .] is particularly helpful as a guide to what is the international understanding of the Convention obligations, as worked out in practice'.[186]

The UNHCR Handbook and subsequent guidelines are indeed often shaped by the relevant practice of states, even if it is fairly difficult to identify which part is a mere codification and which one is a progressive development of the prevailing state practice. Following this cross-fertilizing law-making process, interpretative standards inform states' behaviours and vice versa, before they might eventually become an international practice formally acknowledged by states. Lord Laws concludes in this sense that '[w]hile the Handbook is not . . . itself a source of law, many signatory states have accepted the guidance [so that] it constitutes good evidence of what has come to be international practice'.[187]

At a more general plane, this subtle shift from interpretative guidance to international practice exhibits the porous line between soft law and hard law. It also illuminates the powerful potential of interpretation to bridge the gap between these two opposite forms of normativity. Several instances may be found in domestic case law referring to the UNHCR Handbook. In a reference judgement delivered by the UK Supreme Court in 1996, Lord Lloyd of Berwick characterized the Handbook as an 'important source of law (though it does not have the force of law itself)'.[188] Although his distinction between a source of law and the force of law seems confusing, it shows the difficulty in separating a non-binding interpretation from a binding provision when the former construes and thus gives content to the latter. This also transpires from another important judgement of the US Supreme Court,

---

[184] *U and another v MJELR and another* (30 July 2010) [2010] IEHC 317, para 14. For further discussion, see also SS Juss, 'The UNHCR Handbook and the Interface between "Soft Law" and "Hard Law" in International Refugee Law' in SS Juss and C Harvey (eds), *Contemporary Issues in Refugee Law* (Edward Elgar 2013) 21–67.

[185] *R v Secretary of State for the Home Department, ex parte Adan and Aitseguer* [2001] 2 AC 477 (UK) 516, 520.

[186] *R (on the application of Robinson) v Secretary of State for the Home Department and another* (11 July 1997) [1997] EWCA Civ (Lord Woolf MR).

[187] *R (on the application of Adan) v Secretary of State for the Home Department* [1999] EWCA Civ 1948 (Laws LJ).

[188] *T v Secretary of State for the Home Department* (22 May 1996) [1996] 2 All ER 865.

according to whom the UNHCR Handbook 'provides significant guidance in construing the Protocol, to which Congress sought to conform. It has been widely considered useful in giving content to the obligations that the Protocol establishes'.[189]

Although positivists tend to strictly isolate interpretation from creation of law, the two are practically and normatively intermingled. Any interpretation inescapably adds something to the legal norm by detailing its very content. This is especially true when the creators of the norm, the states, are the authors of its interpretation. But this might happen as well when interpretation is provided by another subject of international law, like an international organization, when it is legitimate and influential enough to shape states' behaviours and create a habit of compliance. As a result of this incremental process, a non-binding interpretation of a binding provision might become mandatory, when it is endorsed by States Parties to the relevant treaty.

As exemplified by not only the UNHCR guidelines, but also the General Comments of UN treaty bodies, among many other similar instances, soft law epitomizes an informal international law-making process, whereby states and international organizations are constantly interacting in a decentralized society. In a sort of normative dialogue between subjects of international law, a non-binding standard adopted by an international organization can generate a consensus and eventually amount to an international practice sanctioned by states. While states formally retain the monopoly of creating international law through treaties and customs, soft law has generated a more inclusive and dynamic law-making process among a plurality of actors. Nonetheless, this structural evolution of the contemporary legal order entails recognition of its own limits. Besides their lack of democratic legitimacy, international organizations are actively engaged in this informal law-making process, following their institutional agenda, in order to justify the relevance of their mandate and the centrality of their own legal categories.

While UNHCR has been particularly prolific and dynamic in developing soft law standards beyond the task assigned by its founding statute to promote the conclusion of new treaties, the same cannot be said about its second function, namely the supervision of the application of international conventions on refugees. The supervisory function of UNHCR is by far the weakest side of its mandate. This is surprising and rather unexpected, given the robust legal framework governing its supervisory responsibility under both its Statute and the 1951 Convention.

According to Article 35(1) of the Refugee Convention, the commitment of States Parties to cooperate with UNHCR specifically includes the obligation to 'facilitate its duty of supervising the application of the provisions of the Convention'.[190] This

---

[189] *Immigration and Naturalization Service v Cardoza-Fonseca* 480 US 421, 107 S Ct 1207 (9 March 1987); reaffirmed in *Immigration and Naturalization Service v Juan Anibal Aguirre-Aguirre*, 526 US 415, 119 S Ct 1439 (3 May 1999).

[190] The same obligation is laid down in art II(1) of the 1967 Protocol and restated in several other instruments, such as art 8 of the OAU 1969 Convention governing Specific Aspects of Refugee Problems in Africa. Türk argued that 'the content of Article 35 of the 1951 Convention could possibly constitute a rule of customary international law': V Türk, 'UNHCR's Supervisory Responsibility' (2002) 14 RQDI 135, 141. This assertion remains highly questionable, for the duty of cooperation is only applicable to States Parties of the Geneva Convention for the very purpose of facilitating the implementation of this particular treaty. A customary obligation of this kind would further presuppose that both the Geneva

duty of cooperation creates a functional link between states' obligation to respect the Geneva Convention and the correlative institutional responsibility of UNHCR to supervise its application.[191] Although all scholars and refugee experts have focused on states' duties concerning its supervisory function, they have forgotten a major variable of the equation: UNHCR is, also and above all, legally committed to supervise the application of the Geneva Convention. Alongside the mandatory wording of its Statute,[192] Article 35(1) makes crystal clear that it is 'its duty of supervising the application of the provisions of the Convention.' Such a duty has been restated in several other instruments, including the New York Protocol of 1967,[193] the ExCom Conclusion N° 57 (XL) of 1989,[194] and the 2001 Declaration of States Parties to the 1951 Convention, and/or its 1967 Protocol relating to the Status of Refugees.[195] In order to enable UNHCR to fulfil its commitment, Article 35(2) of the Refugee Convention requires States Parties to report on the measures they have taken to implement the Convention among other relevant information.[196] Reciprocally, UNHCR is committed by its Statute to obtaining this information from States Parties.[197]

Convention as a whole and UNHCR mandate would be part of customary law—an affirmation that can hardly be defended.

[191] 'The primary purpose of Article 35(1) of the 1951 Convention and Article II(1) of the 1967 Protocol is thus to link the duty of States Parties to apply the Convention and the Protocol with UNHCR's task of supervising their application by imposing a treaty obligation on States Parties (i) to respect UNHCR's supervisory power and not to hinder UNHCR in carrying out this task, and (ii) to cooperate actively with UNHCR in this regard in order to achieve an optimal implementation and harmonized application of all provisions of the Convention and its Protocol.' Kälin, 'Supervising the 1951 Convention' (n 181) 617. See also M Zieck, 'Article 35 of the 1951 Convention/Article II of the 1967 Protocol' in A Zimmermann (ed), *The 1951 Convention Relating to the Status of Refugees and its 1967 Protocol: A Commentary* (OUP 2011) 1508; V Türk, 'The UNHCR's Role in Supervising International Protection Standards in the Context of its Mandate' in J Simeon (ed), *The UNHCR and the Supervision of International Refugee Law* (CUP 2013) 39–58; V Türk, 'UNHCR's Supervisory Responsibility' (n 190) 135.

[192] '*The High Commissioner shall provide for the protection of refugees* falling under the competence of his Office *by* […] promoting the conclusion and ratification of international conventions […] [and] *supervising their application*' (emphasis added).

[193] Protocol Relating to the Status of Refugees (adopted 31 January 1967, entered into force 4 October 1967) 606 UNTS 267 (Protocol) art 2(1).

[194] UNHCR ExCom Conclusion No 57 (XL) 'Implementation of the 1951 Convention and the 1967 Protocol relating to the Status of Refugees' (1989) para 5 (preambular).

[195] UNHCR 'Declaration of State Parties to the 1951 Convention and/or its 1967 Protocol relating to the Status of Refugees' (16 January 2002) HCR/MMSP/2001/09, para 9. See also among other restatements of the UNHCR duty of supervision UNHCR, *Agenda for Protection* (3rd edn, UNHCR 2003) 35.

[196] According to art 35(2), 'the Contracting States undertake to provide in the appropriate form with information and statistical data requested concerning: (a) the conditions of refugees, (b) the implementation of this Convention, and (c) laws, regulations and decrees which are, or may hereafter be, in force relating to refugees'. See also art 2(2) of the 1967 Protocol (n 193). This reporting duty is reinforced by art 36 of the Geneva Convention and art III of its Protocol according to which States Parties shall communicate to the UN Secretary General the domestic law and regulation they adopted to ensure the application of the Convention under.

[197] 'The High Commissioner shall provide for the protection of refugees falling under the competence of his Office by […] obtaining from Governments information concerning the number and conditions of refugees in their territories and the laws and regulations concerning them.'

Contrary to UN human rights treaties, the Refugee Convention does not detail a reporting procedure to be followed by States and UNHCR regarding, notably, the periodicity of the reports and the evaluation process. In this area as in many others, the 1951 Convention paid the price for being the forerunner of the subsequent human rights treaties. Zieck observes that:

Whilst innovative at the time, Art. 35, para. 1, in particular the supervisory role of UNHCR, appears to suffer the drawbacks of being one of the first external supervisory mechanisms in that it is of a rather rudimentary nature … when compared to the supervisory mechanisms of human rights treaties that comprise periodic reporting and corresponding analysis and assessment of performance by an independent body.[198]

This historical context, however, fails to explain the present situation, when viewed in light of the subsequent evolution of international law in this area. As Hathaway rightly acknowledges, '[w]hatever its accuracy, the historical explanation is […] surely insufficient to immunize the Refugee Convention from the contemporary general practice of meaningful independent supervision'.[199] Even more significantly, according to its Statute and the Refugee Convention as amended by its Protocol, UNHCR is committed to supervising the application of these treaties and to requesting the reports of States Parties on their implementation. Accordingly, it is bound to establish a reporting procedure, in order to collect and assess them in accordance with the Refugee Convention. The responsibility of UNHCR is supplemented and reinforced by two correlative obligations of states to facilitate its duty of supervision (Article 35(1)) and to submit their reports on the implementation of the Convention (Article 35(2)).

The fact that the Refugee Convention does not detail the practical modalities of the reporting procedure cannot be a pretext for inaction. Besides the above-mentioned duties of states and UNHCR under this treaty, the very notion of supervision in international law by definition requires a process of monitoring states' compliance with their legal obligations. The term 'supervision' is indeed traditionally understood as 'the process of overseeing the compliance with rules of subjects of law'.[200] It refers to 'a legal process which empowers authorized institutions to apply certain procedures to assure the proper functioning of the legal order by inducing

---

[198] M Zieck, 'Article 35 of the 1951 Convention/Article II of the 1967 Protocol' (n 191) 1508.

[199] JC Hathaway, *The Rights of Refugees under International Law* (CUP 2005) 995. He explains that 'the absence of an independent supervisory mechanism for the Refugee Convention is simply a reflection of the historical reality of the late 1940s and early 1950s, when the entire idea of inter-state supervision of human rights was new, potentially threatening, and not truly accepted by states. Yet with the adoption of the Human Rights Covenants and more specialized treaties beginning in the mid-1960s, the establishment of independent mechanism for inter-state oversight of the human rights treaties has become routine.' ibid.

[200] K Schmalenbach, 'International Organizations or Institutions, Supervision and Sanctions' (2014) Max Planck Encyclopedia of Public International Law, para 4. As far as its objective, '[t]he reasoning behind all supervisory efforts is not purely to expose law-breakers in order to sanction them. Due to the shortage of law enforcement in the realm of international law, the process of supervision is first and foremost designed to enhance compliance with international obligations. International supervision strengthens dialogue and compliance efforts; it sparks public opinion and the shame of the wrong-doer. The ultimate goal is to prevent non-compliance before it occurs': ibid para 6.

subjects to observe obligations incumbent on them. [...] A discussion of international supervision is therefore, a discussion of those procedures through which legal order induces subjects to observe law.'[201]

This seems to be the common understanding within UNHCR as well. Volker Türk, the current Assistant High Commissioner for Protection, acknowledged in 2002 that '[t]he purpose of international supervision relating to the application of provisions of international instruments is, first and foremost, to promote compliance with these rules'.[202] While observing that 'no definition of the UNHCR's supervisory role exists', he admitted that 'supervision by an international institution contains (i) an element of collection of information concerning the application of provisions of the international refugee instruments by the respective contracting states; (ii) the assessment of this information in light of the applicable norms; and (iii) some kind of enforcement mechanism to ensure remedial action and norm compliance by the states concerned'.[203]

However, despite the legally binding framework governing its supervisory responsibility, UNHCR has not adopted any formal and systematic procedure for examining periodical reports of States Parties on the implementation of the Geneva Convention.[204] Its inability or unwillingness to assume the monitoring tasks inherent to its supervisory responsibility is commonly attributed to its structural dependence upon states from both the Global North to fund its activities and the Global South to secure its presence on their territory.[205] As conceded by two senior officials of the organization, 'in delivering protection, UNHCR must work closely on the ground with government partners and is reliant on voluntary state funding. These factors impact on what the Office may say publicly and how it reports its concerns.'[206] In other words, the operational activities carried out by UNHCR on the ground require a close collaboration with its 'government partners', which hampers a more critical stance towards them to the detriment of its supervisory responsibility.

There is, however, nothing irremediable or insurmountable in this, for at least two basic reasons. First, contrary to conventional wisdom, establishing a reporting procedure to assess the implementation of the Refugee Convention shall not be approved by states. It is inherent in the clear-cut duties spelt out in this instrument.

---

[201] TMR Chowdhury, *Legal Framework of International Supervision* (University of Stockholm 1986) 7.

[202] Türk, 'UNHCR's Supervisory Responsibility' (n 190) 139.   [203] ibid 146.

[204] Besides the absence of any proper mechanism, UNHCR has very occasionally requested information from States Parties on an ad hoc and confidential basis concerning specific situations. It made a more comprehensive request to all States Parties through a general questionnaire on only two occasions in 1974 and 1990. See Zieck, 'Article 35 of the 1951 Convention/Article II of the 1967 Protocol' (n 191) 1501–03.

[205] See for instance, ibid, 1507–08; Hathaway, *The Rights of Refugees under International Law* (n 199) 995–98; T Glover and S Russell, 'Coordination with UNHCR and States' (2001) Collaboration of the International Council of Voluntary Agencies and the Program in Refugee and Asylum Law, University of Michigan Working Paper No 7; S Takahashi, 'Effective Monitoring of the Refugee Convention' (2001) Paper Presented at the Refugee Convention 50 Years on; Critical Perspectives, Future Prospects II, International studies Association Conference.

[206] E Feller and A Klug, 'Refugees, United Nations High Commissioner for (UNHCR)' (2014) Max Planck Encyclopedia of Public International Law, para 86.

States are bound by this convention to report on its implementation and, reciprocally, UNHCR is committed to requesting these reports and thus to establishing some kind of process for collecting and examining them. Second, the delicate if not schizophrenic posture of UNHCR towards states can be easily obviated through a monitoring process carried out by independent experts, alongside the reporting procedure under all the other UN human rights treaties. In fact, numerous proposals have been detailed by scholars and most of them converge on the need to resort to an independent process.[207]

The reporting procedure is obviously not a panacea to redress the numerous challenges of states' compliance with international law.[208] Similarly, the fact that such a procedure has not been established does not prejudice the many other tasks falling within the supervisory responsibility of UNHCR, nor does it pay tribute to the concrete achievements of the organization in this area.[209] According to a longstanding practice of the organization, UNHCR undertakes a wide range of activities with the goal of enhancing states' compliance with international refugee law. They include most notably: advising states to design operational activities, strengthening the capacity of state authorities (mainly through training and promotional activities), and commenting upon legislative and administrative reforms; making representations to states' authorities on protection concerns; having access to asylum-seekers and refugees (especially in detention centres and refugee camps); participating in domestic asylum procedures on a consultative basis; and making submissions to international and domestic courts or other quasi-judicial organs (through amicus curiae or statements) and carrying out advocacy activities (through the issuance of public statements).[210]

---

[207] Among the various proposals to enhance the supervisory responsibility of UNHCR, see JC Hathaway, 'Overseeing the Refugee Convention: Taking Refugee Law Oversight Seriously' (2001) Working Paper No UM-ICVA Overview; BS Chimni, 'Reforming the International Refugee Regime: A Dialogic Model' (2001) 14(2) JRS 151–68; Kälin, 'Supervising the 1951 Convention' (n 181) 628–66; AM North and J Chia, 'Towards Convergence in the Interpretation of the Refugee Convention: A Proposal for the Establishment of an International Judicial Commission for Refugees' in J McAdam (ed), *Forced Migration, Human Rights and Security* (Hart Publishing 2008) 225–61; J Simeon (ed), *The UNHCR and the Supervision of International Refugee Law* (n 191); A Blackham, 'A Proposal for Enhanced Supervision of the Refugee Convention' (2013) 26 JRS 392–415; K O'Byrne, 'Is there a Need for Better Supervision of the Refugee Convention?' (2013) 26 JRS 330–59; V Chetail, 'Are Refugee Rights Human Rights? An Unorthodox Questioning on the Relations between Refugee Law and Human Rights Law' in R Rubio-Marin, *Human Rights and Immigration* (OUP 2014) 67–68; J Simeon, 'Strengthening International Refugee Rights through the Enhanced Supervision of the 1951 Convention and its 1967 Protocol' in SS Juss (ed), *The Ashgate Research Companion to Migration Law, Theory and Policy* (Routledge 2013) 103–28. See also from an NGO perspective LM MacMillan, 'Monitoring & Reporting: A Search for New Advocacy Strategies' in AF Bayefsky and Joan Fitzpatrick (eds), *Human Rights and Forced Displacement* (Martinus Nijhoff 2000) 99–119.

[208] The limits of this reporting procedure within existing UN human rights treaties are well documented.

[209] One should never forget that, as a result of its supervisory role, UNHCR's interventions toward states on behalf of individual asylum seekers and refugees are literally saving their lives, even if these actions are not made public for obvious reasons.

[210] Türk, 'The UNHCR's Role in Supervising International Protection Standards' (n 191) 50–53; UNHCR, Global Consultations on International Protection (Cambridge Expert Roundtable 9–10 July 2001) 'Summary Conclusions: Supervisory Responsibility' in E Feller, V Türk, and F Nicholson

Although UNHCR considers that all these activities fall under the label of its supervisory function,[211] they do not. Instead, they respectively refer to capacity-building, protection, and advocacy. This does not undermine the vital importance of these activities or the achievements of UNHCR in these areas. Yet, they have nothing to do with supervision, as it is understood under public international law and in the Refugee Convention, that is, a monitoring process for assessing the application of its provisions by States Parties. Purposely or not, the responsibility entrusted to UNHCR has been denatured to mean nothing more than an advisory rather than a supervisory function.

IOM: a non-normative organization?

In stark contrast with the tasks assigned to UNHCR by its founding Statute, IOM is supposed to be a 'non-normative international organization', as acknowledged in 2015 by the IOM Council in its Resolution 1309[212] and then endorsed the following year in the agreement concluded with the UN.[213] This defining feature still raises more questions than it gives answers. The expression 'non-normative international organization' is not a term of art under international law. It is mentioned neither in the UN Charter nor in the IOM Constitution. When taken literally, a 'non-normative international organization' would mean that IOM is not allowed to set up and enforce legally binding rules towards states without their consent.

The shortcomings of this conclusion are perhaps too obvious to be noted. There is no need to proclaim its non-normative status to acknowledge that IOM cannot create binding rules for its Member States without their specific and explicit consent. It is widely known that no international organization is allowed to adopt legally binding rules for states, with some rare exceptions, such as the Security Council or the EU. These last two counter-examples also embody the very few international organs that have been given the power to enforce binding rules against their Member States.[214] Given this framework, it is fairly difficult to find a coherent legal meaning of the term 'non-normative organization'. This expression is at best redundant, but it adds nothing to what is already known under international law or the IOM Constitution. As demonstrated below, it is particularly hard to determine its legal meaning in a cogent manner. It even seems to be in contradiction with the practice followed by the organization in the last two decades.

When assessed in reference to IOM's practice, this enigmatic expression of 'non-normative organization' says more about what it is not than what it is. Firstly,

---

(eds), *Refugee Protection in International Law: UNHCR's Global Consultations on International Protection* (CUP/UNHCR 2003) 669–70.

[211] ibid.   [212] IOM, 'Council Resolution No 1309' (2015) C/106/RES/1309, para 2(a).

[213] IOM, 'Council Resolution No 1317' (adopted 30 June 2016 at its 1st Special Session) Agreement concerning the relationship between the United Nations and the International Organization for Migration (1 July 2016) C/Sp/1/RES/1317, art 2(3).

[214] Even assuming that enforcement could be interpreted in an extensive way beyond its ordinary meaning of compelling observance of a legal obligation, IOM is not allowed to bring a case before an international court, like the vast majority of international organizations.

although the term 'normative' is obviously broader than legally binding rules, soft law standards should be excluded in this specific context since, as noticed before, IOM has adopted its own soft law guidelines and it has been involved in the drafting process of several other non-binding instruments, including for instance the Global Compact for Migration and the GMG principles and guidelines on migrants in vulnerable situations. Secondly, even circumscribed to legally binding rules, its non-normative nature does not mean that IOM is prohibited from adopting agreements with other international organizations, as exemplified by the one concluded with the UN in 2016. Nor does it imply that it cannot conclude agreements with its Member States, as it regularly adopts host agreements, for instance.[215] Similarly, its so-called non-normative nature does not forbid IOM to be involved, as an observer, in the drafting process of a treaty concluded between states. To mention one obvious example, IOM with UNHCR and other UN agencies addressed their comments and concerns to states regarding the draft protocols on the smuggling of migrants and trafficking in persons.[216] Thirdly, its non-normative status does not mean that IOM is not bound by legally binding rules as a subject of international law or under any specific agreement it may have concluded. As already developed before, as a result of its agreement with the UN, it is committed to undertake its activities in accordance with the principles of the UN Charter and with due regard to the other relevant UN instruments adopted in the field of migration, refugee, and human rights.

If one should find a rationale for this expression, it seems to be more psychological and political than legal. Consciously or not, restating the so-called non-normative nature of IOM is a way to reaffirm its own identity in opposition to UNHCR, and to reassure its Member States that nothing will fundamentally change. In a period of changes, as IOM experienced with its new status as a related organization, the natural inclination to reaffirm its own identity is to do so by opposition to others. Following this stance, the non-normative nature of IOM makes sense only when it is contrasted to UNHCR. Under international law, as acknowledged in its Statute and the Refugee Convention, the supervisory and normative functions of UNHCR represent a unique characteristic when compared to the mandate of IOM.

Nonetheless, as already highlighted, the practice and the meaning of UNHCR's supervisory and normative responsibility have considerably evolved, to such an extent that this distinctive feature might appear more symbolic than real: whatever its achievements in other areas, UNHCR has not initiated the conclusion of any new treaty at the universal plane in the last four decades, and its supervision of

---

[215] Curiously, agreements concluded with its Member States are not available on the IOM website, but they are regularly advertised on the web. See for instance the recent agreements concluded with Turkey in IOM, 'IOM Turkey Newsletter' Issue 6 (IOM, 2017) available at<www.iom.int/sites/default/files/mission_newsletter/file/2017-Winter-IOM-Turkey-Newsletter.pdf> accessed 3 October 2018; and with Morocco in Permanent Mission of the Kingdom of Morocco to the UN and other international organizations in Geneva, 'Host State Agreement between Morocco and IOM' (*Permanent Mission of Morocco*) available at <www.mission-maroc.ch/en/pages/270.html> accessed 3 October 2018.

[216] UNGA 'Note by the Office of the United Nations High Commissioner for Human Rights, the Office of the United Nations High Commissioner for Refugees, the United Nations Children's Fund, and the International Organization for Migration on the Draft Protocols Concerning Migrant Smuggling and Trafficking in Persons' (8 February 2000) UN Doc A/AC.254/27.

the Refugee Convention has proved to be minimalist in practice. Inversely, IOM has been increasingly, albeit timidly, involved in promoting and facilitating the application of international law, even if it is far from forming a core activity of the organization. The fact remains, however, that, since 2007, the IOM Council has heralded 'the effective respect for the human rights of migrants in accordance with international law' as an official priority of the organization.[217] Directly or indirectly, many of its activities, carried out through advisory services, capacity-building support, and humanitarian assistance, are supposed to enhance the effective respect for international law.

Furthermore, although its Member States do not always seem to be aware of it, international migration law is no longer a taboo for IOM. In 2004, it created the International Migration Law Unit 'to strengthen and promote the Organization's involvement in International Migration Law (IML)' through capacity building assistance, legislative support, and policy advocacy.[218] In echo to the activities performed by UNHCR in the field of refugee law, the International Migration Law Unit of IOM 'assists governments to develop and implement migration legislation and procedures consistent with applicable international and regional standards. The objective is to strengthen the capacity of governments to govern migration more effectively and consistent with the rule of law.'[219] Since the establishment of this unit, its work has been tellingly grounded in a 'normative approach to migration' that is typically considered 'from two different, but complementary angles: the principles and standards deriving from state sovereignty [...] [and] the human rights of the persons involved in migration'.[220]

Following this normative approach to migration, IOM has also promoted the ratification of UN conventions on migration and human rights well before its transformation into a related organization of the UN. For instance, IOM has been a member of the International Steering Committee of the Global Campaign for the Ratification of the UN Convention on the Rights of Migrant Workers since its establishment in 1998. This Committee is a unique network composed of four UN agencies (OHCHR, ILO, IOM, and UNESCO, but not UNHCR) and ten civil society organizations (December 18, FIDH, Global Migration Policy Associates, Human Rights Watch, International Catholic Migration Commission, International Trade Union Confederation, Migrants Forum in Asia, Migrants Rights International, Public Services International, and World Council of Churches). Because of its innovative membership, the Steering Committee has been quite proactive in raising awareness of the ICRMW and promoting its ratification.[221] When the Committee

---

[217] See point number 2 under IOM's strategic focus at: 'About IOM: Mission' (IOM) available at<www.iom.int/mission> accessed 3 October 2018.

[218] See the presentation of the IML unit in IOM, 'International Migration Law' (IOM) available at <https://www.iom.int/international-migration-law> accessed 3 October 2018.

[219] ibid.   [220] ibid.

[221] Among other initiatives, the Steering Committee has published a Campaigner's Handbook in International Migrations Rights Watch Committee, *Achieving Dignity: Campaigner's Handbook for the Migrants Rights Convention* (AGL-FM 1998); OHCHR, International Steering Committee for the Campaign for Ratification of the Migrants Convention, *Guide on Ratification: International Convention on the Protection of the Rights of All Migrant Workers and Members of their Families (ICRMW)* (OHCHR 2009).

was created in 1998, this convention counted only nine States Parties. Since then, forty-five other states have ratified it, although this ad hoc committee is clearly not the only actor to be credited for this.[222]

As a member of the Steering Committee, IOM 'sees its role in the global campaign as furthering its own objectives to uphold migrants' rights, as well as a contribution in IOM's quest to translate the Cairo Programme of Action into practice. IOM supports the objectives of the 1990 Convention'.[223] While expressing its official support, the organization underlines that 'the core principles and standards of the Convention clearly link with the principles and objectives of IOM'.[224] Notwithstanding this profession of faith, IOM should be much more proactive in promoting the ratification of the ICRMW among the vast number of its Member States. Its limited involvement in promoting its ratification starkly contrasts with its enthusiastic campaign for ratifying and implementing the UN Protocols against the smuggling of migrants and trafficking in persons.[225]

Whatever the reasons for this double standard, promoting the ratification of UN conventions on migration has become an established practice of the organization. Furthermore and more importantly, since the agreement of 2016, promoting the application of international law and the ratification of UN conventions in the field of migration and human rights should be viewed as an implied power of IOM that is inherent in its recognition as 'an essential contributor [...] in the protection of

---

[222] The recent increase of ratifications is also due to a plurality of other factors, including the support of Mexico and the Philippines as well as the increasing awareness of sending countries to use the Convention as a means for protecting their nationals abroad.

[223] IOM, 'Migrants' Rights: IOM Policy and Activities' 84th Session (13 November 2002) MC/INF/259, para 10.

[224] Ibid. It continues by emphasizing that 'the Convention is a significant move by the international community in the recognition and promotion of migrants' rights. It reflects a growing awareness of the problems and discriminatory treatment that faces many migrant workers, as well as an acknowledgement of the magnitude of the issue of irregular migration. In this way, the Convention is an important and worthy document.'

[225] As acknowledged in an official report of 2013, 'IOM continued to support Morocco, Libya, and Yemen in their efforts to ratify the UN Protocol on human trafficking' in IOM, 'The Middle East and North Africa: Annual Report 2013' (2013), 10. Among other examples, IOM published in 2008 the Caribbean counter-trafficking model legislation to be used by the states of the region and in 2014 a policy guide on criminalizing migrant smuggling for those states involved in the Bali Process. See IOM, *Legal Review on Trafficking in Persons in the Caribbean: The Bahamas, Barbados, Guyana, Jamaica, The Netherlands Antilles, St Lucia, Suriname, Trinidad and Tobago* (2nd edn, IOM 2010), 52; IOM, 'Policy Guide on Criminalizing Migrant Smuggling' in 'The Bali Process on People Smuggling, Trafficking in Persons and Related Transnational Crime: An Introductory Guide for Policy Makers and Practitioners on How to Implement International Legal Obligations to Criminalize Migrant Smuggling at the Domestic Level' (RSO 2014). See also IOM, 'IOM and EU Facilitate the Development and Ratification of a Human Trafficking Legislative Framework in Puntland' (IOM Press Release, 1 September 2018) <https://www.iom.int/news/iom-and-eu-facilitate-development-and-ratification-human-trafficking-legislative-framework> accessed 3 October 2018; IOM provided Costa Rica with guidance and input when the country drafted and enacted legislation on human trafficking, based on the UN Protocol on trafficking (IOM Press Release, 9 February 2009) < https://www.iom.int/news/new-legislation-defines-human-trafficking-costa-rica> accessed 3 October 2018; IOM assisted Kenya in preparing the draft for its domestic legislation based on the Palermo Protocol (IOM Press Release, 15 August 2007) < https://www.iom.int/news/tackling-human-trafficking-through-national-plan-action> accessed 3 October 2018.

migrants'.[226] Despite the silence of its own constitution, the practice followed by the organization during the last two decades has significantly evolved towards a more proactive role in promoting better implementation of international migration law. This, in turn, mitigates its alleged difference with UNHCR.

Nevertheless, the increasing involvement of IOM in these promotional activities falls short of being a key component of its mandate. It does not fundamentally alter the essence of an organization driven by its donors as a service provider for its Member States. This explains several noticeable differences with UNHCR. To mention the most obvious ones, IOM has not criticized so far its Members States for the violations of international law they may commit. It is not involved as an observer within domestic migration procedures, like UNHCR is within national asylum procedures. Similarly, in contrast with the numerous interventions of UNHCR before domestic tribunals, international courts, and UN treaty bodies, IOM has submitted only one single amicus curiae before the Inter American Court of Human Rights.[227]

Additionally, IOM is not allowed to request an advisory opinion of the International Court of Justice. In fact, among all existing related organizations to the UN, IOM is—along with WTO—the only one that is not explicitly habilitated to request an advisory opinion of the International Court of Justice[228] or at least committed to furnishing any information requested by the International Court of Justice.[229] This does not mean, however, that the International Court of Justice has no role to play with regard to IOM. According to Article 26 of the IOM Constitution, any dispute concerning the interpretation and application of its Constitution, which is not settled by negotiation or by a two-thirds majority vote of the IOM Council, shall be referred to the International Court of Justice. By contrast, the UNHCR Statute does not provide such possibility.[230] Furthermore, like IOM, the refugee agency cannot

---

[226] Agreement with the UN (n 18) art 1(2).

[227] IOM, *Amicus Curiae submitted to the Inter-American Court of Human Rights by the International Organization for Migration (IOM): Request for Advisory Opinion on Migrant Children* (17 February 2012) CDH-OC-21/272.

[228] Authorization to the International Atomic Energy Agency to request advisor opinions of the International Court of Justice, GA Res 1146 (XII) (1957); art 7 of the Cooperation Agreement between the United Nations and the Organization for the Prohibition of Chemical Weapons UN Res 55/283 (2001) UN Doc A/RES/55/283.

[229] Art 8 of the Agreement to regulate the relationship between the United Nations and the Preparatory Commission for the Comprehensive Nuclear-Test-Ban Treaty Organization UN Res 54/280 (2000) UN Doc A/RES/54/280; art 5(1)(b)(ii) of the Relationship Agreement between the United Nations and the International Criminal Court (2004); art 4(1)(b) of the Agreement on Cooperation and Relationship between the United Nations and the International Tribunal for the Law of the Sea UN Res 52/251 (1998) UN Doc A/RES/52/251.

[230] By contrast, according to art 38 of the Refugee Convention, any dispute relating to the interpretation or application of the Convention can be referred to the ICJ at the request of any Contracting State. This possibility has so far never been used, thus highlighting the limits inherent to this traditional mechanism of inter-state dispute settlement for ensuring the effective protection of refugees. Grahl-Madsen argued that 'by virtue of Article 35 the High Commissioner may, in given circumstances, ask a Contracting State to intervene with another Contracting State, whose application of the Convention is not agreeable to the High Commissioner, and in case of the intervention being unsuccessful, ask the State concerned to bring the matter before the International Court of Justice according to Article 38'. He still concluded that 'it must nevertheless be kept in mind that one thing is a right of asking—the requested State must be allowed to use its own judgement and to refuse if it finds that this kind of co-operation with the High Commissioner would run contrary to its own interests' in A Grahl-Madsen,

ask for an advisory opinion by the ICJ on its own initiative. Nonetheless, according to Article 96 of the UN Charter, the General Assembly may authorize UNHCR to request an advisory opinion on any legal question arising within the scope of its activities, even if this option has never been used so far.

Beyond all these technical niceties regarding the differences between IOM and UNHCR, the reaffirmation of the non-normative feature of the former was primarily done for internal consumption, in order to reassure its Member States that the nature of the organization, as it is perceived to be, will not fundamentally change. This might also be viewed as a subtle and diplomatically correct way to reiterate the tribute to state sovereignty in the field of migration as contained in Article 1(3) of the IOM Constitution. According to this provision, 'the Organization shall recognize the fact that control of standards of admission and the number of immigrants to be admitted are matters within the domestic jurisdiction of States, and, in carrying out its functions, shall conform to the laws, regulations and policies of the States concerned'.

However, this homage to domestic jurisdiction shall not be understood as a *blanc-seing* for its Member States. They remain legally bound by duly ratified treaties (whether bilateral, regional, or universal ones), general principles of law, and any other rules of customary international law (including the principle of *non-refoulement*, the prohibitions of collective expulsion and arbitrary detention, the right to leave any country, and the right to return one's own country). One should further note that the endorsement of domestic jurisdiction by the IOM Constitution is circumscribed to two specific areas, namely 'the number of immigrants to be admitted' and the 'control of standards of [their] admission'. While international law is largely indifferent to the number of immigrants, it has a role to play in controlling the standards of their admission through, for instance, UN treaty bodies, international courts, or diplomatic protection. Against this background, the endorsement of domestic jurisdiction in the IOM Constitution and the subsequent proclamation of its non-normative stance should be seen as a way of acknowledging that the organization is not a supervisory organ, like UNHCR is perceived to be, for good or wrong reasons.

Commentary on the Refugee Convention 1951 (UNHCR 1997) 153. See also Kälin, 'Supervising the 1951 Convention' (n 181) 653.

Concluding Thoughts on the Future of International Migration Law

The normative and institutional framework governing migration has grown and evolved over the last century to embody a detailed and complex set of international rules and institutions. As discussed in Part I of this textbook, the origins and foundations of international migration law are deeply rooted in the international legal system. As a result of a long incremental process of consolidation, a dense network of both conventional and customary rules currently governs the departure, admission, and stay of migrants. The most emblematic and basic principles notably include the right to leave any country (be it a state of origin, transit, or sojourn), the right to enter, and return to one's own country as a national or a long-term resident, the principle of *non-refoulement*, the positive duty of family reunification, the prohibitions of collective expulsion and arbitrary detention, as well as the principle of non-discrimination. These fundamental principles apply to all migrants and constitute the bedrock of international migration law.

This general normative framework is further supplemented and detailed by specialized treaty regimes, which are analysed in the second part of this textbook, with a focus on the UN conventions devoted to subgroups of people on the move (namely refugees, migrant workers, smuggled migrants, and victims of trafficking). The universal strand of international migration law thus consists of both general principles and instruments, as well as specialized treaty regimes. This normative layer is further entrenched, at the regional level, in numerous agreements endorsing the right to free movement within many continents such as in Europe, Africa, Latin America, and the Caribbean. While migration is regulated by a broad range of legally binding norms under both treaty law and customary law, the proliferation of soft law has become a defining feature of global migration governance. As discussed in the third part of the book, this development is not free from ambiguities: the multiplication of non-binding standards and consultative processes is both a catalyst and a symptom of multilateralism.

Despite its obvious limits, soft law has been an influential vehicle to foster intergovernmental dialogue and build confidence on a traditionally contentious issue alongside the North-South divide. The long and tortuous path initiated at the Cairo Conference of 1994 culminated in 2018 with the adoption of the Global Compacts on Migration and Refugees that have inaugurated a new cycle for global migration governance. Although the two UN Compacts remain largely aspirational, they crystallize the consensus of the international community around a broad range of commitments for a more comprehensive and balanced approach to migration. The UN and its Member States are now embarking upon a vast reform which constitutes a new turning point for multilateralism. Whether this ambitious process will succeed in developing a more coherent and integrated approach is impossible to predict.

The challenges are numerous and require more than ever a global and rational vision grounded on evidence-based knowledge, inclusive dialogue, and the rule of law. At the institutional level, the overall UN framework is arguably bound to remain multilevel and cross-cutting, reflecting the multidimensional nature of migration. The main challenge is to manage the complex and heteroclite array of nested institutions and to improve their efficiency and complementarity. Coordination is crucial; but it can hardly be achieved without revamping IOM and UNHCR as the two leading organizations of the UN system. While IOM has a role to play in enhancing system-wide coordination, it needs a more clear-cut and robust mandate to protect migrants and, like UNHCR, a reform of its funding system to be more predictable and less dependent on voluntary contributions.

The crux of the matter is to establish a more coherent division of labour between UNHCR and IOM in order to mitigate the prevailing duplication and competition. This is by far the hardest task. The most rational, albeit radical, option would be to allocate their responsibility between internal displacement and international migration. UNHCR would be in charge of internal displacement on the basis of its extensive experience in this area, whereas IOM would assume the overall responsibility for international migration, whether forced or voluntary, given the porous nature between the two and the need for a truly comprehensive approach. This option is however unlikely for obvious political reasons. Many powerful states have an interest in maintaining a fragmented institutional framework which reinforces power asymmetries and their correlative margin of manoeuvring. The current patchwork of parallel and overlapping institutions gives them more flexibility and influence to choose the one offering them the best prospects for achieving their own political objectives.[1] This forum-shopping encourages short-term strategy to the detriment of a more coherent and sustainable approach to migration governance.

At the normative level, the challenges of international migration law are equally abundant. The most important one relates to its domestic application by states. Indeed, the main problem is not the lack of international rules governing migration but their poor record of implementation at the national level. The reasons for this enduring gap are well-known: the primitive fear of the stranger is exacerbated by recurrent economic

---

[1] S Angenendt and A Koch, 'Global Migration Governance and Mixed Flows: Implications for Development-centred Policies' (2017) SWP Research Paper, 23. See also A Betts, 'Conclusion' in A Betts (ed), *Global Migration Governance* (OUP 2011) 321; V Guiraudon, 'European Integration and Migration Policy: Vertical Policy-making as Venue Shopping' (2000) 38(2) Journal of Common Market 251–71.

400   *Concluding Thoughts on the Future of International Migration Law*

crises, the spectre of terrorism, the rise of political manipulations and electioneering that have created an environment fertile to violations.

From a conceptual angle, as non-citizens, migrants are structurally vulnerable in the etymological sense of the word, that is to say, they suffer from a 'lack of empowerment'.[2] This structural vulnerability 'derives from the existence of a power structure which empirically shows that in any given national society, some have more power than others'.[3] The distribution of power within the state is shaped and reinforced by the right to vote as the privilege of nationals. Non-citizens as non-voters provide, in turn, an easy target for political electioneering and the perfect excuse to mask the failure of political decision-makers in addressing the social and economic difficulties and anxieties of their nationals. Although this tactic is all but new, it has gained considerable resonance over the last years with the rise of anti-immigrant ideologies and the growing racialization of political discourses.

On a more legal and technical plane, the implementation deficit of international migration law is also due to its limited reception in the domestic legal order. In many states, national legislation is not fully in line with international law or does not incorporate it in a coherent and comprehensive manner. In the prevailing toxic political climate, the application of national migration laws has been mystified by an absolute and outdated understanding of state sovereignty which does not correspond to the current development of international law. The disjuncture between international law and its domestic implementation is, however, not unique to migration and can be observed in many other areas where human rights are at stake. One should add that, in this field as in many others, violations are more visible than compliance. This obscures the fact that, as restated by the Global Compact for Migration, the majority of migrants around the world travel and live in a safe and regular manner.[4] The narrative of abuses has become nonetheless commonplace in the mass media for highlighting—consciously or not—the perils of being a migrant.

While the way to redress this situation is fundamentally political, much remains to be done in order to raise awareness of international migration law and to improve its implementation at the domestic level. The existing panoply of monitoring and enforcement mechanisms still offers some avenues that have not yet been fully exploited. They primarily concern the use of diplomatic protection by countries of origin under the law of state responsibility, as well as individual and inter-state complaints under general human rights treaties. In such a context, two other alternatives are bound to become more prominent.

---

[2] Commission on Human Rights, 'Working Paper Prepared by Mr. Jorge A. Bustamante, Chairman/Rapporteur of the Working Group of Intergovernmental Experts on the Human Rights of Migrants' (8 October 1998) UN Doc E/CN.4/AC.46/1998/5, 9.

[3] ibid. See also Commission on Human Rights, 'Report of the Special Rapporteur on the Human Rights of Migrants, Ms Gabriela Rodríguez Pizarro, Submitted Pursuant to Commission on Human Rights Resolution 1999/44' Fifty-Sixth Session (6 January 2000) UN Doc E/CN.4/2000/82, 15–16.

[4] Global Compact for Safe, Orderly and Regular Migration (13 July 2018) available at<https://refugeesmigrants.un.org/sites/default/files/180713_agreed_outcome_global_compact_for_migration.pdf> accessed 3 October 2018, para 8.

On the one hand, as acknowledged in the Global Compact for Migration,[5] the UN system has a major role to play in supporting the capacity-building of its Member States in order to ensure that they fully implement international law. In addition to the new capacity-building mechanism established by the Global Compact, the well-established expertise of UNHCR and IOM in providing such a support must be reinforced and further developed. However, to be efficient and meaningful, the efforts of the international community to strengthen national capacity presuppose a domestic legal environment where due respect for the rule of law and the human rights of migrants is already acknowledged and endorsed.[6]

On the other hand, persuasion may give way to coercion when violations of migrants' rights result from an open and general policy of a state. In such a case, international criminal law has a role to play in sanctioning the most patent violations. The widespread or systematic policy of unlawful deportations and arbitrary detentions of migrants may amount to a crime against humanity as defined in the Statute of the International Criminal Court.[7] Bringing such cases before the International Criminal Court is obviously not an easy task in light of its limited resources and the broad discretion of its Prosecutor to open an investigation. Whatever the potential role of the International Criminal Court is in the prosecution of large-scale abuses against migrants, the most likely and robust way to enforce international criminal law lies in domestic courts. Criminal prosecutions can be initiated by domestic tribunals, in the states of origin of abused migrants or, when applicable, in any other states in accordance with the principle of universal jurisdiction.

Besides the manifold difficulties related to its domestic implementation, another crucial challenge of international migration law concerns its very substance regarding the admission of migrant workers. Although a significant body of legal norms grounded on treaty law and customary law regulates the stay of migrants in host states as well as their right to leave and to return to their own country, admission for labour purposes represents the main lacuna of contemporary international law. This enduring gap inevitably feeds irregular migration and undermines refugee protection as a side effect. In many instances, submitting an asylum request has become the only lawful opportunity to gain access to a territory. As a result of this vicious circle, refugee law is increasingly implemented by states as a tool of exclusion rather than a means for protecting victims of human rights' violations.

Against this background, legalizing labour immigration represents the new frontier of international migration law that conditions in turn its future development. From this angle, the Global Compact for Migration may be viewed as a positive signal towards a more balanced and comprehensive understanding of labour

---

[5] ibid paras 43–45.

[6] See in this sense Global Commission on International Migration, 'Migration in an Interconnected World: New Directions for Action' Report (Global Commission on International Migration 2005) 64.

[7] Article 7(1) of the Rome Statute of the International Criminal Court (adopted 17 July 1998, entered into force 1 July 2002) 2187 UNTS 3. For further discussion, see notably V Chetail, 'Is There Any Blood on My Hands? Deportation as a Crime of International Law' (2016) 29 LJIL 917; I Kalzpouzos, I Mann, 'Banal Crimes against Humanity: The Case of Asylum Seekers in Greece' (2015) 16 Melb J of Int'l L 1; C Henderson, 'Australia's Treatment of Asylum Seekers: From Human Rights Violations to Crimes against Humanity' (2014) 12(5) JICJ 1161.

migration. Although the tone and content of the Compact is consensual and not ground-breaking, it has the potential to frame the progressive development of international migration law on this issue of common interest. Labour migration is indeed mainstreamed across most of the twenty-three objectives, while several of them are specifically dedicated to this important question.

The most promising avenue is endorsed in objective 5 and lies in the commitment to 'enhance availability and flexibility of pathways for regular migration [...] in a manner that facilitates labour mobility and decent work reflecting demographic and labour market realities'.[8] The actions identified by the Compact to realize this commitment offer a common line of conduct with a view to framing the future development of intergovernmental cooperation. The first three actions agreed on by Member States provide the overall direction and sound like a normative agenda:

- 'Develop human rights-based and gender-responsive bilateral, regional and multilateral labour mobility agreements with sector-specific standards terms of employment';

- 'Facilitate regional and cross-regional labour mobility through international and bilateral cooperation arrangements, such as free movement regimes, visa liberalization or multiple country visas, and labour mobility cooperation frameworks';

- 'Review and revise existing options and pathways for regular migration, with a view to optimize skills matching in labour markets, address demographic realities and development challenges and opportunities, in accordance with local and national labour market demands and skills supply.'[9]

This comprehensive approach based on a combination of domestic, bilateral, regional, and multilateral actions is reinforced by several other objectives focusing on labour migration. They include the following commitments: to facilitate fair and ethical recruitment to guarantee decent work and fight all forms of exploitation (objective 6); to enhance mutual recognition of skills, qualification, and competences of migrant workers (objective 18); and to ensure the portability of social security entitlements and earned benefits (objective 22).

The commitments endorsed in the Global Compact to frame the future development of the international agenda on labour migration are significant and ambitious. However, they are obviously aspirational and, thus, constitute a general guidance which remains prospective in essence. While the Compact has the potential to make the difference on this long-neglected issue, this will heavily depend on whether Member States will honour their commitments and how they will translate them into concrete actions.

In our international system, the state was and remains today the primary subject of international law in every sense of the term. It must, however, now contend with a multitude of other international actors (including international organizations, non-governmental organizations, individuals, and multinational enterprises). Some of

---

[8] Global Compact for Migration (n 4) para 21.   [9] ibid.

them, such as the cities, are increasingly becoming a new counter power. This development is still in evolution and not yet a revolution. It collides with a powerful force of inertia as states continue to create the rules of the international game. Nonetheless, states are more aware than ever of the need for revitalizing multilateralism, because they 'are all countries of origin, transit and destination' and 'no country can address the challenges and opportunities of this global phenomenon on its own'.[10]

While reaffirming their commitment to international law, states have recognized in the Global Compact 'the centrality of a comprehensive and integrated approach' and their shared responsibilities to address the benefits and challenges of migration.[11] The crash test of multilateralism lies in their ability to move from rhetoric to action. If they fail to do so, the recent and unprecedented mobilization of the international community will be remembered as yet another missed opportunity in the long and turbulent history of migration. In this field as in many others, 'the difficulty lies, not in the new ideas, but in escaping from the old ones, which ramify, for those brought up as most of us have been, into every corner of our minds'.[12]

---

[10] ibid paras 11 and 39.   [11] ibid paras 9–14 and 39.
[12] JM Keynes, *The Collected Writings of John Maynard Keynes: The General Theory of Employment, Interest and Money*, Vol 7 (first published 1936, Palgrave MacMillan St Martin's Press for the Royal Economic Society 1973) xxiii.

Bibliography

Abbott K and D Snidal, 'Hard and Soft Law in International Governance' (2000) 54 International Organization 421–56

Abi-Saab G, 'Cours général de droit international public' (1987) 207 Collected Course of the Hague Academy of International Law 9

Abram EF, 'The Child's Right to Family Unity in International Immigration Law' (1995) 17(4) Law and Policy 397–439

Abramson K, 'Beyond Consent, Towards Safeguarding Human Rights: Implementing the United Nations Trafficking Protocol' (2003) 44 Harv Int'l L J 473–502

Acer E and J Goodman, 'Reaffirming Rights: Human Rights Protections of Migrants, Asylum Seekers, and Refugees in Immigration Detention' (2010) 24 Geo Immigr L J 507–31

Acosta Arcarazo D and A Geddes, 'Transnational Diffusion or Different Models? Regional Approaches to Migration Government in the European Union and Mercosur' (2014) 16(1) EJML 19–44

Adeniran AI, *Migration and Regional Integration in West Africa: A Borderless ECOWAS* (Palgrave Macmillan 2014)

Adepoju A, 'Operationalizing the ECOWAS Protocol on Free Movement of Persons: Prospects for Sub-Regional Trade and Development' in M Panizzon, G Zürcher, and E Fornalé (eds), *The Palgrave Handbook of International Labour Migration: Law and Policy Perspectives* (Palgrave 2015)

Adepoju A, A Boulton, and M Levin, 'Promoting Integration through Mobility: Free Movement under ECOWAS' (2010) 29(3) RSQ 120–44

Aga Khan S, 'Legal Problems Relating to Refugees and Displaced Persons' (1976) 149(I) Collected Courses of the Hague Academy of International Law 287

Akinboade OA, 'A Review of the Status, Challenges and Innovations Regarding Temporary Immigration of Labour in the Regional Economic Areas of Africa' (2014) 15(1) Journal of International Migration and Integration 27–47

Aleinikoff TA, 'International Legal Norms and Migration: A Report' in TA Aleinikoff and V Chetail (eds), *Migration and International Legal Norms* (TMC Asser Press 2003)

Aleinikoff TA, 'International Legal Norms on Migration: Substance without Architecture' in R Cholewinski, R Perruchoud, and E Macdonald (eds), *International Migration Law: Developing Paradigms and Key Challenges* (TMC Asser Press 2007)

Aleinikoff TA, 'The Mandate of the Office of the United Nations High Commissioner for Refugees' in V Chetail and C Bauloz (eds), *Research Handbook on International Law and Migration* (Edward Elgar 2014)

Aleinikoff TA and S Martin, 'Making the Global Compacts Work: What Future for Refugees and Migrants?' (2018) The Andrew & Renata Kaldor Centre for International Refugee Law and The Zolberg Institute on Migration and Mobility Policy Brief No 6

Alemayehu G and H Kebret, 'Regional Economic Integration in Africa: A Review of Problems and Prospects with a Case Study of COMESA' (2007) 17(3) Journal of African Economies 357–94

Aljehani A, 'The Legal Definition of the Smuggling of Migrants in Light of the Provisions of the Migrant Smuggling Protocol' (2015) 79(2) JCL 122–37

Allain J, 'No Effective Trafficking Definition Exists: Domestic Implementation of the Palermo Protocol' (2014) 7 Alb Govt L Rev 111–42

Alland D and C Teitgen-Colly, *Traité du droit de l'asile* (Presses universitaires de France 2002)

Alston P, 'Core Labour Standards and the Transformation of International Labour Rights Regime' (2004) 15(3) EJIL 457–521

Alvarez JE, 'Constitutional Interpretation in International Organizations' in J-M Coicaud and V Heiskanen (eds), *The Legitimacy of International Organizations* (United Nations University Press 2001)

Amerasinghe CF, *State Responsibility for Injuries to Aliens* (Clarendon Press 1967)

Amerasinghe CF, *Principles of the Institutional Law of International Organizations* (2nd edn, CUP 2005)

Amerasinghe CF, *Diplomatic Protection* (OUP 2008)

Anderfuhren-Wayne CS, 'Family Unity in Immigration and Refugee Matters: United States and European Approaches' (1996) 8(3) IJRL 347–82

Andrijasevic R and W Walters, 'The International Organization for Migration and the International Government of Borders' (2010) 28 Society and Space 977–99

Angenendt S and A Koch, 'Global Migration Governance and Mixed Flows: Implications for Development-centred Policies' (2017) SWP Research Paper

Angenendt S and N Biehler, 'On the Way to a Global Compact on Refugees: The "Zero Draft"—A Positive, but not yet Sufficient Step' (2018) SWP Comments 18

Anghie A, 'Francisco de Vitoria and the Colonial Origins of International Law' (1996) 5(3) Social and Legal Studies 321–36

Anghie A, *Imperialism, Sovereignty and the Making of International Law* (CUP 2004)

Anker DE, 'Refugee Law, Gender and the Human Rights Paradigm' (2002) 15 Harv Hum Rts L J 133–54

Anzilotti D, 'La responsabilité internationale des Etats à raison des dommages soufferts par des étrangers' (1906) 13 RGDIP 5–29

Arias H, 'The Non-Liability of States for Damages Suffered by Foreigners in the Course of a Riot, and Insurrection, or a Civil War' (1913) 7 AJIL 724–66

Arboleda E, 'Refugee Definition in Africa and Latin America: The Lessons of Pragmatism' (1991) 3 IJRL 185–207

Ashutosh I and A Mountz, 'Migration Management for the Benefit of Whom? Interrogating the Work of the International Organization for Migration' (2011) 15(1) Citizenship Studies 21–38

Atak I and JC Simeon, 'Human Trafficking: Mapping the Legal Boundaries of International Refugee Law and Criminal Justice' (2014) 12 JICJ 1019–38

Augusto Cançado Trindade A, *International Law for Humankind: Towards a New Jus Gentium* (Brill 2013)

Aust A, 'The Theory and Practice of Informal International Instruments' (1986) 35 ICLQ 787–812

Aust A, *Handbook of International Law* (2nd edn, CUP 2010)

Ayoub L and S-M Wong 'Separated and Unequal' (2006) 32(2) Wm Mitchell L Rev 559–97

Bailliet C (ed), *Non-State Actors, Soft Law and Protection Regimes* (CUP 2012)

Baker G, 'Right of Entry or Right of Refusal? Hospitality in the Law of Nature and Nations' (2011) 37 Rev Int'l Stud 1423–45

Bakewell O, 'Conceptualising Displacement and Migration: Processes, Conditions and Categories' in K Koser and S Martin (eds), *The Migration–Displacement Nexus: Patterns, Processes and Policies* (Berghahn Books 2011)

Bagshaw S, 'Benchmarks or Deutschmarks? Determining the Criteria for the Repatriation of Refugees to Bosnia and Herzegovina' (1997) 9 IJRL 566–92

Bagshaw S, *Developing a Normative Framework for the Protection of Internally Displaced Persons* (Transnational Publishers 2005)

Baird T, 'Defining Human Smuggling in Migration Research: An Appraisal and Critique' (2016) EUI Working Papers RSCAS 2016/30

von Bar L, 'L'expulsion des étrangers' (1886) JDI 1–20

Barist J and others, 'Who May Leave: A Review of Soviet Practice Restricting Emigration on Grounds of Knowledge of "State Secrets" in Comparison with Standards of International Law and the Policies of Other States' (1987) 15(3) Hofstra L Rev 381–442

Barnett M and M Finnemore, 'The Politics, Power, and Pathologies of International Organizations' (1999) 53 International Organization 699–732

Barnett M, 'Humanitarianism with a Sovereign Face: UNHCR in the Global Undertow' (2001) 35 International Migration Review 244–77

Barnett M, 'UNHCR and the Ethics of Repatriation' (2001) 10 Forced Migration Review 31–34

Barnes R, 'Refugee Law at Sea' (2004) 53(1) ICLQ 47–77

Barthélemy J, 'François de Vitoria' in *Les fondateurs du droit international* (first published 1904, Edition Panthéon-Assas 2014)

Barutciski M, 'The Reinforcement of Non-Admission Policies and the Subversion of UNHCR: Displacement and Internal Assistance in Bosnia-Herzegovina' (1996) 8 IJRL 49–110

Barutciski M, 'Involuntary Repatriation when Refugee Protection is No Longer Necessary: Moving Forward after the 48th Session of the Executive Committee' (1998) 10 IJRL 236–55

Barutciski M, 'A Critical View on UNHCR's Mandate Dilemmas' (2002) 14 IJRL 365–81

Basdevant S, 'Théorie générale de la condition de l'étranger' in A De Lapradelle and JP Niboyet (eds), *Répertoire de droit international*, vol 8 (Sirey 1930)

Bashford A, 'Immigration Restriction: Rethinking Period and Place from Settler Colonies to Postcolonial Nations' (2014) 9 Journal of Global History 26–48

Bashford A and J McAdam, 'The Right to Asylum: Britain's 1905 Aliens Act and the Evolution of Refugee Law' (2014) 32(2) LHR 309–50

Bast J, 'Commentary on the Annex on Movement of Natural Persons Supplying Services Under the Agreement' in R Wolfrum, P-T Stoll, and C Feinäugle (eds) *WTO–Trade in Services* (Martinus Nijhoff 2008)

Battjes H, 'The *Soering* Threshold: Why Only Fundamental Values Prohibit *Refoulement* in ECHR Case Law' (2009) 11 EJML (2009) 205–19

Battjes H, 'Subsidiary Protection and Other Alternative Forms of Protection' in V Chetail and C Bauloz (eds), *Research Handbook on International Law and* Migration (Edward Elgar Publishing 2014)

Bauloz C, 'The (Mis)Use of International Humanitarian Law under Article 15(c) of the EU Qualification Directive' in J-F Durieux and D Cantor (eds), *Refuge from Inhumanity: Enriching Refugee Protection Standards Through Recourse to International Humanitarian Law* (Martinus Nijhoff 2013)

Bauloz C, *A Comparative Thematic Mapping of Global Migration Initiatives: Lessons Learned towards a Global Compact for Safe, Orderly and Regular Migration* (IOM Migration Research Leaders' Syndicate 2017)

Baxter R, 'International Law in "Her Infinite Variety"' (1980) 29(4) ICLQ 549–66

Bayefsky AF, 'The Principle of Equality or Non-discrimination in International Law' (1990) 11(2) HRLJ 1–34

Beaulac S, *The Power of Language in the Making of International Law: The Word Sovereignty in Bodin and Vattel and the Myth of Westphalia* (Martinus Nijhoff 2004)

Bederman DJ, 'Grotius and his Followers on Treaty Construction' (2001) 3 J Hist Int'l L 18–37

Bederman DJ, *The Spirit of International Law* (University of Georgia Press 2002)

Bederman DJ, *International Law in Antiquity* (CUP 2004)

Bellace JR, 'The ILO Declaration of Fundamental Principles and Rights at Work' (2001) 17(3) IJCLLIR 269–87

Bem K, 'The Coming of a "Blank Cheque": Europe, the 1951 Convention, and the 1967 Protocol' (2004) 16(4) IJRL 609–27

Bentham J, *Introduction to the Principles of Morals and Legislation* (Payne & Son, London, 1789)

Bernal N, MN Prada, and R Urueña, 'Intra-Regional Mobility in South America: The Andean Community and MERCOSUR' in M Panizzon, G Zürcher, and E Fornalé (eds), *The Palgrave Handbook of International Labour Migration: Law and Policy Perspectives* (Palgrave 2015)

Besson S, 'The Principle of Non-Discrimination in the Convention on the Rights of the Child' (2005) 13 Int'l J Child Rts 433–61

Betts A and JF Durieux, 'Convention Plus as a Norm-Setting Exercise' (2007) 20 JRS 509–35

Betts A, 'Conclusion' in A Betts (ed), *Global Migration Governance* (OUP 2011)

Betts A (ed), *Global Migration Governance* (OUP 2011)

Betts A, 'Regime Complexity and International Organizations: UNHCR as a Challenged Institution' (2013) 13 Global Governance 69–81

Bhabha J, 'Internationalist Gatekeepers? The Tension between Asylum Advocacy and Human Rights' (2002) 15 Harv Hum Rts J 151–81

Bhabha J, '"More than their Share of Sorrows": International Migration Law and the Rights of Children' (2003) 22 Saint Louis University Public Law Review 253–74

Bhabha J and M Zard, 'Smuggled or Trafficked?' (2006) 25 Forced Migration Review 6–8

Bhabha J, 'Human Mobility and the Longue Durée: The Prehistory of Global Migration Law' (2017) 111 AJIL Unbound 136–41

Bianchi A, 'Human Rights and the Magic of Jus Cogens' (2008) 19(3) EJIL 491–508

Bjorklund AK and A Reinisch (eds), *International Investment Law and Soft Law* (Edward Elgar 2012)

Black R and others, 'Migration and Development: Causes and Consequences' in R Penninx, M Berger, and K Kraal (eds), *The Dynamics of International Migration and Settlement in Europe: A State of the Art* (Amsterdam University Press 2006)

Blackham A, 'A Proposal for Enhanced Supervision of the Refugee Convention' (2013) 26 JRS 392–415

Blake C, 'Normative Instruments in International Human Rights Law: Locating the General Comment' (2008) NYU Law Center for Human Rights and Global Justice Working Paper Series 17/2008

Blay S and M Tsamenyi, 'Reservations and Declarations under the 1951 Convention and the 1967 Protocol Relating to the Status of Refugees' (1990) 2 IJRL 527–61

Blood CG, 'The "True" Source of the Immigration Power and Its Power Consideration in Elian Gonzalez Matter' (2000) 18 BU Int'l LJ 215–45

Bluntschli JC, *Le droit international codifié* (trans MC Lardy, Guillaumin 1895)

Boed R, 'The State of the Right of Asylum in International Law' (1994) 5 Duke J Comp & Int'l L 1–33

Boeles P and others, *European Migration Law* (Intersentia 2009)

Bogusz B and others (eds), *Irregular Migration and Human Rights: Theoretical, European and International Perspectives* (Martinus Nijhoff 2004)

Böhning R, 'The ILO and the New UN Convention on Migrant Workers: The Past and Future' (1991) 25(4) International Migration Review 698–709

Böhning R, *A Brief Account of the ILO and Policies on International Migration* (International Institute for Labour Studies 2012)

Borchard EM, *The Diplomatic Protection of Citizens Abroad or the Law of International Claims* (Banks Law 1915)

Borgnäs E, 'An Overview of the Model Convention Commentaries' (2017) 56 Colum J of Transnat'l L 238–47

Borrás S and K Jacobsson, 'The Open Method of Co-ordination and New Governance Patterns in the EU' (2004) 11(2) JEPP 185–208

Borschberg P, *'Hugo Grotius's Theory of Trans-Oceanic Trade Regulation: Revisiting Mare Liberum (1609)'* (2006) International Law and Justice Working Papers, New York University School of Law

Bosma U, 'Beyond the Atlantic: Connecting Migration and World History in the Age of Imperialism, 1840–1940' (2007) 52(1) Int'l Rev Soc Hist 116–23

Bosniak LS, 'Human Rights, State Sovereignty and the Protection of Undocumented Migrants under the International Migrant Workers Convention' (1991) 25(4) International Migration Review 737–70

Bossuyt MJ, *L'interdiction de la discrimination dans le droit international des droits de l'homme* (Bruylant 1976)

Bossuyt MJ, *Guide to the 'Travaux Préparatoires' of the International Covenant on Civil and Political Rights* (Martinus Nijhoff 1987)

Bostock CM-J, 'The International Legal Obligations Owed to the Asylum-Seekers on the MV Tampa' (2002) 14(2–3) IJRL 279–301

Boswell C, 'The External Dimension of EU Immigration and Asylum Policy' (2003) 79(3) International Affairs 619–38

Boswell C and J Crisp, 'Poverty, International Migration and Asylum' (2004) UNU World Institute for Development Economics Research (UNU-WIDER) Policy Brief No 8

Bothe M, 'Legal and Non-legal Norms: A Meaningful Distinction in International Relations?' (1980) XI NYIL 65–95

Bourgon S, 'The Impact of Terrorism on the Principle of 'Non-Refoulement' of Refugees: The Suresh Case before the Supreme Court of Canada' (2003) 1 JICJ 169–85

Bouteillet-Paquet D, 'Passing the Buck: A Critical Analysis of the Readmission Policy Implemented by the European Union and Its Member States' (2003) 5 European Journal of Migration and Law 359–77

Bouvé CL, *A Treatise on the Laws Governing Exclusion and Expulsion of Aliens in the United States* (John Byrne and Co 1912)

Bowen HW, *International Law: A Simple Statement of its Principles* (G P Putnam's Sons 1896)

Boyle AE and C Chinkin, *The Making of International Law* (OUP 2007)

Boyle A, 'Soft Law in International Law-Making' in M Evans (ed), *International Law* (OUP 2010)

Brachet J, 'Policing the Desert: The IOM in Libya beyond War and Peace' (2016) 48(2) Antipode 272–92

Bradley M, 'The International Organization for Migration: Gaining Power in the Forced Migration Regime' (2017) 33 Refuge 97–106

Brawley A, *The White Peril: Foreign Relations and Asian Immigration to Australasia and North America 1919–1978* (University of New South Wales Press 1995)

Briggs VM, *Immigration Policy and the American Labor Force* (Johns Hopkins University Press 1984)

Brownlie I, *Principles of Public International Law* (6th edn, OUP 2003)

Brownlie I, *Principles of Public International Law* (7th edn, OUP 2008)

Bruin R and K Wouters, 'Terrorism and the Non-Derogability of Non-Refoulement' (2003) 15 IJRL 5–29

Buckland BS, 'Human Trafficking and Smuggling: Crossover and Overlap' in C Friesendorf (ed), *Strategies Against Human Trafficking: The Role of the Security Sector* (National Defence Academy, Austrian Ministry of Defence and Sports, and Geneva Centre for the Democratic Control of Armed Forces 2009)

Bull H, 'The Grotian Conception of International Society' in H Butterfield and M Wight (eds), *Diplomatic Investigations: Essays in the Theory of International Politics* (Harvard University Press 1966)

Butler PF, '*Legitimacy in a State-System: Vattel's Law of Nations*' in M Donelan (ed), *The Reason of States: A Study in International Political Theory* (Allen and Unwin 1978)

Butterly L, 'Trafficking v. Smuggling; Coercion v. Consent: Conceptual Problems with the Transnational Anti-Trafficking Regime' (2014) 2 UKLSR 45–54

Calavita K, *U.S. Immigration Law and the Control of Labor, 1820–1924* (Academic Press 1984)

Calvo C, *Le droit international: Théorie et pratique* (4th edn, Durand et Pedone-Lauriel/Guillaumin 1888)

Carbonneau TE, 'The Convergence of the Law of State Responsibility for Injury to Aliens and International Human Rights Norms in the Revised Restatement' (1985) 25(1) Virginia J Int'l L 99–123

Carlier J-Y and E Guild (eds), *The Future of Free Movement of Persons in the EU* (Bruylant 2006)

Carlier J-Y, 'Droit d'asile et des réfugiés: de la protection aux droits' (2007) 332 Collected Courses of the Hague Academy of International Law 9

Carty A, *The Decay of International Law? A Reappraisal of the Limits of Legal Imagination in International Affairs* (Manchester University Press 1986)

Carty A, 'Alfred Verdross and Othmar Spann: German Romantic Nationalism, National Socialism and International Law' (1995) 6(1) EJIL 78–97

Carzaniga A, 'The GATS, Mode 4, and Pattern of Commitments' in A Mattoo and A Carzaniga (eds) *Moving People to Deliver Services* (The World Bank/OUP 2003)

Carzaniga A, 'A Warmer Welcome? Access for Natural Persons under PTAs' in JA Marchetti and M Roy (eds) *Opening Markets for Trade in Services: Countries and Sectors in Bilateral and WTO Negotiations* (CUP 2008)

Castañeda C, 'A Call for Rethinking the Sources of International Law: Soft Law and the Other Side of the Coin' (2013) 13 Anuario Mexicano de Derecho Internacional 355–403

Cassese A, *International Law* (OUP 2005)

Cavallar G, *The Rights of Strangers: Theories of International Hospitality, the Global Community, and Political Justice since Vitoria* (Ashgate/Aldershot 2002)

Cavallar G, 'Immigration and Sovereignty: Normative Approaches in the History of International Legal Theory (Pufendorf–Vattel–Bluntschli–Verdross)' (2006) 11 ARIEL 3–22

Cavallar G, 'Vitoria, Grotius, Pufendorf, Wolff and Vattel: Accomplices of European Colonialism and Exploitation or True Cosmopolitans?' (2008) 10 J Hist Int'l L 181–209

Chacon JM, 'Tensions and Trade-Offs: Protecting Trafficking Victims in the Era of Immigration Enforcement' (2010) 158(6) U Pa L Rev 1609–53

Chalidze V, 'The Right of a Convicted Citizen to Leave his Country' (1973) 8(1) Harv CR-CLL Rev 1–13

Chamie J and MG Powers (eds), *International Migration and the Global Community: A Forum on the Report of the Global Commission on International Migration* (Center for Migration Studies New York 2006)

Chamie J and B Mirkin, 'Who's Afraid of International Migration in the United Nations' in R Koslowski (ed), Global Mobility Regimes (Springer 2011)

Chan S (ed), *Entry Denied: Exclusion and the Chinese Community in America, 1882–1943* (Temple University Press 1991)

Chanda R, 'Movement of Natural Persons and the GATS' (2001) 24(5) The World Economy 631–54

Chantre A, *Du séjour et de l'expulsion des étrangers* (Aubert-Schuchardt 1890)

Chapkis W, 'Trafficking, Migration and the Law: Protecting Innocents, Punishing Immigrants' (2003) 17(6) Gender & Society 923–37

Charnovitz S, 'Trade Law Norms on International Migration' in A Aleinikoff and V Chetail (eds), *Migration and International Legal Norms* (TMC Asser Press 2003)

Charney JI, 'Universal International Law' (1993) 87 AJIL 529–51

Chemillier-Gendreau M, 'Un Régime Juridique pour l'Immigration Clandestine' in V Chetail (ed), *Mondialisation, migration et droits de l'homme: le droit international en question*, vol II (Bruylant 2007)

Chetail V and J-F Flauss (eds), *La Convention de Genève du 28 juillet 1951 relative au statut des réfugiés: 50 ans après—bilan et perspectives* (Bruylant 2001)

Chetail V, 'Le principe de non-refoulement et le statut de réfugié en droit international' in V Chetail and J-F Flauss (eds), *La Convention de Genève du 28 juillet 1951 relative au statut des réfugiés 50 ans après: bilan et perspectives* (Emile Bruylant 2001)

Chetail V and V Gowlland-Debbas (eds), *Switzerland and the International Protection of Refugees* (Kluwer Law International 2002)

Chetail V and TA Aleinikoff (eds), *Migration and International Legal Norms* (TMC Asser Press 2003)

Chetail V, 'Le droit des réfugiés à l'épreuve des droits de l'homme' (2004) 37(1) RBDI 155–210

Chetail V, 'La réforme française de l'asile: prélude à la banalisation européenne du droit des réfugiés' (2004) 131(3) JDI 817–65

Chetail V, 'Voluntary Repatriation in Public International Law: Concepts and Contents' (2004) 23(3) RSQ 1–32

Chetail V, 'Le Comité des Nations Unies contre la torture et l'expulsion des étrangers: dix ans de jurisprudence' (2006) 26 RSDIE 63–104

Chetail V, 'The Implementation of the Qualification Directive in France: One Step Forward and Two Steps Backwards' in K Zwaan (ed) *The Qualification Directive: Central Themes, Problem Issues and Implementation in Selected Member States* (Wolf Legal Publishers 2007)

Chetail V (ed), *Mondialisation, migration et droits de l'homme: le droit international en question / Globalization, Migration and Human Rights: International Law Under Review* (Bruylant 2007)

Chetail V, 'Migration, droits de l'homme et souveraineté: le droit international dans tous ses Etats' in V Chetail (ed), *Mondialisation, migration et droits de l'homme: le droit international en question / Globalization, Migration and Human Rights: International Law under Review* (Bruylant 2007)

Chetail V (ed), *Code de droit international des migrations* (Bruylant 2008)

Chetail V, 'Le droit d'avoir des droits en droit international public: réflexions sur la subjectivité internationale de l'individu' in MC Caloz-Tschopp (ed), *Lire Hannah Arendt Aujourd'hui: Pouvoir, Guerre, Pensée, Jugement Politique* (L'Harmattan 2008)

Chetail V, 'Paradigm and Paradox of the Migration-Development Nexus: The New Border for North-South Dialogue' (2008) 51 Germ Yrbk Int'l L 183–215

Chetail V and G Giacca, 'Who Cares? The Right to Health of Migrants' in A Clapham and M Robinson (eds), *Realizing the Right to Health* (Rüffer & Rub 2009)

Chetail V, 'Théorie et pratique de l'asile en droit international classique: étude sur les origines conceptuelles et normatives du droit international des réfugiés' (2011) 115(3) RGDIP 625–52

Chetail V and C Bauloz, 'The European Union and the Challenges of Forced Migration: From Economic Crisis to Protection Crisis?' (2011) Research Report, Florence/Washington, DC, European University Institute, Robert Schuman Centre for Advanced Studies/ Migration Policy Institute

Chetail V and P Haggenmacher (eds), *Vattel's International Law in a XXIst Century Perspective/ Le droit international de Vattel vu du XXIeme siècle* (Martinus Nijhoff 2011)

Chetail V, 'Sources of International Migration Law' in B Opeskin, R Perruchoud, and J Redpath-Cross (eds), *Foundations of International Migration Law* (CUP 2012)

Chetail V, Droit international des migrations: fondements et limites du multilatéralisme' in R Mehdi and H Ghérari (eds) *La société internationale face aux défis migratoires* (Bruylant 2012)

Chetail V and C Bauloz, 'Is Switzerland an EU Member State? Asylum Law Harmonization through the Backdoor' in H Lambert, J McAdam, and M Fullerton (eds) *The Global Reach of European Refugee Law* (CUP 2013)

Chetail V, 'Vattel and the American Dream: An Inquiry into the Reception of the *Law of Nations* in the United States' in V Chetail and P-M Dupuy (eds), *The Roots of International Law: Liber Amicorum Peter Haggenmacher* (Martinus Nijhoff 2013)

Chetail V, 'The Human Rights of Migrants in General International Law: From Minimum Standards to Fundamental Rights' (2013) 28(1) Geo Immigr L J 225–55

Chetail V and MA Braeunlich, 'Stranded Migrants: Giving Structure to a Multifaceted Notion' (2013) Global Migration Research Paper No 5

Chetail V, 'Are Refugee Rights Human Rights? An Unorthodox Questioning on the Relations between Refugee Law and Human Rights Law' in R Rubio-Marín, *Human Rights and Immigration* (OUP 2014)

Chetail V, 'The Swiss Vote against Mass Immigration and International Law: A Preliminary Assessment' (2014) Global Migration Policy Brief 1

Chetail V and C Bauloz (eds), *Research Handbook on International Law and Migration* (Edward Elgar Publishing 2014)

Chetail V and C Laly-Chevalier (eds), *Asile et extradition: Théorie et pratique de l'exclusion du statut de réfugié* (Bruylant 2014)

Chetail V, 'Les relations entre le droit de l'extradition et le droit des réfugiés: étude de l'article 1F(b) de la Convention de Genève du 28 juillet 1951' in V Chetail and C Laly-Chevalier (eds), *Asile et extradition: Théorie et pratique de l'exclusion du statut de réfugié* (Bruylant 2014)

Chetail V, 'The Transnational Movement of Persons under General International Law– Mapping the Customary Law Foundations of International Migration Law' in V Chetail and C Bauloz (eds), *Research Handbook on International Law and Migration* (Edward Elgar Publishing 2014)

Chetail V, 'Armed Conflict and Forced Migration: A Systemic Approach to International Humanitarian Law, Refugee Law and Human Rights Law' in A Clapham and P Gaeta (eds) *The Oxford Handbook of International Law in Armed Conflict* (OUP 2014)

Chetail V, 'Les relations entre droit international privé et droit international des réfugiés: histoire d'une brève rencontre' (2014) 141(2) JDI 447–75

Chetail V, 'The Transfer and Deportation of Civilians' in A Clapham, P Gaeta, and M Sassòli (eds), *The 1949 Geneva Conventions: A Commentary* (OUP 2015)

Chetail V (ed), *International Law and Migration* (Edward Elgar Publishing 2016)

Chetail V, 'Migration and International Law: A Short Introduction' in V Chetail (ed), *International Law and Migration* Vol 1 (Edward Elgar Publishing 2016)

Chetail V, 'Is There Any Blood on My Hands? Deportation as a Crime of International Law' (2016) 29 LJIL 917–43

Chetail V, 'Looking Beyond the Rhetoric of the Refugee Crisis: The Failed Reform of the Common European Asylum System' (2016) 5 European Journal of Human Rights 584–601

Chetail V, P De Bruycker, and F Maiani (eds), *Reforming the Common European Asylum System: The New European Refugee Law* (Brill | Nijhoff 2016)

Chetail V, 'The Common European Asylum System: Bric-à-brac or System?' in V Chetail, P De Bruycker, and F Maiani (eds), *Reforming the Common European Asylum System: The New European Refugee Law* (Brill | Nijhoff 2016)

Chetail V, 'Sovereignty and Migration in the Doctrine of the Law of Nations: An Intellectual History of Hospitality from Vitoria to Vattel' (2016) 27(4) EJIL 901–22

Chetail V, 'The Architecture of International Migration Law: A Deconstructivist Design of Complexity and Contradiction' (2017) 111 AJIL Unbound 18–23

Chetail V, 'Conceptualizing International Migration Law' (2017) ASIL Proc 201–04

Chetail V, 'The Committee on the Protection of the Rights of All Migrant Workers and Members of Their Families' in P Alston and F Mégret (eds), *The United Nations and Human Rights: A Critical Appraisal* (2nd edn, OUP 2018)

Chimni BS, 'The Meaning of Words and the Role of UNHCR in Voluntary Repatriation' (1993) 5(3) IJRL 442–60

Chimni BS, 'The Geopolitics of Refugee Studies: A View from the South' (1998) 11(4) JRS 350–74

Chimni BS, 'Reforming the International Refugee Regime: A Dialogic Model' (2001) 14(2) JRS 151–68

Chimni BS, 'From Resettlement to Involuntary Repatriation: Towards a Critical History of Durable Solutions to Refugee Problems' (2004) 23 (3) RSQ 55–73

Chinedu Okafor O and P Lekwuwa Okoronkwo, 'Re-Configuring *Non-Refoulement*? The *Suresh* Decision, "Security Relativism" and the International Human Rights Perspective' (2003) 15 IJRL 30–67

Chinkin C, 'The Challenge of Soft Law: Development and Change in International Law' (1989) 38(4) ICLQ 850–66

Chinkin C, 'Normative Development in the International Legal System' in D Shelton (ed), *Commitment and Compliance: The Role of Non-binding Norms in the International Legal System* (OUP 2000)

Cholewinski R, P de Guchteneire, and A Pécoud (eds), *Migration and Human Rights: The United Nations Convention on Migrant Workers' Rights* (CUP 2009)

Cholewinski R, 'Evaluating Bilateral Labour Migration Agreements in the Light of Human and Labour Rights' in M Panizzon, G Zürcher, and E Fornalé (eds), *The Palgrave Handbook of International Labour Migration: Law and Policy Perspectives* (Palgrave 2015)

Cholewinski R, *Migrant Workers in International Human Rights Law: Their Protection in Countries of Employment* (OUP 1997)

Cholewinski R, *Study on Obstacles to Effective Access of Irregular Migrants to Minimum Social Rights* (Council of Europe 2005)

Cholewinski R, 'The Rights of Migrant Workers' in R Cholewinski, R Perruchoud, and E MacDonald (eds), *International Migration Law: Developing Paradigms and Key Challenges* (TMC Asser Press 2007)

Cholewinski R, R Perruchoud, and E MacDonald (eds), *International Migration Law: Developing Paradigms and Key Challenges* (TMC Asser Press 2007)

Cholewinski R, 'The Human and Labor Rights of Migrants: Visions of Equality' (2007–2008) 22 Geo Immigr LJ 177–219

Cholewinski R, 'Human Rights of Migrants: The Dawn of a New Era?' (2010) 24 Geo Immigr L J 585–615

Cholewinski R, 'Labour Migration Management and the Rights of Migrant Workers' in A Edwards and C Ferstman (eds), *Human Security and Non-Citizens: Law, Policy and International Affairs* (CUP 2010)

Cholewinski R, 'International Labour Migration' in B Opeskin, R Perruchoud, and J Redpath-Cross (eds), *Foundations of International Migration Law* (CUP 2012)

Cholewinski R, 'Migration for Employment' in R Plender, *Issues in International Migration Law* (Brill/Nijhoff 2015)

Chowdhury TMR, *Legal Framework of International Supervision* (University of Stockholm 1986)

Chowdhury SR, 'Response to the Refugee Problems in Post-Cold War Era: Some Existing and Emerging Norms of International Law' (1995) 7(1) IJRL 100–18

Christov T, 'Liberal Internationalism Revisited: Grotius, Vattel, and the International Order of States' (2005) 10(7) The European Legacy 561–84

Chudinovskikh O, 'Migration and Bilateral Agreements in the Commonwealth of Independent States' in OECD, *Free Movement of Workers and Labour Market Adjustment: Recent Experiences from OECD Countries and the European Union* (OECD Publishing 2012)

Clark T and F Crépeau, 'Mainstreaming Refugee Rights: The 1951 Refugee Convention and International Human Rights Law' (1999) 17(4) NQHR 389–410

Clark T and J Simeon, 'UNHCR International Protection Policies 2000–2013: From Cross-Road to Gaps and Responses' (2014) 33 RSQ 1–33

Clifford J, 'Equality' in D Shelton (ed), *The Oxford Handbook of International Human Rights Law* (OUP 2013)

Cohen R (ed), *The Cambridge Survey of World Migration* (CUP 1995)

Cohn RL, *Mass Migration under Sail: European Immigration to the Antebellum United States* (CUP 2009)

Colella A, 'Les réserves à la Convention de Genève (28 juillet 1951) et au Protocole de New York (31 janvier 1967) sur le statut des réfugiés' (1989) 35 AFDI 446–75

Coleman N, 'Non-Refoulement Revised: Renewed Review of the Status of the Principle of Non-Refoulement as Customary International Law' (2003) 5(1) EJML 23–68

Condinanzi M and others, *Citizenship of the Union and Free Movement of Persons* (Martinus Nijhoff 2008)

Conforti B, 'The Theory of Competence in Verdross' (1995) 6(1) EJIL 70–77

Cornelisse G, *Immigration Detention and Human Rights: Rethinking Territorial Sovereignty* (Brill 2010)

Cortes KE, 'Are Refugees Different from Economic Immigrants? Some Empirical Evidence on the Heterogeneity of Immigrant Groups in the United States' (2004) 86(2) Review of Economics and Statistics 465–480

Costello C, 'Human Rights and the Elusive Universal Subject: Immigration Detention Under International Human Rights and EU Law' (2012) 19(1) Indiana Journal of Global Legal Studies 257–303

Costello C, *The Human Rights of Migrants and Refugees in European Law* (OUP 2015)

Cotler I, 'The Right to Leave and to Family Reunification' (1987) 28(3) Cde D 625–47

Craies WF, 'The Right of Aliens to Enter British Territory' (1890) 6(21) LQR 27–41

Cranston M, 'The Political and Philosophical Aspects of the Right to Leave and to Return' in K Vasak and S Liskofsky (eds), *The Right to Leave and to Return: Papers and Recommendations of the International Colloquium Held in Uppsala, Sweden, 19–20 June 1972* (The American Jewish Committee 1976)

Craven M, 'Non-Discrimination and Equality' in M Craven (ed), *The International Covenant on Economic, Social and Cultural Rights: A Perspective on Its Development* (Clarendon Press 1995)

Craven M, 'The International Covenant on Economic, Social and Cultural Rights' in R Hanski and M Suksi (eds), *An Introduction to the International Protection of Human Rights: A Textbook* (Institute for Human Rights 1999)

Crawley H, *Refugees and Gender: Law and Process* (Jordan Publishing Limited 2001)

Crawley H and others, 'Destination Europe? Understanding the Dynamics and Drivers of Mediterranean Migration in 2015' (2016) Unravelling the Mediterranean Migration Crisis (MEDMIG) Final Report

Crawley H and D Skleparis, 'Refugees, Migrants, Neither, Both: Categorical Fetishism and the Politics of Bounding in Europe's "Migration Crisis"' (2018) 44(1) Journal of Ethnic and Migration Studies 48–64

Crépeau F, *Droit d'asile: De l'hospitalité aux contrôles migratoires* (Bruylant 1995)

Crépeau F and I Atak, 'Global Migration Governance: Avoiding Commitments on Human Rights, Yet Tracing a Course for Cooperation' (2016) 34(2) Netherlands Quarterly of Human Rights 113–46

Crisp J and K Long, 'Safe and Voluntary Refugee Repatriation: From Principle to Practice' (2016) 4(3) JMHS 141–47

Crock M (ed), *Migrants and Rights* (Routledge 2016)

Cunliffe SA and M Pugh, 'UNHCR as Leader in Humanitarian Assistance: A Triumph of Politics over Law?' in F Nicholson and P Twomey (eds), *Refugee Rights and Realities: Evolving International Concepts and Regimes* (CUP 1999)

Daley K and N Kelley, 'Particular Social Group: A Human Rights Based Approach in Canadian Jurisprudence' (2000) 12 IJRL 148–74

D'Amato A, 'Softness in International Law: A Self-Serving Quest for New Legal Materials: A Reply to Jean d'Aspremont' (2009) 20 EJIL 897–910

Dankwa EVO, 'Working Paper on Article 2(3) of the International Covenant on Economic, Social and Cultural Rights' (1987) HRQ 230–49

D'Aspremont J, 'Softness in International Law: A Self-Serving Quest for New Legal Materials' (2008) 19(5) EJIL 1075–93

D'Aspremont J, 'The Systemic Integration of International Law by Domestic Courts: Domestic Judges as Architects of the Consistency of the International Legal Order' in A Nollkaemper and OK Fauchald (eds) *The Practice of International and National Courts and the (De-) Fragmentation of International Law* (Hart Publishing 2012)

Daudet Y, 'Preface' in L Dubin, *La protection des normes sociales dans les échanges internationaux* (Presses Universitaires d'Aix-Marseilles 2003)

Davis GB, *The Elements of International Law* (Harper and Brothers 1908)

Davis K, 'The Migrations of Human Populations' (1974) 231(3) Scientific American 92–105

Dauvergne C, 'Sovereignty, Migration and the Rule of Law in Global Times' (2004) 67(4) The Modern Law Review 588–615

Dauvergne C, *Making People Illegal: What Globalization Means for Migration and Law* (CUP 2009)

Dauvergne C, *The New Politics of Immigration and the End of Settler Societies* (CUP 2016)

Dawson LR, 'Labour Mobility and the WTO: The Limits of GATS Mode 4' (2013) 51(1) International Migration 1–23

Decencière-Ferrandière A, *La responsabilité internationale des Etats à raison des dommages subis par des étrangers* (Rousseau 1925)

Degan VD, *Sources of International Law* (Martinus Nijhoff 1997)

Dembour M-B, *When Humans Become Migrants: Study of the European Court of Human Rights with an Inter-American Counterpoint* (OUP 2015)

Detrick S, *A Commentary on the United Nations Convention on the Rights of the Child* (Martinus Nijhoff 1999)

De Boer T, 'Closing Legal Black Holes: The Role of Extraterritorial Jurisdiction in Refugee Rights Protection' (2014) 28(1) JRS 118–34

De Louter J, *Le Droit International Public Positif,* vol 1 (OUP 1920)

De Schutter O, *International Human Rights Law* (CUP 2010)

Den Heijer M, 'Whose Rights and Which Rights? The Continuing Story of Non-Refoulement under the European Convention on Human Rights' (2008) 10 EJML 277–314

De Wet E and J Vidmar, 'Conflicts between International Paradigms: Hierarchy versus Systemic Integration' (2013) 2(2) Global Constitutionalism 196–217

Devillard A, 'The Principle of Non-Discrimination and Entry, Stay and Expulsion of Foreigners Living with HIV/AIDS' (2009) 11(2) IJMS 91–103

Dinstein Y, 'Freedom of Emigration and Soviet Jewry' (1974) 4 Israel Ybk Hum Rts 266–74

Dinstein Y, 'Discrimination and International Human Rights' (1985) 15 Israel Yrbk Hum Rts 11–27

Di Robilant A, 'Genealogies of Soft Law' (2006) 54 Am J Comp L 499–554

Doomernik J, 'Migrant Smuggling between Two Logics: Migration Dynamics and State Policies' (2013) 48(3) The International Spectator 113–29

Doebbler CFJ, *The Principle of Non-Discrimination in International Law* (CD Publishing 2007)

Doyle MW, 'The Model International Mobility Convention Commentaries' (2017) 56 Columbia Journal of Transnational Law 219–37

Duchatellier M and C Phuong, 'The African Contribution to the Protection of Internally Displaced Persons: A Commentary on the 2009 Kampala Convention' in V Chetail and C Bauloz (eds), *The Research Handbook on International Law and Migration* (Edward Elgar Publishing 2014)

Ducasse-Rogier M, *The International Organization for Migration 1951–2001* (IOM 2001)

Duffy A, 'Expulsion to Face Torture? *Non-Refoulement* in International Law' (2008) 20(3) IJRL 373–90

Dugard J, 'The Application of Customary International Law Affecting Human Rights by National Tribunals' (1982) 76 ASIL Proc 245–51

Dugard J, *International Law: A South African Perspective* (Juta 2011)

Dumas J, 'La responsabilité des Etats à raison des crimes et délits commis sur leur territoire au préjudice d'étrangers' (1931) 36 Collected Courses of the Hague Academy of International Law 183

Dunstan R, 'United Kingdom: Breaches of Article 31 of the 1951 Refugee Convention' (1998) 10 IJRL 205–13

Dupuy P-M, 'L'individu et le droit International: Théorie des droits de l'Homme et fondements du droit International' (1987) 32 APD 119

Dupuy P-M, 'Soft Law and the International Law of the Environment' (1991) 12(2) Mich J Int'l L 420–35

Dupuy P-M, 'L'Unité de l'ordre juridique international: cours général de droit international public' (2000) 297 Collected Courses of the Hague Academy of International Law 1

Edwards A, 'Traffic in Human Being: At the Intersection of Criminal Justice, Human Rights, Asylum/Migration and Labor' (2008) 36 Denv J Int'l L & Pol'y 9–53

Edwards A, 'Human Rights, Refugees, and the Right "to Enjoy" Asylum' (2005) 17(2) IJRL 293–330

Edwards A, 'Back to Basics: The Right to Liberty and Security of Person and 'Alternatives to Detention' of Refugees, Asylum-Seekers, Stateless Persons and Other Migrants' (2011) UNHCR Legal and Protection Policy Research Series, Division of International Protection

Eide A and G Alfredsson, 'Introduction' in A Eide and G Alfredsson (eds), *The Universal Declaration of Human Rights: A Common Standard of Achievement* (Martinus Nijhoff 1999)

Eguiguren M, 'Regional Migratory Policies within the Andean Community of Nations: Crisis vs. Reinforcement of Freedom of Movement within the Region' in S Nita and others (eds), *Migration, Free Movement and Regional Integration* (UNESCO/UNU-CRIS 2017)

Einarsen T, 'Discrimination and Consequences for the Position of Aliens' (1995) 64 Nord J Int'l L 429–52

Elie J, 'The Historical Roots of Cooperation Between the UN High Commissioner for Refugees and the International Organization for Migration' (2010) 16 Global Governance 345–60

Ellerman D, 'Policy Research on Migration and Development' (2003) World Bank Policy Research Working Paper No 3117

Elliott J, '(Mis)Identification of Victims of Human Trafficking: The Case of *R v O*' (2009) 21 IJRL 727–41

Elliott J, *The Role of Consent in Human Trafficking* (Routledge 2015)

Emmer PC and M Mörner (eds), *European Expansion and Migration: Essays on the Intercontinental Migration from Africa, Asia, and Europe* (Berg 1992)

Erasmus E (ed), *MME on the Move: A Stocktaking of Migration, Mobility, Employment and Higher Education in Six African Regional Economic Communities* (International Centre for Migration Policy Development 2013)

Errington EJ, *Emigrant Worlds and Transatlantic Communities: Migration to Upper Canada in the First Half of the Nineteenth Century* (McGill-Queen's University Press 2007)

Falk R, *Human Rights and State Sovereignty* (Holmes and Meier 1981)

Fahrmeir A, O Faron, and P Weil (ed), *Migration Control in the North Atlantic World: The Evolution of State Practices in Europe and the United States from the French Revolution to the Inter-War Period* (Berghahn Books 2003)

Farmer A, 'Non-Refoulement and Jus Cogens: Limiting Anti-Terror Measures that Threaten Refugee Protection' (2008) 23 Geo Immigr L J 1–38

Fauchille P, *Traité de droit international public* (Rousseau 1922)

Fauchille P, 'The Rights of Emigration and Immigration' (1924) 9 Int'l Labour Rev 324–33

Feller E and A Klug, 'Refugees, United Nations High Commissioner for (UNHCR)' (2014) Max Planck Encyclopedia of Public International Law

Fenwick CG, 'The Authority of Vattel' (1913) 7 Am Political Science Rev 395–410

Fenwick CG, 'The New Immigration Law and the Exclusion of Japanese' (1924) 18(3) AJIL 518–23

Fenwick CG, *International Law* (first published in 1924, 3rd edn, Appleton-Century-Crofts 1948)

Fenwick CG, 'The Progress of International Law during the Past Forty Years' (1951) 79 Collected Courses of the Hague Academy of International Law 1

Ferris E, 'In Search of Commitments: The 2016 Refugee Summits' (2016) Kaldor Centre for International Refugee Law Policy Brief No 3

Ferris E and J Bergmann, 'Soft Law, Migration and Climate Change Governance' (2017) 8 JHRE 6–29

Fields H, 'Closing Immigration throughout the World' (1932) 26 AJIL 671–99

Fiore P, *Le droit international codifié et sa sanction juridique* (Pedone 1911)

Fisher MH, *Migration: A World History* (OUP 2014)

Fischer-Lescano A, T Löhr, and T Tohidipur, 'Border Controls at Sea: Requirements under International Human Rights and Refugee Law' (2009) 21(2) IJRL 256–96

Fitzpatrick J, 'Rendition and Transfer in the War against Terrorism: Guantanamo and Beyond' (2003) 25 Loyola Int'l & Comp L Rev 457–92

Fitzpatrick J, 'Trafficking as a Human Rights Violation: The Complex Intersection of Legal Frameworks for Conceptualizing and Combating Trafficking' (2003) 24 Mich J Int'l L 1143–67

Flauss J-F, 'Les droits de l'homme et la Convention de Genève du 28 juillet 1951 relative au statut des réfugiés' in V Chetail and J-F Flauss (eds), *La Convention de Genève du 28 juillet 1951 relative au statut des réfugiés 50 ans après: bilan et* perspectives (Emile Bruylant 2001)

Focarelli C, 'Promotional Jus Cogens: A Critical Appraisal of Jus Cogens' Legal Effects' (2008) 77 Nord J Int'l L 429–59

Footer ME, 'The (Re)turn to "Soft Law" in Reconciling the Antinomies in WTO Law' (2010) 11(2) Melbourne Journal of International Law 241–76

Foster M, 'Responsibility Sharing or Shifting? 'Safe' Third Countries and International Law' (2008) 25(2) Refuge 64–78

Foster M, 'An "Alien" by the Barest of Threads—The Legality of the Deportation of Long-Term Residents from Australia' (2009) 33 Melb UL Rev 483–541

Foster M, *International Refugee Law and Socio-Economic Rights* (CUP 2009)

Foster M, 'Non-Refoulement on the Basis of Socio-Economic Deprivation' (2009) NZLRev 257–310

Foulke RR, *A Treatise on International Law*, vol 1 (John C Winston and Co 1920)

Fourlanos G, *Sovereignty and the Ingress of Aliens: With Special Focus on Family Unity and Refugee Law* (Almqvist and Wiksell International 1986)

Freeman AV, *The International Responsibility of States for Denial of Justice* 507–30 (1st edn, Longmans 1938)

Freeman AV, 'Human Rights and the Rights of Aliens' (1951) 45 ASIL Proceedings 120–39

Friedrich J, *International Environmental 'Soft Law': The Functions and Limits of Nonbinding Instruments in International Environmental Governance and Law* (Springer 2013)

Fudge J, 'The Precarious Migrant Status and Precarious Employment: The Paradox of International Rights for Migrant Workers' (2011) Metropolis British Columbia Centre of Excellence for Research on Immigration and Diversity Working Paper No 11–15

Fuentes CI, *Normative Plurality in International Law: A Theory in the Determination of Applicable Rules* (Springer 2016)

Funk M and others, 'Tackling Irregular Migration through Development: A Flawed Approach?' (2017) EPC Discussion Paper

Gabaccia DR and D Hoerder (eds), *Connecting Seas and Connected Ocean Rims: Indian, Atlantic, and Pacific Oceans and China Seas Migrations from the 1830s to the 1930s* (Brill 2011)

Gabor FA, 'Reflections on the Freedom of Movement in Light of the Dismantled "Iron Curtain"' (1991) 65 Tul L Rev 849–81

Gainer B, *The Alien Invasion: The Origins of the Aliens Act of 1905* (Heinemann 1972)

Galbraith JK, *The Nature of Mass Poverty* (Harvard University Press 1979)

Galbraith J and D Zaring, 'Soft Law as Foreign Relations Law' (2014) 99 Cornell L Rev 735–94

Gallagher AT, 'Trafficking, Smuggling and Human Rights: Tricks and Treaties' (2002) 12 Forced Migration Review 25–28

Gallagher AT, 'Human Rights and Human Trafficking: Quagmire or Firm Ground? A Response to James Hathaway' (2009) 49(4) Va J Int'l L 789–848

Gallagher AT, *The International Law of Human Trafficking* (CUP 2010)

Gallagher AT and F David, *The International Law of Migrant Smuggling* (CUP 2014)

Gallinati C and N Gavazzo 'We Are All MERCOSUR': Discourses and Practices about Free Movement in the Current Regional Integration of South-America' in S Nita and others (eds), *Migration, Free Movement and Regional Integration* (UNESCO/ UNU-CRIS 2017)

Gammeltoft-Hansen T and J Vedsted-Hansen (eds), *Human Rights and the Dark Side of Globalisation: Transnational Law Enforcement and Migration Control* (Routledge 2016)

Garcia-Amador FV, 'State Responsibility: Some New Problems' (1958) 94 Collected Courses of the Hague Academy of International Law 365

Garcia-Amador FV, L Sohn, and R Baxter, *Recent Codification of the Law of State Responsibility for Injuries to Aliens* (Oceana 1974)

Gartner LP, *The Jewish Immigrant in England, 1870–1914* (Allen and Unwin 1960)

Geiger M and A Pécoud, 'International Organisations and the Politics of Migration' (2014) 40(6) Journal of Ethnic and Migration Studies 865–87

Geissler N, 'The International Protection of Internally Displaced Persons' (1999) 11(3) IJRL 451–78

Gent S, 'The Root Causes of Migration: Criticizing the Approach and Finding a Way Forward' (2002) Sussex Migration Working Paper No 11

Georgi F, 'For the Benefit of Some: The International Organization for Migration and its Global Migration Management' in M Geiger and A Pécoud (eds), *The Politics of International Migration Management* (Palgrave Macmillan 2012)

Gil-Bazo M-T, 'The Practice of Mediterranean States in the Context of the European Union's Justice and Home Affairs External Dimension: The Safe Third Country Concept Revisited' (2006) 18(3–4) IJRL 571–600

Gil-Bazo M-T, 'Asylum as a General Principle of International Law' (2015) 27(1) IJRL 3–28

Gilbert G, 'Right of Asylum: A Change of Direction,' (1983) 32 ICLQ 633–50

Glover T and S Russell, 'Coordination with UNHCR and States' (2001) Collaboration of the International Council of Voluntary Agencies and the Program in Refugee and Asylum Law, University of Michigan Working Paper No 7

Gold J, 'Strengthening the Soft International Law of Exchange Arrangements' (1983) 77 AJIL 443–89

Gómez Robledo A, 'Le *ius cogens* international: sa genèse, sa nature, ses fonctions' (1981) 172(III) Collected Courses of the Hague Academy of International Law 9

Gonzaga JAC, 'The Role of the United Nations High Commissioner for Refugees and the Refugee Definition' in S Kneebone (ed), *The Refugees Convention 50 Years On: Globalization and International Law* (Ashgate 2003)

Gonzalez del Pino S, *Rights of Migrant Domestic Workers in Europe* (OHCHR Regional Office for Europe 2011)

Goodwin-Gill GS, *International Law and the Movement of Persons between States* (OUP 1978)

Goodwin-Gill GS, 'AIDS and HIV, Migrants and Refugees: International Legal and Human Rights Dimensions' in M Haour-Knipe and R Rector (eds), *Crossing Borders: Migration, Ethnicity and AIDS* (Taylor & Francis 1996)

Goodwin-Gill GS, 'The Right to Leave, the Right to Return and the Question of a Right to Remain' in V Gowlland-Debbas (ed), *The Problem of Refugees in the Light of Contemporary International Law Issues* (Martinus Nijhoff 1996)

Goodwin-Gill GS, 'Refugee Identity and Protection's Fading Prospect' in F Nicholson and P Twomey (eds), *Refugee Rights and Realities: Evolving International Concepts and Regimes* (CUP 1999)

Goodwin-Gill GS, 'Article 31 of the 1951 Convention Relating to the Status of Refugees: Non-Penalization, Detention and Protection' in E Feller, V Türk, and F Nicholson (eds), *Refugee Protection in International Law, UNHCR's Global Consultations on International Protection* (CUP 2003)

Goodwin-Gill GS, 'Migrant Rights and "Managed Migration"' in V Chetail (ed), *Globalization, Migration and Human Rights: International Law under Review* (Bruylant 2007)

Goodwin-Gill GS and J McAdam, *The Refugee in International Law* (3rd edn, OUP 2007)

Goodwin-Gill GS, 'The Right to Seek Asylum: Interception at Sea and the Principle of Non-Refoulement' (2011) 23 IJRL 443–57

Goodwin-Gill GS and P Weckel (eds), *Migration and Refugee Protection in the 21st Century: International Legal Aspects*, Hague Academy of International Law (Martinus Nijhoff 2015)

Goralczyk W, Statement, in 'Open Session Governing Rules Project: Review and Discussion on the Movement of Persons across Borders' (1991) 85 ASIL Proc 51–63

Gordon E, 'Grotius and the Freedom of the Seas in the Seventeenth Century' (2008) 16 Willamette J Int'l L and Dis Res 252–69

Gorlick B, 'Human Rights and Refugees: Enhancing Protection through International Human Rights Law' (2000) 69(2) NJIL 117–77

Gormley WP, 'The Modification of Multilateral Conventions by Means of "Negotiated Reservations" and other "Alternatives": A Comparative Study of the ILO and Council of Europe' (October 1970–March 1971) 39 Fordham L Rev 413–46

Gosh B, 'New International Regime for Orderly Movement of People: What Will it Look Like?' in B Gosh (ed), *Managing Migration: Time for a New International Regime?* (OUP 2000)

Grahl-Madsen A, *Territorial Asylum* (Almqvist & Wiksell International 1980)

Grahl-Madsen A, 'International Refugee Law Today and Tomorrow' (1982) 20(4) ArchVR 411–67

Grahl-Madsen A, *Commentary on the Refugee Convention 1951* (UNHCR 1997)

Grange M and M D'Auchamp, 'Role of Civil Society in Campaigning for and Using the ICRMW' in R Cholewinski, P de Guchteneire, and A Pécoud (eds), *Migration and Human Rights: The United Nations Convention on Migrant Workers' Rights* (CUP 2009)

Greig DW, 'The Protection of Refugees and Customary International Law' (1983) 8 Aust YBIL 108–41

Groenendijk K, 'The Metamorphosis of Migrant Labour: Will New Rules Help Migrant Workers?' (1999) 1(2) EJML 173–76

Groenendijk K and others, *The Family Reunification Directive in EU Member States: The First Year of Implementation* (Wolf Legal Publishers 2007)

Gross J, *Workers' Rights as Human Rights* (Cornell University Press 2003)

Grotius H, *The Rights of War and Peace* (edited with an introduction by R Tuck, Liberty Fund 2005)

Grotius H, *Mare Liberum 1609–2009* (edited and annotated by R Feenstra, Brill 2009)

Gruchalla-Wesierski T, 'A Framework for Understanding "Soft Law"' (1984–1985) 30(1) McGill LJ 37–88

Guadagno L, 'Human Mobility in the Sendai Framework for Disaster Risk Reduction' (2016) 7(1) International Journal of Disaster Risk Science 30–40

Guani A, 'La Solidarité Internationale dans l'Amérique Latine' (1925) 8 Collected Courses of the Hague Academy of International Law 203

Guggenheim P, *Emer de Vattel et l'étude des relations internationales en Suisse* (Libraire de l'Université 1956)

Guild E, 'The Right to Leave a Country' (2013) Issue Paper by the Council of Europe Commissioner for Human Rights

Guild E, S Grant, and K Groenendijk, 'IOM and the UN: Unfinished Business' (2017) Queen Mary School of Law Legal Studies Research Paper No 255/2017

Guild E, S Grant, and CA Groenendijk (eds), *Human Rights of Migrants in the 21st Century* (Routledge 2017)

Guild E, S Peers, and J Tomkin (eds) *The EU Citizenship Directive: A Commentary* (OUP 2014); MP Broberg and N Holst-Christensen (eds), *Free Movement in the European Union: Cases, Commentaries and Questions* (4th edn, Djøf 2014)

Guiraudon V and G Lahav, 'Comparative Perspectives on Border Control: Away from the Border and Outside the State' in P Andreas and T Snyder (eds), *The Wall Around the West: State Borders and Immigration Control in North America and Europe* (Rowman and Littlefield Publishers 2000)

Guiraudon V, 'European Integration and Migration Policy: Vertical Policy-making as Venue Shopping' (2000) 38(2) Journal of Common Market 251–71

Gungwu W (ed), *Global History and Migrations* (Westview Press 1997)

Guzman A, 'International Organizations and the Frankenstein Problem' (2013) 24 EJIL 999–1025

Guzman A and T Meyer, 'International Soft Law' (2010) 2(1) J Legal Anal 171–225

Gyory A, *Closing the Gate: Race, Politics, and the Chinese Exclusion Act* (University of North Carolina Press 1998)

de Haan A, 'Livelihoods and Poverty: The Role of Migration—A Critical Review of the Migration Literature' (1999) 36 J Dev Stud 1–47

de Hass H, 'Turning the Tide? Why "Development instead of Migration" Policies Are Bound to Fail' (2006) International Migration Institute (IMI) University of Oxford Working Paper No 2

Haggenmacher P, *Grotius et la doctrine de la guerre juste* (Presses universitaires de France 1983)

Haggenmacher P, 'La place de Francisco de Vitoria parmi les fondateurs du droit inter-national' in *Actualité de la pensée juridique de Francisco de Vitoria* (Bruylant 1988)

Haggenmacher P, 'L'Etat souverain comme sujet du droit international de Vitoria à Vattel' (1992) 16 Droits Rev Fr 11–20

Haines R, 'Gender-Related Persecution' in E Feller, V Türk, and F Nicholson (eds), *Refugee Protection in International Law, UNHCR's Global Consultations on International Protection* (CUP 2003)

Haines R, 'National Security and Non-Refoulement in New Zealand: Commentary on Zaoui v. Attorney-General (N°2)' in J McAdam (ed), *Forced Migration, Human Rights and Security* (Hart Publishing 2008)

Hall WE, *A Treatise on International Law* (3rd edn, Clarendon Press 1890)

Handl G and others, 'A Hard Look at Soft Law' (1988) 82 ASIL Proc 371–95

Hannikainen L, *Peremptory Norms (Jus Cogens) in International Law: Historical Development, Criteria, Present Status* (Finnish Lawyers' Publishing Company 1988)

Hannum H, *The Right to Leave and Return in International Law and Practice* (Martinus Nijhoff 1987)

Hannum H, 'The Status of the Universal Declaration of Human Rights in National and International Law' (1996) 25 Ga J Int'l & Comp L 287–397

Hathaway JC, 'The Evolution of Refugee Status in International Law: 1920–1950' (1984) ICLQ 348–80

Hathaway JC, *The Law of Refugee Status* (1st edn, Butterworths 1991)

Hathaway JC, 'Overseeing the Refugee Convention: Taking Refugee Law Oversight Seriously' (2001) Working Paper No UM-ICVA Overview

Hathaway JC, 'Who Should Watch over Refugee Law?' (2002) 45(1) Law Quadrangle 54–57

Hathaway JC, *The Rights of Refugees under International Law* (CUP 2005)

Hathaway JC, 'The Human Rights Quagmire of "Human Trafficking"' (2008) 49 Va J Int'l L 1–59

Hathaway JC, 'Prosecuting a Refugee for 'Smuggling' Himself' (2014) University of Michigan Public Law Research Paper No 429

Hathaway JC and M Foster, *The Law of Refugee Status* (2nd edn, CUP 2014)

Harns C, *Regional Inter-State Consultation Mechanisms on Migration: Approaches, Recent Activities and Implications for Global Governance of Migration* (IOM Migration Research Series (MRS) No 45, IOM 2013)

Harvey C and RP Barnidge, 'Human Rights, Free Movement, and the Right to Leave in International Law' (2007) 19(1) IJRL 1–21

Hatton TJ and J G Williamson, *The Age of Mass Migration: Causes and Economic Impact* (OUP 1998)

Hatton TJ, 'Should We Have a WTO for International Migration?' (2007) 22(50) *Economic Policy* 339–83

Hayes B and T Bunyan, 'Migration, Development and the EU Security Agenda' in *Europe in the World: Essays on EU Foreign, Security and Development Policies* (British Overseas NGOs for Development (BOND) 2003)

Haynes J, 'The Right to Free Movement of Persons in Caribbean Community (CARICOM) Law: Towards 'Juridification'?' (2001) 2(2) Journal of Human Rights in the Commonwealth 57–66

Hein J, 'Refugees, Immigrants, and the State' (1993) 19(1) Annual Review of Sociology 43–59

Henckaerts J-M, *Mass Expulsion in Modern International Law and Practice* (Martinus Nijhoff 1995)

Henckaerts J-M and L Doswald-Beck, *Customary International Humanitarian Law*, vol 1 (ICRC/CUP 2005)

Henderson C, 'Australia's Treatment of Asylum Seekers: From Human Rights Violations to Crimes Against Humanity' (2014) 12(5) JICJ 1161–81

Henkin L, 'International Law as Law in the United States' (1984) 82 Mich L Rev 1555–69

Henkin L, *The Age of Rights* (Columbia University Press 1990)

Héritier A and M Rhodes (eds), *New Modes of Governance in Europe: Governing in the Shadow of Hierarchy* (Macmillan 2010)

Hershey AS, *The Essentials of International Public Law and Organization* (Macmillan 1927)

Higgins R, 'The Right in International Law of an Individual to Enter, Stay In and Leave a Country' (1973) 49 International Affairs 341–57

Higgins R, 'Grotius and the United Nations' (1985) 37(1) Int'l Social Science J 119–127

Hirsch AL and C Doig, 'Outsourcing Control: The International Organization for Migration in Indonesia' (2018) 22(5) IJHR 681–708

Hoerder D, *Cultures in Contact: World Migrations in the Second Millennium* (Duke University Press 2002)

Hofmann R, *Die Ausreisefreiheit nach Völkerrecht und staatlichem Recht* (Springer-Verlag 1988)

Holborn LW, 'The Legal Status of Political Refugees, 1920–1938' (1938) AJIL 680–730

Holland B, 'The Moral Person of the State: Emer de Vattel and the Foundations of International Legal Order' (2011) 37(4) History of European Ideas 438–45

Holmes SM and H Castaneda, 'Representing the "European Refuge Crisis" in Germany and Beyond: Deservingness and Difference, Life and Death' (2016) 43(1) American Ethnologist 12–24

Hudson MO, *International Tribunals: Past and Future* (Carnegie Endowment for International Peace and Brookings Institution 1944)

Humphrey JP, 'The International Bills of Rights: Scope and Implementation' (1976) 17 Wm & Mary L Rev 527–41

Humphrey JP, 'The Implementation of International Human Rights Law' (1978–1979) 24 NYL Sch L Rev 31–61

Hune S, 'Drafting an International Convention on the Protection of the Rights of All Migrant Workers and Their Families' (1985) 19(3) International Migration Review 570–73

Hune S and J Niessen, 'Ratifying the UN Migrant Workers Convention: Current Difficulties and Prospects' (1994) 12(4) NQHR 393–404

Huttenback RA, *Racism and Empire: White Settlers and Colored Immigrants in the British Self-governing Colonies, 1830–1910* (Cornell University Press 1976)

Hyndman P, 'Asylum and Non-Refoulement—Are these Obligations Owed to Refugees under International Law?' (1982) 57 Philip LJ 43

Iglesias Sánchez S, 'Free Movement of Persons and Regional International Organisations' in R Plender (ed), *Issues in International Migration Law* (Brill 2015)

Ingadóttir T, 'Financing International Institutions' in J Klabbers and A Wallendahl (eds), *Research Handbook on the Law of International Organizations* (Edward Elgar 2011)

Ippolito F and S Trevisanut (eds), *Migration in the Mediterranean: Mechanisms of International Cooperation* (CUP 2015)

van Ittersum MJ, 'Preparing *Mare Liberum* for the Press: Hugo Grotius' Rewriting of Chapter 12 of *De iure praedae* in November–December 1608' (2005–2007) 26–28 Grotiana 246–80

Jacobsson J, 'GATS Mode 4 and Labour Mobility: The Significance of Employment Market Access' in M Panizzon, G Zürcher, and E Fornalé (eds), *The Palgrave Handbook of International Labour Migration: Law and Policy Perspectives* (Palgrave 2015)

Jagerskiold S, 'The Freedom of Movement' in L Henkin (ed), *The International Bill of Rights: The Covenant on Civil and Political Rights* (Columbia University Press 1981)

Jagerskiold SF, 'Historical Aspects of the Right to Leave and to Return' in K Vasak and S Liskofsky (eds), *The Right to Leave and to Return: Papers and Recommendations of the*

International Colloquium held in Uppsala, Sweden, 19–20 June 1972 (The American Jewish Committee 1976)

Jastram K, 'Family Unity' in TA Aleinikoff and V Chetail (eds), *Migration and International Legal Norms* (TMC Asser Press 2003)

Jaumotte F, K Koloskova, and SC Saxena, *Impact of Migration on Income Levels in Advanced Economies*, Spillover Task Force (International Monetary Fund 2016)

Jeancourt-Galignani A, *L'immigration en droit international* (Rousseau 1908)

Jennings RY, 'Some International Law Aspects of the Refugee Question' (1939) BYIL 98–114

Jennings RY, 'The Responsibility of States' in 'General Course on Principles of International Law' (1967) 121 Collected Courses of the Hague Academy of International Law 473–514

Jessup PC, *A Modern Law of Nations: An Introduction* (MacMillan 1948)

Johnson KR, 'Open Borders?' (2003) 51 UCLA L Rev 193–265

Johnson TA, 'A Violation of Jus Cogens Norms as an Implicit Waiver of Immunity under the Federal Sovereign Immunities Act' (1995) 19(2) Maryland Journal of International Law 259–91

Jones HH, 'Domestic Jurisdiction—From the Covenant to the Charter' (1951–1952) 46 Illinois L Rev 219–72

Joseph S and J Kyriakakis, 'The United Nations and Human Rights' in S Joseph and A McBeth (eds), *Research Handbook on International Human Rights Law* (Edward Elgar 2010)

Jouannet E, *Emer de Vattel et l'émergence doctrinale du droit international classique* (Pedone 1998)

Juss SS, *International Migration and Global Justice* (Ashgate Publishing 2006)

Juss SS (ed), *The Ashgate Research Companion to Migration Law, Theory and Policy* (Routledge 2013)

Juss SS, 'The UNHCR Handbook and the Interface between "Soft Law" and "Hard Law" in International Refugee Law' in SS Juss and C Harvey (eds), *Contemporary Issues in Refugee Law* (Edward Elgar 2013)

Juss SS and T Zartaloudis, 'Introduction: Critical Approaches to Migration Law, Special Issue: Critical Approaches to Migration Law' (2015) 22 International Journal on Minority and Group Rights 1–6

Kabbanji L, 'Regional Management of Migration in West Africa: The Case of ECOWAS and UEMOA' in S Nita and others (eds), *Migration, Free Movement and Regional Integration* (UNESCO/UNU-CRIS 2017)

Kadidal S, 'Federalizing Immigration Law: International Law as a Limitation on Congress's Power to Legislate in the Field of Immigration' (2008) 77(2) Fordham L Rev 501–27

Kälin W, 'Gender-Related Persecution', in V Chetail and V Gowlland-Debbas (eds), *Switzerland and the International Protection of Refugees* (Brill 2002)

Kälin W, 'Limits to Expulsion under the International Covenant on Civil and Political Rights' in F Salerno (ed), *Diritti Dell'Uomo, Estradizione ed Espulsione* (CEDAM 2003)

Kälin W, 'Supervising the 1951 Convention Relating to the Status of Refugees: Article 35 and Beyond' in E Feller, V Türk, and F Nicholson (eds), *Refugee Protection in International Law, UNHCR's Global Consultations on International Protection* (CUP/UNHCR 2003)

Kälin W, 'Guiding Principles on Internal Displacement: Annotations' (2008) 38 Stud Transnat'l Legal Pol'y 1–171

Kälin W, M Caroni, and L Heim, 'Article 33, para 1 (Prohibition of Expulsion or Return ("Refoulement")/Défense d'expulsion et de refoulement)' in A Zimmermann (ed), *The 1951 Convention Relating to the Status of Refugees and its 1967 Protocol* (OUP 2011)

Kälin W, 'The Guiding Principles on Internal Displacement and the Search for a Universal Framework of Protection for Internally Displaced Persons' in V Chetail and C Bauloz (eds), *The Research Handbook on International Law and Migration* (Edward Elgar Publishing 2014)

Kälin W, 'The Nansen Initiative: Building Consensus on Displacement in Disaster Contexts' (2015) 49 Forced Migration Review 5–7

Kalm S and A Uhlin, *Civil Society and the Governance of Development: Opposing Global Institutions* (Palgrave Macmillan 2015)

Kalzpouzos I and I Mann, 'Banal Crimes against Humanity: The Case of Asylum Seekers in Greece' (2015) 16 Melb J of Int'l L 1–28

Kamminga MT and M Scheinin (eds), *The Impact of Human Rights Law on General International Law* (OUP 2009)

Kapferer S, 'Article 14(2) of the Universal Declaration of Human Rights and Exclusion from International Refugee Protection' (2008) 27(3) RSQ 53–75

Karatani R, 'How History Separated Refugee and Migrant Regimes: In Search of Their Institutional Origins' (2005) 17 IJRL 517–41

Katseli LT, REB Lucas, and T Xenogiani, 'Policies for Migration and Development: A European Perspective' in *Gaining from Migration* (EC/OECD 2006)

Keller H and L Grover, 'General Comments of the Human Rights Committee and their Legitimacy' in H Keller and G Ulfstein (eds), *UN Human Rights Treaty Bodies: Law and Legitimacy* (CUP 2012)

Kelsey J, 'How "Trade in Services" Transforms the Regulation of Temporary Migration for Remittances in Poor Countries' in M Kolsky Lewis and S Frankel (eds), *International Economic Law and National Autonomy* (CUP 2010)

Kennedy DW, 'Primitive Legal Scholarship' (1986) 27(1) Harvard Int'l L J 1–98

Kennedy DW, 'International Law and the Nineteenth Century: History of an Illusion' (1996) 65 Nordic J Int'l Law 385–420

Kent J, *Commentaries on American Law*, vol 1 (11th edn, Little and Brown Company 1866)

Kerr WR, 'U.S. High-Skilled Immigration, Innovation and Entrepreneurship: Empirical Approaches and Evidence' (2014) WIPO Economics and Statistics Series, Economic Research Working Paper No 16

Keynes JM, *The Collected Writings of John Maynard Keynes: The General Theory of Employment, Interest and Money*, Vol 7 (first published 1936, Palgrave MacMillan St Martin's Press for the Royal Economic Society 1973)

King D, *Making Americans: Immigration, Race, and the Origins of the Diverse Democracy* (Harvard University Press 2000)

Kirgis FL, 'Custom on a Sliding Scale' (1987) 81 AJIL 146–51

Kirton J and MJ Trebilcock, *Hard Choices, Soft Law: Voluntary Standards in Global Trade, Environment, and Social Governance* (Routledge 2004)

Kiss A-C, 'La condition des étrangers en droit international et les droits de l'Homme' in *Mélanges en l'honneur de M Ganshof van der Meersch*, vol 1 (Bruylant 1972)

Klabbers J, 'The Undesirability of Soft Law' (1998) 67(4) Nord J Int'l L 381–91

Klabbers J, *An Introduction to International Institutional Law* (2nd edn, CUP 2009)

Klein DF, 'A Theory for the Application of the Customary International Law of Human Rights by Domestic courts' (1988) 13 Yale J Int'l L 332–65

Klein D (ed), *The Paris Agreement on Climate Change: Analysis and Commentary* (OUP 2017)

Klein S, 'International Migration Management through Inter-State Consultation Mechanisms' (2005) Paper prepared for United Nations Expert Group Meeting on International Migration and Development

Kleinlein T, 'Alfred Verdross as a Founding Father of International Constitutionalism?' (2012) 4 Goettingen J Int'l L 385–416

Klekowski von Koppenfels A, *The Role of Regional Consultative Processes in Managing International Migration* (IOM 2001)

Koch A, 'The Politics and Discourse of Migrant Return: The Role of UNHCR and IOM in the Governance of Return' (2014) 40(6) Journal of Ethnic and Migration Studies 905–23

Köhler J, 'What Government Networks Do in the Field of Migration: An Analysis of Selected Regional Consultative Processes' in R Kunz, S Lavenex, and M Panizzon (eds), *Multilayered Migration Governance* (Routledge 2011)

Kolb R, *Peremptory International Law-Jus Cogens: A General Inventory* (Bloomsbury Publishing 2015)

Kolb R, *Theory of International Law* (Hart Publishing 2016)

Koskenniemi M, *The Gentle Civilizer of Nations: The Rise and Fall of International Law 1870–1960* (CUP 2001)

Koskenniemi M, *From Apology to Utopia: The Structure of International Legal Argument* (CUP 2005)

Kothari U, 'Migration and Chronic Poverty' (2002) University of Manchester Working Paper No 16

Kuhn PA, *Chinese Among Others: Emigration in Modern Times* (Rowman and Littlefield 2008)

Kushner T, 'Racialisation and "White European" Immigration to Britain' in K Muri and J Solomos (eds), *Racialization: Studies in Theory and Practice* (OUP 2005)

Lahav G, 'International Versus National Constraints in Family-Reunification Migration Policy' (1997) 3 Global Governance 349–72

Lake M and H Reynolds, *Drawing the Global Colour Line: White Men's Countries and the International Challenge of Racial Equality* (CUP 2008)

Laly-Chevalier C, F Da Poïan, and H Tigroudja, 'Chronique de la jurisprudence de la Cour interaméricaine des droits de l'homme (2002–2004)' (2005) 62 RTDH 459–98

Lauterpacht H, 'The Grotian Tradition in International Law' (1946) 23 BYIL 1–53

Lauterpacht H, 'The Universal Declaration of Human Rights' (1948) 25 BYIL 354–81

Lauterpacht H, *International Law and Human Rights* (Stevens 1950)

Lauterpacht E and D Bethlehem, 'The Scope and Content of the Principle of Non-Refoulement: Opinion' in E Feller, V Türk, and F Nicholson (eds), *Refugee Protection in International Law, UNHCR's Global Consultations on International Protection* (CUP 2003)

Lavenex S and R Kunz, 'The Migration-Development Nexus in EU External Relations' (2008) 30(3) J Europ Integration 439–57

Lavenex S, 'Multilevelling EU External Governance: The Role of International Organizations in the Diffusion of EU Migration Policies' (2016) 42(4) Journal of Ethnic and Migration Studies 554–70

Lavenex S and others, 'Regional Migration Governance' in TA Börzel and T Risse (eds), *The Oxford Handbook of Comparative Regionalism* (OUP 2016)

Leary VA, 'Labour Migration' in TA Aleinikoff and V Chetail (eds), *Migration and International Legal Norms* (TMC Asser Press 2003)

Lee A, 'Aspects of the Working Class Response to the Jews in Britain 1880–1914' in K Lunn (ed), *Hosts, Immigrants and Minorities: Historical Responses to Newcomers in British Society, 1870–1914* (St Martin's Press 1980)

Lee M, 'Human Trade and the Criminalization of Irregular Migration' (2005) 33 Int'l J Soc L 1–15

Lee M, 'Human Trafficking and Border Control in the Global South' in K Franko Aas and M Bosworth (eds), *The Borders of Punishment: Migration, Citizenship and Social Exclusion* (OUP 2013)

Lenzerini F, 'International Trade and Child Labour Standards' in F Francioni (ed), *Environment, Human Rights and International Trade* (Hart Publishing 2001)

Lerner N, *Group Rights and Discrimination in International Law* (2nd edn, Martinus Nijhoff 2003)

Lesaffer R, 'The Grotian Tradition Revisited: Change and Continuity in the History of International Law' (2002) BYIL 103–39

Lord Lester of Herne Hill, 'Non-Discrimination in International Human Rights Law' (1993) 19(4) CLB 1653–69

Lewis C, *UNHCR and International Refugee Law: From Treaties to Innovation* (Routledge 2012)

Lewkowicz N, 'The Spanish School as a Forerunner to the English School of International Relations' (2007) 6 Estudios Humanisticos Historia 85–96

van Liempt I, 'Different Geographies and Experiences of "Assisted" Types of Migration: A Gendered Critique on the Distinction between Trafficking and Smuggling' (2011) 18(2) Gender, Place and Culture 179–93

Lietaert I, E Broekaert, and I Derluyn, 'From Social Instrument to Migration Management Tool: Assisted Voluntary Return Programmes—The Case of Belgium' (2017) 51(7) Social Policy & Administration 961–80

Lillich RB (ed), *International Law of State Responsibility for Injuries to Aliens* (University Press of Virginia 1983)

Lillich RB, *The Human Rights of Aliens in Contemporary International Law* (Manchester University Press 1984)

Lillich RB, 'The Growing Importance of Customary International Human Rights Law' (1995–1996) 25 Ga J Int'l & Comp L 1–30

Lillich, RB 'Civil Rights' in T Meron (ed), *Human Rights in International La*w, vol 1 (OUP 1984)

Linderfalk U, 'The Effect of Jus Cogens Norms: Whoever Opened Pandora's Box, Did You Ever Think About the Consequences?' (2007) 18(5) EJIL 853–71

Lindstrøm C, 'Addressing the Root Causes of Forced Migration: A European Union Policy of Containment?' (2003) Refugee Studies Centre University of Oxford Working Paper No 1

Liss R, 'A Right to Belong: Legal Protection of Sociological Membership in the Application of Article 12(4) of the ICCPR' (2014) 46 NYU JILP 1097–1191

Liu G, *The Right to Leave and Return and Chinese Migration Law* (Martinus Nijhoff 2007)

von Liszt F, *Le droit international: Exposé systématique* (Pedone 1927)

Loescher G, *The UNHCR and World Politics: A Perilous Path* (OUP 2001)

Loescher G, 'UNHCR and the Erosion of Refugee Protection' (2001) Forced Migration Review 28–30

Loescher G, A Betts, and J Milner, *The United Nations High Commissioner for Refugees: The Politics and Practice of Refugee Protection into the Twenty-first Century* (Routledge 2008)

Loescher G, 'UNHCR and Forced Migration' in E Fiddian-Qasmiyeh and others (eds), *The Oxford Handbook of Refugee and Forced Migration Studies* (OUP 2014)

Loescher G, 'Refugees and Internally Displaced Persons' in JK Cogan, I Hurd, and I Johnstone (eds), *The Oxford Handbook of International Organizations* (OUP 2016)

da Lomba S, 'Immigration Status and Basic Social Human Rights: A Comparative Study of Irregular Migrants' Right to Health Care in France, the UK and Canada' (2010) 28 NQHR 6–40

Long K, 'When Refugees Stopped Being Migrants: Movement, Labour and Humanitarian Protection' (2013) 1(1) Migration Studies 4–26

de Los Rios F, 'Francisco de Vitoria and the International Community' (1947) 14(4) Soc Res 488–507

Lucassen L, 'The Great War and the Origins of Migration Control in Western Europe and the United States (1880–1920)' in A Böcker and others (eds), *Regulation of Migration: International Experiences* (Het Spinhuis 1998)

Lucassen L, 'Migration and World History: Reaching a New Frontier' (2007) 52(1) Int'l Rev Soc Hist 89–96

Lucassen J and L Lucassen (eds), *Globalising Migration History: The Eurasian Experience (16th–21st Centuries)* (Brill 2014)

Lyon B, 'The Inter-American Court of Human Rights Defines Unauthorized Migrant Workers Rights for the Hemisphere: A Comment on Advisory Opinion 18' (2003–2004) 28 NYU Rev L & Soc Change 547–96

Lyon B, 'The Unsigned United Nations Migrant Worker Rights Convention: An Overlooked Opportunity to Change the "Brown Collar" Migration Paradigm' (2010) 42(2) NYU J Int'l Law & Pol 389–500

MacDonald E and R Cholewinski, *The Migrant Workers Convention in Europe: Obstacles to the Ratification of the International Convention on the Protection of the Rights of All Migrants and Members of their Families: EU/EEA Perspectives* (UNESCO 2007)

MacLachlan C, 'The Principle of Systemic Integration and Article 31(3)(c) of the Vienna Convention' (2005) 54(2) ICLQ 279–319

MacMillan LM, 'Monitoring & Reporting: A Search for New Advocacy Strategies' in AF Bayefsky and J Fitzpatrick (eds), *Human Rights and Forced Displacement* (Martinus Nijhoff 2000)

Mahalic D and JG Mahalic, 'The Limitation Provisions of the International Convention on the Elimination of All Forms of Racial Discrimination' (1987) 9(1) HRQ 74–101

Mainwaring C and N Brigden, 'Beyond the Border: Clandestine Migration Journeys' (2016) 21(2) Geopolitics 243–62

Mallia P, *Migrant Smuggling by Sea: Combatting a Current Threat to Maritime Security Through the Creation of a Cooperative Framework* (Martinus Nijhoff 2010)

Mann I, *Humanity at Sea: Maritime Migration and the Foundations of International Law* (CUP 2016)

Manning P, *Migration in World History* (Routledge 2005)

Manz JJ, *Emer de Vattel, Versuch einer Würdigung: Unter besonderer Berücksichtigung der individuellen Freiheit und der souveränen Gleichheit* (Schulthess Polygraphischer Verlag 1971)

Marbug T and HE Flack (eds), *Taft Papers on League of Nations* (Macmillan 1920)

Marrus MR, *The Unwanted: European Refugees in the Twentieth Century* (OUP 1985)

von Martens GF, *The Law of Nations* (4th edn, William Cobbett 1829)

Martens J, 'A Transnational History of Immigration Restriction: Natal and New South Wales, 1896–97' (2006) 34 J Imp & Commonw Hist 323–44

Martin PL and JE Taylor, 'The Anatomy of a Migration Hump' in JE Taylor (ed), *Development Strategy, Employment, and Migration: Insights from Models* (OECD Publishing 1996)

Martin P, S Martin, and S Cross, 'High-Level Dialogue on Migration and Development' (2007) 45 International Migration 7–25

Martin SF, *International Migration: Evolving Trends from the Early Twentieth Century to the Present* (CUP 2014)

Marx R, 'Non-Refoulement, Access to Procedures, and Responsibility for Determining Refugee Claims' (1995) 7(3) IJRL 383–406

Massey DS and others, *Worlds in Motion: Understanding International Migration at the End of the Millennium* (OUP 1998)

Maupain F, 'Revitalization not Retreat: The Real Potential of the 1998 ILO Declaration for the Universal Protection of Workers' Rights' (2005) 16(3) EJIL 439–65

Mayer B, 'Migration in the UNFCCC Workstream on Loss and Damage: An Assessment of Alternative Framings and Conceivable Responses' (2017) 6 Transnational Environmental Law 107–29

Mayer B and F Crépeau (eds), *Research Handbook on Climate Change, Migration and the Law* (Edward Elgar Publishing 2017)

Mazumdar S, 'Localities of the Global: Asian Migrations between Slavery and Citizenship' (2007) 52(1) Int'l Rev Soc Hist 124–33

McAdam J, *Complementary Protection in International Refugee Law* (OUP 2007)

McAdam J, 'An Intellectual History of Freedom of Movement in International Law: The Right to Leave as a Personal Liberty' (2011) 12 Melb J Int'l L 27–56

McAdam J, 'From the Nansen Initiative to the Platform on Disaster Displacement: Shaping International Approaches to Climate Change, Disasters and Displacement' (2016) 39(4) UNSW Law Journal 1518–46

McAdam M, 'What's in a Name? Victim Naming and Blaming in Rights-based Distinctions between Human Trafficking and Migrant Smuggling' (2015) 4 International Human Rights Law Review 1–32

McCall-Smith KL, 'Interpreting International Human Rights Standards: Treaty Body General Comments as a Chisel or Hammer?' in S Lagoutte, T Gammeltoft-Hansen, and J Cerone (eds), *Tracing the Roles of Soft Law in Human Rights* (OUP 2016)

McClean D, *Transnational Organized Crime: A Commentary on the UN Convention and its Protocols* (OUP 2007)

McDougal MS, HD Lasswell, and L Chen, 'The Protection of Respect and Human Rights: Freedom of Choice and World Public Order' (1975) 24 Am UL Rev 919–1086

McDougal MS, HD Lasswell, and L-C Chen, 'Protection of Aliens from Discrimination and World Public Order: Responsibility of States Conjoined with Human Rights' (1976) 70 AJIL 432–69

McDougal MS, HD Lasswell, and L-C Chen, *Human Rights and World Public Order* (Yale University Press 1980)

McKean W, *Equality and Discrimination under International Law* (Clarendon Press 1983)

McKeown A, 'Global Migration, 1846–1940' (2004) 15 Journal of World History 155–89

McKeown A, *Melancholy Order: Asian Migration and the Globalization of Borders* (Columbia University Press 2008)

Méchoulan H, *Le sang de l'autre ou l'honneur de Dieu: Indiens, juifs et morisques dans l'Espagne du Siècle d'Or* (Fayard 1979)

Mégret F, 'Transnational Mobility, the International Law of Aliens, and the Origins of Global Migration Law' (2017) 111 AJIL Unbound 13–17

Merin Y, 'The Right to Family Life and Civil Marriage under International Law and its Implementation in the State of Israel' (2005) 28(1) BC Int'l & Comp L Rev 79–147

Merkouris P, *Article 31(3)(c) VCLT and the Principle of Systemic Integration: Normative Shadows in Plato's Cave* (Brill | Nijhoff 2015)

Meron T, *Human Rights and Humanitarian Norms as Customary Law* (Clarendon Press 1989)

Meron T, 'International Law in the Age of Human Rights' (2003) 301 Collected Courses of the Hague Academy of International Law 1

Merrills JG and AH Robertson, *Human Rights in the World: An Introduction to the Study of the International Protection of Human Rights* (4th edn, Manchester University Press 2001)

Meyer T, 'Soft Law as Delegation' (2009) 32(3) Fordham Int'l LJ 888–942

Micinski R and TG Weiss, 'International Organization for Migration and the UN System: A Missed Opportunity' (2016) Future United Nations Development System Briefing 42

Miéville C, *Between Equal Rights: A Marxist Theory of International Law* (Brill 2005)

Milano E, 'Diplomatic Protection and Human Rights before the International Court of Justice: Re-fashioning Tradition?' (2004) 35 Neth Yearbook Int'l L 85–142

Miller DH, *The Drafting of the Covenant* (G P Putnam's Sons 1928)

Mlambo V, 'Cross-border Migration in the Southern African Development Community (SADC): Benefits, Problems and Future prospects' (2017) 8(4) Journal of Social and Development Sciences 42–56

Mohapatra PP, 'Eurocentrism, Forced Labour, and Global Migration: A Critical Assessment' (2007) 52(1) Int'l Rev Soc Hist 110–15

Moch LP, *Moving Europeans: Migration in Western Europe since 1650* (Indiana University Press 1992)

Moeckli D, *Human Rights and Non-Discrimination in the War on Terror* (OUP 2008)

Moeckli D, 'Equality and Non-Discrimination' in D Moeckli, S Shah, and S Sivakumaran (eds), *International Human Rights Law* (2nd edn, OUP 2013)

Molodikova I, 'Two Decades of CIS Coexistence: The Transformation of the Visa-free Movement' in S Nita and others (eds), *Migration, Free Movement and Regional Integration* (UNESCO/UNU-CRIS 2017)

Monsutti A, 'Afghan Migratory Strategies and the Three Solutions to the Refugee Problem' (2008) 27(1) RSQ 58–73

Moreno-Lax V, 'Systematising Systemic Integration' (2014) 12(5) JICJ 907–29

Moreno-Lax V, 'The Legality of the Safe Third Country Notion Contested: Insights from the Law of Treaties' in GS Goodwin-Gill and P Weckel (eds), *Migration and Refugee Protection in the 21st Century: International Legal Aspects* (Martinus Nijhoff 2015)

Moreno-Lax V and E Papastavridis (eds), *'Boat Refugees' and Migrants at Sea: A Comprehensive Approach: Integrating Maritime Security with Human Rights* (Brill | Nijhoff 2016)

Moreno-Lax V, *Accessing Asylum in Europe: Extraterritorial Border Controls and Refugee Rights under EU Law* (OUP 2017)

Moreno-Lax V and E Papastavridis (eds), *'Boat Refugees' and Migrants at Sea: A Comprehensive Approach—Integrating Maritime Security with Human Rights* (Brill 2016)

Mörth U, *Soft Law in Governance and Regulation: an Interdisciplinary Analysis* (Edward Elgar 2004)

Mosler H, *The International Society as a Legal Community* (Brill 1980)

Mooney E, 'The Concept of Internal Displacement and the Case for Internally Displaced persons as a Category of Concern' (2005) 24(3) RSQ 9–26

Moore JB, *A Digest of International Law*, vol 4 (Government Printing Office 1906)

Muir-Watt H, 'Droit naturel et souveraineté de l'Etat dans la doctrine de Vattel' (1987) 32 APD 71–85

Muntarbhorn V, 'Combating Migrant Smuggling and Trafficking in Persons, Especially Women: The Normative Framework Re-appraised' in TA Aleinikoff and V Chetail (eds), *Migration and International Legal Norms* (TMC Asser Press 2003)

Murphy CF, 'The Grotian Vision of World Order' (1982) 76(3) AJIL 477–98

Nafziger JAR, 'The Right of Migration under the Helsinki Accords' (1980) 5 S Ill ULJ 395–438

Nafziger JAR, 'The General Admission of Aliens under International Law' (1983) 77(4) AJIL 804–47

Nakhimovsky I, 'Vattel's Theory of the International Order: Commerce and the Balance of Power in the Law of Nations' (2007) 33 History of European Ideas 157–73

Nanda V, 'Application of Customary International Law by Domestic Courts: Some Observations' (1966) 12(2) NYL Forum 187–244

Nash SL, 'From Cancun to Paris: An Era of Policy Making on Climate Change and Migration' (2018) 9(1) Global Policy 53–63

Nayar MGK, 'Human Rights: The UN and US Foreign Policy' (1978) 19 Harv Int'l LJ 813–44

Neumann L, *Eléments du droit des gens modernes européen* (trans MA de Riedmatten, Rousseau 1886)

Neuman GL, 'The Lost Century of American Immigration Law (1776–1875)' (1993) 93(8) Colum L Rev 1833–1901

Newland K, 'The Governance of International Migration: Mechanisms, Processes and Institutions' (2005) Paper Prepared for the Policy Analysis and Research Programme of the Global Commission on International Migration

Newland K, 'Migrant Return and Reintegration Policy: A Key Component of Migration Governance' in M McAuliffe and M Klein Solomon (Conveners), *Migration Research Leaders' Syndicate in Support of the Global Compact on Migration: Ideas to Inform International Cooperation on Safe, Orderly and Regular Migration* (IOM 2017)

Ni V, 'Study of the Laws and Institutional Frameworks Governing International Migration in North and Central Asia from the Perspective of Countries of Origin and Destination' (2016) UN Economic and Social Commission for Asia and the Pacific, Working Paper 4

Nijenhuis G and M Leung, 'Rethinking Migration in the 2030 Agenda: Towards a De-Territorialized Conceptualization of Development' (2017) 44(1) Forum for Development Studies 51–68

van Nifterik G and J Nijman, 'Introduction: *Mare Liberum* Revisited (1609–2009)' (2009) 30 Grotiana 3–19

Nielson J, 'Labour Mobility in Regional Trade Agreements' in A Mattoo and A Carzaniga (eds) *Moving People to Deliver Services* (The World Bank/OUP 2003)

Niemelä P, 'A Cosmopolitan World Order? Perspectives on Francisco de Vitoria and the United Nations' (2008) 12 Max Planck UNYB 301–44

Nita S, 'Regional Free Movement of People: The Case of African Regional Economic Communities' (2013) 3(3) Regions & Cohesion 8–29

Nita S, 'Free Movement of People within Regional Integration Processes: A Comparative View' in S Nita and others (eds), *Migration, Free Movement and Regional Integration* (UNESCO/UNU-CRIS 2017)

Nobel P, 'Refugee, Law, and Development in Africa' (1982) 3 Michigan YB Int'l Leg Stud 255–87

Noiriel G, *La tyrannie du national: Le droit d'asile en Europe (1793–1993)* (Calmann-Lévy 1991) 45

Noll G, 'Article 31 (Refugees Unlawfully in the Country of Refuge)' in A Zimmermann (ed), *The 1951 Convention Relating to the Status of Refugees and Its 1967 Protocol* (OUP 2011)

Noll G, *Negotiating Asylum: The EU Acquis, Extraterritorial Protection and the Common Market of Deflection* (Kluwer 2000)

Noll G, 'Seeking Asylum at Embassies: A Right to Entry under International Law?' (2005) 17 IJRL 542–73

Noll G, 'The Insecurity of Trafficking in International Law' in V Chetail (ed), *Mondialisation, migration et droits de l'homme: le droit international en question* (Bruylant 2007)

Nollkaemper PA and R Van Alebeek, 'The Legal Status of Decisions by Human Rights Treaty Bodies in National Law' (11 April 2011) Amsterdam Center for International Law, Research Paper No 2011-02

Nolte G, 'From Dionisio Anzilotti to Roberto Ago: The Classical International Law of State Responsibility and the Traditional Primacy of a Bilateral Conception of Inter-State Relations' (2002) 13 EJIL 1083–98

Nonnenmacher S, 'Free Movement of Persons in the Caribbean Community' in R Cholewinski, R Perruchoud, and E MacDonald (eds), *International Migration Law: Developing Paradigms and Key Challenges* (TMC Asser Press 2007)

North AM and J Chia, 'Towards Convergence in the Interpretation of the Refugee Convention: A Proposal for the Establishment of an International Judicial Commission for Refugees' in J McAdam (ed), *Forced Migration, Human Rights and Security* (Hart Publishing 2008)

Northrup D, *Indentured Labor in the Age of Imperialism, 1834–1922* (CUP 1995)

Nowak M, *UN Covenant on Civil and Political Rights CCPR Commentary* (2nd revised edn, NP Engel 2005)

Nowak M and E McArthur (eds), *The United Nations Convention Against Torture: A Commentary* (OUP 2008)

Nugent W, *Crossings: The Great Transatlantic Migrations, 1870–1914* (Indiana University Press 1992)

Nutkiewicz M, 'Samuel Pufendorf: Obligation as the Basis of the State' (1983) 21(1) J Hist Philosophy 15–29

Nyberg-Sørensen N, N Van Hear, and P Engberg-Pedersen, 'The Migration-Development Nexus: Evidence and Policy Options' (2002) 40(5) International Migration 49–73

Nys E, *Le droit international: Les principes, les théories, les faits*, vol 2 (Weissenbruch 1912)

Nys M, *L'immigration familiale à l'épreuve du droit: Le droit de l'étranger à mener une vie familiale normale* (Bruylant 2002)

O'Brien D, 'The Right of Free Movement within Caricom: A Step towards Caribbean 'Citizenship'? Lessons from the European Union' (2015) 42(3) Legal Issues of Economic Integration 233–56

O'Byrne K, 'Is there a Need for Better Supervision of the Refugee Convention?' (2013) 26 JRS 330–59

Obokata T, 'Smuggling of Human Beings from a Human Rights Perspective: Obligations of Non-State and State Actors under International Human Rights Law' (2005) 17 IJRL 394–415

Obokata T, *Trafficking of Human Beings from a Human Rights Perspective: Towards a Holistic Approach* (Martinus Nijhoff 2006)

Obokata T, 'Human Trafficking' in N Boister and RJ Currie, *Routledge Handbook of Transnational Criminal Law* (Routledge 2015)

Ocampo JA and JA Alonso (eds), *Global Governance and Rules for the Post-2015 Era: Addressing Emerging Issues in the Global Environment* (Bloomsbury Academic 2015)

Oger H, 'The French Political Refusal on Europe's Behalf' in R Cholewinski, P de Guchteneire, and A Pécoud (eds), *Migration and Human Rights: The United Nations Convention on Migrant Workers' Rights* (CUP 2009)

Okoth-Obbo G, 'Thirty Years On: A Legal Review of the 1969 OAU Convention Governing the Specific Aspects of Refugee Problems in Africa' (2001) 20(1) RSQ 79–138

Olsson IA, 'Four Competing Approaches to International Soft Law' (2013) 58 Sc St L 177–96

Omelaniuk I, 'Global Migration Institutions and Processes' in B Opeskin, R Perruchoud, and J Redpath-Cross (eds), *Foundations of International Migration Law* (CUP 2012)

Onuf NG, *The Republican Legacy in International Thought* (CUP 1998)

Onuf NG, '"Tainted by Contingency": Retelling the Story of International Law' in R Falk, LEJ Ruiz, and RBJ Walker (eds), *Reframing the International: Law, Culture, Politics* (Routledge 2002)

Opeskin B, 'The Influence of International Law on the International Movement of Persons' (2009) Human Development Research paper 2009/18

Opeskin B, R Perruchoud, J Redpath-Cross (eds), *Foundations of International Migration Law* (CUP 2012)

Oppenheim L, *International Law: A Treatise*, vol 1 (Longmans, Green and Co 1905)

Orellana Zabalza G, *The Principle of Systemic Integration: Towards a Coherent International Legal Order* (Lit Verlag 2012)

Ormonbekova L, 'Freedom of Movement and Labour Migration in the Commonwealth of Independent States Comparative Brief on CIS and EU Legislation' (2012) Comparative Brief on CIS and EU Legislation, Bishkek, Social Research Center

O'Rourke KH and J G Williamson, *Globalization and History: The Evolution of a Nineteenth-Century Atlantic Economy* (MIT Press 1999)

Pagden A, 'Human Rights, Natural Rights, and Europe's Imperial Legacy' (2003) 31(2) Pol Theory 171–99

Paiewonsky D, 'The Feminization of International Labour Migration' (2009) United Nations International Research and Training Institute for the Advancement of Women, Gender, Migration and Development Series, Working Paper 1

Palladini F, 'Pufendorf Disciple of Hobbes: The Nature of Man and the State of Nature: The Doctrine of *Socialitas*' (2008) 34 History of European Ideas 26–60

Panizzon M, 'International Law of Economic Migration: A Menage à Trois? GATS Mode 4, EPAs, and Bilateral Migration Agreements' (2010) 44(6) Journal of World Trade 1207–52

Panizzon M, 'Trade and Labor Migration: GATS Mode 4 and Migration Agreements' (2010) Dialogue on Globalization, Occasional Papers, Friedrich-Ebert-Stiftung

Panizzon M, G Zürcher, and E Fornalé (eds), *The Palgrave Handbook of International Labour Migration: Law and Policy Perspectives* (Palgrave 2016)

Pastore F, 'Europe, Migration and Development: Critical Remarks on an Emerging Policy Field' (2007) 50(4) Development 56–62

Parry C, 'The Function of Law in the International Community' in M Sørensen (ed), *Manual of Public International Law* (Macmillan/St Martin's Press 1968)

Pauwelyn J, RA Wessel, and J Wouters (eds), *Informal International Lawmaking* (OUP 2012)

Pauwelyn J, 'Is it International Law or Not and Does it Even Matter?' in J Pauwelyn, RA Wessel, and J Wouters (eds), *Informal International Lawmaking* (OUP 2012)

Pécoud A and P de Guchteneire, 'Migration, Human Rights and the United Nations: An Investigation into the Obstacles to the UN Convention on Migrant Workers' Rights' (2006) 24 Windsor YB Access Just 241–66

Pécoud A and P de Guchteneire (eds), *Migration without Borders: Essays on the Free Movement of People* (UNESCO and Berghahn Books 2007)

Pécoud A, *Depoliticising Migration: Global Governance and International Migration Narratives* (Palgrave Macmillan 2015)

Pécoud A, 'What do We Know about the International Organization for Migration?' (2017) 44(2) Journal of Ethnic and Migration Studies 1621–38

Peet R, *Unholy Trinity: The IMF, World Bank and WTO* (2nd edn, Zed Books 2009)

Pépin E, *L'Aliens Act de 1905: Causes et résultats* (Rousseau 1913)

Pellet A, 'The Second Death of Euripide Mavrommatis? Notes on the International Law Commission's Draft Articles on Diplomatic Protection' (2008) 7(1) The Law and Practice of International Courts and Tribunals 33–58

Pellet A, 'Article 42 of the 1951 Convention/Article VII of the 1967 Protocol' in A Zimmermann (ed) *The 1951 Convention Relating to the status of Refugees and its 1967 Protocol* (OUP 2011)

Pellonpää M, *Expulsion in International Law: A Study in International Aliens Law and Human Rights with Special Reference to Finland* (Suomalainen Tiedeakatemia 1984)

Perruchoud R, 'From the Intergovernmental Committee for European Migration to the International Organization for Migration' (1989) 1 IJRL 501–17

Perruchoud R, 'Persons Falling under the Mandate of the International Organization for Migration (IOM) and to whom the Organization may Provide Migration Services' (1992) 4 IJRL 205–15

Perruchoud R and K Tomolova, *Compendium of International Migration Law Instruments* (TMC Asser Press 2007)

Perruchoud R, 'L'expulsion en masse d'étrangers' (1988) XXXIV AFDI 677–93

Pesch ST, 'The Influence of Human Rights on Diplomatic Protection: Reviving an Old Instrument of Public International Law' in N Weiss, J-M Thouvenin (eds), *The Influence of Human Rights on International Law* (Springer 2015)

Peters A, 'Soft Law as a New Mode of Governance' in U Diedrichs, W Reiners, and W Wessels (eds), *The Dynamics of Change in EU Governance* (Edward Elgar 2011)

Pettiti LE, 'The Right to Leave and to Return in the USSR' in K Vasak and S Liskofsky (eds), *The Right to Leave and to Return: Papers and Recommendations of the International Colloquium held in Uppsala, Sweden, 19–20 June 1972* (The American Jewish Committee 1976)

Phillimore R, *Commentaries upon International Law*, vol 1 (3rd edn, Butterworths 1879)

Phillimore WGF, 'Droits et Devoirs Fondamentaux des Etats' (1923) 1 Collected Courses of the Hague Academy of International Law 25

Piché V, E Depatie-Pelletier, and D Epale, 'Obstacles to Ratification of the ICRMW in Canada' in R Cholewinski, P de Guchteneire, and A Pécoud (eds), *Migration and Human Rights: The United Nations Convention on Migrant Workers' Rights* (CUP 2009)

Piper N, 'Obstacles to, and Opportunities for, Ratification of the ICRMW in Asia' in R Cholewinski, P de Guchteneire, and A Pécoud (eds), *Migration and Human Rights: The United Nations Convention on Migrant Workers' Rights* (CUP 2009)

Pisillo Mazzeschi R, 'The Relationship between Human Rights and the Rights of Aliens and Immigrants' in U Fastenrath et al (eds), *From Bilateralism to Community Interest: Essays in Honour of Judge Bruno Simma* (OUP 2011)

Phuong C, *The International Protection of Internally Displaced Persons* (CUP 2004)

Piotrowicz R and C Van Eck, 'Subsidiary Protection and Primary Rights' (2004) 53 ICLQ 107–38

Piotrowicz R, 'Victims of People Trafficking and Entitlement to International Protection' (2005) 24 Aust YBIL 159–79

Piotrowicz R, 'States' Obligations under Human Rights Law towards Victims of Trafficking in Human Beings: Positive Developments in Positive Obligations' (2012) 24 IJRL 181–201

Plaetevoet R and M Sidoti, *Ratification of the UN Migrant Workers Convention in the European Union: Survey on the Positions of Governments and Civil Society Actors* (EPMWR 2010)

Plender R, *International Migration Law* (Sijthoff 1972)

Plender R, *International Migration Law* (2nd edn, Martinus Nijhoff 1988)

Plender R (ed), *Basic Documents on International Migration Law* (3rd revised edn, Martinus Nijhoff 2007)

Plender R (ed), *Issues in International Migration Law* (Brill 2015)

Porter B, *The Refugee Question in Mid-Victorian Politics* (CUP 1979)

Potts L, *The World Labour Market: A History of Migration* (Zed Books Ltd 1990)

Preibisch K, W Dodd, and Y Su, 'Pursuing the Capabilities Approach within the Migration–development Nexus' (2016) 42(13) Journal of Ethnic and Migration Studies 2111–27

Price C, *The Great White Walls are Built: Restrictive Immigration to North America and Australasia, 1836–1888* (Australian National University Press 1974)

Prost M, *The Concept of Unity in Public International Law* (Hart publishing, 2012)

Pufendorf S, *The Law of Nature and Nations or A General System of the Most Important Principles of Morality, Jurisprudence and Politics* (first published 1672, 5th edn, J & J Bonwicke 1749)

Rachovitsa A, 'The Principle of Systemic Integration in Human Rights Law' (2017) 66(3) ICLQ 557–88

Raimondi G, 'Réserves et conventions internationales du travail' in J-C Javillier and B Gernigon, *Les normes internationales du travail: un patrimoine pour l'avenir, Mélanges en l'honneur de Nicolas Valticos* (International Labour Office 2004)

Ramcharan BG, 'Equality and Non-discrimination' in L Henkin (ed), *The International Bill of Rights: The Covenant on Civil and Political Rights* (Columbia University Press 1981)

Ramji-Nogales J, 'Undocumented Migrants and the Failures of Universal Individualism' (2014) 47 Vanderbilt J Trans L 699–763

Ramji-Nogales J, 'Moving Beyond the Refugee Law Paradigm' (2017) 111 AJIL Unbound 8–12

Ramji-Nogales J, 'Migration Emergencies' (2017) 68 Hastings Law Journal 609–56

Reale E, *Le régime des passeports et la Société des Nations* (2nd edn, Rousseau 1931)

Reale E, 'Le problème des passeports' (1934) 50 Collected Courses of the Hague Academy of International Law 85

Recchi E, *Mobile Europe: The Theory and Practice of Free Movement in the EU* (Palgrave MacMillan 2015)

Reddie J, *Inquiries in International Law* (2nd edn, Blackwood and Sons 1851)

Rehman J, *The Weaknesses in the International Protection of Minority Rights* (Martinus Nijhoff 2000)

Reisman WM, 'Sovereignty and Human Rights in Contemporary International Law' (1990) 84 AJIL 866–76

Reisman WM, 'The Concept and Functions of Soft Law in International Politics' in EG Bello and BA Ajibola (eds), *Essays in Honour of Judge Taslim Olawale Elias*, vol I (Martinus Nijhoff 1992)

Remec PP, *The Position of the Individual in International Law According to Grotius and Vattel* (Martinus Nijhoff 1960)

Reppy A, 'The Grotian Doctrine of the Freedom of the Seas Reappraised' (1950) 19(3) Fordham L Rev 243–85

Richmond A, 'Sociological Theories of International Migration: The Case of Refugees' (1988) 36(7) Current Sociology 7–25

Rijks B, *Mobility of Health Professionals to, from and within the European Union* (IOM 2014)

Rieter E, *Preventing Irreparable Harm, Provisional Measures in International Human Rights Adjudication* (Intersentia 2010)

Rodley N, 'Human Rights and Humanitarian Intervention: The Case Law of the World Court' (1989) 38(2) ICLQ 321–33

Rogers N, R Scannell, and J Walsh (eds), *Free Movement of Persons in the Enlarged European Union* (Sweet and Maxwell 2012)

Roth AH, *The Minimum Standard of International Law Applied to Aliens* (A W Sijthoff's Uitgeversmaatschappij N V 1949)

Rother S, ' "Inside-Outside" or "Outsiders by Choice?" Civil Society Strategies towards the 2nd Global Forum on Migration and Development in Manila' (2009) 111 Asien: the German Journal on Contemporary Asia 95–107

Root E, 'The Basis of Protection to Citizens Residing Abroad' (1910) 4 ASIL Proceedings 16–27

Rubio-Marin R (ed), *Human Rights and Immigration* (OUP 2014)

Ruddy FS, 'The Acceptance of Vattel' (1972) Grotian Society Papers 177–96

Ruddy FS, *International Law in the Enlightenment: The Background of Emmerich de Vattel's 'Le Droit des Gens'* (Oceana 1975)

Rudolph C, 'Prospects and Prescriptions for a Global Mobility Regime: Five Lessons from the WTO' in B Koslowski (ed), *Global Mobility Regimes* (Palgrave Macmillan 2011)

Rupa C, 'Mobility of Less-Skilled Workers under Bilateral Agreements: Lessons for the GATS' (2009) 43(3) Journal of World Trade 479–506

Ryan B and V Mitsilegas (eds), *Extraterritorial Immigration Control: Legal Challenges* (Martinus Nijhoff 2010)

Ryan B, 'In the Defence of the Migrant Workers Convention: Standard Setting for Contemporary Migration' in J Satvinder (ed), *The Ashgate Research Companion to Migration Law, Theory and Policy* (Ashgate 2013)

Ryan B, 'Policy on the ICRMW in the United Kingdom' in R Cholewinski, P de Guchteneire, and A Pécoud (eds), *Migration and Human Rights: The United Nations Convention on Migrant Workers' Rights* (CUP 2009)

Saito K, 'International Protection for Trafficked Persons and those who Fear Being Trafficked' (2007) UNHCR Research Paper No 149

Sands P and P Klein, *Bowett's Law of International Institutions* (5th edn, Sweet Maxwell Limited 2001)

Santestevan AM, 'Free Movement Regimes in South America: The Experience of the MERCOSUR and the Andean Community' in R Cholewinski, R Perruchoud, and E MacDonald (eds), *International Migration Law: Developing Paradigms and Key Challenges* (TMC Asser Press 2007)

Saroléa S, *Droits de l'homme et migrations: De la protection du migrant aux droits de la personne migrante* (Bruylant 2006)

Saul B, 'Indefinite Security Detention and Refugee Children and Families in Australia: International Human Rights Law Dimensions' (2013) 20 Australian International Law Journal 55–75

Saul B, D Kinley, and J Mowbray, *The International Covenant on Economic, Social and Cultural Rights: Commentary, Cases, And Materials* (OUP 2014)

Sayad A, 'Immigration et "pensée d'Etat" ' (1999) 129 Actes de la recherche en sciences sociales 5–14

Schachter O, 'The Crisis of Legitimation in the United Nations' (1981) 50 Nordisk Tidskrift for International Ret: Acta Scandinavica juris gentium 3–19

Schachter O, *International Law in Theory and Practice* (Martinus Nijhoff 1991)

Shaffer G and M Pollack, 'Hard vs Soft: Alternatives, Complements, and Antagonists in International Governance' (2010) 94 Minn L Rev 706–99

Scheel S and P Ratfisch, 'Refugee Protection Meets Migration Management: UNHCR as a Global Police of Populations' (2014) 40(6) Journal of Ethnic and Migration Studies 924–41

Scheinin M, 'International Mechanisms and Procedures for Implementation' in R Hanski and S Markku (eds), *An Introduction to the International Protection of Human Rights: A Textbook* (2nd edn, Åbo Akademi University Press 1999)

Schmalenbach K, 'International Organizations or Institutions, Supervision and Sanctions' (2014) Max Planck Encyclopedia of Public International Law

von Schmalz T, *Le droit des gens européen* (Maze 1823)

Schloenhardt A and JE Dale, 'Twelve Years On: Revisiting the UN Protocol against the Smuggling of Migrants by Land, Sea and Air' (2012) 67 JPL 129–56

Schloenhardt A and H Hickson, 'Non-Criminalization of Smuggled Migrants: Rights, Obligations, and Australian Practice under Article 5 of the Protocol against the Smuggling of Migrants by Land, Sea, and Air' (2013) 25(1) IJRIL 39–64

Schloenhardt A and KL Stacey, 'Assistance and Protection of Smuggled Migrants: International Law and Australian Practice' (2013) 35 Syd LR 53–84

Schloenhardt A and R Markey-Towler, 'Non-Criminalisation of Victims of Trafficking in Persons—Principles, Promises, and Perspectives' (2016) 4(1) Groningen Journal of International Law 10–38

Scott JB (ed), *The International Conferences of American States 1889–1928* (OUP 1931)

Scott JB, *The Spanish Origins of International Law: Francisco de Vitoria and his Law of Nations* (OUP 1934)

Serdeczny O, *What Does it Mean to 'Address Displacement' Under the UNFCCC?: An Analysis of the Negotiations Process and the Role of Research* (Deutsches Institut für Entwicklungspolitik 2017)

Seidl-Hohenveldern I, 'International Economic "Soft Law" ' (1979) 163 Collected Courses of the Hague Academy of International Law 165

Segatti A, 'The Southern African Development Community: A Walk Away from the Free Movement of Persons?' in S Nita and others (eds), *Migration, Free Movement and Regional Integration* (UNESCO/UNU-CRIS 2017)

Seller MS, 'Historical Perspectives on American Immigration Policy: Case Studies and Current Implications' (1982) 45 LCP 137–62

Sepulveda M, *The Nature of the Obligations under the International Covenant on Economic, Social and Cultural Rights* (Intersentia 2003)

Sexsmith K and P McMichael, 'Formulating the SDGs: Reproducing or Reimagining State-Centered Development?' (2015) 12(4) Globalizations 581–96

Sexton RC, 'Political Refugees, Non-Refoulement and State Practice: A Comparative Study' (1985) 18(4) Vanderbilt J Transnatl L 732–806

Shaw MN, 'Territory in International Law' (1982) XIII NYIL 61–91

Shaw MN, *International Law* (6th edn CUP 2008)

Shearer I, 'Grotius and the Law of the Sea' (1983) 26 ASLP Bulletin 46–65

Shelton D (ed), *Commitment and Compliance: The Role of Non-binding Norms in the International Legal System* (OUP 2000)

Shelton D, 'Prohibited Discrimination in International Human Rights Law' in A Constantidines and N Zaiko (eds), *The Diversity of International Law: Essays in Honour of Professor Kalliopi K Koufa* (Martinus Nijhoff 2009)

Shelton D, 'International Law and Relative Normativity' in M Evans (ed), *International Law* (OUP 2010)

Sherwood Dunn F, *The Protection of Nationals: A Study in the Application of International Law* (The Johns Hopkins Press 1932)

Sibert M, *Traité de droit international public*, vol 1 (Dalloz 1951)

Sibley NW and A Elias, *The Aliens Act and the Right of Asylum* (Clower and Sons 1906)

Simeon J, 'Strengthening International Refugee Rights through the Enhanced Supervision of the 1951 Convention and its 1967 Protocol' in SS Juss (ed), *The Ashgate Research Companion to Migration Law, Theory and Policy* (Rouledge 2013)

Simma B, 'From Bilateralism to Community Interest in International Law' (1994) 250 Collected Courses of the Hague Academy of International Law 217

Simma B, 'The Contribution of Alfred Verdross to the Theory of International Law' (1995) 6(1) EJIL 33–54

Simon H, 'Human Trafficking from an International Protection Perspective: Probing the Meaning of Anti-Trafficking Measures for the Protection of Trafficking Victims, with Special Regard to the United Kingdom' (2009) 28 Penn St Int'l L Rev 633–73

Simpson JH, *The Refugee Problem: Report of a Survey* (OUP 1939)

Sindico F, 'Soft Law and the Elusive Quest for Sustainable Global Governance' (2006) 19 LJIL 829–46

Sinha SP, *Asylum and International Law* (Martinus Nijhoff 1971)

Sitaropoulos N, *Judicial Interpretation of Refugee Status: In Search of a Principled Methodology Based on a Critical Comparative Analysis with Special Reference to Contemporary British, French and German Jurisprudence* (Ant N Sakkoulas 1999)

Sivakumaran S, 'The Rights of Migrant Workers One Year on: Transformation or Consolidation?' (2004) 36 Geo J Int'l L 113–53

Skeldon R, 'Trafficking: A Perspective from Asia' (2000) 38(3) International Migration 7–30

Skeldon R, 'Migration and Poverty' (2002) 17 Asia-Pacific Population Journal 67–82

Skran CM, *Refugees in Inter-War Europe: The Emergence of a Regime* (Clarendon Press 1995)

Slinckx I, 'Migrants' Rights in UN Human Rights Conventions' in R Cholewinski, P de Guchteneire, and A Pécoud (eds), *Migration and Human Rights: The United Nations Convention on Migrant Workers' Rights* (CUP 2009)

Sloan FB, *United Nations General Assembly Resolutions in our Changing World* (Brill 1991)

Sobotka T, V Skirbekk, and D Philipov, 'Economic Recession and Fertility in the Developed World' (2011) 37(2) Population and Development Review 267–306

Sohn LB, 'The Human Rights Law of the Charter' (1977) 129 Tex Int'l LJ 129–49

Sohn LB, 'The New International Law: Protection of the Rights of Individuals Rather than States' (1982) 32 Am UL Rev 1–64

Sohn LB and T Buergenthal (eds), *The Movement of Persons Across Borders* (ASIL 1992)

Spaventa E, *Free Movement of Persons in the EU: Barriers to Movement and their Constitutional Context* (Kluwer 2007)

Spiro PJ, 'The Possibilities of Global Migration Law' (2017) 111 AJIL Unbound 3–7

Starr S and L Brilmayer, 'Family Separation as a Violation of International Law' (2003) 21 Berk J Int'l L 213–87

Stein BN and FC Cuny, 'Refugee Repatriation during Conflict: Protection and Post-Return Assistance' (1994) 4(3) Development in Practice 173–87

Stenberg G, *Non-Expulsion and Non-Refoulement* (University Swedish Institute of International Law, Iustus Förlag 1989)

Stephenson SM and G Hufbauer, 'Labor Mobility' in J-P Chauffour and J-C Maur (eds), *Preferential Trade Agreement Policies for Development: A Handbook* (The World Bank 2011)

Storey H, 'Armed Conflict in Asylum Law: The 'War-Flaw'' (2012) 31(2) RSQ 1–32

Stowell EC, *International Law: A Restatement of Principles in Conformity with Actual Practice* (Henry Holt and Co 1931)

Stoyanova V, 'The Crisis of a Definition: Human Trafficking in Bulgarian Law' (2013) 5 Amsterdam LF 64–79

Strikwerda C, 'Tides of Migration, Currents of History: The State, Economy, and the Transatlantic Movement of Labor in the Nineteenth and Twentieth Centuries' (1999) 44 Int'l Rev Soc Hist 367–94

Sudmeier-Rieux K and others (eds), *Identifying Emerging Issues in Disaster Risk Reduction, Migration, Climate Change and Sustainable Development* (Springer International Publishing 2017)

Suliman S, 'Migration and Development after 2015' (2017) 14(3) Globalizations 415–31

Sybesma-Knoll N, *The United Nations* (Kluwer Law International 2012)

Sztucki J, 'The Conclusions on the International Protection of Refugees adopted by the Executive Committee of the UNHCR Programme' (1989) 1(3) IJRL 287–318

Sztucki J, 'Who Is a Refugee? The Convention Definition: Universal or Obsolete?' in F Nicholson and P Twomey (eds), *Refugee Rights and Realities: Evolving International Concepts and Regimes* (CUP 1999)

Takahashi S, 'The UNHCR Handbook on Voluntary Repatriation: The Emphasis of Return over Protection' (1997) 9(4) IJRL 593–612

Takahashi S, 'Effective Monitoring of the Refugee Convention' (2001) Paper Presented at the Refugee Convention 50 Years on; Critical Perspectives, Future Prospects II, International Studies Association Conference

Takeno Y, 'Facilitating the Transition of Asian Nurses to Work in Australia' (2010) 18(2) Journal of Nursing Management 215–24

Taylor H, *A Treatise on International Public Law* (Callaghan and Co 1901)

Taran P, 'Status and Prospects for the UN Convention on Migrants' Rights' (2000) 2(1) EJML 85–100

Taran P, 'Clashing Worlds: Imperatives for a Rights-based Approach to Labour Migration in the Age of Globalization' in V Chetail (ed), *Mondialisation, migration et droits de l'homme: le droit international en question/ Globalization, migration and human rights: international law under review* (Bruylant 2007)

Tendayi Achiume E, 'The Fatal Flaw in International Law for Migration' (2018) 56 Colum J of Transnat'l L 257–62

Teitgen-Colly C, 'La détention des étrangers et les droits de l'homme' in V Chetail (ed), *Mondialisation, migration et droits de l'homme: le droit international en question/ Globalization, migration and human rights: international law under review* (Bruylant 2007)

Tetsuya T, 'La doctrine vattelienne de l'égalite souveraine dans le contexte neuchâtelois' (2009) 11 J Hist Int'l L 103–24

Tiburcio C, *The Human Rights of Aliens under International and Comparative Law* (Martinus Nijhoff 2001)

Thévenaz H, 'Vattel ou la destinée d'un livre' (1957) 14 ASDI 9–16

Thibert M, 'Emigration et immigration' in A De Lapradelle and J-P Niboyet (eds), *Répertoire de droit international*, vol 7 (Sirey 1930)

Thomas C, 'Convergences and divergences in international legal norms on migrant labor' (2011) 32 Comp Lab L & Pol'y J 405–42

Thomas C, 'What Does the Emerging International Law of Migration Mean for Sovereignty?' (2013) 14 Melb J of IL 392–450

Thomas C, 'Mapping Global Migration Law, or the Two Batavias' (2017) 111 AJIL Unbound 504–08

Thomas J, 'La condition des étrangers et le droit international' (1897) 4 RGDIP 620–45

Thouez C and F Channac, 'Shaping International Migration Policy: The Role of Regional Consultative Processes' (2006) 29(2) W Eur Pol 370–87

Thuo Gathii J, *African Regional Trade Agreements as Legal Regimes* (CUP 2011)

Thürer D, 'Soft Law' in *Max Planck Encyclopedia of Public International Law* (OUP 2015)

Toman J, 'The Right to Leave and to Return in Eastern Europe' in K Vasak and S Liskofsky (eds), *The Right to Leave and to Return: Papers and Recommendations of the International Colloquium held in Uppsala, Sweden, 19–20 June 1972* (The American Jewish Committee 1976)

Torpey J, *The Invention of the Passport: Surveillance, Citizenship and the State* (CUP 2000)

Touzé S, *La protection des droits des nationaux à l'étranger: Recherche sur la protection diplomatique* (Pedone 2007)

Touzenis K, *Free Movement of Persons in the European Union and Economic Community of West African States: A Comparison of Law and Practice* (UNESCO 2012)

Touzenis K and A Sironi, *Current Challenges in the Implementation of the UN International Convention on the Protection of the Rights of All Migrant Workers and Members of their Families* (European Union 2013)

Toyoda T, *Theory and Politics of the Law of Nations: Political Bias in International Law Discourse of Seven German Court Councilors in the Seventeenth and Eighteenth Centuries* (Martinus Nijhoff 2011)

Trachtman JP, *The International Law of Economic Migration: Toward the Fourth Freedom* (WE Upjohn Press 2009)

Trevisanut S, 'The Principle of Non-Refoulement at Sea and the Effectiveness of Asylum Protection' (2008) 12 Max Planck Yrbk UN L 205–46

Trevisanut S, 'The Principle of Non-Refoulement and the De-Territorialization of Border Control at Sea' (2014) 27 LJIL 661–75

Trubek DM, P Cottrell, and M Nance, ' "Soft Law", "Hard Law", and European Integration: Toward a Theory of Hybridity' (2005) NYU School of Law Jean Monnet Working Paper No 2

Truyol y Serra A, 'Verdross et la théorie du droit' (1995) 6(1) EJIL 55–69

Turack DC, 'Freedom of Transnational Movement: The Helsinki Accord and Beyond' (1980-1981) 4 Im&NatL Rev 43–66

Turack DC, 'The Movement of Persons: The Practice of States in Central and Eastern Europe Since the 1989 Vienna CSCE' (1993) 12 Denv J Int'l L&Pol'y 289–309

Türk V, 'The Role of UNHCR in the Development of International Refugee Law' in F Nicholson and P Twomey (eds), *Refugee Rights and Realities: Evolving International Concepts and Regimes* (CUP 1999)

Türk V, 'UNHCR's Supervisory Responsibility' (2002) 14 RQDI 135–58

Türk V, 'The UNHCR's Role in Supervising International Protection Standards in the Context of its Mandate' in J Simeon (ed), *The UNHCR and the Supervision of International Refugee Law* (CUP 2013)

Tzevelekos VP, 'The Use of Article 31(3)(c) of the VCLT in the Case Law of the ECtHR: An Effective Anti-fragmentation Tool or Selective Loophole for the Reinforcement of Human Rights Teleology? Between Evolution and Systemic Integration' (2010) 31(3) Mich J Int'l L 621–90

Valenzuela-Vermehren L, 'Empire, Sovereignty, and Justice in Francisco de Vitoria's International Thought: A Re-interpretation of *De Indis*' (2013) 40(1) Revista Chilena de Derecho 259–97

Vanheule D and others, 'The Significance of the UN Migrant Workers' Convention of 18 December 1990 in The Event of Ratification by Belgium' (2004) 6(4) EJML 285–322

de Vattel E, *The Law of Nations or, Principles of the Law of Nature, Applied to the Conduct and Affairs of Nations and Sovereigns* (B Kapossy and R Whatmore (eds), Liberty Fund 2008)

Varlez L, 'Migration Problems and the Havana Conference of 1928' (1929) 19(1) Int'l Labour Rev 1–19

Varlez L, 'Les migrations internationales et leur réglementation' (1927) 20 RCADI 165

Vecoli R and S Sinke (eds), *A Century of European Migrations, 1830–1930* (University of Illinois Press 1992)

Vedsted-Hansen J, 'Migration and the Right to Family and Private Life' in V Chetail (ed), *Mondialisation, migration et droits de l'homme,* Vol II (Bruylant 2007)

Vedsted-Hansen J, 'Article 28/Schedule: Travel Documents/Titres de Voyage' in A Zimmermann (ed), *The 1951 Convention Relating to the Status of Refugees and its 1967 Protocol* (OUP 2011)

Venzke I, *How Interpretation Makes International Law: On Semantic Change and Normative Twists* (OUP 2012)

Verdross A, 'Les règles internationales concernant le traitement des étrangers' (1931) 37 Collected Courses of the Hague Academy of International Law 323

Verhoeven J, 'Vitoria ou la matrice du droit international' in *Actualité de la pensée juridique de Francisco de Vitoria* (Bruylant 1988)

Vermeer-Künzli A, *The Protection of Individuals by Means of Diplomatic Protection: Diplomatic Protection as a Human Rights Instrument* (Leiden University Press 2007)

Vermeer-Künzli A, 'Diplomatic Protection as a Source of Human Rights Law' in D Shelton (ed), *The Oxford Handbook of International Human Rights Law* (OUP Press 2013)

Vermeer-Künzli A, 'Diplomatic Protection and Consular Assistance of Migrants' in Chetail and Bauloz (eds), *Research Handbook on International Law and Migration* (Edward Elgar Publishing 2014)

Vevstad V, *Refugee Protection: A European Challenge* (Tano Aschehong 1998)

Vierdag EW, *The Concept of Discrimination in International Law* (Martinus Nijhoff 1973)

Virally M, 'La valeur juridique des recommandations des organisations internationales' (1956) 2(1) AFDI 66–96

Virally M, 'Droits de l'Homme et théorie générale du droit international' (1972) 4 René Cassin Amicorum Disipulorumque Liber 323–30

Virally M (rapporteur), 'La distinction entre textes internationaux ayant une portée juridique dans les relations mutuelles entre leur auteurs et les textes juridiques qui en sont dépourvus' (1983) 60(1) AIDI 328–74

de Vitoria F, *On the American Indians* in A Pagden and J Lawrance (eds), *Francisco de Vitoria: Political Writings* (CUP 1992)

Vohra S, 'Detention of Irregular Migrants and Asylum Seekers' in R Cholewinski, R Perruchoud, and E MacDonald (eds), *International Migration Law: Developing Paradigms and Key Challenges* (TMC Asser Press 2007)

Wagner A, 'Francisco de Vitoria and Alberico Gentili on the Legal Character of the Global Commonwealth' (2011) 31(3) Oxford J Legal Stud 565–82

Waldock H, 'Human Rights in Contemporary International Law and the Significance of the European Convention' (1965) 11 ICLQ 1–23

Warner K, 'Human Migration and Displacement in the Context of Adaptation to Climate Change: The Cancun Adaptation Framework and Potential for Future Action' (2012) 30 Environment and Planning C: Government and Policy 1061–77

Weatherall T, *Jus Cogens: International Law and Social Contract* (CUP 2015)

Webber F, 'How Voluntary are Voluntary Returns?' (2011) 52(4) Race & Class 98–107

Weeks G, *Soft Law and Public Authorities: Remedies and Reform* (Hart Publishing 2016)

Weil P, 'Towards Relative Normativity in International Law?' (1983) 77 AJIL 413–42

Weil P, 'Towards a Coherent Policy of Co-Development' (2002) 40(3) International Migration 41–53

Weis P, 'The 1967 Protocol Relating to the Status of Refugees and Some Questions of the Law of Treaties' (1967) 42 British Ybk Int'l L 39–70

Weissbrodt D and A Bergquist, 'Extraordinary Rendition and the Torture Convention' (2006) 46 Virginia J of Int'l L 585–650

Weissbrodt D, 'The Protection of Non-citizens in International Human Rights Law' in R Cholewinski, R Perruchoud, and E MacDonald (eds), *International Migration Law: Developing Paradigms and Key Challenges* (TMC Asser Press 2007)

Weissbrodt D, *The Human Rights of Non-Citizens* (OUP 2008)

Weissbrodt D and S Meili, 'Human Rights and Protection of Non-Citizens: Whither Universality and Indivisibility of Rights?' (2010) 28 RSQ 34–58

Weissbrodt D and J Rhodes, 'UN Treaty Bodies and Migrant Workers' in V Chetail and C Bauloz (eds), *Research Handbook on International Law and Migration* (Edward Elgar Publishing 2014)

Weller M and K Nobbs, *Political Participation of Minorities: A Commentary on International Standards and Practice* (OUP 2010)

Westlake J, *International Law*, part 1 (CUP 1904)

Whelan FG, 'Vattel's Doctrine of the State' (1988) 9 History of Political Thought 59

White ND, *The Law of International Organizations* (3rd edn, Manchester University Press 2017)

Wickramasekara P, *Bilateral Agreements and Memoranda of Understanding on Migration of Low Skilled Workers: A Review* (International Labour Organization 2015)

Williams Jr RA, *The American Indian in Western Legal Thought: The Discourses of Conquest* (OUP 1990)

Wight M, 'Western Values in International Relations' in H Butterfield and M Wight (eds), *Diplomatic Investigations: Essays in the Theory of International Politics* (Allen and Unwin 1966)

Wildman R, *Institutes of International Law*, vol 1 (Benning 1849)

Williams D, *The Specialized Agencies and the United Nations: The System in Crisis* (St Martin's Press 1987)

Wihtol de Wenden C, *Faut-il ouvrir les frontières?* (Presses de Sciences Po 1999)

Wolff C, *Jus Gentium Methodo Scientifica Pertractatum*, vol 2 (trans JH Drake, Clarendon Press/Humphrey Milford 1934)

Wolff C, *Principes du droit de la nature et des gens* (first published 1758, trans S Formey, Université de Caen 1988)

Wouters CW, *International Legal Standards for the Protection from Refoulement* (Intersentia 2009)

Wouters J and B de Meester 'The Role of International Law in Protecting Public Goods: Regional and Global Challenges' (2003) Working Paper No 1, Leuven Interdisciplinary Research Group on International Agreements and Development

Wray H, 'The Alien Act 1905 and the Immigration Dilemma' (2006) 33(2) J L and Society 302–23

Yarris K and H Castañeda, 'Special Issue Discourses of Displacement and Deservingness: Interrogating Distinctions between "Economic" and "Forced" Migration' (2015) 53(3) International Migration 64–69

Yarwood AT, *Asian Migration to Australia: The Background to Exclusion* (Melbourne University Press 1964)

Yepes J-M, 'Les Problèmes Fondamentaux du Droit des Gens en Amérique' (1934) 47 Collected Courses of the Hague Academy of International Law 1

Young MA (ed), *Regime Interaction in International Law: Facing Fragmentation* (CUP 2012)

Zaidi KR, 'Harmonizing Trade Liberalization and Migration Policy through Shared Responsibility: A Comparison of the Impact of Bilateral Trade Agreements and the GATS in Germany and Canada' (2010) 37(2) Syracuse J Int'l L & Com 267–98

Zavodny M and T Jacoby, *Filling the Gap: Less-Skilled Immigration in a Changing Economy* (Immigration Works USA 2013)

Zalewski A, 'Migrants for Sale: The International Failure to Address Contemporary Human Trafficking' (2005) 29 Suffolk Transnat'l L Rev 113–37

Zampogna-Krug A, 'Immigration vs. Emigration: The Internationality of U.S. Immigration Policy' (2012) 27 49th Parallel 1–19

Zanfrini L, 'Migration and Development: Old and New Ambivalences of the European Approach' (2015) ISMU Paper

Zapatero P, 'Legal Imagination in Vitoria: The Power of Ideas' (2009) 11 J Hist Int'l L 221–71

Zemanek K, 'Is the Term "Soft Law" Convenient?' in G Hafner et al (eds), *Liber Amicorum: Professor Ignaz Seidl-Hohenveldern in Honour of his 80th Birthday* (Kluwer Law International 1998)

Zieck M, 'Codification of the Law on Diplomatic Protection: The First Eight Draft Articles' (2001) 14(1) LJIL 209–32

Zieck M, *UNHCR's Worldwide Presence in the Field: A Legal Analysis of UNHCR's Cooperation Agreement* (Wolf Legal 2006)

Zieck M, 'Doomed to Fail from the Outset? UNHCR's Convention Plus Initiative Revisited' (2009) 21 IJRL 387–420

Zieck M, 'Article 35 of the 1951 Convention/Article II of the 1967 Protocol' in A Zimmermann (ed), *The 1951 Convention Relating to the Status of Refugees and its 1967 Protocol: A Commentary* (OUP 2011)

Zilbershats Y, 'The Right to Leave Israel and its Restriction on Security Grounds' (1994) 28 Israel L Rev 626–84

Zimmermann A and C Mahler, 'Article 1A, para 2 (Definition of the Term "Refugee")' in A Zimmermann (ed), *The 1951 Convention Relating to the Status of Refugees and its 1967 Protocol: A Commentary* (OUP 2011)

Zimmermann A and P Wennholz, 'Article 33, para. 2' in A Zimmermann (ed), *The 1951 Convention Relating to the Status of Refugees and its 1967 Protocol* (OUP 2011)

Zolberg AR, 'The Great Wall Against China: Responses to the First Immigration Crisis, 1885–1925' in J Lucassen and L Lucassen (eds), *Migration, Migration History, History: Old Paradigms and New Perspectives* (Peter Lang 1997)

Zolberg AR, *A Nation by Design: Immigration Policy and the Fashioning of America* (Harvard University Press 2006)

Zühlke S and J-C Pastille, 'Extradition and the European Convention—Soering Revisited' (1999) 59 ZAÖRV 749–84

Index

admission
  duty of, 30–31, 43, 50–51, 202–3, 227
    (*see also* asylum; family reunification;
    free movement; non-refoulement;
    right of entry)
  of foreigners, 7, 13, 19, 21, 26–29, 33–34,
    35–36, 38–39, 42, 44–46, 51, 52, 53,
    55, 57, 64, 76–77, 91–144, 169–70,
    186–87, 192–94, 202–3, 204–5,
    207, 212, 227, 236–37, 240–41,
    287, 319, 335, 337–39, 397
  refusal of, 29–30, 33, 35, 36–37,
    42–43, 50, 64
African Economic Community, 109–11
aggression. *See* armed conflict
aliens
  law of, 63, 64, 65, 66, 68, 73–74, 182–84
    (*see also* state responsibility)
  most favoured, 178–79, 180*t*, 182
  ordinary, 178–79, 180*t*, 182–83
Arab-Maghreb Union, 99*t*, 115–16
armed conflict, 44, 46–47, 48–49, 61,
    68, 78–79, 82–83, 115, 129–30,
    147, 149–50, 151, 169, 175–76,
    235–36, 254, 309–10, 371
Asian-African Legal Consultative
    Organization, 87–88, 175–76, 188
Asia-Pacific Economic Cooperation, 99*t*, 100–1
Association of Southeast Asian Nations,
    69–70, 87–88, 99*t*, 101, 251–52
asylum, 26, 134, 178–79, 190–94, 225–26,
    242, 286–87, 336–37, 378, 386, 392.
    See also non-refoulement; refugee
asylum-seeker, 35–193, 198, 225, 226–27,
    242, 264, 275, 300–2, 337, 368–70,
    376–77, 384–85, 391, 395. *See also*
    asylum; non-refoulement; refugee

best interests of the child, 127–29,
    130–31, 136–37, 335, 384–85.
    See also children; detention
bilateral agreement, 40–41, 52–53, 56,
    63, 66, 92, 96–97, 108, 119–20,
    182–83, 203, 214, 218, 245, 250,
    294, 301, 312, 333, 397
bilateral treaty. *See* bilateral agreement
border controls. *See* immigration control

Caribbean Community, 99*t*, 117–18
Central American Integration System, 99*t*, 119
cessation clause (refugee status), 170, 171–72

children, 53, 54, 69–70, 71, 124–32, 136–37,
    155–56, 161, 162–63, 164*t*, 185,
    209, 215–17, 223–24, 233, 235–36,
    238, 245, 253–55, 284–85, 307–8,
    335, 356–57, 358–59, 384–85. *See*
    also best interests of the child
climate change. *See* natural disaster
Common Market for Eastern and
    Southern Africa, 99*t*, 115–16
Commonwealth of Independent States, 107–8
Community of Sahel-Saharan
    States, 99*t*, 115–16
consular protection, 164*t*, 221–22, 332,
    335. *See also* diplomatic protection;
    right to consular access
cooperation, 14, 135, 211–12, 224, 285,
    306, 311, 319, 320–22, 325–27, 328,
    330, 332, 336, 340–41, 344–45,
    355, 358–59, 360, 366–67, 372,
    385. *See also* migration governance
  duty of, 150–51, 228, 327, 385, 387–88
  inter-state cooperation, 52–58, 107–8, 200–1,
    202–8, 227, 228–30, 247, 262–63, 268–69,
    283, 291, 292, 300–2, 304–6, 307–8, 309,
    310–11, 312–14, 315–16, 317–18,
    321–22, 325, 333, 337, 338, 339,
    344, 346, 348, 350, 402
crimes against humanity, 170–71, 254–55, 401
criminalization
  of illegal employment, 205–6, 247
  non-criminalization for irregular
    entry/stay, 178, 179, 192–94,
    206, 232, 263–66, 335
  of smuggling (*see* smuggling)
  of trafficking (*see* trafficking in persons)
customary international law, 13, 49, 63–64, 65,
    76–77, 79, 85–92, 93–94, 119–44, 145–51,
    154–55, 156, 160, 161, 163–64, 164*t*,
    190–91, 209–10, 234–35, 272, 274–75,
    286–90, 372–73, 387–88, 397, 398, 401

departure, 7, 13, 26–27, 76–92, 163, 164*t*,
    193, 201, 223, 331, 398. *See also*
    emigration; right to leave any country
deportation. *See* expulsion
detention, 13, 63, 132, 133–38, 142, 164*t*,
    185–86, 196–97, 226, 231–32, 272–73,
    274, 286–87, 321–22, 332, 335, 358–59,
    378, 384–85, 391, 397, 398, 401
diplomatic protection, 73–75, 149–50,
    236–37, 397